WORLD ERAS

VOLUME 3

ROMAN REPUBLIC AND EMPIRE

264 B.C.E. – 476 C.E.

WORLD ERAS

VOLUME 3

ROMAN REPUBLIC AND EMPIRE
264 B.C.E. – 476 C.E.

JOHN T. KIRBY

A MANLY, INC. BOOK

GALE GROUP

★

THOMSON LEARNING

Detroit • New York • San Diego • San Francisco
Boston • New Haven, Conn. • Waterville, Maine
London • Munich

WORLD ERAS VOL. 3
ROMAN REPUBLIC
AND EMPIRE

264 B.C.E.-476 C.E.

Matthew J. Bruccoli and Richard Layman, *Editorial Directors*

Anthony J. Scotti Jr., *Series Editor*

Library Of Congress Cataloging-in-Publication Data
World Eras vol. 3: Roman Republic and Empire, 264 B.C.E.-476 C.E. /
   edited by John T. Kirby.
      p. cm.— (World Eras)
   "A Manly, Inc. book."
   Includes bibliographical references and index.
   ISBN 0-7876-4504-4 (alk. paper)
   1. Rome—Civilization. I. Title: Roman Republic and Empire, 264
B.C.E.-476 C.E. II. Kirby, John T.

DG77.W726 2001
937'.01—dc21   00-050386

Printed in the United States of America
10 9 8 7 6 5 4 3 2 1

ADVISORY BOARD

FOR MY MOTHER

CONTENTS

Significant People

CHAPTER 7: LEISURE, RECREATION, AND DAILY LIFE

Topics in Leisure, Recreation, and Daily Life

Significant People

CHAPTER 8: THE FAMILY AND SOCIAL TRENDS

Chapter 9: RELIGION AND PHILOSOPHY

Chapter 10: SCIENCE, TECHNOLOGY, AND HEALTH

ABOUT THE SERIES

PROJECT DESCRIPTION

Patterned after the well-received *American Decades* and *American Eras* series, *World Eras* is a cross-disciplinary reference series. It comprises volumes examining major civilizations that have flourished from antiquity to modern times, with a global perspective and a strong emphasis on daily life and social history. Each volume provides in-depth coverage of one era, focusing on a specific cultural group and its interaction with other peoples of the world. The *World Eras* series is geared toward the needs of high-school students studying subjects in the humanities. Its purpose is to provide students—and general reference users as well—a reliable, engaging reference resource that stimulates their interest, encourages research, and prompts comparison of the lives people led in different parts of the world, in different cultures, and at different times.

The goal of *World Eras* volumes is to enrich the traditional historical study of "kings and battles" with a resource that promotes understanding of daily life and the cultural institutions that affect people's beliefs and behavior.

What kind of work did people in a certain culture perform?

What did they eat?

How did they fight their battles?

What laws did they have and how did they punish criminals?

What were their religious practices?

What did they know of science and medicine?

What kind of art, music, and literature did they enjoy?

These are the types of questions *World Eras* volumes seek to answer.

VOLUME DESIGN

World Eras is designed to facilitate comparative study. Thus volumes employ a consistent ten-chapter structure so that teachers and students can readily access standard topics in various volumes. The chapters in each *World Eras* volume are:

1. World Events

2. Geography

3. The Arts

4. Communication, Transportation, and Exploration

5. Social Class System and the Economy

6. Politics, Law, and the Military

7. Leisure, Recreation, and Daily Life

8. The Family and Social Trends

9. Religion and Philosophy

10. Science, Technology, and Health

World Eras volumes begin with two chapters designed to provide a broad view of the world against which a specific culture can be measured. Chapter 1 provides students today with a means to understand where a certain people stood within our concept of world history. Chapter 2 describes the world from the perspective of the people being studied—what did they know of geography and how did geography and climate affect their lives? The following eight chapters address major aspects of people's lives to provide a sense of what defined their culture. The ten chapters in *World Eras* will remain constant in each volume. Teachers and students seeking to compare religious beliefs in Roman and Greek cultures, for example, can easily locate the information they require by consulting chapter 9 in the appropriate volumes, tapping a rich source for class assignments and research topics. Volume-specific glossaries and a checklist of general references provide students assistance in studying unfamiliar cultures.

CHAPTER CONTENTS

Each chapter in *World Eras* volumes also follows a uniform structure designed to provide users quick access to the information they need. Chapters are arranged into five types of material:

- **Chronology** provides an historical outline of significant events in the subject of the chapter in timeline form.

- **Overview** provides a narrative overview of the chapter topic during the period and discusses the material of the chapter in a global context.

- **Topical Entries** provide focused information in easy-to-read articles about people, places, events, institutions, and matters of general concern to the people of the time. A references rubric includes sources for further study.

- **Biographical Entries** profiles people of enduring significance regarding the subject of the chapter.

- **Documentary Sources** is an annotated checklist of documentary sources from the historical period that are the basis for the information presented in the chapter.

Chapters are supplemented throughout with primary-text sidebars that include interesting short documentary excerpts or anecdotes chosen to illuminate the subject of the chapter: recipes, letters, daily-life accounts, and excerpts from important documents. Each *World Eras* volume includes about 150 illustrations, maps, diagrams, and line drawings linked directly to material discussed in the text. Illustrations are chosen with particular emphasis on daily life.

INDEXING

A general two-level subject index for each volume includes significant terms, subjects, theories, practices, people, organizations, publications, and so forth, mentioned in the text. Index citations with many page references are broken down by subtopic. Illustrations are indicated both in the general index, by use of italicized page numbers, and in a separate illustrations index, which provides a description of each item.

EDITORS AND CONTRIBUTORS

An advisory board of history teachers and librarians has provided valuable advice about the rationale for this series. They have reviewed both series plans and individual volume plans. Each *World Eras* volume is edited by a distinguished specialist in the subject of his or her volume. The editor is responsible for enlisting other scholar-specialists to write each of the chapters in the volume and of assuring the quality of their work. The editorial staff at Manly, Inc., rigorously checks factual information, line edits the manuscript, works with the editor to select illustrations, and produces the books in the series, in cooperation with Gale Group editors.

The *World Eras* series is for students of all ages who seek to enrich their study of world history by examining the many aspects of people's lives in different places during different eras. This series continues Gale's tradition of publishing comprehensive, accurate, and stimulating historical reference works that promote the study of history and culture.

The following timeline, included in every volume of *World Eras*, is provided as a convenience to users seeking a ready chronological context.

TIMELINE

This timeline, compiled by editors at Manly, Inc., is provided as a convenience for students seeking a broad global and historical context for the materials in this volume of World Eras. *It is not intended as a self-contained resource. Students who require a comprehensive chronology of world history should consult sources such as William L. Langer, comp. and ed.,* The New Illustrated Encyclopedia of World History, *2 volumes (New York: Harry N. Abrams, 1975).*

CIRCA 4 MILLION TO 1 MILLION B.C.E.
Era of *Australopithecus*, the first hominid

CIRCA 1.5 MILLION TO 200,000 B.C.E.
Era of *Homo erectus*, "upright-walking human"

CIRCA 1,000,000-10,000 B.C.E.
Paleothic Age: hunters and gatherers make use of stone tools in Eurasia

CIRCA 250,000 B.C.E.
Early evolution of *Homo sapiens*, "consciously thinking humans"

CIRCA 40,000 B.C.E.
Migrations from Siberia to Alaska lead to the first human inhabitation of North and South America

CIRCA 8000 B.C.E.
Neolithic Age: settled agrarian culture begins to develop in Eurasia

5000 B.C.E.
The world population is between 5 million and 20 million

CIRCA 4000-3500 B.C.E.
Earliest Sumerian cities: artificial irrigation leads to increased food supplies and populations in Mesopotamia

CIRCA 3000 B.C.E.
Bronze Age begins in Mesopotamia and Egypt, where bronze is primarily used for making weapons; invention of writing

CIRCA 2900-1150 B.C.E.
Minoan society on Crete: lavish palaces and commercial activity

CIRCA 2700-2200 B.C.E.
Egypt: Old Kingdom and the building of the pyramids

CIRCA 2080-1640 B.C.E.
Egypt: Middle Kingdom plagued by internal strife and invasion by the Hyksos

CIRCA 2000-1200 B.C.E.
Hittites build a powerful empire based in Anatolia (present-day Turkey) by using horse-drawn war chariots

CIRCA 1792-1760 B.C.E.
Old Babylonian Kingdom; one of the oldest extant legal codes is compiled

CIRCA 1766-1122 B.C.E.
Shang Dynasty in China: military expansion, large cities, written language, and introduction of bronze metallurgy

CIRCA 1570-1075 B.C.E.
Egypt: New Kingdom and territorial expansion into Palestine, Lebanon, and Syria

CIRCA 1500 B.C.E.
The Aryans, an Indo-European people from the steppes of present-day Ukraine and southern Russia, expand into northern India

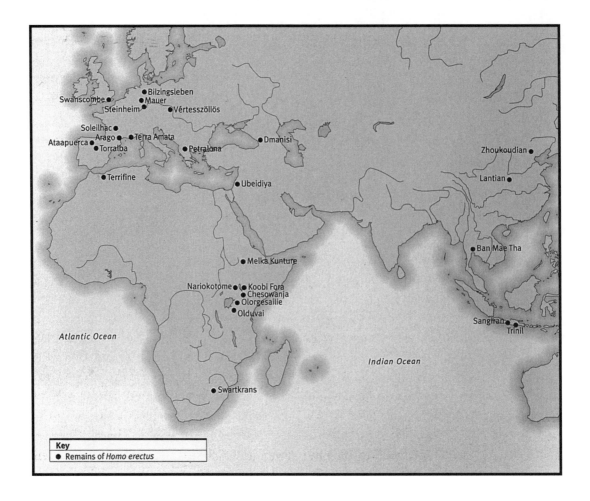

Key
● Remains of *Homo erectus*

CIRCA 1500 B.C.E.
Phoenicians create the first alphabet

CIRCA 1400-1200 B.C.E.
Hittites develop the technology of iron-smelting, improving weaponry and agricultural implements, as well as stimulating trade

CIRCA 1200-800 B.C.E.
Phoenicians establish colonies throughout the Mediterranean

CIRCA 1122- 221 B.C.E.
Zhou Dynasty in China: military conquests, nomadic invasions, and introduction of iron metallurgy

CIRCA 1100-750 B.C.E.
Greek Dark Ages: foreign invasions, civil disturbances, decrease in agricultural production, and population decline

1020-587 B.C.E.
Israelite monarchies consolidate their power in Palestine

CIRCA 1000-612 B.C.E.
Assyrians create an empire encompassing Mesopotamia, Syria, Palestine, and most of Anatolia and Egypt; they deport populations to various regions of the realm

1000 B.C.E.
The world population is approximately 50 million

CIRCA 814-146 B.C.E.
The city-state of Carthage is a powerful commercial and military power in the western Mediterranean

753 B.C.E.
Traditional date of the founding of Rome

CIRCA 750-700 B.C.E.
Rise of the polis, or city-state, in Greece

558-330 B.C.E.
Achaemenid Dynasty establishes the Persian Empire (present-day Iran, Turkey, Afghanistan, and Iraq); satraps rule the various provinces

509 B.C.E.
Roman Republic is established

500 B.C.E.
The world population is approximately 100 million

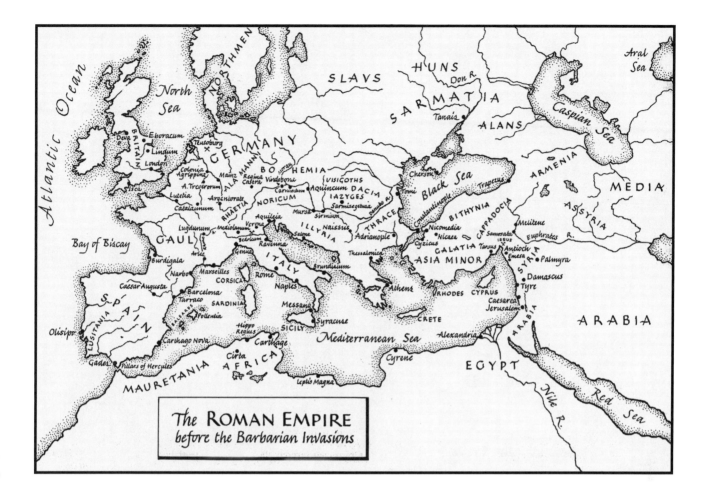

The ROMAN EMPIRE
before the Barbarian Invasions

CIRCA 400 B.C.E.
Spread of Buddhism in India

338-323 B.C.E.
Macedon, a kingdom in the central Balkan peninsula, conquers the Persian Empire

323-301 B.C.E.
Ptolemaic Kingdom (Egypt), Seleucid Kingdom (Syria), and Antigonid Dynasty (Macedon) are founded

247 B.C.E.-224 C.E.
Parthian Empire (Parthia, Persia, and Babylonia): clan leaders build independent power bases in their satrapies, or provinces

215-168 B.C.E.
Rome establishes hegemony over the Hellenistic world

206 B.C.E. TO 220 C.E.
Han Dynasty in China: imperial expansion into central Asia, centralized government, economic prosperity, and population growth

CIRCA 100 B.C.E.
Tribesmen on the Asian steppes develop the stirrup, which eventually revolutionizes warfare

1 C.E.
The world population is approximately 200 million

CIRCA 100 C.E.
Invention of paper in China

224-651 C.E.
Sasanid Empire (Parthia, Persia, and Babylonia): improved government system, founding of new cities, increased trade, and the introduction of rice and cotton cultivation

340 C.E.
Constantinople becomes the capital of the Eastern Roman, or Byzantine, Empire

CIRCA 320-550 C.E.
Gupta Dynasty in India: Golden Age of Hindu civilization marked by stability and prosperity throughout the subcontinent

395 C.E.
Christianity becomes the official religion of the Roman Empire

CIRCA 400 C.E.
The first unified Japanese state arises and is centered at Yamato on the island of Honshu; Buddhism arrives in Japan by way of Korea

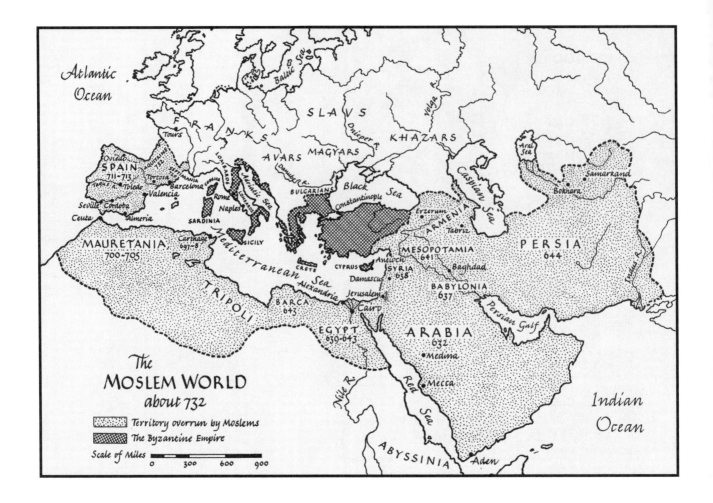

The Moslem World about 732. Territory overrun by Moslems. The Byzantine Empire.

CIRCA 400 C.E.

The nomadic Huns begin a westward migration from central Asia, causing disruption in the Roman Empire

CIRCA 400 C.E.

The Mayan Empire in Mesoamerica evolves into city-states

476 C.E.

Rome falls to barbarian hordes and the Western Roman Empire collapses

CIRCA 500-1500 C.E.

Middle Ages, or medieval period, in Europe: gradual recovery from political disruption and increase in agricultural productivity and population

618-907 C.E.

Tang Dynasty in China: territorial expansion, government bureaucracy, agricultural improvements, and transportation and communication networks

632-733 C.E.

Muslim expansion and conquests in Arabia, Syria, Palestine, Mesopotamia, Egypt, North Africa, Persia, northwestern India, and Iberia

CIRCA 700 C.E.

Origins of feudalism, a political and social organization that dominates Europe until the fifteenth century; based on the relationship between lords and vassals

CIRCA 900 C.E.

Introduction of the horseshoe in Europe and black powder in China

960-1279 C.E.

Song Dynasty in China: civil administration, industry, education, and the arts

962-1806 C.E.

Holy Roman Empire of western and central Europe, created in an attempt to revive the old Roman Empire

1000 C.E.

The world population is approximately 300 million

1096-1291 C.E.

Western Christians undertake the Crusades, a series of religiously inspired military campaigns, to recapture the Holy Land from the Muslims

1200 TO 1400 C.E.
The Mali empire in Africa dominates the trans-Saharan trade network of camel caravans

1220-1335 C.E.
The Mongols, nomadic horsemen from the high steppes of eastern central Asia, build an empire that includes China, Persia, and Russia

CIRCA 1250 C.E.
Inca Empire develops in Peru: Civil administration, road networks, and sun worshipping

1299-1919 C.E.
Ottoman Empire, created by nomadic Turks and Christian converts to Islam, encompasses Asia Minor, the Balkans, Greece, Egypt, North Africa, and the Middle East

1300 C.E.
The world population is approximately 396 million

1337-1453 C.E.
Hundred Years' War, a series of intermittent military campaigns between England and France over control of continental lands claimed by both countries

1347-1350 C.E.
Black Death, or the bubonic plague, kills one-quarter of the European population

1368-1644 C.E.
Ming Dynasty in China: political, economic, and cultural revival; the Great Wall is built

1375-1527 C.E.
The Renaissance in Western Europe, a revival in the arts and learning

1428-1519 C.E.
The Aztecs expand in central Mexico, developing trade routes and a system of tribute payments

1450 C.E.
Invention of the printing press

1453 C.E.
Constantinople falls to the Ottoman Turks, ending the Byzantine Empire

1464-1591 C.E.
Songhay Empire in Africa: military expansion, prosperous cities, control of the trans-Saharan trade

1492 C.E.
Discovery of America; European exploration and colonization of the Western Hemisphere begins

CIRCA 1500-1867 C.E.
Transatlantic slave trade results in the forced migration of between 12 million and 16 million Africans to the Western Hemisphere

1500 C.E.
The world population is approximately 480 million

1517 C.E.
Beginning of the Protestant Reformation, a religious movement that ends the spiritual unity of western Christendom

1523-1763 C.E.
Mughal Empire in India: military conquests, productive agricultural economy, and population growth

1600-1867 C.E.
Tokugawa Shogunate in Japan: shoguns (military governors) turn Edo, or Tokyo, into the political, economic, and cultural center of the nation

1618-1648 C.E.
Thirty Years' War in Europe between Catholic and Protestant states

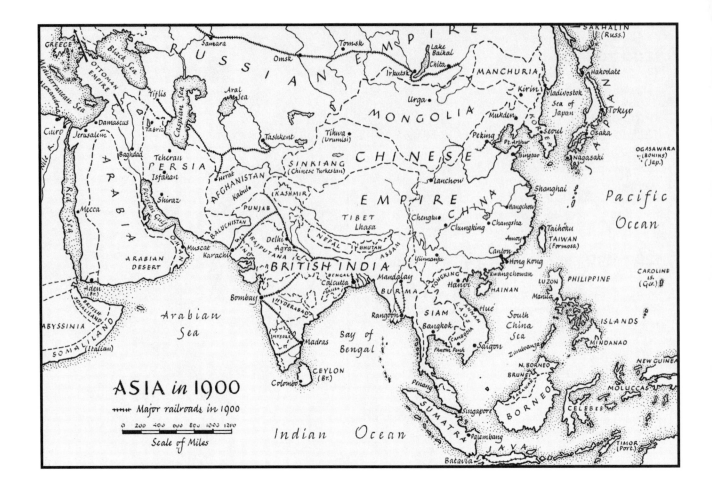

ASIA in 1900

Major railroads in 1900

Scale of Miles

1644-1911 C.E.
Qing Dynasty in China: military expansion and scholar-bureaucrats

1700 C.E.
The world population is approximately 640 million

CIRCA 1750 C.E.
Beginning of the Enlightenment, a philosophical movement marked by an emphasis on rationalism and scientific inquiry

1756-1763 C.E.
Seven Years' War: England and Prussia versus Austria, France, Russia, Saxony, Spain, and Sweden

CIRCA 1760-1850 C.E.
Industrial Revolution in Britain is marked by mass production through the division of labor, mechanization, a great increase in the supply of iron, and the use of the steam engine

1775-1783 C.E.
American War of Independence; the United States becomes an independent republic

1789 C.E.
French Revolution topples the monarchy and leads to a period of political unrest followed by a dictatorship

1793-1815 C.E.
Napoleonic Wars: Austria, England, Prussia, and Russia versus France and its satellite states

1794-1824 C.E.
Latin American states conduct wars of independence against Spain

1900 C.E.
The world population is approximately 1.65 billion

1914-1918 C.E.
World War I, or the Great War: the Allies (England, France, Russia, and the United States) versus Central Powers (Austria-Hungary, Germany, and the Ottoman Empire)

1917-1921 C.E.
Russian Revolution: a group of Communists known as the Bolsheviks seize control of the country following a civil war

1939-1945 C.E.

World War II: the Allies (China, England, France, the Soviet Union, and the United States) versus the Axis (Germany, Italy, and Japan)

1945 C.E.

Successful test of the first atomic weapon; beginning of the Cold War, a period of rivalry, mistrust, and, occasionally, open hostility between the capitalist West and communist East

1947-1975 C.E.

Decolonization occurs in Africa and Asia as European powers relinquish control of colonies in those regions

1948

Israel becomes the first independent Jewish state in nearly two thousand years

1949

Communists seize control of China

1950-1951

Korean War: the United States attempts to stop Communist expansion in the Korean peninsula

1957 C.E.

The Soviet Union launches *Sputnik* ("fellow traveler of earth"), the first man-made satellite; the Space Age begins

1965-1973

Vietnam War: the United States attempts to thwart the spread of Communism in Vietnam

1989 C.E.

East European Communist regimes begin to falter and multiparty elections are held

1991 C.E.

Soviet Union is dissolved and replaced by the Commonwealth of Independent States

2000 C.E.

The world population is 6 billion

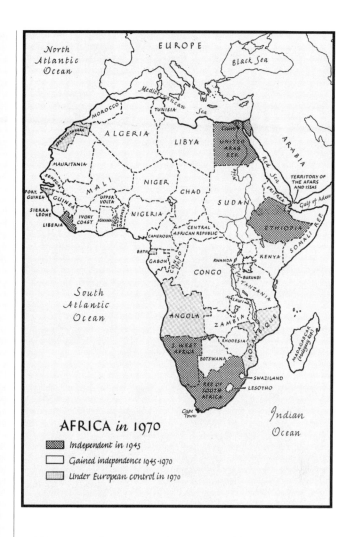

AFRICA in 1970

- Independent in 1945
- Gained independence 1945-1970
- Under European control in 1970

EDITOR'S INTRODUCTION

ROMA ÆTERNA. Rome, The Eternal City. This ancient civilization lives on in its monuments as well as in its impact (in a variety of realms) on western civilization; its grandeur was once obvious to all educated people in our culture. Their military genius made them the undisputed masters of the Mediterranean basin. Throughout the western world, their architecture is to this day echoed whenever an especially impressive public edifice is needed. Their juridical system continues to form the basis of many European legal systems. Their impact on such cultural institutions as rhetoric, philosophy, and poetry has been equally extensive. Their language was once *the* medium of "civilized" scholarly discourse throughout the western world.

Incalculable Debt. Things have changed rather dramatically. No longer can the average student be expected to be familiar with this vanished civilization; on the contrary, to most of us, their customs, their way of life, their language and literature, and many of their interests will doubtless seem alien and remote. And yet, we do indeed owe them a great, an incalculable debt: it is safe to say, in fact, that our own culture would not be what it is if it were not for the ancient Romans. So it behooves us to inquire as closely as possible into the details of their existence.

Many Subdisciplines. Study of the ancient world has traditionally been distributed under two headings: *philology* and *archaeology*. (Other related disciplines, such as history and philosophy, have made use of the combined results of philology and archaeology.) By "philology" I mean not its narrow focus on linguistic scrutiny—although that is surely an important aspect of philology—but its older meaning of textual studies in the broadest sense: the philologist was expected to have competence to work with ancient texts, in every conceivable way. Most widely construed, this includes the actual ability to decode ancient documents. Such work requires expertise in the fields of *papyrology* (the study of papyrus manuscripts) and *palaeography* (the study of ancient handwriting). Johannes Gutenberg did not invent his movable-type printing press until the fifteenth century, so prior to that time virtually all books in the western world were laboriously copied one at a time, by hand, whether onto papyrus, parchment, or (in the case of some mediaeval manuscripts) an early form of paper. It is from such handwritten documents (*manuscript* means, literally, "written by

hand") that our modern printed editions of all ancient authors are made. This process demands skill in *textual criticism*, in which palaeography and/or papyrology may play an important part. More-durable (but generally much briefer) textual remains are those preserved on stone or metal; the field that studies such inscriptions is called *epigraphy*. Aside from the actual matters they discuss, epigraphic texts can also preserve precious information about such things as alphabetic styles and norms of spelling current at the time in which they were produced. A hybrid field, poised midway among philology, epigraphy, and archaeology (on which see below), is that of *numismatics*, the study of coins, which may have not only pictorial images but also verbal inscriptions on them.

Studying the Text. Once palaeographers, papyrologists, epigraphers, and other textual critics have done their work, and a critical text is established and published, the wider community of philologists can set to work studying the text. For Latinists, this of course demands not only expertise in the language—the grammar and linguistic phenomena—but also, ideally, a broad base of knowledge about other texts that were produced in the same time and place. If one is working on a speech of Cicero, for example, it is very helpful to have the greatest possible familiarity with all the other surviving works of Cicero. More than this, one will want to know as much as possible about Roman oratory, both as live performance and as literary artifact; one will want to have access to all the extant fragments of speeches by other orators; and one will try to scout out information about orations that have not survived. One will want to discover as much as one can about how rhetoric was taught in Cicero's day, and how it functioned in Roman society, in the judicial as well as in the political arena. To bring the larger picture into focus, one will want to learn as much as one can about the history of Rome in the late Republic (the period when Cicero lived), and—in order to understand that—the history of the earlier Republic, all the way back to the early kings of Rome. Moreover, since Cicero's oratorical style arguably influenced the entire course of western literature, one may want to know what happened in Europe *after* the time of Cicero, and how his works were received and read. Thus, the history of the transmission of the text—how these works were studied, copied by hand, and handed down for centuries until the invention of the printing press—is a key aspect of the discipline of Classics.

Other Skills. To continue with this imagined study of Cicero: Roman oratory is a very particular type of cultural production, and in order to understand it deeply, the classicist will need some special skills. The vocabulary used in a formal presentation in a court of law, or in the Senate, was more formal than that in ordinary Latin conversation, so the classicist may want to make a lexical study of the text (although to a certain extent there may be some circularity here, as *lexicology* may have played an important part in the process of editing the text for publication). Since Roman orators paid careful attention to the patterns of long and short syllables in their speech, particularly at the ends of sentences, one needs to understand something about *prose-rhythms* and *clausulae*. In order to enrich one's understanding of the text, one will want next to inquire into a number of different realms of knowledge: what guidelines governed jurisprudence in the Roman law-courts? What sort of relationship did an orator have with his client? In presenting a case, what was the balance between evidence and argument? How much of a legal expert did a judicial orator have to be in order to defend a client? What sorts of gestures and intonations were used in delivering an oration? Who could attend orations in the courts, and how did the juries deliberate? The classicist who is interested in this text may find himself hunting down information in any of these areas of study.

Other Genres. There are, of course, many different kinds of text besides oratory; one might want to know, for example, about a work of philosophy, or of drama, or of medical science, or of epic poetry. Each of these genres is a different kind of cultural production; the questions the classicist is going to ask will vary, and differ, not only according to the genre of the text under study but also by virtue of the kind of use he wants to make of it.

Material Culture. The archaeologist is especially interested in the remains of what we call "material culture"—that is, in the physical objects that the ancient Romans left behind, and that have survived to this day. These include such things as buildings (public and private, sacred and secular); works of art, such as paintings, mosaics, and sculpture; pottery, which was often painted with extraordinary skill and beauty; coins; tools and weapons, and machinery of both war and peace; jewelry and other forms of adornment; devices for personal grooming; and so on. The more durable the material, of course, the longer-lasting the artifact (stone lasts longer than wood; metal lasts longer than ceramic; and so forth). One has only to walk around an archaeological site in Italy to get a strong sense of the palpability of the past. Potsherds, which might be two thousand years old, are sometimes just lying on the ground. (Indeed, ironically, while innumerable ancient bronze statues were at some point melted down for the reuse of their metal, the humbler clay pot has often survived to the present day.) Much careful work of recuperation and restoration has been done, especially in the past couple hundred years, and some ancient sites (such as Pompeii) that were literally buried underground have been painstakingly dug out and, as much as possible, meticulously put back together as they once were. The great museums of the world, even those outside Italy itself, contain many artifacts that can shed precious light on the darkness of the past, giving us a glimpse into the humanity of these long-dead peoples.

Art History. That aspect of Classics now known as *art history* is an extension of classical archaeology, studying as it does in stylistic and formal terms the images bequeathed to us by antiquity. The classical art historian will be particularly interested in assessing the development of artistic techniques in the various media, and also in relating these to our larger sociocultural picture of the civilizations that produced them.

Reciprocal Influences. Again the influences are circular: the work of the archaeologist is much illuminated by the information we can glean from ancient texts; conversely, the philologist who does not avail himself of the visual enrichment that archaeological scholarship can provide is an impoverished reader. So each of these subdisciplines nourishes the other in a vital way.

Historical Inquiry. The *historian,* whose job it is to ask questions about the events of the past and their significance, advances the work both of philologists and of archaeologists in order to piece together a coherent narrative about the culture in question. Traditionally, such narratives have focused on matters of government, of warfare, of the grand-scale evolution and devolution of societies. As we move into the twenty-first century, however, we find that ancient historians are inquiring more and more into the life of the ordinary person of antiquity. To a certain extent, this parallels recent trends in cultural-studies programs that focus on current cultures: as the canons of literature and the other arts have been called into question, we are seeing a shift away from "high culture" and toward the everyday. To an extent as well, this reflects the sense (shared by many) that the world is, after all, largely composed of ordinary people leading everyday lives.

Patterns of Scholarship. Such, then, are the parameters of traditional Classics as it was practiced into the twentieth century. Some of these patterns of scholarship were in place before the Enlightenment; indeed, some of them have roots as far back as the Renaissance, or even earlier. And except for some of the very youngest generation, most classicists now alive were trained in this approach. With the extraordinary changes and developments we have seen in the humanities generally over the past few decades, it should not be surprising that Classics too has changed.

Different Approaches, Different Values. The differences have evinced themselves not only in terms of the *topics* that scholars tend to find interesting and important—such as the shift, just mentioned, toward the everyday—but also (and perhaps especially) in terms of *methodology*. More simply put, there have been massive changes, not only in *what* classical scholars tend to study, but also in *how*. As the academic world has become more and more internationalized, there is a good deal of cross-pollination from one culture to another. In the nineteenth century, Classics in America was largely shaped according to English and German styles of scholarship; in the twentieth, the greatest impact came from French theorists, in literary theory and anthropology, especially. These new influences have substantially changed the kinds of questions classicists are likely to ask about ancient peoples (and thus, necessarily, the kinds of answers they are likely to find). As Marxist thought and psychoanalytic theory have entered the critical vocabulary of scholars, for example, recent research has inevitably come to reflect these schools of thought. Issues of class and gender, too, have been much foregrounded in recent work on antiquity; to return again to our sample case: Ciceronian oratory raises many important questions under the rubric of gender studies. What was it like to be a male of the elite class in ancient Rome? Why did women not present orations in the Roman Senate or law courts? What can Cicero's presuppositions, and his explicit statements, tell us about the way men (or women) might have been perceived, represented, or treated in his own day? Other literary schools and approaches, too, will have new light to shed on classical texts. Semiotics, narratology, reader-response criticism—all these, and others as well, promise to open up new vistas for the student of antiquity.

Different Conclusions. In view of all this, it is important to realize that, no matter what approach one takes, the data themselves do not change: that is, the traditionalist will, at the end of the day, have read the same texts, have examined the same vase paintings, as the most avant-garde scholar. Rather, what determines one's findings is (on the one hand) one's worldview, and (on the other) the kinds of questions that one asks of the data.

Why This Volume? There are many books available on ancient Rome, including a number of truly admirable reference works. So why, at the beginning of a new millennium, have we undertaken to compile a new one? The *World Eras* series was conceived with the rationale of providing, in such a way as to reflect changing curricular needs, a cross-disciplinary overview of world history, with a strong emphasis on daily life and social history. Such a project is both difficult and profoundly needed in the study of Roman culture; until recently, because of the way the discipline of Classics was established, the Romans were uniformly put on a pedestal, with the predictable double result that they were not only lionized but also became quite unreachable. In the past few decades we have seen a marked reversal of this trend, but much work still remains to be done, and there are still many things about life in ancient Rome that remain shrouded in mystery for us. It is our hope that *The Roman Republic and Empire (264 B.C.E.–476 C.E.)* will help in this exciting work of discovery.

Triple Goal. I have asked my contributors to keep ever before them the triple goal of *accuracy, clarity,* and *accessibility:* we have made every effort to present the materials in such a way as to avoid factual error, obscurity, or abstruseness. I hope the reader will also find that they have managed to be interesting.

How To Use This Book. It is, of course, impossible to freeze any culture in time. How, for example, could we accurately say what "American culture" is? Is it possible to say what American culture is like, even if we restrict our inquiry to "American culture in the year 2001"? Similarly, the reader should always keep in mind that formulae like "The Romans were X" or "The Romans did Y" are, and can only be, in some sense reductive. Upon reflection it quickly becomes clear that any culture is going to be multifaceted and to look radically different depending on one's vantage point. I would like, just as a point of departure, to suggest three different factors that will radically affect one's perception of any culture, ancient or modern: *place, time,* and *class. Place,* of course, was even more a factor in ancient cultures than it is in modern. Because of the physical and logistical difficulties attendant upon any attempt to travel (see chapter 4), and because the ancients lacked the mass media—television, radio, movies, and the internet—that help to homogenize our culture and make it more instantaneous, a Roman citizen living in the city of Rome itself (for example) would inevitably have a different way of life—many different ways of life—than, say, those living in the province of Bithynia. *Time,* too, plays a crucial role: if Aristotle was right in defining time as the measure of *change,* then it should not be surprising that Roman life in Cicero's day was dramatically different from Roman life in the time of Hadrian. By *class* I mean the socioeconomic factors that divide and distinguish groups of people even when they coexist in the same place and time: poor Hispanics living in downtown Los Angeles have a life unimaginably different from that of the captains of industry whose mansions are only a few miles away in Beverly Hills. A similar class spectrum was in place, for example, in Rome of the first century B.C.E., and can probably be found in all times and places.

Modes of Categorization. With these facts in mind, the reader should consider that a label like "ancient Rome" is, inevitably, an oversimplification. There was no such thing as a monolithic classical Roman civilization. The human mind categorizes relentlessly, if only as a way of facilitating information storage and retrieval, and there are several ways of dividing up the mass of data available to us about Rome. One such is to speak in terms of the Republic and Empire, with the watershed coming at the regime established by Augustus Caesar, also known as the Principate; this, obviously, has been influential in my choice of title for the volume. (We might add yet another division, the "Tetrarchy," a collegiate system of governance instituted by Diocletian in 293 C.E.) But there are other possibilities as well: literary scholars may speak of the development of the Latin language and literature in terms of Old Latin, Latin of the Golden period, and Latin of the Silver period. Of these, the first would refer to the earliest period of Latin literary remains, say from about 450 to 100 B.C.E. The second would refer above all to the great efflorescence of literary production in the first century B.C.E., finding its zenith in the prose of Cicero and Caesar, and in the verse of Catullus, Horace, and Vergil. The third would refer to the literature of the Empire, beginning, say, with Ovid (if you don't like him) or after him (if you do). This approach, it should be clear to my reader, is in many ways unsatisfactory to me: it automatically devalues the literature of the Silver period, and, by association, the culture of that period as a whole. (In this, it may be somewhat indebted to the underlying principle of Edward Gibbon's *The History of the Decline and Fall of the Roman Empire* [1776–1788].) Yet, a third system of organization would be to draw a dividing line before or after the Emperor Theodosius, who made Christianity the official religion of the Roman state in 391 C.E. But we must begin somewhere; and we must find a way of sorting the data into categories of which we can somehow make sense. That is the spirit in which this book has been put together.

Topics. Each volume in the *World Eras* series is scheduled to have the same basic table of contents. This will ensure that the student who wishes to compare details of (say) marriage in a variety of cultures, can do so quickly and easily. It has also meant that the contributors to this volume have, to a certain extent, had their projects arranged for them in advance, and in ways that otherwise might not have occurred to them. But the overall result, I think, has conduced to a volume that is perspicuously structured and easy to consult.

Dates. It may be worth pointing out that dates B.C.E. ("before the common era") count *down*, while dates C.E. ("common era") count *up*. Thus, Cicero was born in 106 B.C.E., and died (63 years later) in 43 B.C.E. Also, centuries are numbered according to the highest year in them: thus, for example, the fourth century B.C.E. spans (counting down) from 400 to 301, while the second century C.E. spans (counting up) from 101 to 200.

Wealth of Material. Readers who want to know details of what life and culture were like in the Roman world between the third century B.C.E. and the fifth century C.E. will find a wealth of material here to reward them. Are you curious about the floor plan of a typical Roman house? Turn to chapter 7. Would you like to know about ancient Roman surgical practices? You will find information about them in chapter 10. Have you ever wondered about different types of Roman money? They are discussed in chapter 5. Do you know what an ancient Roman wedding was like? If not, you can find out in chapter 8. If you would like details on the way law courts were run, look in chapter 6. Chapter 3 describes the arts—verbal, visual, and performing—that have been so profoundly formative of western culture. And if you want to know what Jupiter is telling you when your chickens refuse to eat, check in chapter 9. Chapter 1 provides a summary overview, in chronological format, of major events occurring outside the Roman world during the period covered by the book, while chapter 2 offers a geographical overview of the entire region during this period. We have also added, at the end, a glossary of technical terms and of the Latin words used in the text.

Reference Systems. Classical texts are referred to by numbering systems that may at first seem esoteric and obscure. For the most part, they come either from the earliest printed editions (many of which were produced during the Renaissance) of the author in question, or from the most famous edition of that author. Because of the many scholarly hands that have been involved in this gigantic enterprise of publishing ancient texts in modern editions, the numbering systems are not identical from author to author, although they are usually decipherable once one looks at the actual printed Latin text. For example, a reference to "Livy 21.38" directs the reader to chapter 38 of book 21 of Livy's *Ab urbe condita*. "Lucan, *Civil War* 1.128" refers to line 128 of the first book of that epic. "Juvenal, *Satires* 6.292–5" refers to four lines in Juvenal's sixth *Satire*. Modern translations will usually (though not always) preserve these numbering systems in their printed editions as well, sometimes in the margins or at the head or foot of the page.

Christianity. A special word is perhaps in order about the interplay of Roman culture and the development of Christianity. This is most immediately apparent in the geographical situation of the Roman Catholic Church, which to this day maintains its epicenter, the Vatican City, as a tiny independent state within the city (or "commune," its technical designation) of Rome itself. But its historical ties with Rome go all the way back to the first century: early Christianity's most eloquent expositor, Paul of Tarsus, was born into Roman citizenship (rather than having purchased it), and he exploited that status to spectacular rhetorical effect toward the end of his life. The early emperors took a variety of approaches toward this upstart religion, ranging from bemused tolerance to virulent extirpation, until (beginning with Constantine) they actually began to embrace it themselves. As the era we think of as "antiquity" waned, and what we might call the Middle Ages began, western Europeans—of whose languages several had indeed evolved out of Latin—began to think about what sort of significance the great pagan authors of ancient Rome should hold for them: should they continue to read them at all? Should they handle them only with extreme suspicion? Should they somehow find a way to absorb them into a Christian worldview (and a Christian's library)? Here as well, we find an entire spectrum of responses, ranging from horrified rejection (as in the famous nightmare St. Jerome suffered in Lent of 375 C.E., in which he was accused before the heavenly tribunal of being, not a Christian, but a Ciceronian) to enthusiastic co-optation (e.g. the resolute mediaeval interpretation of Vergil's Fourth Eclogue, which was published around 39 or 38 B.C.E., as a prophecy of the birth of Christ). But in any case, certainly from St. Jerome onward we find Christian writers purposely classicized in their Latin prose style—that is, consciously modeled their vocabulary and syntax on classical pagan models—a practice that was to reach its zenith in the "Ciceronianism" of the Renaissance. In sheerly textual terms, classical antiquity has left its indelible mark on Christian writing.

Pronunciation. We do not know with absolute certainty how the ancient Romans pronounced their language. Moreover, what is certain is that [1] accents would certainly have varied by region, the more so as the Latin language spread around the Mediterranean basin, and [2] patterns of pronunciation appear to have changed, in some cases dramatically, over time. The best that can be done is to offer some recommendations about how Latin words should be pronounced. It should also be mentioned that the spellings found in modern editions of ancient Latin texts have been regularized, and this after centuries of recopying and reprinting; there was no single universal system of orthography in place in the ancient world, and inscriptions on stone that date from this period tell a more motley tale. With these caveats, the following tentative conjectures can be made regarding what might have been the pronunciation of Latin in Rome itself during the first century B.C.E. (Most of what can be known or surmised about this matter may be found in W. Sidney Allen's excellent *Vox Latina: A Guide to the Pronunciation of Classical Latin*, second edition [1989]).

Quantity. A Latin syllable may be "long" or "short," depending on the length of its vowel and/or on certain combinations of consonants. A syllable containing a long vowel or diphthong is long; a syllable containing a short vowel plus two consonants is also (with certain exceptions) counted as long. The quantity of a syllable is significant in determining the *accent* of a word.

Accent. Unlike ancient Greek, Latin appears not to have been a tonal language. Thus, the notion of "accent" has, in Latin, to do with *stressed* syllables. For ease of reference, grammarians refer to the last syllable of a Latin word as the *ultima*; the one preceding the ultima as the *penult* (< *paene ultima*, "almost the last"); and the one preceding the penult, the *antepenult* (< *ante*, "before"). In Latin, the principal stress of a word will fall either on the penult or the antepenult: on the penult, if it is long (see above on "Quantity"); otherwise on the antepenult. Thus, the feminine noun *cupido*, "desire," whose *i* is long, is accented on that syllable (the penult, i.e. *cupído*); the masculine dative singular of the adjective *cupidus*, however, which is also spelled *cupido*, has a short *i*, and would thus be accented on its first syllable (the antepenult, i.e. *cúpido*). Note that the quantity of the ultima, like the quantity of the antepenult, does not come into play here.

Vowels. When we speak of "long" and "short" vowels in Latin, we are speaking primarily of the actual length of time required to pronounce the vowel. However, this also inevitably affected the actual sound of the vowel in most cases. The following rough guide may be offered for pronunciation:

• A, when long, sounded like the *a* in English *father*; when short, more like a schwa sound (cf. the vowel in *cup*).

• E, when long, sounded like the vowel in French *blasé*; when short, more like the *e* in English *get*.

• I, when long, sounded something like the *i* in *prestige*; when short, like the vowel in *dip*.

• O, when long, was like the vowel sound in French *beau*; when short, like the *o* in English *off*.

• V (i.e. U, although the latter form is not found in writing of the classical period itself; handwriting and inscriptions of the first century B.C.E. used only capital letters, and for this sound, always the form V), when long, was like the vowel sound in *food*; when short, like that in *put*.

Semivowels. Latin, like English, sometimes uses the letters I and V (i.e. U) as glides or quasi consonants, comparable to our Y and W respectively.

Diphthongs. A "diphthong" is, essentially, a single syllable composed of two vowel sounds; in pronouncing a diphthong, one glides from the sound of the first vowel to the sound of the second. Here are some of the basic Latin diphthongs:

• AE was pronounced like the *i* in our *high*.

• AV (i.e. AU) was something like the vowel sound in our *how*.

• EI was apparently like the vowel sound in our *vein*.

• EV (i.e. EU) as the ancient Romans appear to have pronounced it is not a sound current in American English; it seems to have been a glide from the *e* of *get* to the *u* of *truth* (imagine Henry Higgins saying "Oh!").

• OE was comparable to the *oi* in *oil*.

• VI (i.e. UI), a rare combination, again has no American English counterpart; it seems to been a glide from the *u* (of French *tu*) to the *i* of *prestige*.

Consonants. The Latin B, C, D, F, G, K, L, M, N, P, Q, S, T, X, and Z were probably pronounced more or less as we would pronounce them (C and G being always hard, as in *cat* and *get*, and S being virtually always unvoiced). At the beginnings of words, C/K/Q, P, and T were probably less aspirated than comparable letters in English.

• It appears that B, before T or S, actually sounded something like our *p*.

• Somewhere in perhaps the fifth century C.E., the letter C (before I and E) became "softened"; this would be the origin of such later Romance pronunciations as French *cent*, Italian *cento*, and Spanish *ciento* (all from Latin *centum*, whose initial consonant would in the classical period have been hard).

• CH, PH, and TH, were aspirated voiceless plosives—i.e, not like the *ch*, *ph*, and *th* in *loch*, *phlox*, and *thin*, but the stop sound followed by an expulsion of breath, as in *cat*, *pot*, and *top*.

• In early inscriptions, we find C used before I and E; K used before consonants and A; and Q used before O and V (i.e. U). Latin QV is usually pronounced, by moderns, like *kw,* i.e. two successive consonants, or a consonant plus separate semivowel. This is probably under the influence of English words such as *quick.* However, it appears that the ancient Romans did not enunciate these two sounds separately; the *u* was probably very lightly pronounced, so that the sound of *qu* was not all that different from *c* or *k*—perhaps with the lips not opened as wide as for those other sounds.

• The combination GN, found in words like *Gnaeus,* seems to have been pronounced not with a hard *g* separated from the *n,* but more like the *ngn* in *hangnail.*

• H in Latin, as in English, represented the exhalation of breath before a vowel. In colloquial Latin, as in Cockney English, it appears that the sound was often lost, and (also as in English) the loss or retention of this sound may have provided some evidence of the speaker's social class. As a rule of thumb, the modern reader should pronounce the sound wherever the letter appears. A few exceptions: *ahenus* (bronze), *humerus* (shoulder), *humidus* (wet), and *humor* (moisture). In fact, it is preferable to spell these *aenus, umerus, umidus,* and *umor.*

• M at the end of a word seems to have been pronounced, not like our *m,* but as a kind of nasalization of the preceding vowel, which was then also typically lengthened. Thus *-am* is really just a nasalized (and typically lengthened) version of *-a.*

• R appears to have been pronounced toward the front of the mouth, and typically trilled as in Spanish or Italian.

Spelling. In this volume we have tried to maintain orthographic consistency throughout, although that has not always been possible, for either Greek or Latin. In the case of Latin, as I have mentioned, this is because the Romans themselves did not have a single official orthography. In the case of Greek, spelling is especially problematic, partly because there is no single universally adopted system of transliterating Greek, and because certain Greek words already have a familiar "look" in English. Eta and omega have been rendered, usually, as *ê* and *ô* respectively. As a rule we have used *k* and *kh* rather than *c* and *ch* to represent the Greek letters kappa and chi. The Greek double consonants GG and GK have usually been transliterated as such, although the reader should know that they were probably pronounced like the *ng* in *angle* and the *nk* in *ankle,* respectively; many scholars will actually transliterate them according to the latter convention. So too the combination gamma-chi, which was probably pronounced like the central cluster in *anchor,* will be represented by *gkh* rather than *nkh.* Some scholars will use *y* to represent upsilon, but where possible we have transliterated the latter as *u.*

Acknowledgments. I have been extremely fortunate to have the collaboration of a skilled and distinguished team of contributors, for whose excellent work I am most grateful. In addition, I would like to express my gratitude for the advice and assistance of Ward Briggs, Lisa and Scott Carson, Keith Dickson, Richard King, David Mirhady, Hans-Friedrich Mueller, Neil O'Sullivan, and Rex Wallace. Richard Layman and Anthony Scotti, of Manly, Inc., have lent their unfailing expertise and assistance; without them this book literally could not have come into existence. Robert Wright has, as always, been an inexhaustible fund of sapience and encouragement. I am especially grateful to my students over the past two decades—at Choate, at Chapel Hill, at Smith, and at Purdue—who, by their unfailing hunger and thirst for knowledge, have enabled me to keep my reading audience clearly in mind as this book came into focus. That audience, esteemed reader, now includes you: and whoever you may be, wherever you are, whenever this book shall come into your hands, I salute you, and invite you in to the captivating world of the ancient Romans.

John T. Kirby
Purdue University

ACKNOWLEDGMENTS

This book was produced by Manly, Inc. Karen L. Rood is senior editor and Anthony J. Scotti Jr. is series editor. James F. Tidd Jr. was the assistant in-house editor.

Production manager is Philip B. Dematteis.

Administrative support was provided by Ann M. Cheschi, Amber L. Coker, and Angi Pleasant.

Accountant is Ann-Marie Holland.

Copyediting supervisor is Sally R. Evans. The copyediting staff includes Phyllis A. Avant, Brenda Carol Blanton, Melissa D. Hinton, William Tobias Mathes, Rebecca Mayo, Nancy E. Smith, and Elizabeth Jo Ann Sumner.

Editorial associates are Andrew Choate and Michael S. Martin.

Database manager is José A. Juarez.

Layout and graphics supervisor is Janet E. Hill. The graphics staff includes Karla Corley Brown and Zoe R. Cook.

Office manager is Kathy Lawler Merlette.

Photography supervisor is Paul Talbot. Photography editor is Scott Nemzek.

Permissions editors are Ann-Marie Holland and Kathy Lawler Merlette.

Digital photographic copy work was performed by Joseph M. Bruccoli.

The SGML staff includes Frank Graham, Linda Dalton Mullinax, Jason Paddock, and Alex Snead.

Systems manager is Marie L. Parker.

Typesetting supervisor is Kathleen M. Flanagan. The typesetting staff includes Jaime All, Patricia Marie Flanagan, Mark J. McEwan, and Pamela D. Norton.

Walter W. Ross supervised library research. He was assisted by Steven Gross and the following librarians at the Thomas Cooper Library of the University of South Carolina: circulation department head Tucker Taylor; reference department head Virginia W. Weathers; Brette Barclay, Marilee Birchfield, Paul Cammarata, Gary Geer, Michael Macan, Tom Marcil, Rose Marshall, and Sharon Verba; interlibrary loan department head John Brunswick; and interlibrary loan staff Robert Arndt, Hayden Battle, Barry Bull, Jo Cottingham, Marna Hostetler, Marieum McClary, Erika Peake, and Nelson Rivera.

WORLD ERAS

VOLUME 3

ROMAN REPUBLIC AND EMPIRE
264 B.C.E. – 476 C.E.

Historical Overview:

Rome in the Earliest Period (753-264 B.C.E.)

by PATRICE D. RANKINE

Tiber River Valley. Scholars use the name *Rome* in both a specific and a more general sense—the latter, to refer to the larger civilization and polity encompassed by the entire Republic and Empire; the former, to refer to the specific confines of the city itself. The evidence for the earliest history of Rome (in this more specific sense) is mainly legendary with some archaeological support, since there are no literary accounts from this period. Archaeological evidence shows that at least three of Rome's seven hills, the Palatine, Esquiline, and Quirinal, were inhabited before 753 B.C.E. settlers took advantage of the Tiber valley. The river valley provided water and pasture for livestock, and the hills surrounding it were protective strongholds against invasion. Archaeological remains also reveal that during the seventh century B.C.E., the area that later became the Roman Forum formed burial sites that resembled those of Alba Longa, the civilization that in legend Aeneas's son, Ascanius, founds. Legend makes Rome a colony of Alba Longa, and settlers might have migrated to the city some time during the eighth century B.C.E.

Romulus and Remus. The founding of Rome itself, as a city and civilization, is again the stuff of legend and myth. Livy tells the story of how the eponymous ancestor Romulus, a descendant of Aeneas, the hero who fled Troy when it fell to the Greeks, slew his twin brother Remus on the city's site. The brothers had departed from Alba Longa when the population began to spill beyond the geographical limits of that city. Because they were twins and thus equal in birthright, they asked the gods which of them should rule the new city:

> For this purpose Romulus took the Palatine hill and Remus the Aventine as their respective stations from which to observe the auspices. Remus, the story goes, was the first to receive a sign—six vultures; and no sooner was this made known to the people than double the number of birds appeared to Romulus. The followers of each promptly saluted their master as king, one side basing its claim upon priority, the other upon number. Angry words ensued, followed all too soon by blows, and in the course of the affray Remus was killed (1.6).

Livy goes on to tell an alternate version of the story, in which Remus is killed for jumping over the newly built city walls.

Establishing Dominance. Livy recounts the various actions that Romulus took to ensure the safety and prosperity of his new city. He not only built protective walls around the city but also established a cult to Hercules (who was worshiped in Alba Longa) and later to Jupiter. He created the *patres,* a council of elders. The legend, moreover, accounts for the interaction of Romans with the various peoples that inhabited central Italy prior to their arrival. In one instance, Romulus and his men seduce the women of neighboring settlements; the women were invited to a harvest festival (the Consualia) and then raped. Without these women, the argument has it, how would the Roman men—colonists without women of their own—continue their lineage? The legend accounts for the settlers' dominance over groups that historically inhabited the region before them, such as the Sabines of the Esquiline hill.

Seven Kings. Romulus begins the legacy of the seven kings of Rome, which ends circa 509 B.C.E. with the expulsion of Tarquin the Arrogant (Tarquinius Superbus) for the rape of Lucretia, the wife of a prominent Roman citizen (Collatinus). The order of early Roman kings after Romulus is as follows: Numa Pompilius (715–673 B.C.E.), Tullus Hostilius (673–642 B.C.E.), Ancus Marcius (642–617 B.C.E.), Tarquinius Priscus (616–578 B.C.E.), Servius Tullius (578–535 B.C.E.), and Tarquinius Superbus (534–509 B.C.E.). Not all of the six kings subsequent to Romulus were of his bloodline. The Tarquins, noted for their excesses, were Etruscans, a people that lived to the north of Rome between the Arno and Tiber Rivers. It is to the Etruscans that Rome owes much of its later culture, including the religious practice of reading the future through an animal's liver (hepatoscopy), observing the flights of birds (augury), and perhaps some aspects of city planning and politics.

Historical Basis. Notable events during the regal period are a mix of legend and history. Legend attributes to Numa Pompilius the creation of a college of priests and a twelve-month calendar. Tullus Hostilius's founding of the Senate-house (the *Curia Hostilia*) and his capture of Alba Longa are likely to be historical facts. Also historical is the rule of Servius Tullius, whose treaty with the Latin League attests to the ongoing struggle between Rome and the *populi Latini,* the communities that inhabited (mainly) Latium.

Origins of the Republic. Rome's history from the sixth through third centuries B.C.E. is marked by a mixture of internal and external tensions that were never to be entirely resolved. Toward the end of the sixth century B.C.E. (circa 509 B.C.E.) Rome had established a Republic to rid itself of the excesses of monarchy. (Tarquin's rape of Lucretia was for the Roman emblematic of the vices of kingship.) Under the Republic, two officials (*consules*) elected (for a term of one year only) were to be the chief magistrates. The new government, however, did not guarantee domestic tranquility. In later years, the consulship itself would become a source of civil strife. (An infamous case from the first century B.C.E. is that of Lucius Sergius Catilina, who, because he was repeatedly unsuccessful at being elected consul, plotted to kill Marcus Tullius Cicero and seize the government.) In addition to this situation, there also arose an ongoing conflict that continued in some form until the government's demise, namely that between the two classes of citizens, the elite patricians (*patres*), or nobles, and the plebeians (*plebs,* a collective-singular noun), or the general body of Roman citizens.

Enemies. Outside of Rome, the stage was being set for military conflicts that would last for centuries. These conflicts would arise from a variety of sources. The *populi Latini* suffered a major defeat at the Battle of Lake Regillus in 496 B.C.E., but the league would not be dissolved until 340 B.C.E. Even after this, Rome would continue to fight the Samnites, the strongest of the Italians, well into the fourth century B.C.E. To the north lived the Cisalpine Gauls, who invaded and sacked Rome in 390 B.C.E. (The Romans would begin to construct new city walls in 378 B.C.E.) By the sixth century B.C.E. the Carthaginians of North Africa were making their presence felt, as is evidenced by their treaty with Rome in 508 B.C.E. They invaded Sicily in 409 B.C.E., destroying the Greek city of Himera, and they sacked Messana in 396 B.C.E. The return of the Carthaginians to Messana in 264 B.C.E. marks the beginning of the First Punic War (ending in 241 B.C.E.).

Greek Influence. Rome's contact with these various and diverse groups would culturally enrich the civilization throughout the centuries. The Greek influence on the Roman way is notable as to modern people as it was to the ancient Romans themselves, and it can be detected in many areas of life, from the arts and literature to religion and architecture. The Greek presence in Italy begins early on. Greeks began migrating to Sicily and southern Italy in the eighth century B.C.E. Today the region contains some of the most magnificent archaeological remains; during ancient times Sicily was actually known as *Magna Graecia*, Great Greece.

Literary Expression. The first Roman literature is Livius Andronicus's translation into Latin of a Greek epic poem, Homer's *Odyssey*. (The earliest performance of Andronicus's work of which modern scholars are aware—a comedy and a tragedy—took place at the Roman Games in 240 B.C.E.) The first works of Roman literature that survive as complete plays are the comic dramas of Plautus, adaptations from Greek New Comedy. Certainly the Latin language existed before these works. The oldest known Latin inscription is on a black stone (the *lapis niger*) discovered by archaeologists in the Roman Forum. It dates from a time (likely as far back as the rule of the kings) when the Latin language was coalescing from the various cultural influences in Italy, such as Oscan, Etruscan, and Greek. Nevertheless, Rome would have to wait until the third century B.C.E. for literary expression; when it arrived, it had a distinctly Greek flavor.

Sources:
Paul L. MacKendrick, *The Mute Stones Speak: The Story of Archaeology in Italy* (London: Methuen, 1960).

John F. Matthews, "Rome," in *The Oxford Classical Dictionary*, edited by Simon Hornblower and Antony Spawforth, third edition (Oxford: Oxford University Press, 1999), pp. 1322–1334.

Aubrey de Sélincourt, trans., *Livy, The Early History of Rome: Books I–V of The History of Rome from its Foundation* (Baltimore & Harmondsworth, U.K.: Penguin, 1960).

T. P. Wiseman, *Remus: A Roman Myth* (Cambridge & New York: Cambridge University Press, 1995).

WORLD EVENTS:
SELECTED OCCURRENCES OUTSIDE OF ROME

by PATRICE D. RANKINE

264–227 B.C.E.	• King Asoka of India sends embassies to the Hellenistic kings.
264 B.C.E.	• The First Punic War begins, pitting Carthage against Rome. The two powers fight for control of colonies on the island of Sicily.
262 B.C.E.	• Eumenes I of Pergamum defeats the Seleucid ruler Antiochus I (Soter) near Sardes.
	• Zeno, founder of the Stoic school of philosophy at Athens, dies. Zeno's philosophy was founded on the idea that the wise man lives in accordance with virtue. Cleanthes succeeds him as head of the Stoic school.
261 B.C.E.	• Antiochus II (Theos) succeeds Antiochus I as the Seleucid king.
260–253 B.C.E.	• Antiochus II regains much of the territories in Asia Minor lost by Antiochus I, during the Second Syrian War against Ptolemy II of Egypt. Pergamum remains independent.
256 B.C.E.	• The Chou dynasty in China ends. The Chou is the longest dynasty in Chinese history, lasting for 771 years.

*DENOTES CIRCA DATE

252-251 B.C.E.

- A citizen of Pontic Callatis (modern-day Mangalia, Romania) travels throughout the country to promote the Pythian games in Delphi, demonstrating the importance of Apollo's cult to the region.

252 B.C.E.

- Carthage and Rome forge a treaty that protects Italy from Carthaginian maritime trade.

251 B.C.E.

- Aratus of Sicyon adds Sicyon to the Achaean Confederacy. He is an aggressive general of the Confederacy and later adds such city-states as Megalapolis (235) and Argos (229).

250 B.C.E.

- Djenné-Jeno, a trading center on the Niger River, is established and flourishes until the eleventh century.

247 B.C.E.

- The Carthaginian naval commander Hamilcar Barca attacks the southern coast of Italy.

- Parthia emerges as an independent kingdom when Arsaces throws off the rule of the Seleucid dynasty. The Parthian (or Arsacid) dynasty eventually rules the area between the Euphrates and the Indus River valleys.

246-241 B.C.E.

- The Third Syrian War is fought between Ptolemy III (Euergetes) of Egypt and the Seleucid king Seleucus II, who had replaced Antiochus II.

244-241 B.C.E.

- Agis IV undertakes sweeping reforms in Sparta, returning to Lycurgus's constitution. He is killed by the Spartan elite after he attempts to cancel mortgage debts.

242-241 B.C.E.

- Arcesilaus, head of the Academy in Athens, dies. The Academy, the school of philosophy that Plato founded, became known for its skeptical doctrine under Arcesilaus.

*DENOTES CIRCA DATE

241 B.C.E.

- Attalus I succeeds Eumenes I of Pergamum. For refusing tribute to the Galatians, he is given the name Soter ("Savior"). Under Attalus, Pergamum becomes an important power and is pivotal to Roman politics in Greece and Asia Minor.

- Hamilcar Barca is defeated by the Romans at the Aegates Islands. The First Punic War ends.

240* B.C.E.

- Masinissa becomes the king of Numidia. He is attributed with transforming the nomadic people who inhabit this region into farmers.

239 B.C.E.

- Demetrius II becomes the Macedonian king. He soon involves Macedon in a protracted war with the Achaean and Aetolian Confederacies.

238 B.C.E.

- Diodotus I of Bactria gains independence for his region from the Seleucid dynasty.

237 B.C.E.

- Hamilcar Barca, accompanied by his ten-year-old son, Hannibal, conquers southern and eastern Spain. The new Punic outposts in the region challenge Roman hegemony.

235-222 B.C.E.

- Cleomenes III rules Sparta; he continues the reforms begun by Agis IV and threatens the Achaean Confederacy with military successes throughout Greece.

232 B.C.E.

- Chrysippus becomes the head of the Stoic school in Athens.
- Ashoka, the Buddhist monarch of the Maurya empire in India, dies.

229 B.C.E.

- Hamilcar Barca drowns during a campaign in Spain. Hasdrubal succeeds him, marries an Iberian princess, and advances across the Spanish frontier as far as the Ebro River (226).

*DENOTES CIRCA DATE

225* B.C.E.

- Ariston of Ceos becomes the head of the Peripatetic school in Athens.

223 B.C.E.

- Antiochus III (the Great) begins his rule over the Seleucid kingdom. He expands the dynasty to Armenia, and he regains Parthia and Bactria.

221 B.C.E.

- Philip V becomes king of Macedon. His vicious expansionist policies alienate many of his Greek neighbors.
- Hannibal takes command of Spain upon Hasdrubal's murder at the hands of a slave.
- The Ch'in dynasty takes complete control of China. Prince Cheng becomes Ch'in Shih-huang-ti, "the First Ch'in emperor."

219-217 B.C.E.

- Ptolemy IV checks the expansion of Antiochus III into Palestine and Egypt in the Fourth Syrian War. He is helped by native Egyptians, who later revolt against him.
- Hannibal seizes Saguntum, a Roman-allied city near present-day Valencia, Spain.

218 B.C.E.

- The Second Punic War begins. Hannibal sets out from Spain in his journey to Italy through Gaul and across the Alps.

216 B.C.E.

- Hannibal defeats the Roman army and cavalry at the Battle of Cannae in Apulia.

215 B.C.E.

- Philip V of Macedon forms an alliance with Hannibal.

214 B.C.E.

- The First Macedonian War begins with Philip V's attack on Messene.
- Construction of the Great Wall of China begins when smaller, pre-existing frontier walls are linked together and strengthened. The purpose of the wall is to keep out the Hsiung-nu, nomads from the north of China (Mongolia).

*DENOTES CIRCA DATE

211 B.C.E.

- Rome joins the Aetolian alliance against Philip V.

- Hannibal marches on Rome. He is later forced to withdraw from Italy through Bruttium as a result of several military defeats.

210 B.C.E.

- Ch'in Shih-huang-ti dies in China. The Ch'in dynasty comes to an end and a three-year revolt ensues.

209 B.C.E.

- Attalus I of Pergamum joins the Aetolian alliance against Philip V.

207 B.C.E.

- Hasdrubal, the younger brother of Hannibal, dies in battle at Metaurus after attempting to join Hannibal's army in northern Italy.

- The first Han dynasty begins in China when Liu Pang (Kao-tzu) becomes emperor.

205 B.C.E.

- The First Macedonian War concludes with the Peace of Phoenice.

- The five-year-old Ptolemy V (Epiphanes) becomes the ruler of Egypt after the death of his father. His reign, which lasts until 180, is marked by a period of revolts and political uncertainty, including the loss of territories throughout the Greek world and the Middle East.

- Croton, a Greek colony in southern Italy known for its culture and learning, falls to the Romans in the Punic War.

204 B.C.E.

- Zeno of Tarsus becomes the head of the Stoic school in Athens.

203 B.C.E.

- The Carthaginian camps at Utica in North Africa are attacked and burned by the Roman general Scipio Africanus.

- Syphax, the chief of a Numidian tribe and an ally of Carthage, is defeated at Campi Magni (Great Plains).

*DENOTES CIRCA DATE

202 B.C.E.

- Hannibal is defeated by Scipio Africanus at the Battle of Zama in North Africa.

202-198 B.C.E.

- Antiochus III annexes Palestine, formerly ruled by the Ptolemies. He fails later in his attempt to conquer Greece.

201 B.C.E.

- The Second Punic War ends. Carthage signs a treaty with Rome, surrendering its navy and its territories in Spain.

200* B.C.E.

- Volcanic islands in the South Pacific are settled by seafaring peoples emigrating from Southeast Asia.

- The Hopewell culture begins to emerge in central North America in what will become the states of Ohio and Illinois; this society is characterized by mound-building.

- The Bastarnae first appear near the lower Danube River; they serve in Philip V's military activities in the Balkans and later are both enemies and allies of Rome.

197 B.C.E.

- The Second Macedonian War between Philip V and Rome concludes with a Roman victory at Cynoscephalae.

196 B.C.E.

- Antiochus III invades Greece but is defeated by the Romans at Thermopylae (191) and Magnesia (189).

191 B.C.E.

- The Boii, a Gallic people living in Bononia between the Po River and the Apennine mountains, are dispossessed of their land by the Romans. They were previously allies of Hannibal.

190 B.C.E.

- The Artaxiad dynasty is established in Armenia under Artaxias (Artashes I).

188 B.C.E.

*Denotes Circa Date

- The peace of Apamea ends Antiochus III's war against the Romans in Greece.

185* B.C.E.

- The Sungas replace the Mauryas as the ruling empire in India. Pusyamitra becomes the first Sunga ruler and returns India from Buddhism to orthodox Hindu.

179 B.C.E.

- Perseus of Macedon succeeds Philip V and renews his father's treaty with Rome.

175 B.C.E.

- Antiochus IV (Epiphanes) becomes the Seleucid king. In addition to his influence in Judaea, he also sought to bring Egypt under Seleucid control.

171 B.C.E.

- The Third Macedonian War begins with Perseus's aggressiveness in Greece. His defeat at the battle of Pydna (168) further extends Roman power throughout Greece.

- Mithradates I begins his rule of Parthia, which will last until 168. Bearing the name of several Parthian kings to follow, he oversees a massive expansion of Parthian rule throughout modern-day Iran and into Babylonia.

167 B.C.E.

- Antiochus IV dedicates the Jewish temple in Jerusalem to the Olympian god Zeus. His attempts to Hellenize Israel cause the Maccabees, of the clan of Joarib and led by Judas Maccabaeus, to begin a revolt. The Pharisees emerge as a political faction.

165* B.C.E.

- The Yuë-Chi, driven out of China, arrive in Bactria. Their arrival forces the migration of the Sakas, a nomadic people in the south of Russia (also called Scyths), who in turn attack India and Iran.

164 B.C.E.

- The Maccabees reconsecrate the temple in Jerusalem. The event is from this date commemorated as Hanukkah.

- Antiochus IV dies.

162 B.C.E.

- The Greek Hipparchus records his first astronomical observation. The geographer, who was born in Bithynia, developed a theory for recording the motion and distances of the sun and moon.

*DENOTES CIRCA DATE

156 B.C.E.

- Han Ching-ti begins his rule of China, which lasts until 140. He quells a rebellion in the second year of his reign through land reforms.

155-130 B.C.E.

- Milinda (Menander) rules the Indo-Greeks. He penetrates into the Ganges Valley and upholds Buddhism against Hinduism in India.

153 B.C.E.

- Carthaginian forces invade Sicily, destroy Himera, and make an unsuccessful attack on Syracuse.

152 B.C.E.

- After the death of his brother Judas Maccabaeus, Jonathan is appointed high priest and then governor of Judaea.

149 B.C.E.

- The Third Punic War begins when Numidian ruler Masinissa, a Roman ally, provokes Carthage into war. Rome then declares war on Carthage.
- Andriscus, a pretender to the throne in Macedonia, invades the country with the help of the Thracians; he wins two victories but is captured and executed by the Romans the next year.

148 B.C.E.

- Micipsa begins his rule of Numidia after the death of his father, Masinissa. He maintains an alliance with the Romans.

146 B.C.E.

- The Fourth Macedonian War ends with the destruction of Corinth by the Romans; Macedonia becomes a Roman province.
- The Third Punic War ends. The Roman blockade of Carthage is lifted, the city is sacked, and the territory becomes a Roman province.

145 B.C.E.

- Aristarchus of Samothrace, an important literary critic most noted for his work on Homer, dies in Cyprus.

*DENOTES CIRCA DATE

141 B.C.E.

- A period of Jewish independence in Judaea begins. Simon Maccabaeus becomes high priest after the murder of his brother Jonathan.

- Han Wu-ti is emperor in China. He is an innovator in education, economics, and defense. He introduces a public granary to China and makes innovations to the cavalry.

140-130* B.C.E.

- The Qumran community is established in Palestine. They separate from the Maccabees and possess an apocalyptic, messianic faith, as demonstrated in the Dead Sea Scrolls.

139-129 B.C.E.

- Antiochus VII Sidetes of Syria conquers territory in Greece, Palestine, and Babylon.

137-136 B.C.E.

- The Greek skeptic Carneades steps down as head of the Academy in Athens.

134 B.C.E.

- John Hyrcanus I of the Maccabees, Simon's son, begins his rule of Judaea. He is an intense rival to Hellenism and expands Jewish rule to the territories of Samaria, Galilee, and Idumaea.

129 B.C.E.

- The death of Antiochus VII marks the end of Seleucid power in the eastern region. The Parthians are left as the major power east of Babylon.

- Rhodian Greek philosopher Panaetius becomes the head of the Stoic school of philosophy, succeeding Diogenes and Antipater of Tarsus. As an admirer of Plato and Aristotle, Panaetius makes Stoicism more accommodating to the Academy and the Peripatetic doctrine.

- The Yuë-chi, a group that the Huns expelled from the borders of China, migrate south, levying tribute from Bactria.

118 B.C.E.

- The Roman colony of Narbo Martius (modern-day Narbonne) is established in Gaul; it becomes an important obstacle to Celtic trade routes and passageways into Spain.

- Adherbal begins his rule of Numidia but is deposed by Jugurtha in 112.

*Denotes Circa Date

112 B.C.E.

- Jugurtha is embroiled in war with the Romans. He is defeated by Quintus Metellus, imprisoned, and executed (105).

110-109 B.C.E.

- Philon of Larissa becomes the head of the New Academy at Athens. He succeeds Clitomachus the Carthaginian.

106 B.C.E.

- Hiempsal begins his rule of Numidia.

103 B.C.E.

- Alexander Jannaeus, John Hyrcanus I's brother, becomes king of Israel. He might have been the first to strike national coins, and he extends Jewish rule from Mount Carmel to Egypt.

102 B.C.E.

- The Germanic Teutones suffer defeat at the hands of the Roman general Gaius Marius.

100* B.C.E.

- The Syrian poet Meleager is active. He is known for his Menippean satires, Cynic discourses, and epigrams, of which only the latter survive.
- The Belgae, a Gallic people, arrive in Britain.
- The city of Teotihaucán, twenty-five miles from modern Mexico City, emerges as a major commercial center; it is the home of the Pyramid of the Moon and Pyramid of the Sun, the latter being the largest building in pre-Columbian America.

96 B.C.E.

- Alexander Jannaeus defeats Aretas II of the Nabataeans, who was making incursions along the Gaza Strip.

95 B.C.E.

- Tigranes I (the Great) becomes king of Armenia.

*DENOTES CIRCA DATE

88 B.C.E.

- A series of three wars (88–85, 83–82, and 76–64) between Mithridates VI Eupator (the Great) of Parthia and Roman forces begins. Mithridates represents one of the strongest challenges to Roman power during this period.

83 B.C.E.

- Quintus Sertorius becomes the governor of Spain. Between 77 and 73 he leads a faction of the Lusitanians against the Roman generals Gnaeus Pompeius Magnus (Pompey) and Caecilius Metellus Numidicus (Metellus). Sertorius also seeks an alliance with the Parthians.

- Tigranes I of Armenia occupies Syria, Phoenicia, and Cilicia.

80* B.C.E.

- Invaders from Central Asia begin to spread throughout the Indus River valley. Chinese silk increasingly becomes a major luxury import to wealthy provinces such as Roman Egypt.

79-78 B.C.E.

- The Greek philosopher Antiochus heads the Academy in Athens. He transforms it from the skepticism of its former proponents, emphasizing the uniting principles of the Stoics, Peripatetics, and the Academy.

76-69 B.C.E.

- Jannaeus's widow, Alexandra Salome, rules Palestine. Her sons John Hyrcanus II and Aristobulus II become rivals after her death.

73 B.C.E.

- Sertorius is killed by Marcus Perperna Veiento; Perperna is later executed when Pompey refuses to accept any terms of compromise.

66 B.C.E.

- The defeat of Mithridates VI Eupator Dionysus marks the decline of many territories in Asia Minor and the rise of Roman rule in those regions. Mithridates commits suicide in 63.

- The Allobroges revolt against Roman control in northern Gaul; the rebellion is crushed in 61.

- Aretas III of the Nabataeans, supporter of John Hyrcanus II, besieges Jerusalem. Roman intervention, under Marcus Aemilius Scaurus, forces him to withdraw.

*DENOTES CIRCA DATE

63 B.C.E.

- Pompey intervenes in Jerusalem. John Hyrcanus II becomes high priest of Judaea, Samaria, Galilee, and Peraea.

61 B.C.E.

- In the Pontic city of Histria, a coalition of Greek and indigenous tribes, such as the Bastarnae and the Getae, defeat the Roman proconsul Gaius Antonius Hybrida.

60–30* B.C.E.

- Diodorus Siculus writes *Bibliothêkê*, forty books of world history that draw upon many lost works.

60 B.C.E.

- Burebistas unites the Dacian social groups and conquers some of the Illyrian people along the Danube River; he begins religious reforms in Dacia under the priest Cecaeneos.
- Juba I becomes king of Numidia.

58 B.C.E.

- The various ethnic groups of Gaul enter a war with Gaius Julius Caesar; the Helvetii, a Celtic tribe in the south of Germany, are pushed out of the region. Suebi king Ariovistus loses power in the area.

57 B.C.E.

- The coalition of the Gallic Belgae succumbs to Caesar.

56 B.C.E.

- Artavazd II, son of Tigranes I, becomes king of Armenia.

55 B.C.E.

- Britain faces a Roman invasion under Caesar.

54 B.C.E.

- A second invasion of Britain under Caesar occurs.

* DENOTES CIRCA DATE

53 B.C.E.

- The Surenas, a Parthian family, defeat the Roman general Marcus Licinius Crassus at the Battle of Carrhae (modern Haran). Crassus and his son, Publius, are killed in the battle.

52 B.C.E.

- Vercingetorix, king of the Arverni, leads a revolt of the Gauls against the Romans; he is defeated at Alesia, modern Alise-Ste Reine.

51 B.C.E.

- Uxellodunum becomes the last town in Gaul to succumb to Caesar. The Roman wars against Gaul end.

51-50 B.C.E.

- The Greek Stoic philosopher Posidonius, who worked in geometry and ethics, dies.

50 B.C.E.

- Burebistas the Dacian exterminates the Boii, a Gallic people, in Bohemia.

49 B.C.E.

- Bogud, who shared the kingdom of Mauretania with his brother Bocchus II, becomes active in Roman politics; he aids Caesar in his struggles against Pompey and later is an opponent of Octavian and ally to Antony.
- Massalia (present-day Marseilles, France) submits to Caesar only after a prolonged, five-month siege.

48 B.C.E.

- Antipater, adviser to John Hyrcanus II, provides mercenary troops to Caesar in Alexandria.

47 B.C.E.

- Ariobarzanes III Eusebes Philoromaios of Cappadocia receives Lesser Armenia from Caesar.

46 B.C.E.

- Numidia becomes the Roman province of Africa Nova.

*DENOTES CIRCA DATE

44 B.C.E.

- Burebistas of Dacia is assassinated; his empire is divided into several kingdoms.

43 B.C.E.

- Antipater is murdered.

42 B.C.E.

- A faction of Geto-Dacians fight in a losing cause with Decimus Junius Brutus at the Battle of Philippi.

40 B.C.E.

- Antigones, son of Aristobulus II, establishes a reign in Jerusalem with Parthian support. John Hyrcanus II is held in exile in Babylonia. Herod (later, the Great), son of Antipater, escapes to Rome.

- Andronicus of Rhodes, a Peripatetic philosopher and later head of the school at Athens, writes an important treatise on Aristotle.

37-34 B.C.E.

- Herod the Great, with Roman support, rules Judaea. Herod promotes the spread of Hellenism throughout the province, which spawns opposition among his subjects, particularly the Pharisees.

35* B.C.E.

- A system of writing is introduced in Guatemala in Central America.

34 B.C.E.

- Artavasdes III, king of Armenia, is deposed and killed by Antony and Cleopatra; Armenia falls under Roman control.

31 B.C.E.

- Bogud dies at Methone in battle against the Roman general Marcus Vipsanius Agrippa.

29-28 B.C.E.

- Dobruja, a city in the Balkans, falls to Crassus; the Bastarnae are brought under Roman control.

*DENOTES CIRCA DATE

27 B.C.E.

- The Four Gauls are established under Roman rule: Gallia Belgica, Gallia Lugdunensis, Aquitania, and Gallia Narbonensis.

25 B.C.E.

- Galatia, the region south of Pontus, becomes a Roman province.
- The geographer Strabo conducts research in Egypt; he later wrote *Geôgraphia*, a world geography in seventeen books.

20 B.C.E.

- Parthia reaches a settlement with Rome and recognizes Roman power over Armenia; Archelaus of Cappadocia becomes ruler of Armenia.

16–13 B.C.E.

- The provinces of Spain and Gaul are reorganized under the Roman emperor Augustus. The emperor subdivides Hispania Ulterior into Baetica (Andalusia) and Lusitania.

15 B.C.E.

- The peoples of the Alps are conquered under the rule of Augustus.

12 B.C.E.

- The Sugambri in Gaul attack the Roman army but are later defeated by the general Nero Claudius Drusus Germanicus.

9 B.C.E.

- The area in central Europe extending as far as the Rhine and Danube Rivers falls under Roman control. The Danube becomes part of the Roman province of Illyricum.

8 B.C.E.

- The Sugambri in Gaul surrender to the Roman general Tiberius.

6 C.E.

- Judaea becomes a Roman province, spawning revolts of Jewish nationalist groups such as the Zealots.
- Pamphlagonia becomes part of Galatia.

*DENOTES CIRCA DATE

7-9 C.E. • Revolts in Pannonia and Illyricum busy the Roman legions in those provinces.

9 C.E. • Under the leadership of Arminius, the Cherusci revolt against the Romans in Germany and annihilate three legions in the Teutoburger Wald; Publius Quinctilius Varus, Roman governor in the region, commits suicide on the battlefield.

9-23 C.E. • Wang Mang rules in China. As with his predecessors, the issues that affect his reign are economic (the resistance of wealthy landowners that leads to famine) and military (continued struggles against the Hsiung-nu in the north).

14 C.E. • Dobruja becomes the Roman province of Moesia.

24 C.E. • The second Han dynasty rules in China for nearly two hundred years. The Hans relied more on the support of wealthy families than previous Chinese dynasties.

26 C.E. • Moesia revolts against Roman rule; the rebellion is put down by the Roman governor of the region, Gaius Poppaeus Sabinus.

30-33* C.E. • The crucifixion of the Jewish religious leader Jesus of Nazareth occurs.

31* C.E. • The monument of Tres Zapotes marks the advent of the calendar and the alphabet for the Olmec civilization in Central America.

35 C.E. • Seleuceia, on the Tigris River, revolts against the Parthian empire. It takes seven years to put down the rebellion.

* DENOTES CIRCA DATE

36 C.E.
- The Surenas crown Tiridates king of Parthia.

38 C.E.
- Cotys, the grandson of Polemo I of Pontus, receives Armenia from the Roman emperor Gaius Caesar (Caligula).

39–40 C.E.
- Philon (Philo Judaeus) is part of a delegation to Rome from the Jewish community in Alexandria. Philo wrote *Legatio ad Gaium* and *In Flaccum*, treatises that would influence both Christianity and Neoplatonism.

41–42 C.E.
- Mauretania is brought under submission to Roman rule by Gaius Suetonius Paulinus.

43 C.E.
- Cunobelinus dies. Suetonius refers to him as "king of the British Isles" because he defied Roman law to form a coalition of the Belgae. Upon Cunobelinus's death the Roman emperor Claudius invades Britain.

45* C.E.
- St. Paul begins his missionary work to bring Christianity to non-Jewish communities throughout Europe.

45–50* C.E.
- Plutarch, the ancient biographer who writes *Parallel Lives*, comparing the morality of various leaders such as Alcibiades and Marcus Antonius, is born.

46 C.E.
- Thrace becomes a Roman province after its ruler, Rhoemetalces, is murdered by his wife.

50 C.E.
- The Ubii, a German tribe, begin to be called the Agrippinenses at the request of Claudius's wife, Agrippina.

*DENOTES CIRCA DATE

58 C.E. • Jewish leaders accuse St. Paul of blasphemy upon his return to Jerusalem. His trial begins.

60-61 C.E. • Boudicca, queen of East Anglia, leads an unsuccessful revolt of the Iceni in Britain against the Romans.

64 C.E. • St. Paul is executed in Rome. The persecution of members of the Christian sect under the Roman Empire begins. In the same year Nero blames the Christians for a fire in Rome.

66 C.E. • An open rebellion, the First Jewish Revolt, begins in Jerusalem against the Romans.

• Tiridates I becomes king of the Armenians. (Nero crowns him in Rome.) The Arsacid dynasty begins in Armenia.

69 C.E. • Natives besiege the German town of Colonia Ulpia Traiana (Xanten); Mainz also revolts.

70 C.E. • Jerusalem is captured by Vespasian, who destroys the Jewish temple.

73 C.E. • Masada, a fort built on a plateau west of the Dead Sea a few centuries earlier by the Maccabees, falls after a six-month Roman siege, resulting in the mass suicide of its defenders. This event ends the First Jewish Revolt.

75-79* C.E. • Flavius Josephus, a Jewish priest, Pharisee, and government official, writes a history of the Maccabean revolt, *Bellum judaicum* (Jewish War).

*DENOTES CIRCA DATE

78 C.E.

- As governor of Britain, the Roman general Gnaeus Iulius Agricola advances into Scotland.

- The Saka era begins in India. Many scholars favor this date for the beginning of the reign of Kaniska, the Buddhist king responsible for having protected the Kushans from Chinese sovereignty.

83-85 C.E.

- The Chatti of Germany are at war with Rome.

85-86 C.E.

- Decebalus leads successful attacks against Roman forces. It takes the emperor Domitian four years to make peace and recognize Decebalus as a client king.

- Moesia is split into two Roman provinces, Moesia Superior and Inferior.

87 C.E.

- Decebalus becomes king of the Dacians and initiates a war against the Romans.

88-89 C.E.

- Lucius Antonius Saturninus leads an unsuccessful revolt at Moguntiacum; the governor of Lower Germany, Aulus Bucius Lappius Maximus, defeats him along the Rhine River.

- The Stoic philosopher Epictetus arrives at Nicopolis after the expulsion of philosophers from Rome.

93-94 C.E.

- Josephus writes *Antiquitates judaicae* (The Antiquities of the Jews), a history of the Jews that begins with the creation of the world.

100* C.E.

- An anonymous Greek merchant in Alexandria writes the *Periplus Maris Erythraei*, which provides the oldest documented account of trade and civilization on the east coast of Africa.

- Traders from Indonesia sail along the coast of Africa, possibly leaving settlers on Madagascar.

- The Funan, a Hindu people that first emerge in Southeast Asia, occupy the Mekong Delta region of present-day Vietnam, as well as portions of Cambodia and Thailand. They trade with both India and China.

- The Anasazi people begin to develop their culture in the deserts of southwest North America. They make baskets, grow corn, and build adobe structures.

*Denotes Circa Date

100 C.E.

- The city of Thamugadi (modern Timgad) is founded in Numidia by the Roman emperor Trajan; it later becomes a center of the African church.

101-102 C.E.

- The First Dacian War is fought. Decebalus faces campaigns against his reign from the Roman emperor Trajan; he temporarily surrenders.

105 C.E.

- The Second Dacian War begins; Decebalus beseiges Roman troops that Trajan left behind in Dacia.

106 C.E.

- Defeat leads to Decebalus's suicide; Dacia becomes a Roman province.
- The land of the Nabataeans in northern Saudi Arabia falls under Trajan's control, becoming the Roman province of Arabia.
- The city of Bostra becomes the capital of the Roman province of Arabia under the emperor Trajan.

108-110 C.E.

- Ulpia Traiana is founded in Dacia; formerly a Roman military camp, a city of veterans grows after Decebalus's suicide.

110 C.E.

- Licchavi rulers, whose people come out of the Ganges River area, establish a kingdom in Nepal.

113-114 C.E.

- Armenia falls under Roman control; earlier, the Parthian king Osroes dethroned the Roman client ruler, Axidares, prompting Trajan's attack on the region.

115 C.E.

- Ctesiphon, the Parthian capital near the Tigris River, falls to Trajan.
- The Jews revolt in Cyrene, Egypt, Cyprus, and the Levant.

*DENOTES CIRCA DATE

116 C.E.
- Southern Mesopotamia revolts against the Roman Empire; the region is subdued by the following year.

118-119 C.E.
- Dacia becomes two Roman provinces, Dacia Superior and Inferior, under the emperor Hadrian.

122-126 C.E.
- Hadrian's Wall, which runs from Wallsend-on-Tyne to Bowness-on-Solway, is built in Britain; it marks the limits of the Roman frontier in the region.

124 C.E.
- Dacia is further divided by Hadrian; the region now represents three Roman provinces.

127-148* C.E.
- The geographer Claudius Ptolemaeus (Ptolemy) rejects the theory, held after the time of Herodotus, that the inhabited world is surrounded by Ocean.

129 C.E.
- The Greek physician Galen is born in Pergamum. Of his many accomplishments, including the proof that veins and arteries carry blood, he is noted for his humanistic (and philosophical) approach to medicine and for his contributions to scientific thinking.

132 C.E.
- Shim'on Bar Cosiba (Bar Kohkba) leads the Second Jewish Revolt against Rome. He is killed in the siege of Jerusalem in 135.

134 C.E.
- Greek politician and historian Flavius Arrianus (Arrian), a student of Epictetus in the Stoic doctrine, defends Cappadocia from the Alans, a Sarmatian people living on the southwestern border of Russia along the Caspian Sea.

138 C.E.
- Evidence of the presence of Moors (or Muslims) appears in Dacia; they occupy the city of Racari.

* DENOTES CIRCA DATE

142 C.E.
- Under the emperor Antoninus Pius, a Roman wall is erected from the Forth to the Clyde in Britain; the attempt to extend the Roman frontier on the island fails by the end of the century.

145-150 C.E.
- Numidian and Mauretanian revolts against Roman rule are put down. Uprisings also occur in Judaea and Egypt.

150* C.E.
- Pausanias, the Greek geographer, writes the *Periêgêsis tês Hellados*, a history and topography of various cities throughout Greece.

150-200* C.E.
- The Goths migrate to the region north of the Black Sea; previous migrations brought them from southern Scandinavia to the area around the Vistula River.

154 C.E.
- A rebellion of the Brigantes and Selgovae results in the first withdrawal of Roman troops from Scotland.

155 C.E.
- Greek theologian St. Justin Martyr, born at Flavia Neapolis in Samaria, writes the first of two *apologiai* (defenses) of the Christian faith.

160 C.E.
- The Costoboci, a social group from northern Transylvania, invade Dacia; they later penetrate into Greece.

162 C.E.
- The Parthian capture of Armenia prompts Roman action.

164-165 C.E.
- Armenia again falls under Roman control after a brief revolt.

*DENOTES CIRCA DATE

165 C.E.

- Smyrna becomes the site of the murder of many Christians; some of the victims, such as St. Polycarp, the bishop of Smyrna, are burned alive.

- St. Justin Martyr is killed at Rome.

165-166 C.E.

- Seleuceia is destroyed by Gaius Avidius Cassius of Rome. The fall of the city ends a major commercial center in Babylonia; Mesopotamia becomes a Roman protectorate.

166 C.E.

- German social groups (such as the Quadi and the Marcomanni) create a disturbance across the Danube River. They later enter into northern Italy.

- Chinese annals record an envoy from Rome during the year. Huan-ti rules China.

168 C.E.

- Dacia is further partitioned and placed in the care of one Roman governor.

170 C.E.

- Flavius Philostratus, author of *Bioi sophistôn* (Lives of the Sophists), which comments on the celebrities of the Second Sophistic movement, is born.

170-174 C.E.

- The Macromanni and Quadi war with Rome; the Danube region is resettled with Roman supporters.

175 C.E.

- The Iazgians, Sarmatian nomads in the Danube region, are temporarily quelled by Marcus Aurelius.

177 C.E.

- Forty-eight Christians are martyred at Lyon including a slave woman named Blandina, who is tortured and given over to wild beasts; they are all later canonized.

- The Macromanni begin a revolt in Dacia.

*DENOTES CIRCA DATE

179* C.E.

- Celsus, a Greek and a Platonist, writes *Alêthês Logos* (The True Word), an attack on the Christian doctrine.

180 C.E.

- Further German revolts in the region of Pannonia are quelled by the Roman emperor Commodus upon Marcus Aurelius's death.
- Tribes in Scotland continue their efforts against Roman occupation and penetrate a frontier-wall in the region.
- The Catechetical School is established in Alexandria. Such noted Christian scholars as Clement and Origen serve as heads of the school.

184 C.E.

- The Romans are forced to cede the frontier in Scotland. The Roman frontier in Britain now extends only to Hadrian's Wall.
- The rebellion of the Yellow Turbans begins against the Han dynasty in China. The peasant revolt is quelled within six years by Ts'ao Ts'ao.

193 C.E.

- The seige of Byzantium begins, lasting about two years. The city supported general Pescennius Niger's revolt against the Roman ruler Septimius Severus.

195 C.E.

- Byzantium and other regions that sided with Niger are punished.
- Syria is divided into two Roman provinces (Coele and Phoenice) because of the civil war.

197 C.E.

- Britain is divided into two Roman provinces.
- The Parthian city of Ctesiphon falls to Septimius Severus.
- The Carthaginian Christian Quintus Septimius Florens Tertullianus (Tertullian) writes his first works, *Ad Martyres* (To the Martyrs), *Ad Nationes* (To the Nations), and *Apologeticus* (Defense). These books are the first Christian writings in Latin; they advance important doctrines of the church, such as the idea of the Trinity.

199 C.E.

- Osroene and Mesopotamia are annexed to the Roman Empire.

*DENOTES CIRCA DATE

200* C.E.

- The Saxons become a more dominant presence along the Elbe River, subduing the Chauci, who formerly inhabited the region.

202 C.E.

- The Athenian scholar and theologian Titus Flavius Clemens (Clement of Alexandria) steps down as head of the Catechetical School of Alexandria; his work includes the *Protreptikos pros Hellênas* (Hortatory Address to the Greeks) and other Christian writings.

203 C.E.

- Origenes Adamantius (Origen) becomes the head of the Catechetical School. The Alexandrian Christian is noted, among other works, for *Contra Celsum* (Against Celsus, circa 248).

204 C.E.

- A Moorish temple is built on the restored Roman site in the Pontic city of Micia.

208-211 C.E.

- Fortifications along Hadrian's Wall in Britain are improved under the Roman emperor Septimius Severus; the Caledonians defend Scotland from Roman attacks.

212 C.E.

- The decree of universal citizenship for all of the Roman world under Caracalla has widespread repercussions for Christians and for other social groups opposed to Roman rule throughout Europe.

213 C.E.

- The Macromanni are involved in a campaign against Caracalla; the emperor offers them money to keep out of Upper Germany.

221 C.E.

- After the fall of the second Han dynasty one year earlier, the period of the Three Kingdoms begins in China. The Wei rule in the north, the Wu in the southeast, and the Shu in the west.

*Denotes Circa Date

224 C.E.

- The Sassanian (Persian) king Artaxerxes (Ardashir) defeats and kills Artabanus V of Parthia at Hormizdagan and enters Ctesiphon.

226 C.E.

- The Sassanians overthrow the Parthian dynasty in Iran. The Parthian empire had covered a great expanse, extending during one period from Iberia (east of the Black Sea) to the Persian Gulf.

230-232 C.E.

- Artaxerxes (Ardashir) engages in an indecisive campaign in Mesopotamia against the Roman emperor Severus Alexander.

233 C.E.

- The Macromanni return to Upper Germany, prompting military action from Alexander.

235 C.E.

- Continuing unrest in Germany results in the murder of the Roman emperor and his mother by the legions on the Rhine River.
- The Thracian peasant and soldier Gaius Julius Maximinus wins a victory in Württemberg after being appointed emperor by his troops some months earlier.

238 C.E.

- Artaxerxes (Ardashir) invades Mesopotamia a second time; he takes the cities of Carrhae and Nisibis.

243-247 C.E.

- The Carpi, a social group in Dacia, raid the Pontic city of Racari.

248 C.E.

- The Goths invade the Balkan city of Moesia and murder the Roman emperor Gaius Messius Quintus Decius (251); they later sack Nicaea and Nicomedia and raid the Ionian cities.

250* C.E.

- The Mayan classical period begins in Mexico and Central America; the dedication of monuments for astrology and mathematics distinguishes this era.

*Denotes Circa Date

252 C.E.

- Sapor I, the Sassanian king, gains control of Armenia and brings the Arsacid dynasty to an end.

254 C.E.

- Barbarian attacks in Upper Germany result in the withdrawal of many Roman troops.

257 C.E.

- The Franks, a coalition of Germanic tribes, invade Lower Germany.

258 C.E.

- The Alamanni of Germany invade Italy; they are defeated by Publius Licinius Egnatius Gallienus, Publius Licinius Valerianus's (Valerian) son, at Milan.
- Bishop Cyprian (Thascius Caecilius Cyprianus) is executed in Carthage during a period of persecution of Christians. He wrote letters on the trials of the early Christian community.

259 C.E.

- Gaul, Germany, Britain, and Spain form a coalition separate from the Roman Empire; Marcus Cassianius Latinius Postumus becomes the independent ruler of the Gallic Empire.

260 C.E.

- Septimius Odaenathus of Palmyra defeats Sapor I after the latter captures the Roman emperor Valerian at Edessa.

262 C.E.

- Franks make incursions into Spain, destroying the city of Tarraco.

263 C.E.

- The Sarmatians of the northern Caspian Sea burn the walls of the Pontic city of Callatis.

265 C.E.

- The Western Chin dynasty, founded by Ssu-ma Yen, begins in China.

*Denotes Circa Date

267 C.E.

- The Heruli, a Germanic people from Scandinavia, sack Athens, Corinth, and Argos; Odaenathus dies of uncertain causes while opposing the invaders.

269 C.E.

- The Goths are defeated by Claudius II in decisive battles at Naissus (in Dacia) and Doberus.
- Septimia Zenobia, widow and perhaps murderer of her husband, Odaenathus, conquers Egypt; during this period she also captures Syria, Bostra, and much of Asia Minor.
- Postumus is killed by his own soldiers.

270 C.E.

- Plotinus, the Neoplationist philosopher from Egypt, dies.

271 C.E.

- Dacia is abandoned by the Roman Empire under the rule of emperor Lucius Domitius Aurelianus (Aurelian); the population shifts to a new province south of the Danube River.
- Zenobia of Palmyra names her son Augustus, inviting open opposition from Aurelian; she is defeated and captured along with her sons.

273 C.E.

- Palmyra revolts; Antiochus, the leader of the rebellion, is unseated by the Roman emperor Aurelian.

274 C.E.

- The Battle of Châlons is fought in Gaul; Aurelian defeats the locally appointed emperor, Gaius Pius Esuvius Tetricus, ending the brief, independent Gallic Empire.

275 C.E.

- The Alamanni, Franks, Vandals, and Burgundians sack Trier (Augusta Treverorum) in Germany.
- Aurelian is killed in the city of Caenophrurium near the Black Sea.

*DENOTES CIRCA DATE

277-279 C.E.

- Efforts are made under the Roman emperor Marcus Aurelius Probus to keep raiding bands out of Germany; the Alamanni, Franks, Burgundians, and others are repelled from the Rhine frontier.

280 C.E.

- The Bastarnae are removed from the Balkans to Thrace by Probus.
- The activity of Saxon pirates in Britain leads to the building of additional forts along the coasts.

286 C.E.

- The Bacaudae, a social group in Gaul, are broken up by Marcus Aurelius Valerius Maximianus (Maximian), one of the Caesars under Diocletian.

287 C.E.

- Marcus Aurelius Mausaeus Carausius, a former Roman admiral, takes Britain and northern Gaul and declares himself emperor.

288-289 C.E.

- The Alamanni in Germany occupy the Roman emperor Gaius Aurelius Valerius Diocletianus (Diocletian).

290 C.E.

- Tiridates III ascends to the throne in Armenia under Roman patronage.

293 C.E.

- Bononia (Boulogne) is blockaded by Caesar Constantius; Carausius is expelled and later assassinated.

294-295 C.E.

- The disturbance in Britain prompts the resettlement of Franks and other Germanic groups in Gaul.

*DENOTES CIRCA DATE

296 C.E.

- Britain, in revolt since Carausius established a British Empire, is reconquered by Caesar Constantius.

- Social groups in Mauretania, including the Quinquegentanei, attempt a revolt from Roman rule; Maximian is sent to check it.

- Egypt revolts under Domitius Domitianus and Aurelius Achilleus.

297 C.E.

- The Egyptian revolt is put down by Diocletian at Alexandria.

298 C.E.

- The Alamanni fall to Constantius at Langres; along with the recapture of Britain, a new period of Roman control in the central European provinces begins.

- Mesopotamia, Armenia, and Iberia (of the Black Sea) are further reduced to the Roman dependents.

301* C.E.

- Christianity becomes the state religion of Armenia, making it the oldest Christian civilization.

303-305 C.E.

- North Africa suffers great losses under the Roman persecution of the Christians.

306 C.E.

- Crocus, king of the Alamanni, convinces the Roman troops in Britain to appoint Flavius Valerius Constantinius (Constantine the Great) as emperor.

308-310 C.E.

- The Franks, Alamanni, and Bructeri suffer defeat along the Rhine River at the hands of Constantine the Great; the Frankish kings Ascarius and Merogaisus are imprisoned in Trier.

311 C.E.

- The Chinese city of Loyang is sacked by Hsiung-nu and the Tartars.

*DENOTES CIRCA DATE

311–383 C.E.

- Ulfilas the Visigoth is responsible for the conversion of many of his people to Christianity; he creates the Moeso-Gothic alphabet and translates the Bible into Gothic language.

313 C.E.

- The Edict of Toleration of Christian Worship is passed in Trier, Germany.

313–316 C.E.

- Constantine frequently visits Germany and Gaul, and Trier gains prominence as the capital of Rhineland.

- The Donatist sect develops in Africa after Caecilian's election as bishop is challenged; the opponents appoint Donatus of Casae Nigrae as rival. A council led by Constantine decides for Caecilian, but the puritanist sect gains momentum.

314 C.E.

- Eusebius becomes bishop of Caesarea. He writes what is probably the first ecclesiastical history of Christianity.

316 C.E.

- The Chinese city of Ch'ang-an falls, and the last Western Chin emperor is imprisoned.

317 C.E.

- The Eastern Chin dynasty begins in China. The rule will eventually succumb to ongoing attacks from the north.

320* C.E.

- King Ezana takes the Axum throne in present-day Ethiopia. He will expand the borders of his kingdom into the Sudan; Christianity is introduced into the region at this time.

320 C.E.

- Candra Gupta I rules in India. He controlled the center of the country by the time of his death, establishing a power base from the Ganges to the coast of Bengal.

- St. Pachomius establishes the first cenobitic community in Egypt.

*Denotes Circa Date

321 C.E. • The construction of the Christian cathedral in Trier begins.

324 C.E. • Byzantium becomes the foundation site of Constantinople, the Roman capital on the Danubian frontier.

325 C.E. • The Council of Nicaea meets to formulate an orthodox Christian doctrine. Known as the Nicaean Creed, the statement of faith directly opposes Arianism, a doctrine that refutes the divinity of Christ and the idea of the Trinity.

332 C.E. • The Goths suffer defeat at the hands of Constantine on the Danube River.

335 C.E. • Samudra Gupta begins his rule in India. He expanded the Indian empire southward and annexes the kingdoms of the rulers in the north.

340-360* C.E. • A mass migration of non-Roman peoples into Dacia occurs.

350 C.E. • Meroe, an ancient city on the upper Nile, is destroyed by Aksumite armies under Ella-Amida.

354 C.E. • Aurelius Augustinus (St. Augustine) is born; he becomes one of the most important authors of the early Catholic Church. His works include *Confessions* (circa 400), *De doctrina christiana* (On the Christian Doctrine, 397–428), *De trinitate* (On the Trinity, 400–416), and *De civitate Dei* (On the City of God, 413–426).

355 C.E. • The Salian Franks gain Toxandria after falling to Flavius Claudius Julianus (Julian the Apostate); both the Alamanni and the Franks cross the Rhine River into Roman territory.

*DENOTES CIRCA DATE

357 C.E.

- The Battle of Strasbourg ends in the defeat of the Alamanni at the hands of Julian.

360 C.E.

- The Franks force a confrontation with Julian near Xanten.
- The Scots take action against Roman rule in Britain.

363 C.E.

- The Persians kill Julian on his way through Armenia.

368 C.E.

- The Roman emperor Valentinian I attacks the Alamanni and consolidates the Rhine frontier.

370 C.E.

- The Huns expel the Ostrogoths from Ukraine. The Ostrogoths are a division of the Goths, who earlier migrated from Scandinavia to the region south of the Vistula River.

376 C.E.

- The Huns expel the Visigoths from the lower Danube.
- Candra Gupta II rules in India. Further expansion in India is made possible by his defeat of the Sakas.

378 C.E.

- The Battle of Adrianople is fought. Under the leadership of Fritigern, the Visigoths cross the Danube River and defeat the emperor Valens.

382 C.E.

- The Visigoths gain a treaty from the Roman emperor Theodosius the Great, who rules in the east; they are recognized as federates of the Romans and are granted land in Thrace.

*DENOTES CIRCA DATE

383 C.E.

- Gaul is occupied by the Spanish general Magnus Maximus, one of the claimants to the Roman Empire.
- The Eastern Chin dynasty defeats a force of foreign invaders at Fei Shui.

386 C.E.

- Persia signs a treaty with the Roman emperor Theodosius the Great; the two kingdoms agree to divide Armenia, previously an area of much contention for the Romans.

387 C.E.

- The Sassanians partition the remainder of Armenia between Parthia and Byzantium.

390 C.E.

- The oracle-site at Delphi is declared a pagan shrine and is officially closed by Theodosius.

395-397 C.E.

- The Visigoths, led by Alaric, defend their territories in Greece against the attacks of the Roman general Flavius Stilicho, who is emperor of the Western Empire.

400* C.E.

- The first settlers, sailing from the Polynesian islands, arrive in Hawaii.
- Pelagius, the British Christian writer, is active during this period. He spends some years in Rome, but the political unrest there leads him to Africa and Palestine; Pelagius's exhortation to Demetrias is called the first British literature.
- The Olmec civilization in Central America ends.

402 C.E.

- Alaric is defeated at Pollentia (Polenza) and the next year at Verona.

405 C.E.

- Radagaisus, leader of the Ostrogoths, invades Italy; the Ostrogoths suffer defeat at the hands of Stilicho.

*DENOTES CIRCA DATE

406-407 C.E.

- The Germanic Vandals occupy the Rhine region after the Huns drive them westward; the nomadic Alans of Russia are also driven to Gaul by the Huns. This expulsion marks the end of Roman rule in Gaul.

409 C.E.

- The Vandals occupy Spain; they join with the Alans.

410 C.E.

- Britain is abandoned by the Roman Empire. The Saxons and other Germanic peoples become more prevalent; Celtic culture also spreads.
- The Visigoths sack Rome after attacking Greek cities; Alaric, the leader of the group, dies in the same year.

414 C.E.

- Kumara Gupta I begins his rule in India. The long-standing peace of the Gupta empire begins to crumble at the end of his reign (455) with the arrival of the Huns.

418 C.E.

- The Visigoths settle in Gaul and Spain, establishing a capital at Toulouse.

420 C.E.

- Eusebius Hieronymus (St. Jerome) dies. His important writings include a chronicle of classical times, a work titled *De viris illustribus* (Concerning Illustrious Men, 392–393), and the *Vulgate*, the Latin translation of the Christian Bible.

421-422 C.E.

- The Persians are defeated in battle by Theodosius II.

422 C.E.

- The Huns begin to exact tribute from the Romans; 350 pounds of gold are given each year, and the amount will later increase.

*Denotes Circa Date

425 C.E.

- The Salian Franks leave Toxandria; the Rhineland Franks cross into Gaul. Within the century, the Roman hold on Gaul will end.
- A university is founded in Constantinople for the teaching of Greek and Latin grammar, rhetoric, philosophy, and law.

428 C.E.

- Gunderic, the ruler of the Vandals, dies; the Asding Vandals and the Alans leave Spain for Africa.
- Artaxias IV, the last Arsacid king in Armenia, is deposed.

429 C.E.

- Gaiseric, king of the Asding Vandals and the Alans, arrives in Africa with eighty thousand of his people.

430 C.E.

- St. Augustine dies.

439 C.E.

- Gaiseric occupies Carthage and denounces Roman rule there.

441-443 C.E.

- Attila leads the Huns against the Eastern Roman Empire; they destroy such cities as Naissus in Moesia.

445 C.E.

- Attila murders his brother Bleda; he is now the sole ruler of the Huns.

447 C.E.

- The Huns, led by Attila, are active in the Balkans and Greece.

*DENOTES CIRCA DATE

451 C.E.

- The Huns are defeated in Gaul by a Roman force, along with the Visigoths, at the Catalaunian plains.

- The Council of Chalcedon establishes the doctrine of diophysitism, the idea that Christ is both human and divine; the council declares any other doctrine heresy.

- The Persians defeat the Armenians at the Battle of Avarayr. The Zoroastrian faith replaces Christianity as the official religion in this region.

452 C.E.

- Attila the Hun invades Italy; he dies in the following year.

454-495*
C.E.

- The Gupta dynasty in India is temporarily restored after the Hun invasion; Skanda Gupta's reign is followed by that of Budha Gupta. His power is curtailed by the rise of subject kings throughout India.

455 C.E.

- The Ostrogoths escape from the rule of the Huns in the Ukraine.

475 C.E.

- Euric of the Visigoths declares an independent kingdom separate from Rome.

476 C.E.

- Odoacer the German deposes Romulus Augustulus in Rome; the Ostrogoths soon establish an empire in Italy. Gaiseric, the king of the Vandals and the Alans, who had captured Rome eleven years earlier, dies the following year.

*DENOTES CIRCA DATE

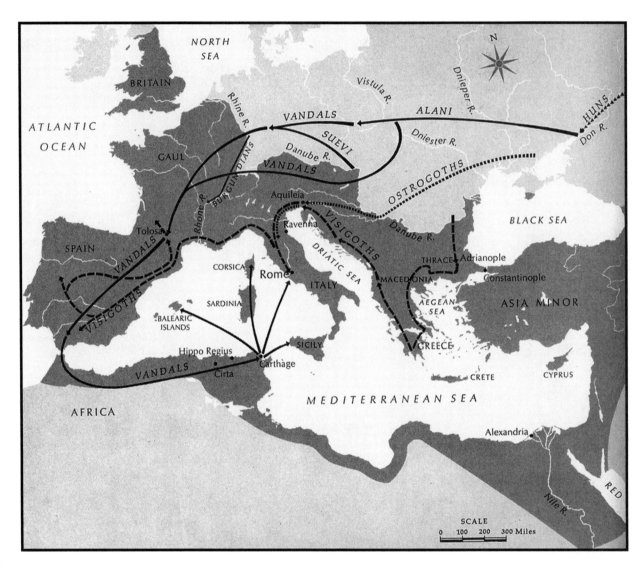

Map of barbarian invasion routes during the fourth and fifth centuries C.E. (from Moses Hadas, *Imperial Rome*, 1965)

GEOGRAPHY

by PATRICE D. RANKINE

CONTENTS

Sidebars and tables are listed in italics.

260* B.C.E.

- The Roman Republic encompasses most of the Italian peninsula.

- Carthage occupies Messana, beginning the series of conflicts against Rome known as the Punic Wars. The Punic Wars bring Romans into increasing contact with North Africa, Spain, and France.

219 B.C.E.

- The Carthaginian general Hannibal captures the Roman-allied city of Saguntum in Spain.

206 B.C.E.

- Rome takes control of Spain during the Second Punic War, defeating the Carthaginian general Hasdrubal.

194 B.C.E.

- Eratosthenes of Cyrene, the librarian at Alexandria, dies. Author of *Peri tês anameirêseôs tês gês* ("On the Measurements of the Earth"), he is the founder of mathematical geography.

168 B.C.E.

- Crates of Mallos visits Rome; the explorer holds the notion that the inhabited world is divided into four sections and that such mythical peoples as the *Perioikoi*, the *Antipodes*, and the *Antoikoi* inhabit the three regions outside of the known fourth.

150* B.C.E.

- Hipparchus of Nicaea revises Eratosthenes' geographical work and develops theories for determining the distance of the Sun and the Moon from Earth.

150 B.C.E.

- Cisalpine Gaul falls under Roman control; the region becomes a wealthy Roman settlement.

146* B.C.E.

- According to Strabo, Eudoxus of Cyzicus is the first Greek trader to use the monsoons to sail to India.

* Denotes Circa Date

100* B.C.E.

- Posidonius of Rhodes makes further advances in mathematical geography; he introduces the idea of the tropics, locations on the globe where the sun once again turns toward the equator.

52 B.C.E.

- Julius Caesar composes *Bellum gallicum,* commentaries on his wars in Gaul and Britain; the work contains geographical and ethnographical information on these regions.

36* B.C.E.

- Agrippa, the chief general of Augustus, writes *Descriptio orbis* and draws a map of the world.

31 B.C.E.

- The Roman Republic now includes Italy, Spain, Gaul, Narbonensis, Cisalpine Gaul, Illyricum, Macedonia, Achaea, Bithynia, Pontus, Phrygia, Pisidia, Cilicia, Syria, parts of North Africa, and various Mediterranean islands.

14 C.E.

- Augustus composes the *Res gestae Divi Augusti* ("The Deeds of Divine Augustus"); the work celebrates the Roman conquest of various regions, including Astures, Rhaetia, Noricum, Pannonia, Moesia, Galatia, Palestine, and Egypt.

21* C.E.

- Strabo composes his *Geôgraphia* in seventeen books; the work is an abundant source of information on earlier geographical advances.

37–41 C.E.

- Pomponius Mela composes *De chorographia* sometime during the reign of the Emperor Gaius. Aside from introducing information on present-day Sweden, he is the only geographical writer of the classical period to compose in Latin.

48 C.E.

- The Emperor Claudius's speech to the senate recorded in Tacitus's *Annales* emphasizes the impact of foreign peoples on the Roman world.

*DENOTES CIRCA DATE

50* C.E.

- The *Periplous maris erythraei* ("Exploration of the Red Sea") is composed; this work, written in Greek, records the peoples and places along a trade route from Roman Egypt to India.

79 C.E.

- Pliny the Elder (Gaius Plinius Secundus) dies of smoke inhalation while researching the eruption of the volcano Vesuvius. His work *Historia naturalis* contains three books on geography that includes information on the Danube River and the interior of Africa.

98 C.E.

- The Roman historian Tacitus composes the *Agricola* and the *Germania*, ethnographical works on Britain and Germany, respectively.

117 C.E.

- With the death of the emperor Trajan, the Roman Empire is at its biggest size; the boundaries are Britain in the North, Egypt in the South, Armenia in the East, and Spain in the West. Major provinces include Cyrenaica, Numidia, Mauretania, Lusitania, Hibernia, Aquitania, Germania, Rhaetia, Pannonia, Dalmatia, Dacia, Cappadocia, Mesopotamia, and Arabia Petraea.

121 C.E.

- The emperor Hadrian visits the German frontier and authorizes the erection of timber walls along certain sections in order to thwart barbarian raids.

122 C.E.

- Hadrian orders the construction of a frontier wall known as Hadrian's Wall in northern Britain. By 126, it stretches from present-day Wallsend-on-Tyne to Bowness-on-Solway (seventy-three miles). Made of stone and turf, its average height is 13.5 feet and its width varies from 10 feet to 19.5 feet.

139 C.E.

- The northern Roman frontier is advanced to Scotland. Construction begins on the Antonine Wall, just north of Hadrian's Wall. When it is completed in 142, it stretches thirty-seven miles between present-day Bridgeness-on-the-Forth to Old Kilpatrick-on-the-Clyde. Unlike Hadrian's Wall, the Antonine Wall is built entirely of turf.

*DENOTES CIRCA DATE

150* C.E.

- Ptolemy (Claudius Ptolemaeus) composes a geographical work in eight books, replete with maps of the inhabited world; he rejects the notion that the known world of Europe, Africa, and Asia is surrounded only by Ocean.

184 C.E.

- The Romans are forced out of Scotland; Hadrian's Wall once again marks the Roman frontier in Britain.

271 C.E.

- The Roman Emperor Aurelian (Lucius Domitius Aurelianus) abandons Dacia (present-day Transylvania), moving its population to a new location south of the Danube River.

406–407 C.E.

- The Vandals occupy Gaul, ending Roman rule in that province.

410 C.E.

- Britain is officially abandoned by the Roman Empire.

* DENOTES CIRCA DATE

The bronze liver of Piacenza, a representation of a sheep's liver with a cosmological map, from the third century B.C.E. (Museo Civico, Piacenza)

OVERVIEW

Spread of Roman Power. Throughout the period beginning in the third century B.C.E. and ending with the fall of the Roman Empire in the West, increase in geographical and topographical knowledge was interchangeable with the spread of Roman power and wealth. Beginning with the Italian peninsula, information about mountain ranges and rivers was one of the most important resources that the Roman general could have. For this reason Caesar's *Bellum gallicum,* written in 46 B.C.E., is much more than a military document. It provides useful geographical, topographical, and ethnographical information about Gaul and its various peoples.

Expanding Knowledge. As their power and resources increased, Roman rulers discovered more about the *orbis terrarum,* the "circle of lands [around the Mediterranean Sea]," which was the inhabited world as they knew it. The westernmost boundary of the inhabited world was Spain, which fell under Roman jurisdiction in 206 B.C.E., after Scipio Africanus's defeat of Hasdrubal and the Carthaginians. The Romans never quite knew exactly how far south the inhabited world extended, although by the second century C.E. they were aware of the vast southern expansion of Africa, particularly along the eastern coast. Wealthy Romans in Egypt profited from the traders that set out from Guardafui (in Somalia) and Dar es Salaam (in Tanzania) during the summers and returned from India at wintertime. About the African interior little was known. Writing in the first century C.E., Pliny mentions a river in Africa called Nigris, which might be the first mention in antiquity of the Niger River, cutting across Nigeria, Niger, and Mali.

Limitations. By the first and second century C.E., geographers knew all they would of the northernmost borders of the inhabited world during the classical period. Pomponius Mela and Ptolemy (Claudius Ptolemaeus) both reported a landmass to the north inhabited by the Suiones; the area is certainly modern-day Sweden. Misinformation, however, persisted. Pliny reported that the Caspian Sea opened into the Northern Ocean and that a journey could be made northward into India exclusively by sea. Ptolemy's refutation of such a notion almost a century later would restore Herodotus's skepticism about the Homeric Ocean surrounding the continents of Europe, Asia, and Africa. Toward the east, Rome would know of China mainly through the trade of silk through India.

TOPICS IN GEOGRAPHY

ANCIENT GEOGRAPHY: QUESTIONS AND ISSUES

Flat or Globular? From the time of the fourth-century philosopher Anaximander, the ancients held to the belief that the earth was a globe. Until the work of Ptolemy in the second century C.E., most writers also believed that the inhabited world was a vast island surrounded by Ocean. The idea was not completely rejected until the time of Ptolemy, who speculated that there must be unknown lands beyond Asia. In the second century B.C.E. Crates of Mallos had already advanced the idea, though with incredible arguments, that the inhabited world of Europe, North Africa, and Asia was not the only inhabitable place on the globe. As Crates's theory had it, the globe could be divided into four regions, of which only one was known by actual exploration, the one that contained the continents of Europe, Asia, and Africa. Although Crates placed unbelievable, mythical people in the remaining three quadrants (which damages his credibility), theories such as his encouraged specula-

tion about the possibility of unexplored places and mythical peoples. So, in the ancient mind the inhabited world constituted only a portion of the globe. The only hindrances to exploring the unknown regions were climate, distance, and resources.

Maps. Owing to the advent of mathematical geography with the writings of Eratosthenes, the mapping of the inhabited world became more precise during this period. Astrological observations led to the innovation of mapping distances through solar and lunar measurements, and although it would take centuries to perfect the tools of land measurement, maps were more precise, or at least useable, because of the advances of mathematical geography. Better maps meant greater knowledge of the inhabited world, and the result of this knowledge was the increased power of the Roman Empire.

Early Geographic Study. Eratosthenes, the third-century B.C.E. geographer, wrote a seminal thesis on geography in three books, which includes the title *Peri tês*

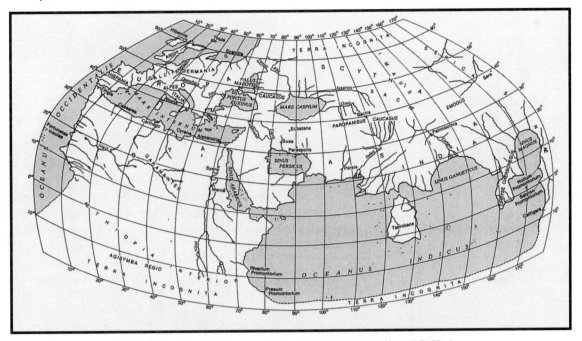

A map of the world as Claudius Ptolemy saw it in 150 C.E. (from J. B. Harley and David Woodward, eds., *The History of Cartography*, volume I, 1987)

anameirêseôs tês gês ("On the Measurements of the Earth"), a work that, although subsequent authors regarded it as pivotal, unfortunately survives through citations of it in other works. Eratosthenes seems to have distinguished between the world of the epic poet Homer, where the fabrication of mythical places limited geographical knowledge, and the *periplous,* a physical exploration of distant places. For Eratosthenes, geography as a study begins with Scylax, whom Darius I sent to explore the Indus River valley (in modern-day Pakistan) at the close of the sixth century B.C.E. Strabo, writing three centuries later, would reject Eratosthenes' thesis in this regard, establishing Homer as the founder of geographical inquiry. Whatever the case, Eratosthenes was an innovator in the study of geography. He pioneered the field of mathematical geography through the use of sundials and land measures, and he estimated the circumference of the earth with these tools. More precisely, Eratosthenes measured the summer solstice at two different geographical points (Syene, present-day Aswan in Egypt, and Alexandria). In this way he was able to determine the degree of latitude between these locations and others. His measurements were based on one central parallel from the Pillars of Heracles (Gibraltar) to India.

The Inhabited World. Like many of his predecessors (with the exception of Herodotus in the fifth century B.C.E.), Eratosthenes conceived of the *oikoumenê gê,* the "inhabited world," as a large island mass surrounded by water called Ocean. He drafted the earth in this way, and the notion was not corrected until the second century C.E. with the research of the geographer Ptolemy. Strabo ultimately faulted Eratosthenes for incorrect measurements. As one example, Eratosthenes apparently elongated the latitude of the inhabited world and underestimated its longitude, shrinking Africa and Northern Europe. He based his measurements on the Greek *stadion* (somewhere between 175 and 200 meters in length); accuracy would depend on the interpretation of a unit of measure.

Ethnography. In addition to his work on the physical proportions and mathematical measurements of lands Eratosthenes also tackles the subject of ethnography in his history of geography. Despite criticizing him for faulty measurements, Strabo does praise Eratosthenes for not indulging in unfounded assertions regarding distant places and people, a vice that he attributes to many other geographers.

Accurate Observation. Another geographical writer whose works survive only in fragments is Hipparchus of Nicaea. Hipparchus's revisions of earlier speculations depended upon the development of more accurate

---

STOICISM AND GEOGRAPHY

Many of the Hellenistic geographers were somehow connected to Stoic philosophy. Eratosthenes was trained by Ariston of Chios, a student of the founder of the philosophical sect of Stoicism, Zeno. Posidonius studied under the noted Stoic philosopher Panaetius, and Strabo, perhaps under Posidonius's sway, converted to the Stoic school of philosophy. The Stoics (named after the *Stoa Poikilê,* a public hall in Athens where Zeno taught) held the doctrine that the *sophos* (Greek) or *sapiens* (Latin), the "wise man," could be virtuous by living in accordance with *phusis* (Greek) or *natura* (Latin), "nature." Originating in the political unrest in Greece that followed Alexander's death in 323 B.C.E., the Stoic doctrine in its first manifestations turned its adherents away from social concerns and toward *aretê* (Greek) or *virtus* (Latin), "virtue," which they argued could be found within the individual and is paralleled in the order of the cosmos. Living in accordance with nature promotes an understanding both of one's own nature, or character, and of nature itself, the physical world that transcends political circumstances. Geography is one of the many academic disciplines that the Stoic ideal of turning inward—and away from politics—encourages.

Stoicism was an important doctrine of the time because, unlike Scepticism or Cynicism, it held that truth could be found in nature, uncorrupted by political circumstances. As a result of this many Stoic philosophers were students of history, astrology, and geography. They believed that these disciplines led to a deeper understanding of nature. In *De vita beata,* Seneca (Lucius Annaeus Seneca), the Roman Stoic that served in Nero's court, writes, "let reason search into external things at the instigation of the senses, and, while it derives from them its first knowledge—for it has no other base from which it may operate, or begin its assault upon truth—yet let it fall back upon itself. For God also, the all-embracing world and the ruler of the universe, reaches forth into outward things, yet, withdrawing from all sides, returns into himself."

Ironically, Stoicism later became a system of involvement with politics, as did the discipline of geography. As the Roman Empire increasingly came to dominate the inhabited world, the order of the cosmos extolled by Stoics became tantamount to the Roman order. In one essay Seneca compared the Roman emperor to the god that is both the world (*mundus*) and the ruler of it. Like this god, the Roman emperor ruled a world that was a microcosm of the universe. Through the study of history, astrology, and geography (among other disciplines), this universe could be known, and the ruler could himself be wise.

Source: Seneca, *On the Happy Life,* in *Moral Essays,* volume 2, translated by John W. Basore (Cambridge, Mass.: Harvard University Press, 1996).

astrological observation, including methods for determining the distance of the sun and the moon (and the variable of motion). Inspired by Eratosthenes' measurement of distances, Hipparchus conceived a map of the world derived from a complete system of parallels and meridians.

Strabo's Critique. Despite Hipparchus's innovations, Strabo was quick to criticize his reliance on formulas rather than actual land-measures and travel. Strabo summarizes the differences between Eratosthenes and Hipparchus in the following way:

> "Now my reply to Hipparchus will be that, although Eratosthenes takes his straight lines only roughly, as is proper to do in geography, and roughly, too, his meridians and his lines to the equinoctial east, Hipparchus puts him to a geographical test—just as if every one of these lines had been taken with the aid of instruments. Neither does Hipparchus himself take everything by the aid of instruments, but it is rather by conjecture that he takes the relations of both 'perpendicular' and 'parallels'"

(2.39, translated by Horace Leonard Jones). He becomes the target of another of Strabo's biases (which were many), namely his bias for factual evidence, but Hipparchus does make important theoretical innovations in the measurement of the inhabited world through astronomy and geometry.

Tropics. Posidonius of Rhodes, an influential political, philosophical, and geographical thinker, developed a method of measuring the inhabited world based on the height of Canopus (a star in the constellation of Argo) from two distinct points. He introduced the idea of the tropics to the study of mathematical geography. Technically speaking, the tropics are the points at which the sun once again faces (or "turns to," hence "tropic" from the Greek *tropos*, meaning "turning") the equator after reaching its greatest distance from it. Posidonius expounded upon the reason for the excessive heat in these regions (namely, their disposition toward the sun). The climate in the tropics, he claimed, would affect the ethnography of the region and its culture. With these ideas Posidonius ushered in the final innovations in geographical studies until the first and second century C.E., when the study of geography fell almost entirely under Roman auspices (even though the authors were often not Roman). The dawn of the Roman Empire would validate the claim of Polybius (made around 150 B.C.E.) that Rome had come to dominate the entire inhabited world.

Geôgraphia. Strabo of Amaseia, the most important single ancient source on geographical matters, wrote his *Geôgraphia*, a seventeen-book treatise, in the early part of the first century C.E. The *Geôgraphia* is divided into seventeen books. The first four books are an overview of the study of geography, including a refutation of Eratosthenes on Homer's role as the founder of the study of geography, a discussion of Eratosthenes' and Posidonius's contributions to mathematical geography, and cartography. The remainder of *Geôgraphia* surveys the inhabited world, beginning with Spain and Sicily in book 3 and ending with North Africa.

Politics of Geography. Strabo shows an interest in the many uses of geography, particularly in its political use. He claims that commanders of armies and rulers "can manage their various affairs in a more satisfactory manner, if they know how large a country is, how it lies, and what are its peculiarities either of sky or soil" (1.1.16, translated by Horace Leonard Jones). He gives the particular example of Rome's recent victory over the Parthians: "But leaving antiquity, I believe that the modern campaign of the Romans against the Parthians is a sufficient proof of what I say, and likewise that against the Germans and the Celts, for in the latter case the barbarians carried on a guerilla warfare in swamps, in pathless forests, and in deserts; and they made the ignorant Romans believe to be far away what was really near at hand, and kept them in ignorance of the roads and of the facilities for procuring provisions and other necessities" (1.1.17, translated by Horace Leonard Jones). From this one sees that geographical knowledge serves a political function; the holder of such knowledge rules with a view toward safety.

New Horizons. Pomponius Mela wrote a work, *De chorographia*, in three books, probably sometime after 43 C.E. He does give details that are not discussed in Strabo's work, such as information on the northeastern coast of Germany beyond the Elbe River. He refers to a large bay north of Germany, beyond which are many islands. The unknown bay would be the Baltic Sea, and the islands to which Mela refers are those of Scandinavia (Codannovia).

Gaius Plinius Secundus. One of the most endlessly engaging sources, not only for matters geographic but also for information on the ancient world in general, is the *Naturalis historia* of Gaius Plinius Secundus (Pliny the Elder), an encyclopaedic compendium that aimed at nothing less than assembling all human knowledge. The political turbulence under Nero curtailed Pliny's public career, evidenced in his diminished military activity, and he spent several years in *otium* (seclusion and absence from politics) from 59 C.E. (the year Nero murdered his mother, Agrippina). Many public figures met their demise during this period, often for writing literature that suggested political dissidence. (The poet Patronius, for example, was forced to commit suicide in 65 C.E. for a satire of Roman life that seems to implicate the Emperor.) In hindsight, Pliny was wise to have chosen an innocuous pursuit during Nero's years: the study of grammar.

Compilation. Pliny emerged again after Nero's death and the Civil War of 69 C.E., becoming governor of Gallia Narbonesis in 70, Africa in 72, Hispania Tarraconensis in 73, and Gallia Belgica in 75. After this period he wrote *Naturalis historia*, which he dedicated to the emperor Titus. The geographical portion of the work spans books 3–6. Surprisingly, despite Pliny's wide travels, in his geographical writing he is unoriginal, a compiler of previous knowledge and not an innovator.

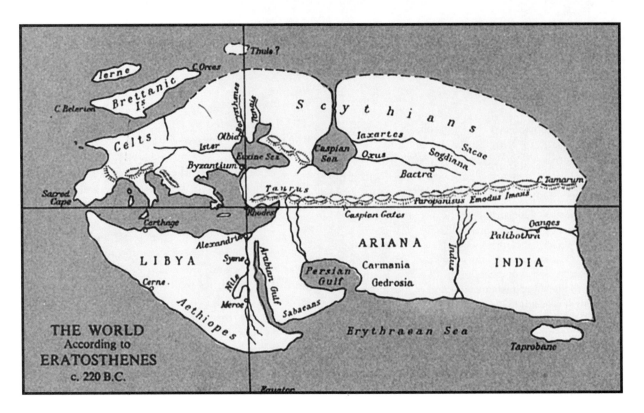

An ancient geographer's interpretation of the world. The "inhabited world" is an island—including Europe, Asia, and Africa—surrounded by Ocean (from O. A. W. Dilke, *Greek and Roman Maps*, 1985).

(Pliny's approach perhaps reveals an ongoing trait of Latin literature, namely the anxiety of rivaling a Greek domain, and this trait is seen in the field of philosophy through such authors as Lucretius and Cicero.) He cites Marcus Agrippa, for example, in his discussion of Spain, but he does not advance knowledge in this area.

Geographical Advances. Despite Pliny's amateur approach, however, some geographical advances are evident in his work. Pliny knows the Danube River, which flows through Austria and southern Germany, and he reports more on the Baltic Sea and Scandinavia (areas about which Mela made mention). He mentions a river in Africa that he names Nigris. The river is possibly the Niger, flowing from the Southern Atlantic Ocean into Nigeria, Niger, and Mali. Pliny's work appears to be the first extant mention of the river or of the region. He speaks about India with a greater degree of clarity than previous writers, and he discusses an overland trade route from India to the Black Sea.

Ptolemy. Another important source for ancient geography is Claudius Ptolemaeus, known to us as Ptolemy. He wrote on astronomical and astrological topics and produced a *Geôgraphikê huphêgêsis* ("Guide to Geography") in eight books, in which he attempted to cover the entire world as it was known at that time. Much of this work consists of lists of place-names and topographical descriptions.

Further Regions. Ptolemy's descriptions can be characterized by increasing knowledge of the further regions, such as Ivernia (Ireland), while he makes many mistakes owing to his flawed measurements. He mistakes the size and shape of Scotland, although he knows several rivers in the area. He speaks about the Suiones (Swedish) on the coast of Germany, and he mentions Scandia (Scandinavia), but he has no real knowledge of the interior of the latter or of Normandy. Toward the east, Ptolemy's knowledge of the Carpathian Mountains shows a greater acquaintance with the Danube region. Because of false measurements, he widens the Caspian Sea. Ptolemy has more knowledge about Asia as far as China (the land of the Sinae). He describes the Taurus mountain range, which extends from Lycia across to the Euphrates River and includes the Himalayas Mountains bordering India and China. He gives accurate details on the Gulf of Siam (Thailand).

Speculations. Like Herodotus, Ptolemy rejected the idea of a Northern Ocean extending beyond the Caspian, or the notion that this Ocean surrounded the inhabited world of the three continents, an area that extended only from Spain to India. Beyond Africa to the south, for example, is not Ocean but the Island of the Blessed. His speculation that there was unknown land beyond Asia, called *Terra Australis*, also goes against the ancient idea of Ocean.

Sources:

Harry E. Burton, *The Discovery of the Ancient World* (Freeport, N.Y. Books for Libraries Press, 1969).

Lionel Casson, *Travel in the Ancient World* (London: Allen & Unwin, 1974).

The Geography of Strabo, 8 volumes, translated by Horace Leonard Jones (Cambridge, Mass.: Harvard University Press, 1917–1932).

Claude Nicolet, *Space, Geography, and Politics in the Early Roman Empire* (Ann Arbor: University of Michigan Press, 1991).

CLIMATE AND TOPOGRAPHY

Persistent Misconceptions. The area around the Mediterranean Sea was already well explored by Homer's time. Nevertheless, misconceptions about the region continued throughout antiquity. Hipparchus, for example, believed that it flowed directly into the Red Sea. Eratosthenes held the notion that the Mediterranean Sea covered one-half of the inhabitable world, of which the Pillars of Heracles (Gibraltar) were the westernmost point. Strabo, writing in the first century C.E., divides the earth's waters into two major bodies (which include the various lakes and seas throughout the world): the Interior Ocean (Mediterranean) and the Exterior Ocean (flowing from the Caspian Sea into the proverbial Northern Ocean).

Climatology. Despite these ongoing misconceptions, knowledge of the Mediterranean basin was fairly detailed by the first century C.E. Strabo knows the rivers of Spain and cites the Guadalquiver and the Ebro flowing into the Mediterranean. Strabo also speaks in great detail regarding the diverse climate of the Mediterranean basin. The middle to southern regions of Italy are generally mild, although winters can be cold, while central Spain is hot and dry. Greece also tends to have a dry climate with seasonal rainfall occurring mainly in the winter. The topography of the region is as diverse as its climate. There are mountainous regions in Greece, such as Parnassus and Olympus, and an active volcano in Thera (Santorini). In Spain and Italy mountain ranges such as the Pyrenees and the Alps form natural borders, but they also create difficulties in climate and modes of production. In addition to the climate and topography of the mountain regions, Italy sees a variety of climates, and there are fertile valleys that allow for the cultivation of a number of different crops, including a variety of fruits, and olives.

Italia. For the inhabitants of the city of Rome, increasing knowledge of the geography of the Italian peninsula and of other regions meant increasingly greater political and economic power. The natural boundaries of the Alps, the mountains that separate the Italian peninsula from Switzerland, and the River Po did not become political boundaries until the second century B.C.E. Before that point, the region between present-day Livorno and the Alps was known as Cisalpine Gaul. The presence of Gallic people south of the Alps was an ongoing threat to Rome, as the sack of Rome in 390 B.C.E. demonstrated. Rome engaged in ongoing military efforts against the Gallic people in Italy, and, as the historian Polybius and others report, by 150 B.C.E. the Gallic presence on the peninsula was minimal. The region received Roman citizenship in 89 B.C.E. (It was known in Cicero's time as a major producer of wool.) From the middle of the second century B.C.E. everything south of the Alps was under the purview of Rome; the region formerly inhabited by the Gauls became a wealthy Roman settlement. The Apennine Mountains also formed natural borders extending along the Italian peninsula. Although they protected inhabitants on either

side from invasion, the mountain regions also prevented widespread cultivation of land.

Tiber River. As for the city itself, there were settlements in at least three of Rome's eight hills by the ninth century B.C.E., although city walls were not erected until 378 B.C.E. (after the Gallic invasion). The Tiber River, which divided the Sabines from their western neighbors, the Etruscans, is another natural border that helped Rome's emergence as a city in the eighth century B.C.E. The river came to serve, as Pliny reports, as a means of transporting goods into Rome from throughout the inhabited world. With the Mediterranean Sea as its source, the Tiber runs from the Roman port of Ostia (established around the fourth century B.C.E.) into the city, linking the Romans to their Italian neighbors as far north as Umbria. By Pliny's estimation the Tiber flows for 150 miles (it is actually 252 miles long).

Imperial Reorganization. After Rome subdued its Oscan, Etruscian, Italian, and Gallic neighbors by the first century B.C.E., one of the great tasks of the nascent empire was that of reorganizing the city. Augustus established fourteen districts, while emperors such as Claudius and Trajan built water supplies from the Tiber, and Nero and Hadrian constructed baths. (The first known baths were found at Pompeii and date from the first century B.C.E.) The last additions to the city of Rome in ancient times were the basilica of Maxentius (in 284 B.C.E.) and the Aurelian Wall (completed circa 275 B.C.E.).

Hispania (Spain). The Pyrenees Mountains form a natural boundary that divides Spain from the rest of Europe. It was in

A marble relief showing a ship in the port of Ostia, circa 200 C.E. The figure of Neptune (central and bearing a trident) represents the sea (Museo Torlonia, Rome).

fact anecdotal before the late twentieth century that Africa began in the Pyrenees. The narrow cross into modern-day Morocco between the Mediterranean Sea and the Atlantic Ocean is less than six miles. (The land on either side of the straits was known in ancient times as the Pillars of Hercules.) Five major rivers cross the Spanish peninsula (the Ebro, Guadiana, Tejo, Duero, and Guadalquivir), and because four of the five rivers flow into the Atlantic Ocean (as opposed to flowing into Spain from the Mediterranean Sea, as the Ebro does), Spain was hard for Roman rulers to administer. They had trouble executing their usual practice of establishing new cities along the river (as they did both in Rome itself and also throughout Britain, for example).

Early Inhabitants. When the Romans encountered Spain toward the end of the third century B.C.E., the peninsula was inhabited chiefly by Celts to the north, Iberians to the south (of whom little is known), and a mixture of the two ethnic groups, the Celtiberians, in the center. The Greeks were also present in Spain until the third century B.C.E., when the Carthaginians of North Africa began to make strong incursions.

Two Provinces. The Romans began to enter Spain when the Carthaginian leader Hannibal captured the Spanish city of Saguntum, an ally to Rome, in 219 B.C.E. After the Roman leader Scipio Africanus defeated Hannibal's brother, Hasdrubal, in Spain in 206 B.C.E., Rome established two provinces, Closer Spain and Farther Spain. The province of Farther Spain, extending southwest on the Spanish peninsula (similar borders to modern-day Andalusia and Portugal), was split in Augustus's time into Lusitania and Baetica. The peninsula took two centuries to subdue, in part because of the difficulty of the terrain, namely the Pyrenees Moun-

tains and the tempestuous rivers. It is certainly possible that ethnography might have played a role; Strabo often speaks of the customs of the Iberians and Celtiberians as inimical to the Roman way of life. Variant methods of warfare (Strabo reports that the Iberian cavalry was well trained for traversing the mountainous terrain) are one factor that would make Roman encounters with the Iberians daunting.

Stable Revenue. By the first century C.E., Spain was providing the Roman Empire with stable revenue. The province also served an important function in the Roman imagination, since its western coast was conceived of as the outer reaches of the inhabited world (as Strabo's account maintains). The domination of Spain meant that Roman power had extended as far westward as was imaginable.

Gallia (France). In addition to those Cisalpine Gauls in the valleys of northern Italy, Gallic tribes (Transalpine Gauls) inhabited the land extending from the Alps to the Pyrenees, and northwest toward the Atlantic Ocean (modern-day France). The Gauls also inhabited the northeastern region of Europe up to (and across from) the Rhine River. (This area includes the southern regions of Britain and Germany). These peoples, who are often discussed interchangeably with the Celts, also extended as far eastward as the Danube River (in the northern part of modern-day Austria). During the conflicts with Carthage, Rome's ally in Transalpine Gaul (namely the Greek city of Massilia, modern-day Marseille) provided access into Spain by land. Some of the Gallic region was already in Roman hands by 121 B.C.E., but Julius Caesar's campaigns brought the Romans a greater knowledge of Transalpine Gaul.

Germania (Germany). Of Germany, Tacitus gives the following description in his *Germania:*

The various peoples of Germany are separated from the Gauls by the Rhine, from the Raetians and Pannonians by the Danube, and from the Sarmatians and Dacians by mountains—or, where there are no mountains, by mutual fear. The northern parts of the country are girdled by the sea, flowing round broad peninsulas and vast islands. . . . The Rhine rises in a remote and precipitous height of the Raetian Alps and afterwards turns slightly westward into the North Sea. The Danube issues from a gentle slope of moderate height in the Black Forest, and after passing more peoples than the Rhine in its course discharges itself into the Black Sea through six channels—a seventh mouth being lost in marshlands.

Under the emperor Domitian (around 90 C.E.), the area to the east of the Rhine was divided into two Roman provinces, Germania Superior in the south and Germania Inferior in the north. Before this time it remained chiefly a military outpost with eight Roman legions.

The *Belgae*. In the territory between modern-day France and Germany were the Belgae, a fierce Gallic people. Caesar reports on them in the first century B.C.E., and Strabo refers to them as the fiercest in Gaul. Caesar gives a general ethnography of the Belgae, some of whom migrated from the Continent to Britain in around 100 B.C.E. He conquered the group that remained in Gaul in 57 B.C.E.

Britannia **(Britain).** In his *Bellum gallicum* ("The Gallic War") Julius Caesar argued for the need to invade Britannia. Such an action, he claimed, was of crucial importance to his campaigns against Gaul. He knew that the Britons across the English Channel helped the Gallic tribes and that the Belgae inhabited both Gaul and Britain. Caesar's reports from his first invasion of Britain in 55 B.C.E. reveal a limited knowledge of the interior. He interviewed traders that traveled into Britain, but "he could not ascertain anything about the size of the island, the character and strength of the tribes which inhabited it, their manner of fighting and customs, or the harbors capable of accommodating a large fleet of big ships."

Description of Britain. By Caesar's second invasion of Britain in 54 B.C.E., he is much more comfortable with his surroundings. He describes the parameters of Britain and its surroundings, characterizing the island as triangular (on this point he was mistaken) and giving details about its three points: one facing Gaul with its tip on the coast of Kent (Dover), the second facing west toward Spain, and the third looking toward the north with no land beyond it. Although relatively ignorant about Britain a year earlier, in 54 B.C.E. Caesar is able to go beyond exterior descriptions of the island: "The interior of Britain is inhabited by people who claim, on the strength of oral tradition, to be aboriginal; the coast, by Belgic immigrants who came to plunder and make war—nearly all of them retaining the names of the tribes from which they originated—and latter settled down to till the soil." The descriptive sections of *Bellum gallicum* might have been written at the time of the invasion, or perhaps Caesar doctored his memoirs when he published them in 52 B.C.E. Whatever the case, the final

result is an increasing acquaintance with Britain and its inhabitants.

Claudius. Further incursions into Britain occurred during the Roman Empire. The Gallic people (the Belgae) in the south of Britannia were ruled by the leader Cunobelinus until his death in 41 C.E., when Rome, under Claudius, invaded the island. Claudius defeated the lower region of Britannia, but he did not accomplish complete domination of the island. Thus, Rome was not quite in control of the territory during the first century C.E.

Agricola. Tacitus's account of the governorship of Agricola (Gnaeus Julius Agricola), which lasted from 78 to 84 C.E., does little to advance knowledge of Britain. In fact, the historian at times shows a striking degree of ignorance. He believes, for example, that Ireland lies between Britain and Spain. Nevertheless, he offers us a view of Britain in the first century. His description is as follows: "Britain, the largest of the islands known to us Romans, is of such a size and so situated as to run parallel to the coast of Germany on the east and to that of Spain on the west, while to the south it actually lies within sight of Gaul. Its northern shores, with no land facing them, are beaten by a wild and open sea."

Scotland. It does appear from fortifications in northern Britain (modern-day Scotland) that Agricola penetrated into Britain as far north as Scotland, although Tacitus gives few geographical details to confirm this. A consortium of the inhabitants from Upper and Lower Britannia eventually drove Agricola out of the island. With Agricola recalled to Rome, many of the inroads made in the upper region of Britannia were eventually relinquished.

Africa. As Pliny reports, the Carthaginian commander Hanno conducted an exploration (*periplous*) around the coast of Africa (Ethiopia), and the historian Polybius did not return from his investigation with information on any human inhabitants. Rome's contact with North Africa begins from the fifth century B.C.E. with attempts to stop Carthage's advances into Sicily. Carthage had attacked Greek cities in Sicily during the fifth century, and by the third century B.C.E. it had strongholds in Spain. The next step to widespread power would be an attempt to destroy Rome's hegemony. In order to do so, however, Hannibal would have to cross the Pyrenees Mountains, traverse the Rhône River in Gaul, and, finally, survive the onset of winter in the Alps.

African Expansion. Despite its presence on the continent of Africa from the second century B.C.E., Rome's incursions into the interior of Africa were limited. Along the western coast of Africa, Mauretania figured in a war with Rome (the conflict with Jugurtha reported by Sallust, 112–106 B.C.E.). Tingi, now the modern city Tangier in Morocco, came under Roman control in the first century B.C.E. Augustus organized the province of Africa Proconsularis, which stretched as far as the eastern border of modern Lybia (Cyrenaica). Claudius established the two provinces of Mauretania, of which Pliny speaks in *Natural Histories,* calling them Tingi and Lixus (Caesarea). (He also relies on mythology for his data, claiming that the mythological character Antaeus, whom Hercules killed, founded the kingdoms.) Caesarea (possibly the city Cherchel in Libya) was an important African port in the early empire.

Roman Reach. Pomponius Mela, writing in the first century C.E., knew that the eastern coast of Africa

A Celtic warrior, from a small golden brooch, circa second century B.C.E. The Celts were a warlike people who posed a great threat to Roman forces in Spain and Gaul
(private collection).

extended further south than the Arabian gulf, but the Romans never seemed to know much about the African interior beyond the Sahara. Pliny, for example, does not believe that any Roman ever penetrated further than the Atlas Mountains (which, from what the maps reveal, they appear to believe were further south than they actually are).

Egypt. Although well known from early antiquity, Egypt never became a Roman province. It fell under the personal management of Roman leaders such as Caesar and Antony in the first century B.C.E. Rome did not control Africa on the eastern coast beyond Egypt, but some cities south of Roman Egypt were outposts for the trade of luxury items among the wealthy classes of the province. The modern cities of Aden in Yemen, Guardafui in Somalia, and Dar es Salaam in Tanzania served as ports for goods to and from India during the early Roman Empire. Strabo knew that beyond Arabia Felix, itself possessing flowing springs of water, the region north of modern-day Yemen across Arabia is desert.

Persia (Iran). The ancients knew of the Caspian Sea (or the Hyrcanian sea, north of modern-day Iran) as early as the fifth century B.C.E., when Herodotus described it as a lake. Ignorance about the region, however, and false speculation prevented Herodotus's view from advancing until the second century C.E., when Ptolemy returned to plotting the

Caspian Sea as a lake. The prevalent (and false) view of the Caspian Sea before the time of Ptolemy was that it was a waterway flowing into the Northern Ocean. The ancients perhaps deduced this from their exposure to the North Sea, since Pythias had sailed to Britain, and Caesar certainly knew of the Rhine River, which flows into the sea. The view that the Caspian Sea flowed into the Northern Ocean was also held by Patrocles, the Greek commander to the region under the Seleucids, who explored the region in 285 B.C.E. The Romans did not travel to Russia, so in the *Natural Histories* Pliny reports that Patrocles sailed north from the Caspian Sea—into India!

Caspian Sea. After 247 B.C.E., the Caspian Sea region was inhabited by the Parthians. Under Roman rule, Augustus's conquest of the region was not complete. To the east of the Caspian Sea was a fertile valley known as Bactria, between modern-day Uzbekistan and Afghanistan. By the third century B.C.E. Bactria was ruled by Greek Bactrians of mixed ethnicity; the Chinese took possession of the Bactrian kingdom in 129–128 B.C.E.

Sources:
Caesar, *The Conquest of Gaul,* translated by S. A. Handford and revised by Jane F. Gardner (London: Penguin, 1982).

Leonard A. Curchin, *Roman Spain: Conquest and Assimilation* (London: Routledge, 1991).

Peter Salway, *The Oxford Illustrated History of Roman Britain* (Oxford: Oxford University Press, 1993).

Tacitus, *The Agricola* and *The Germania,* translated by H. Mattingly and revised by Handford (London: Penguin, 1970).

EFFECTS OF GEOGRAPHY ON HISTORY AND CULTURE

Balance of Power. Throughout Roman history geographical knowledge was of critical importance to maintaining the precarious balance of power. In his *Res gestae* Augustus makes the claim that he brought the inhabited world under Roman rule. It is no coincidence that his assertion was easily visualized on the map that was on display in Rome. The map, which was accompanied by a written commentary, *Descriptio orbis,* was the work of Marcus Agrippa, the general that masterminded many of the emperor's most important military triumph, such as the Battle of Actium in 31 B.C.E., where Antony and Cleopatra met their demise. Agrippa's ability to make political deals in such distant places as the Crimea was directly related to geographical reconnaissance in those regions, and the knowledge of what could and could not be accomplished by the military. Marcus Agrippa's prominence under Augustus's regime demonstrates how Rome maintained political power through geographical knowledge.

Political Diplomacy. Augustus translated Marcus Agrippa's knowledge into political diplomacy. Many regions of the inhabited world, such as Dacia, were not only independent culturally, having their own customs and even coinage throughout their contact with Rome, but they were also powerful. There were known territories in Africa, Asia, and Europe that never came under

A coin depicting the Emperor Trajan (on the right) receiving the *orbis terrarum* (globe), circa 100 C.E.

Roman rule. Nevertheless, Rome had to maintain diplomatic relationships with them. The Nabataeans of Arabia are one example of the diplomatic approach. An independent king ruled the Nabataeans until Trajan made Arabia a province in 106 C.E. Rome's policy was at times simply to control her borders and frontiers. Such a policy meant leaving other cultures in place. Of Armenia, for example, Augustus claims that "When Artaxes was king of Greater Armenia, although I could have made it a province, I preferred to adhere to the example of our ancestors by handing the kingdom over to Tigranes, the son of the king Artavasdes, but also the grandson of the king Tigranes, through Tiberius Nero, who at that time was my stepson."

Reciprocal Influence. Certainly Augustus through his policy wanted to make other cultures lovers of Roman culture. If this could be accomplished, the result would still be the spread of *Romanitas* by force where necessary, and peacefully where possible. Acculturation was not only from Rome outward; Rome adopted many of the customs of other peoples. During the Punic Wars, Rome imported the fertility goddess Cybele from Asia Minor, hoping that she would bring victory. Late in the Empire, Constantine would transform the cult of Christianity into the imperial religion. These instances demonstrated that Rome could be influenced as much as it penetrated other cultures. Once subdued, all of the provinces were vital to the life of Rome, providing not only manpower and natural resources, but also rulers, such as the emperor Hadrian.

Administrative Assets. From Republican times Rome's knowledge of world geography was put to administrative use. The resources of the inhabited world both provided Roman subjects with the necessities of life, such as food, clothing, and shelter, and furnished the aristocracy with its wealth. In the Republican period territories such as Spain, because of its distance and the difficulty of its topography (and, if the historian Livy is to be believed, add to this the unreliable character of the Spanish people), were hard to manage. During the late Republic and Empire territories such as Spain provided Rome with grain and corn. The African provinces offered Rome a continuous supply of grains and cereals. Olives were grown in Tunisia.

Various Resources. Necessities and luxury items alike were also brought to Romans throughout the inhabited world. Consistent with political geography, writers such as Pliny and Caesar were interested in the resources that various provinces would bring to Rome. Pliny cites lead, iron, copper, silver, and gold as some of the resources that Spain provided. Caesar finds tin in

Britain's interior and iron along its coast, and like Gaul, it was rich in timber. Africa also exported marble.

India. Between the third century B.C.E. and the fifth century C.E., India became less and less of a mythical location, and by the first century B.C.E. it provided the Romans access to Chinese silk. In addition to Chinese silk, India imported precious stones such as ivory, perfumes, and spices, although the trade with India reveals that Rome left many trading activities to independent—and international—traders. The trade from Roman Egypt to and from India was dominated by luxury items from India and southeastern Africa, such as precious stones (ivory, marble, onyx, diamonds, pearls), fragrances, and spices (myrrh, frankincense, pepper), and fabrics (fine cotton and silk). In addition to trade to the western coast of India, traders seem to have made incursions into the eastern coast of India. Artifacts have been found in the modern southeastern city of Pondicherry. Traders also knew of the fertile Ganges River Valley.

Dacia. Because of their vast resources, many provinces became civic centers, with great influxes of population from throughout the Roman world. Dacia is one such example. Miners traveled to the Danube, which was also a fertile agricultural region, to mine gold, silver, and iron. Rome could not control Dacia beyond 270 C.E. under the rule of Aurelian.

Sole Parent of All Races. The mandate of Roman culture was to rule. As Pliny boasts, all climates and cultures would inevitably yield to Rome because the gods have blessed the city. Its geographical position in the inhabited world was evidence of its cultural place: "To put it succinctly, Italy was to become the sole parent of all races throughout the world." The view that Pliny articulates is demonstrated both in ethnography, where non-Romans are described as savage and uncivilized, and in policy. While resources were brought into the empire from throughout the inhabited world, environmental legislation protected the mineral wealth of Rome itself. Pliny reports that a decree of the senate forbade mining in Rome.

Geography Is Fate. As the Greek philosopher Heraclitus put it, geography is fate. Geography determined Rome's political and social mission. Control of political geography and knowledge of topography, climates, and customs of peoples throughout the inhabited world reinforced the Empire's power. Romans saw their mandate as that of bringing about the unity of the known world, and they were to accomplish this unity through the influence of customs and language where possible and by sheer military force where necessary.

Sources:

Augustus, *Caesaris Avgvsti res gestae et fragmenta*, edited by Robert S. Rogers, Kenneth Scott, and Margaret M. Ward (Detroit: Wayne State University Press, 1990).

Claude Nicolet, *Space, Geography, and Politics in the Early Roman Empire* (Ann Arbor: University of Michigan Press, 1991).

The Periplus Maris Erythraei, translated by Lionel Casson (Princeton: Princeton University Press, 1989).

Pliny, *Natural History: A Selection*, translated by John F. Healy (London: Penguin, 1991).

DID THE ROMANS VALUE DIVERSITY?

Not only did the provinces enrich Rome with their natural resources: the peoples throughout the Empire also actually influenced Roman culture. In addition to providing military manpower, the provinces also increased the noble class at Rome. Spain gave Rome emperors and philosophers. Many of these territories slowly went from being military outposts to frontiers where inhabitants had rights of Roman citizenship. Under the emperor Claudius (Tiberius Claudius) in 48 C.E. Transalpine Gaul, which became a full colony under Augustus, was given the right to send its noble citizens to Rome to serve in the Senate. Claudius's speech for the occasion, which the historian Tacitus reports in *Annales,* is a remarkable example of the appreciation for what the provinces could offer Roman culture. Claudius celebrates the expansion of the Empire and the peace that the knowledge of diverse peoples had historically brought to Rome:

The day of stable peace at home and victory abroad came when the districts beyond the Po were admitted to citizenship, and, availing ourselves of the fact that our legions were settled throughout the globe, we added to them the stoutest of the provincials, and succoured a weary empire. . . . What else proved fatal to Lacedaemon and Athens, in spite of their power in arms, but their policy of holding the conquered aloof as alien-born? But the sagacity of our own founder Romulus was such that several times he fought and naturalized a people in the course of the same day! Strangers have been kings over us: the conferment of magistracies on the sons of freedmen is not the novelty which it is commonly and mistakenly thought, but a frequent practice of the old commonwealth.

Source: Tacitus, *The Annals,* translated by John Jackson (Cambridge, Mass.: Harvard University Press, 1991).

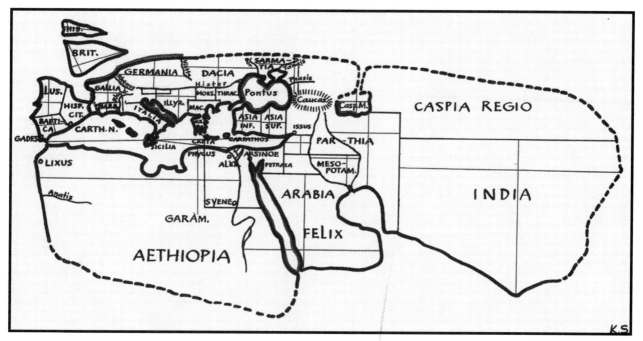

The world in the first century B.C.E. according to Marcus Agrippa (from Susan P. Mattern, *Rome and the Enemy*, 1999)

POLITICAL GEOGRAPHY AND THE ROMAN ECONOMY

Cicero provides an example of the extent to which the Roman economy depended on the control of its frontiers. In 66 B.C.E. he delivered a speech calling for an expansion of power to the general Pompey in his war against Mithridates VI in Pontus (the Black Sea region). Mithridates was gaining control of the region from 120 B.C.E. and threatening Roman stability there. Cicero supported a proposal, advanced by Gaius Manilius, extending power to generals to allow them to handle conflicts such as the one in Pontus with greater power.

In the speech, Cicero emphasizes the economic ramifications of gradually losing control of the region: "Asia . . . is so extraordinarily wealthy and fertile that the productiveness of its soil, the diversity of its crops, the dimensions of its pasture-land and the volume of its exports exceed those of any other country upon earth." Cicero cites previous military losses to Mithridates as detrimental to the Roman economy: "It was a lesson learnt amid direst trouble, since the loss of numerous large fortunes in Asia was immediately followed by a collapse of credit at Rome due to widespread non-payment of debts."

Source: Cicero, *Selected Political Speeches*, translated by Michael Grant (London: Penguin, 1989).

ETHNOGRAPHY AND POINTS OF CONTACT

Increasing Knowledge. The third century marks the point of increasing knowledge about the inhabitants of the lands surrounding the Mediterranean basin. During this period Rome began its intermittent wars with Carthage. The conflict brought further contact with the peoples of Spain and France, since these were the passageways between Rome and Carthage by land. In addition to this contact, the period leading into the first century B.C.E. brought knowledge of Britain and its inhabitants. Toward the end of the fourth century (circa 310–306 B.C.E.) the Greek explorer Pytheas had already claimed to have sailed around the British Isles, reaching as far north as either Norway or Iceland. (Pythias sighted an island, Thule, north of the British Isles). By the first century B.C.E. Caesar would be able to report knowledge of the interior of Britain in his *Bellum gallicum*.

Ethnographical Tradition. Rome's disposition toward the foreign peoples they encountered was often marked by two recurrent phenomena: on the one hand, the desire to spread *Romanitas,* the love of Roman literature and culture, and, on the other hand, a fear (often warranted) of the dangers that un-Romanized cultures might bring. These two factors would stand in the way of a thoroughly scientific ethnography, and they extend to the modern era. As Pliny would report in the first century C.E., Romans held the belief that their city was in the center of the world. The climate and geography of Rome was said to be ideal, and the further away one traveled, the worse the natural environment became. Pliny's descriptions of the Black Sea region or the African interior (beyond the Atlas Mountains) are excellent examples of the tendency. Whereas Rome is "chosen by the divine inspiration of the gods to enhance the renown of heaven itself," the Ripaean Mountains come from a part of the world "condemned by Nature," proven by its extremes of cold.

Stereotypes. Such a division of places as is evident throughout Roman literature has a bearing on ethnography. Although the Roman citizen had knowledge of the outside world, often his view of that world was distorted by stereotypes that served to reinforce either his sense of divine right or his fear. The ancient ethnographer, moreover, worked within a tradition given to fanciful tales. Many of the ethnographical reports of Roman writers are in keeping with a tradition already evident in Herodotus's ethnography, namely the tendency to see others outside of one's own culture as savage, degenerate, and a danger to civilization. Like Herodotus, whose view of other cultures has been likened to a distorted mirror of his own Greek customs, Roman writers exaggerated the differences of non-Roman peoples.

Caesar on the Gauls. The bias of the ethnographical tradition is evident in Caesar's *Bellum gallicum*. Caesar's reports about Gallic peoples are quite stereotypical; the people are savage, fierce in battle. In addition to this report, "wives are shared between groups of ten or twelve men, especially between brothers and between fathers and sons; but the offspring of these unions are counted as the children of the man with whom a particular woman cohabited first." These characteristics tell the Roman that the foreigner's difference is a threat to civilized culture. (The Roman citizen, like men of most cultures, would never dream of sharing his wife with another man.)

Uses of Ethnography. Caesar's ethnographical reports are written in the context of war, and his commentaries on the danger of an unconquered Gaul to Rome's safety would give the Roman Senate justification for continued financing of his efforts. He therefore stresses the importance of Romanization: only by subduing the foreigner can civilization be spread. Some of the ethnographical reports, however, are merely comical. In one instance, Pliny tells of a people in the Atlas mountains in Africa who refuse to name each other, curse the sun, and do not dream when they sleep. While a believer in the supremacy of Roman culture, Pliny tells his tales mainly for the purpose of entertainment.

GEOGRAPHY, ETHNOGRAPHY, AND POWER

It is no coincidence that there is only one geographer in the Roman period writing in Latin: Pomponius Mela. The Roman statesman was generally not interested in science for its own sake; rather, scientific knowledge served political and technological functions. Geography and ethnography were tools of imperialism and the expansion of Roman rule. Historians such as Livy and Tacitus, and prominent statesmen such as Julius Caesar and Augustus, wrote works that contained geographical and ethnographical data, but their main concern was the political usefulness of this information. Caesar's descriptions of the Gallic tribes as fierce, unfaithful, and undisciplined serve a particular end: they justify the conquest of Gaul. Caesar reports, for example, that the tribes living in the interior of Britain do not farm, but live instead on milk (not unlike the mythological Cyclopes, the savage giants in Homeric epic). When his report of the Gallic peoples wearing animal skins and eating only meat is added to information on farming, the result is a composite of a primitive people that have not advanced from the hunter-gatherer stage of human development. Caesar shapes his information to portray a backward people, dangerous and in need of civilization.

Like Caesar's *Bellum gallicum*, the *Res gestae Divi Augusti* ("The Deeds of the Divine Augustus") is rife with information on the world outside of Rome. It is a work of political geography. Augustus's interest is to celebrate the conquest of the inhabited world. By the time of its composition in 14 C.E., Augustus could claim to have subdued peoples that caused his predecessors ongoing concern, such as the Parthians.

The *Res gestae* contains seemingly trivial information, such as Augustus's exhibitions: "I presented the people with hunts of African beasts in my name or in my sons' and grandsons' names twenty-six times, either in the circus or in the forum or in the amphitheater. In those hunts around 3,500 beasts were destroyed." More importantly, the *Res gestae* contains a claim that Augustus often makes of having brought peace to the inhabited world: "I pacified the Gallic and Hispanic provinces, and Germany, which includes the Ocean from Gades (in *Hispania Baetica*) to the port of the Elbe River. I pacified the Alps from the region near the Adriatic Sea to the Tuscan Sea. No war was brought against the people without cause. My ships sailed through the Ocean from the port of the Rhine to the east up to the borders of the Cimbri, where before that time no Roman had gone, either by land or by sea. And the Cimbri, the Charydes, the Semnones, and other German peoples of the same region sought my allegiance and that of the Roman people through envoys." Although his is strictly a political geography, Augustus ultimately claims to advance geographical and ethnographical knowledge.

Sources: Augustus, *Caesaris Avgvsti res gestae et fragmenta*, edited by Robert S. Rogers, Kenneth Scott, and Margaret M. Ward (Detroit: Wayne State University Press, 1990).

Caesar, *The Conquest of Gaul*, translated by S. A. Handford and revised by Jane F. Gardner (London: Penguin, 1982).

Limitations. Despite the tradition of storytelling that marks ancient ethnography, there seems to have been a greater degree of self-consciousness among later writers. Strabo, for example, faulted the irresponsibility of geographers who claimed to travel to distant places but only fabricated their tales. As he puts it, these writers "tell us about the 'men that sleep in their ears,' and the 'men without mouths,' and 'men without noses'; and about 'men with one eye,' 'men with long legs,' 'men with fingers turned backwards'" (2.1.9, translated by Horace Leonard Jones).

Fanciful Storytelling. Although Pliny engages in precisely the kind of fanciful storytelling about which Strabo complains, he seems at times aware that he too is involved in entertainment and not a disciplined study of the customs of foreign peoples. In his discussion of the exploration of Africa, for example, he says the following: "There are five Roman colonies in that province. According to widespread reports it might seem to be an accessible region; but put to the test, this view is found to be almost completely fallacious; persons of rank, although unwilling to track down the truth, are not ashamed to tell falsehoods because they cannot bear to admit their ignorance." The complaints of Strabo and Pliny reveal the limitations of ethnography in the tradition of ancient geography.

Power and Safety. From the comments of Strabo and Pliny it is fair to conclude that the tendency of earlier ethnographical accounts to report fanciful and mythical information about foreign peoples could not be entirely sustained in the world of the Roman Empire. Roman statesmen such as Pliny certainly had a penchant for entertaining accounts of foreign places, but even Pliny realized the limitations of this approach. Political geography was a science that could be used in the interests of power and safety for the Roman people, while ignorance was potentially dangerous. Foreign peoples also brought Rome an abundance of wealth, and in this case ignorance meant the inability to take full advantage of the resources available throughout the inhabited world. Perhaps this is why the trader that wrote the *Voyage of the Red Sea* shows little interest in fanciful or mythical accounts of foreign peoples.

He does comment on the largeness of men along the southeastern coast of Africa and their dark complexion, or the flat faces of people in northeastern India. Unlike some of the accounts of Pliny, however, these comments are simply descriptive. They do not attempt to convince the reader of a set of traits, and they are entirely believable.

Avenues of Contact. Far from adhering to the entertaining but deceptive accounts of foreign peoples, the Roman politician or general had to have somewhat detailed knowledge of the various peoples throughout the inhabited world. Such knowledge meant safety, particularly because there were groups that Rome never fully controlled. Trade routes, for example, such as the one along the southeastern coast of Africa into India, were sometimes independent of the Roman government (that is, unless those goods found their way into the Roman Empire, usually through Roman Egypt). The Empire maintained a complex and fluctuating patron/client relationship with many groups in the inhabited world. The Parthians, for example, recognized Roman rule in Armenia but not in all of their territory. Among the Dacians, Rome was recognized as the dominant power until Decebaus's war against the Emperor Domitian. The Nabataeans were also servants of Rome, although their own kings ruled in Arabia. There were a plethora of social groups throughout the inhabited world, such as the Persis in Iran, the Alemanni and the Marcomanni in Germany, and the Alans north of the Caspian Sea. Peoples outside of the control of the Roman government were either known through contact with traders or generals, or armchair scholars like Pliny speculated about them.

Sources:

Caesar, *The Conquest of Gaul*, translated by S. A. Handford and revised by Jane F. Gardner (London: Penguin, 1982).

Francois Hartog, *The Mirror of Herodotus: The Representation of the Other in the Writing of History,* translated by Janet Lloyd (Berkeley & Los Angeles: University of California Press, 1988).

Pliny, *Natural History: A Selection,* translated by John F. Healy (London: Penguin, 1991).

Strabo, *Geography,* translated by H. C. Hamilton (London: George Bell & Sons, 1903).

Tacitus, *The Agricola* and *The Germania,* translated by H. Mattingly and revised by S. A. Handford (London: Penguin, 1970).

SIGNIFICANT PEOPLE

ERATOSTHENES

CIRCA 285-194 B.C.E.

LIBRARIAN, ASTRONOMER, GEOGRAPHER

Encyclopedic Knowledge. Eratosthenes was born in Cyrene (present-day Libya) and became the librarian at Alexandria during the second half of the third century B.C.E. after studying with the philosopher Ariston of Chios, who himself was a student of Zeno, the founder of the Stoic school of philosophy. The period during which Eratosthenes lived, the Hellenistic period, was one that encouraged eclectic scholars, as many of the personalities connected with the Library at Alexandria demonstrate. In his post as librarian Eratosthenes followed such Hellenistic scholars as Apollonius of Rhodes, who is most noted for his adaptation of classical poetry. (Apollonius wrote the *Argonautica*, a famous poem on the myth of Jason and the Argonauts that brilliantly incorporates allusions to earlier Greek poetry.) Like Apollonius, Eratosthenes demonstrated the encyclopedic knowledge that characterized his time; he wrote on every subject from comedy to philosophy. More importantly, Eratosthenes composed a seminal thesis on geography in three books, which includes the title *Peri tês anameîrêseôs tês gês* ("On the Measurements of the Earth"), a work that, although subsequent authors regarded it as pivotal, unfortunately only survives through citations in other works.

Circumference. Eratosthenes is credited with being the first person to have calculated the Earth's circumference. He observed that at Syene (present-day Aswan) in Egypt, the Sun's rays fell vertically at noon on the summer solstice. Meanwhile, on the same date and at the same time in Alexandria, sunlight fell at an angle of 7° from the vertical. Correctly assuming that the Sun's distance from the Earth is great, he concluded that the rays are nearly parallel when they reach the Earth. Eratosthenes then calculated the Earth's circumference by measuring the distance between the two cities (five hundred miles). Because the exact unit of measurement he used is uncertain, astronomers today believe that his calculation varies anywhere from 0.5 percent to 17 percent from the modern figure.

Sources:
Hipparchus Bithynius, *The Geographical Fragments of Hipparchus*, edited by D. R. Dicks (London: Athlone, 1960).

Peter Marshall Fraser, "Eratosthenes," in *The Oxford Classical Dictionary*, edited by Simon Hornblower and Antony Spawforth, third edition (Oxford: Oxford University Press, 1999), pp. 553–554.

HIPPARCHUS OF NICAEA

CIRCA 190-120 B.C.E.

ASTRONOMER AND GEOGRAPHER

Reputation. Like Eratosthenes, Hipparchus is quoted throughout Strabo's books. Hipparchus, who hailed from Nicaea (a city in Bithynia, in modern Turkey), flourished in the middle of the second century B.C.E, and is considered the greatest astronomer of antiquity. He discovered the precession of the equinoxes, accurately estimated the lunar distance, computed both lunar and solar eclipses, compiled the first catalogue of stars (containing a total of 850), and devised trigonometry. There is also reason to believe that he invented the plane astrolabe, which allowed a user to tell time at night from the stars' positions.

Revising Another's Work. Many of Hipparchus's writings were dedicated to advancing Eratosthenes' mathematical geography. No one can deny Eratosthenes' innovations or his contribution to geography, but subsequent authors such as Hipparchus aimed chiefly to create formulas that would improve Eratosthenes' measurements. For example, Hipparchus developed a crude method of locating geographical positions by their latitude and longitude.

Sources:
Hipparchus Bithynius, *The Geographical Fragments of Hipparchus*, edited by D. R. Dicks (London: Athlone, 1960).

G. J. Toomer, "Hipparchus," in *The Oxford Classical Dictionary*, edited by Simon Hornblower and Antony Spawforth, third edition (Oxford: Oxford University Press, 1999), p. 708.

POMPONIUS MELA

FIRST CENTURY C.E.
GEOGRAPHER

Survey of the World. Pomponius Mela, from Tingentera in the south of Spain, near Gibraltar, probably wrote his geographical work *De chorographia* sometime after 43 C.E. Geographical writers in Latin were a rarity during the Roman period, although authors such as Tacitus and Pliny dabbled in the subject. As is the case both with Strabo's geography in Greek and with later writers in Latin (such as Pliny the Elder), Mela was uninterested in the details of mathematical geography. He was a compiler of physical geography and ethnographical knowledge of his time. *De chorographia* is divided into three books. The first book is an overview of the earth's northern and southern hemispheres, and in it Mela revisits Crates' notion (advanced in the second century B.C.E.) that the earth is divided into five zones, only two of which are inhabited. (Mela still believed in the existence of Crates' *Antichthones,* a mythical people living on an island in the earth's second inhabitable sphere.) After an overview of the four seas that flow into the Ocean (the Caspian, Persian, Arabian, and Mediterranean Seas), the second book of *De chorographia* deals with Greece, Italy, southern Gaul, and Spain, and the third book surveys northern Europe (including Germany) and East Asia.

Sources:
Pomponius Mela's Description of the World, translated by Frank E. Romer (Ann Arbor: University of Michigan Press, 1998).

Nicholas Purcell, "Pomponius Mela," in *The Oxford Classical Dictionary,* edited by Simon Hornblower and Antony Spawforth, third edition (Oxford: Oxford University Press, 1999), p. 1218.

PAUSANIAS

FLOURISHED CIRCA 150 C.E.
TRAVEL WRITER

Greek Tourist. One of the classicist's most important sources on ancient Greece is the *Periêgêsis tês Hellados* ("Description of Greece") of Pausanias. In this work Pausanias, who himself traveled throughout Greece, describes the topography of each region, offering a treasury of precious information about places of interest to the tourist. He opens each account of an important city with a sketch of its history and then discusses its daily life, rituals, and folklore. Even today it is possible to take his work as a useful guide to the archaeological sites in the various parts of Greece. Pausanias offers along the way interesting stories and anecdotes that cannot be found anywhere else in extant ancient literature. He expresses a particular fondness for nature, and throughout the ten books of the *Periêgêsis tês Hellados* are discussions of the tides, the signs of an impending earthquake, the icy seas of the North, and the summer solstice in Syene (Aswan), Egypt, where the noonday sun casts no shadow.

Sources:
Karim W. Arafat, *Pausanias' Greece: Ancient Artists and Roman Rulers* (New York: Cambridge University Press, 1996).

Christian Habicht, *Pausanias' Guide to Ancient Greece* (Berkeley: University of California Press, 1985).

Pausanias, *Description of Greece,* 5 volumes, edited and translated by W. H. S. Jones and Henry A. Ormerod (London: Heinemann; New York: G. P. Putnam's Sons, 1918–1935).

GAIUS PLINIUS SECUNDUS (PLINY THE ELDER)

23/24-79 C.E.
SOLDIER, ENCYCLOPEDIST

Mt. Vesuvius. Gaius Plinius Secundus, or Pliny the Elder, was an Italian native, born in 23/24 C.E. in Novum Comum and educated in Rome. He was from a wealthy background and was therefore able to assume the rank of equestrian. He spent several years in military service in Germany, where he took part (at times as a cavalry commander) in campaigns against the Chauci in Upper Germany. In Lower Germany, Pliny served under an esteemed patron, Pomponius Secundus, whose biography he later wrote. Pliny died on 24 August 79 C.E. during the eruption of Vesuvius. The volcano's eruption destroyed Pompeii, Herculaneum. Pliny died of smoke inhalation in Misenum. His fascinating *Naturalis historia,* in thirty-seven books, was an encyclopedic compendium that aimed at assembling all human knowledge about the world around him.

Sources:
Mary Beagon, *Roman Nature: The Thought of Pliny the Elder* (Oxford: Clarendon Press, 1992).

Roger French and Frank Greenaway, *Science in the Early Roman Empire: Pliny the Elder, His Sources and Influence* (London & Sydney: Croom Helm, 1986).

Paul T. Keyser, "Pliny the Elder," in *Ancient Roman Writers, Dictionary of Literary Biography,* volume 211, edited by Ward W. Briggs (Columbia, S.C.: Bruccoli Clark Layman / Detroit: Gale Group, 1999), pp. 235–242.

POSIDONIUS OF RHODES

MID SECOND CENTURY B.C.E.- 51/50 B.C.E.
POLITICIAN, PHILOSOPHER, GEOGRAPHER

The Athlete. Posidonius, nicknamed the Athlete, was an influential political, philosophical, and geographical thinker. Many people thought him to be the most learned man of his time. He traveled extensively throughout the Mediterranean, visiting Gaul, Spain, Italy, Liguria, Africa, and Sicily. He studied with the philosopher Panaetius, who attempted to adopt the Stoic doctrine for Roman ethics. Like Eratosthenes and Hipparchus before him, Posidonius was not Roman (he was born in Syria), but he figured in the politics of the late Roman Republic. He was brought to Rome to address the political strife of the early first century B.C.E. Cicero (Marcus Tullius Cicero) studied with him in Rhodes in 78 B.C.E., and he was a steady advocate of Pompey (Gnaeus Pompeius Magnus). Posidonius authored many works, and although most of them are now lost, historians do know the titles and subjects of approximately thirty. In addition to philosophy, he was versed in astronomy, meteorology, mathematics, geography, hydrology, seismology, zoology, botany, and history. Posidonius tried to calculate the diameter of the Earth, the influence of the Moon on the tides, and the size of the Sun.

Sources:
Ludwig Edelstein and I. G. Kidd, eds., *Posidonius I: The Fragments* (Cambridge: Cambridge University Press, 1972).

Edelstein and Kidd, eds., *Posidonius II: The Commentary,* 2 volumes (Cambridge: Cambridge University Press, 1988).

A. A. Long, ed., *Problems in Stoicism* (London: Athlone, 1971).

CLAUDIUS PTOLEMAEUS (PTOLEMY)

FLOURISHED 146–CIRCA 170 C.E.
GEOGRAPHER, ASTRONOMER, AND MATHEMATICIAN

Speculations. Claudius Ptolemaeus or Ptolemy, who wrote various works on astronomy and astrology, composed a geographical work (*Geôgraphikê huphêgêsis,* "Guide to Geography") in eight books during the middle of the second century C.E. His method of deriving latitudes and longitudes from itineraries and days' journeys (as opposed to incorporating these with astrological observation) yielded false measurements of the inhabited world. Although he was an astronomer, he depended on speculation rather than measurements of the earth based on astrology. He placed the Equator too far north, and his estimate of the circumference of the Earth was 30 percent less than the more accurate figure that had already been determined. Yet, despite these shortcomings, Ptolemy's geographical work, which is extant, contains no less than twenty-six maps of various regions of the world, and one of the entire inhabited world. Ptolemy is the last notable ancient geographer in Europe before the voyages of Christopher Columbus and was considered a definitive source of geographical information until the fifteenth century.

Sources:
J. L. E. Dreyer, *A History of Astronomy from Thales to Kepler* (New York: Dover, 1953).

Colin A. Ronan, *Discovering the Universe: A History of Astronomy* (New York: Basic Books, 1971).

J. O. Thomson, *History of Ancient Geography* (Cambridge: Cambridge University Press, 1948).

STRABO OF AMASEIA

CIRCA 64 B.C.E.–AFTER 21 C.E.
PHILOSOPHER, GEOGRAPHER

Significant Source. Strabo, who was from Amaseia in Pontus, is by far the most important literary source for ancient geography. His *Geôgraphia* in seventeen books gathers material from many other authors (Eratosthenes, Hipparchus, Polybius, Posidonius, and others) now lost. He studied grammar, geography, and philosophy. He knew Posidonius, and although trained as a Peripatetic philosopher, he later converted to Stoicism. He did not travel a great deal, mainly visiting Egypt and Rome. Rather than an innovator in the field of geography, Strabo serves more as an abundant source of previous geographical writers, whom he brings to bear on one another through an ongoing polemic. He is critical of Eratosthenes for combining astronomical data with coast and road measurements. In his writings he emphasizes the usefulness of geographical knowledge and how it enables generals and statesmen to "bring together cities and peoples into a single empire and political management."

Sources:
The Geography of Strabo, 8 volumes, translated by Horace Leonard Jones (Cambridge, Mass.: Harvard University Press, 1917–1932).

Claude Nicolet, *Space, Geography, and Politics in the Early Roman Empire* (Ann Arbor: University of Michigan Press, 1991).

DOCUMENTARY SOURCES

Agrippa, *Descriptio orbis* (first century B.C.E.–first century C.E.)—Commentaries that accompanied a map of the world.

Caesar, *Gallic War* (52 B.C.E.)—The work recounts the general's war in Gaul and Britain between 58 B.C.E. and 52 B.C.E., with an additional year added by an editor, Hirtius. It contains interesting topographical and ethnographical information.

Eratosthenes, *History of Geography,* which includes *On the Measurements of the Earth* (third/second century B.C.E.)—Summarized throughout Strabo's *Geography.* The three-volume work presented the initial theories of mathematical geography, with measurements of the inhabited world.

Pausanias, *Description of Greece* (second century C.E.)—A history and topography of Greece in ten volumes. The work reads like a modern tour guide.

Pomponius Mela, *De chorographia* (first century C.E.)—Three volumes of geography in Latin. Mela returns to Crates' division of the world into zones, with mythical peoples inhabiting the regions unknown to Europe, Asia, and Africa. Nevertheless, he does know about northern Germany and Scandinavia.

Pliny (Gaius Plinius Secundus), *Natural History* (first century C.E.)—Although this text is not exclusively a work of geography, it does contain significant geographical information. The work demonstrates a fair knowledge about the Danube River, a bit about the interior of Africa, and Scandinavia. Its purpose is primarily entertainment, relating anecdotal tidbits on ethnography.

Claudius Ptolemaeus (Ptolemy) (second century C.E.)—Wrote a geographical commentary that accompanied in excess of twenty-six maps. Ptolemy made the last significant advances in geography before the modern period, and he returned geographical perspective to Herodotus's view that the mythical Ocean did not exist.

Strabo, *Geographia* (first century C.E.)—A seventeen-volume work that provides a general overview of previous geographers and geographical advances. Strabo includes discussions of Eratosthenes and Hipparchus, and he gives important insight on the new geographical perspective under the Roman Empire.

Tacitus, *Agricola* and *Germania* (98 C.E.)—The former work recounts the military career of Gnaeus Julius Agricola, the author's father-in-law, who served as governor in Britain from 78–84 C.E. It includes some topography and ethnography; the latter work is an ethnography of Germany.

The Periplus Maris Erythraei (first century C.E.)—An account of the trade route from Africa to India, including descriptions of sites, difficulties of climate, and items traded.

A portable sundial (circa 120 C.E.) found near present-day Bratislava, a city on the Danube River in Slovakia (Museum of the History of Science, Oxford)

THE ARTS

By MARTIN HELZLE and PATRICK O'SULLIVAN

CONTENTS

239 B.C.E.

- Quintus Ennius, the father of Latin epic poetry, is born. In the *Annales* he not only invokes the Muses by their Greek names, but he also uses for the first time in Latin epic the Greek epic meter, dactylic hexameter. These two related poetic innovations are used by writers of Latin epic poetry for centuries.

211 B.C.E.

- The city of Syracuse is sacked by the Romans, and the general Marcus Claudius Marcellus brings back vast amounts of Greek artworks as spoils.

200* B.C.E.

- Titus Maccius Plautus, the most successful writer of Roman comedy, composes *Stichus,* one of his twenty-one plays. His characters engage in exuberant dialogue and song and also provide valuable information on many aspects of Roman culture.

184* B.C.E.

- Marcus Porcius Cato (Cato the Elder) builds the first basilica (a large, multipurpose public hall), known as the Basilica Porcia.

168 B.C.E.

- Lucius Aemilius Paullus defeats the Macedonians at Pydna and commemorates his victory with a huge monument at Delphi.

160* B.C.E.

- Publius Terentius Afer (Terence) writes six popular comedies characterized by their language of everyday life and moral sentiments.

133 B.C.E.

- Pergamon, a Hellenistic kingdom with a rich artistic heritage, becomes a Roman province.

120-100 B.C.E.

- The Temple of Fortuna Virilis is erected and it is characterized by Ionic columns, a high podium, and a frontal entrance. (Fortuna is the Roman goddess of Chance and Luck.)

*DENOTES CIRCA DATE

100* B.C.E.

- The earliest surviving fresco in Rome is painted.

98 B.C.E.

- The poet Titus Lucretius Carus is born. His great work *De rerum natura* (On the Nature of Things), is a didactic Epicurean poem on physics, psychology, and ethics.

80* B.C.E.

- The poet Gaius Valerius Catullus is active. His most famous work is a series of short poems addressed to a woman called "Lesbia." She is usually identified as the infamous Clodia, sister of the politician Publius Clodius, and the wife of Quintus Metellus Celer, whom she may have poisoned.

- The Sanctuary of Fortuna Primigenia, perhaps the largest temple in Italy, is completed at Praeneste. (Construction had begun in the mid-second century B.C.E.) It is built into the side of a hill with ramps and terraces providing access for worshippers.

80-30* B.C.E.

- Portrait head sculpture becomes popular among the aristocracy.

65 B.C.E.

- Quintus Horatius Flaccus (Horace) is born. He becomes a favorite of the Emperor Augustus and writes poetry ranging from *iambi* (epodes) and *sermones* (satires and epistles) to *carmina* (lyrics).

50-20* B.C.E.

- The architect and engineer Marcus Vitruvius Pollio writes *De architectura* (On Architecture), which is accepted as the final authority on classical architecture for centuries.

43 B.C.E.

- Marcus Tullius Cicero, Rome's foremost public speaker, dies. More than nine hundred of his letters are extant, and his fifty-eight known orations are models of courtroom persuasion.

- Publius Ovidius Naso (Ovid), an irreverent writer of elegy and epic, is born. Among his works are amatory texts (20s B.C.E.–2 C.E.): *Metamorphoses* and *Fasti* (both before 8 C.E..), and *Tristia* (10–12 C.E.).

* DENOTES CIRCA DATE

42-41* B.C.E.

• Gaius Sallustius Crispus, Rome's first significant writer of prose history, composes *Bellum Catilinae* (The War against Catiline). He writes *Bellum Iurguthinum* (The War against Jugurtha) circa 41–40 and *The Histories* after 39 B.C.E.

27* B.C.E.

• Albius Tibullus composes Book I of *Elegies,* which is characterized by a blend of amatory, pastoral, and religious themes.

27 B.C.E.

• Octavian receives the honorific title *Augustus* and institutes the regime of emperors; imperial portraiture becomes prevalent.

20* B.C.E.

• Sextus Propertius composes *Elegies* in four books.

19* B.C.E.

• Publius Vergilius Maro (Vergil) leaves the *Aeneid,* the great epic of the founding of Rome, unfinished at his death.

13-9 B.C.E.

• A large monumental altar known as the *Ara Pacis* is built by Augustus in order to commemorate his safe return from Gaul and Spain. It is surrounded by a walled precinct and decorated with sculptured reliefs on two tiers.

17* C.E.

• The historian Titus Livius (Livy) dies. His *Ab urbe condita libri* (Books from the Foundation of the City) covers Roman history from the origins of Rome to 9 B.C.E. in 142 books.

23 C.E.

• Gaius Plinius Secundus (Pliny the Elder), the chief extant literary source for ancient art, is born. He is best remembered as the author of the thirty-seven-book *Naturalis Historia,* an encyclopedia of all contemporary knowledge on animal, vegetable, and mineral.

35 C.E.

• Silius Italicus is born. His *Punica* is an epic of seventeen books on the Second Punic War (218–201 B.C.E.), and at over 12,000 lines it is the longest poem in Latin.

*DENOTES CIRCA DATE

55 C.E.

- The historian Publius (?) Cornelius Tacitus is born. During his lifetime he writes *Agricola* (98 C.E.), a biography of his father-in-law; *Germania* (Germany, 98 C.E.); *Dialogue on Orators* (circa 101–102 C.E.); *Histories* (circa 109–110 C.E.); and *Annals* (circa 120 C.E.).

60* C.E.

- The first three books of *De bello civili* (The Civil War) by Marcus Annaeus Lucanus (Lucan) are circulated. The grandson of Seneca the Elder and the nephew of Seneca the Younger, Lucan eventually loses favor with the emperor Nero and is forced to commit suicide in 65 C.E.

64 C.E.

- The statesman, Stoic philosopher, and tragic poet Lucius Annaeus Seneca (Seneca the Younger) dies. Some of his most important works include the philosophical *Letters to Lucilius;* the tragedies *Phaedra, Oedipus,* and *Agamemnon;* and a satire called *Apocolocyntosis.*

- A massive fire occurs in Rome. Afterward, Nero builds a new residence called the *Domus aurea* (Golden House). The long portico structure has a domed octagonal hall and uses vaulted concrete construction.

66* C.E.

- Petronius (possibly Titus Petronius Arbiter) composes *Satyrica,* a satirical romance in prose interspersed with verse.

72–80 C.E.

- The *Amphitheatrum Flavium* (Flavian Amphitheater), known later as the Colosseum, is built. The structure measures 205 yards by 170 yards along the axis, and is 170 feet high. The facade has three stories of arcades with half columns of the Doric, Ionic, and Corinthian styles. An estimated 3.5 million cubic feet of travertine blocks are used in its construction. The timber floors of the arena cover rooms for participants, cages for beasts, mechanical elevators, and drains. The Colosseum holds an estimated fifty thousand spectators. On hot days, the audience is protected from the sun by a huge canvas awning pulled across the top of the stadium.

79 C.E.

- Vesuvius erupts, burying Pompeii and Herculaneum in ash, but preserving frescoes, architecture, and various artifacts.

80* C.E.

- The epic poet Valerius Flaccus composes *Argonautica,* which recounts the legend of the quest of the Golden Fleece.

*DENOTES CIRCA DATE

81 C.E.

- The Arch of Titus is built in the Forum. It is dedicated by the Senate and people of Rome to commemorate the deification of Titus Vespasianus Augustus and his suppression of the Jewish revolt ten years earlier.

86-101 C.E.

- Marcus Valerius Martialis (Martial) composes *Epigrammaton libri* (Books of Epigrams), a collection of miscellaneous poems in twelve books. The poems depict, with acute observation but often with obscenity, various aspects of contemporary Roman life.

90* C.E.

- Publius Papinius Statius composes *Thebaid,* an epic poem in twelve books about the war between the sons of Oedipus over the kingship of Thebes. It is possibly the only extant Roman epic that can be said to have been published as a completely finished work by its author.

106-113 C.E.

- Trajan's Column is constructed in the Forum at Rome. The commemorative pillar, made from twenty large blocks of Carrara marble, is almost one hundred feet tall. The outer face has a spiral frieze depicting Trajan's victories in the two Dacian Wars (101–102 C.E. and 105–106 C.E.). The base of the Column contains several small rooms, including Trajan's tomb chamber.

125-128* C.E.

- Hadrian orders the construction of the Pantheon on the site of the original version erected by Agrippa in 27 B.C.E. Completed in 128 C.E., it is roofed by an enormous concrete dome which measures 142 feet across (larger than the dome of St. Peter's in the Vatican).

125-135 C.E.

- An extensive and luxurious villa is built for the Emperor Hadrian at Tivoli, fifteen miles outside of the capital. The different parts of the palace are named after famous places that Hadrian had visited on his various travels. For example, one group of buildings is called the Academia, after Plato's school at Athens, while another set is referred to as the Canopus, after the famous sanctuary near Alexandria.

130* C.E.

- Decius Junius Juvenalis (Juvenal) dies. During his lifetime he wrote sixteen satiric poems, issued in five books, which attacked with brutal frankness the vices of imperial Rome.

*DENOTES CIRCA DATE

146 C.E.

- The biographer Gaius Suetonius Tranquillus (Suetonius) dies. He is the author of *De viris illustribus*, biographies of Roman literary figures, and *De vita Caesarum*, lives of the first eleven emperors.

155* C.E.

- Lucius Apuleius writes *Metamorphoses*, or *The Golden Ass*, the only Roman novel that has survived intact. This work of adventurous, bizarre, and ludicrous episodes provides material for later authors such as Boccaccio and Cervantes.

160 C.E.

- Funerary portraiture becomes popular at Fayum in Egypt.

161-180 C.E.

- Marcus Aurelius is the Roman emperor. A Stoic philosopher and an individual of wide learning, he writes *Meditations*, a collection of moral precepts.

164-166 C.E.

- A bronze equestrian statue of the emperor Marcus Aurelius is made and placed on the Capitoline Hill. The event it was intended to celebrate is unknown.

200-250* C.E.

- The Temple of Venus at Baalbek, Phoenicia (Syria), is erected. Circular in design, it has a concave entablature, a high podium, and Corinthian columns.

203 C.E.

- A triumphal arch is dedicated to Septimius Severus in the Forum at Rome. Four large relief panels portray his victories against the Parthians. The next year a similar arch is finished at Leptis (Lepcis) Magna in North Africa.

211-217 C.E.

- The *Thermae Antoninianae* or Baths of Caracalla are built. The complex is a massive structure made of brick and concrete, and its design is both utilitarian as well as aesthetically pleasing. It has a *frigidarium* (cold room), a circular domed *caldarium* (hot room), *palaestra* (exercise yard), *natatio* (pool), gardens, and a stadium. Meanwhile, the interior has mosaic floors, marble veneer on the walls, and painted stucco on the vaults.

*DENOTES CIRCA DATE

298-306 C.E.

- The Baths of Diocletian are constructed in Rome while a palace-fortress of Diocletian is built at Spalato in present-day Croatia.

313 C.E.

- A colossal statue of Constantine is dedicated to the emperor. Constantine orders the completion of Maxentius's massive basilica in the Forum Romanum.

315 C.E.

- The Arch of Constantine is erected near the Colosseum and commemorates his victory over Maxentius in 312 C.E.

320 C.E.

- The poet and rhetorician Decimus Maximus Ausonius is born. He authors various works of verse such as *Technopaegnion*, *Eclogae*, and *Professores Burdigalenses*.

359 C.E.

- The sarcophagus of Junius Bassus, prefect of Constantinople, is finished. The marble coffin is adorned with scenes from the Old and New Testaments and divided into columns, which is an early example of Christian iconography adapting classical forms.

400* C.E.

- Claudius Claudianus (Claudian), writer of epics and panegyrics, dies. His panegyrics celebrated Theodorus, Honorius, Stilicho, and others.

430 C.E.

- Aurelius Augustinus (Augustine of Hippo), philosopher and early church father, dies. Among his treatises are *Confessions* (circa 397–400 C.E.) and *City of God* (circa 413–426 C.E.).

*DENOTES CIRCA DATE

OVERVIEW

Art and Life. Literature is about life, about what it means to be human in any given place at some time, about human pursuits and aspirations, which may or may not coincide with those of its author. Even a literature that is self-conscious, that is aware of its being literature, tells the reader something about the life and times that have generated it. In the process of reading, readers are engaged in a dialogue with the world of the author, who invites us constantly to compare their own experiences with the ones being presented, whether they be real, fictional, modeled on previous literature or some of all these. Like all the arts, literature at first engages emotion rather than intellect. As the poet Horace said, "The aim of a poet is either to benefit or to please." People "like" or "dislike" a piece of music or a painting; they are "moved," that is, transported from a neutral emotional state to a heightened one, by a statue or a play. The artistic productions humans all over the world have found most satisfying and valuable, however, are also the ones that go beyond the emotional appeal. In order to engage readers' thinking, literature more often than not uses fictional stories and patterned, unrealistic speech that allows detachment from personal worlds with limited viewpoints and catch a glimpse of the larger picture that is human life. Reflection seems to require distance; when looking at the world described by a Roman author, readers are therefore really looking at themselves, their own lives, values, ideals, and sensitivities.

The Challenge of the Greeks. The Roman literary pursuits start at about the time at which Greece was going into a serious decline. Alexander the Great had conquered the known world and exposed it to Greek culture, thus "hellenizing" the entire Mediterranean and Near East. When Roman writers look for models, they naturally look toward Greece and at first absorb Hellenistic literature, for example, works written after Alexander's empire broke apart. Roman writers experienced their encounter with the Greek works of all ages as a major challenge, which led to widespread feelings of inferiority. Reactions to this challenge differ and a growing sense of self-assurance that belies the image of inferiority emerges over time. Early writers such as Livius Andronicus, Plautus, and Terence follow their models much more closely than their successors. While they clearly do not translate, they produce Roman versions of their models. The degree of freedom with which Plautus makes changes to his Greek models—as well as the self-conscious artistry that Terence expresses explicitly in his prologues—indicate, however, that even these writers were not at all overawed by the Greeks. With growing self-assurance Latin *literati* actually invite comparison with their Greek models; examples of this are Vergil in all his works and Horace in his *Odes* and *Epodes*. The *Aeneid* has an obvious Homeric flair, while at the same time telling a Roman foundation myth that is driven by a Roman, teleological view of the world and Roman values such as *pietas* (sense of duty). Horace invites comparison with Greek lyric poetry by his meters and some of his mottoes, but his pragmatic attitude to life and his repeated reflections on recent Roman history, as well as to Roman virtues in the "Roman Odes," show how different he really is. Even in genres that are uniquely Roman, such as satire, the precedence of the Greeks is so powerful that Horace looks back to Greek comedy as well as the poetics of the Hellenistic poet Callimachus when outlining his approach to writing satire (*Sat.* 1.4, 1.10, 2.1). Similarly, the love elegy, for which there is no exact Greek counterpart, uses themes from Hellenistic epigram, comedy, and pastoral poetry as well as Greek myth to form a new and distinctly Roman genre.

Learning. One of the side effects of this continuing obsession with the Greeks stems from the repeated influence of Hellenistic rather than classical Greek literature. The first wave hit Rome when Plautus and Terence used Hellenistic comedy as their models. In the late Republic and early empire, however, poets were looking back to the Alexandrian poet Callimachus to define their own choice of smaller genres and increased formal polish. This second wave brought with it an emphasis on learning as a literary virtue. Callimachus had been the head of the best library of the world at the time—the fabled library of Alexandria, in Egypt—and this showed in his literary works and his idea of what poetry should look like: he preferred short over long works and emphasized learning in poetry. In his wake, Roman writers start to strive for highly artificial word order, they make their meters smoother and more regular, and they pay attention to structural patterns such as framing or ring-composition. Above all else, as voracious readers they unconsciously echo and deliberately refer to the works they have read. Hence, Latin literary criticism is quite obsessed with verbal parallels or "allusions" to this day. The difficulty these days lies not in finding a verbal parallel for what a Roman writer is saying, but in evaluating it. While the trend in recent years has been to claim that any parallel is a meaningful parallel, the pendulum seems to be swinging the other way again since not every parallel needs to be meaningful; it might just be a coincidental echo of a phrase that lingered in the poet's memory. The challenge to readers is in applying their judgment rather than indulging in their own poetic memory.

Use of Greek Myths. Learning also manifests itself in the frequent use of Greek myth in illustrative examples. Callimachus had advocated telling uncommon versions of myths or parts of well-worn stories hitherto unknown. So his friend Theocritus writes about the unrequited love of the man-eating Cyclops Polyphemus from Homer's *Odyssey*. Vergil's *Aeneid* does the same thing by telling the story of Aeneas, who had been just a minor character in Homer's *Iliad*. More than that, he combines the story of Aeneas's travels with that of Dido, Queen of Carthage, thereby giving a mythical explanation or *aition* for the Punic Wars between Rome and Carthage.

Mos maiorum: **The Ways of Our Ancestors.** Such *aitia* pervade Roman literature. What had been a vehicle for displaying mythical learning in Callimachus becomes much more important for the Romans. In general they had an extremely high regard for historical precedent, which they called *mos maiorum*. Anything that would link the past with the present was therefore deeply meaningful to them. It gave them a sense of their own roots and could also be used for purposes of political propaganda, especially if a mythical ancestor was Iulus, as in the case of the family of the Iulii. Stories about the mythical past were therefore highly significant for any writer's present. Even historical narratives acquire the weight of being a guide to life rather than simply an accurate account of what happened. Livy, for instance, tells his history to provide shining examples of senatorial virtue; Sallust gives historical instances of the ruling classes' corruption, which is ruining Rome. Readers are to learn something from history and other genres as well since writers in general are thought to have a didactic effect on their audience.

Patronage. One of the least mentioned but most salient characteristics of almost all the writers to be discussed in this chapter is that hardly any of them are native Romans. Most came from the outlying towns of Italy and were sent to Rome by their aristocratic families to be educated, but then stayed. If they generally came from local nobility in their hometown, they held Roman citizenship and received equestrian status in the capital. It is therefore somewhat surprising that many of them depended in some way or another on a patron, one who is a sponsor of higher social status and greater wealth. Equestrians by definition had to have an estate of at least 400,000 sesterces. If invested in land, this would give an average return of 6 percent or 24,000 sesterces per year. If Martial (*Epigr.* 3.10) makes fun of a young wastrel who has a monthly allowance of 2,000 sesterces per month, then 24,000 must have

been enough money to live on. If a person had a family, little was left for any frills, but even so, the family would survive on this sum. In spite of their own protestations, poets were therefore not "poor"; they just had to live simple lives. They had the free time (*otium*) to do their writing without holding down a job. They did not, however, need a patron to help with their rent or their grocery bills. While it is true that a patron could provide the occasional free meal and arrange an advantageous marriage, their main job was to help disseminate literary works. This duty was extremely important since there was no huge publishing industry like the one that currently exists. In return the patrons received the writers' thanks and often had works dedicated to them. There is, therefore, little evidence of literary works being directly commissioned other than Horace's *Secular Hymn*. Writers dedicated their works to their patrons as tokens of gratitude for past benefits or in expectation of future acts of kindness.

Key Questions in Literature. Latin literature from Ennius to Boethius covers about seven and a half centuries during which the Roman world underwent stunning changes. Providing a survey of Latin material is fraught with difficulties. Rather than mapping all the changes and listing as many writers as possible, this chapter will concentrate on the major figures and among them give most space to those widely read in schools. Recurring questions will be: 1. How do they present the world? 2. What are their main concerns? 3. How do they deal with their Greek or Roman predecessors?

The Spell of Greek Art. As in their literature, so in visual art, the Romans—at least as far back as the third century B.C.E.—fell under the spell of Greek art, and were profoundly influenced by it. A chief indication of this interest is the large numbers of Greek artists that migrated or were brought to Rome from the second century B.C.E. onward. But Roman art involves much more than the mere replication of an older art form, and "influence" need not imply an inability to adapt and select from earlier forms to produce styles and techniques that are distinctive in their own right. To see the Romans' greatest artistic accomplishment as the preserver of a type of art that may be more intuitively appealing to modern romantic sensibilities would be to miss out on their own significant and durable contributions to the art and architecture of the Western tradition.

Cultural Changes. While over several centuries new styles and techniques were developed in media, the fact remains that many practitioners of Roman art were not themselves natives of Rome. This is only to be expected, when we consider the vast expanse of Rome's empire, and especially the political, social, and religious changes within the Roman world. Among these are the shift from a republic to imperial regime, the rise and fall of imperial dynasties (many originating from the provinces), the transition from paganism to the adoption of Christianity as the official religion, and the geographical shift from Rome to Constantinople as permanent imperial residence. Another significant feature at work in Roman art and architecture, of course, is the inevitable stimulus afforded by the expansion of the empire, and contact with art from all over the Mediterranean. Some have, with reason, spoken of the "problem" of identifying what is "Roman" about Roman art, as a result of these factors. But one can identify among the most salient features of Roman art over a period of great changes their technical architectural advances, which develop classical forms on a grand civic scale. We may also consider the important role of private patronage, and the largely commemorative function of artworks in the service of the state or individual. These concepts enable us to grasp with some plausibility many of the main characteristics of the visual monuments and artworks produced under the auspices of Rome from about 180 B.C.E. to the early fourth century C.E.—a period of five hundred years or so.

Christian Art. The accession of Constantine, emperor from 306–337 C.E., and his conversion to Christianity, as well as the shift to Constantinople, all raise the issue of how Christian art is to be dealt with. Detailed treatment of early Christian art is beyond our scope here, not least because such art and its ideological motivations do not come to an end in 476 C.E., when the Roman empire in the West finally fell. More importantly, much in the significance and functions of Christian art can be seen to be separate from the main concerns and motivations behind Roman art of the pre-Christian era. It is true that in stylistic terms, certain features of later pagan Roman artworks anticipate much in early Christian iconography. At the same time, some early Christian artworks maintain Classical pagan forms and techniques of representation. It is also true that the changes under Constantine did not lead to a severance from all things Roman in the East. Indeed, although speakers and writers of Greek, the Byzantines specifically referred to themselves as *Rhômaioi*—Romans. However, in general terms, what does change under Christianity is the increasingly symbolic and didactic nature of art, which, unlike pagan art, depended on a canonical text for its meaning, and which consistently guided the viewer to the next world rather than glorying in this one. Herein lies a significant contrast with major facets of Roman art of all types in preceding centuries, with the result that in Christian imagery important breaks from older narrative techniques emerge. The pagan past was not vanquished under the Constantinian regime, as is attested by the attempts of Julian (emperor from 360–363 C.E.) to revive the religion and customs of pagan antiquity. In fact, the Christian church played a key role in preserving substantial amounts of the literature and philosophy of the Greco-Roman world that would otherwise have been lost forever—a remarkable achievement for a sect once persecuted under pagan Rome. Yet, the long-term changes in the forms and functions of art traceable to Constantine's succession make it plausible to see in his regime a period of major transition.

Etruscan Influences. Important early influences on the art of the Roman world are traceable to other parts of Italy, notably Etruria, the region of the Etruscans. These people were, in fact, the rulers of Rome for a while, and when the Romans established their republic in 509 B.C.E. the king they expelled was an Etruscan. Roman familiarity with Etruscan art thus goes back a long way. When the Romans conquered Veii in southern Etruria in 396 B.C.E., they again would have been confronted with examples of Etruscan art, which had reached sophisticated levels especially in the form of temple architecture, funerary sculpture, and fresco painting in tombs. Etruscan art appears to have grown out of an earlier Italian culture of a people called the Villanovans, some of whose metalwork and pottery were discovered near Bologna in 1853, and which date back to the Iron Age period (circa 1000–700 B.C.E.). A more important strand in the development of Etruscan art, which was to have profound effects more directly on the Romans, was the impact of Greek art, especially from the sixth century B.C.E. onward. Vast quantities of pots were imported into Etruria, and Greek fresco painting as well as sculpture clearly stimulated much in the stylistic development of Etruscan art. It is significant, then, to realize that the Romans, on seeing Etruscan art from an early stage, were also looking at forms frequently adapted from Greek art.

Greek vs. Roman. No treatment of Roman art can afford to ignore what the Greeks had achieved before them. Understanding this not only makes clearer what they borrowed from the Greeks—a debt freely acknowledged by many Romans themselves—but displays more fully what differentiates significant aspects of Roman art from Greek prototypes. Detailed exploration of this important area is beyond the scope of this work, but some very general points should be noted, beginning with the realization that Roman attitudes to visual artworks were often shaped by different motivations to those of the Greeks. Among these are the use (or abuse) of artworks as booty, the explicit commemoration of historical events, and the wish to venerate one's ancestors in the form of portrait sculpture.

Greek Imports. Greek colonies in southern Italy and Sicily from as early as the eighth century B.C.E. would have brought Greek artifacts within early Rome's sphere of influence, independently of the Etruscans. It is chiefly from the third century B.C.E., however, that events in the Roman reception of Greek art take a decisive turn. Conflict with Greek colonies at Tarentum in the 270s B.C.E. and Hellenistic kingdoms, such as that of Pyrrhus of Epirus bring the Romans more fully into direct contact with Greek art and customs in their own environment. Indeed, a watershed in the history of Rome's response to Greek art and culture can be understood in Marcellus's sack of Syracuse in 211 B.C.E., which also exposed the conquerors to the learning and rhetoric of this once-flourishing Greek colony, founded in 733 B.C.E. Masses of artworks were brought to Rome in the form of booty, creating in many Romans a fascination with the Greek world that was to be a marked feature of Roman culture overall. In fact, so strong was this inclination toward Greek art that it sparked outcries from such powerful figures of the day as Cato (234–149 B.C.E.). Nonetheless, Rome's further acquisitions of both mainland Greece by 146 B.C.E. and sophisticated Hellenistic kingdoms such as Pergamon in 133 B.C.E. increased exposure to Greek art. By the late second century B.C.E. a huge market for Greek art had grown, attracting artists from the Greek world to Rome, which by now had become the great power in the Mediterranean. It is also from this time that the earliest significant examples of extant Roman art and architecture appear on a continued basis. As well, this is when the era of copies, private art collections, connoisseurship and even forgeries—an era of which we are the inheritors today—begins.

Danger of Eastern Influences. In a speech that he ascribes to Cato, Livy (34.4.1–4) conveys the conservative reaction of some Romans to the influx of art that came into Rome in the wake of Marcellus's sacking of Syracuse in 211 B.C.E, considered to have degenerate effects:

> You have often heard me complaining about the extravagances of women and often about those of men. . .and how the state suffers from two diverse vices, avarice and luxury, those pests which have overturned all great empires. I come to fear these even more as the fortune of the Republic becomes greater and more pleasant every day and the empire grows—now we have even moved over into Greece and Asia, places which are full of every sort of libidinous temptation, and we are even putting our hands on royal treasuries. For I fear that these will make prisoners of us rather than we of them. They are dangers, believe me, those statues which have been brought into the city from Syracuse. For now I fear too many people praising and marveling at the ornaments of Corinth and Athens and laughing at our terracotta antefixes of the Roman gods. I prefer these gods, who are propitious and will remain so, I hope, if we permit them to remain in their proper places.

Figuring Actuality. Amid all this fascination with Greek art, from an early stage Roman art shows a greater inclination than Greek art toward depiction of actual events and persons. This feature is directly linked to a type of triumphal art designed both to celebrate Rome's ongoing military conquests, and to function as a statement of the personal and political power of the individual who commissioned it. Of course, the Greeks could depict recent historical events in grand public display—Micon's painting in the stoa of Athens of the famous Greek victory over the Persians at Marathon in 490 B.C.E. is an example. But more often famous battles were commemorated by the Greeks in the depiction of mythic battles between, for instance, heroes and centaurs, or Olympian gods and giants. It is no coincidence that such imagery becomes widespread in the wake of the Greeks' defeat of the invading Persian forces in 480–79 B.C.E. For the Greeks, then, military victories seem more often to be celebrated in mythical allegories, whereas the Romans tended to be more explicit and direct in the visual celebration of military triumphs. For instance, we hear that Marcellus commissioned a number of paintings celebrating his conquest in Syracuse; similarly, Aemilius Paullus had a sculptural monument at Delphi made depicting details of his victory at Pydna in 168–7 B.C.E.

Commemorative Monuments. The typically Roman impulse to depict events and figures recent in their history finds famous expression in the Arch of Titus (81 C.E.), commemorating that emperor's destruction of Jerusalem, and presenting him in the company of the allegorical figure of Victory. The *Ara pacis,* or Altar of Peace, set up by Augustus (13–9 B.C.E.) combines further allegorical imagery with depiction of real people, including the emperor and his family. These monuments, among others, incorporate another great Roman contribution to visual art: namely, the mastery of sculptural friezes on a vast scale. Again, great sculptural friezes were produced by the Greeks, such as the Parthenon frieze on the famous temple of Athena on the Athenian Acropolis. But the Romans added elements of their own to this medium, such as the treatment of hugely crowded, multilayered scenes, and the further exploration of spatial depth, as well as the historical subject matter. Over time many public sculptural friezes become somewhat flatter, the figures more frontal and the overall design more openly schematic and symmetrical, anticipating further developments in Christian and Byzantine art. The Arch of Constantine (circa 312–315 C.E.), patched together from earlier imperial arches, has long been regarded as a hybrid of styles. Sculptured friezes can also be found on smaller media such as stone or marble sarcophagi (funeral caskets), which betray the influence of Etruscan art, as well as domestic chests. Yet, perhaps the most striking example of Roman innovation in sculptural relief is the great spiral frieze along Trajan's Column (113 C.E.), which celebrates recent victories over the Dacians, and is a tour de force unparalleled in the Greek world.

Pietas. The veneration felt by pious, mostly aristocratic Romans for their ancestors is a significant feature of the Roman cultural value system, conveyed best in the word *pietas,* origin of our "piety." The word *pius* is consistently applied by Vergil to the central figure of his epic poem, the *Aeneid.* This value also underlies the custom of carrying portraits of the deceased during the funeral procession which, during the Republic, were worn as masks by males within the family who most resembled the dead man being commemorated. These masks were probably wax, so they have not survived, but statues of wealthy Romans carrying ancestral busts, datable to the early first century B.C.E., reveal a desire to commemorate ancestors in more durable materials, as well as in closely realistic detail. In the Classical Greek era (circa 480–323 B.C.E.) portrait sculpture was rarer and tended to be somewhat idealized and for exalted figures of state. Alexander the Great (356–323 B.C.E.) commissioned his favorite sculptor, Lysippos, to produce his portraits in a famously stylized manner, which propagated his image and the idea of ruler-cult throughout his empire. Under some Hellenistic rulers more realistic tendencies emerged, as in the image of the puffy-faced Euthydemos of Bactria (circa 200 B.C.E.). As well, during the Hellenistic period many famous philosophers, such as Socrates, Plato, and Aristotle were commemorated in portraits, which present them as recognizable individuals even if the accuracy of their facial details remains questionable. While the evident wish for genuine realism in Roman sculpture seems to stem from a uniquely Roman ritual, it may have received further impetus from contact with certain Hellenistic regal portraits. In any event, we sometimes find a literally "warts-and-all" realism in many Roman portraits in both the republican and imperial ages, which gives them a striking immediacy. As well, many of these technically accomplished images seem to offer a glimpse of the sitter's personality.

Architectural Advances. In architecture, within Rome and in many parts of the empire, great advances were made both in scale, design, and use of materials. Temple architecture reflected both Etruscan and Greek influences, and, in addition to Greek styles of columns, the Romans used the Tuscan and Composite orders. Moreover, the Romans invented new building types and made innovations to older designs, such as adding multistoried façades behind the acting area of Greek theaters. The amphitheater—literally a "theater on both sides"—was a Roman invention designed to accommodate the masses attending gladiatorial and other kinds of spectacles. Such a building with its tiers surrounding a central arena serves as the prototype of the modern sports stadium, and was most potently embodied by the Colosseum (circa 80 C.E.). The Romans' use of concrete marks another significant shift from earlier building techniques, and enabled the construction of complex vaulting systems in public buildings such as the Sanctuary to Fortuna Primigenia (circa 80 B.C.E.), Imperial Markets of Trajan (circa 100–112 C.E.), and vast public baths like those dedicated by Caracalla (circa 211–17 C.E.). The great dome of the Pantheon (rebuilt 125–8 C.E.) depends largely on the use of concrete, which is exploited to awe-inspiring visual effect in this temple grandly dedicated to all the gods.

Paintings. A further significant element within Roman art is the partial survival of large-scale painting on wood panel and in fresco form. Notable examples come from Rome itself and other areas such as Pompeii and Herculaneum—two cities buried under the volcanic ash of Vesuvius during its eruption in 79 C.E. The disaster for the locals of Pompeii and Herculaneum proved to be an archaeological boon for later ages, since the ash preserved the fragile material from the elements. The almost complete loss of earlier Greek monumental painting makes the Roman survivals all the more precious, and it seems likely that many Roman paintings copy or modify Greek originals. Like sculptors, many successful Greek painters worked for Roman patrons from the late second century B.C.E. onwards. Surviving subject matter includes Greek myths; urban, architectural, and natural landscapes; as well as anonymous scenes of ritual or everyday activity. Here, too, the rich heritage of Etruscan funerary painting seems to have had some influence in style and technique. Four Roman styles have been identified over the 180 years or so covered by this kind of painting, which reveal varying treatment of spatial depth, use of color, and so on. Mosaics remained a popular art form in domestic and more grandiose settings. Many from Pompeii and elsewhere have been unearthed, and show considerable details of workmanship and a diversity of subject

matter similar to that found in painting, as well as stylistic variations over time. Portable paintings beyond 79 C.E. are known elsewhere from the Roman world, most notably the Fayum in Egypt, where many vivid funerary portraits on wood depicting apparently well-to-do men, women, and children have been found, datable from the late first century C.E. and lasting well over a century. Portraits on coins dating from the time of Julius Caesar, and later imperial images in gems and other stones testify to the Romans' use of various media for depicting real people, often with great skill.

Various Sources. Apart from the material remains, information about Roman art and artists can be found in various ancient written sources dating back to the second century B.C.E. These include inscriptions, which tend to be very brief, giving little more than the name of the patron, building, and the consulship or principate at the time of the monument. Literary evidence can sometimes be more informative, especially when so many artifacts are unsigned. As many Greek artists had done, a number of practitioners active in the Roman period wrote about their work, but none of these writings has survived in any form, except for Vitruvius's treatise, *On Architecture.* Written at the time of Augustus, this explains some of the theoretical and practical issues confronting a practicing architect and engineer of the period. The encyclopedic *Natural History* of Pliny the Elder, who died during the eruption of Vesuvius of 79 C.E., is the main source for artists and their work in the Roman period, as indeed it provides detailed descriptions of Greek artists. But Pliny was hardly an "art historian" in the modern sense; rather he was a compiler of various traditions, and likely a preserver of older theories. Other Greek and Latin texts—historiographical, legal, and biographical—provides certain insights into the roles, functions, and receptions of art in the Roman world. Sources as varied as Cicero, Livy, Suetonius, and Cassius Dio provide some idea of what meanings art and architecture could have in the Roman world. These media often employed to express political power and honor individual memory or to glut the megalomania of certain emperors. Artworks reduced to booty by corrupt officials; indeed, Cicero provides evidence not only of this occurrence, but also points to a more reverent attitude to artworks among the Greek residents of Sicily that makes the plundering of their art so hard to bear. In other ancient views, such as Cato's, the lure of visual art is even denigrated as a moral threat to traditional Roman values. By way of contrast or parallel, these and other responses serve as valuable reference points for modern approaches to Roman art. For they can raise awareness of the assumptions underlying contemporary concepts of what art is and what it could or should be.

Loss of Artworks. During a prosecution speech (*Verr.* 2.4.132) Cicero gives an impression of the demoralizing effects of the greed of Verres, who plundered Sicily during his magistracy there, and brought misery to the locals who esteemed their lost artworks:

> Do you think they have been afflicted with only moderate grief? It is not so, judges. First because they are all moved by religious feeling and because they feel that they must maintain and worship diligently those national gods which

they have received from their ancestors; and second, because Greeks delight in this kind of ornamentation, in works of art and artistry, in statues and paintings more than in anything else. And consequently, from their mournful complaints we are able to understand how these things seem so terribly bitter to them which to us might seem less serious and hardly so worrisome.

Legacy. The varied forms and styles of Roman art–the painting, sculpture, and especially architecture produced in Rome or for Roman patrons—constitute one of the great legacies of the ancient Mediterranean world to the modern. And even a brief word on this huge topic is apt here. It is through the Romans that much of Greek architecture and art, especially sculpture, was able to survive at least indirectly, since the Romans adapted Greek architectural forms and copied many (now lost) Greek artworks in vast numbers. A crucial factor affecting Rome's pre-Christian legacy to the world was the renewed interest in antiquity characteristic of the Italian Renaissance of the 1400s and 1500s, which continued unabated for centuries. The rediscovery of statues dating from the Roman period in the 1500s stimulated the development of new sculptural and painted forms for the human figure in the work of major artists of the day. Michelangelo is said to have been present at the unearthing of the famous Laökoon group (probably first century C.E.) in 1506, and was profoundly affected as a result; so too was much of later European art.

Immediate Influence. For hundreds of years, subsequent ages had direct access to Rome and its monuments elsewhere in Italy and scattered throughout its former empire. Thus, the influence of Roman forms became more immediate than was possible for most Greek monuments. These were mostly "off-limits" to western Europeans, due to the Ottoman regime in Greece. In contrast, the tradition of the "Grand Tour" to Italy evolved by the late eighteenth century, further stimulated by the discovery of the "lost" cities of Pompeii and Herculaneum, as well as making Rome a focus for such famous travellers as Goethe, Byron, and Keats and countless artists and architects. This situation remains unchanged today for the Eternal City. During the eighteenth century further renewed interest in the Greco-Roman past became manifest as a result of the political turmoil that culminated in the French Revolution of 1789. The revolutionaries invoked the heroes of the early Roman republic as their role models and had their images disseminated in the suitably austere style of neo-classicism. Nowhere is this more effectively portrayed than in Jacques-Louis David's *Oath of the Horatii* (1784), which he completed in Rome. Across the Atlantic contemporary American revolutionaries would similarly revive Roman styles in architecture, as another way of invoking the "glory" of republican Rome.

Cultural Links. On a different level, the work of J. J. Winckelmann was important. His *History of the Art of the Ancients* (1764) was the first serious attempt to study the arts of Greece and Rome, and is a further manifestation of the inter-est generated by Greco-Roman art and antiquity. He tended to see the arts of these two cultures as linked to the political ideologies of their day, although his dating of Greek art was often hugely incorrect. While many would disagree with his view that Roman art is a decline from the great periods of Greek art, he did much to pioneer the study of ancient art and influenced many subsequent art-historical studies.

Profound Legacy. Rome's most profound material legacy to posterity is its architecture, which has greatly influenced subsequent Western building programs from the Renaissance onward. Filippo Brunelleschi's great dome for the Cathedral in Florence ("Il Duomo," completed 1436), and Michelangelo's dome for St. Peter's Basilica in Rome (completed 1564) would have been impossible without a familiarity with such works as the Pantheon. Indeed, with admirable restraint Michelangelo acknowledged the Romans' achievement by consciously making the diameter of St. Peter's dome 1.5 meters shorter than that of the Pantheon. Less respectful was Urban VIII, a pope from the Barberini family (1623–1644), who ripped out the bronze-work on the ceiling of the Pantheon to make cannons and the *baldacchino* (or canopy) over the altar at St. Peter's. This prompted the famous dissenting remark: "What the barbarians did not do, the Barberini did!" What we know as "neo-classical architecture" of the eighteenth and nineteenth centuries with its temple façades, columns, and pediments echoes both Greek and, more often than not, specifically Roman prototypes. The idea of Rome as the self-professed civilizer of the ancient world endured beyond antiquity, thus making its architectural style suited to a range of civic buildings. Banks, churches, art galleries, museums, libraries, and, notably, law-courts across Europe, the United States, and Australia pay homage to Greco-Roman forms—from the National Gallery in London to the State Library in Melbourne. Many other private and public buildings over the past two hundred years invoke Roman architectural forms and also the sense of authority and tradition of the Roman republic and empire implicit in those forms. For instance, Thomas Jefferson's home, Monticello (1769–1809), testifies to the influence of the Pantheon, as does the domed and colonnaded Capitol Building in Washington, D.C. In the popular imagination today other large scale works like the Appian Way, the Colosseum, or Hadrian's Wall rank highly as some of the best-known monuments of antiquity, even if many would now remain ambivalent about, or reject, the imperial ideology responsible for their construction. An age that can recall the perhaps all too easy appropriation of the Classical Roman past in the form of Mussolini's fascism (a name invoking the *fasces* of the Roman republic) will inevitably have mixed feelings about Roman antiquity. Yet, the profound influence of the Romans' achievements in monumental works, no less than in Western legal and political systems, remains.

TOPICS IN THE ARTS

ARCHITECTURE AND THE LATE REPUBLIC

The Basilica. Roman architecture exists in many forms, including domestic, religious, and civic works such as basilicas. Despite their long-lasting achievements as builders, it is generally recognized that nothing distinctively Roman survives before 200 B.C.E. The earliest known basilica was built around 184 B.C.E. by M. Porcius Cato, who dominated political and cultural life in Rome in the first half of the second century B.C.E. The basic design involved a long rectangular hall with the central part of the roof raised higher than for the peripheral aisles. Internal colonnades supported this central section, and often there was an apse at the end of the hall containing a raised platform for tribunes or magistrates to carry out their duties; at the front was usually a portico and shops. The basic design did not significantly change for centuries and many were commissioned by later emperors. For instance, the architect Apollodorus designed the Basilica Ulpia for Trajan's Forum (112 C.E.) and Constantine completed a basilica begun by Maxentius that was added to the Roman Forum (circa 312 C.E.), which was exceptional in having concrete vaulted roofs.

A reconstruction of the Sanctuary of Fortuna, Praeneste (Archaeological Museum, Palestrina)

Temple of Fortuna Virilis erected in the late second century B.C.E.

The atrium of the "House of the Silver Wedding" in Pompeii, circa early first century B.C.E.

Domestic Buildings. Domestic architecture also remained consistent over time, although, as is the case today, different social classes dwelt in different styles of buildings. The urban underclasses could expect to live in multistoried apartment blocks, known as *insulae,* sometimes five levels high, made of concrete and brick, and with shop fronts on the ground level. Patricians, or members of the wealthier classes, sometimes enjoyed rural villas, which could be quite extensive architectural complexes, with gardens, ponds, and terraced landscapes. The urban dwelling for the rich or better off was called a *domus,* and excavations in Pompeii of the so-called House of the Silver Wedding around the first century B.C.E. have revealed many details of its design. The front wall was usually solid and faced directly onto the street. The entrance led to a rectangular area or *atrium,* whose open roof was supported by four Corinthian columns; a central pool collected rain-water coming in off the inwardly sloping roof, while around the atrium were living rooms and bedrooms. Beyond the atrium was the dining room, reception hall, and often an enclosed colonnaded garden, with further rooms off this as well.

Temples. Like many aspects of their art, temples built by the Romans combine Greek and Etruscan features. Greek orders of columns were used and developed by the Romans, but so too was the Etruscan habit of setting the temple on a high podium with steps approaching it from the front. This front porch was often quite deep and the only part of the temple that had freestanding columns, whereas typical Greek design involved freestanding columns all around, and steps on all sides. The main interior room, or *cella,* housed the cult statue of the god or goddess to whom the temple was dedicated. The temple of "Fortuna Virilis," with its Ionic columns, high podium, frontal entrance, and engaged side columns is a good example of an early Roman temple, dating to the late second century B.C.E. An interesting early variant on this design is the circular, or *tholos,* shaped temple at Tivoli of the Sibyl, an ancient prophetic woman, from the early first century B.C.E. The Greek-style columns are crowned by a frieze showing garlands of flowers and suspended fruit, and have been placed on a podium 2.59 meters high and 14.25 meters in diameter. The Sanctuary of Fortuna at Praeneste, about 25 miles east of Rome, is another significant instance of Roman architectural ingenuity, this time on a grand scale. Building began around the middle of the second century B.C.E., and involved cutting the entire site in flat terraces, on which were colonnades and an open precinct, into the side of a hill crowned by a small circular temple to the goddess herself behind a larger theater-like semicircular area. The terraces were supported by a series of vaults made of concrete containing a kind of volcanic earth called pozzolana, and the main terrace was fronted by a two-storied colonnaded façade with semicircular recesses. The base of this façade was reached by worshippers approaching from below along two opposing ramps, half-covered with a row of Doric columns to support the roofed section; these

The Temple of the Sibyl at Tivoli, early
first century B.C.E.

ramps met in the center of the level. The site afforded magnificent views as one ascended, and added to the sense of pilgrimage each worshipper would have felt in moving gradually closer to the shrine. The overall sanctuary represents a fine example of architecture blending in with the landscape, and develops similar principles of design found in the Greek sanctuary to Asklêpios, god of medicine, on the island of Kos, dating from the third century B.C.E.

Sources:

William L. MacDonald, *The Architecture of the Roman Empire I: An Introductory Study,* second edition (New Haven: Yale University Press, 1982).

MacDonald, *The Architecture of the Roman Empire II: An Urban Appraisal,* second edition (New Haven: Yale University Press, 1987).

Nancy and Andrew Ramage, *Roman Art: Romulus to Constantine,* third edition (London: Laurence King, 2000).

John B. Ward-Perkins, *Roman Architecture* (New York & London: Harry N. Abrams, 1977).

ARCHITECTURE: EARLY IMPERIAL AGE

The Birth of Empire. The accession of Augustus in 27 B.C.E. traditionally marks the end of the Roman republic and a transition to the era of imperial dynasties who present themselves as protectors of the Roman people and true masters of the civilized world. A century of bloody civil wars had only just ended, and Augustus sought to legitimate his claim to power with a series of monuments, as

The Colosseum in Rome, completed in 80 C.E.

well as calling on the services of poets such as Vergil to write his epic *Aeneid,* ostensibly as a panegyric to the new regime. An important consequence of this policy for architecture and visual arts generally is the idea of art in the service of the state—in effect, art as state propaganda. Augustus built his own forum, as well as theaters, arches, aqueducts, and temples, and was said to have boasted that he found Rome made of brick and left it made of marble. At the rear of his forum was a temple to Mars Ultor (the Avenger), which contained a statue to the war god, as well as to Venus, the mother of Aeneas. An image of Julius Caesar, Augustus's adoptive father, was also housed there, as were other statues of former great men of Rome, including Aeneas and Romulus. Pompey had built the first stone theater in Rome in 55 B.C.E., as a way of cultivating popularity with the masses, and Augustus followed suit when he built around 12 B.C.E. the theater of Marcellus, named after his son-in-law. This semicircular building had a more substantial stage building than was usual for Greek theaters and combined on its façade a different order of Greek columns attached to the outer wall for each level, thus setting a major architectural precedent. Beyond Rome, impressive engineering work was also carried out, such as in the famous aqueduct in southern France known as the Pont du Gard, built possibly by Agrippa late in the first century B.C.E. Functional and superbly proportioned with its great rhythm of arches, this construction also suggests the idea of imperial beneficence in providing the provinces with an

NERO'S "GOLDEN HOUSE"

Suetonius (*Nero* 31) outlines the extravagance of Nero's Golden House (*Domus Aurea*) and suggests that the emperor, for all his megalomania, could display a touch of irony at times:

It had a vestibule, in which stood a colossal statue of Nero himself, 120 feet high; the area it covered was so great that it had a mile-long portico with colonnades. It also had a pool which resembled the sea and was surrounded by buildings which were to give the impression of cities; besides this there were rural areas varied with ploughed fields, vineyards, pastures, and woodlands, and filled with all types of domestic animals and wild beasts. All the structures in other parts of the palace were overlaid with gold and were highlighted with gems and mother-of-pearl. There were dining rooms whose ceilings were equipped with rotating ivory panels and with pipes so that flowers could be strewn and unguents sprayed on those below. The foremost of the dining rooms was a rotunda, which rotated everyday and night like the heavens. There were baths through which flowed sea water and medicinal spring water. When the palace was completed . . . he dedicated it and expressed his approval only by noting that he was "at last beginning to be housed like a human being."

Source: *Suetonius,* edited and translated by John C. Rolfe, 2 volumes, Loeb Classical Library (Cambridge, Mass: Harvard University Press, 1913–1914).

The Pantheon in Rome, reconstructed circa 125–128 C.E. to replace the temple first built by Marcus Agrippa in 27–25 B.C.E.

adequate supply of water. Mindful of his own posthumous reputation, Augustus had a circular mausoleum built for himself, just outside the city limits, in keeping with the practice of burying eminent republicans. It was eighty-seven meters in diameter with a colonnade on the upper level and earth atop the lower level, and anticipated later imperial mausoleums such as Hadrian's.

The Julio-Claudians. The successors of Augustus down to 68 C.E. were known as the Julio-Claudians, who continued aspects of public building with aqueducts in Rome and the provinces. Tiberius gave a generous amount of money toward the rebuilding of parts of Asia Minor (modern-day Turkey), which had been hit by an earthquake in 17 C.E. During Claudius's reign two great aqueducts were built: at Segovia in Spain, and the Aqua Claudia, which leads into Rome and whose gate, known as the Porta Maggiore, stands impressively today with its double arches and rusticated (deliberately unfinished) stonework. Near this is an underground basilica, dating from circa 50 C.E. Its function remains a mystery today, but it is notable for its barrel-vaulted stucco ceiling with elegant figures and scenes of abduction and rescue. The fire that hit Rome in 64 C.E., under the reign of Nero, led to attempts to make tenement blocks safer, but the overcrowding and noise seemed to continue as ever. Yet, in the space left in the wake of the fire Nero commissioned his "Golden House," which only survives in sec-

tions today. However, we can see innovations in the use of concrete for the dome of a large octagonal room with a central opening to let in light, which anticipates the great interior of the Pantheon (circa 125–128 C.E.). Suetonius, writing for a later age that had come to despise the Julio-Claudians, gives a fuller account of Nero's "pleasure dome" and of the emperor's self-indulgence.

The Flavians. The Flavian dynasty (69–96 C.E.) was ushered in by Vespasian after Nero's suicide in 68 C.E., and the year of four emperors that followed—Galba, Otho, Vitellius, and Vespasian himself. Under the Flavians two of Rome's most famous monuments were built: the Colosseum and the Arch of Titus. As a soldier of plebeian stock who had worked his to the top through military success, Vespasian was held to be a contrast to Nero. He emphasized the point by building the Colosseum, the grandest amphitheater in the ancient world, for popular spectacles on the site of the former emperor's Golden House. Its dimensions for the oval arena were 188 by 156 meters, and it could hold more than fifty thousand spectators. Below the arena were passages and cages for the lions and other animals brought in to fight with gladiators or kill criminals. The building was made from concrete and travertine stone and its interior was structured by a series of groin vaults and arches on each story; engaged Doric, Ionic, and Corinthian columns on separate levels appeared on the exterior, recalling the theater of Marcellus, built under Augustus.

The Pont du Gard Aqueduct in southern France, possibly built by Marcus Agrippa in the late first century B.C.E.

The Forum of Trajan, Rome, circa 100-112 C.E.

Interior of the Pantheon in Rome

Imperial Zenith. Under the emperors Trajan and Hadrian, whose combined reigns lasted from 98 to 138 C.E., the Roman empire was at its peak, and this is borne out in some of the great monuments constructed at this time. Trajan was a popular and successful general, and on becoming emperor cultivated his image as benefactor by establishing imperial baths in Rome larger than those of Titus. To accommodate the increasing business and commercial needs of the flourishing empire he also had his own markets and forum built. These were designed by Apollodorus and were much admired in antiquity. The markets made of concrete, brick, and travertine were cut into the Quirinal hill on the eastern side of Trajan's forum behind a high wall. They were set in a vast semicircle of three stories accommodating about 150 shops and offices, supported internally by a series of groin and barrel vaults. The entire complex also comprised Trajan's Basilica Ulpia, notable for its two apses. It was located immediately to the north of the markets to the rear of his open triumphal forum, which contained an equestrian statue of the emperor. Behind the basilica were separate Greek and Latin libraries between which is the famous column commemorating Trajan's vic-

tories over the Dacians, still visible today. A notable example of provincial town planning under Trajan's rule is the well-preserved city of Timgad in modern Algeria, originally built to house retired veterans. The plan is a perfect grid system with colonnades, arches, a square forum, and a mostly intact theater, all of which give some idea of the layout of a typical Roman town of the time.

Innovations of Hadrian. Hadrian's interest in architecture led him to embark on his own personal designs, which were dismissed by Apollodorus as "pumpkins"; Apollodorus, it seems, paid for this and other criticisms with his life. Yet, under Hadrian much further building in Rome and beyond continued in often innovative form. While Hadrian's name is associated with the famous defensive wall in northern Britain spanning some eighty miles, other notable works in the provinces were completed during his rule. At Tivoli he established a complex of buildings within a landscaped setting that comprised his villa; among these were vaulted baths, private suites, a so-called maritime theater, a colonnaded courtyard, and two long pools, including one called the Canopus after an Egyptian city visited by the emperor. He built his own

Ammianus Marcellinus (16.10.15) writes of the impact of the Forum of Trajan on the emperor Constantius who visited Rome in 357 C.E., and conveys something of its grandeur:

But when he came to the Forum of Trajan, a structure which, in my opinion, is unique under the heavens, and a marvel which even wins the acceptance of the divine powers, he stopped in his tracks, astonished, while his mind tried to grasp the gigantic complex, which cannot be described by words and could never again be attempted by mortal men. He abandoned all hope of constructing anything of this sort but said that he only wanted to copy, as he was able to do so, Trajan's horse which was situated in the middle of the open court of the forum, and which carried the emperor himself.

Source: *Ammianus Marcellinus,* translated by John Rolfe, 3 volumes, Loeb Classical Library (Cambridge, Mass.: Harvard University Press, 1935–1940).

mausoleum similar to that of Augustus, and outside Rome this philhellene, or Greek-loving, ruler finally completed the great temple of Olympian Zeus in Athens behind the acropolis. This temple had originally been commissioned by Peisistratos, a tyrant of Athens in the sixth century B.C.E., but was abandoned after his death in 527 B.C.E. Antiochus IV (circa 215–164 B.C.E.) resumed the program, employing the Roman architect Cossutius, who changed the original Doric columns to Corinthian, some of which remain today. But the temple had to wait until the second century C.E. for its completion. By far the most spectacular temple built under Hadrian, or arguably any emperor, is the great Pantheon in Rome, reconstructed (circa 125–128 C.E.) over the original version that was dedicated by Agrippa circa 27 B.C.E. Hadrian modestly kept Agrippa's name on the inscription on the new design. The portico with its pediment is supported by sixteen granite columns; beyond this is not a rectangular *cella,* but a vast circular interior, surmounted by a dome with an open *oculus* (eye) of about 9 meters at its center. The rotunda beneath the dome is made of brick-faced concrete externally and has richly colored marble veneer within, as well as niches and columns regularly spaced. The thicker parts of this cylindrical wall act as massive supporting piers for the vast dome, which was constructed of concrete mixed with progressively lighter materials, so that at its base the dome was much heavier and thicker than at the top. The coffered ceiling, once covered with bronze, would also lighten the dome's weight. The interior is wonderfully symmetrical—indeed, spherical—in being 43.3 meters in diameter and height, adding a sense of cosmic harmony appropriate to this temple to all the gods. A brilliantly innovative technical feat of engineering, the Pantheon affords viewers inside an unparalleled visual experience enhanced yet further by the open oculus, and has justly become one of the most influential build-

ings of all time. It seems that Hadrian, undeterred by Apollodorus's slight, had the last word after all.

Sources:

William L. MacDonald, *The Architecture of the Roman Empire I: An Introductory Study,* second edition (New Haven: Yale University Press, 1982).

MacDonald, *The Architecture of the Roman Empire II: An Urban Appraisal,* second edition (New Haven: Yale University Press, 1987).

Nancy and Andrew Ramage, *Roman Art: Romulus to Constantine,* third edition (London: Laurence King, 2000).

John B. Ward-Perkins, *Roman Architecture* (New York & London: Harry N. Abrams, 1977).

ARCHITECTURE: LATE IMPERIAL PERIOD

More Innovations. The period after Hadrian's death in 138 C.E. does not mark a decisive break with the past, but under the Antonines (138–93 C.E.) and Severans (193–235 C.E.) certain differences emerge in Roman art and architecture. Innovations often appear in the provinces, such as in the Market Gate of Miletus (circa 160 C.E.) with its rhythm of recesses and projections that "break" the central pediment, and develop the façades of theatrical backdrops. There is also an increase in plebeian imagery, and generally more schematic, less illusionistic techniques in frieze sculpture that anticipate Christian and Byzantine styles. The Severan period produced more impressive architectural achievements than did the Antonine both within Rome and the provinces. Among these are the arches to Septimius Severus (emperor 193–211 C.E.) and Baths of Caracalla (emperor 211–217 C.E.) in Rome, as well as Severus's arch, forum and basilica at Leptis (or Lepcis) Magna in North Africa, and temple of Venus at Baalbek in Phoenicia. As a native of Leptis Magna who married a Syrian wife (Julia Domna) it is perhaps not surprising that Septimius sponsored many notable buildings in the provinces of

Temple of Venus at Baalbek, Syria, second century C.E.

The restored Market Gate of Miletus, originally built circa 160 C.E. (State Museums, Berlin)

North Africa and the Middle East. Large gateways, gymnasia, amphitheaters, fora, multistoried theaters and innovative temple designs were constructed in places such as Sardis, Palmyra, and Sabratha. At Baalbek in Syria an interesting marble temple to Venus was built, comprised of a circular *cella*, like a Greek *tholos*, surrounded by an ornate concave entablature that was formed by a series of deep niches and supported by Corinthian columns on a high podium that had niches of its own to echo the entablature above; such a design has been labelled an instance of Severan "baroque." The Baths of Caracalla were a vast rectangular and symmetrical complex (220 by 114 meters), characterized by great vaulted ceilings that housed gymnasia, an open air swimming pool, as well as the three standard kinds of bathing rooms: *frigidarium, tepidarium,* and *caldarium.* The baths were probably another imperial exercise in public relations. For in most aspects of his life Caracalla (whose real name was Marcus Aurelius Antoninus) displayed a brutality and cruelty associated with the most despotic of Roman emperors, beginning with the murder in 211 C.E. of his younger brother, Geta, whose image and name were erased from public monuments (a process known as *damnatio memoriae*).

Violent Times. Caracalla's early death at age twenty-nine in 217 C.E. was in keeping with the fates of many of Rome's bloodiest rulers, but the Severan dynasty lasted until 235 C.E. when it was violently ended. For nearly half a century after this termination Rome was ruled by a series of short-lived imperial regimes under men, often from the frontiers of the empire, who had come to power through one military coup after another. An indication of the violence and insecurity of the times can be gauged in the huge wall built under Aurelian, emperor from 270–275 C.E., designed to keep out the northern hordes. This brick and concrete construction was originally 7.5 meters high, and 12 miles long with towers every 30 meters along its face. It is the main architectural building of its time, and was the first defensive wall to be built in Rome since the fourth century B.C.E. The accession of Diocletian in 284 C.E. brought great political changes to the empire to prevent its disintegration. In 293 C.E. he instigated the Tetrarchs—four rulers who shared the empire among themselves, operating from different locations. This organization is likely to have been designed to create the impression of imperial presence throughout the empire and to forestall yet another attempted coup.

A Powerful Regime. Much art and architecture would now serve to emphasize the power and legitimacy of this regime. Notable examples were the Baths of Diocletian in Rome, which follow the designs of Caracalla's baths, and Diocletian's palace in Spalato (in modern Croatia) around 300 C.E. This palace complex (200 by 170 meters) seems to have been like a huge fortress with high surrounding walls and towers on each corner as well as smaller ones between them. The remains of a colonnaded courtyard reveal interesting architectural features such as the series of arches atop the columns, instead of a horizontal entablature. As well, the arch "breaking" the entablature recalls the Miletus Market Gate and echoes the grand doorway that itself carries connotations of a triumphal arch. Under Maxentius, a "second generation" Tetrarch, a grand basilica in the forum (100 by 65 meters) was undertaken from 306–313 C.E., which involved innovations on earlier basilica designs. These included a series of vaults over the central area and three bays on each side whose vaults were lower; of these the bay in the central north wall contained an apse. Constantine took over the construction of this building, where at the west end fragments of the colossal statue to the first Christian emperor were found. Architecture under Constantine, emperor from 307–337 C.E. employs traditional, non-Christian basilica designs for many large churches, such as Old St. Peter's in Rome (circa 330 C.E.). In the mid-fourth century C.E. the mausoleum to his daughter, Constantia, was built in Rome, and later converted into a church. Again it echoes earlier, non-Christian forms in interesting ways with its circular design and arches between the supporting Corinthian pillars, now grouped in pairs.

Sources:

William L. MacDonald, *The Architecture of the Roman Empire I: An Introductory Study,* second edition (New Haven: Yale University Press, 1982).

MacDonald, *The Architecture of the Roman Empire II: An Urban Appraisal,* second edition (New Haven: Yale University Press, 1987).

Nancy and Andrew Ramage, *Roman Art: Romulus to Constantine,* third edition (London: Laurence King, 2000).

John B. Ward-Perkins, *Roman Architecture* (New York & London: Harry N. Abrams, 1977).

CHRISTIAN LITERATURE

Every Ending Is a New Beginning. The first Christian writers, however, take issue with this pagan and philosophical world. Apologists like Minucius or Tertullian attempt to answer head-on the standard Roman accusations against their sect. Contemporary Romans suspected the Christians of immorality and found them to be cliquish. More substantial accusations were the unknowability of the divine, a strange concept of God as a single being, and a rather absurd eschatology. All these (and then some) are refuted individually in Minucius Felix's *Octavius* by the speaker Octavius Januarius.

Jerome, Bible Translator. It took almost two hundred years, however, for the most significant Christian writers to emerge. These were St. Jerome, the translator of the Bible, and St. Augustine, the church father. Jerome's writings show the severity of his ascetic tendencies. He was somewhat remarkable for his time in having mastered both Hebrew and Greek in addition to his considerable Latin erudition; his scholarship still stands out as preeminent in his period. He studied rhetoric, like all educated men of his time, and he spent some time in the desert as an anchorite (hermit). Moving eventually to Palestine, he settled in Bethlehem, where he spent the rest of his life, often engaging in vehement scholarly polemics. He produced an expanded translation of the *Chronicle* of Eusebius of Caesarea, a history of the world, and an historical catalogue of 135 famous writers (mostly Christian), the *De viris illustribus.* His work is classicizing in its style, and frequently alludes to the pagan classics; there is an anecdote about a nightmare he had, in which, standing before the Judgment

Seat, he was accused of being not a Christian, but a Ciceronian.

Vulgate Bible. In Jerome's time the Judaeo-Christian Scriptures, which had been originally composed in Hebrew, Aramaic, and Greek, already existed in Latin translations (known the *Vetus latina,* or "Old Latin" version). It was Pope Damasus who, in the 380s, commissioned Jerome to revise these against the original-language texts. Over time, however, Jerome conceived the project of producing, not just a revision, but an entirely new translation from the original languages. This he did, striving more for an accessible vernacular translation than for a polished style. Over the next several centuries this monumental translation was revised and reworked into what came to be known, by the eighth century C.E., as the "Vulgate" or "common-language" Bible. The Vulgate was the standard version of the Christian Bible until the Reformation. For this achievement alone Jerome would stand as a giant in the history of the Christian church.

Augustine, Church Father. Augustine is the most influential and the most fascinating of the early church fathers, since he combined a thorough philosophical and rhetorical grounding with his Christianity. He could be cerebral or fanatical, philosophical or polemical. His most significant works are his *Confessions,* published in 397/398 C.E., and the *City of God,* written between 413 and 426 C.E. In the first nine books, the *Confessions* provides an autobiography of Augustine until the death of his mother. The last four books present a neoplatonic view of memory, time, creation, and finally an allegorical exegesis of *Genesis* chapter 1. His autobiographical narrative vividly illustrates the theological point of the latter part. In Augustine's view, man has turned away from God and given in to bodily pleasures. Man's soul therefore declines and disintegrates, although it yearns to be made whole again. Only the love of God through the example and mediation of Christ can achieve this. Augustine's own story is therefore emblematic of mankind:

> At last I have come to love You, Beauty so ancient and so new, at last I have come to love You! And behold You were inside me and I outside and there I used to seek You; and I, misshapen, used to rush to those shapely things which You made. You were with me but I was not with You. The shapely things kept me from You which, if they existed not in You, would not exist at all. You called and shouted and broke my silence. You lit, brightened, and chased away my blindness. You emitted a fragrance, I took a breath and I pant for You. I tasted You and now I hunger and thirst for you. You touched me and I burn for your peace. (*Confessions* 10.27)

In describing his own spiritual journey as a paradigm for all of us, Augustine's prose, often reminiscent of Cicero in its style, sometimes rises to poetic heights in his hymnic address to God. These poetic passages re-create an effect in Latin that clearly recalls the repetitive style of the Psalms. And so the last giant of Latin literature is also the first one who already belongs to the subsequent age. Rooted in

Greek philosophy and Latin rhetoric, he combined these traditions with the Bible to argue and spread the message that dominated the next fifteen centuries.

Consoled by Philosophy. The writer Boethius provides a major bridge between antiquity and the Middle Ages. In his philosophical dialogue, *The Consolation of Philosophy*, the prisoner talks to the personified Philosophy. After dealing with chance, God emerges as the essence of happiness, independent of the trappings of this world. Misfortune is a test for the righteous, and each individual depends on his personal attitude toward his own lot. Chance is therefore not without cause, and human free will consists of following God. From a literary point of view, Boethius combines a platonic dialogue with the Roman form of Menippean satire, since he mixes prose and verse passages throughout. However, Boethius's Menippean mixture is injected with a philosophical and theological seriousness never previously associated with this format. Nonetheless, he is firmly rooted in the classical world: his style is surprisingly classical; he quotes with ease from great Latin authors; and his metrical range is astonishing. Following the ancient principle, his manner follows his matter, and great attention is paid to inward unity. Boethius therefore stands on the threshold to a new age: an author writing in thoroughly classical style, but advocating the Christian God as the essence of happiness; a Roman consul at the mercy of a Germanic king. The balance still found in Boethius, however, was destined to tilt in favor of Christianity and the Germanic tribes.

Sources:

Michael von Albrecht, *A History of Roman Literature: From Livius Andronicus to Boethius* (Leiden & New York: E. J. Brill, 1997).

Henry Chadwick, *Augustine* (Oxford & New York: Oxford University Press, 1986).

CICERO AND LATIN PROSE

Roman Hero. Marcus Tullius Cicero is the single figure of Greco-Roman antiquity about whom we know the most—in large part because of the vast literary legacy he has left in a variety of genres. In the Middle Ages his writings were prized as a mirror of the ancient world; in the Renaissance a Ciceronian style in one's use of Latin was the hallmark of an educated man. Essentially conservative in outlook, Cicero was to many of his contemporaries a heroic figure, the one who (as he put it) "saved the Republic" in a time of political crisis. What he could not see, of course, is that the shifting sands of Roman politics meant inevitable change for Rome. As Cicero is arguably the single most important figure in the Roman Republic, and certainly in the history of Latin prose, a summary of Cicero's life and literary legacy is important.

Legal Career. Cicero wrote down his speeches after he delivered them. Sometimes he made revisions; sometimes he even published speeches that ended up not being delivered. Like his Greek model Demosthenes, he published twelve of his speeches delivered during his consulate in 63 B.C.E., which conventionally serves as a watershed for

---

Cicero, consul in 63 B.C.E., has discovered Catiline's plans to overthrow the Roman republic. Having found out that Catiline is organizing his conspirators for an imminent move, he summons an extraordinary meeting of the senate on 7 November of that year—which Catiline himself would have attended—and unmasks the plot before the assembled group in an electrifying speech. By this he succeeds in convincing the Senate that the danger is real; amid the fracas, Catiline actually gets up and leaves the Senate House. For the rest of his life Cicero referred proudly to the way in which he "saved the Republic" by facing down Catiline.

In the name of heaven, Catilina, how long do you propose to exploit our patience? Do you really suppose that your lunatic activities are going to escape our retaliation for evermore? Are there to be no limits to this audacious, uncontrollable swaggering? Look at the garrison of our Roman nation which guards the Palatine by night, look at the patrols ranging the city, the whole population gripped by terror, the entire body of loyal citizens massing at one single spot! Look at this meeting of our Senate behind strongly fortified defences, see the expressions on the countenances of every one of these men who are here! Have none of these sights made the smallest impact on your heart? You must be well aware that your plot has been detected. Now that every single person in this place knows all about your conspiracy, you cannot fail to realize it is doomed. Do you supposed there is a single individual here who has not got the very fullest information about what you were doing last night and the night before, where you went, the men you summoned, the plans you concocted?

Source: Cicero, *Against Lucius Sergius Catalina I*, translated by Michael Grant, from *Cicero: Selected Political Speeches* (London: Penguin, 1969).

---

dividing his corpus. As a newcomer from Arpinum and a nonaristocrat, Cicero celebrated his breakthrough as a lawyer and speaker in 70 B.C.E. in the case against Verres, the corrupt former governor of Sicily. Cicero did his homework as a lawyer, gathering as much evidence of Verres's maladministration as he could. He then delivered his short first speech against Verres, which exposes the defendant's delay tactics as well as his powerful aristocratic backers. Cicero presents himself as being on top of his material, and assumes control of the case by appealing to the judges' Roman virtues. Verres was devastated by the power of Cicero's presentation: he headed for voluntary exile in Marseilles. Cicero had no need for the five following speeches against Verres which he had prepared; nonetheless, having just defeated Hortensius, Rome's most celebrated lawyer of the time, he decided to publish his undelivered material as evidence of his prowess as an orator.

Rising Star. In the following years Cicero's star rose steadily with speeches such as *In Defense of Cluentius* and *On Pompey's Command*. In the former he first formulates his policy of *concordia ordinum* (unity among social classes); in the latter he aligns himself politically with the powerful general Pompey, whose quintessentially Roman qualities of *virtus* (bravery), *auctoritas* (authority), and *felicitas* (timeliness) he praises. In 63 B.C.E. he became consul and faced two challenges: Julius Caesar tried to win popular support and political power by means of a proposed agrarian reform bill, which Cicero in his three speeches on the agrarian law exposed as such and defeated. The second event was the coup attempt by a young nobleman named Lucius Sergius Catilina (Catiline), a minor episode in the civil upheavals of the first century B.C.E., which has received a great deal of attention because we possess not only Cicero's four speeches, the famous *Catilinarians,* but also Sallust's monograph on the series of events. Cicero's first speech against Catiline, held in the senate with many of the coup members sitting in front of him, is nothing short of brilliant. Because the consul had no actual proof of the plot, he bluffs them. In a manner sometimes reminiscent of interrogations staged in TV crime series, Cicero starts out expressing his indignation at Catiline sitting in front of him before telling him that he knows everything. Fortunately, Cicero's language is much more refined than that of modern TV cops. He is also even more devious. Toward the end of the speech, the personified Rome appears to him and asks him "Marcus Tullius, what are you doing?" She questions the wisdom of allowing the conspirators to stay in Rome and suggests that they should be summarily executed, thereby echoing Cicero's own sentiments from the earlier parts of the speech. Cicero's own attitude becomes the same as Rome's attitude and that of every patriotic citizen. In the end, Catiline did run, was declared a public enemy, and was defeated by a Roman army. Cicero also obtained the *senatus consultum ultimum* (declaration of a state of emergency by the Senate), which gave him the power to execute the ringleaders of the plot. He nonetheless had the matter debated in the senate and won a conviction. Cicero managed to defend the freedom of the Roman republic and proceeded to publish twelve of his consular speeches testifying, in spite of their later publication, to his remarkable foresight.

Defense Speech. About seven years after delivering his *Catilinarian* speeches, Cicero, now no longer consul, conjures up another ghost in a speech. This time it is Appius Claudius Pulcher, appearing to his descendant Clodia in the speech *In Defense of Caelius* (34). Marcus Caelius had been accused of inciting public violence, sabotaging an embassy from Egypt and killing one of the ambassadors, and stealing some gold from Clodia as well as hatching a poison plot against her. The ghost of Claudius also asks his descendant "what are you doing?" and goes on to chastise her in a series of rhetorical questions for her immoral escapades. He claims that she has modeled herself after her brother Clodius, Cicero's personal nemesis, rather than after her illustrious ancestors. This voice of Roman *mos maiorum* (ancestral custom) finds its counterpart one paragraph later in an apparition of the good-for-nothing

brother Clodius, who, of course, advises that there are more fish in the sea than Caelius, and that all Clodia has to do is sit in her garden on the Tiber and wait for the willing young men to come to her. But all this is merely a diversion tactic to bypass the (probably not insubstantial) accusations against Caelius. Cicero tries to exonerate his client of the typical moral accusations leveled against him by the prosecution. He also shifts the blame for the entire court case to the jilted Clodia. And lurking behind Clodia is, of course, her brother, who later engineered Cicero's exile. In exposing Clodia's immorality Cicero is, however, treading on dangerous ground because his client Caelius had had an affair with her, and was therefore part of the immoral crowd. But the strategy did not backfire, because Caelius was acquitted.

Exile and Return. Cicero's political opponent Clodius, Caesar's henchman, passed a retroactive law against anyone who had killed a Roman citizen. This measure was of course specifically aimed at Cicero, who fled into exile in Greece, but returned triumphantly less than a year later. Still, his political influence had evaporated in the meantime. Cicero, who had not been able to console himself in exile, turned to rhetorical theory and philosophy, and published three eminent works: *On the Orator, On the Republic,* and *On Laws.* These three works confirm the integrated view Cicero held of statesmanship and oratory: *On the Republic* outlines the mixed Roman constitutions as the ideal; *On Laws* describes the statutes to uphold; and *On the Orator* sketches the ideal public figure who can put all these ideas into action.

Political Changes. Unfortunately for Cicero, after a brief comeback as governor of Cilicia, when he was poised to celebrate a triumph, civil war between Caesar and Pompey broke out and put a nail in the coffin of Cicero's beloved republic. Under Caesar he again found himself politically put on ice. Once again he turned to philosophy, publishing works on ethics such as the *Limits of Good and Evil,* the *Tusculan Disputations, On Old Age, On Friendship,* and *On Duties.* These have become major sources of details of Greek philosophy that would otherwise now be lost. Although Cicero generally favors the line of Plato's successors, *On Duties* develops Stoic thoughts. In it, Cicero overcomes the dichotomy between *honestum* (what is honorable or worthwhile in itself) and *utile* (what is useful): the honorable (e.g. learning Latin) always contains the useful (e.g. Latin builds vocabulary), but the useful does not necessarily contain the honorable.

Final Days. In the aftermath of Caesar's dictatorship, Cicero quickly resurfaced to denounce Caesar's would-be successor Marc Antony in no less than fourteen so-called Philippic speeches, modeled on Demosthenes' speeches against Philip of Macedon. In his first speech, Cicero appealed to Marc Antony to rule the state in such a way that his compatriots might enjoy his presence. Antony retorted in the next senate meeting, which Cicero did not attend, personally attacking the former consul as the major troublemaker of the past

Early-twentieth-century drawing of the Temple of Concord where Cicero delivered his oration against the traitor Catiline (American Academy in Rome)

twenty years. Cicero then wrote his second *Philippic,* which he published (without ever delivering orally) a few months later, after Antony had left Rome. In the first part of the speech, he quickly refutes Antony, then justifies his own political career. In so doing, he sets himself up as the foil for Marc Antony, whom he vitriolically attacks in the remainder with all the rhetorical fireworks of ancient invective. Not only is Marc Antony the real troublemaker in Rome, but he is also a crook, another Catiline whom Cicero will also defeat. The assassins of Caesar have demonstrated what is to be done with all tyrants. Cicero ends with a flourish; he has only two wishes: to leave the Roman people free when he dies, and to see every politician receive his just deserts. Although never delivered, the speech, published as a political pamphlet, encapsulates Cicero's creed: people who use public life for their own ends deserve what Catiline and Caesar got. By this time, Cicero had nothing to lose but his life, which Marc Antony demanded as a condition for the second triumvirate with Octavian and Lepidus. After at least twelve more *Philippics* he had had enough: Cicero, the "most eloquent offspring of Romulus" (Catullus 49.1), was assassinated by Antony's men on 7 December 43 B.C.E. But Marc Antony's reputation as a potential military dictator has never recovered from Cicero's invective.

Sources:

D. R. Shackleton Bailey, *Cicero* (London: Routledge, 1971).

George A. Kennedy, *The Art of Rhetoric in the Roman World* (Princeton: Princeton University Press, 1972).

James M. May, "Cicero," in *Ancient Roman Writers, Dictionary of Literary Biography,* volume 211, edited by Ward W. Briggs (Columbia, S.C.: Bruccoli Clark Layman/Detroit: Gale Group, 1999), pp. 54–67.

J. G. F. Powell, ed., *Cicero the Philosopher* (Oxford: Clarendon Press, 1995).

DRAMA

Early Beginnings. The wellspring of Western drama, of course, was ancient Greece. From the start, Roman writers were fascinated by Greek tragedy and comedy, and they not only zealously translated these into Latin, but eventually began writing original plays of their own, based on these models. We know, for example, that Livius Andronicus (circa 284–204 B.C.E.) wrote both tragedies and comedies, and Titus Livius (known as Livy) tells us that he was the first Roman playwright to use actual plots for his onstage presentations. Gnaeus Naevius (circa 265–190 B.C.E.) not only based some of his Latin-language comedies on Greek originals (the so-called *fabulae palliatae*), but

Roman drama was, from the first, based on Greek models. Plautus, one of the earliest authors writing in Latin whose work has substantially survived the wreck of time, was a master of the stage, creating stories and characters that can still make an audience laugh out loud in the theater. One of characteristic traits of Plautine comedy is his use of "stock characters," or recognizable character-types who recur from play to play: the handsome youth, the nubile maiden, the courtesan, the dour old man, the clever slave. Among these is the *parasitus* or "parasite," the irritating type who lives by sponging off the generosity of others. In this passage we meet one such:

PENICULUS: The boys all call me Peniculus, which may sound ridiculous

But just means *Table Duster* and shows *How Able an Adjuster*

I am to dinner and meticulous in clearing off the table:

You can call me Soft Hairbrush: It seems to be my fate

To be famous as a famished eater and wear such a tail plate.

You know, some men chain down their captives, and they shackle

The legs of runaway slaves. I think *that's* ridiculous,

To load still worse weight on a badly enough burdened crate.

If you put pressure on him, the underdog wants to get up

And take off, and never do another stroke of work.

Somehow, they'll always wriggle loose, file off the link

Or knock the lock to bits with a rock. Are chains worth the pains?

If you'd like to rope someone in, so he doesn't feel

Like escaping, snare him with wine and a meal!

You're putting a ring through his nose when you take him to dinner.

And as long as you keep him well stocked with food and liquor,

Regularly and the way he likes it, he'll stick with you,

Even though he's under heavy sentence. He'll want to serve you;

As long as you're bound to give him food, he's bound to eat it.

The nets and meshes of food are remarkably strong

And elastic, and squeeze even tighter when they get long.

I'm off to Menaechmus's at the moment, where I've signed on

To appear for dinner. I volunteer gaily for a jail

Like his, especially at meals. He doesn't feed; he deals

With his guests, increasing their status; like a good restauranteur

He doesn't diagnose, he offers a cure. This sharp epicure

Puts out a very fine spread; he doesn't spare the courses;

He builds up skyscrapers of dishes—you see something delicious

And have to stand up on the couch and stretch out to reach it

Over all the other things that look nearly as luscious.

I've been out of commission for quite a long intermission,

Not in the preferred position at Menaechmus's house, but at home,

Domiciled and dominated by my own little sweetmeats. Those treats

I provide for myself and my near ones have proved dear [costly] ones,

Thanks to my expensive tastes—and they all go to waist.

So I'm drumming myself out of those ranks, not burning up money

Trooping in with food for the group. Instead, I'm turning tummy

To Menaechmus's place. He may just embrace my company. Here he comes now

Flouncing out of the house—looks like they've had a row.

Source: Plautus, *Menaechmi*, from David R. Slavitt and Palmer Bovie, eds., *Plautus: The Comedies IV* (Baltimore: Johns Hopkins University Press, 1995).

also was the first Roman to write serious plays on topics drawn from Roman history (*fabulae praetextae*). It appears that he may also have written *fabulae togatae,* low comedies on Roman life. Another genre of low comedy in early Rome, relying on the use of stock characters, was known as the *fabula atellana* or Atellan farce, so named after a town in Campania.

Roman Comedy. One of the most successful and visible literary forms in the early Roman Republic was drama, with its main practitioner being Plautus. He based his comedies loosely on Greek "New Comedies," with their limited scope of plots about impediments to true love or mistaken identity. A papyrus fragment of one of his Greek models still exists, which confirms that Plautus adapts the Greek plays freely: he cuts out the tedious moralizing, turns monologues into dialogues, expands the humorous passages, and adds music. In fact, his comedies are more like contemporary musicals than spoken theater. Entertainment was his primary aim, and laughter was his weapon of choice. For the sake of making people laugh he often sacrificed the consistency of the plot and patched scenes from one model play into another, even welding two Greek comedies into one Plautine production, a process commonly referred to as "contamination" (*contaminatio*). In spite of using Greek plays as his blueprint, and of keeping the Greek setting with Greek characters who, for his audience's benefit, spoke Latin and lived largely in Roman circumstances, he had a keen eye for what his Roman audience would like. His favorite type of joke is one that still flourishes today; it follows the pattern of a puzzling question, a pause expressing bewilderment, and finally the punch line. Plautus's favorite stock character was the trickster slave who comes to dominate his aristocratic Roman masters. This, of course, inverts the social roles to which the audience was accustomed. By keeping the Greek setting and names, Plautus creates an illusion of strangeness; this situation allowed the audience to laugh at a comic inversion of their own world, thereby questioning the lives they knew. While Plautine comedy is appealing at first for its sheer fun, one cannot deny that there is also a tendency to refuse to reestablish order at the end of a play. Pseudolus burps in his master's face; Menaechmus sells his own wife! Plautus refuses to reaffirm the hierarchy of Roman society or its marital values, and thereby challenges the audience.

"Contamination" and Sophistication. Plautus's younger contemporary Publius Terentius Afer (Terence) was much more refined than Plautus. As a member of a philhellenic circle centered around Scipio the Younger, Terence followed his Greek models more closely but still reserved the right to adapt freely rather than merely to translate. In his comedies we find much less slapstick and less music than in Plautus. However, Terence also felt the need at times to add some spice to his play by "contaminating," for which he was fiercely criticized in his own day. While his plays feel much more civilized and "Greek" than Plautus's, they are still thoroughly Roman. In one of his best pieces, *Adelphi* or *The Brothers,* two brothers' education methods are pitted against each other: the liberal "Greek" Micio and the tough old "Roman" Demea. Micio has our sympathies throughout most of the play when Demea admits he has been far too restrictive with his son. On the other hand, Demea gets the last word and asserts that Micio has been far too liberal with his boy: "Let me tell you that I may show you the fact that those boys consider you easygoing and jovial does not come from real life nor so much from what's right and just but from humoring them, indulging them and giving them presents, Micio" *(Adelphi 985–8).* Thus Terence preserves at least some Roman ideas about child-rearing by means of advocating a "Greek" middle road. Terence challenges traditional Roman values under the influence of Greek thought. However, he does not replace Roman ideals by Greek ones: rather he aims at merging the two value systems.

Imperial Tragedy. Born almost three hundred years after Plautus was Lucius Annaeus Seneca (commonly referred to by scholars as Seneca the Younger), tutor to the emperor Nero. Seneca wrote a number of tragedies based on Greek originals. The characters in these plays serve as negative examples of the emotions: Medea, Thyestes, and Hercules are deranged by anger, Andromache by fear, Phaedra by desire. These plays are the only complete Roman tragedies we have, and for a long time after the end of antiquity were the only ancient drama available in the West. They have therefore exerted a great deal of influence on people such as Shakespeare, but fell out of favor with the rediscovery of Greek tragedy. They are felt by many to be static and stilted, written for recitation rather than for the stage. While it is certainly true that Seneca was no man of the theater, his plays can be (and have been) successfully put on stage. That does not mean that Seneca ever had any hope of seeing them performed.

Sources:

W. G. Arnott, *Menander, Plautus, Terence: Greece and Rome New Surveys in the Classics* (Oxford: Clarendon Press, 1975).

Gian Biagio Conte, *Latin Literature: A History* (Baltimore: Johns Hopkins University Press, 1987).

E. J. Kenney and W. V. Clausen, eds., *Latin Literature,* volume 2, *The Cambridge History of Classical Literature* (Cambridge: Cambridge University Press, 1982).

EARLIEST LITERATURE

Beginnings. As in most literatures, Roman creative writing began with patterned speech, or poetry. The earliest figure on record is Lucius Livius Andronicus, who

---

FRAGMENTS OF THE EARLIEST EXTANT WRITTEN LATIN: THE TWELVE TABLES

The traditional date of these laws is 450 B.C.E. Legend has it that, when they were being drafted, an embassy was sent to Athens to study the laws of Solon. The Romans' laws were posted on wooden tables (and apparently, later, on bronze tablets) in the forum. Later Romans looked to these laws as foundational of Roman culture. The following fragment concerns ceremonial laws associated with rituals for the dead.

[One] must not bury or cremate a dead man within the city . . . [one] must not do more than this; [one] must not smooth the pyre with an axe . . . three shawls, one small purple tunic, ten oboe-players . . . Women must not tear their cheeks nor raise a lament because of a funeral. One must not gather the bones of a dead man in order to hold a funeral subsequently. (Anointing by slaves is abolished, and so are all) wakes . . . no expensive sprinkling, no long garlands, no incense-boxes . . . When a man wins a wreath, either personally or through a chattel, or as a mark of courage one (is given) to him . . . [one] must not add gold. But if [one] buries or cremates with gold a man with gold dental work, let that be without detriment.

Sources: Gian Biagio Conte, *Latin Literature: A History* (Baltimore: Johns Hopkins University Press, 1987).

Edward Courtney, *Archaic Latin Prose* (Atlanta: Scholars Press, 1999).

HYMN OF THE ARVAL BRETHREN

The *fratres arvales* or "Arval Brethren" (from *arvum*, "ploughed field") were a college of twelve priests in charge of the spring festival of Dea Dia, a goddess apparently connected with the fertility of the harvest. The *Carmen arvale*, though known from an inscription of the early third century C.E., appears to date from 400 B.C.E. or earlier. The Arval Brethren chanted this hymn, it seems, to ensure the purification and fertility of the fields. The text of the hymn, which is so old in form that parts of it are difficult to recognize as Latin, continues to puzzle even the experts; nonetheless a tentative translation is provided here.

Help us, Lares! Help us, Lares! Help us, Lares!

Mars, do not let plague and ruin overrun the people!

Mars, do not let plague and ruin overrun the people!

Mars, do not let plague and ruin overrun the people!

Fierce Mars, be satisfied! Jump over the threshold!

Fierce Mars, be satisfied! Jump over the threshold!

Fierce Mars, be satisfied! Jump over the threshold!

Each of you in turn, invoke all the Semones!

Each of you in turn, invoke all the Semones!

Each of you in turn, invoke all the Semones!

O Mars, help us! O Mars, help us! O Mars, help us!

Triumpe, Triumpe, Triumpe, Triumpe, Triumpe!

*Translation by Denis Bullock

It is possible that parts of the inscription are not part of the actual prayer, but instead stage-directions (so to speak) for the Arval Brethren as they performed the ceremony. The trebling of each formula has a quasi-magical significance in the prayer, as does the assonance in the Latin words for "plague and ruin" (*lue rue*). The gods invoked in this *carmen* are the Lases (i.e. Lares, protective gods); Mars (or Marmar or Marmor; after Jupiter the most important Italian god; in the earliest period he may have had a chthonic connection with the wild land); and the Semones (perhaps related to *semino*, "sow, plant"? — apparently the gods who protected seeds in the earth). The last word of the song is still not entirely understood; its origin was already mysterious to Varro in the first century B.C.E. It may be connected with the Greek *thriambos* (a hymn to the god Dionysus), and, like that word in Greek ritual, it may function here as the epithet of some god (Dionysus was himself a vegetation-god in Greece). Why it is chanted five times, when everything else is chanted thrice, is also still a mystery.

Sources: Edward Courtney, *Musa lapidaria* (Atlanta: Scholars Press, 1995).

Robert Turcan, *Gods of Ancient Rome* (Edinburgh: Edinburgh University Press, 2000).

translated Homer's *Odyssey* into the native Italian Saturnian meter. The principle underlying this verse-form is still disputed, but it apparently relied to some extent on alliteration. Livius Andronicus also wrote tragedies and comedies influenced by contemporary Greek models. One main thread of Latin literature emerges at its beginning, namely the encounter with Greece. Whether it is translated, adapted, used as inspiration or simply rejected, Greek literature provides a constant background for Latin literature even when a writer's primary models are Vergil's epic or Horace's satire. Livius Andronicus's younger contemporary Gnaeus Naevius (circa 265–190 B.C.E.), for instance, followed his precursor's lead, writing drama and an historical epic on the first Punic War, but his drama was set in Rome, not Greece. Furthermore, Greek culture found a vociferous opponent in the elder Cato (Marcus Porcius Cato), who described Rome's *Origins* in seven books, by theme rather than chronologically. In spite of his rejection of Greek culture, this historical work could not help but follow some Greek precedents, such as the inclusion of speeches. His curious blend of Roman lore and Greek "science" is most evident in his work *On Agriculture*.

Father of Latin Poetry. The mainspring of Latin poetry, however, was the dramatist and epic poet Quintus Ennius, whose historical epic *Annales* set the standard for a long time to come. He chose the Greek dactylic hexameter, which became the standard rhythm for long narrative poems. In an early fragment Ennius presents himself as a reincarnation of Homer. This claim tells a great deal about his aims and methods. He wanted to provide a great narrative poem that would define the way in which Rome would think of itself. In this he achieved some success, until Vergil wrote the definitive poem about Rome's understanding of itself, the *Aeneid*.

Sources:
Gian Biagio Conte, *Latin Literature: A History* (Baltimore: Johns Hopkins University Press, 1987).

Edward Courtney, *Archaic Latin Prose* (Atlanta: Scholars Press, 1999).

ELEGY

The Elegiac Tradition. When modern literary critics speak of "elegy" or "elegiac," they generally have in mind a type of poetry characterized by a reflective mood and, often, topics of sadness or mourning. This is quite a different notion from the ancient concept of elegy, which was, first and foremost, a purely metrical designation: elegy was poetry written in elegiac couplets, consisting of a line of hexameter verse (like the meter of Homeric or Vergilian epic) followed by a so-called pentameter line. In ancient Greece, as a matter of fact, elegy was used not only for laments, but also (among other things) for lampoons and other frivolous purposes, for love poems, and for drinking songs. One of the great early Roman poets who used the elegiac couplet for a variety of purposes was Catullus himself.

Roman Developments. Together with their almost entirely lost precursor Cornelius Gallus, the Roman love elegists Albius Tibullus and Sextus Propertius shaped Latin love elegy mostly out of the Hellenistic epigram. The Roman genre also grew out of a rejection of the political turmoil characterizing both the last days of the republic and the public lives of upper-class citizens. While any Roman worth his salt would be engaged in *negotium* (business, whether commerce or public affairs), the elegists require *otium* (leisure) for their pursuits of poetry and love. They are not devoted to a political party or a cause, but wholly "enslaved" by their beloved. This opposition to the values of the day is further mirrored in the fact that many of them were patronized by Messalla Corvinus rather than Maecenas. Some of their works can now be found in the later books ascribed to Albius Tibullus.

Tibullus. In Tibullus's own elegies, we find a consistent yearning for peace (1.10,45–50), a predilection for the country over the city as well as for love rather than war. The latter is the domain of Tibullus's patron Messalla, while the poet devotes his time to his paramours. Love, peace, countryside, and local Italian religion thus form a counterworld to everybody else's rat race. This counterculture contains many autobiographical elements, but also much literary stylization. While scholars today rightly emphasize the latter, it should not be forgotten that these poems aim at persuading the ever-reluctant beloved to accept the poet-lover, often found locked out of her house and serenading on her doorstep. In short, love elegy claims to be something useful to the lover (Tib. 1.4,14).

Propertius. Sextus Propertius took a different track from his contemporary in that he frequently projected his affection into myth, whereas Tibullus had used the peaceful countryside. In addition, he also used the Callimachean refusal to write epic (*recusatio;* see also on Horace) to disassociate himself from the demands made on him after joining the circle of Maecenas. Love elegy is a poetic as well as a lifestyle choice that signals opposition to public life, warfare, and writing long-winded epics. This remains true even if Propertius's beloved Cynthia (pseudonym) is merely a literary construct, as feminist scholars now assert. The focus in elegy is always on the speaker, his emotions, his wishes and dreams. Propertius did, however, change his poetry in his fourth book where he dealt with more Roman themes and Callimachean *aitia*, stories that give a mythical explanation of contemporary features such as a name or a custom.

Ovid. Love elegy finds its culmination in the early works of Publius Ovidius Naso (Ovid), to whom, however, the genre is definitely only a humorous literary game. While Propertius's first book had started with the phrase *Cynthia prima fuit* (Cynthia was the first), Ovid opens his three books of *Amores* with a sequence in which he depicts himself as about to write an epic, until Cupid steals a metrical foot out of every other line, thus forcing him to write elegy. The poet remonstrates that he has no love to write about, whereupon Cupid shoots him with an arrow, thereby making him fall in love (*"Poet' he said, flexing his bow against his knee, / I'll give you something to sing*

A WOMAN SCORNED

Medea helped Jason win the Golden Fleece, which was guarded by a fierce dragon. But now he has abandoned her for a "proper" Greek wife. In Ovid's imaginative elegiac rendition of a letter from her to Jason, she lets loose a torrent of angry remonstrance. She gives only a hint here of the terrible magic by which Jason's new wife will soon perish in agony:

. . . Why did
  we of Colchis see the Argo? Why
did your Greek crew stoop to drink from the [nearby river] Phasis?
  And why did I take so much pleasure
in your golden hair, your fine ways and the lies
  that fell so gracefully from your tongue?

. . .

  I was helpless and the sight of you
enflamed me not with the usual flames but
  like a knot of pine kindled [on the altar] before
some powerful god. While you were wonderful
  to see, fate was rushing me to doom.
The splendour of your eyes robbed mine of vision.

. . .

Then there appeared the unsleeping guardian
  rattling his scales, hissing as he swept
the ground with his coiling body. . . .

. . .

  with my drug, I brought sleep to those eyes
shutting their flaming gaze in harmless slumber
  and I gave the fleece into your hands.
By this act I betrayed my father, gave up
  my throne and the country of my birth,
and my reward for all of this is exile.

. . .

Let her [your new wife] laugh now and be merry at my faults
  while she reclines on Tyrian purple,
soon enough she will weep as she is consumed
  in a blaze that is hotter than mine.
So long as I have poison, fire and weapons,
  Medea's foes will all be punished.

Source: Ovid, *Heroides* 12, translated by Harold Isbell, from *Ovid: Heroides* (London: Penguin, 1990).

about—take that!'" [Am. 1.1.23–4 transl. Lee]). Poetry here comes first, love second. In his *Amores* Ovid does not parody elegy, as is often claimed, but rather makes fun of the absurd situations and arguments of the elegiac lover. Fun was his main aim also in the notorious *Art of Love,* an elegiac instruction manual for would-be lovers, which would have been about as useful in real life as Vergil's *Georgics* would to an Italian farmer. With these works, Ovid, like Tibullus and Propertius, flies in the face of contemporary values, and especially in the face of Augustus's attempt to reform public morality. The *Art of Love* was therefore later used at least as a pretense to banish Ovid to the shores of the Black Sea. While the *Amores* make fun of the male elegiac lover, *The Heroides* present mythical female lovers pouring their hearts out in futile letters to their absent men. Always in search of novelty, Ovid here combined Horace's epistolary form with love elegy written from a different angle.

Ovid's *Fasti*. Even more Callimachean in inspiration than the *Metamorphoses* is Ovid's *Fasti,* a collection of (mostly Roman) myth and lore associated with the calendar. By postclassical readers this has primarily been regarded as a quarry for anthropologists, but in recent years it has been once again appreciated as a poem in its own right. While the *Metamorphoses* is an epic with strong elegiac tones and techniques, the *Fasti* is a narrative elegy in which the genres of epic and elegy are welded together. In spite of its Roman themes, Ovid again cannot keep himself from introducing humorous notes: Romulus is presented as a rapist and tyrant (2.139–142) by contrast with Augustus. If Rome's founder is seen in this light, maybe Augustus's aspirations of being its second founder are therefore not that flattering. As he had made fun of the elegiac lover in the *Amores,* so he makes fun of the voice of the antiquarian who is relating all these stories. And, as in the *Metamorphoses,* eroticism is not absent. For instance, explaining why the priests of Faunus celebrate their rituals naked, Ovid tells the story of how Hercules and his wife Omphale exchanged clothes. Faunus essentially breaks into their house at night and wants to have his way with Omphale while she is asleep (*"He clambers aboard the nearer cot, and lies down,/ his tumescent crotch harder than his horns"* [*Fasti* 2.345–6, translation by Nagle]), but finds that under the soft woman's dress hides the shaggy Hercules, who gives him a beating!

Exile Poetry. Ovid's taste for the salacious evaporates with his exile. Accused of *carmen et error* (a poem and a mistake), Ovid was sent to Tomis (in modern Romania) in 8 C.E. to while away the final ten years of his life. The *carmen* was the *Art of Love;* the *error* remains unknown. From exile he wrote five books of elegy, the *Tristia,* and four of his *Letters from the Black Sea.* Both collections have been historically judged as monotonous complaints about his plight, but recent work has focused on their originality in the use of elegiac verse-epistles as well as their undeniable elements of humor. In a way Ovid inverts themes from love elegy: now he is the locked-out exile, Rome the beloved for whom he yearns. Instead of instructing others in the art of love, he instructs his wife in the art of approaching the emperor's wife. Although he complains about it, his poetic

Statue of Ovid at Sulmona, Italy

powers have not waned. In a long letter to Augustus (*Trist.* 2.), he defends his *Art of Love* by trying to show that all literature is erotic in contents: *"Yet the blessed author of your great Aeneid/ landed 'Arms and the man' in Dido's bed"* (*Trist.* 2. 533–4, translation by Melville). Paradoxically, it was probably his *error* that got him exiled. Whereas he had eroticized myth in earlier years, he is now at pains to "de-eroticize" everything, in order to show that in exile, the world stands on its head. The area of the lower Danube is a veritable mirror image of Rome and Italy as far as climate, people, and economy are concerned. In such an environment, Rome's most celebrated living poet can only become a "bad" author. The pressure to recall him and turn him into a "good" poet is therefore on. Unfortunately, Augustus felt no need for a good poet in Rome.

Sources:

Martin Helzle, *P. Ouidii Nasonis Epistularum ex Ponto liber IV: A Commentary on Poems 1–7 and 16* (Hildesheim, Germany & New York: Olms, 1989).

Stephen Hinds, *The Metamorphosis of Persephone* (Cambridge, U.K.: Cambridge University Press, 1987).

Garth Tissol, *The Face of Nature: Wit, Narrative, and Cosmic Origins in Ovid's* Metamorphoses (Princeton: Princeton University Press, 1997).

EPIC: BEFORE AND AFTER VERGIL

Long Tradition. By no means should one infer that Vergil was the only epic poet of Rome. On the contrary, he worked in a long-established tradition. The *Annales* of Ennius, who died a century before Vergil was born, already borrowed the dactylic hexameter for the recording of year-by-year Roman history (indeed, as an epic poet, Ennius presents himself as the reincarnation of Homer). Even earlier than this, Livius Andronicus had made a translation (although into saturnians) of Homer's *Odyssey*. But the genre was, from the beginning, a complicated one. For one thing, the poems of Hesiod date from approximately the same period as those of Homer, namely, the eighth/seventh century B.C.E., but the *Works and Days* of Hesiod is not a single long narrative about battles or wondrous adventure, like the *Iliad* and *Odyssey*, but rather a work about the practicalities of farming and sailing, cobbled together with proverbs and ritual lore that we classify today as "wisdom literature." The ancients, however, would have classified Hesiod's work as "epic," no less than Homer's, because it was composed in the same meter (dactylic hexameter). The meter was used for various other purposes as well, such as recording the utterances of the Delphic oracle. This flexibility of subject matter was to suit later poets as well, those writing in Latin as well as in Greek.

Important Precursors. Vergil had both important precursors and significant successors in the use of dactylic hexameter verse. Among the former, apart from Homer, Hesiod, and Apollonius Rhodius, we must especially mention Theocritus, the Hellenistic Greek poet who lived in the early third century B.C.E. and wrote his *Idylls* in this meter; Callimachus, whose now-fragmentary Greek poem *Hecale* has been termed by modern scholars an *epyllion* or "mini-epic"; and Catullus, whose poem numbered sixty-four in modern editions is an astonishing tour de force that must have profoundly affected Vergil. Whole books have been written about the putative influences of these authors on the poetry of Vergil, and more still have been written on the influence Vergil had on his successors, some of whom are discussed below.

Ovid's *Metamorphoses*. Ovid's major work—and the only one composed in dactylic hexameters—was his *Metamorphoses*, the first epic written after Vergil. Ovid's catalogue-epic, formally derived from Hesiod's *Theogony*, directly answers the challenge of Vergil. While the *Aeneid* dealt with one hero and one myth, Ovid tells a whole host of stories, loosely organized in cycles. Where Vergil's worldview was teleological, Ovid's world is constantly in flux (*Met.* 15.165, *omnia mutanturi* "everything keeps changing"). One minute you see a young woman, the next moment she is a tree. Although Ovid will never qualify as a philosopher, this constant flux is an expression of a totally different philosophy of life. Nothing is permanent, not even Rome or Augustus. Where Vergil's tone was one of sadness, Ovid cherishes flippant, irreverent wit and humor. (The elder Seneca tells the story that Ovid's friends asked the poet to remove three lines from his entire works. Ovid agreed on the condition that three lines were out of bounds. They were, of course, the same as the ones his friends wanted him to strike. Only two of them have come down to us: "half-human beast and half-beastly human" [*Ars* 2.24] and "both the chilly north-wind and the unchilled south wind" [*Am.* 2.11.10].)

Always Erotic. Above all else, Ovid chooses to eroticize the mythical stories wherever he can. While Daphne, for example, is being turned into the laurel tree, Apollo puts his hand on the newly formed tree trunk under whose bark he can still feel her heart pounding (*Met.* 1.553–4). Clearly he has his hand on her breast. Or take Echo, wooing Narcissus: she can only repeat his last word(s). Ovid has a humorous field day with this speech impediment, despite which the two manage to have a meaningful conversation. The erotic highlight comes at 3.386–7, where Narcissus asks to meet Echo, whom he cannot see. She is said to answer his call *huc coeamus* (let's get together here) more gladly than anything ever by her *coeamus*. She, however, wants to do more than just meet, since the second meaning of the verb *coire* gives us the English noun *coitus!* A further source of humor is paradox: the healing deity Apollo cannot heal his own lovesickness (1.523) and is deceived by his own oracle (1.491). Narcissus, in love with his own reflection in a pond, exclaims "my wealth has made me poor" (3.461)! and wishes to be parted from his own body. Another way of making something funny is by taking it to ridiculous extremes. Pygmalion forges a lifelike ivory statue with which he falls in love, and prays that she may come alive, which with the help of Venus she does. It was commonplace in ancient times to say that an author loves his work. Pygmalion, as Ovid shows us, takes this to an unrivalled extreme: *"Kisses he gives and thinks they are returned; / he speaks to it, caresses it, believes/ the firm new flesh beneath his fingers yields,/ and fears the limbs may darken with a bruise"* (*Met.* 10.256–8, translation by Melville). Another stereotype was that good art was incredibly lifelike. Ovid again takes this theme to its logical and ridiculous extreme. This statue is so lifelike that she does indeed come alive.

Human Suffering. What is disturbing for modern readers is the cavalier manner in which Ovid accepts and describes acts of violence and rape. Actaeon, turned into a deer, is eaten by his own dogs while still feeling like a human: *"But his friends/ with their glad usual shouts cheered*

Bust of Vergil in the Vergilian Park in Naples

on the pack,/ not knowing what they did, and looked around/ to find Actaeon" (*Met.* 3.242–4 translation by Melville). Erysichthon eats himself. Philomela is raped, imprisoned, and has her tongue cut out. There seems to be a complete indifference to human suffering; in fact it often forms the basis of witty paradoxes. What seems distasteful to us is, however, part of the theme of constant flux: one minute we see the wit, the next minute we realize we are laughing at rape. Nothing is what it seems and everything, including our perception, is constantly in flux. This worldview does indeed provide a valid counterpoint to Vergil's *Aeneid.*

Lucan's Anti-Epic. Literature ran in the blood of Seneca's family: his nephew Lucius Annaeus Lucanus (Lucan) wrote an unfinished historical epic on the civil war between Julius Caesar and Pompey the Great. By choosing historical rather than mythical epic, Lucan, like Ovid, avoids direct comparison with Vergil. Instead he strives to invert Vergilian precedents. Where the *Aeneid* gave the foundation myth of Rome, Lucan describes the death of the republic. While the *Aeneid* has one hero, Lucan has three central characters. Caesar, the winner of the historical events, is presented as highly energetic but malicious, while his opponent is more benign but lacks verve. The most positive character in the ten surviving books ends up being Cato ("*The victorious cause pleased the gods, but the vanquished one pleased Cato*" [1.128]), the Stoic sage who fought for Pompey and ended up, like any Stoic facing the loss of his personal liberty, committing suicide at Utica. Lucan's *Civil War* (also known as *Pharsalia*) never gets this far in the plot. The last episodes covered are Cato and his men crossing the Sahara desert and Caesar meeting Cleopatra. The point at which Lucan was going to end remains a fertile ground for scholarly speculation. It seems most likely that Cato's death at the end of a twelfth book would have provided a suitably anti-Caesarian flourish. This work constitutes an "anti-epic": there are no gods, no powerful heroes like Achilles or Aeneas; the winner is the moral loser and vice versa; minor characters like Scaeva in book 6, who would have been whacked over the head by an aristocrat in Homer, become gruesome heroes for short periods of time. Even the style is deliberately more prosaic than is usual in epic. Rhetorical exaggeration becomes evident already in the first line where the war is labeled *plus quam civilia* (more than civil). Equally obvious is Lucan's ardent anti-Caesarianism. After all, the poet was involved in the Pisonian conspiracy against Nero and had to commit suicide upon its discovery in 65 C.E.

Statius's Epic Spectacle. Under the Flavian dynasty literature—especially epic—flourished once more. Perhaps the most accomplished writer of this period was Publius Papinius Statius, who was born circa 40 C.E. as the son of a highly successful rhetoric teacher and poet in Naples. He won various poetry contests staged by the emperor Domitian. In Rome he attached himself to various patrons whom he celebrates in his *Silvae* (Forests). He died back in Naples around 96 C.E. Statius wrote a collection of occasional poems entitled *Silvae* celebrating his patrons, and things dear to them. His main work, however, is the epic *Thebaid* about the dispute between Oedipus's sons Eteocles and Polynices, which culminated in the war between the brothers called "The Seven against Thebes." The theme of fraternal warfare recalls Lucan, but Statius clearly also modeled his work on the *Aeneid*, with his twelve book structure falling into an "Iliadic" second half balanced by some "Odyssean" elements in the first. He also retains the divine apparatus but modernizes it to become an expression of inescapable Stoic fate that is revealed to mankind who do not want to obey it but rather follow fickle fortune. Thus, the curse on the Theban royal house that is familiar from the Greek tragedies, which provided Statius with his subject matter, becomes a more philosophical necessity which governs life. His style tends to be ornate, using descriptive epithets wherever possible. His narrative thereby becomes graphic, both in the beautiful descriptions as well as in the scenes of abominable slaughter in which killing becomes fun for the characters: "*Heavy hooves crush the bodies, while / blood washes the wheels and impedes the hurrying troops. / The men find this road sweet, as if they proudly trampled / Sidonian homes in Thebes herself with bloody feet*" (10.478–80, a translation by Austin and Morse). Maybe there is a hint here of the Roman interest in blood sports. The story as a whole cannot help but remind the reader of the Roman civil war of 69 C.E., the year of the four emperors in which Vespasian emerged victorious. First Galba, who had ousted Nero, was killed by the imperial guard who proclaimed Otho as emperor. However, the general Vitellius was also proclaimed emperor by the legions of the Rhine. He marched against Otho and defeated him whereupon the legions of the East proclaimed Vitellius emperor. He also returned to Italy to defeat Vitellius and found the

Flavian dynasty. In Statius as in history, a brother leaves the city only to prepare an army against his hometown and wage war on it. Peace is finally restored by the benevolent outsider Theseus who comes from Athens to put an end to the bloodshed. Attempts have been made at casting Theseus in a darker light but despite some shortcomings the restoration of peace and the burial of the dead comes as a great relief both to Thebes and to Rome.

Last Gasps of the Epic: Valerius Flaccus. Statius's contemporary Valerius Flaccus directly imitated Apollonius of Rhodes's *Argonautica* in his eight-book epic of the same name and on the same subject, the myth of Jason and the Argonauts. Valerius relies heavily on the Vergilian "personal narrator," telling the story from the perspective of one of the characters in it, which is combined with an interest in human psychology. It presupposes that the reader knows the story. His most notable feature is an unparalleled number of epic similes, which enhance the pathos of the narrative.

Last Gasps of the Epic: Silius Italicus. The longest epic of them all is the *Punica* of Silius Italicus, in seventeen books. His subject matter is taken from Livy's second decade, his seventeen-book form and the annalistic structure probably from Ennius's eighteen books of *Annals*. Avoiding any Ennian archaisms, his main inspiration, however, was Vergil. Thus, the poem forms an intentional bridge between the founding of Rome in the *Aeneid* and the destruction of the republic in Lucan's *Civil War*. Silius presents Jupiter as facing Rome with a hard test that it will pass, thereby proving itself worthy of empire (3.571–629). The main character in this narrative is Hannibal who, of necessity, opposes successive Roman generals. In Hannibal we hear demonizing echoes of Turnus and Lucan's Caesar. It has been said that the epic lacks a positive hero, but Fabius Maximus and Scipio provide an unmistakable counterpoint of Roman *virtus*. Scipio, like Aeneas, descends into the underworld in book 13 to be unofficially instated as Rome's savior ("*Light of Italy, whose martial exploits I have witnessed/ as far too great for one man, who subjects you to descend into the night/ and visit the kingdom one time to be inhabited?*" [13.707–9]). The picture of Scipio Africanus is deliberately blurred with that of his father who, at the beginning of the epic, suffers some hurtful losses to Hannibal. The epic therefore acquires a single artistic hero in the merger of father and son who are tested by initial losses but, after a crucial descent to the underworld, come up triumphant. Reminiscences of Aeneas are surely intentional.

Sources:
Gian-Biagio Conte, *Latin Literature: A History*, translated by Joseph B. Solodow (Baltimore: Johns Hopkins University Press, 1994).

William J. Dominik, *The Mythic Voice of Statius: Power and Politics in the Thebaid* (Leiden & New York: E. J. Brill, 1994).

Martin Helzle, *Der Stil ist der Mensch. Redner und Reden im römischen Epos* (Stuttgart-Leipzig: B. G. Teubner, 1996).

HISTORIOGRAPHY

Caesar. It is ironic that Gaius Iulius Caesar, a contemporary of Cicero and Catullus, and certainly another contender for the title of Most Important Roman of the Republic, is barely studied any more in schools and universities; generations of Latin students have been turned off the subject by having to read about his martial exploits, mostly in the *Gallic War*. He actually came from Rome itself, and his writings are arguably the most Roman of all the literature that survives. His works take the form of a commentary, notes taken down as a basis for a full-fledged history. Since he himself was the protagonist in the warfare he describes, his account is of course necessarily subjective. While some books of the Greek historian Thucydides read like sketches or early drafts of a history, Caesar's "notes" are not obviously modeled on any Greek author and read like a lean but paradoxically finished product, including some of the geographical and ethnographic digressions characteristic of ancient historiography. His style is as remarkable as Cicero's, with a tendency to formulaic expressions. He deserves to be read again as a man of letters and a politician rather than as a general and used as a training ground for translating ablatives absolute or indirect speech.

Critique of the Aristocracy. The historian Gaius Sallustius Crispus (generally called Sallust in English) appeals much more to the modern mind than does Caesar. In his two monographs, *The War with Catiline* and *The Jugurthine War*, written after Caesar's death and Sallust's retreat from public life, consciously echo both the format and the style of the famous Greek historian Thucydides. Even the fragmentary *Histories* in five books seem to have included some quasi monographs within their annalistic structure. Sallust's view of Roman history is highly critical of the Roman aristocracy, which, in the war against the Numidian king Jugurtha, proves itself to be incompetent and corrupt. The sly crook Jugurtha manipulates the Roman aristocrats to his own advantage until Gaius Marius, a man of common origins, puts an end to aristocratic shortcomings and to the war. The Roman revolutionary Catiline (see also under Cicero) exemplifies, for Sallust, everything that is wrong with the young aristocrats: they have all fallen prey to *ambitio* (ambition) and *avaritia* (greed). These two vices have, in Sallust's analysis, taken root since the destruction of Carthage in 146 B.C.E. Like most ancient historians, Sallust therefore sees history as a process of rise and fall. His own period is presented as one of moral and political decline, and the culprits are clearly the ruling Roman noblemen. His abrupt, sententious style, which avoids Ciceronian periods and balance, can be seen as an expression of his dissent.

Ab urbe condita. One of the greatest historical sources for ancient Rome is the massive work of Titus Livius, or Livy, as he is called in English. His annalistic history, referred to as *Ab urbe condita* or *From the Foundation of the City*, begins with Aeneas and, in its final form, ends with the death of Augustus's stepson Drusus in 9 C.E. The work was originally conceived in 120 books, ten times the length of the *Aeneid*, ending with the death of Cicero (and of the republic). This design already indicates Livy's great love for the republican form of government and the glorious days of senatorial rule, a fact apparent to the emperor, who jokingly called him a supporter of Pompey the Great. Livy added the final 22 books to cover the most recent years and presumably acknowledge the achievements of Augustus. It has been argued that Livy's Ciceronian style indicates his overall approval of the status quo, while dissenters such as Sallust and Tacitus choose a terse, cryptic manner of writing. Only books 1–10 (early Rome down to the third Samnite War), 21–45 (second Punic War and war against Macedonia), and a fragment of 120 survive. The contents of the lost volumes are summaries called *periochae*. The vast amount of material is arranged at least in part in chunks of ten books called decades, which may have been the original units of publication. In collecting the material for this huge work, Livy necessarily relied on the accounts of previous historians who often had their own axes to grind. Like his Greek precursor Herodotus, Livy has been judged to be insufficiently critical of his sources. This is not entirely true, as can be seen in the vexed question of Hannibal's route across the Alps (*"I cannot understand why there should be any doubt about the route he followed over the Alps, or why it is often supposed that he crossed by the Pennine Alps."* [21.38 translation by de Sélincourt]). Livy weighs the accounts carefully and then forms his judgment. His guiding principle, however, is not the often biting criticism of Sallust or Tacitus, but rather an interest in what the Greeks called *aitia* (causes, origins), thus connecting the past with the present. Furthermore, Livy seems well informed about Roman army administration and public finances, so he must have used at least some archival material.

Guide to Life. Ancient writers of history conceived of their craft less as a recording of what actually happened than as a guide to lives. Readers were meant to draw lessons for their own lives and times from their accounts. For Livy this means that individuals shape history, standing out as either models of conduct such as Scipio, or negative examples such as Hannibal. The latter is directly characterized in book 21.4 as a godless villain reminiscent of Sallust's Catiline, a man of iron constitution: *"Indefatigable both physically and mentally, he could endure with equal ease excessive heat or excessive cold; he ate and drank not to flatter his appetites but only so much as would sustain his bodily strength. His time for waking, like his time for sleeping, was never determined by daylight or darkness."* (21.4 translation by de Sélincourt). Scipio, on the other hand, is indirectly characterized by his deeds, foremost of which is his carrying his wounded father out of the battle at the Trebia (21.46) as Aeneas had carried Anchises out of Troy. Roman *pietas* (sense of duty toward gods, country, and family) like this cannot help but win out in the end against an opponent who has *nulla religio* (no respect for religious observances, 21.6).

Dramatic Episode. The other building block of Livy's account is the dramatic episode. In a work of this proportion it is difficult to keep the reader's attention. Brilliantly described individual events are Livy's remedy. Who could forget the twin accounts of how the elephants are taken across the river Rhône (21.28)? The version in which they are shipped on rafts symbolically anticipates the Carthaginians' situation in Italy: surrounded by a hostile medium,

Engraved title page for a 1640 edition of Tacitus's history of the Germans and his biography of Agricola, Roman governor of Britain (courtesy of the Lilly Library, Indiana University)

those who lose their cool fall into the river, while those who stay calm in spite of their fear make it to the other side. Another famous episode occurs in 21.37 on the south side of the Alps, where the Carthaginians cut a serpentine path into a rocky precipice to allow their elephants to descend. This is done in four days by heating the rock with fire and then pouring vinegar on it. Whether true or not, this account highlights the extraordinary difficulties of the Alpine crossing in a much more vivid way than logistical considerations would. Consider this: Hannibal used North African elephants, which were smaller than the West African ones in modern zoos. A West African animal eats about 200 kilograms (440 pounds) of vegetation per day. Hannibal managed to get thirty-seven elephants into Italy. Even if his smaller elephants consumed only half of the West African's ration, Hannibal would have had a major supply problem on his hands. This requirement is why he crosses in fall when the harvest has been brought in and stores are generally full. It is also the reason for local opposition to his force: *"Coming to the territory of another mountain tribe, a numerous one for this sort of country, Hannibal encountered no resistance, but fell into a cunningly laid trap. In fact he nearly succumbed to the very tactics in which he himself excelled.”* (21.34, translation by de Sélincourt). Hannibal needed to raid the winter supplies of the mountain dwellers, essentially leaving them to starve. Instead of this dry analysis, Livy gives us colorful episodes of deceiving the local opposition, of men and beasts rolling down mountainsides, creatures slipping and sliding on the ice, breaking through and getting stuck, as well as the rock episode.

Rise and Fall. While the narrative focuses on individual episodes, the overall scheme of Rome's history is the familiar pattern of rise and fall already found in Herodotus. Like Sallust, Livy sees Rome as ascending until the year 146 B.C.E. when Corinth and Numantia were destroyed. The decline of the republic finds its logical end in the death of Cicero, its most vocal champion, in book 120. The scheme of rise and fall, however, allows for a new period of recovery under Augustus which, like the *Aeneid*, ends on a sad note with the death of Augustus's own stepson. In Livy, too, empire has its price.

Astute Observer. A writer of similarly great interest to the social historian is Gaius Caecilius Plinius Secundus (Pliny the Younger), who, in the published version of his speech for the emperor Trajan in the Senate as well as in the nine-book collection of prose letters, offers unrivalled documentation for life around 100 C.E. Literature ran in his family, since his uncle and adoptive father of the same name had written an encyclopedic work called *Natural History* covering all human knowledge about nature. The younger Pliny's published speech, titled *Panegyric*, started a tradition of writing such formal praises of an emperor's virtues. In his published letters he describes Roman life in his day from a detached perspective. The most famous example is his description of the eruption of Mt. Vesuvius in which his uncle dies:

> *"The closer they came, the hotter and thicker the ash that was now falling on his ship. Now black pumice stones and rocks that were burnt and broken by fire were falling. Now the collapse of the mountain and a sudden wave fell on the opposing shore. Hesitating whether he should turn back, he soon told the helmsman who was encouraging him to do just that: 'Fortune favors the brave. Steer towards Pomponianus!' He was in Stabiae cut off by the middle of the bay."* (*Letters* 6.16).

Pliny describes all of this disaster from a safe distance. He laments the deaths of poets Silius Italicus and Martial. Generally, he tries to find something positive to say about the people he describes.

Tacitus's Critique of Monarchy. One of Pliny's closest friends was Publius Cornelius Tacitus, the most unusual historian that Rome produced. Apart from his biography of his father-in-law, Agricola, and his ethnographical account of Germany, he also wrote a work (in Ciceronian style, which he subsequently abandoned) called *Dialogue on Orators*, on the decline of oratory. Of his *Histories*, dealing with the civil war of 68–69 C.E., four books and some fragments have come down to us;

his most famous work, the *Annals*, was probably left unfinished at his death, which is why only books 1–4, part of 5, 6, part of 11, 12–15, and parts of 16 remain. The picture he gives of the principate in his *Annals* is the gloomiest and most critical to be found anywhere. While he claimed to write “without anger or bias” (*sine ira et studio*, 1.1), one cannot help but note that in his view the only good emperor is a dead emperor. Tiberius's reign starts with the devastating phrase *“primum facinus novi principatus fuit Postumi Agrippae caedes”* (“the first crime of the new régime was the murder of Agrippa Postumus,” 1.6). Tacitus's portrait of Tiberius is devastating: A somewhat dark and unapproachable character who would not have done well in the television age, Tacitus sets him up against his nephew Germanicus, whom he had to adopt at Augustus's behest. In Tacitus's account, the able general Tiberius, who had salvaged many potentially disastrous situations for Augustus, can do no right, whereas the inept but popular Germanicus can do hardly any wrong. Germanicus is set up as a check on Tacitus's cruel and violent character, which reveals itself in stages. After Germanicus's death Tiberius becomes slightly less cruel, but hides it behind the even crueler face of Sejanus, his right-hand man and commander of the palace guard: *Of audacious character and untiring physique, secretive about himself and ever ready to incriminate others, a blend of arrogance and servility, he concealed behind a carefully modest exterior an unbounded lust for power. Sometimes this impelled him to lavish excesses, but more often to incessant work.* (4.1, translation by Grant). When Sejanus is discovered as having plotted to become emperor himself, Tiberius finally reveals his true nature in a bloody purge of Sejanus's supporters. Tacitus's picture of Nero is similarly stylized. First, his mother Agrippina manages to control the young monster, then his tutors and advisors Seneca and Burrus, but when he has eliminated all of them, he reveals his childish, conceited, and fiendish true nature. While Tacitus's picture of Nero probably has a great deal of truth to it, Tiberius was much more able as an administrator than Tacitus would have one believe. In his account, anything apparently positive done or said by Tiberius is interpreted as hypocrisy. The emperor is violent by nature and his administration becomes a civil war on his own people. (All this is told in a prose style that sends Latin students screaming for help.) Tacitus cultivated in the *Annals* a remarkable style that avoids parallel grammatical constructions and balance, thereby making the reader pause, reread, and think again. This deliberately difficult style has recently been seen as a hallmark of historiographers who are highly critical of the times they describe, such as Thucydides and Sallust. This picture seems to fit Tacitus quite well, since he had demonstrated that he was perfectly capable of writing like Cicero in his *Dialogue on Orators*.

Suetonius: Lives of People such as Ourselves. Tacitus's contemporary and fellow-historian, Gaius Suetonius Tranquillus, chose a different style, outlook, and format for his works. His preferred genre was biography. Of his *Lives of Famous Men* we only have the ones on teachers of grammar and rhetoric. His *12 Lives of the Caesars,* however, have survived largely intact. Biography had been cultivated in Greece by such authors as Plutarch, but Suetonius develops a different approach: rather than proceeding chronologically he describes different "rubrics," which describe an emperor's personal virtues and vices. His main interest is in the emperor's private lives, delving into court gossip about scandals, and personal shortcomings. Emperors suddenly look like any human being rather than gods on earth: the emperor Claudius, Suetonius says, *hardly ever left the dining room not bloated and drunk so that a feather was put in his mouth for relieving his stomach as he went to sleep immediately and kept his mouth open while asleep* (*Claudius* 33.1). Seeing an emperor as fully human is exactly the effect that Suetonius tried to create.

Sources:

Michael von Albrecht, *A History of Roman Literature: From Livius Andronicus to Boethius* (Leiden & New York: E. J. Brill, 1997).

Ronald H. Martin, *Tacitus* (Berkeley: University of California Press, 1981).

P. G. Walsh, *Livy: His Historical Aims and Methods* (Cambridge: Cambridge University Press, 1961).

A. J. Woodman, *Rhetoric in Classical Historiography: Four Studies* (London: Croom Helm, 1988).

LITERARY SOURCES

Roman Culture, Roman Writers. What is known about the vanished civilization of ancient Rome, aside from the monuments and material culture that remain, comes primarily from literary sources. The range and character of Roman literature is best recognized by considering the work of Rome's most important writers. In some of the topical entries listed, one will read who wrote, what of their writings survives, how it was passed down through time, and who read it.

Ancient Books. Romans accessed their literature on handmade, handwritten papyrus scrolls. (The word "volume" comes from the Latin word for a scroll, which is *volumen,* or, something "rolled up.") These were expensive to produce and cumbersome to use. The "book" as people know it, with turnable pages sewn to a spine, is of the type known as the *codex;* this format gained popularity over the scroll between 200 and 400 C.E. Public libraries had opened in the age of Augustus. The texts we have were taken from these libraries to the monasteries at the end of the Roman era. There they were copied for centuries. Modern text-editions therefore include a "critical apparatus," which list all the major variations (variant readings that the editor deems to be mistakes) in the most important manuscripts.

Sources:

Gian Biagio Conte, *Latin Literature: A History* (Baltimore: Johns Hopkins University Press, 1987).

Edward Courtney, *Archaic Latin Prose* (Atlanta: Scholars Press, 1999).

LYRIC POETRY

Shifting Aesthetic Values. Roman readers were, from an early period, captivated by Greek literary models. For all readers of Greek poetry, of course—whether Greek or otherwise—this meant, above all, Homer. Homeric epic (by which is meant the *Iliad* and *Odyssey*) is vast in conception, grand in execution, and massive in size. Among the Greek *literati* of several centuries after Homer, however, aesthetic sensibilities changed, and what was once seen as grand and admirable came to be regarded as too big, ungainly, ugly. "A big book is a big evil," one of them said, and the new fashion was to write poetry that was characterized by *leptosunê*—delicacy. In practical terms, this new preference meant smaller poems, where each line of verse—indeed each word—was carefully chosen and placed. Key aesthetic values in this poetic trend, besides smaller size, were refinement, subtlety, and allusiveness.

The "New Poetry." A circle of Roman poets in the time of Cicero embraced these new values; the one best known is Gaius Valerius Catullus. Unlike the archaizer Lucretius, he emphasized a terse, highly polished new style; Cicero, who found the fashion distasteful, nicknamed Catullus and his peer group *neoteroi*—"the newer poets." (*Neôterismos* means "revolution" in Greek; hence this nickname indicates a "revolutionary" approach to poetry—not a compliment in this case). Catullus and his friends devoted themselves mainly to short poems and epigrams. His work was lost for much of the Middle Ages; the earliest manuscripts date back only to the 14th century C.E., which raises the question whether the collection is really his or a later arrangement. As usual, scholars cannot agree on this point. His poetic corpus (circa 2,300 verses) clearly falls into three sections: the polymetric poems (1–60), the longer poems (61–68), and the epigrams (69–116, all in elegiac distichs). Within the polymetrics scholars have found so-called "cycles," groups of poems in which one theme (such as his beloved Lesbia, the youth Juventius, or personal invective) predominate, but are interspersed with other poems. Whether he arranged this collection as it is or not, Catullus manages to convey emotions, both positive and negative, with unparalleled immediacy, while exercising a degree of artistic control that should not be underestimated. Even when he adapts a Greek original as he does in poem 51, where he envies a man sitting next to his beloved, he appropriates the passion expressed by the poetess Sappho for himself as the speaker. The first three stanzas therefore constitute not simply a translation, which in itself would be quite a feat considering the metrical complexities of the Sapphic stanza, but he transfers Sappho's burning desire for one of her girls to himself. Sappho's passion becomes Catullus's passion. He as a man can feel every bit as passionate as Sappho. After the third stanza, however, Catullus departs from Sappho's poem, stepping back and addressing himself in the final stanza, in which he expresses the Roman value system: *Leisure, Catullus, does not agree with you. / At leisure you're restless, too excitable. / Leisure in the past has ruined rulers and / prosperous cities.*

"Captive Greece," wrote Horace, "took captive her ferocious captor [Rome]"; Roman writers were deeply influenced by Greek literary models, studying and copying them assiduously. Sometimes they actually translated them into Latin. At the hands of a master such as Catullus, the result can be haunting and powerful. In this example, one sees how he adapts a poem by the Greek lyric poet Sappho, adding personal and cultural references in such a way as to make it not only clearly Roman, but also peculiarly his own. First, an English rendition of Sappho's Greek original, and then a translation of Catullus's version:

Sappho, Fragment 31 [Lobel/Page]

He seems to me to be equal to the gods,

who sits opposite you

and listens nearby to you

sweetly speaking

and laughing alluringly, the laugh that, oh,

sets my heart fluttering in my breast;

since when I look at you, I can

no longer speak,

But my tongue goes silent, and all at once

a filigree of fire runs under my skin,

I see nothing with my eyes, and my

ears are set a-humming,

and a cold sweat grips me, a trembling

seizes me; paler than grass

I turn; a short distance from death

I seem to myself.

But all must be endured, since [...]

Catullus, Poem 51

He seems to me to be equal to the gods,

He seems, if it is *fas* [i.e. without sacrilege, permitted] to say so,

even to surpass the gods,

who, sitting opposite [you], again and again

sees and hears you

sweetly laughing — which robs all

the senses from miserable me: for as soon as I

look at you, Lesbia, nothing is left

[of my voice in my mouth];

but my tongue falls numb; a fine flame seeps down

through [lit. "under"] my limbs; with a sound all their own

my ears ring, my eyes [lit. "lights"]

are covered over with double [lit. "twin"] night.

Otium [leisure, spare time], Catullus, is irksome to you;

you exult in your *otium* and get too eager for it;

otium has been the destruction of ancient kings

and prosperous cities.

*Translations by Denis Bullock

Sources: *The Poems of Catullus*, translated by Charles Martin (Baltimore: Johns Hopkins University Press, 1990).

Sappho: Lyrics in the Original Greek with Translations, edited and translated by Willis Barnstone (Garden City, N.Y.: Doubleday, 1965).

(Poem 51.13–16, translation by Lee). *Otium* (leisure, free time) is the only reason for his passion, and it will ruin him. What a good Roman should be involved in is its implied opposite, *negotium* (business). His emotion is therefore not just controlled by the stringent demands of the meter, but by his own detachment and self-address. This poem has its counterpart in poem 11 in the same Sapphic meter. In the first three stanzas he overemphasizes the fact that Furius and Aurelius would go to the ends of the world for him; then he sends them to Lesbia with the message that she can go to hell with her adulterers, and should not expect Catullus's love, which she has violated as the passing plough mangles a flower on the edge of a field. Furius and Aurelius are really his enemies, appropriate messengers in this case. The flower image recalls Sappho Fragment 105b Voigt, where a bride is compared to a hyacinth trampled on by the shepherds. Sappho's fragment probably refers to the young woman's feeling about being deflowered on her wedding night. Catullus makes the bride's feelings his own: he is the one who feels deflowered by Lesbia. One would expect the most tender moment in the poem to be the most original one, but Catullus uses a literary reference to Sappho to express his feelings in an extremely vivid way.

Poetic Innovations. Everything known about Catullus indicates that he was an extremely innovative poet. His little epic, poem 64 (454 hexameters), gave Rome a taste of Hellenistic Greek epic poetry along the lines of Callimachus's *Hecale:* the story within a story, the dramatic monologue of Ariadne left on Naxos by Theseus, and the sometimes "personal" narrative style, which presents the events as seen through Ariadne's eyes, are all characteristics of this mode of composition. Catullus's poem 64 also paved the way for Vergil's full-scale narrative poem, the *Aeneid.* Just as important is poem 76, placed among the epigrams, but with its twenty-six lines clearly one of the earliest Latin love elegies on record.

Imperial Lyrics. The generation immediately following that of Catullus—during the reign of Augustus—produced one of the greatest of all lyric poets from antiquity, Quintus Horatius Flaccus (known as Horace). Horace, along with his friend Vergil, were part of a circle of poets around a patron named Maecenas, whose purpose it was to groom a writer of an epic. Horace, however, preferred less grand tones and humbler genres. His earliest work he published as a collection of seventeen Epodes, short, invective poems in predominantly iambic meter, modeled after the seventh century Greek poet Archilochus. While Archilochus, a social nobody, had leveled vitriolic attacks against personal enemies of higher status, Horace, son of a freedman, gets at unimportant, nameless, or even fictitious characters and their quirks.

Horace's *Odes*. Horace's greatest achievement, however, consists of the four books of *Odes,* formally inspired by Archaic Greek lyric poets such as Alcaeus, Sappho, and Anacreon, but filled with themes from Hellenistic epigram, popular philosophy, Roman public life, poetics, and Horace's self-irony. The first three books were published together and meant to be a unit, framed by two poems in lesser Asclepiad meter (1.1, 3.30) as well as two poems addressed to his patron Maecenas (1.1, 3.29), which dedicate the collection to him. The guiding principle of arrangement in this, as in other collections arranged by their author, is symmetry with variation which may have originated with the Hellenistic poets, especially Callimachus. Horace put thirty poems in book 3, twenty in book 2, but thirty-eight in book 1. Book 1 starts with eleven "parade" odes in which he chooses a different meter for each. Book 3 opens with six lengthy "Roman" odes, all in Alcaic meter and on Roman virtues (*Manliness, unaware of base defeat, / shines with unsullied glory, / neither puts down nor assumes power / at the whim of popular favor* [*Odes* 3.2.17–3.2.20]). The central book contains predominantly poems of medium length, mostly in Sapphic and Alcaic meter and often on philosophical themes. The middle poem of the second book is devoted to the Golden Mean, which, however, appears in verse five (*Whoever chooses the golden mean / will safely avoid the squalor of a shabby house, / will also avoid an enviable / palace out of moderation* [*Odes* 2.10.5–8]).

Major Themes. As in Sappho, Anacreon, and Hellenistic epigram, love is a major theme. Horace, however, seems quite detached by comparison with other love-poets. Love is a joke that Venus is playing on mortals: A loves B, but B loves C, and C loves none of the others. Horace himself seems to have ever changing paramours, but stays with no one. These women invariably have Greek names which suggests that, if they ever existed, they were slaves, freedwomen, or courtesans. His apparent fickleness indicates that Horace's love-poetry could therefore just be a literary game, inspired by Anacreon, Asclepiades, or Meleager. In fact, the speaker need not be Horace at all but simply some persona he presents. Ultimately there is no way of knowing if Horace had none of these women, some of them, or all of them! The point is that he does not tell about it, since the information he gives about himself is highly selective, intended to create a public image of "Horace," a literary persona in the text that the actual author is adopting.

Poetic Details. Attention to detail regularly pays off when reading a Horatian ode. Ode 3.9 is the only dialogue in the collection. In it, a woman named Chloe (the same as the timid young woman of 1.23?) and the speaker undergo a reconciliation after two stanzas of showing off how well they are doing since they split up. Chloe consistently gets the better of the speaker. In the end, however, she suggest a rapprochement even though the male is "more fickle than cork and more irascible than the cruel Adriatic." Horace elsewhere (*Sat.* 2.3.323) describes himself as prone to anger. The unnamed speaker, who loses every argument to Chloe, could therefore be Horace or at least the image which he wants to project of himself. Obviously this man could make fun of himself. Poem 1.11 contains the now-famous phrase *carpe diem* ("pluck the day," meaning seize the opportunity). In it, human mortality is apparently set against endless time and great forces like the sea. But the sea is specified as the Tyrrhenian and it is churning pumice stones. As David West shrewdly observed, the only place in Italy where this is possible is on the Bay of Naples, where many Romans owned villas, some in chic resorts like Baiae. Whether sophisticated or not, Horace is sitting on this bay, asking Leuconoe to strain some wine for him. She must be a servant or a slave, and Horace's invitation to enjoy the here and now is readily interpreted as an invitation to make love. A similar case has been made by West on 1.9, the lovely Soracte-ode: Thaliarchus there can be seen as the aging speaker's boy-lover, now on the verge of adolescence. The scene implied is that of a male drinking party or symposium at which Thaliarchus is pouring the wine and Horace is explaining to him that with his advancing age he will now pass on from being loved by him to being loved by young women.

Poetic Tact. One of the most outstanding features of Horace's *Odes,* however, is his unquestionable tact. Whether he celebrates Pollio's history of the civil war (2.1) or the return of his friend Pompey, who had fought against Octavian at Philippi with him (2.7), Horace manages to highlight the merits even of opponents of the Augustan régime without attacking the emperor. A case in point is Ode 1.37, the Cleopatra-ode. In the first section (1–21) Horace celebrates Augustus's victory at Actium in suitably exaggerated tone: the opening line "Now we must drink, now shake the earth with free foot" recalls the seventh century B.C.E. Greek poet Alcaeus's celebration of the overthrow of a tyrant (*Frg.* 332 Voigt); after the battle hardly a ship of Cleopatra survived (13), Marc Antony is never mentioned, Augustus chased Cleopatra as a hawk hunts doves or a hunter a hare (17–20). The former simile is taken from Homer's *Iliad* (22.139–42) where the hunter hunts in Thessaly, home of Achilles. Cleopatra, on the

The foundations of Horace's house in
the Sabine Hills near Licenza

other hand, is described as a crazed, drunken, eastern queen surrounded by (venereal) disease-ridden men (6–12), a monster (21). Once the battle is over at verse 21, however, Cleopatra gains in stature in her noble suicide. As a foreign queen, she was a lethal threat to Rome; as a woman she proves to be fearless and not like a woman at all (22). The not unwelcome side effect of this acknowledgment of her nobility is the fact that a victory over a great opponent is always better than one over a weak one. In actual fact, the battle of Actium was probably not much of a fight because Cleopatra panicked and fled too soon.

Poetic Balance. Horace's poetics reveal a similar effort at balancing two sides. Under pressure from Augustus to write an epic, many poets of the time looked back to the Hellenistic poet Callimachus, who had defended himself against recriminations that he had not written an epic. Many Augustan poets used him as a model to forestall the demands made upon them. Their encounter with Callimachus also made them proponents of small, refined genres which include much learning. Horace had used some of these arguments in *Satires* 1.4 and 1.10. They return in *Ode* 1.6 and 4.15, but there the rejection of grand epic subjects (a gesture known as *recusatio*, "refusal") ironically sounds like a celebration of epic topics. Horace is therefore hovering between Callimachean technical skill and anti-Callimachean insistence on inspiration as the mainspring of poetry. This dichotomy is often symbolized by the gods Apollo, invoked in Callimachus's self-defense, and Bacchus, the god of irrational inspiration. It should not come as a surprise that *Ode* 1.6 is mirrored by an ode to Bacchus as the sixth poem from the end of the collection (3.25). In 1.1.29 the poet expresses the wish to be crowned with Bacchus's ivy. In 3.30.16, however, the Muse is instructed to

place a laurel wreath, sacred to Apollo, on his head. Horace therefore successfully manages to balance the dichotomies in his life: technical skill vs. poetic inspiration; public vs. private; humble status but personally acquainted with Augustus; ostensibly involved with lots of women but never married; inspired by Greek poetry but thoroughly Roman.

Sources:
Wendell Clausen, "Catullus," in *Latin Literature*, volume 2, *The Cambridge History of Classical Literature*, E. J. Kenney and W. V. Clausen, eds. (Cambridge: Cambridge University Press, 1982).

Niall Rudd, "Horace," in *Latin Literature*, volume 2, *The Cambridge History of Classical Literature*, E. J. Kenney and W. V. Clausen, eds. (Cambridge: Cambridge University Press, 1982).

David West, ed., *Horace Odes I: Carpe Diem* (Oxford: Clarendon Press, 1995).

Timothy Peter Wiseman, *Catullus and his World: A Reappraisal* (Cambridge: Cambridge University Press, 1985).

MUSIC

Greek Background. It is often said with some justification that music was far less important to the Romans than to the Greeks of the Archaic and Classical periods (circa 750–320 B.C.E.). Although certain Greek musical styles and musicians received adverse criticism by the late fifth century B.C.E., within traditional Greek culture music was generally endowed with divine resonances and profound psychological powers. In Greek culture, music played a central role in poetic and dramatic performances, in religious festivals, and ritual ceremonies, as well as education and even warfare. Indeed, the Greek word *mousikê*, from which the word "music" is frequently derived, conveyed poetry, song, and dance in addition to musical accompaniment. For the Romans, too, music had an important, if less prominent, role in civic and religious activities—public and private—and was also considered worthy of inclusion in an educated citizen's upbringing. The comedies of the early playwright Plautus (active circa 205–184 B.C.E.) included an overture played on the pipes, and a number of Plautine passages have been compared to operatic arias and probably had some musical backing. Patrician boys and girls are known to have sung at the Secular Games of 17 B.C.E., under instruction from the poet Horace. And a number of cults to foreign deities or to gods like Bacchus (Rome's answer to Dionysus) involved hymns of praise to the accompaniment of pipes, cymbals, and percussion. Although some musicians attained great popular success, for most Roman intellectuals, it seems, musical performance of their own times had little of the significance that it had in early Greek culture where it permeated all levels of society. Possible reasons for the relatively marginal position of music in Roman culture, include the fact that most extant Latin poetry was composed without musical accompaniment and was designed instead to be read or spoken. This style is perhaps a natural consequence for a society in which prose and oratory became prime vehicles for public expression in elite circles; such was not the case in Greece until the late fifth century B.C.E. or even later. As well, Roman musical theory tended to focus on older Greek models, which were considered superior to contemporary standards. Even in this sphere one finds criticisms in Roman times, such as in the writings of the Epicurean philosopher Philodemus (circa 110–45 B.C.E.), who challenged the views of Platonic and Stoic philosophers on the ethical and character-building significance of music.

Musical Instruments. In any event, information about the Romans' musical instruments—another instance of their material culture—can be gleaned from ancient literature, inscriptions, depictions in art, and survivals of musical artefacts. The main stringed instrument was the lyre, based on Greek models. Lyres had two arms joined by a crossbar fixed to a sound box of wood or sometimes tortoise shell. Strings of gut, sinew, or flax were stretched over a bridge on the face of the box and secured near its base, and usually struck with a plectrum of wood or bone. There were various types of Greek lyre, such as the *phorminx* and *kithara*. This latter eventually became the prime stringed instrument of antiquity, and with its enlarged soundbox, is the ancestor the modern guitar and zither in etymological and musical terms. This instrument appears in some Roman statues, which show it having tuning-pins with triangular heads. A common wind instrument was the Roman *tibia*, the equivalent of the Greek *aulos*. This instrument was a cylindrical reed instrument, closer to an oboe or clarinet than to a flute, and often played as a pair of pipes with finger holes. A cloth band went around the player's head to keep the pipes in place, as they were held one in each hand. The pipes varied in size and pitch and were deemed to have strongly emotional and expressive effects; thus they were frequently used in dramatic performances and concerts. The Etruscans and Romans introduced a variation on the Greek panpipe, by making connected pipes of different lengths for different pitch whereas the Greeks plugged pipes of the same length with wax to different levels. Bagpipes were known in Italy by the second century B.C.E., as were hydraulically piped organs from the third century B.C.E. Brass instruments such as the straight *tuba* or curved *cornu* (horn) were used by the army and at games for signalling. Percussion instruments such as the *tympanum* (a handheld drum shaped like a tambourine), wooden clappers, and metallic cymbals were used in many contexts. This music could include social entertainment or cult practice, as is attested by a fresco from the "House of the Mysteries" in Pompeii of about 60 B.C.E.

Sources:

Andrew D. Barker, "Music," in *The Oxford Classical Dictionary*, edited by Simon Hornblower and Antony Spawforth, third edition (Oxford: Oxford University Press, 1999), pp. 1003–1012.

Giovanni Comotti, *Music in Greek and Roman Culture*, second edition (Baltimore: Johns Hopkins University Press, 1989).

Curt Sachs, *The Rise of Music in the Ancient World, East and West* (New York: Norton, 1943).

THE NOVEL

The Problem of Genre. When was the "novel" invented in western literature? This is a topic on which the experts cannot agree. Some would say the first novel was *The Princess of Cleves,* a French tale written in the seventeenth century. Others would point to English authors of the eighteenth century. But a case can be made that the genre has precursors, if not actual examples, in the ancient prose writings of such authors as Achilles Tatius, Chariton, Heliodorus (in Greek), and Apuleius (in Latin). For

Ruins of Madauros in North Africa, the birthplace of the philosopher and writer Lucius Apuleius

Apuleius, the last pagan author mentioned in this brief glance at Roman literature, we do not even have a first name. His most famous work is the prose *Metamorphoses* in eleven books, but he also published a collection of samples of oratory and a good number of Platonist philosophical writings.

Greek Borrowings. The *Metamorphoses* of Apuleius is the only completely preserved Latin novel. In it, the protagonist Lucius is mistakenly turned into an ass by a sorceress. He keeps his human faculties and lives to tell of all the extraordinary adventures he experiences until he eats the roses that restore him to human form and is initiated in the rites of Isis. Embedded in this tale is the story of Cupid and Psyche told by an old woman. Venus, jealous of Psyche's beauty, hands her over to a monstrous husband—who turns out to be really her own son, Cupid, who has fallen in love with her. He takes her to a paradise-like place but insists that she must never look at him. She does anyway and is separated from him. She makes up for her lapse by passing many tests, including a descent to Hades. In the end she gets to marry Cupid and becomes a new goddess. The story bears Platonic as well as ritual traits. It can be read as an allegory for the human soul freeing itself from the shackles of this world and finding the divine truth, or it can be read as a story of initiation-myth that connects with Lucius's final initiation into the Isis cult. Both readings have some truth to them and some drawbacks. The gods seem strangely mundane, even more so than in Ovid's *Metamorphoses*. On the other hand, the allegedly philosophical heaven which Psyche finally reaches is also quite worldly, complete with parties. As an author, Apuleius must have been steeped in literature; the effect of his style is that of a mosaic, since he combines archaism with neologisms, epic, and colloquial words, using formulae from previous authors with great ease. The unreal and stylized picture of the world of the novel is made up of small stones drawn from all over Roman literature which, when put together, produce a new and original picture. This description of Apuleius could also be applied to Latin literature as a whole which, to greater or lesser degrees, keeps borrowing from Greek writers of all ages, sometimes from other Roman writers and then, in each case, presents a new and quite original work.

Source:
Gian-Biagio Conte, *Latin Literature: A History,* translated by Joseph B. Solodow (Baltimore: Johns Hopkins University Press, 1994).

PAINTINGS AND MOSAICS

Figural Arts. The remains of monumental painting from the Roman world can be traced back to the second century B.C.E., but it seems that accomplished painters, such as Fabius Pictor, were active as early as the fourth century B.C.E. Many surviving examples of painting come not only from Rome itself, but also from Herculaneum and Pompeii, where distinctive styles continued to develop until 79 C.E., the year of the eruption of Vesuvius. Over this period, too, a number of mosaics were produced which often echo the subject matter, colors, and designs of wall

Portrait of a man from Fayum, Egypt, encaustic on a wood panel, circa 160–170 C.E. (Buffalo Fine Arts Academy, Albright Art Gallery, Acq. No. 38:2)

painting, and may in some instances be copies of lost original frescoes. This has been suggested of the "Alexander Mosaic" from Pompeii depicting Alexander the Great's victory over king Darius of Persia. This mosaic involved the use of *tesserae*—small cubes of cut stone, glass, or terracotta—for greater subtlety and illusionistic effect than was usually possible through older techniques of pebble mosaics. Many paintings and mosaics from the Roman period depict scenes ranging from heroic action in myth and history, to exotic urban and natural landscapes, to images drawn from everyday life. An early instance comes from the floor of the temple of Fortuna at Praeneste, circa 80 B.C.E., where there was a mosaic (5.25 by 6.56 meters) depicting a panoramic view of life on the Nile in a series of vignettes of activity in architectural, mountainous, and maritime landscapes. The inclusion here of animals such as lions, crocodiles, and hippopotamuses would have had an exotic appeal for Romans. Such a mosaic seems to be an important precursor of the panoramic vistas that became fashionable in painting of the Augustan era (27 B.C.E.–14 C.E.).

A mosaic of daily activities along the Nile River, from the floor of the Temple of Fortuna at Praeneste, circa 80 B.C.E. (Archaeological Museum, Palestrina)

Fresco Panels. A house on the Esquiline hill in Rome has yielded eleven fresco panels, from circa 50 B.C.E., depicting scenes from Homer's *Odyssey,* a Greek epic which tells of the return of the hero Odysseus from the Trojan War during a ten year period. These paintings (circa 1.5 meters high) have an almost impressionistic feel to them with their bright hazy colors and confident brushwork, which emphasize the background landscape at the expense of the narrative and diminutive figures. An example is the scene of Odysseus's escape from the cannibalistic giants called the Laestrygonians, one of his misadventures on his way home. Here one sees a shift away from the centrality of the human figure more often associated with classical Greek painting. But the Greek subject matter and varying points of view in different panels have suggested to some that they may be copies of Hellenistic originals, transposed to a new setting in a Roman house. It is also possible that the work may have been done by Greek artists known to be operating in Rome from the second century B.C.E. onward, such as Iaia of Cyzicus and others. Another possible general influence is Etruscan tomb painting from as early as the sixth century B.C.E., some of which reveals an interest in landscape and animals with human activity depicted on a diminutive scale.

INNOVATIONS IN PAINTING TECHNIQUE

Pliny the Elder (35.116–117) tells of the innovations brought to painting by one Spurius "Tadius," active during Augustus's reign, which tally well with remains of wall-painting found in Rome, Pompeii, and Herculaneum.

It was he who first instituted that most delightful technique of painting walls with representations of villas, porticoes and landscape gardens, woods, groves, hills, pools, channels, rivers, coastlines—in fact everything which one might want, and also various representations of people within them walking or sailing, or, back on land, arriving at villas on ass-back or in carriages, and also fishing, fowling, or hunting, or even harvesting wine-grapes. There are also. . . many other lively subjects of this sort indicative of a sharp wit. This artist also began the practice of painting representations of seaside towns on [the walls of] open galleries, thus producing a charming view with minimal expense.

Source: *Pliny: Natural History,* 10 volumes, Loeb Classical Library (Cambridge, Mass.: Harvard University Press / London: Heinemann, 1938–1962).

Fresco of Flagellation, from the Villa of Mysteries, Pompeii, circa 60 B.C.E.

Painting Styles. Wall painting from Pompeii is usually divided up by scholars into four styles, which point to certain differences in this medium over time. The first style from before 100 B.C.E. involved the use of molded plaster, which was painted to imitate architectural forms, mostly marble panels. The second style, beginning circa 80 B.C.E. involved the more detailed and illusionistic treatment of architectural forms and urban landscape at some distance. Sometimes, as in a fresco from the Boscoreale villa in Pompeii, there is more than one vanishing point in these images with receding ledges, colonnades, and balconies. Such features may reflect the painter's interest in perspective, shading, and illusion, which had been the subject of earlier Greek speculation, and which also attracted the attention of the architect Vitruvius (active circa 50–20 B.C.E.) in his treatise *On Architecture*. It is also conceivable that some of these "architectural" frescoes may bear some relation to the work of Pacuvius (circa 220–130 B.C.E.), who was both painter and playwright, and may have painted his own stage scenery. Pompeiian paintings in the "Room of the Great Fresco" from the so-called Villa of the Mysteries, dated circa 60 B.C.E., have attracted much attention for the large-scale depiction of the human form. An array of figures, almost lifesize, appear on a bright red background divided up by painted pilasters, and include Bacchus (god of wine and frenzy), his lover, Ariadne, satyrs, and anonymous men and women. The depiction of a ritual flagellation, possibly an initiation into rites in honor of Bacchus, is a most talked-about image where on adjacent walls a winged female figure prepares to whip a young woman cowering on the lap of another older looking woman. Near them appear two other women, including a nude dancer holding cymbals above her head, understood as a maenad, one of Bacchus's female followers. The figures are dramatically rendered and the scene is one of the most (literally) striking and intriguing images in ancient painting. The "third" Pompeiian style, which appears about the beginning of the Christian era, tends to be more ornamental and floral than other styles, and prettifies the painted surface instead attempting a deeper illusionistic image. Monochrome backgrounds in black, green, or other colors tend to replace the more colorful backdrops of the second style, and the variously active figures and architecture are often quickly and minutely brushed on, adding a spontaneous and delicate effect to the scene overall. Indeed, this imagery seems typical of what Pliny tells us about painting of the Augustan era (27 B.C.E.–14 C.E.). One may also note as an example of this kind of imagery the splendid fresco of the "Garden Room" from Prima Porta in the house of Livia, wife of Augustus, dating from circa 20 B.C.E. The "fourth style" of Pompeiian painting appears around 63 C.E. and sees a return to depicting fuller architectural depth in the frescoes as well as human figures in more monumental form. Frescoes from the house of the Vettii (circa 63–79 C.E.) in Pompeii contain good examples. Treatment of figures and their setting is sometimes called theatrical, and on occasions one does find theater masks and even curtains across the top of a fresco. The subject matter was broad.

A fresco from a house on the Esquiline Hill in Rome, circa 50 B.C.E., depicting a scene from Homer's *Odyssey*
(Vatican Museum, Rome)

Narrative depictions of heroes such as Aeneas, Theseus, Perseus, and Hercules (the Roman name for Heracles) appear around this time, sometimes with or without architectural backdrops. As well there were still lifes, portraits, and even depiction of specific events such as the riot of 59 C.E. between the Pompeiians and Nucerians in the amphitheater at Pompeii, described by Tacitus (*Annales* 14.17).

Funerary Art. Of course, fresco painting and mosaics continued elsewhere in the Roman world after the eruption of Vesuvius. Examples come from Hadrian's villa at Tivoli (circa 130 C.E.), the baths of Neptune at Ostia (circa 150 C.E.), and further afield in the provinces such as the hunting scene frescoes from the baths at Leptis Magna under the Severan emperors (193–235 C.E). But the next most significant achievements in painting from the Roman world can be identified in the funerary portraits from the Fayum in west-central Egypt during the first to fourth centuries C.E. These were painted on a coat of plaster on wooden or linen tablets often in the encaustic technique and placed on the sarcophagus at the height of the deceased's face. There is a marked emphasis on the enlarged dark eyes of the deceased, which stare back directly at the viewer, and the angle of depiction with highlights and shading is consistent from one image to the next. This gives a vivid impression of the subject who is often presented in the prime of life, although child portraits are known, too. There are clear links between these images and portrait frescoes and mosaics from Pompeii and earlier Egyptian funerary images; and the style of the Fayum portraits has rightly been seen to anticipate developments in Byzantine icons of the fifth century C.E. and later.

Sources:

George M. A. Hanfmann, *Roman Art. A Modern Survey of the Art of Imperial Rome* (New York & London: Norton, 1975).

Roger Ling, *Roman Painting* (Cambridge: Cambridge University Press, 1990).

Jerome J. Pollitt, *Art in the Hellenistic Age* (Cambridge: Cambridge University Press, 1986).

PHILOSOPHY

Epicureanism at Rome. One of the major schools of Greek philosophy was that of Epicurus. His views were made more available to Roman readers by Titus Lucretius Carus, whose *On the Nature of the Universe* was said to have been published posthumously by Cicero. In this hexameter didactic poem, Lucretius outlines Epicurean physics. He tries to show that everything in the world is made of matter, made of atoms. There is no afterlife and death is therefore not to be feared. Expressing these doctrines in Latin hexameter was particularly difficult, not just because it meant versifying a branch of Hellenistic Greek philosophy that today would be called natural science. In addition to this challenge, Latin simply lacked a philosophical vocabulary; Lucretius says, *I know / new terms must be invented, since our tongue / is poor, and this material is new* (1.137–8 translation by Humphreys). The end result has to be considered something of a tour de force, since Lucretius combines plain, philosophical exposition with beautiful descriptions of nature that have a high poetic appeal. While asserting that there are no gods, he repeatedly invokes Epicurus, the master, in hymnic style as a quasi-deity: *O glory of the Greeks, the first to raise / the shining light of tremendous dark / illuminating the blessing of our life, / you are the one I follow; in your steps / I tread, not as a rival, but for love / of your example* (3.1–6 translation by Humphreys). On the one hand, his meter and language are reminiscent of Ennius; they have something of an archaic flair, which Cicero much appreciated even though he disagreed with Lucretius's Epicureanism. On the other hand, Lucretius was undoubtedly also influenced by his more modern contemporaries, such as Catullus, and consequently paved the way for Vergil's *Georgics* as well as the *Aeneid*. While embracing Greek philosophy for his subject, Lucretius pushed the Latin language as far as he could, and expanded the potential of the Latin hexameter.

"The Most Eloquent Offspring of Romulus." The most important expansion of the Latin philosophical vocabulary was, however, accomplished by Marcus Tullius Cicero, the acknowledged master of Roman oratory and Latin prose style who found a golden mean between the two entrenched rhetorical camps of his time, namely "Asianism" (which advocated a flowery, dramatic, elaborate style) and "Atticism" (which delighted in plainness, austerity, and simplicity). Cicero also briefly reunited philosophy, rhetorical theory, and practical oratory in a manner reminiscent of the Greek Sophistic movement. To him, an orator (whether lawyer or politician) had to have a thorough grounding in the liberal arts, especially philosophy and rhetoric: this allows him to adapt his style and contents to his audience, thus becoming as effective as possible.

Stoicism in the Empire. One of the most important literary figures under the emperor Nero was the emperor's own tutor, the younger Lucius Annaeus Seneca. As the son of a rhetorician who had written a collection of *suasoriae* and *controversiae*, Seneca cultivated a terse, sententious style, which he uses both in his philosophical writings and in his tragedies with plots similar to well-known Greek plays. His main love was Stoic philosophy, which he communicated in pragmatic ways to his countrymen (*You are afraid to die? So what? Isn't that kind of life death?* [*Epist.* 77.18]). Without Seneca one would know substantially less about this Greek school of thinking. Besides a number of treatises traditionally mislabeled *Dialogues*, he wrote a collection of literary prose epistles, addressed to his friend Lucilius, but meant primarily for publication. In these he gives advice on such topics as friendship, the use of time, the fear of death, the avoidance of passions, and even the treatment of slaves whom he sees as unfortunate fellow humans who share in the same divine reason as a free man (*'They are slaves.' Actually, they are humans. 'They are slaves.' Actually, they are our companions. 'They are slaves.' Actually, they are our humble friends. 'They are slaves.' Actually, our fellow slaves, if you consider that Lady Luck has as much power over each of us.* [*Epist.* 47.1]). Passions such as fear, desire, or anger are to be avoided because they render a person insane. The rational man transcends them.

Sources:

C. D. N. Costa, ed., *Seneca* (London: Routledge & Kegan Paul, 1974).

Simon Hornblower and Antony Spawforth, eds., *The Oxford Classical Dictionary*, third edition (Oxford: Oxford University Press, 1996).

SATIRE

All Ours. "Satire is all ours," wrote Quintilian, by which he seems to mean that this was a competitive arena in which the Romans beat even Greek writers hands down. And indeed, some of the most memorable Latin literature is in this genre. While scholars are not able to agree on the origin of the actual word "satire," one is able to discern two major strains of Roman satire: the Lucilian, that stemming from the tradition established by the early Roman writer Lucilius, and the Menippean, that is, satire written in the style of the Syrian writer Menippus (third century B.C.E.). Menippus wrote in Greek, in a mélange of prose and verse, and taking a seriocomic narrative approach; writers such as Varro and the Greek author Lucian worked in this genre, and we might say that the *Satyrica* of Petronius falls into the Menippean tradition. The Lucilian tradition, by contrast, reflects the influence of Gaius Lucilius (circa 180–102 B.C.E.), a member of the Scipionic Circle, who wrote purely in verse. The satires of Lucilius, known only in fragments, were composed in dactylic hexameter, like Greek and Roman epics, and took the form of informal philosophical discourses; they show the influence of Stoicism. The most significant follower of Lucilius in Roman satire is, of course, Horace.

Human Foibles. Small targets representative of human foibles recur in Horace's *Satires*. These poems aim to be "conversations" advocating common sense mixed with some Epicurean philosophy. Moderation and contentment are set forth as keys to human happiness, while greed, social climbing, adultery, and other excesses are gently made fun of. In *Satire* 1.9, for instance, the bore who tries to get an introduction to Maecenas from Horace vividly dramatizes the social climber who will sacrifice even his own defense in a court case in order to get the chance at making the right connections. But some humor is also aimed at the speaker. At pains to get away from the sycophant, Horace's friend Fuscus leaves the poet in the lurch. Only the bore's legal opponent manages to haul him away. Horace's conclusion raises the encounter to the level of an epic fight: "Thus did Apollo save me" (78). The otherwise skeptical Horace, having been rid of a pest of epic proportions, humorously attributes his salvation to a divinity. Only a god could have achieved this! The often strong autobiographical element recedes in the second book where dialogue plays a significant role in which the poet seems to yield to his conversation partner. Paradoxically, each speaker has strong and weak points to make and a positive code of behavior is not always clear. Things become clearer again in the much later *Epistles*, which continue in the prosaic hexameter style of the *Satires*, but now Horace gives advice to friends and acquaintances. In the second book of

A NOUVEAU-RICHE HYPOCHONDRIAC

Petronius, author of the *Satyrica*, is a master of narrative and of mischievous humor. Of the portion of this work that remains, the most famous section is known as the *Cena Trimalchionis*—the "Banquet of Trimalchio." Here Trimalchio, a freedman who has become vulgarly wealthy, has staged a party of unimaginable lavishness. After letting all his guests arrive, he stages a late and ostentatious entrance. His frank and crass conversation shows that it takes more than money to elevate one's social class:

. . .Trimalchio waltzed in, mopped his brow, washed his hands in some scented water, and, after pausing a moment, said: "My friends, forgive me, but my stomach has been unresponsive for many days. The doctors are lost. Nonetheless, a concoction of pomegranate rind mixed up with pine sap boiled in vinegar has loosened things up a bit. I hope my stomach remembers its manners now; otherwise it's as noisy as a bull. And if anyone of you wants to relieve himself, there's nothing to be ashamed about. None of us was ever born solid inside. I don't think there's any greater torment than holding yourself in. This is the one thing Jove himself cannot deny us. . . .

I don't object to your doing anything here in the dining room if it makes you feel better. Even doctors forbid holding it in. And if more comes out than you expected, well, there are facilities just outside—water, chamber pots, and little sponges. Believe me, those vapors go right into your brain and upset the whole body. I personally know many, many men who've died because they wouldn't admit the truth to themselves.

When the food is served, the spectacle becomes more and more extraordinary. In his powers of phantasmagoric description, Petronius shows himself the rival of such authors as Rabelais and Lewis Carroll.

. . . looking intently at the pig, Trimalchio exclaimed, "What is this? Has this pig been gutted? No, it hasn't, by god! Get that cook in here now!"

A contrite looking cook appeared in front of our table and admitted that he'd forgotten to gut the pig. "What? Forgotten!" shouted Trimalchio. "You'd think he'd forgotten to add the salt and pepper, the way he says it; off with his shirt!" In no time the poor man was stripped and flanked by two executioners. Everyone tried to get him off the hook saying: "This happens all the time. Please, let him go. If it happens again, no one will speak up for him."

. . .[Trimalchio's] face relaxed into an hilarious grin as he said, "O.K., since you've got such a bad memory, gut him right here in front of us." The cook donned his tunic, again, grabbed his butcher knife, and sliced the pig's belly every which way with a quivering hand. The slits immediately gave way to the pressure from inside and roasted sausages and giblets gushed out of the wounds!

Source: Petronius, *Satyrica*, translated by R. Bracht Branham and Daniel Kinney (Berkeley: University of California Press, 1997).

this new genre of verse-letters, whose third letter is commonly called *Ars Poetica*, Horace extends his advice to the writing of poetry.

The Pumpkinification of Claudius. In Seneca's *Apocolocyntosis*, or "Pumpkinification" of the dead emperor, Claudius, who is presented as asking to be admitted among the Olympians but is sent to Hades, ends up serving under a freedman. The work is a mixture of prose and verse satire in which Seneca makes fun not only of the emperor who had banished him in his youth but also of literary genres and styles, including possibly his own tragedies.

Arbiter elegantiarum. The date of birth of Gaius Petronius is unknown. He was consul before 66 C.E., which would put his birth in the 30s at the latest. Nero held him in high esteem as a judge of good taste (*arbiter elegantiarum*, hence "Arbiter"). He committed suicide in 66 C.E. It has been doubted whether he is the author of the work we know as *Satyricon* whose proper name is *Satiricon* or *Satyrica*. However, the work fits well in the middle of the first century C.E. and is therefore likely to be his. Of the *Satyricon* only some of books 14 and 16 as well as all of book 15 remain. What the reader has is a fantastic story of the adventures of a young man named Encolpius in successive homosexual triangle relationships. This work inverts the plot of Greek novels in which a pair of separated lovers overcome many hazards in order to be united. It is also written in the Roman tradition of Menippean Satire, a mixture of prose and verse passages like Seneca's *Apocolocyntosis*. This form gives Petronius many opportunities to parody literary styles including Lucan and Homer. The most famous passage is the so-called *Trimalchio's Dinner Party*, where riches and bad taste are satirized.

Master of the Epigram: Martial. A totally different note is struck by the epigrammatist Marcus Valerius Martialis, known in English as Martial. From his pen we have twelve books of epigrams from the years 86–102 C.E. plus a separate, earlier one called *Book about the Spectacles* and two books of two-liners to accompany gifts (*Xenia*) or party-favors (*Apophoreta*). Epigrams started their life as Greek inscriptions but in Hellenistic times were cultivated as an art form, often associated with specific occasions. Catullus picked up the genre in the latter third of his collection and it is to him that Martial looks back. Unlike the Catullan epigrams we have, Martial's poetry is of mixed meter and varied length. Martial aims mainly at giving lively impressions of contemporary Roman life. Although he provides celebrations of imperial events as well as funerary poems, he tends to be more humorous (and even satirical) about life in Rome than his Greek precursors and Catullus. He certainly cultivates the tendency to end an epigram with a witty final line, which had already been apparent in Hellenistic epigram, and which became the hallmark of this genre after him. Martial's epigrams work rather like a joke: he starts by setting up the situation or character, thus heightening the reader's suspense. This tension is then released at the end by a witty, unexpected, often paradoxical punch line called *aprosdoceton* (Greek for

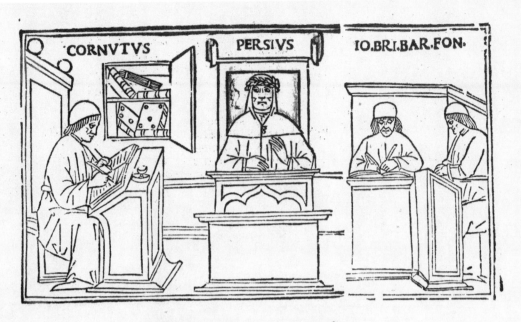

CORNVTVS   PERSIVS   IO.BRI.BAR.FON.

❡ Persius cum tribus comentariis.

❡ Cornuti phylosophi eius preceptoris cometarii.

❡ Ioannis Britannici Brixiani comentarii.

❡ Bartolomei Foncii comentarii.

Illustration from the 1499 Venetian edition of Persius's *Satyrae* (courtesy of the Lilly Library, Indiana University)

"unexpected"): *You ask me what I get / out of my country place. / The profit, gross or net, / is never seeing your face.* (2.38, translation by Mitchie). However, witty and even salacious pieces are varied by more somber, serious, or encomiastic ones, thereby giving the reader interesting insights into all facets of late first-century life.

Satire: Persius. Verse-satire in this age was written by Aulus Persius Flaccus. Born on 4 December 34 C.E. into a family of Etruscan descent in Volterra, north of Rome, Persius went at the age of twelve to Rome for his education. At sixteen he joined the Stoic philosopher Cornutus, and got to know Seneca and Lucan. He died of a stomach ailment before turning twenty-eight on 24 November 62 C.E. He left his estate to his mother and sister, his books to Cornutus. In his writings, Persius aims at drastically reforming the morals as well as the literature of his day. In harsh and often cryptic terms he tries to shake his reader out of his complacency and turn toward the life of the Stoic sage.

Satire: Juvenal. Equally scathing but less obscure are the fifteen satires of Decius Junius Juvenalis. Born around 67 C.E. in Aquinum near Naples, Juvenal made a living as a speech writer (*declamator*). His main creative period was under the emperor Hadrian (117–38 C.E.) to whom he dedicated satire 7. Accounts that he was banished in old age are highly suspect. He died sometime after 127 C.E. Juvenal chastises pretty much everything in his day, from declamation via legacy-hunting, social climbing, and sexual depravity to the life in the city in general: *More deadly than armies, / luxury has fallen upon us, avenging the world we conquered. / Every crime and act of lust has become familiar / since the demise of Roman poverty* (*Sat.* 6.292–5, translation by Rudd). Rather than attacking living contemporaries, he uses the dead as examples of vice. This attitude of rage mellows with satire 10, where he becomes a more detached observer of the irredeemable wickedness of the world. In his case, not even Stoic apathy can mend his disgust.

Sources:
Gian-Biagio Conte, *Latin Literature: A History*, translated by Joseph B. Solodow (Baltimore: Johns Hopkins University Press, 1994).

SCULPTURE: FRIEZES AND RELIEFS

Triumphal Art. The victory of the general Aemilius Paullus over the Macedonians at Pydna in 168 B.C.E. is significant not least for the uses of artworks in the celebrations that followed. A triumph was held in Rome during which paintings of the battle by Greek artists were paraded—a typical example of Roman interest in using historical events as a basis for representation in art. As well, Paullus paraded vast amounts of statues and

Interior frieze from the Arch of Titus, Rome, 81 C.E., depicting the removal of spoils from the temple in Jerusalem

paintings looted from Greece in the wake of his victory, which apparently filled 250 wagonloads. In Greece he had a sculptured monument set up at Delphi (168–167 B.C.E.), the location of the most famous oracle in the ancient world, and a sanctuary of great significance. This monument was a column 9.5 meters in height supporting a bronze equestrian statue of the general; at the top of the column were marble relief sculptures (31 centimeters high and 6.5 meterssmeters long), which depict specific moments of the battle that are also spoken about by ancient historians. For instance, Livy (44.40.4–10) and Plutarch (*Aemilius Paullus* 18) write that the battle began when a riderless horse broke loose from the Roman ranks, causing both sides to clash as they tried to catch it. A rearing riderless horse conspicuously appears on the frieze, as do Romans and Macedonians elsewhere who are made clearly distinguishable from each other by their dress and armor. The idea of depicting actual battles in monumental sculpture was not unknown to the Greek artists. Alexander the Great had commissioned Lysippos to make a vast monument to celebrate an early victory over Persia at Granikos; and the artists who worked on Paullus's monument were probably Greek. But already in Paullus's monument one sees imagery drawn from real events (or events taken to be real), which was a recurrent feature in later sculptural memorials in the Roman world. More mundane subjects also appeared in Roman marble relief sculpture, such as the rather static depiction of census-taking on the so-called altar of Domitius Ahenobarbus from the temple of Neptune (circa 100 B.C.E.). This contrasts in style and subject matter from the more assured and flamboyant rendering of the wedding of Neptune and Amphitrite in the same building.

Ara Pacis. From the Augustan age the most significant sculptural monument is the *Ara Pacis* (13–9 B.C.E.), a marble rectangular enclosure (11.6 by 10.6 meters) surrounding an altar on raised steps. Aspects of its overall design recall on a smaller scale the great altar of Zeus at Pergamon, (circa 180 B.C.E.) which celebrates Pergamene military victories. This earlier monument was set on a high podium approached by twenty-four steps, with an Ionic colonnade on three sides, below which is the famous frieze depicting the battle of gods and giants. The Ara Pacis was set up on the Campus Martius to commemorate Augustus's safe return from Gaul and Spain and further participates in the Augustan propaganda campaign, as did, for instance his Prima Porta statue. Within the enclosure are sculpted wreathes hanging from ox skulls (*bucrania*) above vertical fluting. Externally, on the lower panels were sculpted complex ornamental acanthus leaves, while above are scenes propagating messages of peace, prosperity, and the piety of the imperial entourage who are engaged in a sacrificial procession. Augustus was presented as supreme priest (Pontifex Maximus), echoing an image of Aeneas on another part of the frieze in the role of a priest conducting a sacrifice. The grand civic procession of figures recalls that of the Parthenon frieze (circa 448–32 B.C.E.), and the use of shallow relief to suggest figures at a slight distance on the *Ara Pacis* recurs notably on later monuments such as the arch of Titus (81 C.E.). Allegorical figures appear on the altar, too, such as the female figure, usually seen as Earth (Tellus) or Peace (Pax) who embraces two babies and is surrounded by contented animals in a pastoral setting flanked by two other female figures who may represent the elements. These figures owe something to the fine sculptures of aristocratic Athenian women on tombstones that date from

Detail of Trajan's Column, erected in the Forum and dedicated in 113 C.E. to celebrate the victories over the Dacians

the late fifth century B.C.E. That peace leads to prosperity and fecundity is a commonplace of ancient thought, and here is seen as a direct consequence of the Augustan regime. On a smaller scale, the *Gemma Augustea* of circa 14 C.E., a large piece of onyx (19 by 23 centimeters) divided into upper and lower pictorial sections likewise invokes allegorical as well as historical imagery to disseminate the glory of Augustus and his successors. Above, Augustus is depicted as a deified figure about to be crowned and attended by the goddess Roma; below defeated enemies of Rome await their fate as soldiers hoist the victory spoils tied to a pole into the air.

Arch of Titus. Imperial arches date from the early first century C.E. such as that of Tiberius at Orange (26 C.E.). But the marble arch built to commemorate Rome's victory in the Jewish war under Titus, Vespasian's successor, (circa 81 C.E.) has become widely known as a classic example of triumphal Roman art. It is located toward the eastern end of the Roman forum and is comparatively small, measuring 15 by 12 meters. Its main inscription reveals that it was built by Titus's brother, Domitian, but its chief points of interest are in the reliefs in its passageway. These depict the actual triumphal procession itself in both realistic and allegorical ways. One panel shows Titus riding a chariot with a winged personification of Victory behind him, as attendants appear below wielding fasces. A sense of spatial depth is suggested by the fuller carving of figures in the foreground compared to the shallower carving for figures behind, and the fine carving of the horses in profile and three-quarter views recalls sculptures from the treasury of the Siphnians built at Delphi (circa 525 B.C.E.). The panel on the opposite side has less of the slow decorum of the panel depicting Titus in glory. It shows the plundered objects from the Jewish temple, especially the menorah (the great lampholder) being carried by a crowd of wreathed men, some of whom also carry trumpets and placards, possibly describing the booty. This procession appears to move forward and then turns toward an arch in the background with foreground figures more fully carved than those behind—again emphasizing a sense of depth here. The Corinthian pilasters and coffered vault of the arch make the figures seem more lively, and as one moves through the arch into the forum a palpable feeling of being part of the procession itself, or reliving it, is evoked.

Trajan's Column. Victory monuments could take a number of different forms apart from arches. Trajan's column was set up in 113 C.E. in his imperial forum to celebrate his recent successes over the Dacians. It is 28.9 meters in height, set on a podium of 6.2 meters with a continuing spiral frieze 200 meters long and varying in height from 85 cm to 1.45 meters. This monument—which was originally surmounted by a statue of the emperor—is one of the grandest examples of Roman sculpture. In very general terms the design owes something to the monument to Aemilus Paullus of 168–7 B.C.E., but there is, of course, nothing on the older monument that comes close to the great frieze on Trajan's column. The episodes from Trajan's

The Arch of Titus in Rome, built in 81 C.E. to commemorate the recent conquest of Judaea

campaign are carved in shallow relief (about 5 centimeters) on hollow drums of marble placed on top of each other. The scenes are not formally divided from each other and comprise detailed images of battles, the army on the march, transportation of goods, Trajan sacrificing or addressing the troops, as well as architectural and natural backdrops. Depth is suggested through the diminishing size of background figures as well as their being placed on a higher level than foreground figures. The "realism" of the scenes does not preclude the presence of gods and personifications such as the winged Victory, or the Danube River in the form of a bearded giant. As might be expected on a frieze of such vast proportions telling a basic story, a number of stock images are repeated and human types are presented with an artificial uniformity. Certain conventions such as depicting Trajan as taller than the surrounding figures are also employed. It would be mistaken to view the frieze as an accurate record of the campaign, although it may give some generic information about equipment and so on. Its prime function is imperial propaganda, and through its sheer size, range of imagery, and sculptural virtuosity, Trajan's column achieved a lasting impact on subsequent ages in antiquity and beyond. While other impressive monuments to Trajan's regime appeared in Rome and elsewhere—such as the arch at Benevento or the friezes on Trajan's trophy at Adamklissi in Rumania—Trajan's column stands apart in more ways than one. It not only inspired columns to later emperors such as Antoninus Pius and Marcus Aurelius (which depict his battles with German tribes), but was considered a worthy resting place for

Detail from the Arch of Constantine in Rome, dedicated in 315 C.E. to celebrate his victory at Milvian Bridge three years earlier

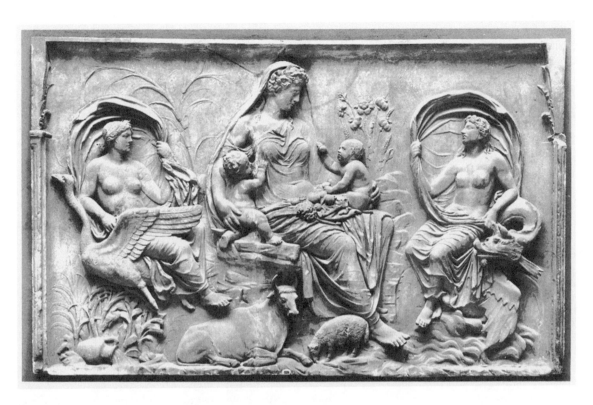

Relief of Tellus (Earth) or Pax (Peace) holding two babies on the monument *Ara Pacis* in Rome, completed in 9 B.C.E.

A reconstruction of the *Ara Pacis*, or Altar of Peace (from George M.A. Hanfmann, *Roman Art*, 1964)

the emperor's ashes by the senate, though not originally intended for this purpose. It is mostly intact today, surmounted by a statue of St. Peter, erected in 1588.

Severan Arches. One of the best-preserved monuments of the Roman forum is the arch of 203 C.E. honoring Septimius Severus. At 20.6 meters in height it is much larger than that of Titus. As well, there are three arches to this Severan monument—one main central arch is flanked by two smaller ones. It commemorates victories over the Arabs and Parthians as recorded in the inscription atop the arches, and its relief sculptures depict the emperor and his sons along with images of Victory, river gods and lines of the defeated enemy as captives. Like many Roman monuments, then, it combines allegorical as well as historic figures. The Severan arch at Leptis Magna, erected in 203 C.E. was a four-way monument—two sets of arches set at right angles—at a major intersection of the city. It has richly ornate Corinthian pillars and pilasters and is decorated with triumphal friezes of the emperor and his retinue. There is less attempt at illusionistic depth in these images than, for instance, in the arch of Titus. These figures are often frontal, and those understood to be in the background are raised to a slightly higher level; also drapery is rendered by deeper thin incisions than before. Some of these techniques would be designed to accommodate the viewers below, but they also led to a style that was to become steadily more schematic.

Old and New Styles. As an amalgam of old and new sculptural styles with various panels recycled from older monuments, the arch of Constantine (312–15 C.E.) is a fit-

ting embodiment of his regime, which saw the transition to Christianity as the official religion, while still retaining much of the classical past. The arch commemorates his defeat of his main rival Maxentius at the Mulvian bridge, and borrows from works dedicated to Trajan, Hadrian, and Marcus Aurelius. Ideology as well as artistic convenience would be the motives here, as Constantine would be attempting to legitimate his regime and its changes by presenting them as being in a tradition consistent with these former emperors who had left a favourable legacy to posterity. The three-way arch is similar in design and dimension to that of Septimius Severus at the other end of the forum, and notable borrowings from Trajanic monuments are the Dacian figures sculpted in the round, standing on plinths atop the Corinthian pillars supporting the arch. Two sculpted roundels above the peripheral arches show the fuller "classical" style of sculpture from the time of Hadrian, and these contrast in clear stylistic terms with images from Constantine's own time which show the emperor making a speech (*Oratio*) in the forum and distributing gifts (*Donatio* or *Liberalitas*). These images develop trends seen in the arch of Septimius Severus at Leptis Magna. The figures now are more squat than earlier with narrow lines signifying drapery folds, and the overall design is more symmetrical and openly schematic than, for instance, the frieze on the Ara Pacis. As well, distant figures in the *Oratio* scene appear as more or less severed heads above foreground figures, and the gaze of most of the characters toward the center emphasizes the symmetry of design. The frontality of key figures is explicit in the central figure of the emperor himself (now decapitated) and in the two enlarged seated figures at each end of the podium, identified as Hadrian and Marcus Aurelius. Many of these later scenes verge on the symbolic in their design and execution and convey a clear message of imperial authority to the laity. Such techniques would, of course, feature more emphatically in the heavily didactic, or message-driven, art of Christianity of successive centuries.

Sources:

Diana E. E. Kleiner, *Roman Sculpture* (New Haven & London: Yale University Press, 1992).

Jerome J. Pollitt, *Art in the Hellenistic Age* (Cambridge: Cambridge University Press, 1986).

Nancy and Andrew Ramage, *Roman Art: Romulus to Constantine,* third edition (London: Laurence King, 2000).

Donald E. Strong, *Roman Imperial Sculpture* (London: A. Tiranti, 1961).

Mario Torelli, *Typology and Structure of Roman Historical Reliefs* (Ann Arbor: University of Michigan Press, 1982).

SCULPTURE: FUNERARY IMAGERY

Honoring the Dead. Many Roman relief sculptures survive in the form of sarcophagi for private patrons. Cremation seems to have been the dominant means of disposing of the dead from the time of the late republic to about 100 C.E., but by the time of Hadrian's rule a change in burial customs led to the use of large stone or marble caskets on a more widespread basis than before. While some late republican examples are known, such as the tomb of the Gessius family (30–13 B.C.E.), most funerary sculptures date from the second century C.E. onward. These give further glimpses of sculptural forms and techniques within the

Roman world, and may well have been produced by the same workshops that worked on public monuments. Subjects varied widely, and Greek myths seem to have been popular, as do generic scenes of war, hunting, marriage, sacrifices, and so on, which likely refer to events in the deceased's life or reflect his or her perceived attributes or station in life. Some imagery seems obscure and hard to relate to an individual's life—for instance, the appearance of minor sea gods and goddesses known as Tritons and Nereids. It has been suggested that such imagery is of perhaps allegorical relevance, signifying a journey to the next world, but this is not certain. It is quite possible the images are part of the stock repertoire of sculptors' workshops; again, they may signify something lost forever to modern eyes.

Sarcophagus Styles. Two types of sarcophagi are generally identified. There is the so-called Attic type, which involves sculptures on three sides of the coffin and across the front of the lid and which was set against the wall of a tomb. The Asiatic type had sculpture on all four sides often set up in cemeteries by the road. Asiatic reliefs are sometimes more ornate than Attic ones and are notable for the inclusion of sculpted columns all the way around which divide the action into specific episodes; the events in the life of a hero like Hercules performing his twelve labors fit well into a medium like this. As well, figures in Asiatic reliefs are often depicted in classical style in even higher relief than found in Attic reliefs; sometimes they are almost in the round. So-called strigil sarcophagi were widely in use in the second century C.E. and later, too. These have few, if

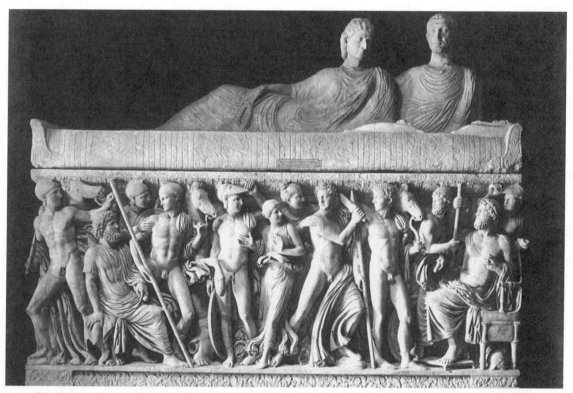

Marble sarcophagus (circa 250 C.E.) depicting Achilles at the court of Lycomedes (Capitoline Museum, Rome)

any, human or animal forms, but instead are dominated by a series of wavy lines like an elongated "S" that resemble a curved instrument used by ancient athletes to scrape off oil and dirt after exercise. These sarcophagi could be mass produced and made more affordable to a larger market aside from aristocratic patrons. Indeed, many sarcophagi have been found in shipwrecks in various parts of the Mediterranean, which testifies to their wide dissemination in antiquity, despite their bulky and unwieldy nature.

Relief Carvings. Scenes from the life of Achilles appear on a marble "Attic" sarcophagus dated circa 250 C.E. once thought to belong to the emperor Alexander Severus, who ruled from 222–35 C.E. The main relief (1.3 meters in height) depicts the discovery of Achilles at the court of Lycomedes, where he had been sent by his mother, Thetis, to live in disguise as a girl because she knew he would die at Troy. Achilles gives himself away by wielding the sword that has been laid aside for him when Odysseus goes to find him—the moment depicted here. The figures are elegantly carved with complex overlaps and varied poses in a crowded scene, yet with a clear focus on the central action. Also of interest are the two figures on the lid who are naturally taken to represent the deceased couple. Their presence and, indeed, their pose recalls the Etruscan habit of depicting reclining figures on sarcophagus lids, as typified by a terracotta sculpture from Cerveteri, datable to the sixth century B.C.E.; this feature is found in later models down to at least the second century B.C.E. Many aristocratic sarcophagi from about the mid-second century C.E. depict complex battle scenes replete with figures on a number of different levels, and with energetic, almost chaotic action. Some of these recall the action and energy of the Alexander Sarcophagus (made for the king of Sidon circa 325–311 B.C.E.), which depicts battle scenes and lion hunts. As well they seem to parallel scenes on the Column of Marcus Aurelius which depict the chaos of battle with arguably greater ferocity and immediacy than do the images on Trajan's Column.

Two Traditions. Just as official art produced under Constantine contained much that was embedded in the pagan past as well as looking forward to developments in later Christian iconography, so too the sarcophagus of Junius Bassus (circa 359 C.E.) is comprised of elements from both traditions. The status of this man who was prefect of the city, and second only to the emperor, is clearly reflected in this elaborate marble coffin, measuring 1.17 meters in height and 2.41 meters in length. The design develops the Asiatic technique of dividing scenes with columns, and replaces pagan content with Christian and biblical imagery, while retaining forms from the classical past. Scenes from the Old and New Testaments are represented: moments from the life of Christ, Adam and Eve, St. Peter, St. Paul, Abraham, and Isaac appear between elaborate Corinthian columns, and ornate architectural frames. The figures are deeply rendered, and although more squat than on earlier monuments such as the *Ara Pacis*, the drapery is typically Roman as are the faces and many of the poses— for instance, St. Peter under arrest. The central image of Jesus on

the upper panel recalls the image of Constantine on his imperial arch in the frontality of the sitter and symmetry of the vignette. And the allegorical appearance of Heaven beneath Jesus' foot is akin on one level to the figure of the Danube on Trajan's Column. In this rich and elaborate sarcophagus is an early glimpse of the legacy of pagan Roman art, which is now being adapted to preach the message of canonical texts and is conveying new meanings through a tried and trusted technique of visual allegory and narrative.

Sources:
Diana E. E. Kleiner, *Roman Sculpture* (New Haven & London: Yale University Press, 1992).

Jerome J. Pollitt, *Art in the Hellenistic Age* (Cambridge: Cambridge University Press, 1986).

Nancy and Andrew Ramage, *Roman Art: Romulus to Constantine*, third edition (London: Laurence King, 2000).

Donald E. Strong, *Roman Imperial Sculpture* (London: A. Tiranti, 1961).

Mario Torelli, *Typology and Structure of Roman Historical Reliefs* (Ann Arbor: University of Michigan Press, 1982).

SCULPTURE: PORTRAIT STATUES

Realistic Style. A major Roman achievement in the sphere of sculpture from the republican age is what is known as a "veristic," or realistic, style that aims at a genuine, if sometimes unflattering, likeness of a real individual. An early instance of Etrusco-Roman sculpture with realistic tendencies is the life-size bronze statue of Aulus Metellus of about 100 B.C.E. in the *adlocutio* (speaking) pose of an orator. With his "unidealistic" features—cropped hair, furrowed brow, arched eyebrows and thin mouth—and inclusion of prosaic details such as the lacing on his boots, the statue has an air of realism and directness absent from much Classical Greek sculpture. A key

PORTRAIT-SCULPTURE AND THE DEAD

Polybius (6.53) describes the ritual significance behind early Roman portrait-sculpture used in aristocratic burial ceremonies:

The portrait is a mask which is wrought with the utmost attention being paid to preserving a likeness in regard to both shape and contour. Displaying these portraits at public sacrifices, they honor them zealously, and when a prominent member of the family dies, they carry them in the funeral procession, putting them on those who seem most like [the deceased] in size and build ... The men so dressed also wore the togas and carried the insignia of the magistracies which had been held by the person whom they were impersonating. One could not easily find a sight finer than this for a young man who was in love with fame and goodness. For is there anyone who would not be edified by seeing these portraits of men who were renowned for their excellence and by having them all present as if they were living and breathing? Is there any sight that would be more ennobling than this?

Source: *The Histories of Polybius*, translated by Evelyn S. Shuckburgh, 2 volumes (Bloomington: Indiana University Press, 1962).

A patrician carrying portrait–busts of ancestors, circa first century B.C.E.–first century C.E. (Conservatori Museum, Rome)

motivation behind "realism" in Roman sculpture is the commemoration of one's ancestors in funeral ceremonies as outlined by the historian Polybius (circa 202–120 B.C.E.). While these masks were probably wax and may have been specifically "death masks" molded from the face of the deceased, it is clear that many Romans wished to commemorate their ancestors in more permanent materials. To meet this expense would be a typically patrician custom and is evident in a statue of a Roman nobleman of the first century B.C.E. (or C.E.) carrying portrait-busts, presumably of his ancestors. While much Roman portrait sculpture is closely linked to a specific ritual, it may also reflect some of the more or less "realistic" tendencies in the portraiture of Hellenistic monarchs from the third century B.C.E. onward. These images continue a trend of

ruler-cult through image-making propagated especially by Alexander the Great, who wished to be immortalized in the works of his favorite artists Lysippos the sculptor, Apelles the painter and Pyrgoteles the engraver. Later Roman men of power similarly had their images disseminated as a form of self-promotion to bulwark their political ambitions, among them Pompey and Julius Caesar. While these are obviously stylized, their real point is presentation of recognizable individuals to convey something of their forceful character. Stone and marble were not the only media used for such purposes. As had been the practice of Hellenistic monarchs, during the late Roman republic and throughout the empire, coins were struck with profile-portraits of the most powerful figures of the day, among them Caesar, Marc Antony, and Octavian (later Augustus).

Greek Influence. Under Augustus imperial portraiture took on certain trends reminiscent of Classical Greek art but put to political ends to glorify his family and regime. The famous marble, over-lifesize "Prima Porta Augustus" (circa 20 B.C.E.) presents the emperor in armor gesturing forward as if leading his people to a new era of peace and prosperity. Although recognizable as an individual—not for the last time would jutting-out ears be a conspicuous feature in depictions of members of royal families—Augustus's face has become simplified compared to the detail of other portraits. He has become "classicized" as a result, with an emphasis on the wide brow and deep set eyes. His pose recalls that of idealized and

Prima Porta Augustus, circa 20 B.C.E., an oversized marble portrait statue of the Emperor Augustus (Vatican Museum, Rome)

Bronze statue of Marcus Aurelius completed in 166 C.E. and now located outside the Capitoline Museum in Rome

heroic Greek statues, such as the great Doryphorus (Spear-bearer) made by the famed sculptor Polyclitus (circa 440 B.C.E.). In both images weight is shifted onto one leg, and the head tilted slightly to the right, and facial expression is calm and contemplative. This seems to add a sense both of understated movement and repose to Augustus, whose heroic status is further implied in the fact that he is barefoot—a contrast to the detailed footwear of Aulus Metellus. Political allegory is included with the figures on Augustus's armor depicting the defeated Parthians returning the standards to a Roman soldier, which recalls actual recent victories over these enemies. Thus, in this impressive work of propagandistic art Greek form meets Roman function. Similar facial features and pose in another famous image of Augustus as priest, with toga drawn over his head, likewise convey the idea that he is at once pious and dignified—like the hero of Vergil's *Aeneid* so often called *pius*—and that the Augustan reign ushers in a new age of order and civilization.

Imperial Portraiture. More or less grandiose portraits of the Julio-Claudians are known, such as the perhaps incongruous statue of Claudius as Jupiter (the supreme Roman god), as well as fairly distinctive images of Caligula and Nero. Under the new dynasty of the Flavians (69–96 C.E.) a range of sculp-

Porphyry statue of the Tetrarchs at St. Mark's Cathedral, Venice, carved circa 305 C.E.

tural styles emerges. One finds a more earthy type of imperial portraiture for the self-made man Vespasian, whose evidently practical, no-nonsense approach to life radiates from this statue of circa 75 C.E. The tough but not brutal facial features contrast with the "idealism" of Augustan imagery and suggest that Vespasian wished to be perceived as different in more ways than one from the previous regime which had come to be despised by this time. Other notable images from the Flavian period include elegant portraits of aristocratic women with elaborate coiffures of high-stacked curls. This style is likely to have followed a fashion set by imperial wives, and here one sees intricate carving skills and use of deep drills for the hairstyle that gives off interesting effects in the contrasts of light and shade. Such effects recur in later imperial portraits. As the first emperor to wear a full beard as part of his official imagery, Hadrian ushers in a different style for depiction of male rulers, previously beardless. His "beardedness" is a likely expression of his interest in Greek culture and is designed to assimilate him to figures from the Greek past. At the same time this also allows scope for depicting his beard and sometimes full, heavy locks of hair in ways which develop techniques pioneered for portraits of women in the Flavian era. Apart from fuller details in rendering male coiffures, two major sculptural innovations of around this time (117–138 C.E.) are the incision and drill used to render the iris and pupil of the eye, often to striking effect, especially in later imperial portraits. Hadrian was besotted with a Bithynian youth, Antinous, whose early death led to his deification and, consequently, frequent depiction in sculpture and painting which drew comment from the traveller Pausanias (second century C.E.). In many statues of Antinous one sees a recurrence of Greek ideals of male beauty from the classical period (circa 480–320 B.C.E.). Poses and facial expressions are similar to those found in images produced by Polycli-

Marble portrait of a woman of the Flavian era, circa 120 C.E. (Museo Capitolino, Rome)

tus and others, but now with softer musculature and fuller, wavier hair to emphasize the youth and charm of the subject.

Impressive Monuments. One of the most impressive surviving monuments from antiquity is the bronze equestrian statue of Marcus Aurelius of 164–66 C.E. This image, much admired in the Middle Ages and Renaissance, was long thought to represent Constantine, but comparison with other portraits confirms identification with the earlier emperor. With one arm raised to address a crowd in the *adlocutio* (speaking) pose, Marcus Aurelius sits astride a powerful horse that originally had a barbarian under its foot. The emperor's hair and beard are fully modelled, perhaps suggesting his philhellene disposition, and his expression is far from brutal. He does not ride in full armor as might be expected of an ostensibly military statue. Instead a more restrained and even humane presence seems to be in evidence in the image, which is perhaps fitting for a ruler who also happened to leave a philosophical tract, written in Greek, called *The Meditations*. Of the imperial portraits under the Antonine and Severan dynasties, some interesting developments include the appearance of full-scale nude statues, of, for instance, Lucius Verus (circa 160–9 C.E.) and Septimius Severus (circa 200–210 C.E.). These, it seems, might not have been suited to all Roman

tastes and were not produced in Rome, but rather in the provinces, chiefly the Greek parts of the empire. Further variants in imperial imagery can be found in the portraits of the demented Commodus (emperor circa 180–92), who not only fancied himself a gladiator (where he had no fear of being defeated), but also as the incarnation of Hercules. Thus he is depicted with the hero's characteristic lionskin and club. While some sculptures reveal the self-delusions of certain emperors, other imperial portraits expose something of the brutality and insecurity of their subjects. Caracalla's menacing persona is consistently evoked in a series of scowling, bull-necked images where his heavy eyebrows, harsh stare, lined forehead, and rough beard add a sense even of paranoia to his presence. Indeed, many emperor portraits of the post-Severan period up to the time of Diocletian (235–84 C.E.) represent men who seem anxious and world-weary, far removed from Augustan idealism or the calm of a Marcus Aurelius. In stylistic terms, one notable change is in the hair, which is now more of a cap rather than a series of deep bushy curls. Many of these later figures, whose short-lived reigns were often instigated and ended by bloody coups, are distinctly human, and evidently weighed down by mundane matters. One often sees worried or scowling expressions in their fur-

Marble portrait of the Emperor Vespasian, circa
75 C.E. (private collection)

make one figure distinguishable from the next. The facial features are animated by lines across the forehead and apparently anxious expressions, but overall the faces have little detail, without much depth of sculptural modeling. Notable features are the enlarged eyes, which protrude more than previously, being set less deeply in the head. While some of these features can be seen to anticipate later Christian imagery, portraiture under Constantine, emperor of the Roman west and himself a former Tetrarch, retains some elements closer to older styles. The chief example is, of course, his colossal marble portrait (circa 313 C.E.) which sat in his basilica. Now only fragmentary, the head itself is 2.9 meters high and its overall dimensions recall the great colossal statues of the Greek world, such as Pheidias's gold-and-ivory Zeus at Olympia (circa 435 B.C.E.), which became one of the Seven Wonders of the World. Constantine's face shows greater depth of modeling than does the Tetrarch's image in his protuberant nose, jutting chin and huge, deeply set eyes, implied in other portraits of him. These features are also

A bronze statue of Aulus Metellus, early first century B.C.E.
(Museo Archologico 249, Florence)

rowed brows, sidelong glances, and circles under the eyes. Attempts at self-glorification through full-length nude bronze portraits, such as that of Trebonius Gallus (emperor 251–253 C.E.), seem simply unconvincing or absurd in the light of his facial details and awkward proportions. A fine example of imperial portraiture from this age is the image of Philip the Arab (244–249 C.E.), an emperor who hailed from Syria. His heavily lined face, large, apparently once-broken nose, and distant, melancholy gaze under his broad brow convey a palpable physical presence and a sense of resignation and foreboding, which seem appropriate for an age of insecurity.

Visual Changes. With the regime of Diocletian, different elements in the depiction of powerful figures emerge again, that were to have long-lasting effects, beyond the era of pagan antiquity. The new rule of the Tetrarchs was to be propagated in visual imagery in such a way as to emphasize the idea of unified power which they represented, even though, as one commentator put it, they seem to cower like nervous monkeys in this depiction. As was beginning to happen in other types of sculpture, figures were becoming more schematic with less emphasis on features that might mark them out as individuals. Drapery becomes more openly patterned, and here the costumes of each figure are identical. Thus, in the porphyry image of the Tetrarchs (circa 305 C.E.) at St. Mark's Cathedral in Venice, there is nothing really to

A colossal marble portrait of Constantine, circa
313 C.E. (Palazzo dei Conservatori, Cortile 2,
Inv. 1692, Rome)

VERGIL AND LATIN POETRY

The Classic Text. As Cicero is to Latin prose, so Vergil is to Latin poetry: for many readers he epitomizes the greatest and most beautiful artistic achievement of Roman civilization. Indeed, his *Aeneid* is regarded by many as *the* classic text *par excellence.*

Vergil's Earliest Work: The *Eclogues.* The earliest, definitely authentic poems of Publius Vergilius Maro, the *Eclogues,* were published shortly after Sallust's works in 39 B.C.E. In these ten pastoral poems modeled on the Hellenistic Greek poet Theocritus, Vergil combines an idyllic, rustic world, inspired by Greek poetry and apparently dominated by peace and love, with contemporary Roman events such as land expropriations or civil war. The great yearning for peace after almost one hundred years of intermittent civil strife finds its climax in the fourth *Eclogue,* in which this hope is connected with the birth of a child, either Marc Antony's and Octavia's or Octavian's (the later emperor Augustus's) and Scribonia's.

The *Georgics.* The *Georgics,* Vergil's second work, purports to be a didactic in four books on the topic of agriculture. Hellenistic poets such as Nicander and Aratus had specialized in this genre but Vergil looks back beyond them to Hesiod's *Works and Days.* His language as well as the pairing of books (arable farming, arboriculture—husbandry, beekeeping) and the internal proems also recall Lucretius. Vergil's poem could, however, never serve as a handbook for farmers. Its main aim is the exposition of a natural order in the world: Octavian is in the middle (3.16) and Italy represents the land with ideal geography and inhabitants (2.136). With its praise of the farmer's life (2.458) Vergil's poetic version of agriculture is also in accordance with later attempts by Octavian/Augustus to return Rome to its agricultural roots. Some scholars have, of course, seen the poem as a dark reflection on the Augustan regime. While nothing in life is clearcut, this view surely tells more about the current age than it does about Vergil.

The *Aeneid:* Rome's National Epic. Opinions similarly differ about Vergil's Homeric epic, the *Aeneid.* The poet left it unfinished at his death in 18 B.C.E. after ten years' work on it. In his will, he asked for it to be burned, but Augustus had it published anyway by two friends of the deceased. The arguments over a "dark" or "optimistic" reading of the work may therefore be completely moot, since this ending may not be what the poet had in mind. After all, his main models, Homer's *Iliad* and *Odyssey,* both end on notes of reconciliation.

Long Tradition. Vergil was relying on a long tradition of writing narrative poems about heroic deeds in the past. First and foremost is, of course, Homer. Already the structure of the epic as a whole reflects the two Homeric works: books 1–6 form the "Odyssean" half, followed by the "Iliadic" 7–12. This bipartite arrangement is anticipated in the first two words *Arma virumque* (Arms and the man), with *arma* foreshadowing the Iliadic wars of the latter half, and *virum* the wanderings of Aeneas, modeled on Homer's Odysseus. However, the Latin word *arma* sounds more like the Greek word *Andra* (the man—for example Odysseus), which was the first word of the *Odyssey.* The first sentence in Vergil takes up the first seven

likely to have been slightly exaggerated to facilitate viewing from below or at some distance, as this seated statue was over 9 meters high. The expression is impassive and distant, the gaze far beyond the viewer, and the overall pose—more rigid than that of the Prima Porta Augustus—conveys the idea of power in almost iconic or abstracted terms. The image of grandeur aims at a sense of permanence beyond this world. Here, one sees something of the transcendentalism of Byzantine imagery of later ages.

Sources:
Diana E. E. Kleiner, *Roman Sculpture* (New Haven & London: Yale University Press, 1992).

Jerome J. Pollitt, *Art in the Hellenistic Age* (Cambridge: Cambridge University Press, 1986).

Nancy and Andrew Ramage, *Roman Art: Romulus to Constantine,* third edition (London: Laurence King, 2000).

Donald E. Strong, *Roman Imperial Sculpture* (London: A. Tiranti, 1961).

Mario Torelli, *Typology and Structure of Roman Historical Reliefs* (Ann Arbor: University of Michigan Press, 1982).

lines, as did the first sentence in the *Iliad*. After stating his two themes as "Arms and the man," Vergil then goes on to repeat and vary them in the following six and a half lines, beginning with the "man" theme in verses 1b to 4 and finishing with the "war" theme (5–7). In these six and a half lines of summary, the reader moves from Troy (the first word after the initial thematic announcement) to Rome, the last word in the first sentence, thus anticipating the entire development of the epic. The storm scene in which we first meet the protagonist (1.8–296) then forms a third, symbolic anticipation of the entire narrative. This storm is whipped up by Aeolus, god of the winds, at Juno's behest. When the reader first meets the hero at 1.94–101 he is in deep emotional turmoil which corresponds to the external upheaval caused by the storm. The turning point comes at verse 124, when Neptune raises his head out of the sea and calms the waves. The storm symbolically anticipates both Aeneas's personal trials in books 1–6 and the wars of 7–12. In the end, however, order and calm will prevail as Jupiter prophesies to Venus in 1.257–96. While the real storm is calmed by the sea god, the symbolic storms will be faced and overcome by Aeneas, who grows into the type of Roman statesman with whom Neptune is compared (1.148–153).

Hapless Dido. Vergil, however, also drew on Hellenistic epics such as the *Argonautica* of Apollonius of Rhodes, especially in the love story between Dido and Aeneas in books 1 and 4, which bears a resemblance to the Jason and Medea narrative in Apollonius. In Vergil, the episode is set up as a tragedy within the epic. When Aeneas lands in North Africa, he puts to shore in a bay remarkably shaped like a Roman theater, complete with stage (*scaena* 1.164) and seats (*sedilia* 1.167). After addressing his comrades and a divine interlude, he meets Venus, his mother, who delivers a quasi-Euripidean tragic prologue (1.338–368). As Aristotle had outlined in the *Poetics*, this tragedy contains a reversal of fortune for Dido (*peripeteia*) and a final catastrophe, including Iris coming down as *deus ex machina* to set Dido's soul free (4.694), leading to a quiet ending. The question, however, remains where Dido went wrong: what is her *culpa* or *hamartia*? This Aristotelian concept refers to a "missing of the mark," a mistake that a character makes which entails his/her downfall, not a tragic flaw of character. Dido's unique characteristic is her devotion to her dead husband Sychaeus, her *univiritas*. This, however, is exactly what she loses when she gives up the female virtue of *pudor* (shame: 1.55 *solvitque pudorem)* and when she celebrates a quasi marriage with Aeneas after the hunt (4.166–172). The poet states that she is hiding her *culpa* (guilt) under the name of marriage (1.172). On another reading, however, Dido ignores the many prophecies related to her by Aeneas in his long narrative in books 2 and 3, which predict that he will have to move to a land called Hesperia. She acts as if these prophecies did not exist, and therefore pretends that she is married to him, while he does not interpret their relationship in this way.

Realistic Characters. One should, on the other hand, also consider that Dido and Aeneas communicate with each other remarkably like modern people. Women prefer to talk in private in order to establish closeness; men talk a great deal in

Vergil, perhaps the greatest poet in all Roman history, wrote what became the national epic of the Roman people during the rule of Augustus Caesar. In it he tells of the end of the Trojan War and the escape of the Trojan Aeneas to found a new nation in Italy after many trials and tribulations. At the beginning of the poem, Vergil invokes the Muse's help as he attempts to undertake the massive task of narrating this heroic story:

I sing of warfare and a man at war.

From the sea-coast of Troy in early days

He came to Italy by destiny,

To our Lavinian western shore,

A fugitive, this captain, buffeted

Cruelly on land as on the sea

By blows from powers of the air — behind them

Baleful Juno in her sleepless rage.

And cruel losses were his lot in war,

Till he could found a city and bring home

His gods to Latium, land of the Latin race,

The Alban lords, and the high walls of Rome.

Tell me the causes now, O Muse, how galled

In her divine pride, and how sore at heart

From her old wound, the queen of the gods compelled him —

A man apart, devoted to his mission —

To undergo so many perilous days

And enter on so many trials. Can anger

Black as this prey on the minds of heaven?

… Saturnian Juno, burning for it all,

Buffeted on the waste of sea those Trojans

Left by the Greeks and pitiless Achilles,

Keeping them far from Latium. For years

They wandered as their destiny drove them on

From one sea to the next: so hard and huge

A task it was to found the Roman people.

Source: *Virgil: the Aeneid,* translated by Robert Fitzgerald (New York: Random House, 1981).

public with a view to establishing their status. Furthermore, modern sociolinguists have shown that women often "switch off" when men give long, instructive accounts on matters about which they did not ask them. Aeneas gives exactly such a "lecture" (3.717 *docebat*) in books 2 and 3. The queen asked him about the fall of Troy and the vicissitudes of his survivors

Vergil's tomb (upper left) near the entrance to the Neapolitan tunnel

him to meet his helmsman Palinurus (6.337), Dido (6.450) and Deiphobus, Hector's brother (6.495). These episodes are modeled on Odysseus's encounter with Elpenor (*Odyssey* 11.51), Aias (*Odyssey* 11.541), and Agamemnon (*Odyssey* 11.385). In the case of Palinurus, Vergil has added an *aetion*, a mythical explanation of a contemporary name, custom, or geographical feature, thus connecting myth with his contemporary world. Deiphobus, on the other hand, was the heir to Priam's throne after Hector's death. He tells the story of his own death on the night on which Troy was taken, and then he sends Aeneas on with the phrase "Go, glory of us all! Use your better fate!" (6.547). In this way he makes Aeneas, who comes from a sideline of the Trojan royal family, his legitimate successor. In between these events he meets the ghost of Dido who, like Aias in the *Iliad,* remains silent and gives Aeneas the cold shoulder. This episode inverts the situation in book 4, where Aeneas had been silent. Now he weeps, just as Dido had wept at their parting. Now she is hard as a rock, as he had been earlier. After one last meeting with these figures from his past, he leaves the Golden Bough and moves on to the future in the show of heroes. Based on the Platonic theory of reincarnation, his father Anchises points out the future Romans for whom Aeneas is doing all this. The list is basically chronological, beginning with the kings of Rome's predecessor settlement, Alba Longa. After Romulus, the first founder of Rome, the chronological order is broken to highlight Augustus, its "second founder." He is likened to the god Bacchus and the legendary hero Hercules, two comparisons frequently found in encomia of Alexander the Great. The show proceeds with republican noteworthies and culminates in three famous lines summarizing Rome's understanding of itself (851–853) as the ruler of peoples and bringer of peace. Rome's mission is "to spare the conquered, battle down the proud." This stirring assertion of Roman imperialism is, however, immediately tempered by one last figure, an appendix to the show. This figure is Marcellus, a young nobleman who had won great renown and was singled out by Augustus as a potential successor, but died young. This situation is the downside of empire: individuals pay a high price for it. Patriotism is inextricably linked with sadness because young people die on behalf of Rome and its empire.

***Sunt lacrimae rerum:* Life Is Sad.** This sadness is a constant current in the epic. Almost every book ends with a death, most notably the last one, thus leaving the reader with a sad final impression. Turnus has finally fought Aeneas and been beaten. At this point he admits that he has deserved his lot and claims he will not try to avoid it by begging (931), but he does so anyway (932–938). Aeneas is about "to spare the conquered" (940–941) when he sees the sword belt of his young protégé Pallas on Turnus's shoulder. This makes him fly into a rage and kill Turnus. Many modern scholars feel that Aeneas falls short of the ideal of sparing the conquered in this episode. While any death is profoundly sad, this interpretation is not without its difficulties. When he is faced with the "reminders of his severe grief" (945-946), that of Turnus killing young Pallas, he is outraged that Turnus can have the temerity to ask for clemency when he granted none to a younger and inferior opponent. This is arro-

(1.753–6). Aeneas dutifully tells her about these, but also includes a great number of prophecies in book 3 in which Dido had not expressed any interest. Maybe she simply let her mind wander for some time while allowing the male to try and impress her with his account. Seen from this point of view, Aeneas's taciturnity in book 4 is neither cold nor hostile, just male, since most of the book takes place in the privacy of Dido's palace. Dido's incessant talk in the same stretch is not "hysterical," but simply her female attempt at establishing closeness with those around her. Her *hamartia* could then consist of something as little as not paying attention to those parts of Aeneas's narrative that did not interest her. On top of this love story, one can also detect Hellenistic techniques such as the personal narrator, who slips into one of the characters and presents a particular point of view. This technique has been shown to be the case in the footrace in book 5, where the epic narrator presents the events from the perspective of Nisus, one of the contestants.

The World Below. The descent to the underworld in book 6 provides the pivot of the *Aeneid.* In it Trojan Aeneas "dies" and Roman Aeneas is "born." In order to go down, he has to bury his friend Misenus and find the Golden Bough, a symbol of death and rebirth which he ends up depositing on the threshold of Hades, god of the underworld. Before being shown Rome's future by his father Anchises, the Sibyl guides

gance, and Aeneas consequently "battles down the proud." Turnus had made war when king Latinus wanted peace; he attacked the Roman camp in Aeneas's absence, killed the young and vulnerable Pallas, and needed to be rescued by Juno. He is not the kind of man with whom one can work to found a city. Furthermore, there is evidence that he constitutes the human sacrifice often performed in connection with city foundations. His plucking of the Golden Bough in book 6 also associates him with the *Rex nemorensis,* the priest of Diana at Aricia, who is challenged by his successor to fight to the death after plucking a branch off a certain tree. Turnus must die in order for one unified people to grow out of this struggle.

General Themes of the *Aeneid*. Turnus is part of a whole set of dichotomies that run through the work: he is pitted against Aeneas, his lack of piety against Aeneas's piety and Juno against Jupiter, to name but a few. Turnus also provides a mythical counterpart to Marc Antony in the Roman civil war, since Aeneas represents Augustus. Unlike Homer's *Iliad* and *Odyssey,* the mythical past in the *Aeneid* is always a means of talking about the present. Prophecies within the epic always predict events that have already occurred by Vergil's own time.

Since Aeneas's ancestor Dardanus originally came from Italy (3.167), the war with the Latins reflects the civil war, Dido's curse (4.625–9) generates the Punic Wars, and even individual Trojans anticipate their historical descendants, such as Sergestus in the ship race, who is as mad as his putative descendant, L. Sergius Catilina. What is missing, of course, is the future. All prophecies, including the pictures on Aeneas's shield in book 8, necessarily end with Augustus.

Sources:
Michael von Albrecht, "Die Kunst der Spiegelung in Vergils Aeneis," *Hermes* 93 (1965): 54-64.

C. M. C. Green, "The Slayer and the King: *Rex Nemorensis* and the Sanctuary of Diana," *Arion* 7 (2000): 24–63.

E. L. Harrison, "The Tragedy of Dido," *Echos du Monde Classique,* n.s. 8 (1989): 1-22.

Martin Helzle, *Der Stil ist der Mensch. Redner und Reden im römischen Epos* (Stuttgart-Leipzig: B. G. Teubner, 1996).

Brooks Otis, *Virgil: A Study in Civilized Poetry* (Oxford: Clarendon Press, 1964).

Viktor Pöschl, *The Art of Vergil: Image and Symbol in the* Aeneid (Ann Arbor: University of Michigan Press, 1962).

T. P. Wiseman, *Remus: A Roman Myth* (Cambridge: Cambridge University Press, 1995).

SIGNIFICANT PEOPLE

Note: Roman names can be quite long, and well-known figures of Roman history are sometimes known in English by shorter, anglicized names: for example, Marcus Tullius Cicero is now almost always known in English as "Cicero" (though a few hundred years ago he might have been referred to as "Tully"). In certain cases, the full Latin name has been included (where that is known) of each individual, followed in parentheses by the name by which he is commonly referred to in English.

Almost nothing is known about the lives of any artists or artisans working in the Roman world. The situation is not much better for most Greek artists, but for certain figures such as Pheidias (chief sculptor of the Parthenon) some details about his life beyond his works are known. Many Roman monuments visible today were, however, unsigned and unascribed, and much of the work involved in producing large-scale buildings would have come from slave labor. Occasionally one finds references to particular artists, but often these are only names to which certain works are ascribed. In a few exceptional cases there is a little more information to go on.

APOLLODORUS

ACTIVE EARLY SECOND CENTURY C.E.
ARCHITECT

Relationship with the Emperors. Apollodorus carried out many of Trajan's building projects, including his forum, and may have been the chief designer for the famous column dedicated to that emperor. As was the case with Vitruvius, Apollodorus probably had a military background designing machinery for warfare, on which he wrote a treatise, as did many practitioners in the visual arts in antiquity. He seems to have been on close terms with Trajan, with whom he was in regular contact, but had a less fortunate association with his heir, Hadrian. Cassio Dio (69.4.1–5) tells how Apollodorus dismissed some architectural plans drawn by Hadrian before he was emperor as mere "pumpkins"—possibly a reference to Hadrian's fondness for vaults and domes, which are evident in his palace buildings at Tivoli and in such monuments as the Pantheon, rebuilt under his regime. In any event, Hadrian certainly took his own drawings seriously, according to ancient sources. Later, when Hadrian was emperor, Apollodorus stridently criticized in detail his plans for a temple to Venus and Rome. Hadrian resented this criticism and, not forgetting the earlier insult, is said to have banished Apollodorus, eventually having him executed.

Sources:

Jacob Isager, *Pliny on Art and Society* (London: Routledge, 1991).

K. Jex-Blake and Eugenie S. Sellers, eds., *The Elder Pliny's Chapters on the History of Art* (Chicago: Argonaut, 1968).

Jerome J. Pollitt, *The Art of Rome c.753 B.C.–337 A.D. Sources and Documents* (Englewood Cliffs, N.J.: Prentice-Hall, 1966).

APULEIUS OF MADAURA (APULEIUS)

125-AFTER 170 C.E.

LAWYER, PRIEST, WRITER

Under Suspicion of Witchcraft. Born in Madaura in North Africa, Apuleius was educated in Carthage and Athens. Having used up his estate, he moved to Rome and worked as a lawyer. Back in Africa he was tried for allegedly practicing witchcraft, but he was acquitted. He never held any political office, but he did become a priest of the imperial cult. He died some time after 170 C.E. Apuleius is remembered primarily for his *Metamorphoses,* or *The Golden Ass.*

Sources:

Gerald Sandy, "Apuleius," in *Ancient Roman Writers, Dictionary of Literary Biography,* volume 211, edited by Ward W. Briggs (Columbia, S.C.: Bruccoli Clark Layman / Detroit: Gale Group, 1999), pp. 17–25.

Carl C. Schlam, *The Metamorphoses of Apuleius* (Chapel Hill: University of North Carolina Press, 1992).

ANICIUS MANLIUS SEVERINUS BOETHIUS (BOETHIUS)

CIRCA 476-524 C.E.

STATESMAN, PHILOSOPHER

Treason by Association. Boethius was born into a noble family. His father held the consulate in 487 C.E. but died prematurely. It was during his lifetime that the last Roman emperor was deposed, leaving the city ruled by a native senate at the mercy of Theodoric, king of the Goths. Initially, Boethius was held in high esteem by Theodoric. Boethius held the consulate in 510 on his own, and his sons served in 522. On this occasion he delivered a panegyric on the barbarian ruler. But when one of the Roman patricians was accused of treason with the Eastern Roman empire, the delicate arrangement exploded. Boethius rushed to Verona to defend his compatriot but found himself accused of treason by association. After a lengthy imprisonment in which

he wrote the *Consolation of Philosophy,* Boethius was condemned without trial and executed in 524.

Sources:

Henry Chadwick, *Boethius: The Consolations of Music, Logic, Theology, and Philosophy* (Oxford: Clarendon Press / New York: Oxford University Press, 1981).

Margaret T. Gibson, ed., *Boethius: His Life, Thought, and Influence* (Oxford: Blackwell, 1981).

GAIUS VALERIUS CATULLUS (CATULLUS)

BEFORE 80-AFTER 54 B.C.E.

POET

The New Poets. Catullus was born in Verona into a wealthy family, probably in the late 80s B.C.E. He owned estates in Tibur and the Peninsula Sirmio in Lake Garda. His father, who was personally acquainted with powerful Roman figures such as Metellus and Julius Caesar, sent Catullus to Rome for his education. Having little or no political ambition, he joined a group that Cicero called the "new poets" (for their innovative approach to poetry), and fell in love with a woman whom, in his passionate love poems, he calls Lesbia. According to an ancient source she was Clodia, the wife of Metellus and sister of Cicero's nemesis, Clodius. At one point Catullus traveled to Asia Minor, where he also visited his brother's grave near Troy. The theory that he turned to writing mime for the stage in the 50s B.C.E. is attractive. He died some time after 54 B.C.E.

Sources:

William W. Batstone, "Catullus," in *Ancient Roman Writers, Dictionary of Literary Biography,* volume 211, edited by Ward W. Briggs (Columbia, S.C.: Bruccoli Clark Layman / Detroit: Gale Group, 1999), pp. 41–53.

Micaela Janan, *"When the Lamp is Shattered": Desire and Narrative in Catullus* (Carbondale: Southern Illinois University Press, 1994).

Timothy P. Wiseman, *Remus: A Roman Myth* (Cambridge & New York: Cambridge University Press, 1995).

QUINTUS ENNIUS (ENNIUS)

239-169 B.C.E.

SOLDIER, POET

Simple Life. Ennius was born in Rudiae in Calabria. As the descendant of an indigenous Italian family, he also encountered Greek theater in Tarentum. He was proud to be fluent in the Oscan, Greek, and Latin languages. In 204 B.C.E. he met the elder Cato on military service in Sardinia. Cato brought Ennius to Rome, where he made a living teaching Greek and Latin grammar. As a poet, he was patronized by Roman noblemen, especially Publius Cornelius Scipio Africanus. However, he accompanied another patrician, Marcus Fulvius

Nobilior, on a military campaign. With the help of Marcus's son Quintus Fulvius Nobilior, Ennius subsequently won Roman citizenship in 184 B.C.E. He lived a simple life on the Aventine hill in Rome. He probably did not die of gout, as alleged by one anecdote. He was cremated in Rome and his ashes taken to his native Rudiae.

Sources:

Richard L. S. Evans, "Ennius," in *Ancient Roman Writers, Dictionary of Literary Biography,* volume 211, edited by Ward W. Briggs (Columbia, S.C.: Bruccoli Clark Layman / Detroit: Gale Group, 1999), pp. 79–83.

H. D. Jocelyn, *The Tragedies of Ennius: The Fragments* (London: Cambridge University Press, 1967).

Jocelyn, "Quintus Ennius," in *Oxford Classical Dictionary*, edited by Simon Hornblower and Antony Spawforth, third edition (Oxford: Oxford University Press, 1999), pp. 525–526.

FABIUS PICTOR

ACTIVE CIRCA 300 B.C.E.
PAINTER

Aristocratic Family. Fabius Pictor, known as Fabius "the Painter," was born into an aristocratic family called the Fabii. He was famous for his paintings in the temple of Salus (Health), which eventually burned down during the reign of Claudius (41–54 C.E.). It seems that his painting was admired for the precision of its outlines and the brightness and mixture of its colors, which refrained from being gaudy (at least in Roman eyes). Fabius Pictor is an interesting example of a trend in the Roman republic and early empire whereby certain members of the aristocracy found fame as painters. This fame, however, brought with it some controversy. Some considered that his occupation as painter fell short of the pride of his family, which had won honors with consulships, priesthoods, and triumphs. Yet, Fabius proudly signed his works and apparently compared himself to the great Greek sculptor Pheidias, who moved in high political circles, and is said to have depicted his own portraits on one of his works.

Sources:

Jacob Isager, *Pliny on Art and Society* (London: Routledge, 1991).

K. Jex-Blake and Eugenie S. Sellers, eds., *The Elder Pliny's Chapters on the History of Art* (Chicago: Argonaut, 1968).

Jerome J. Pollitt, *The Art of Rome c.753 B.C.–337 A.D. Sources and Documents* (Englewood Cliffs, N.J.: Prentice-Hall, 1966).

CORNELIUS GALLUS (GALLUS)

69-26 B.C.E.
POET, STATESMAN

New Genre. Born in southern France in 69 B.C.E., Gallus became quite involved in Augustus's new administration. He may have helped Vergil win back his expropriated farm. In the 40s he wrote a four-book collection of *Amores* in which he sings about his beloved Lycoris. All but eleven lines of this work are lost; historians think that he drew on Hellenistic love epigram, scenes from comedy, Hellenistic pastoral poetry, and narrative elegy to form the new genre of love-elegy. After the defeat of Cleopatra and Marc Antony he became the first governor of the new province of Egypt, the first governor to report directly to the emperor rather than the senate. In 26 B.C.E. he committed some indiscretion that upset Augustus so much that Gallus committed suicide. His books were removed from the public libraries and were subsequently lost.

Sources:

Carl Deroux, ed., *Studies in Latin Literature and Roman History, volume I* (Bruxelles: Latomus, 1979).

David O. Ross, *Backgrounds to Augustan Poetry: Gallus, Elegy, and Rome* (Cambridge: Cambridge University Press, 1975).

QUINTUS HORATIUS FLACCUS (HORACE)

8 DEC. 65-27 NOV. 8 B.C.E.
SOLDIER, ADMINISTRATOR, POET

Financial Independence. Horace, as he is known in English, was born on 8 December 65 B.C.E. in Venusia in southeast Italy as the son of a freedman. Nonetheless, he was sent to Greece, like many noblemen, to finish his education. There he joined Caesar's assassin, Marcus Brutus, and followed him into Asia Minor. As military tribune he fought on the losing (republican) side at Philippi. He returned to Rome, where he obtained an administrative position. He got to know Vergil and Varius, who introduced him to Maecenas. Horace became Maecenas's protégé and lifelong friend. In 32 B.C.E. Maecenas gave him a farm in the Sabine country, which made the poet financially independent. Maecenas also introduced him to Augustus, who offered him a post as his secretary, but Horace declined. Shortly after the battle of Actium in 31 B.C.E. he published his *Epodes,* which included some of his earliest works. The first book of *Satires* was actually published earlier, in 35 B.C.E., the second book in 30. This work was followed by the first three books of *Odes,* which were published as an artistic unit in 23 B.C.E. Since this work was not a success, Horace returned to hexameter poetry with his verse *Epistles.* The first book of these appeared in 20 B.C.E.; the second book, including the so-called *Ars Poetica,* appeared maybe as late as 10. He was commissioned to write a hymn for Augustus's celebration of a new century, which he followed up by a fourth book of *Odes.* He died on 27 November 8 B.C.E., only months after his friend Maecenas.

Sources:

David Armstrong, *Horace* (New Haven: Yale University Press, 1989).

S. J. Harrison, *Homage to Horace: A Bimillenary Celebration* (Oxford: Clarendon Press / New York: Oxford University Press, 1995).

David H. Porter, *Horace's Poetic Journey* (Princeton: Princeton University Press, 1987).

Matthew S. Santirocco, *Unity and Design in Horace's Odes* (Chapel Hill & London: University of North Carolina Press, 1986).

IAIA

ACTIVE CIRCA LATE SECOND-EARLY FIRST CENTURIES B.C.E.

PAINTER

Portraits of Women. Iaia was a painter from Cyzicus, a Greek city on the coast of Asia Minor. Although little is known about her, she rates mention not only for the praise that Pliny bestows on her—including the fact that she was a virgin all her life—but as one of the very few female artists of antiquity whose name is actually known. In fact, she seems to have enjoyed considerable success in her lifetime. She is said to have specialized in portraits of women, including a self-portrait, and worked on ivory and other surfaces with brush and spatula in the encaustic technique. She won fame for the high quality of her work in Naples and elsewhere and was said to have had a quicker hand than any other painter. She commanded higher prices than many celebrated artists of the same period, such as Dionysius and Sopolis.

Sources:

Jacob Isager, *Pliny on Art and Society* (London: Routledge, 1991).

K. Jex-Blake and Eugenie S. Sellers, eds., *The Elder Pliny's Chapters on the History of Art* (Chicago: Argonaut, 1968).

Jerome J. Pollitt, *The Art of Rome c.753 B.C.–337 A.D. Sources and Documents* (Englewood Cliffs, N.J.: Prentice-Hall, 1966).

TITUS LIVIUS (LIVY)

69 OR 54 B.C.E.-CIRCA 17 C.E.

HISTORIAN

A Typical Paduan. Little is known about Livy's life. He was born in 59 or 64 B.C.E. in Patavium, now Padua, a wealthy city because of its wool trade. The Paduans were also renowned for their moral puritanism. Maybe this puritanism is what a contemporary of Livy's referred to when he called him a typical Paduan. There is no sign of his ever having held office in Rome, although he clearly knew his way around the city and around Italy. It seems most likely, therefore, that he came from a wealthy municipal family and moved to Rome only after Augustus had ended the civil war and established himself as the ruler. Livy wrote not just history but also philosophical dialogues and a treatise on rhetorical style, the titles of which are now lost. He died back in Padua, probably in 17 C.E., having obtained such great fame in his lifetime that one of his admirers traveled all the way from Cadiz to Rome just to see him.

Sources:

T.A. Dorey, *Livy* (London: Routledge & Kegan Paul, 1971).

James Lipovsky, *A Historiographical Study of Livy, Books VI–X* (New York: Arno, 1981).

Gary B. Miles, *Livy: Reconstructing Early Rome* (Ithaca, N.Y.: Cornell University Press, 1995).

LUCIUS ANNAEUS LUCANUS (LUCAN)

3 NOV. 39-65 C.E.

STATESMAN, POET

Rising Star. Born on 3 November 39 C.E. in Cordoba as the son of Marcus Antonius Mela, Lucan was Seneca's nephew. Like most members of the upper class, he received an excellent education in Rome, where his talent attracted the attention of the emperor Nero, who befriended him. As a result he became Quaestor before the required age and then Augur. In 60 C.E. he took part in the Neronian games. Soon after this time the first three books of his *Civil War* were circulated, which strained Lucan's relations with the jealous emperor, who forbade him to write poetry. Lucan joined the Pisonian conspiracy, which was discovered before it could come to fruition. He was forced to commit suicide on 30 April 65 C.E.

Sources:

Frederick Ahl, *Lucan: An Introduction* (Ithaca, N.Y.: Cornell University Press, 1976).

R. T. Bruère, "The Scope of Lucan's Historical Epic," *Classical Philology*, 45 (1950): 217–235.

M. P. O. Morford, *The Poet Lucan* (Oxford: Blackwell, 1967).

TITUS LUCRETIUS CARUS (LUCRETIUS)

CIRCA 96-55 B.C.E.

POET, PHILOSOPHER

Rumors of Insanity. Lucretius was born between 98 and 94 B.C.E.; nothing certain is known about his life. He is the author of *De rerum natura*, "On the Nature of Things," a hexameter poem in six books which is one of the most important sources for Epicurean philosophy. Saint Jerome states that Lucretius wrote his poetry between bouts of insanity, having been driven mad by a love potion given him by his wife, and also that he eventually committed suicide; these are probably legends. He died on 15 October 55 B.C.E.

Sources:

Gian Biago Conte, "Lucretius," in *Latin Literature: A History*, translated by J. B. Solodow, revised by Don P. Fowler and G. W. Most (Baltimore: Johns Hopkins University Press, 1994), pp. 155–174.

E. J. Kenney, *Lucretius, Greece and Rome: New Surveys in the Classics*, no. 11 (Oxford: Oxford University Press, 1977).

David West, *The Imagery and Poetry of Lucretius* (Edinburgh: Edinburgh University Press, 1969).

MARCUS VALERIUS MARTIALIS (MARTIAL)

CIRCA 39/40-103/104 C.E.
POET

Status without Wealth. Born in the late 30s C.E. in Bilbilis in Spain, Martial moved circa 64 to Rome, where he was initially patronized by the family of the Senecas, his compatriots. He found favor at court and was raised to the status of a Roman knight, but he never managed to gain full financial independence. He knew the leading *literati* of his time, such as Silius Italicus, Juvenal, and the younger Pliny. He wrote the *Epigrammaton Liber,* as well as the two collections of couplets, *Xenia* and *Apophoreta.* Having praised the tyrant Domitian in fulsome terms, he came under suspicion during the principates of Domitian's successors, Nerva and Trajan, and in 98 at the earliest he moved back to his home in Spain. There some friends gave him a farm, which supported him until his death in 103 or 104 C.E.

Sources:
Walter Allen Jr. and others, "Martial: Knight, Publisher, and Poet," *Classical Journal,* 65 (1970): 345–357.

J. P. Sullivan, *Martial: The Unexpected Classic. A Literary and Historical Study* (Cambridge: Cambridge University Press, 1991).

PUBLIUS OVIDIUS NASO (OVID)

20 MAR. 43 B.C.E.-18 C.E.
POET

Banishment. Ovid was born on 20 March 43 B.C.E. in Sulmo in the mountains southeast of Rome. His family belonged to the local aristocracy, which meant they held the status of knights (*equites*) at Rome, and he was sent to Rome itself for his education. He also toured Greece and Asia Minor. After holding a minor post as a public official, he turned to writing poetry fulltime. Although financially independent enough to enter the senate, he joined the circle of poets around Messalla Corvinus and wrote elegies. This step was obviously not welcomed by his father, who, according to an anecdote, had given young Ovid a beating when he wrote poetry as a boy. Ovid's promise never to write verse again, however, could be scanned as a verse of dactylic hexameter! His first work was five books of *Amores* in circa 18 B.C.E., later reduced to a three-book edition. This work was followed by fifteen *Heroides*, fictional letters from mythical heroines to their absent lovers, then two books of a lover's instruction manual titled *The Art of Love.* This work, in turn, was followed by a third book as sequel, and the *Remedies for Love* for those who want to get over being rejected.

Between the years 2 and 8 C.E., he wrote his major works: fifteen books of *Metamorphoses,* six books of *Fasti* (on stories associated with the Roman calendar), and six double *Heroides* (letters and their responses). This period of time is when disaster struck in the form of Ovid's banishment. He was tried in closed proceedings by the emperor himself, which indicates that the charge was something Augustus wanted to keep secret. Probably Ovid saw the emperor's granddaughter Julia commit adultery and did not tell. Ovid had to leave Rome and report to the garrison at Tomis, modern Constanza, on the Black Sea coast of what is now Romania. He did not lose his property, and he took about a year to get there. From there he kept writing personal appeals (in verse) to the emperor, his friends, and his wife to get him back. These appeals were published in nine books of elegies. Ovid, however, was never recalled and died in exile in 18 C.E. He had been married three times and had a daughter from his second marriage.

Sources:
Barbara Weiden Boyd, *Ovid's Literary Loves: Influence and Innovation in the Amores* (Ann Arbor: University of Michigan Press, 1997).

G. Karl Galinsky, *Ovid's Metamorphoses: An Introduction to the Basic Aspects* (Berkeley: University of California Press, 1975).

Sara Mack, *Ovid* (New Haven: Yale University Press, 1988).

PACUVIUS

CIRCA 220-130 B.C.E.
DRAMATIST, PAINTER

Prestige. Pacuvius was both a stage poet and a visual artist of South Italian birth and was nephew and pupil to the poet Ennius. Pliny tells that, next to the work of Fabius Pictor, the paintings by Pacuvius in the temple of Hercules in the *Forum Boarium* were the most renowned of their day. He wrote at least thirteen tragedies based on Greek myths and was heavily indebted to Greek playwrights such as Sophocles and Euripides. References to satires and a comedy by him are known. He seems to have had relations with L. Aemilius Paullus, consul in 182 B.C.E. and victor over the Greeks at Pydna in 168, which led to the building of his monument in Delphi (168–167). Pacuvius's work *Paulus* seems to have dealt with an episode in the life of that figure. Pacuvius's dramas were admired especially in the first century B.C.E. and, according to Pliny (*N.H.* 35.19), he seems to have made painting a more distinguished occupation through "the glory of the stage." This statement could mean that he painted scenes for his own dramas and, as a result, made his artworks more famous, or that his prestige as a poet increased that of his paintings and painting in general—or both. Apparently after his time, however, painting was not seen as a respectable occupation for the elite.

Sources:
Jacob Isager, *Pliny on Art and Society* (London: Routledge, 1991).

K. Jex-Blake and Eugenie S. Sellers, eds., *The Elder Pliny's Chapters on the History of Art* (Chicago: Argonaut, 1968).

Jerome J. Pollitt, *The Art of Rome c.753 B.C.–337 A.D. Sources and Documents* (Englewood Cliffs, N.J.: Prentice-Hall, 1966).

PASITELES

ACTIVE 106-48 B.C.E.
SCULPTOR, SILVERSMITH

Special Audience. Pasiteles, who hailed from southern Italy, was given Roman citizenship. He was active as an artist at the time of Pompey the Great (106–48 B.C.E.). His works were admired by contemporaries in antiquity, including the great polymath Varro (116–27 B.C.E.). He placed much emphasis on modeling, for working sculpture in metal and for carving statues. Pliny records an ivory statue he made depicting Jupiter in the temple of Metellus at the approach of the Campus Martius. He was also noted for sketching from life, and he appears to have been interested in animal as well as human or divine subjects. He wrote five volumes on famous artworks throughout the world and seems to have been part of the tradition of the artist cum theorist/scholar known from the Hellenistic world, but probably traceable to classical Greece. A statue support is the only surviving work signed by him, but examples from younger sculptors in his workshop are known, including a neoclassical youth signed by "Stephanus, pupil of Pasiteles" and a pair known as Orestes and Electra, signed by "Menelaus, pupil of Stephanus." Pasiteles and his influence represent an important redirection in Greek sculpture, in producing images specifically for Roman tastes, which often involved revivals and adaptations of earlier styles in an environment of connoisseurship.

Sources:
Jacob Isager, *Pliny on Art and Society* (London: Routledge, 1991).

K. Jex-Blake and Eugenie S. Sellers, eds., *The Elder Pliny's Chapters on the History of Art* (Chicago: Argonaut, 1968).

Jerome J. Pollitt, *The Art of Rome c.753 B.C.–337 A.D. Sources and Documents* (Englewood Cliffs, N.J.: Prentice-Hall, 1966).

TITUS MACCIUS PLAUTUS (PLAUTUS)

CIRCA 250-184 B.C.E.
MILLER, PLAYWRIGHT

Success. Plautus was probably named Titus Plautus ("Maccius" being a nickname). He was the most successful writer of Roman comedy, with at least twenty-one plays to his name. Born in Sarsina in Umbria, maybe before 250 B.C.E., he came to Rome as a stagehand. The story goes that he made a small fortune, which he lost in a speculative deal. He then got a backbreaking job in a mill, and there started writing comedies, including *Stichus* (200 B.C.E.) and *Pseudolus* (191 B.C.E.).

Sources:
William S. Anderson, *Barbarian Play: Plautus' Roman Comedy* (Toronto: University of Toronto Press, 1993).

Timothy J. Moore, *The Theater of Plautus: Playing to the Audience* (Austin: University of Texas Press, 1998).

SEXTUS PROPERTIUS (PROPERTIUS)

CIRCA 47-2 B.C.E.
POET

Classic Example. Propertius was born circa 47 B.C.E. in Assisi. He lost his father early and as a youth witnessed the Roman civil war that was raging around his home area. Like Vergil and Tibullus, he lost his land in the expropriations of 41–40. His first book of elegies, which appeared in 28 B.C.E., became the classic example of Latin love elegy. It also won Propertius the patronage of Maecenas. Two further books of love elegies came from his pen, both published in the 20s. Book 2, however, contains thirty-four elegies, which Propertius had published as two books (since he refers to his having written three in all). The original book break falls somewhere between 2.10 and 2.13. In his fourth and final collection, published after 16 B.C.E., love is displaced as a theme by Roman mythical topics. Propertius died by 2 B.C.E. at the latest date.

Sources:
Margaret Hubbard, *Propertius* (London: Duckworth, 1974).

J. P. Sullivan, *Propertius: A Critical Introduction* (Cambridge: Cambridge University Press, 1976).

GAIUS SALLUSTIUS CRISPUS (SALLUST)

1 OCT. 86-13 MAY 34 B.C.E.
STATESMAN, SOLDIER, HISTORIAN

Friend of Caesar. Sallust came from a family of knights in Amiternum, east of Rome. For his education he was sent to Rome, where his family owned a house. After some military service in the 60s, he fell on hard times and had to sell his family's home in the capital. Subsequently, he is on record as Quaestor in 55 or 54, when he either delivered or wrote an invective speech against Cicero. During his first stint in the senate he was caught committing adultery with Fausta, Sulla's daughter, the wife of an Annius Milo. In the late 50s he joined Julius Caesar, which may be why Caesar's opponents had him expelled from the senate in 50 (ostensibly for his adultery with Fausta). He unsuccessfully held command of a legion of Caesar's in 49. In 48 he was Quaestor again, thus being readmitted to the senate. In 47 he was almost killed in a mutiny, but in 46 he was Praetor and accompanied Caesar to Africa. He was rewarded by the governorship of Africa. After his return in 45 he was sued for gouging the provincials, but Caesar stopped the case. After Caesar's death he retreated to private life and wrote his historical works, *The War against Catiline* (circa 42–41 B.C.E.), *The War against Jugurtha* (circa 41–40 B.C.E.), and *The Histories* (after 39 B.C.E.).

Sources:
Donald C. Earl, "Sallust," in *Ancient Writers: Greece and Rome*, volume 2, edited by T. James Luce (New York: Scribners, 1982), pp. 621–641.

Sir Ronald Syme, *Sallust* (Berkeley: University of California Press, 1964).

TIBERIUS CATIUS ASCONIUS SILIUS ITALICUS (SILIUS ITALICUS)

CIRCA 35-100 C.E.
STATESMAN, POET

Punic Wars. Silius Italicus came from a wealthy senatorial family and held senatorial offices himself, including the consulate in 68 C.E., followed by a governorship in Asia Minor circa 77 C.E. He died circa 100 C.E. He is remembered for his *Punica*, a long epic that recounts the Punic Wars.

Source:
Denis C. Feeney, "Tiberius Catius Asconius Silius Italicus," in *The Oxford Classical Dictionary*, edited by Simon Hornblower and Antony Spawforth, third edition (Oxford: Oxford University Press, 1999), p. 1407.

GAIUS SUETONIUS TRANQUILLUS (SUETONIUS)

CIRCA 70-AFTER 122 C.E.
HISTORIAN, ADMINISTRATOR

Poor Etiquette. Suetonius was born in Hippo Regius in North Africa. He went the usual course of education in Rome, followed by legal practice. The younger Pliny supported him, helped him buy a small farm near Rome, and pushed for giving him a favorable tax status. After 114 C.E., Suetonius received official, imperial administrative jobs under Trajan. From around 99 to 122 C.E., Suetonius composed his major work, *De vita Caesarum* (On the Life of the Caesars). In 121 he was dismissed for not having observed the proper etiquette concerning the empress. He died some time after 122 C.E.

Sources:
Barry Baldwin, *Suetonius* (Amsterdam: Hakkert, 1983).

Andrew Wallace-Hadrill, *Suetonius: The Scholar and His Caesars* (New Haven: Yale University Press, 1983).

PUBLIUS [?] CORNELIUS TACITUS (TACITUS)

56/57-AFTER 117 C.E.
HISTORIAN

Germanic Tribes. Tacitus was born in southern France or northern Italy. While he was studying in Rome, his talent was noticed and admired by many, including Pliny; the two men became friends. In 78 Tacitus married Julia, daughter of Gnaeus Iulius Agricola; he wrote an encomiastic biography of his father-in-law, which was published probably in 98

C.E. The same year his *Germania* was published, an ethnographical and geographical survey of the Germanic tribes and their territory. This work is unique in Roman literature and defies classification in a particular genre. It reads like a long digression in an historical account. It is generally thought that Tacitus partly, but not totally, idealized the Germanic tribes as a mirror-image for contemporary Rome. In the years following the two publications, Tacitus entered the senatorial career (*cursus honorum*) on which, in 88, he reached as high as the praetorship. The following four years were spent away from Rome in unknown locations. He resurfaced under Nerva as consul in 97. In 100 C.E. he and Pliny sued a former provincial governor for maladministration. Around 112–113 Tacitus himself acted as governor in Asia Minor. The year of his death is unknown.

Sources:
Ronald H. Martin, *Tacitus* (Berkeley: University of California Press, 1981).

B. Walker, *The Annals of Tacitus: A Study in the Writing of History* (Manchester: Manchester University Press, 1952).

A. J. Woodman, *Tacitus Reviewed* (Oxford & New York: Clarendon Press, 1998).

PUBLIUS TERENTIUS AFER (TERENCE)

CIRCA 185-159 B.C.E.
FREED SLAVE, PLAYWRIGHT

Good Fortune. Born 185 B.C.E. or earlier in Carthage, brought to Rome as a slave, educated and set free by Titus Terentius Lucanus, Terence was befriended by Publius Cornelius Scipio Aemilianus Africanus Numantinus. Scipio championed Greek literature at Rome and included a number of authors among his group of friends, which came to be known as the "Scipionic circle." Terence wrote six comedies between 166 and 160 B.C.E., which met with less success than Plautus's. His *Hecyra* failed twice before its final production in 160 B.C.E. He died in 159 B.C.E. on a study tour of Greece and Asia Minor, allegedly in a shipwreck. Although he is the first Roman author of whom there is an ancient biography, wild anecdotes about him abound: Terence is said to have translated 108 Greek comedies on his final voyage; another story tells of his bequeathing a property to his daughter so that she could marry a Roman knight. It is even claimed that his friend Scipio wrote all his comedies.

Sources:
Walter E. Forehand, *Terence* (Boston: Twayne, 1985).

Sander M. Goldberg, *Understanding Terence* (Princeton: Princeton University Press, 1986).

ALBIUS TIBULLUS (TIBULLUS)

CIRCA 55-19 B.C.E.
SOLDIER, POET

Expressions of Love. Tibullus was born in the 50s B.C.E. into a family of knights who may have lost their lands in the expropriations of 41–40 B.C.E. He joined the entourage of Messalla Corvinus, whom he followed on one of his campaigns. He published his first book consisting of ten elegies in 26 or 25 B.C.E. In it he expresses his love for a woman he calls Delia and a boy he names Marathus. This work established him as the major figure in the circle of poets surrounding Messalla Corvinus; his friends' work was collected under Tibullus's own name in his third and fourth book. In his second, authentic collection of just six poems, he addressed a new woman called Nemesis. This book was published around the year 18, shortly before the poet's death.

Sources:

Francis Cairns, *Tibullus. A Hellenistic Poet at Rome* (Cambridge: Cambridge University Press, 1979).

F. Solmsen, "Tibullus as an Augustan Poet," *Hermes*, 90 (1962): 295–325.

GAIUS VALERIUS FLACCUS SENTINUS BALBUS (VALERIUS FLACCUS)

DIED CIRCA 95 C.E.
POET

Epic Tale. Virtually nothing is known about the life of the epic poet Valerius Flaccus. Historians think that he was of senatorial rank and that the opening of his epic was written circa 75 C.E. The only thing that is certain is that he is mentioned as having recently died in about 95 C.E. (Quint. *Inst.* 10.1.90). He is remembered principally for his *Argonautica*, an epic (based on the *Argonautica* of Apollonius of Rhodes), which tells the story of Jason and the Argonauts.

Sources:

Debra Hershkowitz, *Valerius Flaccus'* Argonautica: *Abbreviated Voyages in Silver Latin Epic* (Oxford: Oxford University Press, 1998).

P. R. Taylor, "Valerius' *Flavian Argonautica*," *Classical Quarterly*, 44 (1994): 212–235.

PUBLIUS VERGILIUS MARO (VERGIL)

15 OCT. 70-21 SEPT. 19 B.C.E.
POET

Last Request. Vergil (also spelled Virgil) was born on 15 October 70 B.C.E. in Andes near Mantua in northern Italy. His father sent him to Cremona and Milan to be educated. Later he went to Rome to study rhetoric. His attempt at representing someone in a lawsuit was a complete failure since he proved to be a clumsy speaker. Therefore, he went to Naples to study Epicurean philosophy. His family lost their farm in Octavian's land expropriations of 41 B.C.E. Vergil later received some reparations for it. By 38 he had been introduced to Maecenas, the famous patron of poets. Together with Horace, he accompanied Maecenas on a diplomatic mission to Brindisi in 37. Two years later he published his *Bucolics,* consisting of 10 Eclogues. The next ten years were spent writing the *Georgics,* which he read to Augustus in 29. The final eleven years of his life he spent writing the *Aeneid,* of which he read books 2, 4, and 6 to Augustus in 23 B.C.E. In 19 he intended to take a three-year sabbatical in Greece to finish the work, but he fell ill and was taken back by Augustus to Brindisi. There he died on 21 September 19 B.C.E. In his will he asked for the unfinished *Aeneid* to be burned, but Augustus commissioned two of Vergil's friends, Plotius Tucca and Varius Rufus, to edit and publish the work.

Sources:

Jasper Griffin, *Virgil* (Oxford: Oxford University Press, 1986).

S. J. Harrison, *Oxford Readings in Vergil's* Aeneid (Oxford: Oxford University Press, 1990).

Richard Heinze, *Vergil's Epic Technique,* translated by Hazel and David Harvey and Fred Robertson (Berkeley: University of California Press, 1993).

Nicholas Horsfall, *A Companion to the Study of Virgil* (Leiden Holland: E. J. Brill, 1995).

L. P. Wilkinson, *The Georgics of Virgil* (Cambridge: Cambridge University Press, 1969).

DOCUMENTARY SOURCES

Notes on Literary Sources:

Earliest Latin authors: Many of these are known only from references in other, later authors, and/or from mere fragments of their work. The latter are edited in collections such as Jürgen Blänsdorf's *Fragmenta Poetarum Latinorum* (1995) or E. H. Warmington's *Remains of Old Latin* (1979). These sources are the places to find texts of early authors such as Livius Andronicus. Warmington's edition includes the Latin with English translations on facing pages.

Works listed: Some of the authors included here wrote many works besides those listed. The aim is to include the major works of the major Latin authors, and to suggest publication dates for these where possible.

Apuleius (Lucius [?] Apuleius), *Metamorphoses*, or *The Golden Ass* (circa 155 C.E.)—This novel, the only Roman one that has survived intact, is eleven books long and includes the famous story of Cupid and Psyche.

Augustine (Aurelius Augustinus), *Confessions* (circa 397–400 C.E.), *City of God* (circa 413–426 C.E.)—A formidable early Christian theologian and philosopher (subsequently canonized) who could also write with great tenderness.

Anicius Manlius Severinus Boethius, *The Consolation of Philosophy* (523–524 C.E.)—The last great writer of antiquity and the first great writer of the Middle Ages. *The Consolation of Philosophy* is a prison dialogue that mingles prose and verse, offering an explanation of divine providence that owes debts to Stoicism and Neoplatonism.

Gaius Julius Caesar, *The Gallic War* (not before 52 B.C.E.); *The Civil War* (not before 48 B.C.E.)—An outstanding general and politician, as well as a polished writer.

Gaius Valerius Catullus, *Poems*—One of the greatest poets of the late Roman Republic, Catullus was a master at packaging great emotion in polished small verse forms.

Marcus Tullius Cicero, *Speeches; Rhetorical Works; Letters; Philosophical Works*—Rome's greatest orator, and a central political figure of the late Republic, as well as a significant philosopher. His letters are a wonderful source for the social historian.

Ennius, *Annales*—Ennius might be considered the father of Roman poetry; his Annales collected, in versified form, a history of Rome from its beginnings to Ennius's own day.

Valerius Flaccus (Gaius Valerius Flaccus Setinus Balbus), *Argonautica* (first century C.E.)—A follower of Vergil in epic, renowned for his many similes.

Horace (Quintus Horatius Flaccus), *Epodes* (circa 30 B.C.E.); *Satires* (circa 30 B.C.E.); *Odes* (books 1–3, 23 B.C.E.; *Carmen saeculare*, 17 B.C.E.; book 4, circa 13 B.C.E.); and *Epistles* (book 1, 21 or 19 B.C.E.; book 2, circa 19–16 B.C.E.)—Friend of Vergil, member of the circle of Maecenas, and Rome's greatest lyric poet, Horace was successful at adapting Greek models to Latin verse, but also at composing that peculiarly Roman genre, satire.

Jerome (Eusebius Hieronymus)—Saint Jerome is most famous for his translation of the Hebrew and Greek scriptures into Latin (late 4th–early 5th century C.E.), which came to be known as the Vulgate Bible.

Lucan (Marcus Annaeus Lucanus), *On the Civil War* (circa 62–65 C.E.)—Lucan was a prodigious young talent who wrote an anti-epic about the demise of the Roman republic.

Titus Lucretius Carus, *On the Nature of Things*—Lucretius, Rome's most significant poet/philosopher, produced a long hexameter poem that is one of the principal sources for Epicurean philosophy.

Martial (Marcus Valerius Martialis), *Epigrams* (86–101 C.E.)—A prolific writer of epigrams with a satirical streak.

Ovid (Publius Ovidius Naso), Amatory works (20s B.C.E. to 2 C.E.); *Metamorphoses* and *Fasti* (before 8 C.E.); *Tristia* (10–12 C.E.); *Letters from Pontus* (books 1–3, 13 C.E.; book 4, 18 C.E.)—Rome's most prolific and irreverent poet.

Petronius (possibly Titus Petronius Arbiter), *Satiricon* or *Satyrica* (after 66 C.E.)—Writer of a rather bizarre but often hilariously funny satire.

Titus Maccius Plautus, *The Comedies*—Plautus was Rome's most successful writer of comedy. His plays were adaptations of Greek originals; they were aimed at entertainment, even included many sung passages, and often sacrificed consistency to get an extra laugh.

Pliny the Elder (Gaius Plinius Secundus), *Naturalis historia* (published posthumously, after 79 C.E.)—Natural historian, soldier, statesman, and polymath, his intellectual appetite was insatiable.

Pliny the Younger (Gaius Plinius Caecilius Secundus), *Letters* (early second century C.E.)—A perceptive chronicler of life in his own time.

Sextus Propertius, *Elegies* (20s B.C.E.)—Tibullus's contemporary and colleague in the field of love-elegy. His first book of love poems was extremely popular.

Gaius Sallustius Crispus, *The War against Catiline* (circa 42–41 B.C.E.); *The War against Jugurtha* (circa 41–40 B.C.E.); *The Histories* (after 39 B.C.E.)—An historian critical of Rome in the late republic.

Lucius Annaeus Seneca [the Younger], Philosophical works, letters, tragedies, *Apocolocyntosis, Naturales quaestiones* (37–65 C.E.)—A poet, politician, and Stoic philosopher all in one.

Publius Papinius Statius, *Thebaid* (90 or 91 C.E.)—*Silvae* and *Achilleid* (90s C.E.)—The most significant of the Flavian epic poets.

Silius Italicus (Tiberius Catius Asconius Silius Italicus), *Punica* (late first century C.E.)—Another follower of Vergil, Silius Italicus wrote the longest Latin epic poem that has come down to the modern age.

Publius (?) Cornelius Tacitus, *On Agricola* (98 C.E.), *On the Germans* (98 C.E.), *Dialogue on Orators* (circa 101–102 C.E.), *Histories* (circa 109–110 C.E.), *Annals* (circa 120 C.E.)—Rome's most acerbic and powerful historian.

Publius Terentius Afer, *The Comedies*—Plautus's more sophisticated but less successful younger contemporary, Terence wrote several plays (also based on Greek originals) that display a refined and subtle wit.

Albius Tibullus, *Elegies* (book 1, circa 27 B.C.E.; book 2, unknown)—A sensitive writer of love elegy in whose corpus the work of other poets from his circle are preserved.

Vergil (Publius Vergilius Maro), *Eclogues* (circa 42–35 B.C.E.); *Georgics* (36–29 B.C.E.); *Aeneid* (circa 19 B.C.E.)—Vergil, Rome's greatest composer of epic verse, came to be regarded as Rome's national poet. His *Aeneid* rivals the works of Homer.

Note on Visual Sources: The following selection is a brief overview of some noteworthy ancient literary figures who inform the modern reader something about art in the Roman world and Roman attitudes to it.

Ancient Ecphrases—The term *ekphrasis*, which in Greek means "description," is usually applied in literary studies to a lengthy verbal description of a work of art, real or imaginary, found in ancient writings. These are themselves important as sources for ancient ideas about art and artistic production. Ecphrasis was a popular literary form and lasted throughout antiquity, beginning with Homer, poet of the Greek epic, the *Iliad*, which features a description of the shield of Achilles, the central hero of the poem. In book 8 of the *Aeneid*, Vergil, the great poet of the Augustan age, develops Homeric ideas in his ecphrasis of the shield of his own hero, Aeneas, on which is depicted the future history of Rome. Two writers of the third and fourth centuries C.E., Philostratus and Callistratus, discuss statues and paintings (some famous, others imaginary), sometimes putting them into their mythological contexts. The *Greek Anthology*, a collection of short poems from the seventh century B.C.E. to tenth century C.E., is comprised of epigrams, epitaphs, and such, arranged in sixteen books, and contains some ecphrases. The detailed and sometimes fanciful descriptions found in ancient ecphrases vary widely in their tone and points of emphasis, but overall they can provide further insight into ancient attitudes to artworks and their perceived powers and ideological functions.

Polybius—In the course of his history of the rise of Rome from the First Punic War (264 B.C.E.) to its conquests in Greece in the mid-second century, he gives some insight into early Roman uses of art (for instance, portraiture).

Cicero (Marcus Tullius Cicero)—Provides evidence, to varying degrees of detail, of ancient Roman attitudes on art by, for instance, outlining the greed and devastating effects of the corrupt governor of Sicily, Verres, whom he prosecuted for plundering that province of much of its artistic treasures (70 B.C.E.). Elsewhere, Cicero displays an interest in Greek art in speaking of an evolution in painting and sculpture in which each medium progressively depicts "reality" more beautifully. His highest praise seems to go to the sculptor Pheidias (active in the fifth century B.C.E.), whom he portrays as a kind of artistic visionary.

Dionysius of Halicarnassus—A rhetorician, historian, and literary critic active in the late first century B.C.E., he draws stylistic comparisons between various types of orators and visual artists—a kind of criticism found in other ancient writers. He had a specific interest in early Roman culture and his *Roman Antiquities* in twenty books discussed the institutions of Rome down to the time of the first Punic war.

Vitruvius (Vitruvius Pol(l)io)—A Roman architect active under Julius Caesar and Augustus. His treatise *On Architecture* is an important source for Roman and

Greek building techniques as well as philosophical attitudes relevant to the field. The work became very influential in antiquity and beyond and includes famous anecdotes such as the great inventor Archimedes' shouting in the bathtub "Eureka" (Greek *heurêka*, "I've found it!") on discovering the proportions of silver and gold in a wreath made for a tyrant of Syracuse. Leonardo da Vinci's "Vitruvian Man" is a canonical representation of the human figure based on bodily proportions enumerated by Vitruvius.

Livy (Titus Livius)—Author of a history of Rome in 142 books from the foundation of the city to the accession of Augustus, at whose behest he undertook the task. Only 35 books and some fragments survive, but periodically in Livy's account one can see the longstanding Roman link between military conquest and the various roles of art, either as victory spoils to be put on public display, or as a means of commemorating success on the battlefield.

Pliny the Elder (Gaius Plinius Secundus)—Books 33–36 of *The Natural History* comprise the fullest source for the history of Greek and Roman painting and sculpture, but his real subjects in these books are the uses made by humans of metals, minerals, and types of stone. The achievements of the Greeks and Romans in the visual arts are extensively treated as examples of such usages. Despite these difficulties, Pliny is still of much value to understanding ancient art history, for he had access to a great amount of material and ancient evidence (he mentions using more than two thousand sources!) which have since become almost entirely lost. He lists in his sources the writings of many artists, and it is apparent that he is using a number of ancient art theories in many of his accounts of ancient art. Books 33–36 contain, then, not necessarily Pliny's own personal tastes, but seem to preserve information and ideas traceable to various periods and authors who are often closer in time to the artworks being described.

Plutarch—His *Parallel Lives* compares the achievements of eminent Greeks and Romans and for centuries has been an important source for the history and character of many illustrious figures such as Alexander the Great and Julius Caesar.

Suetonius (Gaius Suetonius Tranquillus)—He wrote a series of biographies of the "Twelve Caesars" (from Julius Caesar to Domitian), which has long been acknowledged as emphasizing the scandalous and personal aspects of its subjects' lives sometimes at the expense of overall reliability. He includes a number of interesting anecdotes, nonetheless, which involve the uses and abuses of art and various building programs by certain emperors.

Pausanias—His *A Description of Greece* focuses largely on much earlier Greek painting, architecture, and sculpture, but does include accounts of works commissioned in Greece under certain emperors such as Hadrian and Antoninus Pius, and the local benefactor, Herodes Atticus. Like Pliny, he relies on older sources (many lost to scholars now), but also inscriptions, eyewitnesses, and what he saw with his own eyes (autopsy). He is generally reliable, as later discoveries have confirmed, and he includes much important information in his records by locating many monuments in their historical and religious contexts. He tends to give fairly clear and dispassionate accounts of what he sees, and his preference for the art of Archaic and Classical Greece is in many ways typical of his time.

Cassius Dio—His eighty-book history of Rome from the city's foundation to 229 C.E. is only very partially preserved. He moved in high civic Roman circles and held the consulship with the emperor Alexander Severus in 229, then retired to Bithynia. The history is arranged as a series of annals with many digressions and a focus on the shift from the republic to life under imperial monarchies.

Ammianus Marcellinus—A soldier of high rank from Antioch who saw service in many parts of the empire, and the last of the great pagan Latin historians of Rome. There he settled to complete his history in thirty-one books (now only partially preserved) that cover Roman imperial history from the accession of Nerva (96 C.E.) to events datable to circa 390 C.E., and include many antiquarian excursuses along the way.

Cameo with profiles of Emperor Claudius and his wife, Agrippina the Younger, superimposed over profiles of Germanicus and his wife Agrippina the Elder, circa first century C.E. (Kunsthistorisches Museum, Vienna)

COMMUNICATION, TRANSPORTATION, AND EXPLORATION

by JOEL ALLEN

CONTENTS

Sidebars and tables are listed in italics.

312 B.C.E.	• The *Via Appia*, running from Rome to Capua, is built by Appius Claudius Caecus.
264-241 B.C.E.	• The Romans fight the First Punic War with Carthage. Their first naval victory comes in 260 at the Battle of Mylae off the coast of Sicily. After the war they make Sicily a province ruled directly by a Roman magistrate.
229 B.C.E.	• The Illyrian queen Teuta is believed to have supported piracy of the Roman Adriatic coast; she is ultimately defeated by the growing Roman fleet.
220 B.C.E.	• Work is begun on the *Via Flaminia*, a road connecting Rome and Rimini on the Adriatic coast.
218-202 B.C.E.	• The Romans fight and win the Second Punic War with Carthage, surviving an attempt by Hannibal to turn their Italian allies against them.
210* B.C.E.	• The scholarly geographer Eratosthenes is active in Alexandria.
187 B.C.E.	• Work is begun on the *Via Aemilia*, an extension of the *Via Flaminia*, stretching from Rimini to Cisalpine Gaul.
179 B.C.E.	• The first stone bridge, the pons Aemilius, is built over the Tiber River.
168 B.C.E.	• The Roman victory at Pydna over Perseus, king of Macedon, ensures Roman power in Greece. One thousand prisoners of war, including the historian Polybius, are brought to the city of Rome.

*DENOTES CIRCA DATE

146 B.C.E.

- The cities of Corinth and Carthage are destroyed.
- Polybius explores the west coast of Africa beyond the Strait of Gibraltar.

133 B.C.E.

- King Attalus III of Pergamum dies, leaving in his will his political power and wealth to the Romans.
- Tiberius Gracchus enters upon a campaign to break up large senatorial estates and redistribute their land to dispossessed Roman soldiers. He is assassinated during a riot.
- Work is begun on the *Via Egnatia*, beginning on the Adriatic coast and leading to Byzantium.

121 B.C.E.

- The *Via Domitia* is built in southern France, connecting the Alps with the Iberian peninsula.

104 B.C.E.

- The Alexandrian geographer Artemidorus explores the western coasts of Spain and Gaul. His written work also includes research on Ethiopia and India.

67 B.C.E.

- Pompey rids the Mediterranean Sea of pirates.

63 B.C.E.

- Cicero becomes consul and quashes the conspiracy of Catiline. The record of his private correspondence begins in 62 B.C.E. and lasts until his death in 43 B.C.E.

60 B.C.E.

- The first triumvirate of Gnaeus Pompeius Magnus (Pompey), Marcus Licinius Crassus and Julius Caesar is formed. Caesar gets the command of the armies in Gaul and spends the next eight years conquering the Gallic tribes up to the English Channel and writing to Rome of his accomplishments and observations.

44 B.C.E.

- Caesar plots a campaign against Parthia but is assassinated on the Ides of March.

*DENOTES CIRCA DATE

38 B.C.E.

- Agrippa begins work on a road in Gaul connecting Lugdunum (modern Lyons) with the English Channel.

31 B.C.E.

- Octavian defeats Mark Antony and Cleopatra at Actium and then embarks on a journey around the entire empire.

27-14 C.E.

- Augustus reigns as the first emperor of Rome.
- Juba II writes of his travels to the Canary Islands, the source of the Nile, and through Parthia.
- Gaius Caesar, grandson and heir of Augustus, embarks on a campaign to the East, passing through Arabia, Parthia, and Armenia before being fatally wounded.
- Augustus builds the Altar of Peace and a large sundial in celebration of the stability, prosperity, and international prestige of his reign.
- Strabo is at work on his seventeen-book study of geography.

44* C.E.

- The emperor Claudius turns the coastal city of Ostia at the mouth of the Tiber River into a major harbor by digging out a large basin and canal and by constructing a lighthouse.

44 C.E.

- Pomponius Mela writes his description of the world, similar in form to the work of Strabo and other geographers, but he is primarily concerned with the mythological and the bizarre.

70 C.E.

- The Jewish rebellion ends with the sack of Jerusalem. The historian Josephus is taken prisoner at Jotapota and enters the patronage of the emperor.

83 C.E.

- Agricola, the governor of Britain, orders an expedition to circumnavigate the island and to explore the Shetland Islands.

*DENOTES CIRCA DATE

98-117 C.E.

- In his wars against Dacia, Trajan has his architect, Apollodorus, construct a large bridge across the Danube River.
- The *Via Traiana*, built by the emperor Trajan, replaces the old *Via Appia* as the primary route from Rome to Brundisium.
- Trajan improves Claudius's harbor at Ostia with the addition of a large hexagonal basin.
- Pliny the Younger is active in his letter writing.
- The Vindolanda tablets, letters inscribed on wood on the British frontier, are written.

160* C.E.

- Ptolemy is at work on his spherical map of the world, with latitude and longitude as markers of locations.
- Pausanias is at work on his travelogue of Greece.

212 C.E.

- Caracalla grants citizenship to all free residents of the empire.

257 C.E.

- The city of Dura-Europos, on the caravan route between Rome and the East, falls to the Persians.

267 C.E.

- Small kingdoms begin to separate from the empire. Zenobia, queen of Palmyra, and Postumus, a governor in Gaul, make a bid for independence but are ultimately defeated.

293 C.E.

- The emperor Diocletian reorganizes the Roman provinces and establishes a tetrarchy of four emperors who share power.

312 C.E.

- Constantine becomes sole emperor of Rome and legalizes Christianity.

378 C.E.

- The Romans are defeated by the Goths at the Battle of Adrianople, beginning a long series of migrations of northern populations into the empire.

*DENOTES CIRCA DATE

392 C.E.	•	Symmachus is active in his letter writing.
400 C.E.	•	Christian pilgrims such as Eutheria and Melania the Younger travel throughout Egypt and Judaea in search of biblical sites.

A relief of a Roman trireme, late first century B.C.E., found at Palestrina, Italy (Vatican Museum, Rome)

OVERVIEW

Agricultural Foundations. From its very beginnings in prehistory, Rome was a place of travelers and transients. Long before the city acquired its empire, it was a collection of small, independent, hilltop settlements situated around a river crossing about sixteen miles inland from the sea. An island and a broad marsh broke up the current of the Tiber River and made it relatively easy for farmers, herdsmen, and merchants to traverse there; it became a crossroads for those traveling either along the east-west route of the river or along the north-south axis. An early road, the *Via salaria* (Salt Road), which followed the course of the river, provided access to the precious commodity found at the mouth of the river, and an agricultural marketplace emerged that served several distinct tribes of central Italy: the Etruscans, Sabines, and Latins. Archaeological evidence suggests that individual outposts at the site, over time, grew together and merged—a phenomenon called *synoecism*. The result was a single city, with agricultural origins, composed of different ethnic groups and located, like a bull's-eye, in the center of several distinct tribal regions. Archaeologists estimate that the unified city emerged around the middle of the seventh century B.C.E.

Mythology. Legends concerning the foundation of the city place its origins about one hundred years earlier, in 753 B.C.E.; nonetheless, they reflect the same kind of cultural blending that is attested by archaeological evidence. In Roman historical myths one finds a multinational character for the early society of the city hidden underneath the obvious attributes of literary epic, such as the divine lineage of the first king, Romulus, and his miraculous rescue from exposure by a kindly she-wolf. As the story goes, in order to populate his fledgling city, Romulus, who was from Latium, accepted renegades and bandits from all over Italy, and then, in order to fill out the lopsided male population, kidnapped the women of the neighboring Sabines. When the Sabine king came to the rescue of the stolen women, Romulus negotiated a system of shared rule between them, and for the next few generations of mythical kings, the ethnic identities of the monarchs seesawed between Latin and Sabine. Etruscan kings also appeared later. The picture of early Roman society provided by myths and legends, in keeping with the material remains of archaeology, is one of intense cultural mélange and inclusiveness.

Language. Linguistic evidence also betrays the multiethnic origins of Rome. The many languages of the early hilltop communities and tribes must have posed initial challenges for communication. The Etruscan language, which has yet to be fully understood by modern scholars, does not belong to the same linguistic family as the other Italian dialects that were also spoken in and around the Tiber. Nevertheless, Etruscan loan words exist in Latin, in much the same way as some French and Spanish words have become standard in English. Several examples have to do with writing: *litterae*, the Latin word for letters, and *stylus*, a type of writing instrument, derive from Etruscan. Some Sabine words also worked their way into Latin: *bos* for cow and *scrofa* for sow. The evidence of language thus suggests not only the close habitation of disparate groups, but also extensive interaction and even acceptance during the period of the Roman monarchy. Bilingualism, with all its attendant understandings and shared experiences between two cultures, must have been common, though Latin ultimately became the dominant tongue.

"Justified" Warfare. Most of what is known about Roman travel and communication following the period of the monarchy comes in the arena of warfare and military activity. Sources become more numerous and more reliable after the foundation of the Republic in 509 B.C.E., when Rome survived a political revolution and a series of wars against Etruscan opponents. After their territory was secure, the Romans began to look beyond their borders to the rest of the central Italian peninsula; through nearly constant warfare, their territory grew. Expansion into non-Roman land, however, required a just cause and consultation with the Roman gods. In early Rome, special priests, called *fetiales* (singular, *fetial*), were responsible for carrying out religious rites of diplomacy in the declaration and conduct of wars. When Roman honor had been challenged, the priest would go to the enemy state and ask for retribution; if he received no response after thirty-three days, he approached the border between the two territories and hurled a spear across, ceremonially marking the start of the war. The gods also played a role in the aftermath of war. In a famous episode following a defeat of the Etruscans in 396 B.C.E., a boy asked the patron goddess of the city if she wanted to come to Rome, and the statue reportedly nodded yes (Livy, 5.22.5). She was then carried to Rome and given a new temple—the growth of the city included the absorption of foreign religions, and according to the Roman etiquette of diplomacy, it had to have the approval of the gods, both old and new.

Conquest and Incorporation. The status and treatment of the defeated depended on their behavior during the war. Roman responses to their enemies ranged from harsh enslavement, or even capital penalties, to benign incorporation of the conquered. In terms of the former, those who had fought the Romans tooth and nail, once they surrendered, were labeled as *dediticii,* meaning that they were entirely offered up to the Roman will, losing all measure of local autonomy. For the communities that surrendered with less of a fight, the Romans were willing to make extensive concessions in areas of local government and daily life. They conferred upon certain communities the so-called Latin rights, which meant that they could trade and intermarry with Romans, but did not, initially, hold the right to vote. Once Rome granted them suffrage, they could run for magistracies. The Romans also sent out new settlements, called "Latin colonies," which were autonomous, but closely allied with Rome. In the course of the fourth century B.C.E., the Roman sphere of influence spread to include all of central Italy, most notably, the territory of the Samnites; part of the explanation for the success of Rome belongs to this system of alliances and shared rule.

Romans in Italy. As more and more Italians beyond the city of Rome gained privileges within the Republic, there arose a greater need to travel to and from the capital city. People might have to cover great distances to cast a vote, visit new in-laws, engage in trade, or participate in military endeavors. At the end of the fourth century the first great Roman road was constructed under the leadership of Appius Claudius. The *Via Appia* covered 132 miles from Rome southward into Samnite territory; it was later extended to Brundisium on the eastern coast for a total of 366 miles. At first, the surface was gravel; in the third century, broad, flat paving stones made the surface smoother. The *Via Appia* was the first of many high-quality, paved roads that facilitated the critical communications between the central Roman authority and the peripheral allies. By the end of the second century B.C.E., a web of Roman roads held Italy together.

Romans Overseas. The record of international relations in the early Republic shows that the Romans kept abreast of the Mediterranean world beyond their Italian sphere of influence. They traded with the Greeks who had settled in southern Italy, Sicily, and southern France, as well as with the Gauls to their north. They formed diplomatic agreements with Carthage, the great naval power on the northern coast of Africa. Despite these increased ties overseas, the Romans had yet to develop a strong navy, and they suffered as a result. It was not until the First Punic War (264–241 B.C.E.) that the Romans became experts in seafaring. In the course of that twenty-year struggle with Carthage,

they managed to capture and copy an enemy vessel and quickly fitted out their first permanent navy. When a band of pirates, allegedly at the command of the Illyrian queen Teuta, attacked Roman ambassadors and harried the Roman coastline shortly thereafter in 229 B.C.E., the Romans were able to respond swiftly.

Provinces. The First Punic War also yielded an innovation in the management of the defeated: the use of the *provincia* (province) rather than the colony or the grant of Latin rights. Once Rome won the islands of Sicily and Sardinia from Carthage, they were in need of a means of control that was more efficient than their Italian network. In response to this challenge, they overruled local control by installing permanent Roman institutions of administration. Romans who had already completed terms as high-ranking officials within the city became governors abroad and were put in charge of a battery of soldiers, scribes, judges, and engineers. Individual cities within a province might still retain nominal freedom, and the native aristocracy still retained their prestige and position, but they were increasingly encouraged to "become Roman" themselves. Citizenship was granted to select provincials in a piecemeal way. Soon a confusing array of social statuses, each with unique rights and privileges in Roman law, applied to residents of the Roman territories: Roman citizens, Italian allies, and varying ranks of provincial natives. An intricate bureaucracy was necessary to maintain order; a steady traffic in letters, edicts, and other sorts of correspondence began to move throughout the new empire.

Hannibal. The logistics of communication, recruitment, and troop deployment were determining factors in the outcome of the Second Punic War (218–201 B.C.E.). In their second war with Carthage, the Romans experienced an innovative assault by Hannibal, who decided, rather than sailing to the Italian peninsula, to embark on an overland march through Spain, southern France, the southern Alps, and down into Italy. His journey, recorded in Livy, reveals much of the dangers and risks of travel. It was an exceedingly slow process, subject to natural disasters—storms, blizzards, and strong winds—and was complicated by an imperfect knowledge of local geography. Once Hannibal was in Italy, his plan was to convince the Italian allies to abandon Rome and to fight for him. Most, as a result of generations of incorporation and communication within Italy, felt their interests were inextricably interwoven with those of Rome; only a few defected to Hannibal's side. When Hannibal did not receive the support he had counted on, the great size of his army quickly became a detriment; it had to keep always on the move in search of food and supplies to sustain itself. An army in ancient Rome operated without the benefit of a map or reliable intelligence; mass movement was always something of a gamble.

The Hellenistic Mediterranean. With the success of the Second Punic War and the acquisition of new provinces in Africa and Spain, the Romans, irreversibly, became members of an international community. They next came into contact with the great Hellenistic kingdoms in the East: the remnants of the conquests of Alexander the Great in Greece, Asia Minor, and Egypt. Complex games of diplomacy, as well as several violent wars, involved a frequent practice following the signing of treaties during the first half of the second century B.C.E.: as part of their diplomatic negotiations, the Romans would demand possession of adolescent or preadolescent royal heirs as hostages. The role of the hostages differed from that of the modern world in that their safety was never threatened; they were never used to coerce certain behavior from the defeated. Rather, their value was in their potential to learn a Roman way of life and to take it with them when they returned home following their period of detention. Hostages, with their non-Roman languages and customs, were highly visible in the city, and though the intent may have been to introduce Rome to them, they also had the effect of exposing the Romans to others. They could be a source of intelligence for Roman tacticians as well as "teachers" of non-Roman cultures to Roman "students." The hundreds of hostages taken from all over the Mediterranean—from Macedonia, Sparta, Syria, Egypt, Spain, and other countries—were instrumental in the creation of a multicultural empire.

Philhellenism. A hostage's first view of Roman citizens, and vice versa, typically came as part of a triumphal procession, when victorious generals paraded through the city streets with all the loot they had brought back from their campaigns. Works of art, piles of precious metals, posters of exotic locales, and throngs of prisoners of war, in addition to the hostages, were marched through the forum, broadcasting the glory of Rome to all spectators. Most Romans would never have seen Greece, Egypt, or Syria, and the images of the defeated lands would have been their only source of information about new Roman gains. The festivals became ever more elaborate and ostentatious, until the influx of Greek art and educated hostages and prisoners of war brought about in Rome a fascination for the cosmopolitan world of the East. As Romans increasingly traveled throughout the Greek world, they became enamored of Hellenistic history and the artistic and scientific accomplishments of the Greeks. Greek writers introduced the Romans to new genres of expression, as epic poetry, dramatic comedy, and annalistic history became popular in literary circles. The historian Polybius, who was taken as a hostage to Rome after the battle of Pydna in 168 B.C.E., boasted that he had become a tutor to his captor's sons, who were eager to learn about Greek culture. In the end, it became both necessary and fashionable to speak Greek, and many Romans at the upper echelons of society took pride in their bilingualism. Horace, observing the phenomenon from a later period, remarked that Greece, though captured, had itself captured Rome.

Service Abroad. Escalating military campaigns exposed more and more Romans to the thrill—and danger—of travel and exploration in foreign lands. The triumphal processions that wove through the streets of Rome heaped great honors upon the handful of aristocratic families that controlled the generalships. The *triumphator* held a quasidivine status: he wore the purple of a king and was permitted to sit enthroned in the temple of Jupiter. Adding a new kingdom to the Roman empire became a virtue, and the political and financial value of provincial commands made service abroad an absolute necessity for any ambitious politician. Generals took huge armies to the frontier to fuel further expansion; these armies might remain overseas for years. Thousands of Roman soldiers were thus exposed to a world away from home on a scale that was unrivaled in the ancient world for their tenure of service and breadth of travel. In the late second century B.C.E., the consul Marius reformed the army in order to admit soldiers from the lowest ranks of society, who had previously been unable to serve. Romans from all classes were leaving Italy in huge numbers. Constant military activity changed the course of Roman social history and was instrumental in making the Roman world one of close overseas ties, with territorial borders diminishing in significance. There was a sharp increase in foreign trade, and Roman merchants could be found crisscrossing the Mediterranean Sea. Julius Caesar gave the citizenship to entire communities in Gaul, where large numbers of Roman veterans and merchants had settled, in return for their support of his causes. Roman soldiers who were permanently stationed abroad might marry into the local population, although such unions were not recognized in Roman law, and their children did not have, at first, the right of Roman citizenship.

Corruption and Civil War. Aristocrats began to compete viciously in their conquests, which were the keys to political success. Rivals secured nontraditional military commands in order to keep their armies employed on their side. Marius held multiple consulships in a row, ignoring the rule that a decade had to elapse between offices; Sulla acquired a command in the East by marching on Rome and forcing the senate to give it to him. In the next generation, the popularity of both Pompey and Julius Caesar depended on their conquests of non-Romans. The Roman people were ever hungrier for spectacle and for the display of the unknown, proof of their destiny to rule. So much wealth and power was caught up in the Roman provinces that corruption was perhaps inevitable. Some Roman provinces might be overtaxed to the point of exhaustion by their governors, as Sicily was by Verres in 73–71 B.C.E. To express their dissatisfaction, indigenous peoples might take aim at highly visible Roman populations of merchants, soldiers, and the like. Roman settlers in North Africa, for example, were butchered by supporters of the local king, Jugurtha, when war erupted with Rome.

Correspondence. In the midst of the civil conflict, missives of various sorts were sent back and forth, reporting late-breaking news of alliances and betrayals. Caesar, from his command in Gaul, wrote commentaries describing his conquest and, to add the element of the exotic, reported on the new cultures and religions he encountered. These letters were designed with a public readership in mind, similar to a modern public-relations campaign. Thousands of letters of Cicero survive from the turbulent period of the late Republic; a principal topic of these communications is the unfolding political maneuvering of his associates. He also wrote of the state of his meager military campaigns while he was in his province, Cilicia, and after he was exiled to Macedonia he sought forgiveness from the Senate and the Roman people by means of publicized written correspondence. Cicero's letters also preserve, amid his political commentaries, aspects of his private life at home and with his friends; his correspondence with his wife and brother, and with his close confidant, Atticus, provide readers with a glimpse of his life away from the public eye.

Augustus. The constant civil war that had raged for nearly a century was brought to a close when Octavian defeated his rivals for power, Mark Antony and Cleopatra. He appears to have immediately recognized the difficulties inherent in controlling such a broad and far-flung empire. Without maps or reliable documentary evidence to describe the reality of Roman rule abroad, he was at a disadvantage, and accordingly, he set out to examine the provinces first-hand. He spent years after his victory at Actium circumnavigating the empire, lingering for a time in the particularly vexing trouble spots. Lest any political rivals try to challenge him again, Octavian, soon to be renamed Augustus, needed to impress upon his subjects that he had achieved great military victories. His public image relied heavily on fostering in the Roman populace a warped sense of what the world was like beyond Rome. The official record of his travels, propagated in a variety of media, presented him as a great and perpetual *triumphator,* even when his accomplishments against foreign enemies had included only a diplomatic agreement. One of his trusted generals, Agrippa, set up a public map for all Romans, for the first time, to track the growth of their domain; on his own public monument, the *Ara pacis* (Altar of Peace), the emperor portrayed children from the East and from the West taking part in a procession of the royal family and Roman senators.

Discoveries and Disasters. Augustan art seemed to fan the fire for exploration of the unknown, and there developed in his regime a fascination for the exotic. Writers in the period published theories of what lay over the horizon, and ethnography became a salient feature of literature. Authors such as Strabo, writing under Augustus, and Pomponius Mela, writing under Claudius, described what the outer world was like, or at least what they thought the outer world was like. Mela described a race of people whose faces were down below their shoulders, and Strabo wrote of a land that had flying scorpions, enormous tarantulas, and three-foot-long lizards. Ethnographies such as these typically privileged the Romans themselves as superior and civilized. Despite their claims to understand remote civilizations, imperfect knowledge was, in fact, the rule, and ignorance of reality could lead to serious problems. Believing that German tribes had been pacified, and that the distance from the Rhine to the northern European coast was shorter than it was, Quintilius Varus took his army northward in 9

C.E. The locals were not at all ready to submit; the distance to be covered was not as short as he had thought; and he walked into a trap. Thousands of soldiers were killed because of the error.

Propaganda. Losses of this magnitude made deep cuts into an emperor's prestige. Success over the unfamiliar was a hallmark of rule, and without it an emperor could be on shaky ground. Playing upon the fascination with the unusual, emperors would stop short of explorative campaigns, yet communicate to the people that they had continued. Instead of conquering Britain, Caligula, the third emperor and the great-grandson of Augustus, collected seashells from the English Channel to show the folks back home in a triumph, passing them off as loot that was legitimately seized by force of arms. He also dressed up prisoners of war as hostages in order to suggest that these victories might provide an investment in future generations. Nero compelled an Armenian king, Tiridates, to travel to Rome to receive his crown, so that the world would know that he could make or break a foreign regime—never mind that he exercised little true control over Tiridates thereafter. Representation of conquest through false communications and fanciful reports of exploration were as important as reality.

Client Kingdoms. Although alliances that were struck with nonprovincial kingdoms on the Roman frontier may have been depicted, misleadingly, as military feats, they still held a strong geopolitical significance. The Romans continued to lend support to Roman-friendly regimes and to back resistance movements against their enemies. The result was a network of client kingdoms, whose monarchs owed informal, but powerful, obligations to the Romans; in some cases, they became more reliably Roman than formal provinces. Juba II, a former hostage from Numidia in North Africa, was made king of Mauretania and was a loyal vassal to Augustus throughout his nearly fifty-year reign. Several sons of Herod the Great, while ruling Judaea, were beholden to the imperial throne because of the favors granted their father and because they were protected from their domestic rivals by Roman intimidation. The Romans tried several times in the first century C.E. to install client-kingdoms in Parthia, further East, but had less success.

Infrastructure. Trajan revived the moribund Roman army when he took the throne in 98 C.E. No longer relying on the rhetoric of conquest, he sought it out with deliberate intent. His conquest of Dacia faced many of the same logistical obstacles encountered by Hannibal in his overland route to Italy, but Trajan's preparedness and wealth made his experience vastly different. Confronted with the raging current of the Danube, he had his engineer, Apollodorus, build a massive bridge in little time. He told his subjects back in Rome all about it on his column: a sculptured, narrative frieze that depicted the Dacian campaign spiraled up a massive trophy, standing in the bay between two libraries he had constructed. The empire reached its furthest extent under Trajan, and a period of relative stability ensued. Infrastructure throughout the empire improved at the behest of the emperors and local aristocrats, particularly during the reign of the well-traveled Hadrian, Trajan's successor. New bridges and roads were built, along with aqueducts, which channeled water to cities and made drier areas habitable by larger numbers of people. For some projects, the emperors paid; for others, the expense was shared by indigenous grandees. Euergetism, or the voluntary contribution of funds by the wealthy for projects that benefited the people at large, was widespread; the public works sponsored by Herodes Atticus, a wealthy Athenian of the second century, include an aqueduct in Troy, a covered theater on the south slope of the Acropolis in Athens, and a large fountain at Olympia.

The Concentration of Power. Political power became more concentrated in the person of the emperor; his orders radiated outward to the periphery like the spokes of a wheel. Communication through letters was of the essence in the success of this system. An imperial postal service conveyed messages quickly back and forth from the provinces, and imperial edicts were carved in stone and put up in public places for all to read. The emperor's decisions had the force of law. A vast, international bureaucracy was in place, which was intended to keep the docket functioning smoothly. Records of an emperor's daily routine mention that he typically rose early to work and spent a good amount of time hearing petitions or meeting with judicial advisers. The emperor personally certified *diplomata*, which were permits or licenses guaranteeing an individual's special rights and privileges, such as a soldier's veteran status or an ambassador's right to use certain imperial roads.

Internationalism. Tourism flourished in the empire, and the emperors themselves increasingly traveled for personal pleasure. Nero went to Greece to attend and participate in the Olympic Games; Hadrian toured the pyramids of Egypt. A travel writer, Pausanias, wrote a guide to Greece that suggested sight-seeing excursions and described the history of various landmarks. The Severan dynasty, which ruled from 193 to 235 C.E., is a vivid testimony of the ease of travel and the relaxing of the significance of territorial borders. The first emperor of the dynasty, Septimius Severus, was of North African descent; his wife, Julia Domna, was Syrian. Together they ruled from Italy, and Septimius raised their sons while on campaign in northern Europe. Multiethnic families such as these were common at every level of society, especially among the military, whose careers took them over great distances. The identity of "Roman" was changing; it came to have little to do with Italy proper. Caracalla, Septimius's son and successor, formalized the trend in 212 C.E. when he granted citizenship to all free residents of the provinces.

The Devolution of Power. The Roman prosperity, which had lasted for so long, began to break down in the third century C.E. Smaller kingdoms sought to break free from the empire and become independent. Zenobia, queen of Palmyra in the East, ruled apart from Rome from 267 to 272 C.E.; Postumus, a Roman general in Gaul, established a separate kingdom at roughly the same time. They, and others like them, were eventually subdued, but not without great disruption in the general workings of imperial administration and the economy. One emperor, Diocletian, recognized that the empire was simply too large and too complex for power to rest in the hands of one man. In 293 he created a tetrarchy—a hierarchy of four separate rulers—whereby the empire was divided into four parts, each with its own "emperor" or "vice-emperor." Diocletian, out to micromanage the empire back to solvency, redrew the boundaries of provinces and increased the size of government. His system was later overturned by Constantine, who reverted back to a system of one-man rule but retained the new provincial framework.

Fragmentation. Toward the end of the fourth century C.E., the Roman world gradually began to collapse under its own weight. Large non-Roman populations from the North were forced by their own difficulties—overpopulation, hunger, and invasion—to descend into Roman territories. At the battle of Adrianople in 378 C.E. they overwhelmed a Roman army that was sent to stop them; the emperor, Valens, was killed. Mass migrations continued apace thereafter; Goths, Vandals, Huns, and Franks crossed the Rhine and Danube Rivers in droves. In many cases they took up the preexisting Roman way of life: letters continued to be written, travelers continued to move from place to place, and Latin remained the dominant language. But the separate tribal identities of the European migrants persevered, and the empire was increasingly fragmented. Ever since its prehistory at the Tiber crossing, Rome had been an umbrella covering many different cultures and ethnicities; even after the empire broke into its constituent parts, the shadow still lingered.

TOPICS IN COMMUNICATION, TRANSPORTATION, AND EXPLORATION

DISCOVERIES

Philosophers. Ignorance of the landscape did not come about for the Romans from lack of trying. Travelers of all varieties—generals, merchants, tourists, and so forth—studied the geographic texts and theories that were available to them from Hellenistic scholars. Most of these earlier philosophers at least had realized that the world was round; Eratosthenes even calculated the length of the equator; his estimate of 252,000 stades (approximately 27,967 miles) is a little over the true measurement (24,902 miles), despite his complete ignorance of the Americas. Many of the Hellenistic geographers also believed that their plot of inhabited land was surrounded by a great ocean on all sides; technically correct if one thinks only of the three continents—Europe, Africa, and Asia—that each branch off from the central Mediterranean (central, that is, to their understanding). One influential account in particular was that of Ptolemy (Claudius Ptolemaeus) of the second century C.E., who carefully plotted his map on a sphere with the use of latitude and longitude lines as markers. His ideas were used in the Arab world and Byzantine empire for centuries after the fall of Rome. Dissenting opinions, which stated that the world was either flat or cylindrical were rare by the Roman period, but even in these cases, the theory of a huge perimeter ocean and a tripartite division of land, based loosely on what is now known to be three continents, prevailed.

Explorers. As early as the Republic, Romans were sponsoring expeditions to learn more about the territories beyond their scope. In the 140s B.C.E. the historian Polybius, with the financial support of Scipio Aemilianus, traveled beyond the Strait of Gibraltar to explore the West African coastline. He returned safely, but it is not known what he saw or how far he went. Later, during the Principate, emperors regularly supported missions of discovery in every corner of the empire. Augustus sent explorers to Dacia to learn the nature of the major rivers there, and he sent Juba II, the king of Mauretania, eastward to study

Parthia before his grandson, Gaius Caesar, was to embark on a campaign into the region. Juba also wrote of the Canary Islands in the Atlantic and the source of the Nile in Nubia. At the request of Claudius, Gaius Suetonius Paulinus traversed, for the first time, the Atlas Mountains in northwest Africa, and Nero had the regions around the Red Sea carefully mapped by his own praetorians. The explorative journeys often took the form of *periploi* (singular, *periplus*, a Latinization of the Greek *periplous*)—literally, "sailing around" an unknown territory.

Army Scouts. Roman legions, each with officers responsible for reconnoitering, gathered much of the reliable and systematic information about geography, as their forays into uncharted territory had the benefit of large numbers of witnesses (soldiers) and the strength of arms. The fact-finding voyages listed in the preceding paragraph each served a direct military purpose; to them one could add the explorations of Britain and the Shetland Islands by Agricola, the governor of Britain who ordered a battery of ships to circumnavigate the islands in 83–84 C.E. and to map the results. Epigraphic evidence shows that the position of *explorator*, or scout, became a regular post in a military career. They were organized into special units, each with their own centurions and, in the case of the land north of Hadrian's Wall, their own camp.

Merchants. The incentive of profits inspired many merchants to become the vanguard of Roman exploration, venturing abroad even before the army. Trade moved in both directions: Roman goods and currency were useful to non-Romans, while it was also affordable for Romans to acquire raw materials from abroad, and even fashionable to own a piece of a non-Roman culture. Julius Caesar, when he plotted a crossing of the English Channel from Gaul in 55 B.C.E., first turned for information to Roman merchants, whom, he said, had gone well beyond the coast. Much knowledge of India, especially its cycle of monsoons, was disseminated under Augustus by merchants who had conducted business there, and under Nero, merchants were

In 44 C.E., Pomponius Mela published a description of the lands that surround the Mediterranean Sea and what is now known to be the Atlantic coast of Western Europe. At times, he lists the sources of his information, but nevertheless is frequently vague or completely inaccurate. Such was the nature of Roman geography and the perpetual incentive for continued exploration.

The following excerpt from his work describes the waters and coasts of the Caspian Sea, which he erroneously believed was connected to the north Atlantic. The anxieties felt by his readers for the dangers of far-away places are obvious.

The Caspian Sea first breaks into the land like a river, with a strait as small as it is long, and after it has entered by its straight channel, the sea is diffused into three bays. Opposite its very mouth, it passes into the Bay of Hyrcania; on the left, into Scythian Bay; and on the right, into the one they call by the name of the whole, Caspian Bay. The sea as a whole is violent, savage, without harbors, exposed to storms everywhere, as well as crowded with sea-monsters more than any other sea is, and for all these reasons it is not fully navigable. To the right as you enter, the Scythian Nomads occupy the shores of the strait. To the interior, beside Caspian Bay, are the Caspians and the Amazons . . . . The forests also bear other fierce animals, but they even bear tigers—Hyrcanian ones, to be sure—a savage breed of wild animal so swift that they easily, and typically, track a mounted rider, even one passing at a distance; and they do it not once only but several times, even when the trail is retraced each time right from where it began. . . . For quite some time it was unclear what lay beyond the Caspian Bay, whether it was the same Ocean or a hostile, cold land that extended without a border and without end . . . Metellus reported it as follows: when [he] was proconsul of Gaul, certain Indians were presented to him as a gift by the king of the Boii. By asking what route they had followed to reach there, he learned that they had been snatched by storm from Indian waters, that they had traversed the intervening region, and that finally they had arrived on the shores of Germany. Therefore, the sea is continuous, but the rest of that same coast is frozen by the unremitting cold and is therefore deserted.

Source: *Pomponius Mela's Description of the World*, translated by F. E. Romer (Ann Arbor: University of Michigan Press, 1998).

the first to understand parts of northwestern Europe, owing to their quest for new sources of amber, a precious commodity in Roman jewelry manufacturing. After the Roman armies had established a foothold in certain territories, merchants often were the first nonmartial residents there. It was a risky endeavor: families of traders in North Africa were slaughtered by Jugurtha in 112 B.C.E. and in Asia Minor by Mithridates in 89–88 B.C.E. Hoards of Roman coins have been found in places strangely remote from the Roman center—from Britain, to Romania, to Sri Lanka.

Embassies and Diplomacy. The Romans might have gotten their information indirectly by waiting for and interrogating non-Romans who came to them. In the Republic, international diplomacy was well developed, and ambassadors from around the Mediterranean came to Rome to negotiate alliances or to plot betrayals. The Romans would not have passed on the chance to inquire about their native lands. According to Augustus's *Res gestae*, the emperor received ambassadors from India, China, Parthia, Armenia, Spain, Britain, and Germany, and the custom continued well into the empire. In 39 C.E. the emperor Caligula interrogated an embassy of Jews in Rome; he asked not just about their petition, but also about their cultural practices, such as their refusal to eat pork. Part of the diplomatic process in the ancient world was the exchange of young men and women between the center and the peripheral communities. A prominent non-Roman who might want to align himself with the new imperial power might send his son to Rome for an education, or offer a daughter or sister in marriage, or encourage other youths to fight for the Roman armies. From conversations and daily interactions with these individuals, the Romans could learn more about geography and foreign cultures. Women such as the Italian Thesmusa, who married the Parthian king Phraataces during the reign of Augustus, and the imperial princess Galla Placidia, who married the Gothic king Athaulf centuries later in 410 C.E., would have been valuable sources of knowledge to both sides. The German brothers Flavus and Arminius, who were recruited to the Roman soldiery and even rose through the ranks, could have taught their new comrades about aspects of German language, religion, and geography. When neighbors of the empire did not volunteer to submit such wards, the Romans might demand them and later use them for information. Juba II, a Numidian prince who was taken as a hostage when an infant, wrote a treatise on Africa that received wide distribution in the Roman world. Josephus, a Jewish general who was seized in the Jewish revolt at Jotapota, wrote a history of the Jews for Roman consumption.

Sources:

N. J. E. Austin and N. B. Rankov, *Exploratio: Military and Political Intelligence in the Roman World from the Second Punic War to the Battle of Adrianople* (London & New York: Routledge, 1995).

A. D. Lee, *Information and Frontiers: Roman Foreign Relations in Late Antiquity* (Cambridge & New York: Cambridge University Press, 1993).

DISCOVERIES: SYMBOLS OF THE UNKNOWN

Public Display. For most Roman citizens the only way to learn about the new discoveries made abroad was through the triumphal displays made by victorious generals upon their return from some exotic locale. The parades put forth not only the loot taken from the defeated but also descriptive media, such as paintings of the faraway lands and rivers, or placards with slogans describing the conquered. Prisoners of war and hostages would also take part, wearing the clothing of their native land and speaking among themselves in languages incomprehensible to their spectators. An understanding of the nature of this first outlay of new information helps the modern student to understand the Roman attitudes toward, and motivations for, exploration. The Arch of Titus, celebrating the sack of Jerusalem, shows a triumph in progress; the Jewish menora is immediately recognizable—an emblem not only of the Jews, but also of superiority of and physical taming by Rome over the unfamiliar.

Ethnography. Written texts also catered to this interest, and a proliferation of ethnographies in Rome can be matched against various major conquests. Texts that described the topography and habits of northern European civilizations were integral parts of Julius Caesar's explanations of his victories in Gaul and of Tacitus's laudatory biography of his father-in-law, Agricola, the governor of Britain. The fascination with the exotic was coupled with the fear of defeat. The result was a paradox of respect and loathing. Northern Europe was a depressingly bleak place of constant chill and its people, milk-drinking peasants (wine was viewed as the drink of the civilized). Yet, in the same breath, the historian expresses admiration for their courage. Easterners emerge as soft, feminine, and cowardly; however, they are educated and admire Greek learning. A Roman received mixed signals from ethnographies, which have more to do with their own ethnocentrism than with reality.

Poetry. Several popular songs of ancient Rome—metrical compositions that are read today as poetry, without music or singing—give a further indication of how the Romans, broadly defined, might have found out about the world at large. The conquest of Parthia and Armenia was frequently exploited as a literary theme by Augustan writers. Commissioned by Augustus, several poets implied that a great military victory had either already been achieved or was simply around the corner, just a matter of time. Horace proclaimed that Armenia had fallen to Rome and that Phraates was on his knees shortly after 20 B.C.E. Ovid, writing later in the *Fasti*, used the language of warfare and conquest: Italy was protected by the "powerful arms of Caesar," Parthian "bows had been broken," and their "swift horses" rendered useless. The *Ars amatoria* heralded the physical revenge to be wrought against Armenia by Gaius Caesar in 2 B.C.E., as he left to place Ariobarzanes as the new ruler; despite the previous recovery of the standards, the Parthians "will pay" (again) for their past crime against Crassus, they will be "conquered by arms," victory will belong to Gaius, and Augustus will be Mars incarnate. By all accounts, Parthia and Armenia had been thoroughly cowed by the *princeps*—evidence of his nearly unprecedented *auctoritas*.

Monuments. A Roman could also turn to monuments to find out more about non-Romans, both friends and enemies, but the information, of course, would be only one version of the truth. Physical memorials were just as much texts to be read as ethnographies, and as such, were equally susceptible to the propagandistic manipulation of their creators. The *Ara pacis* of Augustus (Altar of Peace) included portraits of young children in foreign dress, holding hands with adults in a procession. One wears the dress and ornaments of an eastern prince, and two more wear what seem to be Germanic costumes. Their happy inclusion in a Roman context not only informed viewers of the monument of their aspect, but also implied that their acceptance of Rome was peaceful and enthusiastic. The motif is repeated elsewhere in Augustan art; gold cups from the Italian village of Boscoreale show non-Romans happily hoisting up babies in offering to the emperor. But Augustus also showed foreigners in a negative light: a triumphal arch

---

BARBARIANS IN ROMAN EYES

Cassius Dio, like most historians from ancient Rome, included ethnographic descriptions of foreign civilizations, whether they had firsthand knowledge of them or not. In the first excerpt, he reports on the residents of Pannonia (roughly modern day Hungary) whom he had governed earlier in his career:

[T]hey are the most wretched of men. . . . They cultivate neither olives nor wine, except a very little and very bad at that, because they live most of their lives in the harshest winter . . . but they are considered the bravest men of whom we know. For they are spirited and murderous. . . . This I know, not just because I heard it or read about it, but I learned it also from experience when I governed them.

In the second excerpt, he describes the residents of Scotland, whom he could never have seen himself:

They live in wild and waterless mountains and desert, marshy plains, having no walls, cities or agriculture. . . . They live in tents, naked and barefoot, having the women in common, and raising all the children in common. They practice democracy for the most part, and they love to plunder. . . . They are able to bear hunger, cold, and all kinds of hardship, for they go down into the swamps and endure there for many days, having only their heads out of the water.

Sometimes, ethnographers clearly skew the representation of foreign regions, even when they know better. As Susan P. Mattern has pointed out, "[in the account of Pliny the Elder, who served in a Roman army in Germany,] the climate is described as unimaginably cold, though he must have experienced summer there."

Source: Susan P. Mattern, *Rome and the Enemy: Imperial Strategy in the Principate* (Berkeley: University of California Press, 1999).

The *Gemma Augustea,* a cameo depicting Rome and Tiberius, late first century B.C.E. (Kunsthistorisches Museum, Vienna)

celebrated the defeat of the Parthians and depicted them in their traditional dress and wielding their native weapons in an attitude of submission. A similar image of cultural difference comes in the column of Trajan, erected about a century after Augustus. A continuous band of sculptures spirals up the column, depicting Trajan's conquest of Dacia, modern-day Romania. Along the way it illustrates rivers, mountains, bridges, and other physical landmarks, as well as the Dacians themselves. This depiction is not what they really looked like, but rather how the emperor wanted them to look to the Romans: hoary, ragged, and defeated. At a less monumental level, individual sarcophagi were carved with scenes of warfare, with non-Romans cast in pathetic situations.

Coins and Gems. Roman currency largely echoed these images of conquest. Coins of Augustus show Parthians kneeling before him, and those of Trajan show him posing with one foot resting on the decapitated head of a Dacian. Cameos were decorated with similar images of despair and destitution on the part of the non-Romans. Artists frequently juxtaposed the defeated with peculiar animals. Coins celebrating the defeat of

Judaea show a crocodile in chains, and others marking the annexation of Arabia show a female personification of the region with a camel walking by her side. The empire was for show and for entertainment as much as it was for imperial power.

Exclusion and Inclusion. Romans, as they fiddled with the coins in their hands before making a payment, or as they walked among the urban monuments, or as they heard the popular songs of the day, would have learned about different peoples, places, and cultures in bits and pieces. Artists and writers tended to present their audiences with examples of the bizarre and the extraordinary. The average Roman would have been bombarded with a riot of images that, considered together, offered a confusing mixture of messages. Far-away places were, at times, beautiful and welcoming, yet at others, dangerous and foul. The Romans tolerated difference among their subjects but also reviled them as barbarians. An individual could only discover his/her own version of the truth through travel and firsthand inspection, which was widespread, but not universal, or he/she could arrange a measured and informed appraisal

Boscoreale cup showing the Emperor Augustus receiving Gallic children, early first century C.E. (Louvre, Paris)

of what they read in public and in private. The thrill of new things, and pursuit of them through exploration, was pushed to its very limits. Patriotic fervor and the limits of technology competed with the political benefits and financial profits of inclusion and the innate desire for new things. The cultural mélange of the Roman world was much like that of modern-day America, with all its enlightening advantages coexisting uneasily with its darkening suspicions.

Sources:

J. P. V .D. Balsdon, *Romans and Aliens* (Chapel Hill: University of North Carolina Press, 1979).

Carlin A. Barton, *The Sorrows of the Ancient Romans: The Gladiator and the Monster* (Princeton: Princeton University Press, 1993).

Niels Hannestad, *Roman Art and Imperial Policy* (Århus, Denmark: Århus University Press, 1986).

H. S. Versnel, *Triumphus: An Inquiry into the Origin, Development and Meaning of the Roman Triumph* (Leiden: Brill, 1970).

GEOGRAPHY

Maps. Any study of Roman history, particularly topics such as foreign policy, international relations, and multiculturalism, must begin from the assumption that the Romans had only a rudimentary understanding of where they were in relation to others. Their knowledge of geography—the distances between two points, the bend and flow of rivers, the compass directions among regions—was as limited as one might expect for a culture without access to aerial observation. The Romans did try to make maps of their empire, but none survive; what little is known about them suggests that they were terribly inaccurate. Nonetheless, some were posted in promi-

nent places. As early as 174 B.C.E. the Roman conqueror of Sardinia put up a map of the island in the Temple of Mater Matuta to illustrate his accomplishments. In the reign of Augustus, the general Agrippa had a map of the world painted in his public colonnade for curious onlookers to contemplate, as news of victory after victory piqued the interests of the untraveled citizens of the city. It was not a passive display; Agrippa's map served a political purpose: it was part of the propaganda campaign that glorified the new emperor as the unknown became known as a result of his deeds. The Peutinger table, a map of the world that dates to the thirteenth century but was made from a Roman copy, shows how a public map might look. Since the rectangle on which it was cast was low and broad—probably just like Agrippa's mural—the north/south axis is greatly compressed, and the east/west is stretched, so that the result is an elongated distortion of reality. By contrast, maps that covered a smaller, more manageable region were more accurate. A stone map of just the city of Rome survives from the third century C.E. (the so-called *forma urbis*, or "shape of the city"), whose conception of space in a two-dimensional abstraction is rendered with some precision.

Misconceptions. Narrative maps survive, where authors attempted to explain the position of cities, continents, and bodies of water with words. In these works ambiguities and mistakes abound. According to descriptions of northern Europe in Strabo, who wrote under Augustus, and Tacitus, who wrote a hundred years later under Trajan, the British isles were sandwiched *between*

With some questions of geography and mapping, the Romans might swear that they had it right: perhaps they had seen a particular region themselves, or they knew people who had been there, or they had read accounts from more than one author. Even so, the state of knowledge was never perfect, as can be seen in the following unequivocal assertion of the historian Tacitus that *he*, at last, will be the Roman who gives an accurate description of Britain:

Although the geographical position and the inhabitants of Britain have been described by many authors, I shall describe them once again, not to match my industry and ability against theirs, but because the conquest was only completed in this period. Where my predecessors relied on graces of style to make their guesswork sound attractive, I shall offer ascertained fact. Britain, the largest of the islands known to us Romans, is of such a size and so situated as to run parallel to the coast of Germany on the east and to that of Spain on the west, while to the south it actually lies within sight of Gaul. The general shape of Britain has been compared . . . to an elongated diamond or a double-headed axe. Such indeed is its shape south of Scotland, and so the same shape has been attributed to the whole. But when you go farther north you find a huge shapeless tract of country, jutting out to form what is actually the most distant coastline and failly tapering into a kind of a wedge. . . . The climate is wretched, with its frequent rains and mists, but there is no extreme cold. Their day is longer than in our part of the world. The nights are light, and in the extreme north so short that evening and morning twilight are scarcely distinguishable.

Tacitus's father-in-law was the governor of Britain, and he himself hailed from a Gallic family, yet he argued that Spain was *west* of Ireland. With the description of the weather, however, he perhaps could not be further from the truth!

Source: Tacitus, *The Agricola and the Germania*, translated by H. Mattingly (London: Penguin, 1948).

Spain and France, so that sailing due west from Ireland, one would eventually run aground in the Basque region. Julius Caesar, plotting a campaign against Parthia in the East shortly before his assassination, believed that if he set out from Macedonia, keeping the Black Sea on his right and conquering indigenous peoples as he went, he would reach Parthia through a shortcut. He would have grossly underestimated not only the length of such a route but also the numbers of people to defeat and the sharply mountainous terrain in which to pull it off. One imagines that Hannibal had made similar errors of judgment in his trek to Italy when, two hundred years prior, he led a cohort of desert elephants through the snowy Alps. The history of Roman foreign wars is riddled with misconcep-

tions that jeopardized thousands of soldiers' lives. A Roman general lost three legions in Germany because he misunderstood the depth of the Black Forest, and Strabo tells of a general in Arabia who was deliberately misled by the natives to take a path through a dry and impossible desert, which resulted in the gradual annihilation of his troops through starvation, dehydration, guerilla attack, and disease.

Sources:
O. A. W. Dilke, *Greek and Roman Maps* (Ithaca, N.Y.: Cornell University Press, 1985).

Susan P. Mattern, *Rome and the Enemy: Imperial Strategy in the Principate* (Berkeley: University of California Press, 1999).

Claude Nicolet, *Space, Geography, and Politics in the Early Roman Empire* (Ann Arbor: University of Michigan Press, 1991).

IMPERIAL ADMINISTRATION

Legal Texts. Another common type of public inscription is the legal text, whose author might be the Roman senate or, during the Principate, the emperor himself. For particularly thorny matters of public law, a provincial community might appeal to the emperor for a decision. Whether or not they accompanied their petition to Rome, the request was read out loud in a hearing. The emperor would not, from such a distance, be able to verify the facts of the case, but he would nonetheless make a decision based on stipulations concerning the true circumstances, which would be referred to the local courts. Having made his ruling, the emperor might specifically order that it be carved in stone and set up in a public place in the community in question. Such rescripts, as the replies were called, thereafter had the force of law in analogous cases, until the decision was overruled or modified by a later rescript, or imperial edict. The practice was in use as early as Augustus but became more prevalent under Hadrian; many rescripts were collected by jurists as codes of law.

Edicts and Decrees. Similar in form and content were the laws that the emperor or senate issued on their own initiative without having first heard an appeal from below. Laws such as these could pertain to the empire at large or to specific communities, in which case their publication would be more limited. Dates of publication on some of the edicts show the speed, or lack thereof, with which they traveled. An edict of the emperor Caracalla, posted in Italy in July of 212, was copied in Egypt in January of the next year and not finally installed until February. In 303 the emperor Diocletian issued an edict concerning the illegality of Christianity in February, which was set up in Palestine in March of that year and in Africa in June. Edicts took time to travel; the process might seem slow, but in the ancient world, with limited information technology, the delivery time was a result of careful organization and extreme relative efficiency. The emperor was in close contact with the administration of every corner of his realm, and a resident even of the remotest province would be expected to keep his eyes open for new decrees.

Diplomata. Certificates and permits, issued by the imperial authority and inscribed on thin bronze sheets,

Even today, with modern information technology, rumor has an inestimable power. Vergil noted its features and horrors during the reign of Augustus, when he described how the story (Rumor = *Fama* in Latin) of Dido and Aeneas's secret love affair become known among the citizens of Carthage:

Rumor instantly moved through large Libyan cities. No other evil we know is faster than Rumor, thriving on speed and becoming stronger by running. Small and timid at first, then borne on a light air, she flits over ground while hiding her head in a cloud-top. Mother Earth, they say, deeply provoked by the Sky-Gods, bore this daughter last: Enceladus' sister and Coeus', light on her feet and agile at flying, but broad and fearful: a monster whose bodily plumage matches her numerous leering eyes (amazing to hear of), her many mouths, upraised ears and jabbering accents. At night she flaps between earth and sky in the shadows, buzzing—her eyes won't yield to the pleasure of sleeping. By day she squats on a house roof like a watchman high in his tower, scaring eminent townsmen, telling some truth but clinging to lies and distortion. Now she filled people with various gossip, gladly singing both her fact and her fiction: Aeneas had sprung from a Trojan bloodline and come here, lovely Dido accepting the man as her husband, now they passed a long winter together in pleasure, thralls of a shameless desire, forgetting their kingship. The Goddess spread her dirt on the lips of the people.

Source: Virgil, *The Aeneid/Virgil,* translated by Edward McCrorie (Ann Arbor: University of Michigan Press, 1995).

---

were used for a variety of purposes. The word, *diploma* (plural, *diplomata*), meaning folded in two, refers to how they were closed and bound to maintain a measure of security and privacy for the owner. They might allow individuals to use the official imperial postal service and requisition horses and other supplies, or grant other types of privileges. Soldiers who had been legitimately discharged from the army were entitled to certain rights as veterans. In order to certify a former soldier's status, *diplomata* would be issued to them upon their release from duty, listing the promotions and positions of the man's career. They would become a passport of sorts, which a veteran would carry on his person and guard closely.

The News. Not all public communication was written on stone or bronze. Public announcements that had only a temporary value, such as the time and location of a certain public meeting, or the news of certain events from abroad, would be made on removable posters or circulated in brief pamphlets. The *Acta diurna* (Daily Happenings), for example, were placards that were set up in the forum of Rome, serving the same function as newspapers do today. While scholars know these documents existed (the historian Tacitus's sources had used them in their histories), none survived from antiquity, owing to their transcription on perishable materials. One exception, however, are the commentaries of Julius Caesar on his campaign in Gaul, which were copied down by and circulated among enough people that the texts have survived to the modern day. The texts, written by Caesar himself, or else closely monitored by him, were reports that the general sent back to the people of Rome from his campaign. They described what he had done, how he had done it, and how the deed enhanced the greater glory of Rome. They told the Romans what the unknown people of the north were like, whom they worshiped, what they ate, and what they wore. They are perfect illustrations of the kinds of messages that the people of Rome might receive from their leaders and the state of information about the unknown.

Imperial Post. The physical need to transport important documents quickly and efficiently, in order to maintain the empire, led to the creation of an official postal service at the order of Augustus. Called the *cursus publicus,* it carried not just news of appeals and decisions, but of troop movements or other crises that needed attending to. It was made up of roads, with marking posts describing destination and distance, and inns or stations where the traveler could change horses. Later in its development, officials began to use the network for uses other than sending messages. Supply trains traveled along the roads, and individual governors, with special permits, might use them for personal reasons. Pliny the Younger, for example, issued an emergency permit for his wife to visit a grieving aunt in the early second century C.E.

Rumor and Hearsay. Arguably, most information that passed among individual Romans was conveyed by the much less reliable, less organized, and less sensible medium of rumor. In a world without the instantaneous broadcast of words, let alone pictorial images such as is common with modern technologies, stories had a way of changing as they

Coin depicting the personification of the *Via Traiana,* a highway built by order of Trajan, circa 109 C.E.
(Hunterian Museum, Glasgow)

spread over great distances. Two modern metaphors apply: they might grow in some aspects, like snowballs, or they might shrink in others, like the moss that falls from rolling stones. The falsity of rumors might have major political ramifications. In the 70s and 80s C.E., it was spread about that Nero had not really died, but had gone into hiding and was now gathering troops to make a run at the throne. One man, claiming to be Nero, went a long way before he was ultimately exposed as an impostor and removed; provincials who had never seen the emperor but for his idealized portraits on coins or public monuments could not possibly have known better. The Romans themselves understood the vagaries of the phenomenon of rumor, and one author developed his own metaphor: rumor was a great, ugly bird, who had eyes hidden under every feather and who grew as it flew; much more eloquent, elaborate, and appropriately terrifying than snowballs and rolling stones.

Sources:

Fergus Millar, *The Emperor and the Roman World: 31 BC–AD 337* (Ithaca, N.Y.: Cornell University Press, 1977).

O. F. Robinson, *The Sources of Roman Law: Problems and Methods For Ancient Historians* (London & New York: Routledge, 1997).

LOGISTICS OF TRAVEL AND TRANSPORTATION

Space and Time. The Roman empire was roughly the same size as the continental United States. The distance from the far northeastern corner to the southwestern one, when the empire was at its height, was roughly the same as from Boston to Los Angeles, with one big and obvious difference: the Romans had in their center a huge sea, the Mediterranean, meaning, literally, "in the middle of the lands." This large body of water, with its predictable periods of relative calm during the summer and its lack of tides, greatly facilitated movement within the empire. The central location of the capital city, in the middle of a peninsula that jutted out into the middle of the sea, makes it no surprise that the Romans frequently referred to the Mediterranean as *mare nostrum* (our sea). They were never more than a two-week voyage from any coastal location under their domain, provided the weather cooperated. Overland travel was much slower; the furthest one could go, comfortably, on a given day would have been about forty miles. Travel for armies, with their baggage, equipment, and large numbers of soldiers, was more cumbersome; they could make no more than twenty-five miles a day. Under pressure, a single messenger, riding on horseback and stopping along the way to change horses, could, at most, cover 150 miles in a day, as one did in 9 C.E. in order to report to Augustus the destruction of his army in Germany.

Efficiency. From just these basic pieces of geographical information, one could almost guess the history of Roman travel and transportation. The importance of seafaring was paramount, and the problems of overland travel were severe, and at times, devastating. If an army on campaign in, for example, Parthia, had suffered a defeat, it would take about five days to carry the message to the coast and then fifteen more days to get it to the emperor in Rome. If he responded immediately, the emperor's orders would return in slightly less time, owing to the direction of the winds; that would mean a total of about thirty-five days after the initial defeat before the emperor's intentions could be known. A neighboring army from the area, since it was closer than the emperor, may have found out about the problem sooner and marched to relieve them, but even so, it would have taken weeks for help to arrive. Early on, the Romans recognized the threats posed by the obstacles of travel and responded to them with the same efficiency and administration that was in evidence for their modes of communication. Their roads, bridges, harbors, and aqueducts were miracles of ancient engineering and are a vivid testament of their careful planning and organization. Though slow by modern standards, the Romans were able to travel greater distances more quickly than people in any other previous period of human history. The relative ease of travel was partly responsible for the cultural mélange that so defines the Roman empire.

Sources:

Lionel Casson, *Travel in the Ancient World* (London: Allen & Unwin, 1974).

Tim Cornell and John Matthews, *Atlas of the Roman World* (New York: Facts on File, 1982).

OVERLAND TRAVEL

Roads. Contrary to the popular saying, all roads did not actually lead to Rome. The empire had a web of highways in almost every province, connecting cities and army camps, stretching across deserts, winding through mountains, and plunging deep into forests. Like President Dwight D. Eisenhower's system of interstate highways in 1950s America, Roman roads were built with security in mind; they allowed the free and efficient movement of armies. Army engineers designed them while on campaign, and soldiers, during times of peace, constructed them, thus keeping busy and fit when not on campaign. Roads were also built as populist measures that assisted in general travel and trade. In building the *Via appia* in 312 B.C.E., Appius Claudius was making it possible for rural populations to participate in the civic life of the city, as well as employing large crowds of workers who would remain indebted to him thereafter. Augustus was particularly proud of his roads; he set up a gilded milestone in the forum, which recorded the distances from that spot to the most important cities of the empire. The average width of a major country road was about twelve feet, which provided ample room for Roman carts, averaging four feet in width, to pass each other. Limestone paving required extensive organization for the quarrying and transport of stones. It was not universal; packed gravel often sufficed.

City Streets. Urban streets were built in much the same way as country roads, with large, flat paving stones. They were narrow and alleylike, as shops and houses were built up to their very edge. Gullies were dug along their sides in order to collect aboveground sewage; raised stones at the corners of city blocks gave pedestrians the means to step over the offal. There were few wide-open spaces in the

The Bridge of Tiberius at Rimini, early first century C.E.

ancient city, and traffic on the city streets could become tight, particularly when large stone buildings were being constructed in the city center, which required laborers and suppliers to clog up throughways already crowded with litter and hurrying pedestrians. The satirist Juvenal complains of the noises of wagons and stonemasons and the danger of being crushed under collapsed carts of heavy building materials (3.236–261). The streets were dark at night; the fire necessary to keep them well lit must have posed a significant fire risk, given the closeness of buildings.

Bridges and Tunnels. Roads outside the cities had to deal with what could sometimes be tricky terrain. Bridges could range from small wooden affairs to huge, complicated structures, set atop series of trademark Roman arches and traversing deep river gorges and valleys. The first stone bridge in Rome was the pons Aemilius, built in 179 B.C.E.; it was soon followed by the pons Mulvius in 109 B.C.E. and the pons Fabricius in 62 B.C.E. All bridges had Janus as their patron god, whose two faces, looking in opposite directions, vividly represented their function. Some were expensive to build, and their sponsors took great pride in their accomplishments; Trajan's bridge across the Danube gets attention on his coinage and in the histories of Dio: "it has 20 piers of stone, 150 feet high, excluding the foundations, and 60 feet wide." The bridge was dismantled shortly after it was built to keep the Dacians from attacking the Roman side, but many other stone bridges are still in use

throughout the former Roman provinces. Sometimes, rather than succumbing to the landscape, the Romans took great expense in altering it to fit their needs. Near the Bay of Naples, the emperor Trajan had an entire cliff chopped up and removed to make way for a much-needed new road. When the geography was more accommodating, Roman roads were easier to build but were still technically sophisticated; in a level part of Germany, a Roman road extends for miles without even the slightest bend.

Conveyances. The variety of wagons and chariots for use by merchants and the military matches the array of different kinds of ships in the Roman world. The basic wagon, with its tall wooden wheels, shallow bed, and yoke for horses or oxen, is a universal design that was used to carry commercial cargo or supplies for legions on campaign. Chariots on two wheels—and thus faster, lighter, and more maneuverable—were used in warfare for high-ranking officers. They also had a high entertainment value; chariot-racing in the circus (a long racetrack) drew huge numbers of spectators. Luxury conveyances transported the wealthy both within the city and along country roads. A special chariot, decked out in royal colors and drawn by special horses, carried victorious generals in their triumphal processions. The *carpentum* used by the empress Livia, the wife of Augustus, and other women of the imperial dynasty was reproduced on coins. Some may have chosen to travel by sedans, which were chairs or chambers set

Some time in the second half of the first century B.C.E., the poet Horace made the journey from Rome to Brundisium. He later wrote a verse account of his trip in a book of Satires, in which he lampooned, among others, the slaves and boatmen, the annoying animals along the way, and his fellow travelers, some of whom he liked and some of whom he despised. The following excerpt is just the first twenty-nine lines of an immensely entertaining tale, describing not only what an Italian journey might be like, but the attitudes of the travelers, as well:

Departing mighty Rome, I took lodging / in a modest inn at Aricia. / My companion there was the rhetorician / Heliodorus, by all odds the most / learned of the Greeks. Thence to Forum Appi / boiling with boatmen and rascally tavern-keepers. / Lazily we spent two days on this stretch alone. / A single day would have sufficed for swifter souls. / Here, owing to the water which was villainous / I declare war against my stomach, waiting / (and not with good will, either) while my companions / roistered over their dinner. Already night / was preparing to spread its shadows over the earth / and sprinkled the sky with stars and constellations. / And now the slaves are shouting insults at the boatmen, / the boatmen at the slaves; '—Tie up here! / Pile in three hundred! Ahoy! That's / plenty now!' — While they are dickering over fares, / harnessing the mule, an hour slips by. / Impossible to sleep what with cursed / mosquitoes buzzing, frogs croaking from the swamp, / while the boatmen, drunk with too much wine, / together with a passenger sing in wretched / competition of their distant loves. At last / the weary voyager begins to snooze, and / the lazy boatman turns his mule out to graze, / tying his reins to a rock. Then, supine, / he too stretches out and snores away.

Source: Horace, *The Complete Odes and Satires of Horace,* translated by Sidney Alexander (Princeton: Princeton University Press, 1999).

A coin depicting *a carpentum,* or imperial cart, from the reign of Domitian in the late first century C.E. (Hunterian Museum, Glasgow)

kinds of grain from the surrounding farmland, and fish from the river. The position of the town on the border between two major empires—two different worlds, in effect—led to the frequent and regular passage of people from various ethnic backgrounds, and as a result, the remains of the city preserve an international and even cosmopolitan feel. Several religions were practiced in close proximity to each other within the mere four square miles of the town. A Jewish synagogue is a few blocks down from a Christian church, which is a few blocks down from a temple to the eastern god, Mithras. A short distance away was a shrine to the imperial cult, as well as temples to both Zeus, a conventional Greco-Roman deity, and Atargatis, a native eastern goddess. The town is a vivid illustration of multicultural quality of the empire, aided and abetted by the revolutionary ease of travel and communication.

Discomfort. Travel over long distances, according to many sources, was not pleasant. The poet Horace, again, wrote of an overland journey between Rome and Brundisium in the south of Italy, which was supremely uncomfortable. Not only had he to deal with poor water quality; loud frogs that kept him awake; the monotonous, nonperishable foods that one would pack for days of travel, but with boredom and the unbroken company of overbearing fellow travelers. Long journeys were dangerous in that people might be susceptible to unsanitary conditions or to illnesses in a strange land, to which their bodies were unaccustomed. The student of ancient Rome frequently comes across famous figures who died of sicknesses while away from home or en route: for example, the emperors Augustus, Marcus Aurelius, and Septimius Severus, and the poet Vergil. A traveler had to plan carefully, since he/she might be on the road for days before encountering an adequate

across poles and carried by slaves. In most cases, however, animals provided the labor: horses, cattle, elephants, and camels. The poet Horace even talks of children who hooked miniature toy chariots to teams of mice.

Dura-Europos. Towns that were located on major trading routes stood to gain much from the economy of overland trade. Those that controlled a bridge or passage along a certain road might charge a direct toll to all users, or simply benefit from the services and markets that travelers required. A perfect example of the latter is the desert town of Dura-Europos, located on the Euphrates River and on the caravan route between Palmyra and Parthia. It was a trading post and military station of the Romans until 257 C.E., when it fell to the Persians; its ruins were covered over by the sands of the desert until it was excavated by archaeologists in the 1930s. The town appears to have supported a diverse economy, with evidence of trading in silks and other cloths, bronze tools and implements, slaves, various

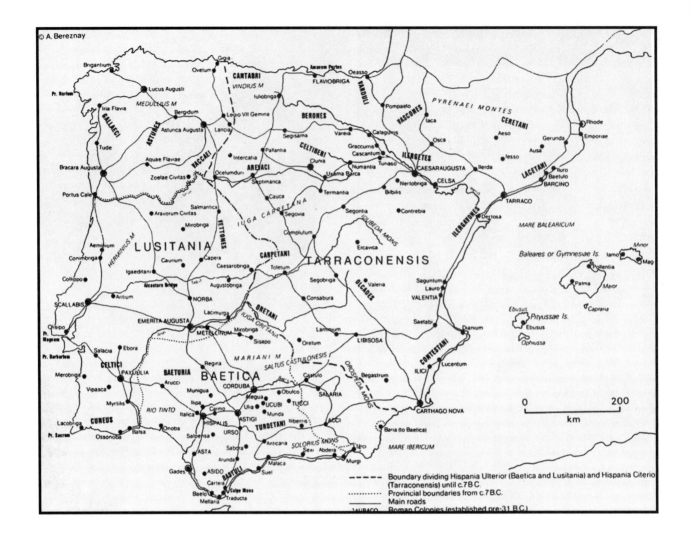

Map of Roman roads in Spain, circa 200 C.E. (from Richard J.A. Talbert, ed., *Atlas of Classical History,* 1985)

market for supplies. A papyrus from Egypt, dating to the early fourth century, preserves the various daily expenditures made by a man named Theophanes on a round-trip overland journey from Egypt to Antioch in Syria. His purchases include food, not only for himself but also for slaves and animals, as well; he also bought nonedible supplies: wood for building fires and snow for chilling his wine (making the most of what Horace considered an unappealing situation).

Bandits. Just as seafarers had to contend with pirates, overland travelers risked confrontations with bandits. These criminals could be as carefully organized and numerous as pirates; one example is the bandit named Bulla in the reign of Septimius Severus, who planned his attacks well in advance by using information about an individual traveler's itinerary. Stories of the violence of bandits could be gruesome; the *Boukoloi* of Egypt allegedly practiced human sacrifice and cannibalism. Sometimes those who are classified as bandits in ancient sources were actually rebels who disliked Roman rule; their activities were not so much robberies for personal gain as guerilla tactics employed in pursuit of freedom. "Bandits" such as these often required the

attention of Roman armies in full-blown campaigns. The punishment for captured robbers was frequently crucifixion along the very roads they terrorized.

Sources:

Lucinda Dirven, *The Palmyrenes of Dura-Europos: A Study of Religious Interaction in Roman Syria* (Boston: Brill, 1999).

Ray Laurence, *The Roads of Roman Italy: Mobility and Cultural Change* (London & New York: Routledge, 1999).

Colin O'Connor, *Roman Bridges* (Cambridge & New York: Cambridge University Press, 1993).

Brent Shaw, "Bandits in the Roman Empire," *Past and Present,* 105 (November 1984): 3–52.

PRIVATE CORRESPONDENCE

Letter Writing. Not all correspondence was meant for public consumption; the sending and receiving of messages in private also flourished in ancient Rome. Some writers kept their letters and later published them, so that, from a vantage point centuries later, one can peer into the daily lives of even apolitical figures, whom most primary sources ignore. Perusing some of the letters that survive from antiquity, a modern reader might be reminded of the range of his/her own correspondence, whether by letters or e-mail. Private correspondence from Rome covered many of the same areas: requests to purchase particular items on credit, wishes for a happy birthday, condolences for relatives of the deceased, descriptions of a new house, recommendations of one friend to another, and general gossip and rumor. If the sender was a high-ranking official, he might get to use the imperial post; otherwise, letters would be given to any traveler who seemed reliable and who was headed in the direction of the intended recipient. The texts would be sealed with a waxen impression that was unique to the sender, impressed with a signet ring. These letters are a treasure trove for historians who want to find out more about ordinary aspects of the daily life of ancient Rome in realms other than politics, the law, or diplomacy (although they preserve information for these areas, as well).

Cicero. The most prolific of correspondents whose works survive is the orator and statesman of the late Republic, Cicero (Marcus Tullius Cicero). His letters span a twenty-year career following his consulship in 63, the earliest being from 62 B.C.E. and the latest being from 43, just before his execution. They discuss the politics of the day, and demonstrate his pride and success as a former consul who had risen from humble origins to the highest office of the land. In the heady days, he was ordering works of art to be purchased in Greece, discussing works of literature with friends, and commenting on the suitors of his daughter, Tullia. Twice Cicero had to spend time abroad: first, as an exile in Macedonia, and later, as a governor of Cilicia. Exile and provincial assignments are plentiful in Roman history, but it is not until one reads the letters of Cicero that one can develop an appreciation for what life abroad was like for a man of Cicero's station. In both cases, he dearly missed Rome and expressed an eagerness to return. His letters were directed not just to his political associates, but also to his wife, Terentia, whose letters mainly concern the family's financial situation. From exile, Cicero bemoaned his absence from his former life. Perhaps somewhat bombastically, he complained that writing was difficult because his tears were excessive and made it difficult to function.

Pliny the Younger. Another active letter writer, coming some 150 years after Cicero, was Pliny the Younger, a friend of the emperor Trajan and an eventual governor of Bithynia in Asia Minor. Again, in his letters one has a multidimensional source for a Roman's private life; they cover a broad range of topics. He wrote to the historian Tacitus to register his eyewitness account of the eruption of Vesuvius; with another friend he shared a ghost story about a haunted house in Athens; he wrote to Aefulanus Marcellinus, otherwise unattested, to console him on the death of a thirteen-year-old girl, the daughter of a mutual friend. By far his most-famous epistolary exchange was with the emperor himself, asking him for advice on how to handle Christians who refused to sacrifice to the emperor. Many of his letters, however, are more mundane. His works include formulaic letters of recommendation, where he

THE VINDOLANDA TABLETS

In 1973 several Latin letters were found in the most unlikely of places—a damp excavation of Vindolanda on Hadrian's Wall in Britain. Almost all of ancient writing on perishable materials, up to that year, had been found in Egypt, where the dry climate was naturally conducive to the preservation of such documents. But peculiar, anaerobic conditions of certain layers of deposits at Vindolanda allowed for the survival of these letters. Further excavations in the 1980s and 1990s have yielded more fragments that now number in the thousands.

The most famous letter from the collection has to do with an invitation to a party:

Claudia Severa to her Lepidina greetings. On the third day before the Ides of September, sister, for the day of the celebration of my birthday, I give you a warm invitation to make sure that you come to us, to make the day more enjoyable for me by your arrival, if you are present. Give my greetings to your Cerialis. My Aelius and my little son send him their greetings. [second hand] I shall expect you, sister. Farewell, sister, my dearest soul, as I hope to prosper, and hail. [back to first hand] To Sulpicia Lepidina, wife of Cerialis, from Severa.

Source: Alan K. Bowman, *Life and Letters on the Roman Frontier: Vindolanda and Its People* (New York: Routledge, 1998).

might return the favors of an associate by encouraging a high-ranking official to hire his son.

Other Senatorial Writers. These letters are not the kinds of messages that belong on stone, destined to last for ages. Sometimes the letters preserve a slice of life that their authors may not have expected or wished to last for posterity. When Fronto and Marcus Aurelius wrote to each other, they both frequently complained of various pains and ailments throughout their bodies, betraying the hypochondria of one of the most memorable Roman emperors. More weighty concerns, however, are conveyed in the letters of Symmachus, a senator in Rome in the fourth century C.E. As Rome became increasingly Christianized, Symmachus, an old-style pagan, had cause to worry about the demise of his religion. One of his most-famous letters is an appeal to the emperor not to allow the altar of the goddess Victory to be taken down. More than two hundred years after Pliny sought to define the status of Christianity through his letters, Symmachus was endeavoring to limit it through the same medium.

The Vindolanda Archive. The largest cache of *original* letters written in Latin (all the correspondence of Cicero, Pliny, and others copied and recopied many times over the centuries) was found at Vindolanda, a Roman fort in Britain. The letters were written with ink on thin wooden tablets, and they provide a window into the types of day-to-day activities that would require letter writing. Since they are in a fragmen-

Pompeiian wall painting of a husband and wife with writing utensils, early first century C.E. (Museo Archeologico Nazionale, Naples)

The Epigraphic Habit. Inscriptions, chiseled in stone, were a highly visible and durable means of conveying information to the general public. The process of writing in stone or bronze, or on any other hard and permanent medium, was a well-advanced science in Rome; more than three hundred thousand inscriptions survive today, a fraction of what originally existed, and the study of them is called epigraphy. They range in length from one or two words to long passages that would fill many pages of modern publications; one of the longest, a philosophical text of Diogenes of Oenoanda, was carved on stone tablets that stretched for eighty-seven yards. So prevalent was the practice, and so formulaic was its aspect, that the Romans have been said to function according to an epigraphic habit that outpaced earlier civilizations, including the Greeks, particularly during the turn of the second century C.E. A widespread expectation prevailed that important documents were to be cast in stone and in accordance with certain patterns and language. Like any other kind of text, inscriptions had an author, or group of authors, and an audience. The audience for an inscription was simple: it included any literate passerby who chose to stop and read it, or illiterates who asked someone to read it for them. The authors of inscriptions were, of course, more specific, and a wide range of people might engage in epigraphy, regardless of their social position or ethnic origins. Their access to the reading population depended only on the location and prominence of their carved, immobile texts.

Tombstones. The bulk of public inscriptions that survive are funerary epitaphs for the deceased. These works were set up outside of tombs, which themselves were typically positioned along a well-trafficked road outside of the sacred boundary of the city. They could take the form of conventional slabs, such as are common in modern cemeteries, or they could be written on altars, upon which offerings to the spirits of the dead were made. The more busy the thoroughfare, the more valuable was the funerary real estate. The *Via appia*, leading south from Rome, was a popular site for memorials early in the Republic, and its tombs have yielded some of the oldest Latin epitaphs. The clan of the Cornelii Scipiones, which produced several generals and consuls, including Scipio Africanus of the Second Punic War (218–201 B.C.E.), had a complex of tombs there, beginning, at least, in the third century B.C.E. Their epigraphic dedications are written in meter and some are addressed to the Roman people generally, using the second person plural. Most funerary inscriptions share certain characteristics, in keeping with a basic pattern, no matter the time period or location. Authors of the memorials would usually record the age of the deceased, often down to the number of months and days; his/her career and occupation, including the most significant promotions and accomplishments; the children or other family members who remained; and perhaps a description of the deceased's personality or moral rectitude. By

tary state, it can be difficult to determine their message or purpose, but lists of food and clothing appear to be supply inventories or requisitions. Some have specific military applications: records of the state of the native population, requests for leave, and reports to superiors. There is also a letter between brothers about money and mutual friends, and one letter preserves an invitation to a birthday party.

Curse Tablets. Letters, like tombstone inscriptions, could carry messages between the realms of the living and the dead, the mortal and the divine: archaeologists have found many lead tablets on which the writer has appealed to some supernatural spirit to harm an adversary in some way. They make reference to a variety of conflicts, including athletic competitions and law court disputes. The sheets, called *defixiones*, were folded and pierced with a nail and then tossed into wells or buried in the ground. Magic incantations were thought to be more effective if written down and not merely spoken. In all areas of life, the Romans, in keeping with their epigraphic habit, felt compelled to give substance, literally, to their language. To the Roman mind, words had real power; written evidence throughout the Roman world shows that they sought to harness this power through writing.

Sources:

Alan K. Bowman, *Life and Letters on the Roman Frontier: Vindolanda and Its People* (New York: Routledge, 1994).

Cicero, *Cicero's Letters to His Friends*, translated by D. R. Shackleton Bailey (Harmondsworth, U.K. & New York: Penguin, 1978).

Finley Hooper and Matthew Schwartz, *Roman Letters: History from a Personal Point of View* (Detroit: Wayne State University Press, 1991).

Augustus's epitaph is a prime example, writ large, of the formulae that typically appeared on Roman tombstones. The style is prosaic and clipped, and the confidence that it exudes is unabashed.

At the age of nineteen on my own responsibility and at my own expense I raised an army, with which I successfully championed the liberty of the republic when it was oppressed by the tyranny of a faction. . . . I drove into exile the murderers of my father, avenging their crime through tribunals established by law; and afterwards, when they made war on the republic, I twice defeated them in battle. . . . When foreign peoples could safely be pardoned I preferred to preserve rather than to exterminate them. . . . I captured 600 ships, not counting ships smaller than triremes. . . . In my triumphs nine kings or children of kings were led before my chariot. At the time of writing I have been consul thirteen times and am in the thirty-seventh year of tribunician power. The dictatorship was offered to me by both senate and people in my absence and when I was at Rome, . . . but I refused it. I did not decline in the great dearth of corn to undertake the charge of the corn-supply, which I so administered that within a few days I delivered the whole city from apprehension and immediate danger at my own cost and by my own affairs. At that time the consulship was offered to me, to be held each year for the rest of my life, and I refused it. . . . I restored the Capitol and the theater of Pompey, both works at great expense without inscribing my own name on either. I restored the channels of the aqueducts, which in several places were falling into disrepair through age, and I brought water from a new spring into the aqueduct called Marcia, doubling the supply. . . . In my seventh consulship I restored the Via Flaminia from the city as far as Rimini, together with all bridges except the Mulvian and the Minucian. . . . I gave three gladiatorial games in my own name and five in that of my sons and grandsons; at these some 10,000 men took part in combat. Twice in my own name and third time in that of my grandson I presented to the people displays by athletes summoned from all parts. . . . I made the sea peaceful and freed it of pirates.

Source: P. A. Brunt and J. M. Moore, eds., *Res gestae divi Augusti: The Achievements of the Divine Augustus* (London: Oxford University Press, 1967).

way of example, the following excerpt from an inscription from Rome demonstrates the kinds of attributes that one might want remembered, as well as the conversational, almost casual, nature of communication between the realms of the dead and the living, as preserved on stone:

Stranger, my message is short. Stand by and read it through. Here is the unlovely tomb of a lovely woman. Her parents called her Claudia by name. She loved her husband with all her heart. She bore two sons; of these she leaves one on earth; under the earth she has placed the other. She was charming in converse, yet gentle in bearing. She kept house, she made wool. That's my last word. Go your way.

Another example, taken from the *Via appia*, demonstrates the careful guarding of rights to use the tomb by others:

Stranger, stop and turn "your gaze towards this hillock on your left," which holds the bones of a poor man "of righteousness and mercy and love." Wayfarer, I ask you to do no harm to his memorial. Gaius Atilius Euhodus, freedman of Serranus, a pearl merchant of the Via Sacra is buried in this memorial. Wayfarer, good-bye. By last will and testament: it is not permitted to convey into or bury in this memorial anyone other than those freedmen to whom I have given and bestowed this right by last will and testament.

The *Res gestae*. One career inscription has received considerable attention from historians because of the honoree. The *Res gestae* (the Accomplishments), often called "the queen of Latin inscriptions," is a long description of the deeds of the first emperor, Augustus, written in a first person, autobiographical style. It had a broad readership: the original was set up in Rome outside the emperor's new family tomb, which he had constructed in the middle of a large public park, and copies of it were distributed throughout the provinces and translated into different languages. The inscription details Augustus's conduct in the recent war against Mark Antony and enumerates the foreign enemies he had conquered or subdued. It also discusses the benefactions of the emperor, from major buildings to public gladiatorial combats, for which he had paid from his personal funds for the enjoyment of the people. The object was to impress all readers, from all walks of life, with the stature and magnanimity of their leader, regardless of whether it was true or not.

Auctoritas **and Propaganda.** Prestige counted for a lot in antiquity; the Latin term, *auctoritas,* loosely translated as "authority," stood for a virtue that carried real political significance. The level of one's *auctoritas* determined his/her ability to command favors from supporters or to influence decisions by others, either through intimidation or attraction. It was important not just to the emperor: all people were measured by how others perceived and remembered them. *Auctoritas* was a nonquantifiable virtue—an intangible entity—meaning that one's prestige was simply a "gut feeling" on the part of the populace. Public inscriptions were manipulated in such a way as to elevate or improve one's public image. Honorary inscriptions did not just come upon a person's death but were also employed in order to mark a momentous occasion—a military victory or the construction of a large public building, aqueduct, or bridge. In the case of the *Res gestae,* some of Augustus's claims are known to have been illusory; yet, in a world that dealt heavily in the value of images, reality was not as important as its perception, even if it were mistaken. It is a never-ending

Funerary relief of a Roman family, with inscription, from the late first century B.C.E. (North Carolina Museum of Art, Raleigh)

task of the student of Roman history to uncover what in public memorials is fact and what is fiction, or rhetoric.

Damnatio Memoriae. The power and significance of how positively one was remembered can be demonstrated by how greatly the Romans feared its reverse: a negative opinion, or complete oblivion. One form of punishment that the Romans saw as particularly heinous was the *damnatio memoriae* (condemnation of one's memory). In such a penalty, a public figure's name was to be erased from all documents—inscriptions, coins, contracts, and so forth—and his images were to be recarved or painted over. His first name, the *praenomen*, was never to be used again by anyone else in his family. It was a negative sort of propaganda, visited upon a sitting emperor's worst enemies. Victims of *damnatio memoriae* include emperors, such as Nero, Domitian, and Commodus, who were viewed as despotic by those who followed.

Sources:

Lawrence Keppie, *Understanding Roman Inscriptions* (Baltimore: Johns Hopkins University Press, 1991).

Naphtali Lewis and Meyer Reinhold, eds., *Roman Civilization: Selected Readings*, two volumes (New York: Columbia University Press, 1951–1955).

Ramsay MacMullen, "The Epigraphic Habit of the Roman Empire," *American Journal of Philology*, 103 (Fall 1982): 233–246.

Paul Zanker, *The Power of Images in the Age of Augustus*, translated by H. Alan Shapiro (Ann Arbor: University of Michigan Press, 1988).

PURPOSES OF TRAVEL

Trade and the Military. The responsibility for the ease of travel in the ancient world was shared by the twin incentives of profit and security. Harbors such as Ostia and outposts such as Dura-Europos teemed with merchants hocking their wares and with soldiers maintaining their emperor's brand of order. Military and administrative travel included more than the movement of troops: ambassadors, sometimes with significant entourages, had to visit separate kingdoms and empires; news and information had to move efficiently among leaders. Commercial travel was also multifaceted: the archaeological evidence of shipwrecks and storefronts show all varieties of goods moving through desert caravans or coastal convoys. Soldiers and tradesmen made up a large portion of the total population of the empire, and it is fair to assume that from them alone unprecedented numbers of individuals were broadening their horizons: encountering new gods, new languages, and new cultures.

Tourism. These were not the only type of travelers, however; other reasons for travel developed, making use of the paths forged by merchants and generals. Under the security and prosperity of the middle Roman empire, tourists began to travel for traveling's sake. Despite the discomforts, risks, and expense of overseas or overland journeys, they nonetheless desired to see great, faraway, and storied landmarks of the civilizations that preceded them. Egypt and Greece were both popular tourist destinations for those who could afford them. Julius Caesar, in the middle of fighting a civil war for his very survival, took time to cruise down the Nile with Cleopatra on her royal barge and see the sights: the pyramids and temples of the pharaohs who ruled millennia before him. Other Romans highly revered the cultural achievements of the Greeks and sought out their famous temples, schools, sanctuaries, oracles, and athletic sites at places such as Athens, Olympia, and Delphi. Pausanias, in the late second century C.E., published a guidebook of Greece, giving his readers directions to various sites and descriptions of their history. His works survive and are a valuable source for the look of major sites that were ancient even in his day. The list of seven wonders of the ancient world, canonized in the second century

A mosaic, from the port of Ostia, depicting a lighthouse, merchant ships, and dolphins, circa 200 C.E. (Foro delle Corporazioni, Ostia)

B.C.E. by Antipater, was popular: essentially a checklist for adventurous and historically minded tourists.

Pilgrimage. One subcategory of tourism was religiously inspired. People covered great distances to visit a particular holy place, either to ask advice, to seek some kind of healing, or just to pay respects to the divine. Religious sites, both pagan and Christian, did a brisk business with their visitors, accepting their donations and gifts and selling them miniature replicas of their buildings or statues as souvenirs. Glass bottles in the shape of the famous cult statue of Tyche of Antioch look much like the kitsch one might find in tourist traps. Early Christians made pilgrimages to the Holy Land, especially Jerusalem. Women, such as Etheria in the late fourth century and Melania the Younger in the early fifth, spent years traipsing around biblical sites in Egypt and Palestine; the former even re-created the Exodus of the Jews. Christian emperors and members of their families built shrines and monasteries there that further inspired the wanderlust of contemporary Christians.

Exile. Some forms of travel were the opposite of leisurely, fulfilling, or joyous. A severe penalty in the Roman world was exile, when citizens would be forced to leave the city forever, unless later pardoned. It was forbidden for anyone to shelter or feed them; they lived in remote, poorly inhabited places, under guard. The initial journey to the place of exile would have been the dangerous phase of banishment: Augustus considered it a great act of clemency just to grant his exiles passage on imperial Roman roads. Their experiences upon arrival to their new homes were reportedly miserable. Various members of the imperial dynasties were carted off to islands where they often starved to death. Cicero complained bitterly of his situation in Greece, and Ovid wrote a series of poems from Tomis on the Black Sea called *Tristia* (The Sadnesses), in which he bemoaned, among other things, the lack of food and his inability to understand the language of the locals. Exiles also endured the torturous fear that an order for their execution might arrive from the emperor at any time.

Migration. Sometimes entire communities would have to abandon their homes and move to a new land because of poor crops, warfare, or overpopulation, all of which could be interrelated. Mass migrations of Gallic populations presented a serious threat to Roman populations in southern France in the end of the second century B.C.E., which required the extraordinary measure of repeating Marius's consulships so that he could deal with the problem with

A TOURIST'S GUIDE TO GREECE

Pausanias's description of his travels through Greece provides modern archaeologists with valuable information about the location of particular monuments. His anecdotes concerning the buildings and monuments he visited are also a useful resource for historians. Any nonacademic travelers going to Greece today for a simple vacation might find him useful for the very reasons he originally wrote: to explain the sights, as a tour guide, to curious tourists. The following representative excerpt suggests that the ancient Olympic Games could be as scandalous as they sometimes are today, and stories of a landmark's past had a ready audience among ancient travelers:

[If you are walking through the sight of the athletic competitions at Olympia] "on the way to the racing-track from the Mother's sanctuary, on the left at the edge of Mount Kronion, there is a stone platform against the mount itself, with steps that go up through the platform; bronze statues of Zeus have been dedicated against this platform, made from the money paid in penalties by athletes fined for dishonoring the games. . . . The first six were set up at the 98th Olympics, when Eupolos of Thessaly bribed the boxers who entered, . . . who won the boxing at the previous Olympics. This is said to have been the first crime that athletes ever committed in the games. . . . Apart from the third and fourth of these statues, they all have couplets inscribed on them. The first couplet is meant to show that you win at Olympia with the speed of your feet and the strength of your body, and now with money; the one on the second statue says it was put up out of respect for religion and by the pious practice of the Eleans, and to frighten crooked athletes. . . . They say the next offender was Kallippos of Athens, who bought off his opponents with bribes when he was competing in the pentathlon.

Source: Pausanias, *Guide to Greece*, volume 2, translated by Peter Levi (Harmondsworth, U.K.: Penguin, 1971).

SEAFARING

Routes. Roman sailors were never adept at handling the high seas and always maintained a profound fear and respect for the potential violence of the Mediterranean. They, like most sailors from other periods of antiquity, preferred to stick to the coast, leaving the sight of land only when it was necessary. To the best of their ability, they limited their journeys to the calmer summer seasons and avoided travel during the unpredictable winters. Cities that were located on excellent natural harbors thus grew quickly in population, as the business of sheltering ships, both military and commercial, required and attracted a large amount of manpower. Two of the three next largest cities of the empire, after Rome, were harbor towns: Alexandria and Ephesus; the third, Antioch, was just fifteen miles from the sea, connected by the Orontes River. Inland population centers, naturally, were also located on water; navigable rivers and lakes sustained a steady flow of traffic. Where such rivers were lacking, the Romans on occasion dug canals for transportation, examples of which can be found in the Po River valley in northern Italy and in Greece, across the Isthmus of Corinth.

Types of Ships. By modern standards, the ships and boats of ancient Rome were quite small. The largest vessels were, naturally, those meant for seagoing travel and were on average forty feet in length. (One extraordinary exception was a 180-foot cargo ship, mentioned by Lucian.) Ocean-going ships can be subdivided into those made for trade, for war, and for luxury. All were rigged with some kind of sailing apparatus, while merchantmen had wider, deeper keels for storage and fewer oars than battleships. Battleships, or triremes, were built for speed, maneuverability, and strength; they were fitted out with three banks of oars, a battering ram with which to sink their opponents, and, occasionally, a large crane, which could be lowered on the enemy to trap them while soldiers boarded across long planks. Quinqueremes, or ships with five banks of oars, are also attested, though less frequently. Sources for the imperial period describe luxury barges that had all manner of amenities, including running water, bathing complexes, banquet halls, and temples. Two of the emperor Caligula's large floating palaces were discovered on the floor of Lake Nemi in Italy (they were housed in a lakeside museum until being destroyed by the Nazis). These ships were evidently stationary and not meant for travel at sea, but the bronze pipes, elaborate sculptures, and mosaics on board suggest that sources for highly advanced nautical engineering do not exaggerate. One story about the emperor Nero even claims that he had shipbuilders design a collapsible luxury yacht for his mother, whom he despised, so that it would appear seaworthy to her, but then fall apart when she was away from shore.

The Tiber. River-going vessels were much smaller. On the Tiber they were used to transport goods from the sea to the city. The flow of the river could be swift and heavy, and shallow craft had to be dragged against the current by animals up to the warehouses and storage facilities constructed

authority. In the twilight of the Roman empire, large groups of people from northern Europe crossed the rivers that had, in effect, formed the northern border of Rome: the Rhine and the Danube. These groups—Visigoths, Ostrogoths, Vandals, and Franks—moved in droves. In the long run, Roman culture remained largely intact, though in an obviously altered form.

Sources:

Mary T. Boatwright, *Hadrian and the Cities of the Roman Empire* (Princeton: Princeton University Press, 2000).

Lionel Casson, *Travel in the Ancient World* (London: Allen & Unwin, 1974).

Jo-Marie Claassen, *Displaced Persons: The Literature of Exile from Cicero to Boethius* (Madison: University of Wisconsin Press, 1999).

E. D. Hunt, *Holy Land Pilgrimage in the Later Roman Empire, AD 312–460* (Oxford: Clarendon Press, 1982; New York: Oxford University Press, 1982).

Emperor Caligula's palace barge, excavated when Lake Nemi was drained in 1928–1932
(from Lionel Casson, *Ships and Seafaring in Ancient Times,* 1994)

just south of the city. Larger ships attempting to travel up the river would have run aground, as did one that arrived in 205 B.C.E. bearing the new goddess, Magna Mater, from the East. According to legend, the Vestal Virgin, Claudia Quinta, tied her hair around the bow and yanked it free with the help of the goddess; regular merchants obviously could not count on such assistance! River-borne transportation was also widespread elsewhere in the empire. The Euphrates, Nile, and Rhine Rivers were heavily used by merchants, fishermen, and armies on campaign.

Ostia. The main harbor of Rome during the empire was the city of Ostia, located at the mouth of Tiber, sixteen miles from the capital. The earliest prosperity, before Rome acquired its empire, was based on its wide, low, salt flats; Ostia did not originally have a naturally well-defined harbor. In keeping with Roman ingenuity and craft, various attempts were made to construct one, first by building a breakwater to guard against the direction of the surf, and later by digging out wide basins, at great expense, just inland along the river. Because of its value to Rome, the town frequently received the beneficence of the emperor: Claudius built a lighthouse there and the emperor Trajan carved out a large hexagonal bay, which he proudly depicted on his coinage. As Rome grew, so did Ostia, until it became quite wealthy in its own right, with richly decorated townhouses, temples, and baths. An elaborate marketplace survives in which the merchants' stalls, opening onto a large square, were decorated with mosaics that described their product or the region they traded with. The Ostians, though, were perpetually fighting a losing battle against the silt brought down from the Appennine mountains by the Tiber, and when the empire fell and Ostian population declined, the town was slowly buried. Archaeologists, as a result, have found it to be well preserved, much like a second Pompeii.

Cargo. Hundreds of Roman-era shipwrecks have been explored by underwater archaeologists. From these finds one is able to learn much about the ancient Roman economy, trade routes, and produce. Most ships bearing cargo, for example, carried their products in large earthenware jars called *amphorae* (singular, *amphora*), which could carry dry goods, such as various types of grain, or valuable liquids, such as wine, olive oil, and *garum,* a fish sauce that was a popular condiment in the Roman diet. Shipwrecks with cargo of art, coins, and other kinds of treasure have been fewer, although they have attracted much attention. In 1972 an ancient shipwreck was discovered off the coast of southern Italy, which yielded several masterpieces of Greek bronze sculpture, including life-size statues of athletes or heroes, which presumably had been destined for sale in Rome. No ships were built exclusively to carry human cargo; there were no modern passenger vessels. People traveling for personal reasons hitched rides on ships that were headed in the right direction, though with different principal missions, military or commercial.

Shipwreck. Travelers and merchants must have greatly feared the possibility of shipwreck, if one is to appreciate the epic description of the horrifying waves that sank the ships of the founding hero of Rome, Aeneas. As Vergil says:

A HARROWING SHIPWRECK

One of the best firsthand accounts of a shipwreck from the ancient Roman world is that of Paul, the author of Acts in the New Testament of the Christian Bible. Death by drowning or exposure was a real risk for the ancient traveler, as was financial loss from the abandonment of cargo in such situations.

When a southerly breeze sprang up, they thought that their purpose was as good as achieved, and, weighing anchor, they sailed along the coast of Crete hugging the land. But before very long a violent wind, the Northeaster as they call it, swept down from the landward side. It caught the ship and, as it was impossible to keep head to wind, we had to give way and run before it. As we passed under the lee of a small island called Cauda, we managed with a struggle to get the ship's boat under control. When they had hoisted it on board, they made use of tackle to brace the ship. Then, afraid of running on to the sandbanks of Syrtis, they put out a sea-anchor and let her drift. Next day, as we were making very heavy weather, they began to lighten the ship; and on the third day they jettisoned the ship's gear with their own hands. For days on end there was no sign of either sun or stars, the storm was raging unabated, and our last hopes of coming through alive began to fade. . . . The fourteenth night came and we were still drifting in the Adriatic Sea. . . . When day broke, [the sailors] did not recognize the land, but they sighted a bay with a sandy beach, on which they decided, if possible, to run ashore. So they slipped the anchors and let them go; at the same time they loosened the lashings of the steering paddles, set the foresail to the wind, and let her drive to the beach. But they found themselves caught between cross-currents and ran the ship aground, so that the bow stuck fast and remained immovable, while the stern was being pounded to pieces by the breakers. The soldiers thought they had better kill the prisoners for fear that any should swim away and escape; but the centurion was determined to bring Paul safely through, and prevented them from carrying out their plan. He gave orders that those who could swim should jump overboard first and get to land; the rest were to follow, some on planks, some on parts of the ship. And thus it was that all came safely to land.

Source: *The Oxford Study Bible* (Oxford: Oxford University Press, 1992).

winds, like volleys of soldiers given an opening, rushed out to blow through the countryside, twirling. They fell on the sea: they roiled its bottom completely. Eastwind joined the Southwind; Southwesterly, crowded with squalls, ran out and rolled huge tumblers on the beaches. Cables creaked on the ships. Crewmen were yelling. Clouds had suddenly stolen the brightness of heaven from Trojan eyes, and a black night sat on the water.

The Romans, of course, did not have satellite technology with which to track and predict weather patterns, and storms could easily overwhelm entire fleets with no warning. The First Punic War (264–241 B.C.E.) was nearly lost by the Romans as a result of an inundation of their fleet.

Merchants who had to transport goods by sea took out insurance policies to guard against loss as a result of shipwreck; the insurance contracts survive on stone. As a storm worsened, all hands would help to secure the ship; Paul, in the New Testament book of Acts, joined the crew in tossing the cargo overboard. Sailors sought to alleviate the pressure of the unknown by prayer to the gods of the sea and by other superstitious observances. Sneezing as one boarded a ship was considered bad luck, as was setting sail on certain days: 24 August, 5 October, and 8 November. If one dreamed of an owl before a voyage, it meant that either a storm or pirates would wreck the ship.

Piracy. Another risk of sea travel was attack by pirates. In the popular literature of the Romans, such as comedies in the Republic and novels in the Principate, the pirate was a stock figure; an archetypal hero/villain of melodramatic proportions, whose bumbling could be cast as amusing. The reality of piracy, however, was no laughing matter. Bands of marauders lived in groups that, in some cases, rivaled whole towns in terms of size and organization. According to Strabo, agents of pirates would spy on merchants on land in order to discover their route, destination, and time of travel, and then set a trap for them down the coast. Julius Caesar, in his youth, was kidnapped by pirates and held for ransom; after he won his freedom, he later returned to kill his former captors. The problem became serious enough to warrant the attention of full-blown military campaigns. Pompey, in 67 B.C.E., received a formal charge by the Senate to rid the Mediterranean of pirates.

Sources:

Lionel Casson, *Ships and Seamanship in the Ancient World* (Princeton: Princeton University Press, 1971).

Russell Meiggs, *Roman Ostia*, second edition (Oxford: Clarendon Press, 1973).

John S. Morrison, *Greek and Roman Oared Warships* (Oxford: Oxbow Books, 1996).

Henry A. Ormerod, *Piracy in the Ancient World: An Essay in Mediterranean History* (Liverpool: University Press of Liverpool; London: Hodder & Stoughton, 1924; reprint, Chicago: Argonaut, 1967).

WRITING AND LANGUAGE

Necessity. Communication in the Roman empire was expensive, slow, unreliable, and yet, utterly crucial. Emperors, generals, soldiers, tax collectors, priests, businessmen, and women, and any other kind of traveler, had to send and receive information in order to function and survive. An accurate knowledge of events was necessary to preserve order at all levels of society: news of a military victory or failure would affect the subsequent decisions of an army on campaign; the yield of an individual's farm in an unpredictable season would affect his credit, either positively or negatively, in commercial transactions abroad; the political maneuvering of a provincial magnate would have to be reported with accuracy to his rival elsewhere; a matter of law that had been settled by the emperor would have to be made known to all residents of the empire. Written documents were needed to carry information into the future, as well: the marriage of a relative, divorce of a spouse, birth of a child, manumission of a slave, conviction for a crime, acquittal from a charge, all of which could alter an individual's status or testament, would have to be recorded in an organized and verifiable way. Communication, broadly defined in all its styles and ranges of effectiveness, across space and time, affected millions of lives. Yet, in the diverse world of ancient Rome, one had to deal with dozens of competing languages, varying degrees of literacy, the high cost of writing materials, and irregularities in the physical delivery of messages. A mastery of communication was an indispensable key to success, yet it did not come easily.

Materials for Writing. Written communication, in all its forms, was a costly undertaking. The closest equivalent to use of paper was the *papyrus* (plural, *papyri*), which was made from the Egyptian plant of the same name. The papyrus plant was a reed that grew along the Nile, whose stalks, when cut and layered in crisscross patterns on top of each other, would dry into stiff, yet pliable, sheets. A quill dipped in ink was the primary writing utensil. Given the proper conditions of dryness and heat, documents on papyrus could and did last for thousands of years; archaeologists have found large numbers of papyri in excavations throughout Egypt. The method was widespread, but it was not cheap; the cost of single sheet of quality papyrus was nearly the same as that of a daily wage for an unskilled worker. An alternate means of writing—one that was recyclable and thus more cost-effective—was on shallow wooden tablets that held a thin layer of wax. The writer could carve letters into the wax with a *stylus* and later erase them by heating the tablet slightly. Still cheaper was writing on broken pieces of pottery called *ostraka*, although this method was unwieldy. The most-expensive and least-portable forms of writing were carving on stone and painting on walls, yet these methods had the benefit of permanence.

Literacy. Writing was everywhere in the Roman world. On just the briefest of excursions through the ruins of Pompeii (a town buried by the eruption of Mt. Vesuvius in 79 C.E.), one is surrounded by honorary inscriptions, public edicts, campaign posters, price lists, and graffiti. Writing is in evidence for all contexts—social, political, diplomatic, and so forth—and for all levels of society. The ubiquity of the written word, however, belies the modern understand-

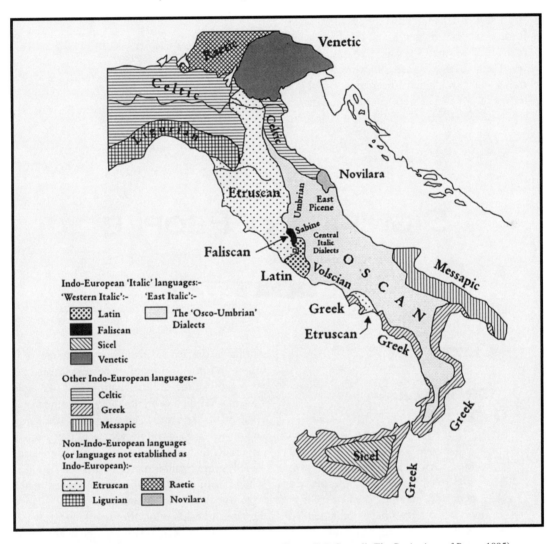

A map of the languages in Italy, circa 450–400 B.C.E. (from T. J. Cornell, *The Beginnings of Rome*, 1995)

ing of literacy rates of the time. Education in reading and writing was limited only to those who could afford formal tutors or who had the time and devotion to learn it on their own. For those who could not write, a hired scribe or an educated slave could lend assistance. Papyri from Roman Egypt, which record contracts of marriage, trade, and other types of transactions, frequently are signed on another's behalf, when the person was unable to make out its meaning on his or her own. For those who could write, their knowledge was something to brag about; some portraits from various parts of the Roman world, both painted and sculpted, show the sitter with tablet and stylus in hand, demonstrating their possession of this highly valuable skill.

Latin and Greek. As opposed to reading and writing, spoken communication, of course, was universal, yet it was, at times, no less complicated. The principal languages of the empire were Latin and Greek, the former being dominant in the West and within the Roman army; the latter being prominent in the discourse of literary artists and intellectuals and in the East, where Alexander the Great had transported Greek culture before Rome came on to the scene. Remnants of the Latin language in western Europe demonstrate its inertia: Italian, French, Spanish, Portuguese, and Romanian—called the Romance Languages because of their link to the Romans—are all directly descended from Latin. Many Romans, however, particularly of the ruling elite, would have been fluent in both Latin and Greek, and provincials who had not been reared speaking either of these languages would have striven to learn them if they had ambitions to rise in the empire in any field of endeavor—commerce, politics, or the arts.

Bilingualism. Other languages besides Latin and Greek continued to be spoken long after the arrival of the Romans. As an imperial power, Rome thrived in part because of its willingness to let provincial communities retain many aspects of their culture, language included. Archaeologists have found thousands of Roman-era inscriptions and papyri from around the Mediterranean that demonstrate the wide variety of languages: Punic in Carthage, Demotic in Egypt, Aramaic in Palestine, and so forth. Authors who wanted to direct their messages at as many people as possible might write the same text in more than one language; bilingual inscriptions have been found throughout the empire. Interpreters were valuable to Roman armies as they negotiated with natives or sought intelligence from deserters and hostages from the other side. Some leaders understood the value of being able to communicate freely with others in their native tongue and the honor it paid to their conversers: Cleopatra reportedly spoke seven languages and was the first Hellenistic monarch of Egypt to learn the local dialect.

Sources:

Roger S. Bagnall, *Reading Papyri, Writing Ancient History* (London & New York: Routledge, 1995).

Raffaella Cribiore, *Writing, Teachers, and Students in Graeco-Roman Egypt* (Atlanta: Scholars Press, 1996).

William V. Harris, *Ancient Literacy* (Cambridge, Mass.: Harvard University Press, 1989).

SIGNIFICANT PEOPLE

CLEOPATRA

69-30 B.C.E.
QUEEN OF EGYPT

Learned Leader. Although the men, her two brothers and her son, who ruled Egypt alongside her are generally forgotten, the name Cleopatra conjures images of a seductress and schemer. A descendant of the Macedonian rulers who came to Egypt during the invasion of Alexander the Great (323 B.C.E.), Cleopatra was the second daughter of Ptolemy XII. She was bright and intelligent and reportedly learned multiple languages, including the native tongue of her subjects. When Ptolemy XII died in 51 B.C.E., she ascended to the throne along with her brother and husband, Ptolemy XIII. The real power in Egypt, however, were the Romans, who had essentially dictated policy since 168. Cleopatra was determined to use Roman power and saw an opportunity when Julius Caesar arrived in 48. A union of mutual benefit was established, and Cleopatra used the Roman emperor to reestablish her place on the Egyptian throne. Caesar soon left to return to Rome, although he may have left behind a son by Cleopatra. She made lavish expenditures on her fleet and personal transports and impressed the Roman men with whom she pursued her imperial ambitions. Cleopatra followed Caesar to Rome in 46, but the emperor was assassinated in 44, and she returned to Egypt.

The Logistics of Power. Perhaps better than any other political rival or ally of her day, with the possible exception of Caesar, Cleopatra understood the importance of communication, public image, the movement of wealth and troops, and the knowledge of geography in the acquisition of political power. She soon decided to cast her fate with Mark Antony, who was consolidating his power on the Roman throne. When Antony came east to pursue a campaign against Persia, Cleopatra seduced and entranced him. In Rome, however, Octavian was gaining power. Antony later married Cleopatra (37), but Roman sentiment was against the union. She managed to get Antony to give her lands that formerly belonged to Herod the Great of Judaea, but she created an implacable enemy. Octavian turned against Antony and defeated a fleet commanded by Antony and Cleopatra in 31 at the Battle of Actium. Antony killed himself, but Cleopatra tried again to use her wiles, but this time failed to capture another Roman emperor. Rather than suffer humiliation, she also committed suicide, and was buried beside Antony. She was remembered by future Romans as a dangerous public enemy in the negative propaganda of Augustus.

Sources:
J. P. V. D. Balsdon, *Julius Caesar and Rome* (London: English Universities Press, 1967).

Michael Grant, *Cleopatra* (London: Weidenfeld & Nicolson, 1972).

Julia Samson, *Nefertiti and Cleopatra: Queen-Monarchs of Ancient Egypt* (London: Rubicon Press, 1985).

Dorothy J. Thompson, "Cleopatra VII," in *The Oxford Classical Dictionary*, edited by Simon Hornblower and Antony Spawforth, third edition (Oxford: Oxford University Press, 1999), p. 347.

JULIA DOMNA

DIED 217 C.E.
EMPRESS

Syrian Roots. Julia Domna, the daughter of a Syrian priest, was born in Emesa. In 187 C.E. she married the North African Septimus Severus, who was appointed governor of Pannonia Superior in 191. In 193 he was proclaimed emperor, and they became the first rulers of the Severan dynasty. During their rule Severus fought off domestic rivals and was successful in battle in Parthia and Britian. He lavished honors and posts on their two sons, Caracella and Geta, but after his death in 211, a sibling rivalry resulted in the assassination of Geta in 212. Domna supported her son and even ruled in his absence.

An International Family. The empress was interested in intellectual matters and reportedly sponsored a circle of writers and thinkers with whom she discussed matters of philosophy and history. She was a patron of Flavius Philostratus and commissioned him to write *The Life of Apollonius* (circa 220), possibly as a counter to the growing influence of Christians in the empire. A literate woman herself, while working for Caracalla, Julia Domna oversaw his correspondence. After her death in 217, her sister and nieces from Syria became just as active as she had been in public life and imperial administration.

Sources:
Graham Anderson, *Philostratus: Biography and Belles Lettres in the Third Century A.D.* (London & Dover, N.H.: Croom Helm, 1986).

Anthony R. Birley, "Iulia Domna," in *The Oxford Classical Dictionary*, edited by Simon Hornblower and Antony Spawforth (Oxford: Oxford University Press, 1999), p. 777.

Birley, *Septimus Severus: The African Emperor* (London: Eyre & Spottiswoode, 1971).

PUBLIUS AELIUS HADRIANUS (HADRIAN)

76-138 C.E.
EMPEROR

Provincial Beginnings. Born in 76 into a family of Italian settlers who lived in Spain, Publius Aelius Hadrianus was educated in Rome, and after the death of his father, he came under the influence of a paternal cousin, the emperor Trajan. He served in political and military posts in the provinces, especially along the Danube and in Macedonia. He followed his patron into the upper echelon of imperial politics and even married his grandniece. Hadrian rapidly advanced to greater positions of power, gaining the consulate in 107, only to suffer a decade of lesser political appointments when he lost political favor after the death of Licinius Sura, a powerful supporter of Trajan.

On the Road. In 117 C.E., Hadrian inherited a stable and prosperous empire from his adoptive father, Trajan, but he departed from his predecessor's policy of rapid expansion and expensive conquest. He effectively froze the borders of the empire and directed his attentions to the defense of the frontiers and the infrastructure of the provinces. During his far-flung travels throughout the empire, he often paid for or ordered others to pay for major improvements in waterworks, road construction, and other civic amenities. His wall in Britain—a sharp line separating Roman from non-Roman—illustrates the inward focus of his policies. A consummate tourist, his interest in the history and culture of Roman territories was representative of others of his time. Even as he was dying, in 138, he took time to pen a letter describing his emotions.

Sources:

Anthony R. Birley, "Hadrian" in *The Oxford Classical Dictionary*, edited by Simon Hornblower and Antony Spawforth (Oxford: Oxford University Press, 1999), pp. 662–663.

Birley, *Hadrian: The Restless Emperor* (London & New York: Routledge, 1997).

Mary T. Boatwright, *Hadrian and the Cities of the Roman Empire* (Princeton: Princeton University Press, 2000).

POLYBIUS

CIRCA 200–AFTER 118 B.C.E.
HISTORIAN AND EXPLORER

Politics and Servitude. Polybius belonged to a powerful political family in Greece that resisted the growing influence of Rome in the early second century B.C.E. He served in several political positions, including one stint as an envoy to Alexandria. After the Roman victory at the Battle of Pydna in 168, he was taken to Rome, where he soon developed a strong relationship with his captor, Scipio Aemilianus. He accompanied the Romans in their defeat of Carthage and subjugation of Greece. He was later given a ship and crew with which to explore the coast of Africa beyond the Strait of Gibraltar. He lived into his eighties and died after falling off a horse.

Historical Works. His histories, written while he was in Rome, were aimed at a Greek audience to whom he prescribed a reasoned accommodation of Roman imperial rule. His earlier works, including a history of the Numantine War (133), have been lost. The remaining portions of his major work, a history of the rise of Rome to imperial status, were based on his documentary research, eyewitness accounts, and geographic and political knowledge. He was an innovator in writing history that attempted to explain causation and processes.

Sources:

Peter Sidney Derow, "Polybius," in *The Oxford Classical Dictionary*, edited by Simon Hornblower and Antony Spawforth (Oxford: Oxford University Press, 1999), pp. 1209–1211.

Kenneth Sacks, *Polybius on the Writing of History* (Berkeley: University of California Press, 1981).

F. W. Walbank, *Polybius* (Berkeley: University of California Press, 1972).

DOCUMENTARY SOURCES

Augustus (Gaius Julius Caesar Octavianus), *The Accomplishments of the Divine Augustus* (14 C.E.)—A long, autobiographical inscription, first set up outside the emperor's tomb and later copied and circulated throughout the empire. As propaganda, it presented the civic benefactions and foreign ties and victories of the emperor in an exaggerated light.

Julius Caesar (Gaius Julius Caesar), *Commentaries on the Gallic War* (58–50 B.C.E.)—A collection of the general's missives to the people of Rome, describing, from a Roman point of view, elements of Gallic culture and geography, amid a record of interaction, both peaceful and warlike, with non-Romans.

Cicero (Marcus Tullius Cicero), *Letters to His Family and Friends* (62–43 B.C.E.)—The personal correspondence of the Roman statesman with his wife, daughter, brother, and political colleagues.

Pomponius Mela, *Circumnavigation of the Empire* (44 C.E.)—Geographic and ethnographic observations of mythological and fantastic phenomena, perhaps originally accompanied by a map.

Pausanias, *Description of Greece* (circa 150 C.E.)—A travelogue of several tourist destinations in Greece.

Pliny the Younger (Gaius Plinius Caecilius Secundus), *Letters* (99–109 C.E.)—Personal correspondence of a wealthy Roman senator and governor of Bithynia in Asia Minor.

Strabo, *Geography* (circa 5–20 C.E.)—A geographer's treatise outlining the layout of the world, region by region, and the customs of the people who lived in it.

Tacitus (Cornelius Tacitus), *Germania* and *Agricola* (98 C.E.)—The first is an essay on all aspects of Germany, written from a Roman perspective and catering to a Roman audience. The second is a history of the governorship of Agricola in Britain, with digressions on the exploration of Britain.

CHAPTER FIVE

SOCIAL CLASS SYSTEM AND THE ECONOMY

by WILFRED E. MAJOR

CONTENTS

Sidebars and tables are listed in italics.

215 B.C.E.
- The *Lex Oppia* is introduced, which restricts the overt signs of extravagance of the rich.

176 B.C.E.
- The *tributum,* a property tax on Roman citizens, is suspended.

149 B.C.E.
- As part of attempted reform aimed at restraining corrupt Roman governors who abused the people in their provinces, the Romans establish permanent courts.

133 B.C.E.
- Tiberius Gracchus is elected tribune, attempts broad reform of land ownership, and is killed.

129 B.C.E.
- The equestrians officially become distinct from the senatorial order.

125* B.C.E.
- The *cursus honorum* (course of honors), the path of upward mobility for senators, becomes more regulated.

123-121 B.C.E.
- Gaius Gracchus follows his brother to the office of tribune. He pushes through further reforms and is murdered.

107 B.C.E.
- Marius becomes the first general to enlist volunteers, regardless of wealth, into the Roman army.

89 B.C.E.
- Roman citizenship is extended to all Italians.

87-86 B.C.E.
- Marius initiates a violent dictatorship at Rome but dies shortly thereafter.

*Denotes Circa Date

81-79 B.C.E.	• Sulla takes over Rome as dictator, retiring from the position after a few years.
80* B.C.E.	• Sulla begins minting coins in gold.
72-71 B.C.E.	• Spartacus leads a massive slave revolt, forming an army that roamed Italy for eighteen months.
67 B.C.E.	• The *lex Gabinia* authorizes Pompey to clear pirates from the Mediterranean.
63-62 B.C.E.	• After unsuccessful attempts to reach the consulship, Catiline attempts a conspiracy to seize Rome, but Cicero thwarts him.
50* B.C.E.	• The office of the praetor is reduced in power during Republican infighting.
44 B.C.E.	• Julius Caesar is assassinated.
31 B.C.E.	• Octavian defeats Antony at Actium.
27 B.C.E.- 14 C.E.	• Octavian rules as Augustus. His reign traditionally marks the beginning of the Empire (or Principate). Augustus reconstitutes the Senate, transfers control of the treasury to his court, stabilizes coinage, and establishes new positions for freedmen, among many other reforms.
2 B.C.E.	• The *lex Fufia Caninia* restricts the number of slaves a master can free in his will.

*DENOTES CIRCA DATE

54-68 C.E.	• Nero is Emperor. Among other reforms, he revalues coinage.
96 C.E.	• The public distribution of grain is limited.
97* C.E.	• A system of imperial endowment for the feeding of poor children, called the *alimenta*, is established.
200-300* C.E.	• The Empire experiences a period of frequent political instability and repeated economic crisis.
200* C.E.	• Caracalla issues a new coin called the *antoninianus*.
212 C.E.	• Citizenship is extended to all free persons residing within the Roman Empire.
250* C.E.	• Primary school is mandated for all children.
284-305 C.E.	• Diocletian serves as emperor (with Maximian from 286 onward).
301 C.E.	• Diocletian issues his edict on prices. He also establishes a new gold coin, the *solidus*, restores the *denarius*, and starts a new series of bronze coins.
306-337 C.E.	• Constantine serves as co-emperor (solo 323–337).
395 C.E.	• The Roman Empire is permanently divided into eastern and western portions.

*DENOTES CIRCA DATE

430 C.E.	• The Roman Empire is divided into three monetary zones.
476 C.E.	• Romulus Augustulus is the last emperor of the west.

*Denotes Circa Date

Basalt portrait of Octavian's third wife, Livia, circa 40–30 B.C.E. (Louvre, Paris)

OVERVIEW

The Roman Classes. At any time in Roman history, individual Romans knew with certainty that they belonged to a specific social class: Senator, Equestrian, Patrician, Plebeian, Slave, Free. In some cases they were born into that class. In some cases, their wealth or the wealth of their families ensured them membership. Sometimes a political honor could gain them entry to a class. In other cases, Romans could move from one class to another during their lifetime. Over time, the requirements for some classes and moving between classes changed, but at any given moment, there was never any doubt over which Romans belonged to which class. Because the members of one class might enjoy a standard of living far better, or far worse, than members of another class, struggles or even wars could break out over the rights and powers of a given class. One key to the Romans' great success was keeping stability and order among the classes of their own people.

Economics of Empire. As they built and expanded their empire, the Romans earned, or at times demanded, the respect of the peoples, communities, and nations they incorporated into their empire. For hundreds of years, the Romans surpassed every other people they encountered in at least two respects: their military prowess and their ability to organize their empire in times of peace. The Roman economy, then, consisted of the millions of workers across the Roman Empire and beyond, who farmed, built, crafted, traded, educated, enjoyed, and managed a network of products and services in an organized system. This system became so vast and complex that wealthy Romans could purchase clothes made of silk from China, although the person who bought them might never have known where they came from or how they were made.

Rome: World Trade Center. As huge and diverse as the Roman economy became, however, no one could ever doubt what was the center for the entire system: the city of Rome itself. Aelius Aristides, a professional Greek lecturer in the second century C.E., described the network at its height:

> Whole continents lie all around the Mediterranean Sea, and from them, to you, Rome, flow constant supplies of goods. Everything is shipped to you, from every land and from every sea, the products of each season, each country, each river and lake, the handiwork of the Greeks and other foreigners. Consequently, anyone who wants to see every

one of these items must either travel over the whole world or just live in this city. Not only is everything grown or made by every nation available here, but it is available in abundance. So many ships dock here bringing their cargo from everywhere, during every time of the year, after every harvest of crops that the city seems like the downtown market for the entire world! You can find so much cargo from India, or, if you like, from Arabia, that the trees in those countries have been stripped bare and that the inhabitants in those countries would have to come to Rome to beg for their own products. Clothes from Babylon and decorations exported from farther away arrive here in greater amounts and more easily than the imports from the Greek islands of Naxos and Cythnos to Athens, just on the coast of their sea! Egypt, Sicily, and the cultivated lands of Libya in North Africa are your farmlands. Ships never stop coming and going, so it is amazing there is enough room on the sea, to say nothing of in the harbor, for them all. . . . Everything comes together *here:* trade, commerce, transportation, agriculture, metallurgy, every skill that exists or has ever existed, everything that is made or grows. [Translations by Wilfred E. Major]

Class Structure and the Economy. Because the city of Rome itself dominated and directed the form and function of the huge international economy, the class structure at Rome exerted a huge influence on the operation of the network throughout the empire. Usually, an official appointed at Rome governed a province and would inevitably expect the economy and class system of the sort with which he was familiar. Furthermore, he had the authority to shape and guide the local economy so it would fit the Romans' plans. The Romans recognized several different classes in their society. While Romans of the various classes were not legally bound to particular professions or barred from others, the force of tradition and social pressure meant that in practice Romans of a particular class would most often occupy certain positions and perform specified types of work. Moreover, in many cases, membership in a particular class might legally require a specific level of wealth, which in turn would affect what professions the members of that class engaged in.

Patricians. The patrician class consisted of Roman nobles from the earliest days of the city. To be a member of the patrician class, one had to be born into it. Throughout much of the Republic, patricians dominated the important political and religious offices of government. Patrician families were historically prestigious, and through these offices and membership in the Senate they would have had control and influence over many financial dealings. By the end of the Republic, many of the patrician families had died out. The Roman emperors, beginning with Julius Caesar, were given the power to designate new patrician families, but within a few hundred years even this practice faded, and the entire class disappeared. Finally, the Emperor Constantine used the title *patricius* to recognize an individual's service to Rome, but the ties to the hereditary Roman nobility no longer existed.

Senators during the Republic. As Roman power expanded through military conquest, the Senate became the most powerful and prestigious governing institution of Rome. The specific requirements for belonging to the Senate changed over time, but the Senate regularly included men who had served in some government office, such as quaestor, and all members were wealthy men who owned large amounts of land in Italy. The Senate controlled the finances of Rome and so was the most powerful single entity in the Roman economy. Theoretically, the members of the Senate were supposed to direct and make the best decisions for Rome without directly participating in business ventures. Strictly speaking, senators could not bid on the state contracts the Senate set up, nor could they own the large ships used for bigger trading ventures. Senators were also supposed to represent traditional Roman values, which meant in part playing the role of humble but hardworking farmers, and soldiers when necessary. Consequently, senators were not supposed to engage in menial labor or commerce. In practice, however, senators amassed and maintained their fortunes by doing favors for their friends and clients, as well as acting as secret partners in business ventures.

The Emperor. The emperor maintained direct control of Roman finances and assumed ultimate authority over financial decisions. This control dated to the formation of imperial administration under Augustus. He restructured state revenues so the taxes collected from provinces went directly to his coffers. Every emperor, therefore, controlled an enormous personal fortune with which he could gain leverage with individuals, such as senators, or whole groups, such as the military. Especially at times of crisis, it was the emperor and his court that had the responsibility and authority to institute and modify economic and monetary policy.

Senators during the Early Empire. By the end of the civil wars and the collapse of the Republic, the ranks of the Senate had swelled to its highest number, around one thousand. As Augustus gradually set up an imperial administration, the duties and membership of the Senate changed. When the rolls stabilized at six hundred, it became easier for sons to inherit their fathers' senatorial positions, and the property requirement became one million sesterces (a Roman monetary unit). While in some ways these reforms stabilized the membership, the emperors controlled the membership substantially. An emperor could ensure the Senate consisted of his friends and supporters by manipulating the membership. The emperor could, for example, give or loan money to a supporter in order to meet the minimum property requirement to enter the senatorial order. The composition of the order also changed. Whereas at the start senators came almost exclusively from Italy, during the course of the early empire the makeup of the Senate began to reflect the expanding empire, and eventually the majority came from outside Italy itself. The Senate no longer served as the ultimate authority on finances and economic policy, but it was an important political body, and it controlled many key positions and offices from which senators wielded economic power, in addition to being wealthy and powerful individuals in their own right.

The Senate in the Late Empire. Beginning in the third century C.E., Diocletian, Constantine, and other emperors profoundly modified and weakened the power of Roman senators. Political and military offices previously available only to senators opened up to Equestrians. Over the course of a series of reforms, the order both expanded to more than two thousand members and lost what concentrated power it had. The Emperor Valentinian I even divided the Senate into three ranks. Economically, members of the Senate belonged to the wealthy but did not wield special economic force as senators.

Equestrians. The *equites*, "cavalry," derived their origin from the earliest days of Rome in the military horsemen of the Roman army and their honorific positions. By the end of the Republic, however, the order had a property requirement of four hundred thousand sesterces and possibly called for additional qualifications as well. Unlike senators, equestrians tended not to seek or hold political office. On the other hand, where senators were forbidden or discouraged from engaging in commerce, equestrians often built their fortunes in trade or projects contracted by the Senate. Under the empire, the equestrians became more formally an aristocratic order second to the Senate. Equestrians occupied a wide range of posts, especially in local governments. As a class in which wealth was traditionally concentrated, indeed wealth was consistently the defining characteristic, the equestrian order was always an economic force.

Plebeians. The remaining freeborn population of Rome was called the *plebs* because in the earlier history of Rome, any citizen not born a patrician would be a plebeian. This class included people of a wide range of economic means. The wealthier constituents among the *plebs* in fact struggled for and won the right to certain political offices during the middle years of the Republic. Many economic struggles continued for the plebeians, however. Since most wealth was rooted in land and property ownership, the plebeians clashed with the wealthier classes over the distribution and use of public and private lands. While the wealthier plebeians could border on the lifestyle of the aristocracy, some small landowners and farmers lived in harsh, destitute conditions.

Roman Citizens. A person was not necessarily a Roman citizen simply because he resided in Rome or within the Roman Empire. Roman citizenship was a formal, legal status that an individual had either by birth or was granted at some point. Official Roman citizenship granted critical rights and protections. For example, citizenship during the Republic meant the right to vote. Even more importantly, citizenship meant legal protection of a person's body: a citizen would be subject to less violent penalties under the law and could not be executed for a crime. Consequently, peoples who allied themselves with the Romans or were conquered by them desired and even fought for citizen rights. Gradually, the Romans extended citizenship status to more and more people. In 89 B.C.E. all Italians officially became Roman citizens. In 212 C.E. all freeborn residents within the borders of the Roman Empire automatically became citizens.

Honestiores and *Humiliores.* All Roman citizens were not equal, however. An informal distinction existed between *honestiores,* which included prestigious individuals such as senators, equestrians, political officials, and military officers, and *humiliores,* individuals of lower rank. While no formal legal definition of these two groups is known, by the time that all freeborn inhabitants of the Roman Empire were granted citizenship status, the distinction had serious legal consequences. Roman law called for differing levels of punishment according to these categories for those found guilty of the same crime, and the punishments for *humiliores* were always more severe.

Slaves. Slaves constituted a huge portion of the population and their numbers increased as Rome conquered more and more territories and people. Romans consistently enslaved foreigners but not native Italians. Prisoners of war, children of slave mothers, and victims of piracy replenished the slave population throughout the history of ancient Rome. While all slaves lacked the protection and basic rights granted to Roman citizens and suffered the oppression characteristic of slavery, in terms of quality of life and economic means, slaves could live in a wide range of circumstances.

Freedmen and Freedwomen. Slaves could never acquire formal Roman citizenship, nor could they ever enter the senatorial, equestrian, or even plebeian classes. Some slaves could, however, acquire their freedom, at which point they became free (*libertini*). Whether a slave became free was entirely up to the slave's owner. Masters freed slaves for a variety of reasons, some altruistic, and some selfish, and often a mixture of both. A few individuals achieved their freedom for their considerable skills in management and business and became extremely wealthy in their own right, although a freedman always owed his allegiance to his former master. Freedman or freedwomen retained their status for the rest of their lives, but their children would be born free.

Types of Economic Activity. What jobs did ancient Romans perform? How did the Romans make money? It may seem obvious that when the Roman military conquered an area, they profited by acquiring the wealth of the people who live there, but the Romans could conquer a town or country and make it even wealthier. How did a farmer in Italy make money from a military conquest hundreds of miles away? Why did millions of people pay money to the Roman emperor even though he was just one man? Moreover, while the Romans aggressively pursued wealth and power, they also expected that everyone always worked. Indeed, they always retained some suspicion of anyone at any time who was not working. Even "retirement" was a suspicious thing! So it is worth keeping in mind the general areas in which Romans worked and what classes of people in general did this type of work.

Agriculture. Although the Romans have earned great fame for their military, engineering, and cultural achievements, basic agriculture remained the foundation of the Roman economy. Ownership of farmland was the prerequisite for becoming a senator, for example, and hence for wielding large-scale economic and political power. The sizes of farms could vary widely. Some Roman citizens owned small plots of land and barely survived on what they could grow and sell. Some senators ran gigantic farming businesses on huge tracts of land and turned enormous profits. These senators would hire (or purchase, in the case of slaves) people to do the labor, as well as overseers, accountants, and others as necessary to maintain the business.

Infrastructure. The Romans consistently displayed their famous practicality by devoting many of their resources to establishing a basic infrastructure to meet fundamental human needs. When they conquered or annexed a city, they would build roads, buildings, and do more to establish or strengthen the infrastructure of the city and incorporate it into the network of the Roman Empire. Many people had to work together to set up the structures to acquire and distribute the basic needs of food, water, shelter, health, and safety. The agricultural base of the economy tried to keep foodstuffs in adequate supply. The Romans built miles and miles of aqueducts, many of which survive to this day, to supply water to individuals and also to irrigate farmland. They constructed temples, buildings, theaters, arenas, and other public works. All such works required architects, suppliers, and laborers in huge numbers. Brickmaking, for example, became an enormous industry. In the process of establishing networks to supply these basic needs and for transporting building materials, the Romans also made the transport and procurement of luxury items easier.

Public Administration. As the empire expanded, there was more need for people to devote their time just to making sure all the projects, whether military, public, or other, ran efficiently. Likewise, networks for moving materials, goods, and specific items became larger and more complex. Wealthier Romans, although the foundation of their wealth lay in their farmland, dominated these positions and used them to increase their wealth even more.

Trades and Crafts. Romans all over the empire and of every class needed, wanted, and used a wide variety of items that an individual could manufacture and supply. These products could range from small items such as spoons and clothes to household furniture and decorations. Romans also went to restaurants, hired skilled labor, and sought out a variety of services. As with many jobs, many people struggled to manage a subsistence living while some managed decent livings. Slaves and free citizens could work the same job, even side by side. Nevertheless, class distinctions mattered. Aristocratic Romans, even though they respected the industriousness of farming, despised the menial physical labor that went into many of those jobs, and despised those who performed them as well.

The Military. Whereas in the earliest days of Rome, wealthy Romans enlisted in the army and provided their own equipment, as Rome expanded through conquest, the army needed systematic funding. The army needed equipment and the soldiers had to be paid. Moreover, veterans, after they had completed their service, needed homes to return to or other benefits. On one hand, through conquest and other works, the army brought wealth and economic opportunities to Rome. On the other hand, because of the sheer power of the army, no one, not even the emperor, could risk ignoring the economic demands of the military.

Models of the Roman Economy. So far as it is known, no one among the Romans formally analyzed the economic system of Rome, so it can be difficult to describe more than a thousand years later how the vast network operated as a unit and how it changed over time. Moreover, while the Romans kept financial records and recorded elaborate contracts for work, only a handful of such documents have survived. Therefore, it is impossible for modern scholars to measure the activity of the Roman economy as they can modern ones. Still, it is useful to employ models in order to understand the system and talk about how the Roman economy all worked together. Finally, while the Romans employed mechanisms and techniques that today would be associated with a specific type of economy (for example, "capitalism"), most scholars would agree that the Roman economy was a unique type.

The Consumer City. While Rome and other cities within the empire were centers of power and wealth, they played a different role in the economy from modern cities. Many modern cities acquire economic power because they have factories or companies that generate wealth in and for the city. Because the economic power of the Roman economy derived ultimately from agriculture, urban areas were locations more for consumption than for production. For this reason, a city such as Rome in an ancient economy is called a "consumer city." A consumer city is a hub for products, consumers, and exchange.

Investment and Banking. Wealthy Romans certainly invested. They would buy land or put money into trading ventures, for example. Nevertheless, some scholars argue that the Roman economy lacked a true investment and banking system with which to keep the economy expanding

and improving. The economy remained static and was subject to crises. Other scholars argue that the investments the Romans made accomplished the same goals as a formal banking and investment system.

Subsistence. The Roman Empire clearly expanded in terms of people, territory, and resources, but this expansion does not necessarily mean the economic system grew. While the Romans devoted many resources to the establishment of a basic infrastructure to provide food, water, shelter, and other basic needs, some scholars believe that the Roman economy never grew enough to allow the bulk of its inhabitants to live much beyond what they needed to survive, that is, beyond the subsistence level.

Growth and Invention. The Romans accomplished many great feats of engineering. They built and created many structures and devices that still amaze people today. Still, the Romans did not invent or use inventions in many ways that seem commonplace today. Some historians believe that the Roman economy was geared toward stability rather than expansion. Consequently, the Romans did not foster invention nearly as much as they could have and even failed to capitalize on inventions that they did have.

Economic Policy. With any model of the Roman economy, one has to wonder whether the Romans ever looked at their economic network and tried to make decisions about it as an economy. They definitely made many financial decisions and established, for example, a far-reaching monetary system. Still, any attempt to model the Roman economy must wrestle with the question of whether the Romans simply did not think about their economic system, or whether they accomplished economic goals without overtly making economic policy, or whether they conceived of their system in some way quite different from modern economists. Unless someone can somehow discover the records and ideas of many of the key figures who made large-scale decisions for Rome, people may always have to speculate about this question.

A Multicultural and International Economy. The Romans commanded an empire and economy involving more people, more territory, more resources, and more different types of nations than perhaps any empire in ancient history, and they managed it for centuries. Whether through conquest or alliance, they constantly worked on ways to make new territories and peoples part of the empire, and yet they were quick to recognize the differences and value of the people and communities they encountered. They faced differences in language, religion, culture, tradition, as well as economic system. Today the world is increasingly developing a global economy, involving different peoples and nations literally all around the globe. The successes and failures of the Romans as they endeavored to create the largest and most complex economy the world had ever known still have much to teach about uniting a world in peacetime growth.

TOPICS IN SOCIAL CLASS SYSTEM AND THE ECONOMY

ECONOMIC ACTIVITY: CULTIVATION AND RESOURCES

Agriculture. Agricultural production formed the foundation of the entire Roman economy. Most ancient historians even believe that agriculture all but eclipsed other economic activity. Certainly Roman tradition favored such a view. The most respectable wealth was was based on property and derived from farming. On the other hand, the Romans knew very well that farming did not generate the largest fortunes. Still, agriculture provided an established, stable, and profitable economic base.

Polyculture. Three agricultural products dominated trade and have been labeled the "Mediterranean Triad": grain, wine, and olive oil. The demand for grain was constant and estate owners considered it a dependable investment. Grapevines represented a riskier market, but with a higher potential return. More importantly, grapevines and olive trees have different soil requirements and harvest times from grains, so farmers could grow all three different crops on the same farmland. "Polyculture" refers to farming the triad in this way. This efficient use of arable land provided a reliable source of food, which in turn permitted more permanent settlements. The development of this polyculture took place over several thousand years in prehistoric times, and scholars believe it was the key ingredient allowing civilization to flourish around the Mediterranean Sea. Consequently, by the time of the Romans, polyculture had a long and venerable history of providing the most basic needs for survival and growth, which may explain why the Romans esteemed farming so highly. In turn, the value and prestige associated with farmland meant that land throughout Italy in particular was parceled and farmed much more thoroughly than in modern times. Many small and large farms filled out all the land. The value of crops beyond the Mediterranean Triad is more difficult to determine, but the elder Cato once suggested a list of nine farming prospects in order of desirability: grapevines, irrigated gardens, willow, olives, grazing meadows, grain, timber, orchard trees, and nuts.

Ranch and Farm Animals. The life of a shepherd in particular had a literary tradition of being peaceful and idyllic. Few who idolized the shepherd's life actually lived it, however, or would have been willing to do so. Thieves and rustlers were problems for herders of all sorts, the work was always demanding, and the profits perhaps not so promising. Romans rarely discussed the reality of raising animals for meat and other by-products, so it is difficult to know the scale or details about this activity. Archaeological evidence indicates that Romans throughout the empire fattened and slaughtered cattle, pigs, and sheep. Meat production was strong enough to support a fairly complex industry in butchery. Cases in Roman antiquity of raising poultry successfully, including thrushes and peahens have been known. Cows and goats could be kept not only for their milk, but also for the production of cheese, which was more easily stored and transported than fresh milk (and so had broader economic advantages). The Romans did not limit the exploitation of animals to edible products. The ever-increasing population of the Roman Empire meant a constant need for huge amounts of wool for clothing and leather for a variety of implements (for example, for much of a soldier's equipment), needs met by ranch farmers throughout the empire and beyond.

Working on the Farm. While the Romans held up the farmer's life as something of an ideal, the reality of practice varied. Some small farm owners worked their own land, though hired help must always have been a component. Especially as Rome conquered Italy, small farms struggled against much larger and better-organized plantations. Handbooks about how to manage such plantations survive, and these provide the most detailed knowledge about work on farms. In such circumstances, slaves did most of the physical labor. Farming, as always, was demanding labor. Clearing, planting, and maintaining land, then harvesting, processing, and storing crops all require constant, intense work. Slaves in urban households might consider work in the farm fields as banishment or punishment.

Fishing and Fish Farming. The Mediterranean region does not provide a consistent and reliable source of fish. Since fish provided an excellent source of protein in the ancient Mediterranean diet, it was worthwhile to stockpile fish as much as possible, so an industry in salting fish to pre-

Funerary relief of men with poles stomping on grapes to extract the juice for wine production, circa first century C.E. (Museo Archeologico Nazionale, Venice)

serve and transport them flourished. Another strong demand supported the fish industry: one of the most popular ingredients in many dishes was *garum,* a fish sauce (perhaps somewhat similar to modern Worcestershire sauce). In fact, cities with or near supplies of fish are known to have had factories devoted to the production of *garum.* This constant demand for fish made it possible to support fish farming in large tanks, dams, and channels around the coast of the Mediterranean Sea. The most desirable fish, however, came from open sea fishing, but the dangers and difficulty of this enterprise meant such fish, especially fresh, were a quite expensive luxury.

Forests and Timber. As with raising animals, only scattered information is known about how the Romans harvested trees and to what extent. The wood required for ships and buildings alone meant a huge, consistent need for lumber and would have called for timbers of particular types, sizes, and quality. Archaeological evidence indicates that the Romans planted, fenced, and managed forested land to produce the wood necessary. Whenever possible, of course, Romans would acquire wood from nearby forests rather than have to transport heavy timbers over long distances, and so forestry remained mostly a local industry. In some cases, clearing forests could have motives other than economic ones. For example, Roman armies would clear forests for

military purposes and use the wood to build their camp. Forests could also support a neighboring industry. There is evidence that in Roman Britain, pottery industries were set up near woods so as to be closer to their primary source of fuel, even if it meant transporting their finished products greater distances.

Mining. Italy itself provided relatively little metal to be mined. As the Romans conquered and absorbed their rivals around the Mediterranean, they took control of many mining operations. Mining could be extremely lucrative since valuable metals such as gold and silver not only were valuable in themselves but acted as the measure for most economic exchange. Less valuable metals were still in great demand for metalworking across the empire. On the other hand, mining itself was expensive, because it required huge numbers of laborers and a great many skilled workers. The Romans did not concentrate as much on starting new mines as expanding already operational ones. New sources of ore, when found, tended to be located by noticing traces of veins on the surface. The Romans would exploit a mining site by employing three basic methods, in order of increasing cost. First, ore discovered in gravel or sediment was uncovered by flushing the looser materials away with water. Nearby waterways could be diverted to wash away the lighter elements and leave the heavier, desirable metals and ores to be pulled up (similar to "panning" for gold). Next came "opencast" mining, which involved digging huge pits and clearing the necessary area to reach the desired metal. Although the Romans did not have modern explosives for blasting, they did have effective ways of clearing areas. They could, for example, set an area on fire and quickly flood it with cold water, causing rocks and hills to explode in the sudden temperature shift. Workers could then clear and dig out the rubble. The final and most-expensive method was shaft mining. Dropping shafts required intensive and hazardous labor along with excellent engineering. Nonetheless, Roman mine shafts deeper than one thousand feet have been discovered. As well as digging and maintaining the shafts themselves, mining would often involve draining subterranean water, for which the Romans devised and used an array of tools and techniques. Especially at this last stage, mining became extremely hazardous work for the miners (as it is in modern mines) and mines earned a comparably notorious reputation. Mine owners and supervisors were known to have used recalcitrant slaves, forced labor, and criminals for the most dangerous work. On the other hand, the enormous profits involved also supported an entire local economy around the mine. Workers had to be fed, clothed, cared for, and sheltered during their work. The distances some men traveled to work at a mine may suggest the wages were high enough to attract workers. Many skilled workers and engineers were always involved. Some records of lease agreements and labor contracts that indicate the complexity of these arrangements and even show that there were safety regulations have survived. The enormity of the work, the complexity of the organization, and the value of the projects meant that many mines were state owned and operated, but there always remained some private individuals who owned and ran mines.

Sources:

Kevin Greene, *The Archaeology of the Roman Economy* (Berkeley: University of California Press, 1986).

Jo-Ann Shelton, *As the Romans Did: A Sourcebook in Roman Social History*, second edition (New York: Oxford University Press, 1998).

ECONOMIC ACTIVITY: MANUFACTURING AND PRODUCTION

Metallurgy and Metalworking. The huge and increasing mining of metal ores precipitated a comparable industry in metallurgy. The Romans found most metals alloyed together when they mined, so separating the ore into the desired individual metals was a constant activity. Gold and silver went primarily for coinage, jewelry, and luxury items. Bronze, lead, iron, and other metals served a host of needs from piping to weapons to tableware to statuary. As in other areas, the Romans increased the scale and range of metallurgy, incorporating the industry into the vast network of the empire.

Stone and Stoneworking. Many of the most famous images and artifacts of ancient Rome, from the Coliseum to the aqueducts, are built of stone. Given that for the most part only the basic structures and cheaper stones survive of such structures, we should remember the enormous quantities of stone involved in the construction of the many buildings, homes, streets, and infrastructure all around the Roman Empire. The use of stone began always with retrieving the stone from where it was buried. Quarrying was labor-intensive work, and it did not become much easier until the nineteenth century C.E. with modern blasting techniques. Because stone is so heavy, and hence difficult to transport, Romans preferred not to carry it any farther from its source than necessary. In different regions of the empire, therefore, people tended to use the types of stone available locally. On the other hand, the demand for attractive stone such as marble was high and those who could would pay to have stone shipped to them on barges. Demand was such that eventually the Romans built up a stockpile of types and sizes of marbles so as to make ordering and delivering stone easier and more efficient. As with different types of wood, the Romans took pains to use suitable and attractive types of stone according to the needs of their construction. Basic stonework formed the foundations of structures ranging from temples to roads, but more meticulous stonework would decorate buildings, streets, tombs, and gardens. In addition to the quarrymen and stoneworkers needed to recover, deliver, and lay basic stoneworks, repair work was always necessary, especially in areas that suffered earthquakes.

Bricks and Tiles. The raw materials for bricks and tiles, clay and loose stone, were available in abundance. The production of red-clay roof tiles constituted one of the earliest industries in Rome, and it would remain a fixture of Italian production throughout the history of the Roman world. In 64 C.E., after a great fire raged through Rome, brickmaking soared. The rebuilding of the city called for bricks on a

Relief of a knife-maker in his shop with a customer, circa first century C.E. (from Anna Maria Liberti and Fabio Bourbon, *Ancient Rome*, 1996)

Wall painting of Cupids working as goldsmiths, from the House of the Vetii, Pompeii, probably done as part of the redecoration following the circa 62 C.E. earthquake

greater scale than had ever been used before. The potential profits led to increased production and also left a record unlike other Roman industries. For some reason, elite Roman families willingly associated themselves with the brick factories they owned, although wealthy partners usually avoided public affiliation with any source of income other than agriculture. It is possible that the Romans associated the production of clay bricks and tiles with the production of terra-cotta roof tiles on a farm, and so it had a respectable air. In any case, especially following the great fire in Rome, bricks bore stamps indicating what factory produced them, the owner of the company, and even other workers. These stamps provide rare evidence of the production and history of a Roman industry. The Emperor Marcus Aurelius inherited a large part of the brick industry, and then factories gradually came under imperial control.

Glass. While the use of glass for opaque bottles, beads, and other decoration goes back thousands of years, the invention of glassblowing in Syria during the first century B.C.E. transformed glass production. The glass industry, which now included vessels of a variety of shapes in highly desirable transparent form, spread across the Roman Empire. Ancient authors comment that glass products became rather inexpensive. As early as the first century C.E., window glass is known and later becomes widespread.

Pottery. No artifact survives in greater numbers from ancient sites than pottery. Broken pieces of pottery can exist in the millions on just one site. Like other ancient peoples, the Romans used pottery wares constantly on a daily basis.

Pottery included standard tableware such as plates and bowls. Many goods were stored and transported in types of pots called "coarse" or "kitchen" ware, much as they are in boxes today. Wealthy people could also have fancy and elaborate pottery for their table or home. Pottery was so prevalent in the Roman world that ancient writers rarely comment on it; they could not imagine anyone would ever need to know anything about it! Meeting such a huge demand meant that production had to be constant and efficient. Since everyone used pottery, production centers existed in every part of the ancient world. Except for luxurious and expensive types of pottery, there was little reason to produce pottery in one area and ship it away (except when it was being used as a container). Trade in pottery wares, then, rarely extended beyond a particular region. While talented potters and craftsmen could make the more expensive, elaborate, and decorated pots, common types could be produced in assembly-line fashion. For example, a common pottery type called *terra sigillata* ("sealed earth," for example, clay marked with a seal-stamp) is known to have been produced in stages by different workers. Some surviving examples have as many as three different signature stamps. The craftsman who designed a mold for a certain type of pottery might put his name on the mold to be reproduced on each of the items produced from that mold. A workshop, company, or factory would often incorporate their name or some form of advertisement for themselves into the design. Finally, the worker who added the last molding to the pot could sign it. Such "signatures" served the purpose of trademarks and barcodes on modern products. Once a pot or series of pots was

An assortment of Roman glassware from the first century C.E. (Yale University Art Gallery, New Haven, Connecticut)

TECHNOLOGY AND THE ROMAN ECONOMY

The Romans left a legacy of technological achievements rivaled by few peoples until the advent of the Industrial Revolution. And yet, in view of the Industrial Revolution and the many technological advances to follow, scholars have been divided about evaluating the success of the Romans. As archaeological work continues to show, the Romans employed an astounding array of devices and methods in building up the empire, in architecture, weaponry, mining, medicine, harvesting, and more. At its peak, the empire also brought widespread stability and economic success. Most of the innovations in technology, however, such as blowing glass, belonged to other peoples and the Romans would expand or intensify the use and production of such items. In some cases, a new technology was known (such as the principle for the steam engine) but the Romans never developed it. Some scholars also believe that by privileging agriculture, the Romans kept the economy of the empire just barely above the subsistence level. Other scholars point out, however, that production, trade, and even the sophistication of available technology peaked during Roman domination and would not be matched again or exceeded for over a thousand years. Further complicating the problem is that Roman writers rarely express the kind of interest or provide the kind of information about technology and economic advancement which we would expect today, so comparison of Roman practice with modern achievements is difficult. Is it fair to judge the Roman economy by later economic systems? How should we decide?

Source: K. D. White, *Greek and Roman Technology* (Ithaca, N.Y.: Cornell University Press, 1984).

molded, it still had to be fired in a kiln. Surviving records from kiln operators show that a workshop might take its dried pots to kilns elsewhere to be fired and completed. The "signatures" could then be helpful for accounting in this process.

Pottery as an Economic Indicator. The quality and variety of pottery at a given home or community often suggests the economic health of the area as well as its ties to other parts of the empire. While particular pots would not normally be sold in and of themselves, the distribution of pots, especially *amphorae* used for transportation, help scholars trace the network of trade in the Roman economy. The results are impressive. The distribution of pottery as a result of trading suggests a thriving trade network that would not be rivaled again until the height of the British Empire many centuries later. Types of pottery can also contribute to understanding how the quality of life of the wealthy compared to poorer folk. While at some times and places, wealthy and more modest homes might all use comparable tableware, at other times the wealthy might use distinctively more elaborate and expensive ware. Toward the end of the empire, wealthy homes even started using metal tableware.

Clothes Manufacture. Traditional Roman ideals called for the women of the house to make all the clothes for the household. *Lanam fecit,* "she made wool," a traditional epitaph for wives on tombstones, meant she upheld this ancient virtue. In urban areas, however, an industry of clothes production existed. As the Roman world expanded, people enjoyed experimenting with fashions from far-off and exotic places. A full range of clothiers, tailors, and textile workers existed, both men and women. Jobs included importing wool, leather, linens, and other fabrics; tailoring the material; weaving; dying materials with all sorts of colors; designing; shoemaking, and many more. With so much labor going into producing clothes, people were more prone to have their clothes repaired and patched than dispose of them. Workers involved in every type of patching existed, as well as shoe repair. The final process for some clothes was fulling (a method of shrinking and thickening the woolen cloth by means of wetting, heating, and pressing it). Fullers also operated the laundries of the ancient world. They cleaned and pressed clothes. One of the stages involved working the clothing in a mixture that included stale urine. For this reason, the Emperor Vespasian actually passed a tax on urine! This upset the fullers, of course.

Jewelers. Although despised by many Romans who felt jewelry was a sign of decadence, many types of jewelry were popular in the Roman world. Goldworking in particular had a long history. The Etruscans (who lived in southern Italy, were important in the early history of Rome, and eventually were absorbed into the Roman population) had a long, splendid history of goldsmithing. Some surviving Etruscan jewelry has goldwork so fine that even modern goldsmiths cannot match it. Both Roman men and women wore rings. Necklaces and earrings were also popular. Often slaves and foreign craftsmen did the work, or their pieces were imported. As with many other arts and crafts, the Romans could appreciate the products but not respect their creators.

Sources:

Kevin Greene, *The Archaeology of the Roman Economy* (Berkeley: University of California Press, 1986).

Jo-Ann Shelton, *As the Romans Did: A Sourcebook in Roman Social History*, second edition (New York: Oxford University Press, 1998).

ECONOMIC ACTIVITY: SERVICE SECTOR

Tabellarii. Slaves and freedmen were employed as postal carriers, *tabellarii*, by the Roman state and by private individuals. Publican companies also supplied couriers available for private individuals. Such individuals often wanted to be sure of the security of their personal mail. *Tabellarii* were known to cover more than sixty Roman miles in a day. Augustus initiated a massive postal communication system for government purposes, which came to be known as the *cursus publicus*. This system depended on a series of stations (the larger *mansiones* and changing posts, or *mutationes*) and local provision of animals and supplies. These local provisions proved burdensome, unpopular, and prone to abuse, and there were constant efforts to reform the system.

The interior of a thermopolium ("hot spot"), a street-side restaurant, in Pompeii, circa first century C.E. When archaeologists excavated the site, they found the last day's earnings (683 sesterces in small coins) in a jar on the counter.

Restaurants and Bars. In ancient cities, restaurants and bars throve. While wealthier residents with large homes could have a kitchen and kitchen staff at home, and others would hope for a dinner invitation in such a house, most people ate outside the home. The huge portion of the population who lived in apartment complexes had no kitchens, for in antiquity they were dreaded as fire hazards, and apartment buildings were susceptible to fire as it was. Restaurants were everywhere, offering food, hot meals, and drinks. Such establishments would have employed cooks, servers, and other staff. Roman houses did not have front façades, but only small entryways. Often, then, the space around the entrance to a house was rented out for a shop or small tavern, thus providing extra income for a houseowner. It also meant city blocks became an amalgam of residences and businesses.

Cooks and Caterers. Wealthier residents or officials could have held private dinners or even had other meals of the day at home. Cooks and other kitchen staff could have been among the household slaves. Cooks and catering staff could also be hired for special occasions, such as weddings, funerals, meetings, and the like. As with some other professions, although food preparation was crucial for important gatherings such as formal dinners, the cooks themselves were usually slaves, foreigners, and often objects of scorn or mockery.

Grocers. In a world without refrigeration, regular access to grocers was essential. Except on larger farms where the ideal was for the property to be self-sufficient, people shopped for their meals probably on a daily basis. While some crops, especially grains, could be bought and stored, many items such as fruits, vegetables, and meats would be bought and prepared the same day. Even in wealthy residences, the kitchen staff would have to shop for ingredients daily or have them delivered. Restaurant owners would require a regular supply of foodstuffs.

Public Games. Perhaps no image of ancient Rome dominates the imagination like the wild ancient spectacles and games. Many *ludi*, "games," were, in origin at least, religious festivals, although even many sacred games became more entertainment than ritual as time went on. Such games involved play acting and shows, as well as the more notorious gladiatorial combats, chariot races, and other spectacles. Such productions cost huge amounts of money and admission was free. The sponsors of the games had to pay and provide for the hundreds of construction workers, trainers, engineers, and other workers to put on such shows. Of course, sellers of snacks, drinks, and memorabilia (for example, mugs with a favorite athlete on them) peddled their stock at the arenas as well. Gambling on the contests was also a thriving industry, as surviving records of bets show.

Hotels and Tourism. Travel in the ancient world could be slow and difficult. The stability of the Roman Empire and the remarkable system of roads made it much easier than at other times and places, but travel could still be expensive and dangerous. Wealthy travelers ideally would stay only with friends on their journeys, but for most travelers, hotels, motels, and inns were a necessity. Such stops did not enjoy a good reputation. They were often simple, dirty, and attracted a rough clientele. A basic inn would consist of bedrooms (guests would be locked into their rooms for security) and a tavern. Romans went on vacation and visited tourist attractions. The supposed site of the Trojan War, for example, remained a popular tourist attraction for centuries. Several coastal cities became resort towns for Romans looking to get away from it all. They provided fine accommodations and the most lavish of accoutrements.

Brothels. Prostitution was legal in the Roman world. In fact, it was a thriving industry. Prostitutes, and especially the procurers who supplied them, had an unsavory reputation. Nonetheless, brothels were not hidden or restricted to marginal parts of a city. They competed openly and frankly for

MONEY-CHANGERS

Today, when people travel between different countries which use various forms of currency, there is a fairly secure and standard system for exchanging money. Financial experts maintain and participate in an intricate global system for determining the relative values of the currencies of countries all over the world. In the Roman world, as in many ancient civilizations, exchanging currencies was a more problematic process. Often individual cities issued their own coinage. A traveler needing the coinage of a new city had to go to someone known as a "money-changer." This individual would compute how much the coin of one city or country was worth in terms of the coin of another city or country. Since the value of coins was determined by the value of the metal used in them, money-changers would weigh the coins and try to compute how much the metal was worth. Such computations could be difficult because coins might be made of several types of metal at once. Governments would sometimes issue coins that were not worth as much as they claimed. They might, for example, put a silver coating around a cheaper metal and claim it was a silver coin. Money-changers would have to keep up with these technicalities. Moreover, money-changers themselves could try to take advantage of the difficulties. Money-changers charged their customers a fee for their services but they might also try to trick their customers and make an extra profit. They could fudge on the exchange rate or distribute poor quality coinage. Money-changers, in fact, had a notorious reputation for cheating people. Because of all these problems, the establishment of government mints and the gradual universal acceptance of Roman coinage made life easier and more secure for many people in the Roman world.

Source: Richard Duncan-Jones, *Money and Government in the Roman Empire* (Cambridge & New York: Cambridge University Press, 1994).

"Wounded Aeneas," a house painting from the House of Siricus at Pompeii showing a doctor healing an injured soldier, circa first century C.E. (Museo Nazionale, Naples)

business. Because many people did not read, businesses often used picture signs for advertisements. A fish shop would have a placard with a fish on it, for example. Brothels also seem to have catered to nonliterate clientele. Appropriate signs or carvings indicated a given building was a brothel. Decorations inside may have suggested available services. Tokens with drawings may have allowed customers to make a selection even if they did not know the language.

Teachers and Schools. The Romans never instituted mandatory public schooling, although by the middle of the third century C.E., primary school was provided all over the empire. Generally, teachers charged fees and attracted what students they could. They did not necessarily have a permanent building or location, but they might rent space or, to save money, simply hold class outside. A lot of education and training probably took the form of apprenticeships. Wealthier Romans could afford tutors or more-expensive schools. Wealthy sponsors could also endow schools to make them more accessible. Under the influence of the Greeks, several types and levels of teachers developed. Full-time pedagogues, basically in-home tutors, might be qualified Greek slaves bought by the family. Elementary teachers seem to have been

the most affordable (and conversely least well-paid) instructors, as well as the most plentiful. The *grammaticus* provided the first formal education, generally with an emphasis on language and literature. A *rhetor* provided a higher level of training, most especially for those pursuing careers in law or statesmanship. The Emperor Vespasian, toward the end of the first century C.E., provided the first known state sponsorship of education. Quintilian held one of Vespasian's endowed chairs and wrote an elaborately detailed treatise on educating Roman statesmen, which still survives, called the *Institutio oratoria*, circa 95 B.C.E.

Doctors. Practitioners of medicine enjoyed an ambivalent reputation in antiquity. While some excellent physicians lived in this period, many doctors evidently did not serve their profession well. Much of what is known of Roman medicine derives from Greek practice, and most doctors seem to have been Greek, but new knowledge is arising about distinctly Roman practices. Doctors pervaded the Roman world, especially in cities and accompanying armies. They were not among the wealthiest in the Roman world and far from the most respectable. The first Greek doctor to come to Rome, Archagathus, earned the nickname *carnifex*, "butcher." Cruel

The remains of a bakery at Pompeii, circa first century C.E.

Frieze of a produce market in Rome, late second century C.E. (Ostia Museum, Ostia)

The Romans are as famous for their holidays as for anything else. The massive spectacles they put on constitute the "circuses" in "bread and circuses," a phrase still used to denote functions put on to gain favor crassly with a mass population. Courts were closed, and certain types of work were restricted. The sheer number of such festival holidays (*ludi*) has also become notorious. While in the first century B.C.E., 57 days were devoted to *ludi*, in the fourth century C.E. as many as 177 days had *ludi*. With nearly half of the year devoted to holidays, when did people work? Holidays did not mean everyone got off work. Many people would still have to work to maintain their living, and slaves would be at their masters' whim. Games required a large number of people to work just to put them on. Holidays would not necessarily all be celebrated in all places around the empire. Many modern days off from work would also be foreign to the Romans. They did not have weekends, for example, so there are 104 holidays built into the modern calendar that the Romans never had. They also did not recognize the forty-hour workweek, paid vacations, sick leave, or child-labor laws. No wonder they looked forward to the games!

Source: H. H. Scullard, *Festivals and Ceremonies of the Roman Republic* (London: Thames & Hudson, 1981).

jokes about the inefficacy and hazards of doctors abounded. The poet Martial joked about a doctor who became a mortician, without changing jobs! Julius Caesar, however, wished to grant citizenship to doctors for their skill and service. By and large, little is known about the many doctors who maintained their practices and offices around the Roman world.

Legacy-Hunting. Especially in the early days of the empire, the Romans recognized the phenomenon of "legacy-hunting." This referred to befriending and ingratiating oneself with a wealthy person in the hopes of being included in their will. Death, divorce, childlessness, or other difficulties could leave someone with control of an estate and no clear heir. A young man might romance a wealthy widow or a young woman might pursue a wealthy widower, for example, to try to get in on the fortune. Slaves were suspected of flattering their masters in the hopes of being freed and otherwise compensated in their masters' wills. It became a dark joke that an elderly person with a fortune and a cough (a sign they might be ill and near death) was attractive. Petronius in his novel *Satyricon* describes Croton as a place where the dominant occupation was legacy-hunting! How much Romans exaggerated the problem of legacy-hunting cannot be known. Wealthy Romans feared legacy-hunting because they generally preferred that wealth be kept within a family and handed down from generation to generation. Thus, some aristocratic Romans probably were somewhat anxious about wealth being passed on to lower classes, slaves, freedmen, or foreigners.

Sources:

Kevin Greene, *The Archaeology of the Roman Economy* (Berkeley: University of California Press, 1986).

Jo-Ann Shelton, *As the Romans Did: A Sourcebook in Roman Social History*, second edition (New York: Oxford University Press, 1998).

ECONOMIC ACTIVITY: TRANSPORTATION

Transportation. Any product an individual, household, or community does not produce on their own, they must acquire from somewhere else and have it transported. This principle remains true for basic necessities, desirable items, or luxuries. Transport thus stands as an essential mechanism of any economy. Efficiency and reliability of delivery in turn are necessary for a functioning economic system to flourish and grow. Three basic types of transport existed in the Roman world: by boat across a sea, by boat along a river, or by cart across land. Land

Tomb painting from Ostia depicting porters loading grain into the "Isis Giminiana," a small merchant ship, from the third century B.C.E. (Vatican Museum, Rome)

and Black Sea to the Southeast, and northward around the Western coast of Europe on the Atlantic Ocean. Cargo ships constantly traveled on the seas. To be most profitable, a ship would not simply cross a sea but would make multiple stops along the coast, selling and buying cargo at each stop. Such constant shipping would support full-time sailors, crewmen, captains, navigators, and others.

Piracy. Seaborne cargo offered a mechanism for profit that the carrier did not intend. Pirates made their living by capturing ships at sea and stealing their cargo, both material and human. While writers would romanticize the plight of sons and daughters ransomed or enslaved by pirates, real piracy posed a serious threat to sea travel and trade in Classical times. Pirates established coastal bases and resold the merchandise they captured, sold the people they captured as slaves, and sold or used the ships they took. As Rome solidified its empire, however, Roman efforts gradually suppressed pirate activities. Pompey earned fame for cleansing the Mediterranean basin of pirates in the 60s B.C.E. When the Roman Empire fragmented centuries later, piracy once again rose in the Mediterranean.

Shipbuilding. The use of so many ships by merchants, as well as by the military, provided for a robust industry in shipbuilding. Every ship required a vast amount of material and a huge number of workers. First, workers needed wood from several different types of trees for the keel, hull, frame, and treenails. The keel was shaped and laid first and then the hull built up with tightly fitted planks. Only with the hull completed did the workers add the internal supports (the "skeleton"). The mast and decking came last. Metalworkers labored throughout the process, adding joints, fittings, rigging, and a lead covering around the hull to guard against sea worms. The demand for ships, the constant risk of loss and damage to ships while sailing, and maintenance also would have supported units of carpenters, builders, and metalworkers.

Ports and Harbors. Larger freighters require protected, safe harbors and fixed dockworks so that they can pull to shore safely and securely for loading and unloading. The Romans used some relatively large freighters. Cargo ships for grain regularly could carry more than one hundred tons. Many ships could carry three hundred to five hundred tons, and a few super-size freighters had the capacity to carry more than a thousand tons. Few harbors could dock these largest ships, but smaller Roman harbors circled the Mediterranean. The Roman invention of concrete that sets under water advanced the design and construction of moles (protective walls that keep the waters near the harbor calm) and quays (reinforced banks where loading and unloading take place). Building such harbors called for designers, engineers, and construction workers. The regular dockwork of loading and unloading supported work crews. In addition, as in all areas and times, port cities provided lodgings, entertainment, and other support services for seamen while they were between voyages.

River Travel. The scale of trade along a particular river depended on its navigability and its proximity to settlements

Funerary stele of the shipbuilder Publius Longidienus, circa first century C.E. The inscription reads: "Publius Longidienus hastens to get on with his work" (Ravenna Museum, Ravenna).

transport was the most expensive, costing five to ten times what river transport cost. River transport in turn could cost five times as much as sea transport, so Roman businessmen tried to use water transport as much as possible. For example, merchants would use several different rivers to reach their destination, or would have their merchandise carried from one river to another in order to capitalize on the cheaper shipping. As the Romans added to their conquests and expanded their empire, trade expanded and transportation became a larger and more complex industry in its own right.

Sea Transport. Travel over the sea meant predominantly transportation across and around the Mediterranean Sea. "We sit around a pond," Plato had said once, "like frogs," referring to the way peoples clustered around the borders of the Mediterranean. When the Roman Empire was at its broadest, trade could also include routes on the Black Sea to the Northeast, the Caspian Sea to the East, the Persian Gulf

The *Via Appia* (Appian Way), started in 312 B.C.E. on orders of the censor Appius Claudius, was the first paved road in Rome.

or other waterways. Travel along rivers ran the range from small freighters to simple rafts. Rivers served as the highways for trade to and from the coast and between destinations away from coastal waters. Transport by river was vital enough to the Roman Empire that the state, especially for military purposes, would sometimes organize traffic on rivers or dig and construct canals to facilitate travel and commerce. Locals also organized, however. For example, boatmen formed guilds. Trade did not provide the only economic opportunity. Because travel over land was slow and uncomfortable, people would also travel in a boat along the river when they could. The poet Horace (65–8 B.C.E.) describes part of a trip he makes by boat, in this case a small barge pulled by a mule walking along the shore. Unfortunately, Horace does not find his trip going well:

> Slaves hurled insults at the boatmen, and boatmen back at the slaves. "Put in here!" "You must have three hundred! That's enough!" By the time the fare was paid and the mule hitched up, a whole hour had gone by. Evil mosquitoes and frogs in the marsh made sleep impossible. Meanwhile, a boatman and one of the passengers, both drunk from way too much cheap wine, took turns serenading their absent girlfriends. Finally, the passenger wore out and fell asleep. The slacker boatman let the mule go grazing, hung the harness on a rock, and commenced snoring on his back. It was already daylight before we noticed that the boat wasn't moving. So one hothead jumped out of the boat and beat the mule (and the boatman, too) on the head and crotch with a willow stick. We barely arrived four hours after sunrise. (Horace, *Satires* 1.5.11–23).

"All Roads Lead to Rome." The city of Rome represented the economic hub of the Roman world every bit as much as

the center for political and military power. With regard to road building, the Romans justly earned their fame. Their massive system of roads linked important sites wherever the Romans held control. Originally, the road system had the purpose of facilitating troop movement and making communication as efficient as possible (by a system of couriers). Like the interstate system in the modern United States, these roads had economic benefits as well. In times of peace and stability, trade and communication along these roads became reliable to a degree entirely unprecedented in the Mediterranean world. Even though water transport was cheaper and always remained more desirable, the lengthy trade routes, sometimes stretching hundreds or thousands of miles, could never have developed without the Roman system of high-quality roads. The Roman state initiated and maintained the best and most important roadways, but local communities and even wealthy individuals added to the complex. During the years of expansion under the Republic, the Romans linked together the entire Italian peninsula. Later, emperors continued the practice of constructing and maintaining large stretches of roadwork all over the empire. Moreover, the Romans made a show of the way they would maintain straight roads even across or through difficult obstacles rather than divert the path of the road. Many roads had such strong foundations and construction that they still form the basis for important modern roads, and even some abandoned ones can be followed to this day.

Horses, Mules, and Oxen; Carts and Wagons. Large shipments always had to be delivered by boat, and water travel always remained much less expensive. Still, at some point carts and wagons had their part to play in delivery, and the dependability of Roman roads assisted economic development in this area. In urban areas, carts and wagons congested streets every bit as much as cars in cities today. As in modern times, related businesses flourished, such as rental companies, insurance, and legal wrangling over accidents. Between urban areas, carts and wagons drawn by oxen could transport loads, and indeed pack animals by themselves could carry substantial loads. Horses were more expensive and were used more for rapid transit, such as for postal couriers, who could ride horseback or in a small, light chariot. People could also travel in passenger chariots, though such travel had a reputation for being slow and uncomfortable.

Sources:

Kevin Greene, *The Archaeology of the Roman Economy* (Berkeley: University of California Press, 1986).

Jo-Ann Shelton, *As the Romans Did: A Sourcebook in Roman Social History*, second edition (New York: Oxford University Press, 1998).

MONEY

The Roman Monetary System. In the most general terms, money is an agreed upon measurement for the economic value of items. If a seller and a buyer agree that one item is worth twenty dollars and another is worth ten dollars, the agreement says less about how much a dollar is worth than about the relative value of the two items. More importantly, both individuals are agreeing to use dollars to measure the relative worth of both items, as well as probably their own incomes, estates, and so on. In this sense, money can facilitate economic exchange through coinage, paper money, property, loans and interest, credit, or a variety of other goods. As in many areas, the Romans did much to standardize and make monetary systems efficient. Monetary value operated in exchanges of all scales, from buying food at the market to meeting the financial requirements to be a senator. Monetary value was articulated in terms of coinage, which was in turn based on the relative values of the metals used to produce them: gold, silver, bronze, copper, tin, and occasionally other metals. Via this standard expressed through coinage, the Romans assessed

THE PRICE-EDICT OF DIOCLETIAN

The many changes in currency during the third century C.E. fueled rampant inflation. People wanted to use up the coins they had before they lost their value. The emperor Diocletian (ruled 285–305) published an edict in 301 C.E. that initiated reforms that would eventually stabilize the currency, but prices continued to soar in the meantime. To combat skyrocketing inflation, Diocletian soon published a Price Edict, copies of which have survived. It lists strict price controls for a variety of items and stiff punishments for selling anything for prices in excess of those given. In the end, the Edict itself failed, for sellers preferred not to sell items rather than sell them at the prices demanded by the Edict, and eventually the order was simply ignored. Still, it provides a fascinating glimpse of the relative prices of different items.

Food Prices (per *modius*, about one-fourth of a bushel; all prices in *denarii*):

wheat 100, barley 60, rye 60, millet (whole) 50, millet (ground) 100, beans (whole) 60, beans (ground) 100 , lentils 100, peas 60, split peas 100, chick-peas 100, vetch 100, oats 30, fenugreek 100, lupines (raw) 60, lupines (cooked) 40, dried beans 100.

Wine Prices (per *sextarius*, about a pint or half-liter; all prices in *denarii*):

Picene 30, Tiburtine 30, Sabine 30, Falernian 30, aged (high grade) 24, aged (second grade) 16, ordinary 8.

Oil Prices (per *sextarius*, about a pint or half-liter; all prices in *denarii*):

olive oil (fresh) 40, olive oil (second grade) 24, vinegar 6, *liquamen* (fish sauce, high grade) 16, *liquamen* (second grade) 12, salt (per *modius*) 100, honey (high grade) 40, honey (second grade) 24.

Meat Prices (per Roman pound, about 327g or .72 pounds; all prices in *denarii*):

pork 12, beef 8, goose 100, goose (fattened) 200, chicken 60, lamb 12, goat 12.

Fish Prices (per Roman pound, about 327g or .72 pounds; all prices in *denarii*):

fish (second grade) 16, freshwater fish (high grade) 12, freshwater fish (second grade) 8

Shoe Prices (all prices in *denarii*):

high grade workboots (mule drivers, farmworkers) without hobnails 120, soldiers' boots without hobnails 100, patrician shoes 150, senatorial shoes 100, equestrian shoes 70, women's shoes 60

Daily Wages (all in *denarii* and expect meals to be provided):

farm laborer 25, wall painter 75, picture painter 150, carpenter 50, baker 50 camel/donkey driver 25, shepherd 20, sewer cleaner 25

Wages for teachers (all in *denarii* per student per month):

elementary teacher 50, arithmetic teacher 75, *grammaticus* (Greek or Latin instruction, geometry) 200, teacher of rhetoric and public speaking 250, teacher of architecture 100.

Other Wages (all in *denarii*):

veterinarian (for trimming hoofs) 25 per animal, (for bleeding and cleaning the head) 20 per animal, barber 2 per man, tailor (for high grade hooded cloak) 60, (for second grade hooded cloak) 40, (for pants) 20, (for socks) 4, guard of clothes at a public bath 2 per customer, attendant at bath 2 per customer.

Source: Simon Corcoran, *The Empire of the Tetrarchs: Imperial Pronouncements and Government, AD 284–324* (Oxford: Clarendon Press, 1996; New York: Oxford University Press, 1996).

the monetary value of all property, material, and anything else of economic value.

Coins and the Republic. Roman coins, which survive to this day in the thousands in the hands of scholars and collectors, provide the most accessible and tangible remains of the Roman economy. In fact, however, the Romans were late in utilizing coins. In earlier times, the Romans had a basic system for assigning values by metal weights and issued some rudimentary coins, but neighboring peoples around the Mediterranean, such as the Greeks and Carthaginians, already used much more elaborate systems and coins. Following the costly Second Punic War at the end of the third century B.C.E., however, the Roman economy flourished in general and the system of coinage stabilized. The *as* became the standard unit of bronze coinage, and the *denarius* ("tenner," from *decem* "ten"; originally ten times an *as*) remained the standard for silver coinage for five hundred years. Whereas at the beginning of this process, bronze was the dominant metal for coinage and Roman coins were yet another system of coins circulating among the peoples of the Mediterranean, within fifty years, silver overtook bronze and Roman coinage became a dominant currency. By the end of the Republic in the 30s B.C.E., the entire region around the Mediterranean (except Egypt) used Roman coins as standard currency.

Coins and the Emperor. The last fifty years of the Republic saw coin issues reflect the civil unrest of the times. The dictator Sulla began minting coins in gold during the late 80s B.C.E., and later rivals for control of Rome competed to issue their own coins and encourage their use. After Augustus emerged victorious, stability returned to both the Roman state and its coinage. Augustus standardized the gold issue (*aureus*), minted *asses* in copper rather than in bronze, and introduced two new standard coins in bronze, the *sestertius* and the *dupondius* to fill the gap between the *as* and the *denarius*. Their ratios give some idea of the relative values of their constituent metals:

1 *aureus* (gold) = 25 *denarii* = 100 *sestertii* = 400 *asses*

1 *denarius* (silver) = 2 *quinarii* = 4 *sestertii* = 8 *dupondii* = 16 *asses*

1 *sestertius* (bronze) = 2 *dupondii* = 4 *asses*

1 *dupondius* = 2 *asses*

1 *as* (copper) = 2 *semisses* = 4 *quadrantes*

The emperor, in turn, fixed standard weights and amounts of the key metal. For example, Augustus decreed that *aureii* be produced forty to one pound, *denarii* eighty-four to a pound, and later Nero modified the ratios to forty-five *aureii* and ninety-six *denarii* to the pound.

Changing Monetary Policy. In the third century the Roman Empire faced several crises, and coinage once again reflected the instability. The imperial reaction to the economic crisis also illustrates the Roman version of monetary policy. Either from lack of control or by policy, the actual silver content of the *denarius* declined steadily, leading people to consider it worth less and less. In an attempt to raise

revenues, the Emperor Caracalla (ruled 198–217 C.E.) issued a new coin called the *antoninianus,* which was supposed to be worth two *denarii* but had only the silver weight of one and a half *denarii.* It could have happened, therefore, that people would pay their taxes to the emperor in older, more valuable *denarii* while the state mint was actually generating less valuable silver coins, and so the imperial treasury could turn a profit in the process. It turned out, however, that people were not fooled, and instead paid their taxes with the new, cheaper coins and melted down their old coins for the silver! Later emperors tried various means to restore faith in the coinage by guaranteeing silver levels or other means. It was Diocletian (ruled 285–305), however, who set the direction of Roman coinage for the future. He established a new gold coin, the *solidus,* restored the *denarius* to its Augustan proportion of silver, and started a new series of bronze coins. The gold *solidus* later supplanted silver as the standard by which other coins were measured. Eventually, as the empire split and fragmented, Roman coinage lost the backing it received from the stability of the empire. Scholars remain divided on an important question, however. Did the Roman Empire have a formal monetary policy? Some scholars look at actions such as those of Caracalla as evidence the imperial court had no coherent understanding of monetary policy. Other scholars believe that earlier emperors had solid, formal control over coinage and monetary policy and that the crisis of the third century C.E. reflects other problems in the empire and, in some cases, simply poor management rather than lack of management. Since there are very few economic records from the imperial court, no one can be sure what the various emperors thought they would accomplish or why they took the steps they did with respect to coinage and other economic reforms.

Collapse of the Monetary System. The fifth century saw a general breakdown of Roman administration and military. The chasm between the wealthy few and the poor masses widened considerably. The division of imperial authority initiated by Diocletian later turned into a schism between eastern and western empires. The capital moved east to Byzantium, refounded as Constantinople (modern Istanbul in Turkey). Central authority in the western empire evaporated, paving the way for later European nations. The eastern empire struggled but eventually rebounded and prospered for centuries as the Byzantine Empire. Coinage reflected all these broad changes. The empire shifted completely to a gold standard in the fifth century. The gold *solidus* became the coin of choice for state revenues. Silver disappeared into private hands. Bronze and copper coins, now known as *nummi minimi* ("the tiniest coins"), were worth so little that people needed whole bags of them to complete simple transactions, and counterfeiting ran rampant. The reliability of imperial coinage disintegrated across the empire as invaders captured the territories where mines and mints had produced coins. Attempts to restore the quality of and faith in impe-

Relief of a construction project under way, circa 100–110
C.E.; a human-powered treadmill is depicted at the
lower left (Lateran Museum, Vatican, Rome)

rial coinage were as fleeting as the attempts at recapturing the prosperity and stability of the classical Roman Empire. Never since, not even in modern times, have all the lands that once belonged to the Roman Empire ever shared a common and reliable currency.

Sources:

Kevin Greene, *The Archaeology of the Roman Economy* (Berkeley: University of California Press, 1986).

Allen M. Ward, Fritz M. Heichelheim, and Cedric A. Yeo, *A History of the Roman People,* third edition (Upper Saddle River, N.J.: Prentice-Hall, 1999).

OCCUPATIONS: THE ELITE

Senators. Tradition always maintained that a Roman senator should be a farmer who did public service when called upon to do so and for him to generally act as a model of Roman industriousness. In practice, a senator's working day varied from individual to individual and changed a great deal in the course of the history of the empire. During the Republic, when the Senate held the greatest power in the Roman state, senators had many responsibilities. The Senate directed all of Rome's finances, made crucial decisions about deploying the military, and guided all diplomatic missions. To enter the Senate, and as members, many also took administrative jobs or governed the territories they conquered. In earlier times, too, senators were more likely to be or have been officers in the military. By contrast, in spite of their wealth, senators were not supposed to engage in commerce or invest in trade. Such activity was unbecoming to a senator and legal measures, such as those prohibiting a senator from owning a merchant ship, were put in place to discourage such activity. In practice, however, the profits to be made from such investments were great, and senators found ways to put their money into trade anyway. They would have friends or clients handle the business for them and would be "secret" partners in such ventures. After the emperor started assuming the senate's previous responsibilities, senators still led vital, public lives. Some emperors relied on the Senate more than others, but individual senators still held important offices and many emperors emerged from the ranks of the Senate. The property requirement instituted by Augustus insured that all senators had substantial estates of their own to manage. Senators also remained voices of authority in the courts and were regularly called upon to testify or support those involved in litigation. At all times, membership in the Senate carried prestige with it, and its members always bore the responsibility of embodying Roman ideals in all their activities.

The *Cursus Honorum*. For men on the senatorial career track, there existed a set of laws and customs governing the sequence of public offices they should hold in order to advance, known collectively as the *cursus honorum* (course of honors). Few rules are known about this sequence from the earlier days of the Republic, other than the expectation of military service and certain restrictions on repeating terms in the same office. By the early part of the second century B.C.E., the *cursus* was more regulated, generally for the purpose of slowing down the ambitious. The standard sequence ran: quaestor, praetor, and consul. The tribuneship of the *plebs* might be held after the quaestorship. The position of censor was open usually only to former consuls. Later, the vigintivirate magistracies (and, unofficially, the post of military tribune) were added to the beginning as prerequisite to the quaestorship.

Viginti(sex)viri. Six boards comprising twenty-six magistracies were collectively known in the late Republic as the *vigintisexviri* ("Twenty-six Men"). Half of the positions belonged to the Board of Ten for Judging Lawsuits (*decemviri stlitibus iudicandis*). Four were Prefects for Campania (*praefecti capuam cumas*). The three-man board *tresviri capitales*, also known as the *tresviri nocturni,* had limited police functions, such as guarding prisoners. Another three-man board, the *tresviri monetales* ("Monetary Board of Three"), also known as the *tresviri aere argento auro flando feriundo* ("Board of Three for Smelting and Casting Bronze Silver and Gold"), supervised the minting of coins. A board of four men (*quattuorviri*) governed the maintenance of streets in the city of Rome (*viis in urbe purgandis*) and another of two (*duoviri*) handled street maintenance around the city (*viis extra urbem purgandis*). The Emperor Augustus abolished two of these boards (the four prefects to Campania and the two offices in charge of streets around Rome), and the group became known as the *vigintiviri* ("The Twenty Men"). These boards became important by the Late Republic as precursors (along with, unofficially, the post of Military Tribune) for the quaestorship and hence to a senatorial career.

A first-century B.C.E. frieze showing the census being conducted in Rome. While one citizen is being registered (on the left), the others are preparing to perform sacrifices (Louvre, Paris).

Quaestor. The quaestor primarily controlled finances and served under the praetor. Quaestors governed the treasury (*aerarium*). Provinces, as they were created, also had one or more Roman quaestors to supervise their finances. Eventually the number of quaestors reached stability at twenty. When called upon, a quaestor was expected to act in place of his supervisor, as *propraetor* (from *pro*, "on behalf of"). After Augustus transferred control of the public treasury to the emperor's court, the office of quaestor accordingly moved and candidates were chosen by the emperor. The quaestorship was traditionally the least of the public magistracies, but it was nonetheless the beginning of the *cursus honorum* and a senatorial career. At times, holding the office could gain, but not guarantee, admission to the Senate. Later, the holding of one of the lesser magistracies (the *vigintisexviri*) became a prerequisite for quaestor.

Aedile. The office of Aedile originated in the supervision of the temple (*aedes*, hence *aedilis* "of/pertaining to the temple") of the *plebs*, and in support for the tribune of the *plebs*. As the office developed, Aediles had three main areas of responsibility: *cura urbis*, *cura annonae*, and *cura ludorum sollemnium*. *Cura urbis*, "care of the city," referred to maintaining the city and public events within it, including public cultic rituals, streets, water supply, markets, and so on. *Cura annonae* referred specifically to maintaining the grain supply. Finally, *cura ludorum sollemnium* called upon the aedile to provide religious and spectacular games for the public. Because these games generated much publicity for their sponsors, aediles came to spend more and more lavishly on them to further their own careers. Under the empire, aediles surrendered many of these functions to other officials but still held authority over markets. Provinces and municipalities outside Rome also had aediles with analogous responsibilities. While

never a strict requirement along the *cursus honorum*, the aedileship was a frequent step after the quaestorship.

Tribune. Two classes of tribunes, *aerarii* (of the treasury) and *militum* (of the military) were traditionally associated with the equestrian order (see below). The *tribunus plebis*, the tribune of the *plebs*, could be held after the quaestorship along the *cursus honorum* toward a senatorial career. The origin and growth of the office coincides with the long struggle of the plebeians against the patricians for power in the Roman state. The first secession of the *plebs* traditionally created the office, which gradually acquired the power of veto against other magistrates and became a full public magistracy itself. Broadly speaking, the tribune was responsible for communicating and enacting the will of the *plebs* or of the people generally. Tribunician authority came to be subsumed by the emperors, but the office still remained on the path of the potential senator until the third century C.E.

Praetor. The praetorship was the one of the most powerful offices in Republican Rome, second only to the consulship. Originally, praetors were elected annually with consular powers, only in lesser degrees. In the absence of the consuls from the city of Rome, the praetor was the chief magistrate in the city, president of the Senate, and in charge of the legal system. A praetor could also lead armies. In the third century B.C.E., two praetorships developed, the *urbanus* ("of the city") and *peregrinus* ("of/for foreigners"). The number of praetorships rose as high as eight, in order to provide enough governors and commanders for new provinces during Rome's expansion. The urban praetor became increasingly responsible for the law courts, but late Republican civil strife led to the collapse of the Praetorian office in the 50s B.C.E. During the empire, praetors governed principally over law courts and also took over production of public games. In all periods, the praetorship was a highly sought-after office, being one of the most powerful

The Romans developed a complex legal system that has influenced and served as the foundation, directly or indirectly, of many legal systems around the world. They established the principle whereby legal experts (Jurists) would interpret and reinterpret the proper application of laws. Included in Roman law was the basic mechanism for one individual to sue another for damages. This type of lawsuit was called "delict," based on a law called the *lex Aquilia,* and is similar to American torts. Surviving legal writings include fictional cases that jurists use to illustrate legal principles. These sample cases provide a glimpse of the common events and disputes of people in the Roman world. Many disputes, for example, involve people who rent work animals, much as someone today might rent a car or equipment. One famous case asks how to award damages when some children are playing ball in the street and a stray ball hits the hand of a barber, who then, because he is hit, cuts the neck of the slave whom he is shaving. The slave's master sues for the value of the dead slave. Should the barber pay up?

Source: Bruce W. Frier, *A Casebook on the Roman Law of Delict* (Atlanta: Scholars Press, 1989).

magistracies. In the Republican *cursus honorum,* it was the stepping-stone to the consulship.

Consul. The two consuls were the most powerful individual officials in Republican Rome. Traditionally, the consulship was developed when the monarchy was abolished in 509 B.C.E. Two consuls were elected each year, insuring that no one man would have the power of monarchy (literally, "sole rule"). A consul was invested with a supreme power called *imperium,* and restricted in his authority only by (1) the limit of his office to one year; (2) the veto power (Latin *veto,* "I forbid") of the other consul, who also had *imperium;* and (3) an appeal-procedure called *provocatio.* The two consuls could share responsibilities or alternate them. For example, on military campaigns the consuls traditionally each held overall command on alternate days. The consulship represented a key stage in the *cursus honorum* in a senatorial career, and except for the senate itself, no institution was more identified with the Roman Republic. Under the empire the office of consul continued to exist, but the emperor held the consular *imperium,* and the position entailed more prestige than power.

Censor. The office of the two censors was created in the early days of the Republic. The censors had the primary responsibility of maintaining the official list (*census*) of Roman citizens. Censors served originally for four years, and later for five, but terms and elections varied in actual practice. The power of the censors extended beyond the *census* itself. Censors had the right and responsibility to inspect the moral health of the Roman citizenry. Censors could exclude citizens from their tribe and thus deprive them of the right to vote. Censors also served as gatekeeper to the Senate, from which censors could also exclude members. Censors reviewed the suitability of members of the cavalry (*Equites equo publico*). Censors were also in charge of leasing public properties and selling public contracts, such as those for tax collection. Reserved for former consuls, the censorship represented the pinnacle of the *cursus honorum* in a senatorial career. Under Augustus, the emperor absorbed the duties of the censors.

Occupations of Equestrians. The equestrians (*equites,* "horsemen" or "cavalry") originated with, as their name suggests, a segment of the military. Certain rights and prestige seem to have belonged to them from the earliest days, even in the monarchy. By the end of the third century B.C.E., their role in the military had all but vanished but the prestige remained and wealth was the primary key to gaining admittance. In 129 B.C.E., the equestrians officially became distinct from the senatorial order, when senators were forbidden to enroll in the equestrian order. At the end of the

Statue of a praetor signalling the start of a chariot race, circa fourth century B.C.E. (Bildarchiv Preussischer Kulturbesitz, Berlin)

decade, Gaius Gracchus included in his reforms that jurors in corruption trials be composed of equestrians, and this change may mark the beginning of the later order as it is now known. The juror-function was returned to the senate fifty years later, but the identity of the equestrian order remained. They were traditionally wealthy and prestigious, but involved in business ventures and commerce in a way not officially permitted to senators. Because senators often formed "secret" partnerships with equestrians in business ventures, the equestrian order could influence the senate. Augustus more clearly defined the order as an aristocratic class second only to the Senate and restored their identity as jurors. Emperors during the third century C.E. increasingly appointed equestrians to positions traditionally held by senators. As more and more officials of lower rank were granted the status of equestrian, by the end of the fifth century C.E., the equestrian order ceased to be a recognizable element. During the most prosperous and historic epochs in Roman history, however, while equestrians could and did run for political office, they were better known as the large capital investors and management executives of the Roman world.

Tribunes. Two types of tribuneships are associated with the Equestrian order. The *tribuni aerarii* (treasury officials) were early officials in charge of collecting tribute from foreign nations and disbursing military pay. This office disappeared, but the title was later applied to a class of jurors (third after the senators and equestrians) who met the census requirement of equestrians but were not members. After Julius Caesar abolished this category of jurors, the title disappeared. *Tribuni militum* (military tribunes) originally commanded tribal contingents of the Roman army. A quota of six tribunes became the norm, with four elected to command legions and two others appointed and acting in rotation. In the later empire, the term applied to a wider variety of commands. At all periods, equestrians dominated these posts, but some men of senatorial families might also serve as military tribunes, as this post was customary (but not required) between a stint among the *vigintisexviri* and the quaestorship.

Publicans: Contractors and Construction Companies. Much collection of public revenue and many public construction projects were sold to private individuals and companies known as *publicani*. The Senate would approve a project and allot the funds for it. The censors would offer a contract for the project for sale. Publicans, represented by a bidder called the *manceps*, bought the contracts and made their profit by spending less on the project than the contract cost them. In the case of contracts to collect taxes, this situation could lead tax collectors to extort extra taxes to increase profits. Offices of publican companies consisted of *magistri* ("chiefs") who ran the companies, and staffs (*familiae*), which ran into the hundreds in some instances, consisting generally of slaves and freedmen. Gaius Gracchus seems to have greatly expanded the scale of publican activity by arranging for the taxes from the province of Asia (corresponding to the southwestern part of modern Turkey) to be sold by the censors. The partners (*socii*) in a publican company put up the money to buy a contract and then expected their money returned plus a share of the profits when the contract was completed. Equestrians dominated these companies. Senators were forbidden to be partners, but they certainly found ways to skirt the law. By the end of the Republic, such companies had become so successful that they even acted as bankers for the Roman government. Corruption and conflict of interest (especially when senators were illegally involved in these companies) became serious problems. At times, too, some companies offered public shares of stock (*partes*), compounding the difficulty. The civil wars engulfing the Republic hurt publican companies, and they were sharply curtailed under the empire.

Sources:
Lionel Casson, *Everyday Life in Ancient Rome* (Baltimore: Johns Hopkins University Press, 1998).

Jo-Ann Shelton, *As the Romans Did: A Sourcebook in Roman Social History*, second edition (New York: Oxford University Press, 1998).

MAKERS OF WOMEN'S FINERY

People today know the trades and details about ordinary workers mostly from paintings, carvings, and occasional inscriptions. Some professions existed, but scarcely more than that is known. This is certainly the case with professions devoted to making and repairing items for women. For example, the comic playwright Plautus includes a monologue that helps us learn what sort of professions existed in the Roman Republic of his day. A character is lamenting what happens when a man gets married and moves to the city. He speaks of the days when the wife's bills come due:

These days you'll find more delivery-wagons in front of buildings in the city than you'd see in the country when you go to your remote villa. But even that's a nice view compared to when your expenses track you down. Up pops the dry-cleaner, the embroiderer, the goldsmith, woolsmith, salesmen, hem-makers, negligee-makers, veil-makers, purple-makers, yellow-makers, or sleeve-makers, or slipper-scenters, linen sellers, shoe-makers, shoe-shiners, slipper makers, sandal-makers, all right there waiting. The pink makers!—right there waiting. The dry-cleaners look for you. The patch-makers look for you. The scarf-makers are right there waiting. At the same time, the belt-makers—right there waiting! And just when you figure you've got them all taken care of, they leave—and three hundred more show up! Countless numbers of them, ready with the bills, stacked up in the hallway, frilly-fringe-makers, jewelry-box-makers. You let them in. You think you've taken care of it—the yellow-robe-makers stroll in, or some other dead man walking who wants something!

Source: *Plautus*, 5 volumes, translated by Paul Nixon, Loeb Classical Library (Cambridge, Mass.: Harvard University Press, 1916–1938).

Remains of a building in Pompeii belonging to a woman named Eumachia and possibly used by cloth-workers for meetings, circa first century C.E.

OCCUPATIONS: THE NON-ELITE

Working Lives. The elite senatorial and equestrian orders, and later the imperial court, added up to a relatively small proportion of the whole population of Rome and the Roman Empire. Most of the population worked in the growing, building, moving, service, and military operations required to make the Roman world function on a daily basis. They worked at their jobs, receiving wages or barter as compensation. They formed unions, groups, and clubs. They went to religious services and to entertaining spectacles. The quality of life for them and for their families varied as much as it does in any modern country.

Slaves. Although barred from the elite orders, political office, and the military, slaves could otherwise hold nearly any occupation. Because many slaves came as prisoners of war, they often would take on jobs comparable to what they had done before the Roman conquest. The Romans were perfectly willing to use huge amounts of slave labor in brutal conditions, but fortunate, skilled, and educated slaves could hold fairly powerful managerial and authoritative jobs. Tutors were generally slaves. Property managers and accountants were often slaves. Because many free citizens also did such jobs, slaves and free persons could work side by side, even under the authority of another slave.

Manual Labor and Craftsmanship. Elite Romans expressed disdain for many types of professions. While they idealized the rustic farming life, they mostly scorned jobs requiring manual labor. Even labor involving considerable skill and intelligence could still be viewed as demeaning. Painters and sculptors, for example, were lower-class occupations. Wealthy Romans would willingly praise a painting, sculpture, or mosaic, but give the credit to the patron who commissioned and paid for it, rather than the artist who created it. This attitude does not mean, of course, that the artists and workers themselves shared this attitude toward themselves and their work. Evidence suggests that they took pride in their own work and in themselves despite the condescension of snobbish Romans. Artists and craftsmen often signed their works, partly as advertising for their skills but also as a mark of pride.

Labor Unions and Clubs. People who worked in the same occupation in the same community naturally associated together and organized, though one cannot always know now just how formal or organized such groups were. The clearest evidence for labor groups are the election notices at places such as Pompeii. Many inscriptions and remains of painted signs saying that a certain group of workers supports a particular candidate for a given office have been found. "All the carpenters ask you to elect Cuspius Pansa as aedile," says one, while

TREATMENT OF SLAVES

No one can say simply or easily how the Romans treated their slaves. Different Romans at different times or places felt and acted differently about the issue. In a notorious case in 61 C.E., a slave master named Pedanius Secundus was killed by one of his slaves. The Senate debated the matter and voted that all four hundred slaves in the household be executed in response. On the other hand, several emperors before and after this case had taken steps, through legislation and personal influence, to curtail the abuse of slaves by their masters. Even an individual Roman might express complex views about the treatment of slaves. The Roman senator Pliny (called Pliny the Younger, to distinguish him from his uncle, Pliny the Elder) published letters that survive, including some about slaves in his household and in the news of his day. In one, he expresses deep compassion for his slaves. He considers it a basic human trait to have compassion, and to be emotionally concerned for one's slaves. When two of his slaves die, he is very upset. He adds that he at least has the consolation that he did two things for them: he set them free before they died, and he let them draw up wills and executed their wishes (although slaves had no legal claim to the making a will). Yet, in another letter, Pliny describes with horror how some slaves murdered their cruel master, beating him up, then burning his body on the hot floor of a bath. It took several days for him to die. Pliny says the master lived to get revenge, for the murderous slaves were killed the same way. Pliny adds that slaves are not ruined by their masters, but rather ruin themselves. Thus Pliny himself expresses some rather different views on slaves at different times. To add to the irony, the cruel master in this last case was the son of a former slave, but apparently had no compassion for his own slaves. It is well documented that slaves and former slaves in the ancient world routinely owned slaves themselves. Such is the complex, and sometimes paradoxical, reality of slavery in the Roman world.

Source: Betty Radice, *The Letters of the Younger Pliny* (Harmondsworth, U.K.: Penguin, 1963).

---

another says, "All the fisherman say 'Elect Popidius Rufus as aedile.'" No one knows know how a group of workers agreed to such endorsements nor exactly what a candidate might have done to secure it. No one has evidence that such groups used collective bargaining to negotiate contracts, as modern labor unions do. Working-class people might also belong to a funeral-club (*funeraticum collegium*). Funerals could be expensive, so a club would form. Members would pay a fee and regular dues. The club then paid for, and attended, the member's funeral. Funeral-clubs also met at monthly dinners to pay dues, which provided a regular social occasion as well. In places or times of civil unrest, Roman governors would be sus-

picious of clubs and unions, fearing they would support revolution. Even a group of firefighters might be seen a potential source of danger!

Soldiers. Military service in the early days of Rome fell to those wealthy enough to supply their own provisions, weapons, armor, and anything else required (for example, a horse, if the soldier was in the cavalry). Military service was required for advanced command or for high political office. Gradually, as conquests and expansion continued, the army grew and the Romans recruited from a broader spectrum of the population. In the first century B.C.E., Gaius Marius finally removed entirely the property requirement for enlisting. Henceforth, military pay and provisions for retired veterans became crucial economic issues, for a discontented army could wreak havoc in the political realm. The army provided huge economic boons when it captured and returned booty from conquests. An army also became an economic asset during times of peace, when they could be used on construction projects.

Sources:
Lionel Casson, *Everyday Life in Ancient Rome* (Baltimore: Johns Hopkins University Press, 1998).

Jo-Ann Shelton, *As the Romans Did: A Sourcebook in Roman Social History*, second edition (New York: Oxford University Press, 1998).

THE SOCIAL CLASSES

Roman Class Distinctions. The Romans never shied away from grouping themselves—and others—into social classes. While the origins and motivations for the oldest classes remain obscure, historical sources reveal how the classes shifted, disappeared, and were invented over the centuries. The change and growth of Rome brought about many realignments of classes. The conservatism of the Romans and the Roman elite, by contrast, tended to retard changes among the social classes and retain class designations well after they had much purpose. Class distinctions tended to be functional, practical, and measure social worth rather than derive from beliefs about race, biology, or philosophy. Ultimately, since class distinctions affected the quality of life, respect, and power of the individuals belonging to a particular class, members of the different classes would come into conflict with other classes. The Romans themselves would even associate the history of their culture with the actions of particular classes.

Class-Structure of Early Rome. During the early days of Rome, when it was a city-state headed by a king, class divisions that would become important later in history were just developing. At the earliest stages, the privileged class was referred to as the *patricians*. The patricians controlled the religious and political offices of the city. The rest of the citizens were by default the *plebeians*. These two classes became fixed and hereditary for centuries. The only slavery mentioned during this period is debt bondage (for example, citizens under the dominion of someone to whom they owed a financial debt). The origins of the Senate also seem to reach back to this earliest period, though little can be known for certain. The Senate was probably an advisory council to the king. Both patricians and plebeians could belong to the Senate at this time. Roman legend told that the founder of Rome, Romulus, had founded the Senate with one hundred members and later increased it to three hundred, but scholars today doubt this report.

Conflict of the Orders during the Republic. After the last king was expelled, Rome officially became a republic. The duties of the king fell to a new office, that of consul, two of whom served at any time and only for a year. The Senate, however, accumulated the most power during this period, as well as came increasingly under control of the patricians. The distinction between patrician and plebeian also became sharper, which fueled a conflict called the Conflict of the Orders. This struggle continued intermittently for more than two hundred years while Rome grew as a military power in the region. As the patricians solidified their control over Rome and enjoyed the benefits of an aristocracy, the plebeians organized themselves to defend their own rights and interests.

Early Organization and Secession of the Plebeians. The conflict between the patricians and plebeians seems to have started within decades of the foundation of the Republic. With the patricians in control of the government through the Senate and public magistracies, the plebeians needed other means to assert their power. They organized themselves as a political body and elected their own leaders at their own assemblies (called the *comitia plebis*). Their first priority was to make the patricians recognize the leaders the plebeians had elected for themselves. The plebeians chose two types of officials, tribunes and aediles. The tribunes had the task of leading the *plebs* and pursuing the needs and wishes of the order. Aediles were originally temple officials (Latin *aedes* "building"), but they started to judge disputes in commerce and served as general support for the tribunes. These officials were sacrosanct, which meant that the plebeian assembly had sworn to defend and protect the men in office from harm if the patricians attempted to arrest or threaten them. It was of primary importance, then, for the patricians to recognize and respect these officials. The Roman military depended on the participation of plebeians, and this military importance proved to be a bargaining weapon. The plebeians threatened to withdraw from Rome (Latin *secessio*) and thus take their military force away, too. The first secession eventually compelled the patricians to recognize the plebeian tribunes in 471 B.C.E.

The Second Secession and the Twelve Tables. The early to middle years of the fifth century brought economically hard times for Rome. The plebeians wanted codification of the laws to prevent arbitrary abuse of authority by patrician officials. Plebeian tribunes began pushing for a written legal code, and, finally in 451 B.C.E., a decemvirate (board of ten men) consisting entirely of patricians convened to draft a legal code. They completed ten tables of laws, and then a second commission, including five plebeians, met to continue the work. Controversy broke out, however, when the patrician members, led by Appius Claudius, tried to force through the ratification of two additional tables of harsh laws considered oppressive to the *plebs*. The plebeians protested

and seceded again. Eventually, constitutional order was restored, and a new slate of tribunes and consuls put in place. Difficulty surrounds the Romans' own historical accounts of the creation of the Twelve Tables, and some parts were quickly repealed (such as the ban on intermarriage between patrician and plebeian), but in the long run the Tables were a breakthrough. The Twelve Tables (mostly lost to scholars today) provided the foundation for the Roman legal system until the end of the empire (and the Roman legal code in turn has influenced legal systems all over the world). Gradually, over the remaining decades of the fifth century, the plebeians maintained their established institutions, gained certain legal rights, and acquired access to some magistracies. The patricians retained the greater power, however, through the Senate, assemblies, and religious offices.

Continued Class Conflict and the *Lex Hortensia*. Economic difficulties, especially following the costly wars Rome engaged in, continued to fuel the conflict between the patricians and plebeians. Over the course of the fourth and early

---

FEEDING THE STOMACH

The Roman historian Livy provides a dramatic account of the first secession of the *plebs*. When the plebeians had withdrawn and thus threatened the military stability of Rome, fear gripped the patricians. A man named Menenius Agrippa, himself a plebeian, was sent to address the crowd. He used a famous parable to convince the seceding plebeians that it was best to negotiate an agreement for the good of Rome as a whole:

> There was a time when everything in the human body did not, as they do now, work together, but each part had its own ideas for itself and its own way of expressing them. The other parts resented that their own stress, efforts, and service should go to providing everything for the stomach, while the stomach sat in the middle of all this, with nothing to do but enjoy all the pleasures given to it. So they swore that the hand should carry no food to the mouth, that the mouth should take nothing that was offered, and that the teeth should not chew. In their anger, while they intended to subdue the belly by starvation, they themselves and the whole body nearly wasted entirely away. Hence it became clear that the belly, too, has no lazy job to perform: it is no more nourished than it nourishes, returning back to all parts of the body—distributing it fairly through the veins once the food is digested—that very thing upon which our life and health depend, blood.

Agrippa explained how the anger of the *plebs* paralleled the internal rebellion of the body. His speech persuaded the plebeians to negotiate, and as a result of these negotiations the first tribunes were recognized, who would represent and protect the *plebs*.

Source: *Livy*, translated by B. O. Foster and others, Loeb Classical Library, fifteen volumes (Cambridge, Mass.: Harvard University Press, 1919–1967).

third centuries B.C.E., the plebeians won a series of legal and political battles to gain ground with the patricians. Two victories stand out. The plebeians finally won the right to be elected as one of the two annual consuls, the most powerful of the individual magistracies. The *lex Hortensia* was passed in 287 B.C.E. after the final secession, and gave the resolutions (*plebiscita*) of the *concilium plebis* (assembly of the *plebs*) the full force of a law (*lex*), binding all citizens including the patricians. The *lex Hortensia* traditionally marks the end of the Conflict of the Orders.

Isolationism. The end of the Conflict of Orders did not, however, mean democratic equality. The reforms served the interests of the wealthier component of the plebeians, while the entire class of plebeians included many much poorer members. The Romans continued to take control of the Italian peninsula militarily and refine their internal political system. During this process, the Romans remained economically and socially conservative. With their military conquests, they engaged in the slave trade enough that they taxed the process of manumitting slaves, but they do not seem to have substantially incorporated slaves into the city or the workforce until later. Indeed, economically, Rome lagged behind some of the other cities that they had conquered in Italy.

The *Nobiles*. The *plebs* had struggled long and hard for equal political rights with the class of patricians. By the close of the third century B.C.E., when the Conflict of the Orders was effectively over, it became possible for a "new man" (*novus homo*) to join the ranks of the elite by gaining admission to high office and to the Roman senate. Wealthy plebeians took advantage of this new opportunity, and their ranks began to fill the Senate, but over the next two hundred years these few plebeians closed ranks as much as the patricians had before them. The families who constituted this new aristocracy were known as the *nobiles* ("nobles").

The Senatorial Class in the Republic. After the abolition of the monarchy in 509 B.C.E., the Senate arose as the dominant authority in Republican Rome. Once a man was admitted to the Senate, he remained a member for life. Moreover, many members had experience in public office, so the Senate as a political body became a knowledgeable and powerful entity. Membership in the Senate was the measuring stick of power in the Republic and the power of the Senate was identified with the security of the Republic itself. Through the Conflict of the Orders and the realignment of the aristocracy, the Senate guided the Roman state through the stunning conquests of Italy and the entire Mediterranean region by the end of the second century B.C.E. By virtue of the enormous influence and prestige of the Senate, the senators constituted a class from this time onward in Roman history.

Patrons and Clients. The system of patronage during the days of the Republic served as the mechanism for organizing alliances and maintaining clear hierarchies in daily business. Patronage operated when an individual sought a wealthier, more educated, or more powerful individual for advice, protection, or assistance. The person seeking assistance was the *cliens* and the one from whom he sought help was the *patro-*

nus. In accepting the patron's help, the client became bound to reciprocate at the patron's command. The system was complex and pervasive in Roman public life. The patron acquired power and prestige through the number and standing of clients he held. The client in turn gained access to the means and favor of a more powerful patron. The ritual of *salutatio* openly demonstrated the phenomenon. A patron would begin the day by greeting, dispatching, or listening to the various clients who had gathered at his home. This patron could in turn be a client of a still more powerful patron. The patrons competed with one another in terms of the clients they maintained. Patronage could also continue across generations. While patron and client were not legal distinctions, a patron might expect a client to support him in court or in a campaign for office.

Sources:

M. I. Finley, *The Ancient Economy* (Berkeley: University of California Press, 1973).

Allen M. Ward, Fritz M. Heichelheim, and Cedric A. Yeo, *A History of the Roman People*, third edition (Upper Saddle River, N.J.: Prentice- Hall, 1999).

SOCIAL REVOLUTION AND PROGRESS

Tiberius Gracchus and the Roman Revolution. Internal domestic politics had remained relatively stable at Rome since the *lex Hortensia* in 287 had effectively settled the Conflict of the Orders. The end of the Third Punic War and the sack of Carthage in 146 B.C.E. announced the domination of Rome over the Mediterranean region. Internal dissent quickly resurfaced and would eventually engulf the Republic over the next hundred years. This period, referred to as the "Roman Revolution," traditionally begins with the proposals and fate of one Tiberius Sempronius Gracchus. Tiberius was himself a plebeian through his father (also named Tiberius Sempronius Gracchus), but was related to one of the most prestigious patrician families, the Scipios, through his mother, Cornelia. In 133 B.C.E., Tiberius was elected tribune and proposed new legislation governing the distribution of land. No one can be absolutely sure now what Tiberius hoped or planned to effect with his reform, but his proposals affected several problematic issues at the time. Wealthy Romans had illegally been amassing large amounts of land (including territory won in military conquests) and using more slave labor to maintain huge farms. Land ownership was a prerequisite to military service and the basis for much Roman wealth, so farmland gathered in the hands of a few men weakened the military reserves and generally impoverished many citizens. In addition, the dependence on slave labor led to the fear of slave revolt. Tiberius Gracchus proposed restricting land lots to their traditional limit of five hundred Roman acres (roughly three hundred modern acres) with related restrictions and compensations, including a new commission that would ensure the continued fair distribution of parcels of land. Wealthy members of the Senate objected to having their own land holdings restricted or reduced. Tiberius bypassed the Senate on a legal technicality to propose his reforms, which set off a

TRIMALCHIO: A FAT-CAT FREEDMAN

No more vivid account of the stereotype of the wealthy freedman survives from the Roman world than the account of Trimalchio from the *Satyricon*. The author of the *Satyricon*, Petronius, worked under the Emperor Nero and was in charge of entertainment. Some scholars believe the portrait of Trimalchio also includes characteristics of Nero. Wild stories seep through about Trimalchio's fantastic wealth. He has estates everywhere, rather like a small country, raising everything he needs all over the world. Most of Trimalchio's guests are other wealthy freedmen, which provides further opportunity for more satire as well as a fascinating portrayal of the unique world of the freedman. In the novel, Trimalchio is hosting a dinner party—and what a party! Before the feast even begins, the guests receive a pedicure from singing slaves. Trimalchio enters late and starts dinner by playing a board game with gold and silver coins, grinding his teeth on a silver toothpick. Appetizers begin with eggs, actually egg-shaped pastries, containing a seasoned oriole. As a further demonstration of Trimalchio's impossible wealth, when a servant accidentally drops a silver platter, Trimalchio has it swept out with the trash instead of picked up. Between courses, a skeleton with silver joints is brought in and Trimalchio recites poetry to it. At another intermission, when acrobats begin tumbling around the room and one of them lands on Trimalchio's arm, Trimalchio sets the boy free (so that he would not have been hurt by a slave) and recites extemporaneous poetry on the subject. After a live performance of some Trojan War scenes from the epic poetry of Homer, Trimalchio has a cook, dressed like the mythical warrior Ajax, cut up a calf (Ajax, the story goes, had cut up sheep in a mad fit). As the party and foods continue coming, Trimalchio reads out his will and makes plans for his burial monument. After the meal, the whole party moves to the baths, which the wealthy Trimalchio has right in the house! (The norm in a Roman town was to bathe at the public baths.) The evening ends only when Trimalchio dresses up for his own funeral, which everyone starts to perform, but the chaos and racket cause the fire department to come, which finally stops the party.

Source: Petronius, *The Satyricon and the Fragments*, translated by John P. Sullivan (Harmondsworth, U.K.: Penguin, 1965).

incident would be far from the last to shed blood in the name of controlling the Republic.

Gaius Gracchus Continues the Revolution. The younger brother of Tiberius Gracchus, Gaius Sempronius Gracchus, served on the land commission, which remained in power even after Tiberius's murder. Gaius, however, would go much farther than his brother had. When he was elected Tribune in 123 B.C.E., he worked for a series of significant reforms. These reforms included solidifying the land bill of his elder brother, establishing a means for distributing grain to the masses at Rome, providing some relief and public works for the poor and for Italians outside of Rome, and forming a colonization plan for the Romans. Gaius also attempted to extend the right of full citizenship to Italians outside of Rome, who had supported Rome in its wars but still did not have full rights. This measure failed, however, and Gaius's popularity began to wane, scarcely two years after being elected tribune. When Gaius lost the election to his third term, tensions rose. The new tribune promptly repealed one of Gaius's reforms, and Gaius chose to take up arms in revolt. The Senate, in turn, declared a state of emergency (which came to be called the *senatus consultum ultimum*, "final decree of the senate") and empowered magistrates to take drastic measures to protect the state. In the ensuing conflict, Gaius and some three thousand followers were killed or executed.

Legacy of the Gracchi: *Populares* **and** *Optimates*. Although unsuccessful, the Gracchi permanently changed the nature of political and class struggle in ancient Rome. Judgment of the Gracchi has been mixed. On one side, they were themselves nobles who tried to bring about much needed reform. On another side, they took steps that undermined the very Republic such reforms would protect. They also tragically set the precedent for spilling Roman blood in civil conflict. In spite of their deaths, their legislation and methods had a profound impact. Whereas previously the plebeians had gradually (and through threat of secession) won a series of concessions, the Gracchi demonstrated it was possible to defy the Senate openly while pursuing reform or power. Henceforth, those who pursued their goals backed by support of the people (*populus*) against the Senate became known as *populares*, while backers of the aristocracy were the *optimates* (from Latin *optimi*, the "best"). This schism led to dire consequences over the next century.

The Power of the *Equites* **and** *Publicani*. Some Gracchan legislation also had long term reverberations. Gaius Gracchus passed legislation to reduce corruption by Roman governors who ruled over provinces in newly conquered territories. These governors became notorious for wrecking their territories and securing wealth for themselves. These activities were illegal, but, because those accused would be tried by their fellow senators, who themselves had or desired to acquire wealth from governorships, they would rarely be punished. Gaius instead made the juries of such trials drawn not from the Senate but from the class of *equites* ("cavalry," traditionally the second-wealthiest class in Rome). This move increased the power and influence of

series of questionable tactics by both Tiberius and the Senate until the bill was finally enacted. The commission was formed and began its work. Tiberius then sought to be reelected as tribune, an unprecedented action that alienated many of Tiberius's own supporters. Eventually, a senator named Scipio Nasica led a charge that killed Tiberius and some three hundred of his backers. Unfortunately, this

the *equites*. In another reform, Gaius Gracchus raised money to support his proposals by selling taxes in a new Roman province, Asia (corresponding to the southwestern part of modern Turkey). Unlike modern governments, Rome did not collect taxes directly. Gaius set up a system where tax collectors (*publicani*) bid on the right to collect taxes. The Roman government would award the contract to whichever publican promised to deliver the most money. The publican, meanwhile, would make a profit by extracting as much money as possible in the process of collecting the tax, which inevitably led to abuse. Gaius Gracchus likely did not realize the power he was giving to the publican corporations at Rome, since he generally supported the rights of residents in the provinces.

Marius and the New Military Class. The Gracchi had recognized areas in the Roman Republic where tensions could break out into violence and disaster. Tiberius understood the disparity of land ownership and related weakness in recruits for the Roman military. Gaius tried to extend political franchise to the citizens of Italy. The assassinations of the Gracchi meant that the drastic need for reform went unfulfilled. The Romans had been struggling to recruit forces for their military campaigns, for landowners were reluctant to leave on military service only to have their homes lost or otherwise devalued in their absence. A general named Gaius Marius finally took the necessary step to solve the problem. When he was consul and was put in charge of a campaign in Africa in 108 B.C.E., he recruited vast numbers of poorer citizens who owned no property. Marius's move solved the problem of providing sufficient manpower for the army, but it also had far-reaching consequences for the relationship between Rome and the soldiers. Previously, soldiers enlisted for a limited number of campaigns and expected to return home to their farms after completing their service. Many of the new recruits, without their own homes, made careers of military service. They needed to be provided for while in the army (not having their own wealth to provide supplies and equipment) and expected to have some land when they finally retired. Moreover, career soldiers devoted their loyalty more to the general who led them and looked out for their interests rather than the Senate or aristocracy back at Rome. Both the standing army and veterans remained a power in politics and economic decisions throughout the history of Rome, although Marius certainly could not have envisioned such long-reaching consequences of his solution to a recruitment problem.

The Social War and the Dictatorships of Marius and Cinna. Marius scored many military successes, including in what is called the "Social War" (*socius* being Latin for "ally," so "War with the Allies"), when the peoples of the Italian peninsula revolted. This war concluded when the Senate finally granted citizenship to all of Italy in 89 B.C.E. It is typical of the chaos of the time that the Social War served to delay yet another crisis. The ensuing struggle for supreme power at Rome involved armies loyal to their generals rather than to Rome, to say nothing of to the Senate.

First-century B.C.E. marble bust of Gaius Marius (Antikensammlung, Munich)

Lucius Cornelius Sulla became the first person to capitalize on the new power derived from troops loyal to himself and he attacked the very city of Rome in order to unseat Marius. Marius, joining his army with that of Cornelius Cinna, drove Sulla out of Rome and initiated a reign of terror against his enemies. Marius died in 87 B.C.E. before actually ruling and Cinna was thus left in charge for the next few years. Throughout these conflicts, the Roman senate ranged from being utterly helpless to trying delicately to negotiate among fierce military rivals, a role far from the absolute dominance the Senate held over financial, military, and political affairs for several centuries.

Sulla the Temporary Dictator. By 83 B.C.E., Sulla was openly mobilizing his troops to recapture the city of Rome by force. By the end of 80 he had thoroughly destroyed all those who opposed him, although he was already legislating as victor in early 81 B.C.E. Sulla's actions showed the brutal consequences of Marius's reforms in the army and the reality of the new military power. Sulla had made huge financial promises to his supporters and owed his troops land to settle. He fulfilled these obligations by drawing up long lists of men (conscriptions) to be killed and property confiscated. This move at once demonstrated the dominance of military leaders and also led to long-term changes in the social and cultural makeup of the Italian territories. On the political front, Sulla demanded from the Senate the title of *interrex* ("Acting King"), which had not been used since the days of the monarchy more than four hundred years earlier. Sulla's *de facto* ("in fact") authority as a military leader and *de iure* ("in law") power as dictator enabled him to push through reform on a scale others had been trying to accomplish since the days of the Gracchi. He increased the power of the Senate overall, including adding three hundred new members, notably introducing members of the equestrian order from Italy outside Rome, in order to dilute the old entrenched aristocracy. At the same time, he reduced the office of Tribune, where the *plebs* had once struggled for power and from where activists such as the Gracchi had attempted reform. He also put the *cursus honorum* (literally "course of honors," for example, the sequence of political offices for nobles to attain) in its canonical form to control the later membership of the Senate. Sulla held the dictatorship for three years and then retired, entirely of his own desire, in 79 B.C.E. He had attempted to restore the Republic by reasserting the power of the Senate, which had guided Rome through its glory years, and by reestablishing a ruling class that reflected more broadly the Italian constituents of the empire. Sulla's accomplishments with his army and through the conscriptions, however, would not fade.

Slave Revolt of Spartacus. Symptomatic of the social and economic instability of the period was the revolt in southern Italy led by the slave gladiator Spartacus. Spartacus had military training in the Roman auxiliaries and in 73 B.C.E. began a slave revolt in Capua in which he crisscrossed Italy over the next few years. At their peak, Spartacus's troops numbered in the tens of thousands and drew in sympathizers from the oppressed free population as well. His forces defeated several Roman military attempts to stop them. Finally, M. Crassus mustered sufficient forces to defeat Spartacus and subsequently crucified thousands of the participating slaves along the Appian Way. No slave revolts on such a scale are known after that of Spartacus's. Some thoughtful Romans realized from this revolt, and from their long history of class struggle, that brutal oppression leads to catastrophe; some others simply concluded (on a crude practical level) that forced servility is a waste of human talent. But the suitable treatment of slaves remained a controversial matter for a long time to come, often with deadly results. In the decades following Spartacus's uprising, as the Republic continued to disintegrate, such bloody chaos would envelope more and more of the Roman population.

The Fall of the Republic. The next several decades found the Roman Republic repeatedly in turmoil. Taking their cue from the military dictatorships of Marius and Sulla, individuals vied with each other for supremacy. Such individuals would make promises of financial reward to their followers and attempt to appeal to one class or another (for example, the senate, the equestrians, the soldiery) to gain their support. No individual or situation lasted for long, from the failed conspiracy of Cataline, to Cicero's hope of a "harmony of the orders" (*concordia ordinum*), to the First Triumvirate of Crassus, Pompey, and Caesar, with Caesar winning out and then being assassinated, to the Second Triumvirate of Lepidus, Antony, and Octavian, with Octavian finally emerging victorious after the Battle of Actium in 31 B.C.E. Throughout the decades of civil war, the Roman economy was generally anemic, although it is perhaps amazing under the circumstances that it did not collapse. The agricultural base for the economy did experience some change. The various land reforms meant a great amount of land changed hands, but the large farm estates continued to exist. Slave revolts such as that of Spartacus caused some Romans to rethink their use of slave labor. Free workers known as *coloni* would rent and work farmland, but the fact that some of these individuals joined Spartacus's army suggests their standard of living might not have been any better than that of the slave workers. For all the societal upheavals, orchard cultivation seems to have thrived at this time. Trade inevitably suffered with the instability, but there were fortunes to be made for traders who succeeded in this high-risk environment, for competing armies meant high demand for supplies of every kind. Rome itself, ever the heart of political and economic activity, experienced growing pains typical of urban centers. The wealthy few mustered a luxurious lifestyle in the city, although some would feign a preference for a simpler life in a country home (*villa*). Population growth led to cramped and dangerous slums. Crises would leave the food supply and public safety unreliable. When Octavian had completed his military coup, he had much work to do as the Emperor Augustus.

Augustus and the New Order. Over the course of his forty-year reign (27 B.C.E. to 14 C.E.), Augustus established the political and economic infrastructure that would remain a successful engine of the Roman Empire for more than two hundred years. He reduced the Senate to a fixed membership of six hundred and also asserted some control over who remained and who was purged from the rolls. He set a requirement that a senator must possess property in excess of one million sesterces, and he could thus further manipulate membership by providing the necessary funds to individuals he wanted included in the Senate. It also became easier for a son to inherit his father's position in the senate, which allowed for greater hereditary stability in the body as a whole. Control over financial and military affairs moved to the emperor, but the Senate retained its prestige as a political organ and social class. Augustus assigned men to administrative posts for permanent or lengthy terms, which gradually allowed for a pool of knowledgeable, professional imperial administrators. The Senate remained the source for the highest of these positions. The equestrian class now had a property requirement of four hundred thousand sesterces and became clearly defined as the pro-

The Romans consistently restricted most elite offices to men. All military positions, magistracies, enrollment in the Senate, and so on, allowed only men. Nevertheless, elite political activity was always intertwined with familial relationships, and women of powerful families could be formidable in their own right. Indeed, several women played powerful roles at key turning points in Roman history. For nonelite occupations, the division of roles between gender might vary. For example, in the honorable professions associated with agriculture, women worked alongside men even in management positions. In their guides to farming, Varro and Columella recommend women in part because the women make the men work better! Other professions, sailing for example, were certainly exclusive to men. Working women are known in scattered jobs, but often historians cannot know whether or how many women worked at certain kinds of jobs. A tombstone indicating a women's occupation (clothesmaker, fishseller, and the like), in some cases paid for by someone else because the woman herself was too poor, may sometimes be the only clue to jobs that women held.

Source: Jane F. Gardner, *Women in Roman Law & Society* (London: Croom Helm, 1986).

fessional and social class second to the Senate. Augustus generally left the tax structure and administration of the provinces as they were, but with his own accounting officials in charge, he was able to balance out the revenues of the new empire. At times he contributed from his personal wealth (more than a billion sesterces) to ensure solvency. Toward the end of his reign he established a public fund to provide retirement benefits to veterans (the *aerarium militare*) and so began making the military dependent on, and hence more loyal to, the Roman state rather than to individual commanders. At his death, Augustus left his successor a more sound financial system and clearer class structure than had been in place since before the days of Marius.

Economy during the Early Empire. The first and second centuries C.E. can generally be considered a time of economic prosperity and expansion for the empire. Agriculture was still basic to the economy and remained stable, but trade and commerce exploded during this period. The stability of the empire meant that trade routes could be relied upon and extended. Trade extended north as far as the British isles, south into Africa, and east as far as China; the Roman intellectual Seneca (in the first century C.E.) even predicted a trade route sailing west across the Atlantic Ocean to India. In general, financial administration became centralized in the imperial court, building progressively on the structure established by Augustus. Better emperors in this time were even able to reduce tax rates and to expand public programs. The Roman bent for practicality ensured that in every corner of the empire basic infrastructure needs—food, water, shelter, and public safety—

were a priority, and provinces mostly prospered economically under Roman rule. Provisions for the provinces and cities across the empire also included a public dole to relieve the distress of the poor. The famous shows in amphitheaters across the empire became a substantial part of public funding. Political rights also expanded. Provinces gradually acquired the rights of Roman citizenship until 212 C.E., when all free people within the borders of the empire were declared Roman citizens.

Freeing Slaves. Roman slaves could be freed by their masters, at which point they acquired the status of freedman or freedwoman, an intermediate phase between slavery and freeborn. Freedmen could vote, but could not run for public office or enroll in the equestrian or senatorial orders (even if they met the financial requirements for admission to these orders). Freed slaves still had legal obligations to their former masters; for example, the former slave continued to be have a patron-client relationship with his former master. The terms of manumission could also include the freed slaves providing a certain amount of labor or services (*operae*) per year. The act of manumission itself took the form of a ritual before an official and, after 357 B.C.E., required the payment of a special tax. Romans seemed to have practiced manumission more than other peoples around the Mediterranean, but the extent of it cannot be exactly determined. Motivations, methods, and results varied every bit as much as the whole complex system of slavery. A Roman ideal held that masters freed slaves as a reward for honest, hard work, and such a slave was then supposed to be a valuable client to his patron, the former master. In reality, of course, other motivations prompted manumission, too. Masters had an obligation to provide food, shelter, and medical help for their slaves, but might free an old, sick, or otherwise troubled slave rather than provide for an unproductive worker. Because slaves could legally be tortured to yield official testimony in a court case—in fact a slave's testimony was not legally valid *unless* delivered under torture—a master might free slaves to prevent them from providing incriminating testimony. Masters might, of course, have nobler motives as well. A master might fall in love with one of his slaves and free her so they could marry. A common method of manumission was for a master to free slaves in his will. The relationship between a slave and former master could also vary widely. Some freedmen or freedwomen were legally adopted by their former master. Some had extremely warm, close relationships. Some relationships turned bitter. Slaves could hold a wide range of jobs, and the likelihood of manumission probably differed according to their positions. Most surviving evidence about freed slaves refers to wealthier slaves involved in business, who were more likely to leave behind records or monuments of their achievements. Slaves in harsher roles (such as that of farm laborer or mineworker) were probably less likely to be freed when they could simply be sold instead. The children of freed slaves were born free and had all the rights of free citizens.

Freedmen, Provincials, and Patronage. As the Roman Empire expanded and grew more prosperous, social change permeated Roman culture as more individuals from all around the empire participated in political and business life. Some Romans expressed discomfort with the changes in the institutions they had venerated, often expressing it in terms of decline from the glory days of the Republic (although most Romans who expressed this disdain had never experienced the Republic themselves nor the chaos that engulfed it). The system of clients and patrons was one such institution. Whereas during the Republic wealthy patrons needed clients for the purpose of campaigning in elections, under the empire such elections fell away to imperial authority and so the nature of the client-patron relationship changed. Some Romans felt it decayed into a system where clients simply fawned on wealthy patrons in order to garner money, gifts, or a dinner invitation, while the patron simply relished the flattery. At times they would blame "foreigners" for such changes, as Rome became increasingly cosmopolitan with peoples from provinces well beyond Italy. Another type of patronage also increased, or was more noticed, that between master and former slave. Slaves, when freed, automatically and legally became a client of their former master. Talented and skilled freed slaves of a well-connected patron could become rather wealthy and powerful in their own right (and thus, that much more beneficial to their former master). The creation of certain official positions by the Emperor Augustus enhanced the visibility and status of successful freedmen. Certainly compared with the entire slave population, relatively few slaves became wealthy. Other Romans of free status (but perhaps not as well off in finances or authority) stereotyped these wealthy freed slaves as tasteless, crude, and unsuited to their new position. Despite these reactions, the Roman Empire continued to diversify and reflect the broad range of peoples within its borders. Gradually, even prestigious and conservative groups such as the Senate had a majority of members from outside Rome and Italy. Such was the melting pot of Rome.

Crisis in the Third Century. A combination of invasions and problematic emperors promoted radical instability following the death of Marcus Aurelius in 180 C.E. and through much of the third century. The military once again became the practical force that determined who would be emperor, but conflicts between different armies meant that, at times, emperors ruled with little or no certain authority. This period also saw the traditional Roman sites of authority lose what power they had left. The Emperor Septimius Severus, for example, openly stripped the Senate of authority and promoted equestrians where he could. The military chaos that dominated much of the century brought on comparable economic chaos, including uncontrolled inflation.

Diocletian and Constantine. The chaos of the third century found some respite under the rules of Diocletian and Constantine. Diocletian hoped to stabilize the empire by dividing the responsibilities, first between two people (himself and Maximian), and then among four rulers (the *tetrarchy*). He initiated many economic reforms, including a new mechanism for assessing taxes and a failed Price Edict to bring inflation under control and restore some fairness and trust to imperial finances. Diocletian decided it was best to resign after ruling for twenty years, and the problematic succession meant that one of the heirs, Constantine, took nearly another twenty years before reuniting the rule of the Roman Empire. Most famous for his conversion to Christianity and for moving the capital of the empire to Constantinople, Constantine continued to advance the reforms begun by Diocletian and laid the foundations for the prosperity of the Roman Empire, at least in the East. By this time, however, the venerable institutions of the Roman Republic remained in name only. The Senate declined to little more than a prestigious council for the city of Rome. Constantine would revive a title such as "patrician" from the early days of Roman history, but now it became an honorary designation rather than a statement of class or distinction.

Sources:

M. I. Finley, *The Ancient Economy* (Berkeley: University of California Press, 1973).

Allen M. Ward, Fritz M. Heichelheim, and Cedric A. Yeo, *A History of the Roman People*, third edition (Upper Saddle River, N.J.: Prentice-Hall, 1999).

SIGNIFICANT PEOPLE

CRASSUS

CIRCA 115 B.C.E.-53 B.C.E.
ENTREPRENEUR AND POLITICIAN

Financial Wizard. Marcus Licinius Crassus lost his brother and father in the civil strife during the early part of the first century B.C.E. To carry on his family's aristocratic heritage and to be a substantial player in politics, he needed to build up his finances. In this pursuit he excelled. He not only made money off of farmland (the traditional financial base for a Roman senator), he also invested in mining and loaning operations. He was also unusual for having made money off of urban real estate in Rome, where he would buy at a low price properties that burned (a common phenomenon) and then salvage them. He maintained a skilled workforce of slaves whom he would rent out. Because such open interest in finances was considered degrading for a Roman senator, Crassus earned a reputation for greed. He rose to join Julius Caesar and Pompey in the First Triumvirate but was killed in battle in 53 B.C.E.

Sources:
B. A. Marshall, *Crassus: A Political Biography* (Amsterdam: Hakkert, 1976).

Allen Mason Ward, *Marcus Crassus and the Late Republic* (Columbia: University of Missouri Press, 1977).

DIOCLETIAN

CIRCA 240 C.E.-CIRCA 312 C.E.
ROMAN EMPEROR

Through the Ranks. Although little is known of his origins, Gaius Aurelius Valerius Diocletianus was probably born in Dalmatia. He served in the personal bodyguard of the Emperor Numericanus in Persia. After Numericanus was murdered by the prefect Apev,

Diocletian was proclaimed emperor. He defeated several rivals and returned to Rome.

Trying to Stabilize the Empire. Diocletian rose to the position of emperor by 285 C.E. He hoped to stabilize the empire, then in chaos, by dividing the responsibilities first between two people (himself and Maximian) and then among four (the *tetrarchy*). He initiated many economic reforms. One was a new mechanism for assessing taxes based on production and labor rather than simple land area. His Currency Edict was meant to stabilize and unify the value of coinage. The Price Edict was supposed to bring inflation under control and restore some fairness and trust to imperial finances. Neither of these edicts had much success. Diocletian decided to resign after ruling for twenty years and retired in 305 C.E. He died in his castle several years later.

Sources:
Timothy D. Barnes, *The New Empire of Diocletian and Constantine* (Cambridge, Mass.: Harvard University Press, 1982).

Stephen Williams, *Diocletian and the Roman Recovery* (London: Batsford, 1987).

FRONTINUS

CIRCA 30 C.E.-104 C.E.
CITY OFFICIAL

Technical Writing. Sextus Julius Frontinus served successfully as a governor and general in Britain during the 70s C.E. In the more difficult days under the Emperor Domitian he turned to technical writing. His book on military strategy, *Strategemata*, survives, which collects techniques employed by military commanders throughout history, including some relatively recent ones from his own day. Only parts of his work on land surveying survive, which covered measuring, categorizing, marking of land, along with resolution of property disputes. His most famous and popular work, however, is *De aquis urbis Romae* (The Water Supply of Rome). In it he collects and synthesizes a vast amount of technical information about building, administering, and maintaining one of Rome's architectural wonders, the aqueduct system. Included among his topics is keeping the system secure from those who tried to build illegal siphons into the aqueducts and acquire free water. Throughout, Frontinus displays the sort of the expertise and pride which Roman officials used to keep the empire, at its peak, running on a daily basis.

Sources:
Peter J. Aicher, *Guide to the Aqueducts of Ancient Rome* (Wauconda, Ill.: Bolchazy-Carducci, 1995).

Harry B. Evans, *Water Distribution in Ancient Rome: The Evidence of Frontinus* (Ann Arbor: University of Michigan Press, 1994).

TIBERIUS GRACCHUS

(163-133 B.C.E.)
TRIBUNE AND POPULAR REFORMER

Revolution and Assassination. Tiberius Sempronius Gracchus, and his younger brother Gaius Sempronius Gracchus, were plebeians on their father's side but were related through their mother, Cornelia, to one of the most prestigious patrician families, the Scipios. He fought against Carthage during his military service and later was made a quaestor in Spain. Tiberius was elected tribune of the *plebs* in 133 B.C.E. and pushed hard to change laws about land ownership, particularly as they related to military service and slave ownership. His proposals had popular support but faced opposition from wealthy landowners who stood to lose some of their land. His proposals were defeated by the Senate, but he continued to resubmit them. Despite his popular efforts, when Tiberius ran for reelection, he and many of his supporters were killed by a mob. Tiberius's younger brother later attempted to continue and expand the reform program. He was elected Tribune in 122 B.C.E. and pushed through a more extensive revolutionary program than his brother had ever considered. He failed to win a third term, and his enemies managed to have him assassinated in 121 B.C.E. The Gracchi became famous as martyrs for the cause of popular reform. Their actions (and bloody failures) also set the course for the civil wars that were to consume the Republic in the next hundred years.

Sources:
Alvin H. Bernstein, *Tiberius Sempronius Gracchus: Tradition and Apostasy* (Ithaca, N.Y.: Cornell University Press, 1978).

Keith Richardson, *Daggers in the Forum: The Revolutionary Lives and Violent Deaths of the Gracchus Brothers* (London: Cassell, 1976).

TERENTIA

CIRCA 95 B.C.E.-CIRCA 8 C.E.
HOUSEHOLD ESTATE MANAGER
AND WIFE OF CICERO

Shrewd and Wealthy. Terentia became Cicero's first wife (circa 77 B.C.E.), and they had two children, Tullia and, later, Marcus. She was wealthy in her own right and a powerful force in Cicero's household. She incited Cicero to action against political enemies such as Catiline and Clodius Pulcher. During Cicero's exile (58–57 B.C.E.), she managed the whole estate. Ten years later, however, they divorced over a dispute about how Terentia handled the finances. Cicero believed she handled the money *too* much and that she stole some for herself. It was Cicero, though, who faced financial hardship after the divorce. Terentia had two subsequent husbands, one of them the historian Sallust. She lived to be 103 years old.

Sources:
Ernst Badian, "Terentia," in *The Oxford Classical Dictionary*, edited by Simon Hornblower and Antony Spawforth (Oxford: Oxford University Press, 1999), p. 1484.

Elizabeth Rawson, *Cicero: A Portrait* (London: Allen Lane, 1975).

VESPASIAN

9 C.E.-79 C.E.
ROMAN EMPEROR

Reasserting Fiscal Stability. Titus Flavius Vespasianus took command of the Roman Empire after the chaotic year following the death of Nero, during which he was the fourth man to act as emperor. Vespasian brought discipline and control back to imperial finances. He instituted a thorough *census* (counting) of the resources of the empire and discovered many untapped resources for bringing in more money to the public treasury. Some places that had previously been exempt from Roman taxes (such as Byzantium and Rhodes) he now taxed. He also found ingenious ways to raise money, such as by taxing latrines for their urine (fullers—cloth cleaners—used the urine in their businesses). Vespasian ran a tight financial ship but also invested in many large-scale public building projects, including a new forum (a downtown business area) and, most famously, the Colosseum. He also endowed the first state-sponsored academic position, given to the orator and educational theorist Quintilian.

Sources:
P. A. L. Greenhalgh, *The Year of the Four Emperors* (London: Weidenfeld & Nicolson, 1975).

Barbara Levick, *Vespasian* (London & New York: Routledge, 1999).

DOCUMENTARY SOURCES

Apuleius, *Metamorphoses* (or, *The Golden Ass*, circa 160 C.E.)—The vivid story of a man transformed into a donkey. He travels the Roman world, seeing the lives of folks at all levels of society.

Cato, *De agri cultura* (2nd or 3rd century B.C.E.); Varro, *De re rustica* (37 B.C.E.), Columella, *De re rustica* (first century C.E.)—These guidebooks provide technical information about the agrarian component of the Roman economy, as well as insight into the aristocratic perspective on farming. Columella's is the most ambitious of the three, comprising twelve books (inspired by Vergil's *Aeneid*), one of which is in the epic meter of dactylic hexameter.

Cicero (Marcus Tullius Cicero), *Letters to His Family and Friends* (62–43 B.C.E.)—Some of Cicero's correspondence provides a wealth of information about the finances and politics in the final days of the Republic.

Frontinus, *De aquis urbis Romae* (The Water Supply of Rome, circa 100 C.E.)—This technical treatise provides a look at both the finances involved with this topic and the vast knowledge required of a magistrate at Rome.

Livy, *Ab urbe condita*, Books 1–10 (written in the 20s B.C.E.)—The first ten books of this majestic history of early Rome cover the founding of the city through approximately 289 B.C.E. It remains the standard, though at points still controversial, account of the monarchy and rising Republic, covering the Struggle of the Orders and more.

Petronius, *Satyricon* (mid-first century C.E.)—This satirical novel includes an outrageous but fascinating portrayal of classes of Roman society (especially freedmen) not often written about elsewhere.

Pliny the Younger (Gaius Plinius Caecilius Secundus), *Letters* (99–109 C.E.)—This collection of letters provides the most detailed information about the finances of a Roman senator.

Roman sestertius made of brass, 37–38 C.E., with three sisters (Agrippina, Drusilla, Julia), each holding a cornucopia (British Museum)

CHAPTER SIX

POLITICS, LAW, AND THE MILITARY

by ANDREW M. RIGGSBY

CONTENTS

Sidebars and tables are listed in italics.

264 B.C.E.

- The Roman Republic is administered by two consuls who each rule for one year and are invested with the power of *imperium,* the right to issue commands. Financial officers, called *quaestors,* assist them in their duties. Like the early Roman kings, the consuls lead the army, serve as judges, and perform certain religious duties.

- The First Punic War begins, pitting Rome against the North African city-state of Carthage. The war ends in 241 when Carthage agrees to relinquish control of Sicily and to pay a war indemnity in ten annual installments.

241 B.C.E.

- This year is the last one in which the Roman people are divided for administrative purposes into thirty-five *tribus* (tribes), four of which are urban and thirty-one rustic.

233 B.C.E.

- For the next one hundred years, twenty-six Roman families will provide 80 percent of the consuls, with ten families alone accounting for almost 50 percent. These same families also dominate the Senate.

218 B.C.E.

- Political machinations in Spain cause Rome and Carthage to engage in the Second Punic War. The next year a large Roman army is defeated at Lake Trasimene in central Italy.

216 B.C.E.

- At the Battle of Cannae in southeastern Italy, the Romans suffer the worst defeat in their military history. An entire army of eighty thousand men is either killed or captured by the Carthaginians under Hannibal. Many of the Roman allies in southern Italy and Sicily defect.

214 B.C.E.

- The First Macedonian War begins, pitting Rome against Macedon after the Macedonian king Philip V forms an alliance with Carthage. The conflict lasts until 205.

202 B.C.E.

- At the Battle of Zama in present-day Tunisia, the Roman Publius Cornelius Scipio (later called Africanus) defeats Hannibal. The Second Punic War ends, and Rome now rules the entire Mediterranean coast from Italy westward.

* Denotes Circa Date

200 B.C.E.

- The Second Macedonian War begins.

197 B.C.E.

- At the Battle of Cynoscephalae in northeastern Greece, a Roman army under Titus Quinctius Flamininus crushes a Macedonian army under Philip V. This battle demonstrates the flexibility of Roman military doctrine over the more rigid Macedonian phalanx (a rectangular tactical formation). The Second Macedonian War ends, and Flamininus declares the Greek city-states to be autonomous.

171 B.C.E.

- The Third Macedonian War begins. It ends three years later, after a Roman force commanded by Lucius Aemilius Paullus defeats the Macedonians under King Perseus at the Battle of Pydna in northern Greece. Macedon is now divided into four separate republics.

149 B.C.E.

- The first standing criminal court for *repetundae* (recovery of money) is created.
- The Third Punic War begins. It ends in 146 after the city of Carthage is sacked and the population is sold into slavery.

139 B.C.E.

- For the first time, secret ballots are allowed for certain votes in the Assembly. Later laws in 137, 131, and 106 expand the use of secret ballots.

133 B.C.E.

- Tiberius Sempronius Gracchus becomes tribune, an official elected by the plebeians and charged with the defense of those people and their interests. His program of land reform—restoring the class of peasant farmers by restricting the amount of public land a citizen might own and redistributing small lots—arouses great hostility. After he attempts to be reelected a riot ensues and a mob of senators and their supporters kill Tiberius and three hundred of his followers.

123 B.C.E.

- Gaius Sempronius Gracchus becomes tribune and attempts to implement his brother Tiberius's agrarian reforms. He also proposes measures to limit the powers of the Senate and courts and to grant citizenship to the Latins.

*DENOTES CIRCA DATE

111 B.C.E.

- The Jugurthine War begins, growing out of a dispute over the succession to the throne of Numidia, a Roman client kingdom near Carthage. Jugurtha seizes control and massacres Roman merchants. He is eventually betrayed to the Romans and executed in 104.

100* B.C.E.

- The consul Gaius Marius introduces a series of military reforms. These so-called Marian reforms include an end of property qualifications for military service, as well as a new tactical structure for the legions. A typical legion now has 4,800 men subdivided into ten cohorts, each containing six centuries of 80 men. There are six professional officers, known as centurions, in each cohort. Also during this time the *aquila* (eagle) is adopted as the symbol of each legion.

91 B.C.E.

- The "Social War" begins between Rome and its Italian allies (*socii*). By the end of the strife in 88, all free Italians are made Roman citizens.

88 B.C.E.

- The Mithridatic wars, three intermittent conflicts between Rome and Pontus, begin and last until 64. Although a formidable opponent, Pontus is defeated and the Roman frontier is extended to the Euphrates River.

80* B.C.E.

- The dictator Lucius Cornelius Sulla implements conservative political and judicial reforms. Most of his limits on individual office holding are dismantled within a decade, but his version of the criminal courts remains in force for many years.

73 B.C.E.

- The Thracian gladiator Spartacus leads a revolt of runaway slaves. His followers eventually grow to ninety thousand strong, and it takes two years to finally crush the insurrection. Spartacus is killed in battle and six thousand slaves are crucified by Marcus Licinius Crassus along the Appian Way.

63 B.C.E.

- Marcus Tullius Cicero becomes consul. He foils the conspiracy of Lucius Sergius Catilina to assassinate leading politicians and plunder Rome.

*Denotes Circa Date

60 B.C.E.

- Gaius Julius Caesar returns to Rome from his governorship of Spain. He forms the First Triumvirate, an informal agreement with two other leading politicians, Marcus Licinius Crassus and Gnaeus Pompeius Magnus (Pompey). The next year, Caesar becomes consul.

58 B.C.E.

- Cicero is banished through the efforts of Publius Clodius but is recalled the next year.
- Caesar initiates a military campaign to subdue Gaul, and Vercingetorix unites the various tribes in the region to thwart the Roman invasion. The climactic event of the Gallic Wars is the siege of Alesia (52), where Vercingetorix is captured.

53 B.C.E.

- At the Battle of Carrhae (in present-day Turkey), an army commanded by Crassus is surrounded and annihilated by the Parthians.

49 B.C.E.

- A civil war begins between Caesar and senatorial forces under Pompey. Caesar and his army cross the Rubicon River and march into northern Italy.

48 B.C.E.

- Caesar defeats Pompey at the Battle of Pharsalus in eastern Greece.

45 B.C.E.

- Caesar defeats Pompey's sons at the Battle of Munda in Spain; the civil war ends and Caesar becomes the sole leader of Rome.

44 B.C.E.

- A conspiracy led by Gaius Cassius Longinus and Marcus Junius Brutus gathers strength and includes approximately sixty senators. On 15 March they assassinate Caesar. The next year Gaius Octavius (now called Gaius Julius Caesar Octavianus), grandnephew and adopted heir of Caesar, marches on Rome with an army and has Brutus and Cassius declared outlaws. The Second Triumvirate is formed with Octavian and two of Caesar's former supporters, Marcus Aemilius Lepidus and Marcus Antonius (Mark Antony).

42 B.C.E.

- At the Battle of Philippi in Macedonia, the forces of Brutus and Cassius are defeated by the triumvirs. Afterward, Lepidus is placed in charge of Africa, Antony receives control of the eastern provinces, and Octavian administers the western provinces.

*DENOTES CIRCA DATE

31 B.C.E.

- The Second Triumvirate dissolves. Octavian defeats Antony in a naval battle at Actium off the coast of western Greece. The Roman Republic comes to a close and the Roman Empire begins with the installment of Octavian as virtual monarch.

27 B.C.E.

- The Senate confers on Octavian the title *Augustus*, i.e. "revered, majestic, venerable."

- Augustus establishes a permanent force to act as the emperor's bodyguard. The Praetorian Guard consists of nine cohorts, each containing anywhere from five hundred to one thousand men, recruited mainly from Italy and the Romanized provinces. As elite troops, the guards receive three times the regular legionary pay and are housed in special barracks. Over time the Praetorian Guard becomes heavily involved in the appointment of emperors.

- The Pax Romana (Roman Peace), a period of comparative tranquility and prosperity throughout the Mediterranean world, begins. It ends with the death of Emperor Marcus Aurelius in 180.

6 C.E.

- A city watch (a system of police and fire patrols) is created in Rome.

9 C.E.

- Three legions commanded by Publius Quintilius Varus are wiped out at Teutoburger Wald (Teutoburg Forest) in western Germany by Arminius, war chief of the Cherusci.

14 C.E.

- There are twenty-five Roman legions in service. The size of each legion has increased to 5,400 infantrymen and 120 cavalrymen. Before the end of the first century, the term of service for a legionnaire is increased to twenty-five years.

- Augustus dies and is succeeded by his stepson, Tiberius.

37 C.E.

- Caligula becomes emperor. Erratic and cruel, he is murdered by members of the Praetorian Guard in 41.

41 C.E.

- Claudius becomes emperor.

*DENOTES CIRCA DATE

56 C.E. • Imperial appointees replace the *quaestors* and assume control of the treasury.

60 C.E. • A rebellion led by Queen Boudicca of the Iceni begins in Britain and is suppressed by the next year.

64 C.E. • A great fire ravages the city of Rome. It breaks out near the Circus Maximus and quickly spreads. Although Nero blames the Christians, many people become convinced that the emperor himself started the blaze in order to clear land for his new Golden House.

68 C.E. • Nero, the last of the Julio-Claudian emperors, dies. During the course of the next year, Rome has three emperors—Servius Sulpicius Galba, Marcus Salvius Otho, and Aulus Vitellius.

69 C.E. • Vespasian is the first of the Flavian emperors.

85 C.E. • Over the course of the next three years, the Dacians, a group of people from present-day Romania, mount raids across the Danube frontier.

96 C.E. • Domitian, the last emperor of the Flavian dynasty, dies. The next four emperors—Nerva, Trajan, Hadrian, and Antoninus Pius—have no surviving sons and their successors are chosen by adoption. The Adoptive Emperors provide the empire with eighty years of stability.

98 C.E. • Trajan comes to the throne. The first non-Italian emperor, he was born near Seville in present-day Spain. Under his nineteen-year rule, the frontiers of the Roman Empire are pushed to their widest extent.

101 C.E. • The First Dacian War begins. Trajan leads an expedition into the heart of Dacian lands, and the Dacian king Decebalus sues for peace the next year.

*DENOTES CIRCA DATE

105 C.E. • The Second Dacian War begins. A Roman army captures the Dacian capital of Sarmizegethusa and the kingdom of Dacia becomes a Roman province in 106.

114 C.E. • The Parthian War begins, an inconclusive two-year struggle between Rome and Parthia.

132 C.E. • The Praetor's Edict governing civil law is revised by the jurist Salvius Julianus on behalf of the Emperor Hadrian.

138 C.E. • Antoninus Pius is the first of the Antonine emperors.

167 C.E. • The Marcomanni and Quadi, Germanic peoples living north of the middle Danube River, begin a series of raids into Roman territory.

192 C.E. • With the assassination of Commodus, the Antonine Dynasty ends. Following a brief period of civil unrest, Septimius Severus becomes the first Severan emperor in 193.

200 C.E. • There are thirty-three Roman legions in service.

212 C.E. • In the Antonine Constitution, the Emperor Caracalla extends Roman citizenship to all free men and women living in the empire. While the edict strengthens the concept of the empire as a unified entity rather than a mere group of provinces dominated by Rome, it also widens the obligation for public service as well as increases the imperial tax base.

235 C.E. • The Severan dynasty ends with the murder of Alexander Severus. During the next fifty years the Roman Empire has a series of short-reign emperors, many of whom are chosen from the army and meet violent deaths.

*DENOTES CIRCA DATE

260 C.E. • Marcus Cassianius Latinius Postumus, the governor of Lower Germany, revolts from Roman rule and establishes a breakaway empire made up of Gaul and the two Germanies. Within a year Spain and Britain are also incorporated. The Gallic Empire survives as a separate state for almost fifteen years before being reabsorbed by the Roman Empire.

284 C.E. • Diocletian becomes emperor. Because of the past decades of civil war and turmoil, Diocletian reorganizes the empire and divides power territorially. (His ultimate goal is to provide a peaceful succession.) In 286 he names a co-emperor, Maximian. Seven years later two subordinate leaders are given the title *Caesar:* Galerius and Constantius I. Diocletian controls the provinces of Thrace, Asia, and Egypt, while Maximian administers Italy, Africa, and Spain. Galerius receives the Danube frontier and the Balkans, and Constantius I supervises Britain and Gaul.

300 C.E. • The number of Roman legions in service has increased to sixty-seven. Much of the manpower comes from the provinces and foreign nations.

305 C.E. • Diocletian retires and compels his co-emperor Maximian to do the same; five claimants to the thrones emerge, and a civil war ensues.

307 C.E. • Constantine, the son of Constantinus I, becomes emperor of the West.

312 C.E. • At the Battle of Milvian Bridge in northern Italy, Constantine defeats Maxentius, son of Maximian.
• Constantine disbands the Praetorian Guard.

313 C.E. • In the Edict of Milan, Constantine declares official toleration of Christianity.

324 C.E. • Constantine becomes sole emperor and founds a new capital on the site of the existing city of Byzantium. In 330 he renames the city Constantinople.

*Denotes Circa Date

364 C.E. • Valentinian I becomes emperor. Within a month he appoints his younger brother Valens joint Augustus. Valentinian rules Illyricum and the western provinces, while Valens administers the rest of the Balkans and the East.

376 C.E. • The Visigoths, a Germanic people pushed out of their homelands by the Huns, receive permission to settle in the Roman Empire. Although they defend the eastern frontier as *foederati* (special allies of the empire), they also plunder the Balkan provinces.

378 C.E. • Valens is killed in battle with the Visigoths and Ostrogoths at Adrianople in Thrace.

379 C.E. • Theodosius I becomes emperor in the East.

382 C.E. • Under a new treaty the Visigoths are allowed to settle south of the Danube River.

395 C.E. • With the death of Theodosius I, the final division of the Empire between East and West occurs. He leaves the eastern provinces to his eldest son, Arcadius, seventeen years old, and the western regions to his second son, Honorius, who is only ten years old.

397 C.E. • The Visigoths raid as far south as the Balkans and Greece.

401 C.E. • Alaric, king of the Visigoths, ravages Italy until he is repulsed by Roman forces under Flavius Stilicho in 403.

406 C.E. • The Vandals, Alans, and Sueves cross the Rhine River and ravage Gaul; within three years they settle in Spain.

* DENOTES CIRCA DATE

410 C.E. • Alaric besieges, occupies, and sacks the city of Rome.

412 C.E. • Athaulf leads the Visigoths into Gaul.

415 C.E. • The Visigoths invade Spain but withdraw three years later and establish a settlement at Tolosa (present-day Toulouse, France).

429 C.E. • The Vandals cross into Africa from Spain and conquer the North African provinces; by 439 Carthage falls to them.

447 C.E. • Attila the Hun begins a series of raids into the Balkans and Greece that lasts for three years.

450 C.E. • Attila the Hun claims Honoria, sister of Emperor Valentinian III, for his wife and demands one-half of the Western Empire as her dowry.

451 C.E. • A combined army of Romans, under Flavius Aetius, and Visigoths, under Theodoric and Thorismond, defeats the Huns at the Battle of the Catalaunian Plains in Gaul.

476 C.E. • Odoacer, a German general in the Roman army, deposes the Emperor Romulus Augustulus and sacks Rome. The Western Roman Empire collapses.

*Denotes Circa Date

OVERVIEW

Roman Law. One of the most distinctive features of Roman culture was its large and elaborately articulated legal system. There were three layers of what might today be called "laws." First, there were laws in the narrow, Latin sense: statutes passed by one of the legislative assemblies. These laws were fewer and less systematic than modern legal codes. Second, there were the decrees ("edicts") of the various magistrates, particularly the so-called urban praetor. The praetor's edict provided for most of the law in many areas such as contract, inheritance, and property rights. Other edicts governed, for instance, certain commercial transactions and any legal matters in the provinces. Third, there were interpretations of both the statutes and the edicts by legal professionals called "jurists." In some cases these interpretations were merely clarifications of the law, but in other cases they completely rewrote the original intent. Jurists had no formal legal status, but they were brought in as advisers to judges and writers of laws (as well as private individuals) and their consensus was usually treated as authoritative.

Public and Private. The Romans divided their legal system into the "private" and "public." Private law corresponds fairly closely to what would now be called civil law. It includes areas such as contract, property, inheritance, marriage and divorce, defamation, and slavery. It also encompasses some areas considered criminal today—generally matters that affect only individuals—such as theft and most assaults. Private law cases were tried in front of a single judge. This judge was a prominent citizen rather than a legal professional, and he was given only the most general legal direction from the magistrate in charge of the legal system. The public offenses were generally things that would be considered crimes today: homicide, forgery, racketeering by provincial governors, electoral bribery, and sedition. Cases were heard by large juries. Again, these were prominent citizens instead of legal professionals. Both public and private trials were conducted with little intervention by the government; both sides made whatever speeches and presented whatever evidence they thought would advance their case without interference from the presiding officer. Even criminal offenses were pursued by private citizens rather than a state prosecutor.

Transition. These procedures changed somewhat under the Empire. In criminal matters, members of the elite Senate came to be tried before that body rather than by the courts. Other cases were heard more and more by a delegate of the emperor in a process known as *cognitio*. This procedure was more inquisitorial (rather than adversarial), more professionalized, and allowed for the possibility of appeal, which had not existed before.

Shortcomings. Equality before the law was not a fundamental property of the legal system. Slaves had no rights. Women, the blind, the deaf, and those officially judged morally inferior (including felons and members of certain professions) were openly discriminated against. Members of the elite had small but overt advantages. Certain legal procedures were also financially risky for potential litigants; this risk would have discouraged the poor from protecting their rights in court. This formal inequality was probably reinforced by corruption and influence. Nonprofessional judges were particularly open to influence. Even when specific favors were not exchanged, the people who ran the system were all of the upper class and seemed to have looked after their own peers. Bribery was apparently much more common then and would have been in favor of the rich as well. And in an openly hierarchical society, even a judge who thought of himself as honest might well have found elite litigants or witnesses more trustworthy than ordinary people.

Convoluted System. The legal "system" was not particularly systematic. Statute law, edicts, and juristic interpretation were not well coordinated and sometimes even contradictory. Even individual rules were not written with the same regard for coherence and comprehensiveness as modern legal codes. Processes of amendment and abrogation made laws more confusing over time, not more refined. Earlier precedent was not a standard for judging later cases, nor was there a system of higher and lower courts, so the same case could be decided differently in different places or at different times.

Law and Order? The Roman government was surprisingly uninterested in "law and order" and the suppression of crime. There was no police force to prevent crimes or catch criminals. There were no state prosecutors, and the most common "crimes" of today were not treated as such in Roman law.

Republican Government. The government of the Roman Republic can be thought of as having five branches. One is the judiciary, or the court system. The second is the executive branch, which was composed of a number of elected magistrates. Magistrates served for a year at a time. At any given time there were several incumbents of each office. Although each office had characteristic areas of responsibility, they formed a hierarchy. The ranking of each office was both one of authority and the order in which they had to be held by a given individual. There were a variety of devices for small numbers of magistrates (even individual ones) to block positive actions by others. The third branch, the assemblies, might be described as "legislative," though that term is not accurate. There were several assemblies with largely overlapping powers. They passed the laws, elected the magistrates, and, in a few cases, acted as courts. The assemblies were composed of all adult male citizens who showed up in person (at Rome) to vote on any given matter. The assemblies practiced group voting, like the American electoral college, instead of directly counting the votes of those present (the differences between assemblies were primarily in how the voters were divided into groups). Individual voters were not allowed to amend or debate laws or propose candidates. They could only vote on proposals put before them by the magistrates. The fourth (and perhaps most distinctive) element of the government was the Senate. This element should not be confused with the American institution of the same name. The Roman Senate was composed, roughly, of all former magistrates, who served for life. The Senate had little or no formal legal authority (only the assemblies could pass laws), but the magistrates usually took directions from it. Arguably a fifth branch of the government was the various state priesthoods, especially once these came to be elected by the same assemblies that voted for the magistrates.

How Democratic? Ancient and modern writers on the Roman government have disagreed considerably on how democratic it was. On the one hand, little could be done legally without the consent of the people. On the other hand, the assemblies could not initiate action without a magistrate. These magistrates were all members of the upper classes. Senate and magistrates sometimes acted without consulting the people first. Votes could be bought or manipulated in a variety of ways. The group structure of the assemblies gave the relatively well off (if not the super-rich) disproportionate voting power. If the elite held together, they could probably dominate the political process. When they were divided, whether out of genuine differences of opinion or to exploit popular sentiment for popular gain, then a much broader segment of society might have had a say in particular decisions.

Growth and Development. The Romans did little to distinguish "levels" of government, unlike the city, county, state, and nation arrangement in the contemporary United States. The apparatus was both the city government of Rome, and the government of Italy (which was entirely Roman territory from about 90 B.C.E.) and of the entire Empire. As the size of the Roman world grew, the govern-ment grew somewhat and positions became more specialized. In particular, more flexible means for creating and assigning provincial governors were developed. The Romans did not, however, really keep up with the demands of empire either in scale or in sophistication.

Imperial Government. When Augustus (then named Octavian) took the throne as the first emperor in 31 B.C.E., there were great changes in the government but not a complete revolution. The Senate continued to exist and gained some formal legal authority, primarily over its own members. The assemblies soon ceased to meet, but the magistracies continued to exist. (Some were essentially appointed by the emperor and some were chosen within the Senate.) These old offices became largely honorary. Most of the power began to shift to a parallel set of positions that were answerable directly to the emperor. The emperor's own position was complicated by the pretense for the first several decades that there was no such person. There was no title or office of "emperor." Instead, the emperor held (simultaneously) a large number of traditional offices, as well as novel offices and powers derived from traditional Republican ones. This fact made the succession inherently unstable. Some emperors were able to set up succession by a son (often adopted) by sharing power while they were still alive. But quite often military struggles and/or bribery of the troops proved decisive.

Imperial Control. The emperor's rigid control of power at the top forced competition among aristocrats into other arenas. There were still elections, and so support to be gathered, whether among their peers or from the emperor. Local governments remained democratic (at least to the extent that the Republican Roman government had been democratic). Some shifts even occurred in spheres that might not seem obviously political. So, for instance, public benefactions moved from Rome to the municipalities. Literature became a more popular arena.

Bureaucracy and Division. The imperial government developed a larger and more professional bureaucracy. In part this bureaucracy was made up of the emperor's subordinates, in part from the use of the emperor's own household as the framework for a permanent staff. There were more administrators, many of them served longer, and career paths were somewhat more regular than under the Republic. Eventually, the empire was broken up into a larger number of relatively small provinces, grouped into dioceses. This division gave a little more depth to imperial administration. At about the same time, military and civilian administrations were made completely separate for the first time. The later empire also saw changes in the character of the emperor's position itself. It became more open and more "despotic" almost from the beginning, but especially after the first two centuries. So, for instance, the emperor and everything surrounding him became increasingly sacred (a change surprisingly unaffected by the Christianization of the later Empire).

Armed Forces. The Roman army was divided into two parts: the legions and the auxiliaries. The legions were composed of citizens. They were large units (around five thousand men) of heavily armed and armored infantry (subdivided into units of about five hundred and one hundred). The auxiliary troops were made up of foreign allies. They comprised many different kinds of forces. Some were equipped more or less as the legions, though in somewhat smaller units. Others were cavalry, archers, slingers, skirmishers, or other specialized troops. In addition to strictly military duties, most troops (especially the legions) also had engineering tasks (e.g., roads, bridges) as well as keeping up fortifications and practicing siege warfare.

Nature of the Army. During the Republic, the army was essentially a militia. Most adult males were liable for service during time of war (which was most of the time), though in practice they were only called up a year or a few years at a time. There were originally property qualifications to serve in the army, but these were dropped over the course of time. The imperial army was much more professionalized. Service in the army was for a long, fixed term. Nearly all soldiers were volunteers. The number and identity of individual units were stabilized, instead of varying by yearly need. Higher officers at all periods were not promoted from the ranks, nor were they even professional soldiers. The intermediate officers ("centurions," something like modern noncommissioned officers) were a combination of veteran soldiers promoted for their skill and experience and members of well-to-do but nonaristocratic families who got their positions through connections.

TOPICS IN POLITICS, LAW, AND THE MILITARY

ADVERSARINESS AND ADVOCACY

Attempting to Win. American courts today are highly adversarial (most European ones less so). That is, the two parties gather and present the evidence they want and tell the stories they want in an attempt to win. The court's role is primarily to decide between the two positions they offer. There are certain exceptions. The sides can have witnesses compelled by the court's subpoena. "Discovery" procedures require some sharing of information. Evidentiary rules constrain what can be offered in court (e.g., no hearsay). The judge makes authoritative decisions on questions of law (as opposed to those of fact). Lawyers are bound by canons of ethics. In the Roman courts the procedure was almost purely adversarial. Romans also had nothing like the rules suppressing the results of an improper search. One of the few countervailing factors, at least in private trials, was that the *iudex* might seek his own legal or other advice. The praetor (magistrate) did direct the *iudex* of a private case by means of the formula. It, however, gave only the most general guidance. *Iudices* in public cases apparently did not get even this treatment. Many have held that this extreme adversariness was a relatively "primitive" feature of the Roman legal system.

Public Speakers. Romans in both public and private cases, both prosecuting and defending, ordinarily came into court with one or more advocates to speak for them. These advocates should not be confused with the modern "lawyers" they superficially resemble. Advocates were primarily public speakers and only exceptionally had more legal expertise than they happened to pick up on the job. (Conversely, only occasionally most jurists argued cases in court.) The other thing an advocate might be hoped to bring to the table was personal prestige. Thus, in celebrity public cases each side would try to sit as many former chief magistrates (and the like) as possible. Another striking difference from modern practice is that, for most of Roman history, advocates were not allowed to accept pay for their services. This practice is connected to the desire for prestigious advocates. They were meant to personally guarantee the characters of their clients more than provide technical skills. In any case, the ban seems to have been easily evaded. The reliance on advocacy is in striking contrast to some other well-known legal systems of antiquity (such as that of Athens).

Sources:
John Anthony Crook, *Law and Life of Rome* (Ithaca, N.Y.: Cornell University Press, 1967).

Crook, *Legal Advocacy in the Roman World* (Ithaca, N.Y.: Cornell University Press, 1995).

APPEALS PROCESS

A Second Chance. Originally, verdicts of public and private law courts were not subject to appeal. It has been suggested that public law trials themselves were originally thought of as appeals from a magistrate's decision, but this situation was never the case for, at least, private law cases. The only remedy for a defeated party in the Republic was a special law passed by an assembly, and of these there are only a few known examples. Emperors, beginning with the first one, began to exercise an appellate jurisdiction. This exercise was obviously valuable to victims of dishonest or incompetent judges. It was also valuable to the system in that it provided a central, authoritative source of legal interpretation. This was particularly true since many such cases were probably settled by high-powered jurists in the emperors' courts. Finally, the judging of appeals was a source of patronage. Regular judges were significantly constrained by existing law. Emperors could change the law or make ad hoc exceptions whenever it seemed desirable. Thus, the emperor could make himself a figure of mercy and common sense.

Sources:
John Anthony Crook, *Law and Life of Rome* (Ithaca, N.Y.: Cornell University Press, 1967).

Fergus Millar, *The Emperor in the Roman World (31 B.C.–A.D. 337)* (Ithaca: Cornell University Press, 1977).

THE ARMY

The Legion. The core of the Roman army of the Republic and most of the Empire was made up of formations of heavily armed and armored infantry. The largest standing unit was the legion, theoretically composed of about five thousand men. (The legion and all of its subdivisions were ordinarily smaller in practice than on paper.) This legion was divided into ten numbered "cohorts," the first being about twice the size of the others. Each cohort in turn consisted of six "centuries" made up of about eighty men. Finally, centuries were divided into *contubernia* of eight men. The century was commanded by a centurion; he was often an experienced soldier promoted from the ranks, but sometimes a political appointee instead. He was assisted by a standard-bearer and two other officers. The cohorts did not have officers of their own but appear to have been in the charge of their senior centurion. The legion was commanded by two or more military tribunes (no relation to the magistrate of similar name). In practice,

however, the tribunes often served as staff officers for the magistrate or promagistrate in command of a whole army rather than directing a particular part of the army. Tribunes were often, in fact, young aristocrats who needed military experience more than the army needed them. Also attached to the commander could be a number of *legati*. These were also aristocrats, but normally of more experience, and they might be dispatched with a force of their own if the army needed to be in more than one place at a time. Also attached to the legion as a whole were a small group of cavalry, some artillery, and an "eagle-bearer" carrying the legion's standard.

Equipment. These soldiers were equipped in uniform fashion. They wore armor from shoulders to waist made of scale, mail, or bands (and the famous protective leather skirt below this). There was also a large helmet, a heavy, partly cylindrical shield with a central boss, and greaves. The main weapons were fairly heavy throwing spears and short, broad swords. The former were cast at modest range to injure but also to disorganize the enemy; the latter were primarily thrusting weapons. Some may also have carried some kind of knife, and the heavy shield could be used effectively to strike an enemy. Cavalry were equipped more lightly than infantry and often carried a stabbing spear or lance. Legionary cavalry were often more important for communications and scouting than for battle.

Auxiliary Forces. Around the legions, and sometimes even outnumbering them, were "auxiliary" troops provided by Rome's allies. Sometimes this situation was a matter of mutual interest, but more often it was a condition of peace with Rome. Republican auxiliary troops were equipped in national fashion. For Italians, this gear was essentially Roman. For Gauls and Africans it could vary considerably. Under the Empire, auxiliary infantry was generally organized like the Roman forces, but the largest unit was the cohort, not the legion. This unit was commanded by a Roman prefect. Most of these units also used arms and tactics like those of the legions. However, others provided the Roman army with its light-armed troops and missile-firers (archers, slingers). Nearly all of the "Roman" cavalry were actually auxiliary. The main unit was the *ala* (wing) of about five hundred men, commanded by a Roman prefect or indigenous leader. This unit was divided into sixteen *turmae* (squadron, singular *turma*), each lead by a decurion. Some auxiliary cohorts of the imperial army also combined a full compliment of infantry with a substantial number of cavalry.

Recruitment and Service. All able-bodied male Roman citizens between seventeen and forty-six (older in emergencies) were liable for service in the Republican army. At the beginning of a campaign the consul (or other responsible official) would hold a levy to which the potential soldiers were summoned. From these he chose enough men to fill the number of legions to be filled. Originally levies were held at Rome, but as Roman citizenship spread, regional levies were also added in times of need. A man was liable for sixteen years of service, but would not normally have to

Toward the end of his conquest of Gaul (52 B.C.E.), Julius Caesar cornered the leader of a major uprising in the hilltop town of Alesia. His troops built a ring of fortifications to contain the Gauls in the city, then built another around themselves to fend off the huge relief force that arrived soon. He describes the works himself in his memoir of the Gallic campaign.

Both construction material and food supplies had to be gathered and great fortifications be built at the same time, despite our reduced forces, which were going further and further from camp. Occasionally, the Gauls tested our defenses and attempted sallies in full force from the town from several gates at a time. As a result, Caesar thought these works needed to be reinforced so they could be defended by a smaller force. Tree trunks and strong branches were cut off and their ends were smoothed and sharpened and continuous trenches of five-foot depth were dug. The stakes were set into the trenches, fastened at the bottom so they could not be removed, and the other end was allowed to stick up. Five ranks of these were joined and bound together so that anyone who entered would impale himself on very sharp points. This they call "boundary markers." In front of these, arranged like the dots on a "five" on a die, three-foot deep pits were dug, narrowing at the bottom. Into these were set smoothed sticks, thick as a man's thigh, sharpened and fire-hardened at the end, and projecting only a few inches from the ground. To firm and stabilize them, the ground was trampled down for a foot from the bottom of the pit; the rest of the pits were covered in twigs and branches to hide the trap. There were eight rows of these, three feet apart from each other. These were called "lilies" from their resemblance to the flower. In front of these lilies, foot-long sticks with iron hooks attached were completely buried in the earth and scattered everywhere at modest intervals. They call these "spurs."

Source: *Caesar: The Gallic Wars*, translated by Henry John Edwards, Loeb Classical Library (London & Cambridge, Mass.: Harvard University Press, 1979).

serve more than six years consecutively. For most of the Republic there was a minimum property qualification to serve in the army, though its value declined over time. (The theory was apparently that the best soldiers were those with *something* to fight for.) The general Marius seems to have been the first to recruit among the landless as a matter of course, at the end of the second century B.C.E. It soon became common practice.

Professionalization. Poorer soldiers had less economic motivation to return to civilian life. Rome's wars grew increasingly distant over time and so there was greater need to keep the troops away. Thus, it was probably not surprising when Augustus shifted the army to a more professional basis. The term now, apparently, became sixteen years plus four more of special veteran service. Troops stayed in the army for the full term even when not campaigning and received a substantial cash bonus on discharge. Units of the

army also developed continuing histories; some can be traced for two centuries. The levy was never actually abolished, but the career was attractive enough that volunteers were normally sufficient. Auxiliary service also came to be more professionalized. There was a standard term of service (twenty-five years) and a conventional grant of Roman citizenship at its end.

Engineering. The Roman army had no separate corps of engineers, but most of the soldiers were taught construction skills of various sorts. The most basic was construction of the field camp set up at the end of each day's march during war. This bivouac was not a heavy fortification, but it prevented easy infiltration or sneak attack by an enemy. It must also have been valuable as a symbol of Roman discipline and occupation. When occasion demanded they could also construct much more elaborate defenses as well. Soldiers also needed to be able to build and use various devices of siege warfare: ramps, mobile towers and shelters, rams, and tunnels. Special needs might also require unusual items: Julius Caesar's bridge across the Rhine, field fortifications to guard the army's flanks, fences to protect a naval beachhead. Additionally, legionary soldiers operated artillery—both large, crossbow-like bolt-throwers and even larger, catapult-type stone-throwers. Either would have been used primarily in sieges or against packed groups of men.

Military Law. Roman soldiers were citizens and thus subject to ordinary law except when some specific exception was made. This exception happened primarily in two areas: criminal and family law. A soldier accused of a criminal offense, including theft and violations of military discipline, was subject to the commander's summary judgment rather than a trial. The soldier also lacked the citizen's normal immunity to corporal punishment. Minor offenses could be punished correspondingly—loss of pay, reduced rations, or the like. More serious infractions, however, were met with beatings or death. Violations of military discipline were often punished at the unit level as well as the individual level. Most famously, a unit might be "decimated." That is, one tenth of the soldiers were to be clubbed to death by their fellows. Under the Empire, steps were taken to weaken the legal ties of soldiers to their families. For the first two centuries C.E., soldiers could not form legal marriages, though the rule seems to have been widely ignored. Soldiers with living fathers were given the exceptional ability to hold and bequeath property independent of those fathers.

The Early and Late Armies. The Roman army remained remarkably stable over its history, but there are a few significant differences at the beginning and end of the period. The armies that fought the Punic Wars were based on the "maniple" of two centuries, not the cohort of six. This maniple was a slightly more mobile unit, but too small to operate on its own as well as the cohort did. There was also a little variation in equipment within the legion. There were skirmishers up front, and the back rank had thrusting (not throwing) spears. The army of the late

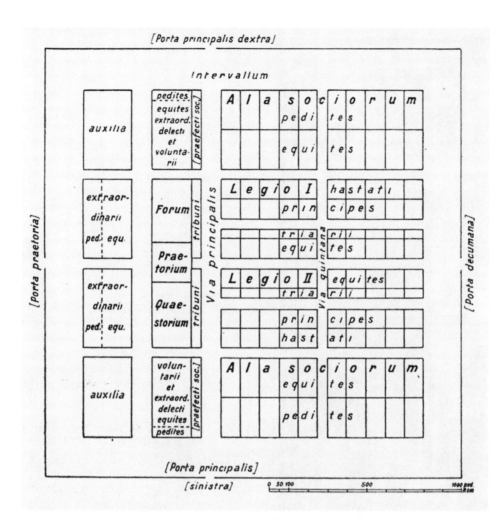

Diagrammatic plan of a typical Roman legion encampment of the second century B.C.E. (from E. Fabricius, "Some Notes on Polybius' Description of Roman Camps," *Journal of Roman Studies,* 1932)

Empire changed rather more. Emperors created more and more legions and auxiliary units, but these were much smaller than before. A legion might have as few as one thousand men. Cavalry became more prominent (though infantry was always more numerous). Finally, from time to time "barbarian" forces were absorbed into the army for political reasons. Unlike Republican auxiliaries, these were large groups and not well integrated into the Roman command structure.

The Army in Battle. The structure of forces was actually more flexible than the century/cohort/legion scheme might suggest. Field commanders made free use of "vexillations" (*vexillum*, or "military standard")—temporary, ad hoc units. These might be single cohorts, segments of one or more legions, combinations of legionary and auxiliary troops, or even groups of picked individuals. The importance of such vexillations even grew under the late Empire. Whether permanent or temporary, units had considerable freedom of action in battle. This freedom was not so much a matter of deliberate choice as poor communications and surveillance. A general essentially had to choose between a position in the rear from which he could see the whole battle (but give orders only inefficiently) or one closer in where he could direct the surrounding troops (but not tell what else was going on).

Infantry and Cavalry. Most Roman battles were contested primarily by masses of infantry that collided and fought. If a clash was not decisive, they would pull back briefly, then try again. Eventually, one side would usually start to flee long before most were actually killed. If a hole opened up in the center or end of an enemy's line, it was much easier to roll up the rest by attacking from two directions at once. Cavalry could be used to charge enemy infantry, but only if they did not hold their ground well. Otherwise, it could attack stragglers or those in flight and protect the flanks of an infantry formation. The military effectiveness of fire and (except in special circumstances) archery was much less than it is portrayed to be in modern television and movies.

The Army and Society. Except perhaps for the church of the later Empire (which had as yet no central authority), the Roman army was the largest organization in the ancient world. Naturally it had effects on the larger society of which it was a part. First, Rome was at war, often on multiple fronts and far from Italy, for almost the whole of the Republic. The militia-style organization of the army and

Ivory relief carved after 395 C.E. showing Flavius Stilicho, commander in chief of the Roman army from circa
393–408 C.E., and the son of a Vandal chieftain (Monza
Cathedral, Italy)

the extent of this effect is debated). The soldiers were paid
in coins and so had cash to spend. Taxes to pay them were
collected in coin, so taxpayers had to have at least some
cash as well. Before the coming of Rome, much of the
eventual empire was dependent on barter and traditional
entitlements to move goods, a much less efficient system
than one that uses money. Under Roman rule even small
farmers had to be part of the money economy. While the
army's purpose was certainly not to lead Rome to a monetary economy, that must have been one of its effects in at
least some degree.

Sources:

Frank E. Adcock, *The Roman Art of War under the Republic* (New York:
   Barnes & Noble, 1960).

Averil Cameron, *The Later Roman Empire, AD 284–430* (Cambridge,
   Mass.: Harvard University Press, 1993).

J. B. Campbell, *The Roman Army 31 B.C.–A.D. 337* (London & New York:
   Routledge, 1994).

Arther Ferrill, *The Fall of the Roman Empire: The Military Explanation*
   (London: Thames & Hudson, 1986).

Adrian K. Goldsworthy, *The Roman Army at War 100 B.C.–A.D. 200*
   (Oxford & New York: Clarendon Press, 1996).

Michael Grant, *The Army of the Caesars* (New York: Scribners, 1974).

L. J. F. Keppie, *The Making of the Roman Army: From Republic to Empire*
   (London: B.T. Batsford, 1984).

EARLY ROME: THE REPUBLIC AND ARISTOCRATIC COMPETITION

Controlling Elite. One consequence of the way the government was organized was that a small elite could exercise
considerable control, especially negative control, as long as it
presented a relatively united front. However, this control was
not always the case. Consider the elections. Romans did not
call political "offices" by the Latin word *officia* ("duties"); they
called them *honores* ("honors"). For the aristocrats engaged in

the extensive needs of this massive warfare combined to put
massive demands on the ordinary citizenry. A large per-
centage of men of military age were in service every year,
often for years at a time. This service created massive social
and economic disruption at home, even for families whose
members survived. Second, the legions contributed to the
"Romanization" of the Empire. When legions fought or
were stationed far from Italy, they brought with them the
Latin language and other aspects of Roman culture. Under
the Empire they often settled in the same areas after retirement. Moreover, the auxiliary forces were a good career
path for those who wanted (or could tolerate) a Romanized
lifestyle. None of these things forced anyone to become
more Roman, but they certainly encouraged it. Third, the
army encouraged a more sophisticated economy (though

POLITICAL INVECTIVE

In fourteen orations known as *Philippics*, Cicero
attacked Mark Antony following the assassination of
Julius Caesar.

How many days you held your sickening orgy in that
house! From ten in the morning there was drinking,
fooling around, and vomiting. . . . Once you and your
crew of squatters took over, the halls echoed with the
voices of drunks, the floors were swimming with wine,
even the walls were soaked, free boys were mixed up
with rented ones, matrons with hookers. . . . You took
on a man's toga and turned it into a whore's. At first,
you were a common prostitute and your price was fixed
(and not small either). But soon Curio turned up, drew
you away from your meretricious trade and, as if he had
given you a matron's robe, established you in lasting and
stable matrimony.

Source: Cicero, *Philippics,* translated by D. R. Shackleton Bailey (Chapel
   Hill: University of North Carolina Press, 1986).

Section of a painting titled *The Triumph of Caesar: The Triumphal Car,* by Andrea Mantegna, circa 1475. It illustrates Caesar's victory procession following his defeat of the Gauls in the first century B.C.E. (Royal Collection, Hampton Court Palace).

politics, much of it was about the search for honors and, in particular, competition with their peers. This situation could lead to considerable disunity. How were political battles conducted? Most of the same devices aristocrats used to separate themselves from the masses could also be used against political foes. Superiority could be claimed by a bigger gift to the people or a better speech. If positive approaches such as this did not work, Roman politicians were quick to "go negative" and attack each other personally in a type of speech known as "invective." If the opportunity presented itself, one could sometimes have one of his opponents prosecuted in the public courts. Doubtless many Roman politicians also held genuine policy positions, but they are often difficult to separate out of the struggles for individual supremacy. Moreover, there were at least a couple of factors that helped keep the elite together. First, their own material interests were similar. All were wealthy landowners. They also shared an interest in the notion of inherited right to rule. Most families relied on this notion directly, and the few upstarts could use it to pull the ladder up after them once they had entered the Senate. Second, the Senate itself was a moderating influence. Even a wildly successful politician was likely to hold office for less than ten years out of a career of decades. For most of his career he would be a sena-

tor giving advice, not a magistrate receiving it. Thus, it was in his long-term best interest to advance the institutional authority of the Senate.

Sources:
Mary Beard and Michael Crawford, *Rome in the Late Republic* (Ithaca, N.Y.: Cornell University Press, 1985).

Fergus Millar, *The Crowd in the Late Roman Republic* (Ann Arbor: University of Michigan Press, 1998).

Lily R. Taylor, *Party Politics in the Age of Caesar* (Berkeley: University of California Press, 1949).

EARLY ROME: THE REPUBLIC AND DEMOCRACY AT ROME

Differing Evaluations. In some respects, the Roman government was highly democratic. Magistrates were popularly elected, and even individual laws were all voted on only by the people. Yet, at least one contemporary observer saw it a little differently. The Greek historian Polybius, who lived in Rome for many years in the mid-second century B.C.E., described it as a mixture of democratic, aristocratic, and monarchical elements. Some modern scholars, noting that the magistracies were largely held by the same powerful families for generations, have gone even farther. They see Rome as run by a thinly disguised oligarchy—rule by the few. Some of the dif-

W hile the ordinary citizen did not have a chance to speak in the official processes of government, a certain amount of gossip circulated and some of this gossip eventually had its effect even on the rich and powerful.

Publius Scipio Nasica, the light of political power, who as consul had declared war on Jugurtha, who with his own sacred hands received the Idaean Mother from her home in Phrygia when she came to our home, who crushed many dangerous seditions by the force of this authority, in whose leadership the senate had gloried for many years, was seeking the aedileship in his younger days, and took firm hold of a farmer's roughened hand in the way candidates do. As a sort of joke he asked him whether he tended to walk on his hands. Once bystanders heard this remark, it flowed out to the rest of the people and caused Scipio's defeat.

Source: Fergus Millar, *The Crowd in the Late Roman Republic* (Ann Arbor: University of Michigan Press, 1998).

ference of opinion seems to come from how people feel about their own political systems, but there are legitimate questions as well. If modern elections have proved nothing else, it is clear that elections alone do not make for democracy. One must also consider what choices even appear on the ballot and what external pressures are put on voters. Asking these questions about ancient Rome reveals a variety of antidemocratic forces. There is no consensus at present as to the balance between these forces and the opportunities for popular participation. It is perhaps best, then, merely to note the individual forces and assess their impact in individual cases rather than rendering a once-and-for-all verdict on democracy at Rome. (It must also be recalled that there was a more general and profound aspect to the Roman political process: its total exclusion of women and slaves.)

Who Speaks? One crucial issue is what topics are ever allowed to come up for a vote. Recall that the average citizen could not propose a measure, only a magistrate could, and magistrates were all members of the upper classes. Support of a magistrate was even required to participate in the public debates of the *contiones*. Thus, popular proposals could arise only with some support among the elite. Once a bill was proposed, the voting itself was biased. The wealthy could position themselves in various tribes and could afford to come to Rome, the only site for voting. Thus, they had disproportionate influence. When consuls and praetors were elected, the grouping of the centuriate assembly exaggerated this effect further.

Obstruction. Many officials had the power to slow or stop legislation single-handedly. Consuls could summon the people away from other meetings. Any of the tribunes could veto a magistrate's proposal. Omens could be found (some would say manufactured) that would force the suspension of public business. In addition, the Senate was normally given a chance to review legislation before it was formally proposed. Even if it had been evenly distributed,

such individual grants of authority would strengthen the hand of minority groups such as the rich. As it was, these powers were entirely in the hands of the officeholding elite.

Shaping the Vote. When a proposal (or candidate) came before the people, did they vote according to what one would consider their best interests, or were other factors in play? The elite used two sets of strategies to win over voters. One came down to buying votes. Sometimes, particularly in elections, this vote buying was done by simple bribery. This practice was illegal but hard to prove. Also, the candidates kept ahead of the law by providing benefits, such as meals, other than cash. Sometimes aristocrats made gifts to the entire people rather than to individuals—say, public games or a temple or a semipublic park. This practice is called "euergetism." Such gifts were not necessarily tied to a particular vote, but aided the giver's long-term reputation. Each aristocrat also served as a "patron" to a number of long-term supporters called "clients." Clients received advice, legal support, and occasional material goods in return for attending to the great man, thus making his importance publicly visible. The clients of any given candidate were not numerous enough to be an electoral force, but they could form the basis of a much larger network of support on particular occasions.

Other Strategies. The other set of strategies included ways of making accidents of birth and inheritance seem like personal virtues. For instance, noble families displayed ancestor portraits (*imagines*) in their homes and at their public funerals. These portraits reminded the people of how they had in the past elected many of this current generation's ancestors to

Miniature model of an Etruscan *fasces* dating from 600 B.C.E. This ax bundled with rods was the symbol of authority of the Roman kings and later the consuls and praetors (Soprintendenza alle Antichità dell'Etruria Meridionale, Rome).

office. If the choice of the old, tried and true families had worked in the past, why not continue it? *Euergetism* (gift giving) worked similarly. The continued success of the family promised continued material rewards for Rome. The elite also tried to maintain advantages in public speaking, the only mass medium in the Roman world. An education in rhetoric (like the gift of a public building) was possible only for the wealthy. In fact, in 161 and 92 B.C.E. the government made legal attempts to limit the teaching of rhetoric.

Sources:

Mary Beard and Michael Crawford, *Rome in the Late Republic* (Ithaca, N.Y.: Cornell University Press, 1985).

Fergus Millar, *The Crowd in the Late Roman Republic* (Ann Arbor: University of Michigan Press, 1998).

Lily R. Taylor, *Party Politics in the Age of Caesar* (Berkeley: University of California Press, 1949).

EARLY ROME: THE REPUBLIC AND GOVERNMENT STRUCTURE

Three Branches. Much like the modern U.S. government, most of the government of ancient Rome can be divided into three branches: legislative, executive, and judicial. There are, however, some differences in function, and the Roman government had at least one important component (the Senate) which does not fit this scheme well.

Legislative Branch. The legislative bodies were two popular assemblies with largely overlapping authority. In addition to lawmaking, these assemblies also elected the magistrates and, in a few instances, sat as courts of law. All adult male Roman citizens were eligible to vote in these assemblies, but they had to be present in person (at Rome) to do so. Both assemblies used group voting. That is, the electorate was divided into a number of groups, and the majority in each of these subunits determined its one vote. Thus the "tribal" assembly, which was divided into thirty-five tribes, produced votes like 19-to-16 or 21-to-14 even if tens of thousands of people voted. Voters are not necessarily equal in group-voting systems; if one is in a smaller group, his individual vote counts for more. Also the influence of a large minority of the population could be reduced if they were confined to a few groups (and so they could only affect those groups). The tribal assembly was arranged to be biased automatically in favor of rural voters and in practice also the wealthy. It was used to pass most laws and elect the lower magistrates. The other assembly

(called the "centuriate") was openly tilted in favor of older voters (forty-six and up) and the wealthy; former slaves were discriminated against. Laws were occasionally passed in the centuriate assembly, but its normal function was to elect men to the highest magistracies. These voting assemblies were both called *comitia*, and must be distinguished from assemblies for debate called *contiones* (singular *contio*). Either kind of meeting could be called only by an elected magistrate. In *comitia*, the magistrate laid a question before the people, such as whether they approved of a proposed law (which was read aloud) or whom they wished to elect; then there was a vote. At a *contio* the magistrate and anyone else he invited addressed the people on an issue of public interest, often a bill which would shortly be voted on in *comitia*. Note that the ordinary citizen had no automatic right to speak at any point in this process, nor to offer amendments. In fact, amendments could only be made by back-room negotiation before the assembly met.

Executive Branch. The executive branch consisted primarily of a number of magistrates elected by the people. They administered justice, commanded armies, supervised public works, checked major disturbances of public order, conducted state sacrifices, and the like. There were five ranked major magistracies, all of whom shared several characteristics. The term of office for each was one year, and reelection was rare. All offices were collegial; that is, several men held each office at once. (The number in any given office varied over time, usually increasing.) Responsibilities of each office were generally divided into separate spheres (*provinciae*). So, for instance, one praetor might be in charge of the *ambitus* court and another in charge of the *repetundae* court; another, the

While the main functions of the magistrates were quite routine and traditional, some chance incidents illustrate that their potential authority (at least that of the consuls and praetors) was much expansive. In the early 80s B.C.E. the praetor Gratidianus responded to problems in the currency with a series of measures not supported by any law. He changed their value (by changing either the composition or the official exchange rate) and established a board to test coins already in circulation and punish, apparently, forgers. In 58 B.C.E. Cicero was exiled with the support of the consuls of that year. Many of his senatorial and equestrian allies staged demonstrations of sympathy by dressing in mourning clothes. One of the consuls forbade them to dress this way and banished at least one knight from the city altogether. When Cicero returned the following year, he complained that these measures were immoral and abusive, but even he did not suggest that they were illegal.

Source: Thomas N. Mitchell, *Cicero the Senior Statesman* (New Haven: Yale University Press, 1991).

urban praetor, controlled the private law courts. In emergencies, though, colleagues could step in for each other. Qualifications for office varied over time but included minimum age and wealth, military service, and (for higher offices) service in the lower ones. The two consuls were the chief magistrates. In addition to supervising the other officials, they commanded armies and proposed legislation. The two main functions of the praetors, the next highest magistrates, were the administration of justice and of Roman provinces. Beneath the praetors were quaestors. They were often in charge of treasury and other bureaucratic functions; many were specifically assigned to assist praetors and consuls. Between the praetorship and aedileship were two magistracies, of which aspiring politicians usually held at most one. Four "aediles" were in charge of the city's markets and much of its public infrastructure. The ten "tribunes" were originally not magistrates, but the elected representatives of the "plebs"—the lower and larger of the two castes in the early city. Though soon absorbed into the regular government, the tribunes always retained an activist, populist image. They could veto laws, senatorial decrees, and acts of magistrates and intercede to protect individual citizens from the government. They also proposed most Roman legislation.

Other Elected Officials. These "major" magistrates made up the core of the government, but there were also two other classes of elected officials. On the one hand, a number of "minor" magistrates were elected each year from the ranks of young aristocrats not yet eligible for the major offices. These included control of the mint, supervision of punishments, care of the roads, and some military staff positions. On the other hand, there were also extraordinary offices that were not occupied at all times. For eighteen months every five years or so there were two censors, elected by the centuriate assembly. They conducted a cen-

sus—a count and property evaluation—of the entire populace. They were responsible for assigning persons to (or rejecting them from) the higher ranks of society such as the Senate. The censors were also responsible for awarding contracts for services such as constructing public works and collecting taxes. In times of crisis up until the late third century B.C.E. a dictator was chosen. He served for up to six months with absolute authority and was assisted by a "master of the cavalry." The office was twice revived in the first century B.C.E., by Lucius Cornelius Sulla and by Julius Caesar, both times to institute a "dictatorship" in the modern sense. In addition to these elected positions, there were also so-called promagistrates. When a consul or praetor was carrying out an important task, usually a war, outside of Rome that outlasted his term of office, he was often authorized to continue until he was done. Such an official was then said to be a proconsul or propraetor, that is, "in the place of" the regular magistrate. In the later years of the Republic, when Rome was involved in complicated foreign adventures in many places, there was demand for many field commanders. Even consuls and praetors who had served their terms at Rome came systematically to be sent out as promagistrates.

Judicial Branch. The judicial branch of government consisted of the courts. Except for the praetor's initial hearing, Republican trials were conducted by private citizens, not public officials.

The Senate. One major component of the government—the Senate—has no close parallel in modern democracies, and even professional scholars disagree considerably over just what its role was at Rome. Its members were not directly elected, though its numbers were essentially all former magistrates. (Over time the censors were given less and less flexibility in including former magistrates.) Once admitted, senators served for life unless convicted of a crime or expelled by the censors for moral turpitude. Unlike the assemblies, the Senate could not pass laws. Also unlike them, its decrees (called *senatus consulta,* singular *consultum*) normally took the form of instructions to one or more magistrates to take certain actions. While not binding, these were often followed. In fact, magistrates often convened the Senate preemptively to ask direction before proposing legislation or taking other action. In certain areas it was particularly common to take the Senate's judgment as a necessary and sufficient decision of policy: declarations of war, treaties, expenditure of public funds, honors for triumphant generals, and allocation of provinces. In the last case (and a few others) a law was passed by the assembly that specifically granted authority to the Senate to make such decisions.

Custom vs. Constitutionality. Almost all of the structure was based on customary practice rather than any written law. The inherent fuzziness of this situation could lead to crises. For instance, a tribune named Gaius Gracchus tried to have a colleague unelected by the assembly for opposing some popular measures. This unelecting had never been done before, but there was no specific rule

Not all senators were equal. There was an order of precedence within the Senate based on the highest office to which individual senators had been elected (and, within those groups, on the judgment of the presiding consul). In addition to the official gradations, there was a group of lesser senators colloquially called *pedarii*, "footmen." Even the Romans debated exactly what this meant. Some thought it alluded to a right, purportedly won by men who had held the higher offices, to come to the Senate in a chariot. The most popular theory today is that the *pedarii* were far enough down the line of seniority that they voted but were rarely called on to give their opinions. Voting was conducted by gathering on different sides of the Senate house. Thus *pedarii* only spoke with their feet.

Source: John C. Rolfe, trans., *The Attic Nights of Aulus Gellius* (Cambridge, Mass.: Harvard University Press / London: Heinemann, 1946–1952).

against it either. If this issue were valid, there was no problem, but if it were not, then much of Gracchus's later activity was arguably also illegal. Without a consensus, which was never formed on this issue, the legitimacy of the government was in question and could not be resolved by any well-defined process. Moreover, even for what had been written down, there was not a special level of constitutional law. In principle, the assemblies could have voted the entire structure out of power with a single law. (Arguably, they were compelled to do just this at the end of the Republic.) In practice, however, structural changes tended to be gradual when armed force was not brought to bear.

Sources:
Frank F. Abbot, *A History and Description of Roman Political Institutions* (New York: Biblo & Tannen, 1963).

Herbert F. Jolowicz and Barry Nicholas, *Historical Introduction to Roman Law* (Cambridge: Cambridge University Press, 1972).

Andrew W. Lintott, *The Constitution of the Roman Republic* (Oxford: Clarendon Press / New York: Oxford University Press, 1999).

EARLY ROME: THE REPUBLIC AND LIMITED GOVERNMENT

The Powers That Be. It is hard for a citizen of any modern nation to grasp how little government Republican Rome had. The assemblies were quite clumsy and passed laws only occasionally. Magistrates had much more freedom of action but were remarkably few in number. Including promagistrates, the total in the late Republic was in the low hundreds. And recall that this government was not only of a city of hundreds of thousands of people but also of an empire whose population was in the tens of millions. These magistrates were, of course, supported by a bureaucratic staff of so-called *apparitores*. But these officials had little or no independent authority and were still few in number. Lack of information also made it harder to exercise systematic authority. The government had

only a rough idea of where its citizens were and what they were doing; records of the government's own actions were sometimes hard to find or nonexistent. One device to make up for this weakness was the reliance on local governments. Another was the contracting out of government functions such as tax collection. In sum, however, the government did little policing, little building except for the largest projects, little consumer protection, no education, and no direction of the economy. The average Roman was less burdened and far less protected by the state than persons today.

Sources:
Frank F. Abbot, *A History and Description of Roman Political Institutions* (New York: Biblo & Tannen, 1963).

Andrew W. Lintott, *The Constitution of the Roman Republic* (Oxford: Clarendon Press / New York: Oxford University Press, 1999).

EARLY ROME: THE REPUBLIC AND MUNICIPALITIES

Administration. Under the Republic no clear distinction was ever made between local and national levels of government. Yet there were many other governments within the empire. Most of that empire was governed not by officials sent out from the capital city but by local city magistrates and councils. Even though a Roman governor had the ultimate authority in his province, most administration was done by the municipalities. Technically, cities could have many different statuses. None were truly independent of Rome, but few were really run by it. As long as taxes were paid and a minimum level of public order and loyalty was maintained, the central government was usually satisfied. The local communities raised their own funds through taxation and gifts, took care of most local jurisdiction, saw to public buildings and resources (such as water), and celebrated their own religious festivals.

Miniatures of the Great City. Rome was most comfortable dealing with governments like its own in miniature—elected magistrates and a permanent council, all drawn from the elite. So, for instance, many cities of Italy had two *duoviri* (local equivalents of the consuls), aediles, and a board of "decurions" (essentially the local Senate). As at Rome there was competition for these *honores*. It often involved substantial private expenditure (both voluntary and compulsory) on public projects. When, however, a civic constitution predated Roman rule (especially common in the eastern empire), it was normally allowed to persist. Over time, there was some drift toward Roman forms, as in the civil law, but it was not strictly required by the central authorities.

Sources:
Michael Grant, *History of Rome* (London: Weidenfeld & Nicolson, 1978).

Andrew W. Lintott, *Imperium Romanum: Politics and Administration* (London & New York: Routledge, 1993).

EARLY ROME: THE REPUBLIC AND VIOLENCE IN POLITICS

Strong-arm Tactics. Crime was probably common on the streets of Rome. Men were killed as spectacle in the arena. The Republic collapsed in a famous series of civil wars. It is easy to imagine, then, that Roman politics was always conducted by force, but for most of the Republic this idea was surprisingly false. There are perhaps traces of uprisings and riots in the early years after the fall of the kings, but these are hard to pin down. For periods about which more is known—the third and most of the second century B.C.E.—there is nearly no political violence. The problems started around the time when two brothers, Tiberius and Gaius Gracchus, became tribunes in 133 and 123 B.C.E., respectively. Both wanted to redistribute the use of some publicly owned land from the wealthy to the poor. There was resistance from some but not all of the other nobles. Both brothers pressed proposals through the assemblies by means that were probably legal but contrary to some interpretations of political custom. Both were then lynched by followers of conservative nobles. In both cases one should note the haphazard forces that were gathered and their improvised weaponry (e.g., broken benches). The conservative ringleaders were tried; one was exiled, the other acquitted. Even when violence had been introduced, it was hardly normalized. After several further decades marred by only a few killings (and, some say, abuse of the courts against political enemies) the stakes were raised dramatically. Lucius Cornelius Sulla, an already famous general, used his army to seize power in 88 B.C.E. and reconfirm it in 82. He had himself named dictator but retired after a few years, and the government was not permanently altered. Such a direct seizure of power did not occur again until Julius Caesar took Rome in 49 B.C.E., but the lesson was not forgotten in the interim. At several points between 71 and 50, Gnaeus Pompeius (Pompey "the Great") kept forces near the city as an implicit threat. On a lower level, but more directly active, were the gangs of Titus Annius Milo and Publius Clodius Pulcher. Both used groups of thugs throughout the 50s to intimidate political opponents in the assemblies and the courts. This came to a head in 52 when Clodius was killed in a clash with Milo's men. Pompey was then authorized to come in with his soldiers and restore order—and not incidentally to take sole control over the government.

Sources:
Michael Grant, *History of Rome* (London: Weidenfeld & Nicolson, 1978).

Andrew W. Lintott, *Violence in Republican Rome* (Oxford: Clarendon Press, 1968).

Wilfried Nippel, *Public Order in Ancient Rome* (Cambridge & New York: Cambridge University Press, 1995).

THE EMPIRE: THE AUGUSTAN SETTLEMENT

Formal Conservatism. When the first emperor, Augustus (then called Octavian), came to power in 31 B.C.E., it was mainly on the strength of superior military force. During the next fifteen years or so, however, steps were taken to put his reign on a legal or at least legalistic footing. On the one hand, nearly the entire apparatus of the Republican government was preserved. There were still courts and a Senate and consuls and praetors and the rest. Many provinces continued to be governed by proconsuls, and municipal governments continued to flourish. Only the assemblies were really eliminated, and even those continued to meet sporadically and symbolically for a time. There were, of course, certain changes to the traditional institutions. The emperor "recommended" candidates for half of the offices, and these men took office unopposed. The effective number of annual consulships actually increased. Under the Republic a "suffect" consul could be chosen if there were a vacancy in mid-year. Under the Empire it became customary for several pairs of consuls to

A coin minted in 137 B.C.E. with a depiction of a Roman citizen dropping a stone tablet into a voting urn (Bibliothèque Nationale, Paris)

ELECTIONS UNDER THE EMPIRE

Not only were elections themselves still sometimes hotly contested under the Empire, but also supporters of the various candidates were eager to use these contests to prove their own political clout. Pliny writes this letter to ask support for one of his protégés:

My friend Sextus Erucius' campaign has me in a state of worry and anxiety. I am pained, and any worry I don't feel on my own behalf, I suffer for my other self. My sense of shame, my reputation, and my worth are being put to the test. . . . I grab my friends, I beg, I canvass, I wander people's homes and hang-outs, and I try to cash in all my authority and favors by my prayers. And I beg you think it a favor to relieve me of some of my burden. I'll pay you back whether or not you demand it. . . . Only show that you are willing, and there'll be plenty of people who will make your wish their command.

Source: Betty Radice, *The Letters of the Younger Pliny* (Harmondsworth, U.K.: Penguin, 1963).

Statue of Augustus dressed in a religious ceremonial robe, from Via Labicana after 27 B.C.E. (Museo dell Terme, Rome)

Concentration of Power. On the other hand, many other institutions were created or radically transformed. The emperor assumed the powers of several different magistracies without technically holding the offices themselves. He had tribunician power and proconsular authority (*imperium*) that was officially described as "bigger" than anyone else's. Among other things this power gave him ultimate command of Rome's armies. From time to time the emperor also took up the censor's powers. In addition to the elected magistracies, several appointed posts were created, directly responsible to the emperor. So, for instance, most important provinces came under the control of *legati* (deputies) of the emperor. *Legati* were not a new creation, but previously they had stayed in the same province as the officials they served. The process of *cognitio* also fell under the purview of imperial appointees and so tended to bring the administration of justice into the emperor's hands. The offense of *maiestas* was reshaped to cover treason against the emperor personally, not the state in general. On paper, the powers of the Senate were increased. It could elect and try its own members. Its decrees, rather than acts of the assemblies, became a central source of statute law. Of course, much of this power could be given to the Senate because its activities could be monitored closely.

Terminology and Ideology. The first Roman "emperors" were not usually called by that word (from the Latin *imperator*, successful general), but were described instead as *princeps*. This term had long been used for the "leading man" of the Senate. Augustus's general strategy, followed in varying degrees by his successors, was to assume as much power as he needed without advertising the fact. Even if he was really more than first among equals, he did not claim to be above normal aristocratic standards of behavior and judgment (in contrast to European absolutist monarchs, Egyptian pharaohs, and Chinese and Japanese emperors of various periods, who claimed to be the representative or even embodiment of some god on earth.) A major factor in Julius Caesar's assassination seems to have been his open disregard for his fellow aristocrats. Augustus learned from this example. While his superiority was unquestioned, other nobles were allowed some share of position and honor as well.

Sources:
Karl Galinsky, *Augustan Culture: An Interpretive Introduction* (Princeton, N.J.: Princeton University Press, 1996).

K. A. Raaflaub and M. Toher, eds., *Between Republic and Empire: Interpretations of Augustus and His Principate* (Berkeley & Los Angeles: University of California Press, 1990).

Ronald Syme, *The Roman Revolution* (Oxford: Oxford University Press, 1939).

Colin M. Wells, *The Roman Empire* (Stanford, Cal.: Stanford University Press, 1984).

THE EMPIRE: CONTINUITY AND COMPETITION

New Rules. The Republican elite spent most of its energy in internal competition, both within and outside the political arena. To a considerable extent this situation

resign and be replaced in the course of a year. The emperor might also take multiple offices (including state priesthoods) for himself simultaneously.

remained true for the imperial elite, but the presence of a monarch changed the rules by which the game was played. Certain areas of competition remained more or less open. Elections continued to be held and contested hotly, even if the candidates were now canvassing a narrow elite instead of the whole populace. Moreover, there were now competitions for imperial favor, which could secure both appointed and formally elected office. A new, if unofficial, wrinkle also appeared in the early empire. The emperors apparently tried to distinguish a "prestige set" and a "power set" among the elite. The former were already of noble birth and tended to be given honorific posts. The latter, only recently of social and economic prominence, were given the powerful posts, especially military commands. Separating power and prestige allowed ongoing competition without allowing potential rivals to the emperor from challenging him on both grounds at once. Many kinds of informal competition continued as well. Conspicuous consumption seems actually to have increased as the elite grew wealthier under the Empire. Patronage also continued to be at least equally important, as many resources trickled down from the greatest patron of all—the emperor.

Restrictions. In other areas, however, the emperor ended competition by claiming a personal monopoly. He was always the *pontifex maximus,* or chief priest. Only he (or members of his immediate family) was awarded public ceremonies of triumph, and only they could be given the title *imperator.* In fact, this title eventually became part of the emperors' names. Eventually the emperors also took over most *euergetism* (gift giving) at Rome. Public buildings were all in their or their families' names, and they gave most public games. Sometimes these imperial monopolies extended beyond the realm normally thought of as political. Some emperors tried to ban astrologers (except their own) from the city. The emperor Nero took first place in 1,808 Olympic events and other international competitions, including ones he never actually entered. The emperor's official patronage also gave him unmatched opportunities. He appointed most major government officials, had the last word in all legal cases, and controlled much of the state's wealth as his private possession.

Election slogans on the wall of a building in Pompeii, circa 79 C.E.

New Arenas. These imperial inroads into traditional aristocratic competition pushed the elite to open up new areas of competition. If oratory was no longer so central to active politics, then declamation—giving speeches on imaginary topics—became an opportunity for displaying skill in public speaking. Composition and public recitation of many kinds of literature became more respectable for and more important to the elite. And if they could no longer build or give other public gifts at Rome, they were allowed (and even encouraged) to do so in the rest of Italy and in the provinces.

Sources:
Keith Hopkins, *Death and Renewal* (Cambridge & New York: Cambridge University Press, 1983).

Fergus Millar and Erich Segal, eds., *Caesar Augustus: Seven Aspects* (Oxford & New York: Clarendon Press, 1984).

K. A. Raaflaub and M. Toher, eds., *Between Republic and Empire: Interpretations of Augustus and His Principate* (Berkeley & Los Angeles: University of California Press, 1990).

THE EMPIRE: GOVERNMENT BY PETITION

Special Requests. The Republican government was not a particularly proactive one. Its weak systems of information-gathering and administration and short terms of office made planning and anticipation difficult. Still, individuals might sometimes try to adopt farseeing policies to increase their own domestic patronage or military glory. The incentives for such individual innovations dropped under the Empire, without much growth in the state apparatus. The emperor could make new laws by various devices including direct decree. Yet, most imperial decrees came in the form of decisions on appeals or other such petitions. It has been argued that this situation illustrates the basic operation of the imperial government in general: the emperor (and his staff) received requests, from both subordinates and private citizens, and responded to them. Sometimes the decisions were broader than absolutely necessary to settle the issue presented, but most imperial action was in reaction to a specific outside request. The most famous instance of public policy being set this way is probably Pliny's correspondence with the emperor Trajan in the early second century C.E. on the treatment of Christians in Pliny's province in Asia Minor (*Letters* 10.96–7). Trajan directed him to take a "moderate" course on the persecution of Christians, but the important point is that Pliny had to ask. The policy did not begin in Rome, but on the periphery.

Sources:
Michael Grant, *The Roman Emperors: A Biographical Guide to the Rulers of Imperial Rome, 31 B.C.–A.D. 476* (New York: Scribners, 1985).

Fergus Millar, *The Emperor in the Roman World (31 B.C.–A.D. 337)* (Ithaca, N.Y.: Cornell University Press, 1977).

THE EMPIRE: GROWTH OF THE BUREAUCRACY

Administrative Positions. The Republican government was minimal by modern standards and remained so under the Empire, but some growth did occur. On the one hand, the emperors created or regularized several hundred posts for knights and senators. These were short-term, salaried positions in both the military and civilian sectors. Examples include the procurators of small provinces, prefects of the

city and the imperial bodyguard, *iuridici* to dispense justice, and the officials in charge of the imperial roads. There was a hierarchy to these jobs insofar as these were recognized career paths, but the organization remained flat. That is, almost everyone still reported to the emperor. On the other hand, there were long-term staff of lower (slave or former slave) status. These included secretaries in charge of the emperor's accounts, correspondence (Greek and Latin separately), petitions, and other departments. At the heart of this group was the emperor's own household. There was often tension between the top imperial freedmen and slaves and socially superior aristocrats who envied their power. Over time, most of the top positions shifted from freedmen to equestrians.

Sources:
Peter Garnsey and Richard Saller, *The Roman Empire: Economy, Society, and Culture* (Berkeley: University of California Press, 1987).

Fergus Millar, *The Emperor in the Roman World (31 B.C.–A.D. 337)* (Ithaca, N.Y.: Cornell University Press, 1977).

THE EMPIRE: SUCCESSION AND THE ARMY

Flaw. One weakness of the "principate"—Augustus's disguised monarchy—was that it did not deal well with the problem of succession. Officially, there was no emperor, just a man who happened to hold an extraordinary set of powers and offices. As a result, there could be no official rules for succession (contrast, for example, the elaborate scheme that can tell who is twelfth in line for the British throne today). Many emperors were able to choose a successor, usually a son, and have him granted a similar package of powers in advance. But what if there were no designated successor? Several emperors and would-be emperors were acclaimed by the Praetorian Guard (the imperial bodyguards) or various armies in the field. The candidates could be members of the existing imperial family or simply men who happened to be in charge of a large military force. When there were several competing factions, as in 68–69 and 193–195 C.E., fierce civil wars ensued. Occasionally, aspirants to the throne might not even wait for the death of the old emperor if they thought they had enough support to seize power. Whatever the case, it became crucial to political survival to pay the troops

---

DIDIUS JULIANUS

The lowest point of the succession problems was actually not during the long troubled years, but in 193 C.E. After the emperor Commodus was assassinated (by a professional wrestler), there was no obvious successor. The Praetorian Guard auctioned the throne off to a senator named Didius Julianus. Unfortunately for Julianus, he had no military support and was killed a few months later in the face of the advance of Septimius Severus, a real general.

Source: Chris Scarre, *Chronicle of the Roman Emperors* (London: Thames & Hudson, 1995).

A second century C.E. bas-relief of the Praetorian Guard, the household troops of the emperors (Louvre, Paris)

well and especially to give large bonuses at times of transition. The system, such as it was, broke down almost entirely during the middle half of the third century C.E. There was nearly constant struggle between potential emperors, both in the field and by assassination. Even in peaceful times the fluidity of the rules led to considerable intrigue (and rumors of even more). So, for instance, the emperor Claudius (possibly) and his son Britannicus (certainly) were murdered to ensure the succession of Claudius's stepson Nero. One of the most stable periods of the Empire covered the first three-quarters of the second century C.E. This period required several fortunate trends. None of the emperors died young, whether naturally or otherwise, which required both luck and popularity. Each emperor but the last had no biological son and thus found and adopted a skilled man as son and heir.

Sources:
Chris Scarre, *Chronicle of the Roman Emperors: The Reign–by–Reign Record of the Rulers of Imperial Rome* (London: Thames & Hudson, 1995).

Colin M. Wells, *The Roman Empire* (Stanford, Cal.: Stanford University Press, 1984).

JUDICIAL CORRUPTION

Bad Reputation. Many have claimed that the Roman courts were staggeringly corrupt. The Roman advocate and politician Marcus Tullius Cicero noted three sources for this corruption: personal favoritism, the influence of the powerful, and bribery (*Defense of Caecina* 73). It is certain that such problems existed, but one must keep in mind two other points. First, complaints about particular cases always come from the losing side; no one ever sees favoritism at work when he wins. Second, the idea of "corruption" is more complicated than it first appears. Romans openly depended more on personal authority and less on objective evidence than most moderns do in arriving at the truth. What, then, is the line between legitimate authority and corrupt influence? For Romans, it was probably a matter of which side one supported in a case. From a modern point of view, however, the system was certainly biased in favor of the wealthy and powerful.

Sources:
Peter Garnsey, *Social Status and Legal Privilege in the Roman Empire* (Oxford: Clarendon Press, 1970).

John M. Kelly, *Roman Litigation* (Oxford: Clarendon Press, 1966).

THE LATE EMPIRE: GOVERNMENT STRUCTURE

Defining Moment. There is no single, sharp dividing line between periods of the empire as there was between Republic and Empire. Nonetheless, one may identify certain trends particularly characteristic of the later Empire. This period may be said to start in the third century C.E. or even after the period of near-collapse that took up much of that century. It runs until 476, when Rome was sacked and the last emperor there, Romulus Augustulus, was deposed.

Growth of Despotism. The position of the emperor changed (though early signs of this change can be traced back almost to the beginning of the Empire). He became more distinct from his subjects, even those of high rank. *Dominus* (lord) became a conventional title—this term was the word for a slave's master or, later, the Christian God. Emperors also came to associate themselves with their patron divinities and take on divine attributes themselves. For instance, things connected to the emperor (e.g., his bedchamber) came to be called "sacred." Some emperors took on names derived from those of gods. In practice this trend was accelerated by the Christianization of the empire in the fourth century C.E. If the emperor was put on the throne by the creator of the universe, then he was not to be questioned or contradicted by mere mortals. Beginning around 300 C.E. those meeting the emperor were to prostrate themselves. This gesture had previously been associated with the open despotism of near-eastern kingdoms such as Persia. Minor deviations from imperial orders became treasonous and subject (at least in theory) to increasingly violent penalties. There was less deference to the Senate as a legislative and judicial body, however tightly controlled, and even in its advisory capacity. Ranks and honors remained important within the general population but were no longer commensurable with the ruler's position.

The Imperial Court. Along with this increasing focus on the person of the emperor came the creation of an imperial court. Already under the Republic, magistrates and judges had sought the advice of a *consilium*, an informal body of advisors, in making decisions. The early emperors naturally adopted the practice. They could also command

Septimia Zenobia (in Syriac called Bathzabbai) was the wife of Septimius Odaenatus, a Roman ally/vassal king of Palmyra (in Syria) and later of "the Orient." From his death in 267 C.E. she effectively ruled the kingdom. In 270 she began to encroach on Roman territory in Egypt. Eventually, she titled herself Augusta, putting herself on a level with the Roman emperors. The emperor Aurelian retook the captured Roman territory and seized her and her capital in 272. She may at one point have been a student of the Greek philosopher Longinus.

Source: Paul de Rohden and Hermann Dessau, *Prosopographia Imperii Romani* 3.217–218 (Berlin: George Reimer, 1898).

the attention of poets, actors, scholars, and other diverting hangers-on. What is striking about the later Empire is the vastly increased size and regularization of the court. There were the emperor's chamberlain, secretary, chief-of-staff, and their respective staffs. Many of the financial and military officers of the government and the emperor's multi-purpose couriers also attended him. Favorites might simply be appointed "companions" of the emperor. All of these positions were, technically, military ones and so carried official ranks and salaries, support, and tax-exemption. What most distinguishes this group as a "court" is their mobility. They were attached to the emperor personally, not to the capital of Rome. When the emperor traveled, even the mint and much of the treasury went with him.

Division of the Empire. Such travel became more important and more common as the empire and its government grew increasingly subdivided. A crucial figure here was the emperor Diocletian (ruled 284–305 C.E.). First, he set up the "tetrarchy," in which there would be two senior emperors (*Augusti*) in the East and West, assisted by two junior emperors (*Caesares*). The full system did not survive his own time in office, but some features were long-lived: de facto division of east and west, multiple emperors co-ruling cooperatively. Diocletian also divided the empire into much smaller provinces. Then he created a middle level of administration by grouping these provinces into twelve "dioceses." Finally, he made a nearly-complete break between the civil and military sectors of the government. (These changes, as well as the growth of the court, eventually produced a government perhaps fifty times as large as it had been in 100 C.E., though still small by modern standards.) The special status of Italy and even Rome itself continued to fade. Emperors and the court went where the action was (or where it was likely to be). This gave rise to a whole set of new imperial residences, sometimes called "capitals." There were also divisions of the empire that had nothing to do with the emperor's policies. There was a breakaway state in Gaul from 258 to 274 C.E. and another centered on Palmyra in Syria in the 270s. This situation was partly a symptom of the third century crisis (nothing

directly comparable happened after Diocletian), but in the end the emperors may merely have defeated the separatists by joining them.

Military and Financial Crises. Since the end of the Second Punic War (202 B.C.E.) Rome had expanded for several centuries and Roman wars were almost entirely fought on foreign soil. The expansion, however, stopped in the second century C.E., and the pressure of war soon began to grow inward instead of outward. This pressure took two forms. There were the "barbarians." These were a series of migratory tribes coming generally from the north and east of the empire: Goths, Huns, Vandals, and others. Then in the near east there was ongoing warfare with the kingdom of Persia, another organized state like Rome itself. In the long term these wars produced little territorial gain for either side but were a considerable drain of men and material. It was the tribes who actually made significant incursions into Roman territory. This process was long and involved. The various tribes were not responsible to each other and often not internally united. The Romans themselves had a variety of responses: going to war, bribery (in cash or land), diplomacy (to turn tribes against each other), or attempting to absorb some within the empire. Choosing strategies was one of the major political tasks of the later emperors. All of them cost, directly or indirectly, a lot of money, and led to the other primary task: collecting taxes sufficient to fund the government.

Rising Expenses. The problem was that expenses were rising without a corresponding increase in government. Peasant farmers, sharecroppers, and the like lived so close to subsistence levels that it was hard to extract any more from them. Worse, the Romans long felt that persons of high status (generally the wealthiest) should be exempt from taxation. This problem was exacerbated by the growth of the imperial government and by the extension, in 313 C.E., of certain tax exemptions to Christian clergy. Thus, a growing tax burden was born by a shrinking middle group. This group was not a "middle class" in the modern sense but was made up of local elites who had not managed to work or buy their way into the central government (or the church). There were various responses to this problem and its economic consequences. Coins were minted with ever-decreasing amounts of precious metal. Some inroads were made in tax privileges. People were forced to stay in ancestral homes and occupations to keep them paying. Diocletian even attempted universal wage and price controls briefly. Lack of economic knowledge and the power of outside forces doomed these moves. The empire continued to suffer from inflation and partial demonetization. That is, exchanges and taxes were more likely to use barter than cash. These factors, in turn, just made the empire's financial position worse.

Christianity. Except, perhaps, for its eventual fall, the most famous trend of the later Empire was its Christianization. Like the fall, this trend was not really a single event but an ongoing process. Official persecution of Christians was first practiced by Nero (64 C.E.) but carried on by only a few of his successors, and not always systematically at that. Nonetheless, the official toleration of Christianity, declared by Constantine and his co-emperor in 313, must have been a great boon to its followers. Constantine went on to help the church in other ways: tax exemptions for clergy, building and endowment of churches. Pagan worship was not yet attacked, and an official temple was even built to Constantine himself. On the other hand, there would be only one more pagan emperor (Julian, 361–363). For the rest of the century, state support for Christianity grew, and pagan worship was defunded or stopped in places. This trend accelerated toward the end of the fourth century, and pagan temples began to be closed and even destroyed. In 391 the emperor Theodosius ended the Olympic games after more than a thousand years since they were held in honor of the god Zeus. Most of the above has to do with public activity. Private, individual conversion to Christianity was also slow, especially in rural areas. On the winning side, however, there were immediate internal disagreements. There were divisions, both theological and administrative, among professed Christians as to just what Christianity meant. Constantine to some extent put the state's power at the disposal of the faithful to resolve these disputes (though he clearly would have preferred a peaceful consensus). Christians thus began to persecute each other more quickly and more severely than they did the pagans. Moreover, Constantine's own intervention in these controversies set another example. Church (especially in the persons of the bishops) and state (the emperor) became entangled without the establishment of a clear hierarchy. It became a matter of ongoing negotiation for the remainder of the empire.

Sources:
Averil Cameron, *The Later Roman Empire, AD 284–430* (Cambridge, Mass.: Harvard University Press, 1993).

Donald Kagan, ed., *The End of the Roman Empire: Decline or Transformation* (Lexington, Mass.: D.C. Heath, 1978).

H. M. D. Parker, *A History of the Roman World from A.D. 138 to 337* (London: Methuen, 1958).

LAW AND ORDER

Lack of Police. By almost any modern standard Roman politicians look like a tough and moralistic lot. It is surprising, then, that they seem to have had almost no interest in what one would think of as crime fighting. "Law and order" appears neither as a campaign promise nor as a subject for more abstract political theorizing. There were nearly no state prosecutors nor police, and the minor exceptions prove the rule. Under the Republic, several magistrates had the authority to prosecute wrongdoers before the assemblies. But these magistrates all had many other duties, and this trial procedure was too clumsy to have been used except in a few important cases. Under the Empire a city-watch was founded, but it was small (six thousand men in a city of roughly one million) and included no detectives to investigate crimes already committed. And even if the Romans had had a police force, it would presumably have been interested mainly in what were thought of as "public" offenses—i.e., not most of what one calls crime.

Reliance on Symbolic Order. How then did Romans respond to crime? Members of the law-writing class, that is of the elite, were protected by fortresslike houses and private security. Armed bodyguards were common, especially in the dangerous countryside. Ordinary citizens had to rely on less systematic forms of self-help: dress or chants designed to shame offenders, private prosecution, presumably sometimes direct violence. To keep discrete private disputes from turning into a general breakdown of social order, Romans depended on the stabilizing force of a few, mostly official, authority figures. Magistrates had special dress, attendants, and insignia, including the *fasces*, an axe bundled with rods symbolizing the state's power to punish. Potential alternative sources of authority—from astrologers to would-be usurpers—were dealt with in harsh, exemplary fashion. This system seems to have worked to some extent, but had at least two weaknesses. The authorities' tenuous grasp on order produced a fear of alternative authorities, a fear that gave rise to seemingly paranoid conspiracy theories. Even when "proper" authority remained unchallenged, it only worked locally. In particular, the spaces between towns went largely ungoverned in a "wild West" fashion. Bandits roamed the

---

SYMMACHUS AND AMBROSE ON THE ALTAR OF VICTORY

Most of the last vestiges of official paganism were eliminated during the reign of the Emperor Theodosius, including eliminating privileges for the Vestal Virgins and removal of the altar of Victory from the Senate house. Even at this date, however, there was resistance from pagan elements of the Senate. Symmachus pleaded with the emperor (unsuccessfully) against St. Ambrose for the restoration of the altar. Interestingly, both sides argued more in practical than theological terms:

Who is so allied to the barbarians as not to demand the altar of Victory? A place of honor should at least be returned to the name (*nomen*) if not to the spirit (*numen*). Your eternal reputation already owes much to Victory and will come to owe still more. Others who do not benefit from it may shun this power, but you cannot refuse patronage so friendly to triumphs. . . . Where will we swear allegiance to your laws and decrees? What religious scruple will discourage false testimony? That altar contains the concord of all, that altar keeps individuals true to their word, and nothing else gives greater force to our words than the fact that our order [the Senate] makes its decisions as if under oath.

Source: *Prefect and Emperor: The Relationes of Symmachus,* translated by R. H. Barrow (Oxford: Clarendon Press, 1973).

The Tullianum Prison in Rome

countryside in some numbers and were a prominent danger in the Roman imagination. It was a problem the Romans never really solved.

Sources:
Tim J. Cornell, "Police," in *The Oxford Classical Dictionary,* edited by Simon Hornblower and Antony Spawforth, third edition (Oxford: Oxford University Press, 1999), pp. 1204–1205.

Michael Grant, *History of Rome* (London: Weidenfeld & Nicolson, 1978).

Wilfried Nippel, *Public Order in Ancient Rome* (Cambridge & New York: Cambridge University Press, 1995).

LEGAL EQUALITY: WHO COUNTS?

Official Discrimination. The central political principle behind most modern legal systems is equality before the law. Neither individual cases nor legal rights in general are supposed to depend on the identity of the persons involved. While there are exceptions in practice (e.g., for minors, aliens, and the mentally ill), the ideal is well established. For the Romans, legal equality was more suspect in theory and the practical exceptions were more numerous and more serious. There was inequality both in substantive rights and in procedural access to the justice system. It may be useful, then, to consider in turn the various categories of people who did not have the full rights of the adult male Roman citizen.

Women. Women not under paternal control were subject to a limited form of guardianship (called *tutela*). The guardian (tutor) only had authority over will making and the sale of certain kinds of property (mostly farmland and large animals). Even in these cases he could only veto a transaction, not require it. Women's financial competence seems not to have been the central issue. Originally, the tutor was a male relative of the woman's father and probably was meant to act in the interests of her paternal family. Over the latter centuries of the Republic and early part of the Empire, devices arose so that a woman could choose and even replace her own tutor. This device eliminated the practical effects of *tutela* in most cases. Women were at various times prohibited from engaging in certain kinds of multiparty transactions: they could not offer security for a nonrelative's business deal, and they could not represent another person in court. The idea here seems to have been that in these situations women became public rather than private actors, and public activity was to be the domain of men. In fact, in the fully public sphere (officeholding, voting), women had no rights at all. In private matters such as commerce or inheritance women had full legal rights (with the exceptions above). They could even go to court themselves to enforce those

The fear of conspiracies led the Roman govermnent to drastic action that included use of slave informers (thus overcoming another deep-seated fear), mass execution of citizens, and even execution without trial.

Over the course of the first half of the second century B.C.E. there was a series of at least four mass trials of Roman matrons charged with poisoning. Little is known of the details, but it is virtually certain that these were "witch-hunts" rather than the reflection of waves of poisoning. This is a stereotypical conspiracy story in at least two respects. Wives were supposedly murdering their husbands—the ultimate betrayal from within. Poisoning was appropriate both because it is inherently sneaky and because in primitive technological circumstances it can never be disproved. Any woman whose husband died of illness or natural causes could be suspect.

Rome was home to many imported religious practices and made sporadic attempts to suppress or control some of them. The most dramatic of these attempts was a move in 186 B.C. to crush the followers of the god Bacchus (the Greek Dionysus). It was alleged that the religious movement concealed a conspiracy to corrupt and take over the state, as well as concealing simpler criminal and sexual offenses. Thousands of worshippers were tried and killed; places of worship were destroyed. The cult was not banned entirely, but further worship could only take place under tight regulation and supervision from the Roman government. The text of one of the Senate's decrees on the matter, inscribed on a bronze tablet, has survived to this day:

Let no one wish to hold Bacchic rites. If there are any people who say that they do need to hold Bacchic rites, they should come to the Urban Praetor at Rome, and the Senate should vote on the matter when their application is heard.

Sources: Wilfried Nippel, *Public Order in Ancient Rome* (Cambridge & New York: Cambridge University Press, 1995).

E. H. Warmington, ed. and trans., *Remains of Old Latin*, volume 4 (Cambridge, Mass.: Harvard University Press, 1959).

never changed fundamentally, but over time some of the law of persons came to be applied to them in addition. Under the empire they could be tried for crimes (and receive especially harsh punishments). At some point the killing of someone else's slave became punishable as homicide. Slaves even gained the ability in practice to hold property. The master kept a fund (*peculium*) for the slave, which was technically his property but from which he could be held liable for the slave's debts. Slaves even "owned" other slaves in this way. Since they had essentially no rights, it is not surprising that slaves could not file suits. Even if someone wished to assert that he had been wrongly enslaved, a free person had to make the claim in court. Slaves could testify in legal proceedings, but only under torture (a procedure whose wisdom even the Romans were divided on). They were allowed to testify against their own masters only in exceptional circumstances.

Minors. The Roman treatment of minors was fairly complicated, with full adult rights coming in several stages and varying ages. The most important distinction was not a strictly chronological one. Any child of any age and of either sex with a living father (or paternal grandfather) had essentially no private law rights in his or her own right. Such a child could not make binding agreements or even own property. (They could, however, be allotted *peculium* just like a slave.) The father could technically even execute his own children, though this practice seems to have been extremely rare. A child could be "emancipated" by the father and would then be treated more or less as if the father had died.

Levels of Minority. In terms of chronological age, there were several levels of subadulthood. If a court found that a person under twenty-five years of age had been tricked in a business deal, it could order restitution. This

Romans wanted to believe that their slaves were all loyal members of the family, but they were also aware that they were independent, thinking beings. One result of this was fear. This was especially true for the elite, who were vastly outnumbered in their homes by their slaves. One result of this fear was the *senatus consultum Silianum*, a senatorial decree dealing with slaves whose master had been murdered or died under suspicious circumstances. Those who had been in the house at the time were to be interrogated under torture, and if they were complicit (or had simply failed to help), they were to be executed.

As no home can be safe except if slaves are compelled and guard their masters both from members of the household and from outsiders at the risk of their own lives, decrees of the senate have been introduced concerning the questioning on public authority of the household slaves of those who have been killed.

Source: Alan Watson, *The Law of the Ancient Romans* (Dallas: Southern Methodist University Press, 1970).

rights, though they might face informal prejudice if they did not employ a male advocate.

Slaves. Roman society practiced slaveholding on a large scale. In legal terms this practice was "chattel" slavery; that is, nearly all the normal law of property applied to slaves. They were subject to whatever use, abuse, sale, lease, or other treatment their owners desired. Originally the law of property was essentially the only law that applied to slaves. So, for instance, the situation was the same if one's ox or one's slave damaged a neighbor's farm. A person could either make good the damage or hand the offending "animal" over to the injured party. The character of the Roman slave as property

Sandstone relief (circa 200 C.E.) of provincials paying taxes to a tax collector (Landesmuseum, Trier)

court ruling provided some protection but may also have discouraged others from doing business with young men and women. Girls under twelve and boys under fourteen were largely under control of a tutor. This tutor had more control than that of an adult woman. His approval was needed for any of the child's transactions, and he could also initiate transactions himself. He was not allowed to get rid of certain large assets, but the main check on his authority was a legal duty to act in the minor's interest. If he failed to do so, then he could be sued when the child left his guardianship. Finally, children under seven could not be legal actors at all; they depended entirely on their tutors. Note that none of these age-based restrictions is relevant to children with a living father; they have no property in the first place, and thus no guardians.

Peregrini. *Peregrini* is the Roman term for citizens of other nations, whether under Roman political domination or not. The usual ancient understanding was that a person was subject to the law of his own people, not of the territory he happened to be in at a given time. (This understanding did not leave one free to commit crimes, since one lacked the legal protections of citizens as well.) This situation is the source of the problems of provincial justice discussed above. It also raised questions about aliens in Roman territory. One thing that helped close the gap was that the principle was applied only to laws (*leges*) in a narrow technical sense. The

praetor could and did grant actions in cases involving noncitizens. Hence, *peregrini* had access to most of Roman commercial law. In other areas, such as family law, they were on their own, but this situation may have been in everyone's best interest. Aliens could bring prosecutions in the public, criminal courts, though they seem usually to have preferred to engage a Roman patron as an advocate.

The Disabled. The deaf had full substantive rights but could not represent themselves (or anyone else) in court because the proceedings in general and the magistrate's orders in particular were oral. (The derivation of "edict" from the Latin for "speak out" shows that even that text was notionally oral.) The blind were also prohibited from representing others in court.

Status. Even among adult, able-bodied, male Roman citizens, there were officially recognized distinctions of rank or status. These differences were primarily of significance to the political system, but in a few instances they were relevant in the courtroom as well. Through most of Roman history certain individuals were in an official state of disgrace, today called by the Latin term *infamia*. Those suffering *infamia* included members of certain professions (e.g., prostitutes and gladiators), persons convicted of major crimes or abuse of the legal system, and persons who had violated certain special trusts (e.g., by stealing from a child who was their ward). Whatever the source of their disgrace, such people

VISTILIA

Modern justice systems depend primarily on material penalties—fines and/or imprisonment—but Romans seem to have taken the shame of *infamia* seriously. Sometimes, however, they did exploit what look like loopholes in the law. In 19 C.E. a woman named Vistilia figured out that she could avoid the penalties for adultery by registering with the aediles as a prostitute. Prostitutes, whose business was perfectly legal, were naturally allowed to have sex with whomever they pleased. The case became quite notorious because Vistilia was from a prominent family, and the Senate decided that she should be punished regardless of the law and that noblewomen should in the future be prohibited from registering. Still, they seem to have been surprised that the more concrete penalty was needed.

Source: *The Annals of Tacitus,* translated by D. R. Dudley (New York: New American Library, 1966).

were generally prohibited from holding public office and from representing others in court. Thus their legal position was like that of women (though women technically could suffer *infamia* as well). Perhaps of more significance was a distinction that arose only during the Empire. The aristocracy, including senate, *equites,* and down to decurions (members of town councils) were lumped together in a group called the *honestiores* ("the more honorable"). All others were *humiliores* ("the more lowly"). Criminal offenses came to have a dual set of penalties. The *honestiores* got a more lenient sentence for a given offense; *humiliores* suffered the more severe (and often corporal) one.

Sources:

John Anthony Crook, *Law and Life of Rome* (Ithaca, N.Y.: Cornell University Press, 1967).

Bruce W. Frier, "Sociology of Roman Law," in *The Oxford Classical Dictionary,* edited by Simon Hornblower and Antony Spawforth, third edition (Oxford: Oxford University Press, 1999), pp. 823–825.

Michael Grant, *History of Rome* (London: Weidenfeld & Nicolson, 1978).

PRIVATE LAW

Substance. Even a cursory review of all of Roman private law would be too long to provide. Instead, it may be more useful to consider selected aspects of Roman law in a few important areas. This selection may give some idea of the strengths and limitations of the Roman legal system concerning contracts, property damage, ownership, and "crimes" within the private law.

Contracts. Roman law recognized a variety of different kinds of contract, some defined by their forms (e.g., an oral question and answer using certain key words) and others by substance of the underlying transaction (e.g., sale or rental, but not barter or lending at interest). Among the latter group were the "consensual" contracts; these did not require any written or oral expression at all, merely the consent or agreement of both parties. These formless contracts were conve-

nient ways of conducting the transactions they covered, such as sale, rental, hiring, and formation of partnerships. Thus, they seem to have been created in the interest of more efficient commerce. A later development, perhaps of the first century B.C.E., was the inclusion of certain implied warranties. So, for instance, it became part of the definition of a sale that the seller guaranteed to the buyer that no third party had a legal claim to the item being sold. If a dispute over one of these contracts came to court, the judge decided what each party should pay "in accord with good faith." Many other legal systems (and, indeed, early Roman law) preferred an all-or-nothing system in which, for instance, a buyer could be liable only for the full purchase price or nothing at all. The "good faith" standard is clearly better, among other things, in accounting for partial performance, as when the seller delivers some but not all of the other promised goods.

Transactional Limitations. This system was not without its problems. Not all transactions were covered by consensual contract. There was no sale of generic items or sale without a fixed price. Generic items could be, say, any ten bushels of wheat instead of a particular ten bushels. Note that this means there could be no sale of items not yet manufactured or (except in certain circumstances) crops not yet grown. The other rule means that one could not sell at a price to be determined later (contrast modern adjustable-rate loans, which vary with the prime rate). For dealings between individuals, these limitations were not necessarily big problems. For larger and more sophisticated businesses, however, the difficulties were greater. Note how hard it would be to make long-term arrangements with suppliers or set up lines of credit. There was a way around these limitations. All of these transactions could be carried out by one or more formally defined contracts such as the *stipulatio* (the oral question and answer). This contract, however, brought its own disadvantages. Unlike the consensual contract, it required the parties to meet face-to-face. Moreover, *stipulatio* did not have the same implied warranties, nor was it judged on a good faith basis. Thus, many transactions, even some fairly simple ones, would force the parties to use relatively unpredictable forms, and unpredictability discourages people from doing business at all.

Property Damage. The Aquilian Law of perhaps the third century B.C.E. provided that a property owner should be compensated if someone "wrongly killed his slave or herd animal (whether male or female)" or "caused him loss by burning, breaking, or rending" other property. Over the next two centuries or so, the scope of the law was expanded so that it could cover damage to any property by any means. In the course of this expansion, many significant refinements were also introduced. To establish liability, one had to show the defendant's malice or negligence. He, in turn, could argue your contributory negligence as a defense. Outside the scope of the Aquilian Law, provisions were made in some cases for preemptive action before damage occurred; for instance, the owner of a dilapidated house could be required to fix it or else offer a guarantee to his neighbor against any damage its collapse might cause. In this area, too, there were gaps in the law. Most notably, there was no way to collect damages for accidental injury to one's own person, only property.

Ownership. "Ownership" seems like a simple enough idea, but in fact it potentially includes a number of distinct rights: the use of a thing, selling or giving it away, destroying it, preventing others from doing any of these things. Roman law distinguished a number of different rights over property. Ownership proper (*dominium*) gave broad rights but was potentially difficult to prove. Thus the law also came to protect someone in possession (*possessio*) of property against most challengers. It was possible (and common) to transfer the use (usufruct) of property (and ownership of its products, if any) to someone else without transferring title. For instance, husbands commonly left usufruct of the family homes to their surviving widows, but they could not sell the property because ownership had been transferred to the children. Individual pieces of land could also bring with them specific rights and responsibilities, for instance, the right to carry water across one farm to another. Once established, these so-called "servitudes" were no longer matters of contract between the two owners personally; they were inherent in the property. In fact, Roman law developed the ability to treat entirely nonphysical rights as property. For instance, one could sell a debt he owned or the right to sue someone in a given matter.

"Crime." Roman private law corresponds roughly with what is now called civil law. However, it also covers a number of situations which would be the province of criminal law today. For instance, virtually all forms of theft were treated this way, including burglary, embezzlement, and fraud. Most assaults and batteries were also private offenses. In fact, for much of Roman history, most homicides were private offenses as well. The one early exception was murders within the family. Over time, killings by poisoning and by armed gangs moved from private to public jurisdiction. Finally, perhaps in the first century B.C.E., all homicides became public offenses (with a few exceptions, such as killing one's own slave, which were not illegal at all).

Sources:

Bruce W. Frier, *A Casebook on the Roman Law of Delict* (Atlanta: Scholars, 1989).

Barry Nicholas, *An Introduction to Roman Law* (Oxford: Clarendon Press, 1962).

Andrew M. Riggsby, *Crime and Community in Ciceronian Rome* (Austin: University of Texas Press, 1999).

Alan Watson, *The Law of Obligations in the Later Roman Republic* (Oxford: Clarendon Press, 1965).

Watson, *The Law of Property in the Later Roman Republic* (Oxford: Clarendon Press, 1968).

PUBLIC LAW

Offenses. Public law comprised both the bulk of Roman "criminal" law and the rules that structured the government. The criminal offenses were few in number and many of them were "political" insofar as they were connected to the opera-tions of the government. Two different offenses (*perduellio, maiestas*) are conventionally translated as "treason." Neither, however, focuses on direct betrayal to a military enemy. They extend to usurpation of government authority, exceeding one's own authority in public office, and, in a few extreme cases, military incompetence. Bribing voters and other forms of electoral corruption were prosecuted as *ambitus*. *Vis*, literally "force," was prosecutable as a public offense under the Republic only when it involved seditious violence. Under the Empire, the definition of the crime was expanded to include purely private violence. *Repetundae* is generally described as "extortion" but was only a crime in limited circumstances. It originally covered provincial governors who took money from their subjects and was later extended to a variety of public officials who demanded or took bribes. The other public offenses were various forms of homicide, forgery of coinage or wills, theft of state property, and (under the Empire) adultery and interfering with the state grain supply.

Penalties. For most offenses the punishment was set by law, and so there was no need for a separate penalty phase of the trial. One exception was *repetundae*. The defendant was required to repay a multiple of the amount of money extorted, so a second hearing was held to determine the precise amount. Under the Republic there was some attempt to make punishments fit the specific offenses in kind, not just in severity. Those guilty of *repetundae* had to pay back money; those who committed *ambitus* were prohibited from holding office. Several offenses, including homicide, carried a "capital" penalty. In practice, however, the guilty party was allowed to go into exile, stripped of his citizenship, and prohibited from return on pain of actual execution. Only those guilty of the murder of a family member were actually killed; such a "parricide" was sewn into a sack with a snake, a dog, a rooster, and a monkey, then thrown into the sea as part of a ritual purification. Imperial punishments were not so closely tied to individual crimes: fines, floggings, internal exile, loss of rank, actual execution. Members of the upper classes remained exempt from corporal punishment, even as it came to be used for the bulk of the population. Criminals at all periods might be detained before trial or execution of their sentence, but imprisonment was never a punishment in its own right.

Sources:

John Anthony Crook, *Law and Life of Rome* (Ithaca, N.Y.: Cornell University Press, 1967).

Andrew M. Riggsby, *Crime and Community in Ciceronian Rome* (Austin: University of Texas Press, 1999).

O. F. Robinson, *The Criminal Law of Ancient Rome* (Baltimore: Johns Hopkins University Press, 1995).

ROMAN LAW AS A SYSTEM

Lack of Codification. While there was a lot of Roman law, especially by ancient standards, it was never systematically organized by modern standards. Neither the laws (*leges*) nor juristic decisions were ever collected before the fall of Rome. Much less did Roman law ever become a "code"—a set of laws all composed and enacted as a body. There are several reasons for this development. First, the

American and British legal systems are self-organizing because of their reliance on precedent: later courts are required to follow the decisions of earlier ones. Roman courts were not similarly bound. In fact, since decisions were not published, precedent was hardly even available. The emperors had the authority to make binding interpretations but in practice could do so in only relatively few cases. Second, the jurists were not interested in a system. They worked in a strictly "casuistic" (case-by-case) manner; this manner presented the *iudex* with many models for judgment in a new case, but few general rules. Finally, the legislative process itself was unhelpful. Romans tended not to repeal or emend outdated laws. Often they would simply ignore them or reinterpret them beyond all recognition. Thus, the "paper trail" of the law could be quite confusing or misleading.

Legal Implications. This disunity was doubtless confusing for the aspiring jurist or prospective litigant. It may, moreover, have had deeper implications for the law itself. Without much legal theory the Romans appear never to have solved certain problems simply because they never entirely recognized them. For instance, Roman jurists agreed that a person had to be at "fault" to be legally liable for damage to another's property. They never agreed, however, whether this fault was subjective (one was not as careful as one could be) or objective (one was not as careful as the ordinary person would be). They never decided this fault because they did not define their terms so abstractly. But the abstract difference can make a huge difference in individual cases. In modern terms this distinction between subjective and objective fault is what makes "negligence" much easier to prove than "recklessness" and means the former is almost never sufficient to convict someone of a crime. Similarly, they never discussed in general what it means to "cause" something. This lack of fault made it tricky to assign responsibility in complicated cases such as a multiple car pileup. Who "caused" which collisions?

Sources:

Bruce W. Frier, *A Casebook on the Roman Law of Delict* (Atlanta: Scholars, 1989).

Alan Watson, *The Spirit of Roman Law* (Athens: University of Georgia Press, 1995).

ROMAN LAW: THE PARAMETERS

Extensive Scope. One of the most distinctive features of ancient Rome as compared to any of its contemporaries is its extensive legal system. Of course, many Greek and near-eastern civilizations had had law codes long before the Romans. Some have even speculated that the roots of the Celtic "Brehon" laws antedate the origins of Rome. None of these legal systems, however, nor any that were to appear for another thousand years (except the religiously based Jewish Talmud), had anything like the scope of Roman law. A consequence (and cause) of this large system was the Romans' interest in establishing legal rules not just for the most common or most general situations, but for every eventuality.

Criminal and Constitutional Law. In contrast to this interest in legal particulars, the Romans were not generally interested in grand theories of the law. Still, one can stay fairly true to Roman thinking by dividing the law into three parts: private, public, and sacred. Private law covered disputes between individual parties. (These were normally individual people, since Roman law did not really create "artificial persons" such as corporations.) This area is like modern "civil" law, though somewhat broader. Private law touched on areas such as commerce, property disputes and damage, family and inheritance, marriage and dowry, slavery, and defamation. It also included some matters that would be considered crimes today. Public law deals with matters which interest not just the parties but the whole community. It can be divided into two main branches. One includes most of what is called "criminal" law today. The other might be described as "constitutional." It controls the structure and functioning of the government, including standards of eligibility for office or rules for advance notice of pending legislation. Some parts of sacred law could be considered "merely" religious, such as requirements for holding priesthoods or rules for repeating sacrifices in case of ritual errors. Other parts of the sacred law could have a more dra-

---

ROME VS. GORTYN

In the early days Roman law was not any more sophisticated than their Greek neighbors'. For instance, the Twelve Tables (Rome, 450 B.C.) and roughly contemporary code of the Greek city of Gortyn have comparable rules of inheritance:

If someone provides for his estate or guardianship by will, let this be legally valid. If someone dies without a will, and he has no *suus heres* (direct descendant), let the nearest "agnate" [relative traced only through male lines] have the property. If there is no agnate, let the members of the clan have the property. (*Twelve Tables* 5.3–5)

When a man or woman dies, if there are children or grand-children or great-grand-children, they get the property. If there are no such people, then the brothers (or their descendents) get it. And if there are none of these either, the sisters (or their descendants) get it. . . . And if there are no others entitled, the serfs of the property get it. (Gortyn 5.9–28)

But the law of the later empire covers far more exotic circumstances:

If a man with two grandsons has emancipated one of them and adopted him in place of a son, we must see whether he alone may be admitted to the estate as per a son. This is the case if he has been adopted as the father of the grandson who had been kept in power, but the better view is that he alone can come into possession of the estate. (Ulpian, *Digest* 37.4.3.1)

Source: *The Civil Law, Including the Twelve Tables,* edited and translated by S. P. Scott (New York: AMS, 1973).

Bronze tablet inscribed with Julius Caesar's "Lex Cisalpina" of circa 48 B.C.E. that defined the legal powers for the province of Cisalpine Gaul, whose inhabitants he had made citizens of Rome (Parma Museum, Parma)

matic impact on the human world. Consecration to the gods or use for burial took land out of the realm of human ownership. A Roman noble was once forced to tear down his house because it blocked the view of the priests whose job was to watch for omens in the sky. Others had to resign from the state's highest office when it was later discovered that rituals had not been carried out properly at their elections.

Elaborate Apparatus. Roman law was created both by legislative bodies and by individual magistrates in the government. It also received a substantial contribution from private legal specialists known as "jurists." The state had an elaborate apparatus for resolving disputes according to the law. Parties (usually represented by professional advocates) argued their case and presented their evidence before a court. Their cases were then judged by a single judge or set of jurors. This similarity in outline to the modern legal system makes it easy to use many of the same terms when speaking of the Romans. However, the detail of each part of the Roman system turns out to be much different from modern

custom. Therefore, one must be careful not to take too much for granted on the basis of similar terminology.

Sources of Law. In modern nations of the "common law" tradition (including the United States and England) there are two primary sources of law. First, there is "statute" law—the enactments of legislative bodies such as Congress, Parliament, local councils, state legislatures, and the like. Second, there are judicial precedents—interpretations of these statutes and of long-standing conventions by judges. The sources of Roman law were similar, but not identical. Moreover, the balance of importance between sources was radically different.

Statute Law. The Romans had statute law called *lex* (plural *leges*). *Leges* were the enactments of the various popular assemblies. Compared to any modern nation, however, they passed few of these laws. Those that were passed tended to be concentrated in certain areas such as governmental structure and procedure, declarations of war and peace, and distribution of land. Other areas, notably including most private law, were neglected.

Magisterial Edicts. By contrast, the role of the executive was much more important in shaping the law. The chief magistrate in charge of the administration of justice was called the urban praetor. At the beginning of his term, he would publish an edict listing the actions he would allow to be brought in court, that is, the circumstances in which someone could be sued in a Roman court. In a few instances these actions were mandated by statute law, but most were allowed solely on the basis of the praetor's authority. In principle the praetor was free to include or reject whatever he wished. In practice the edict tended to evolve slowly, with each praetor deviating only slightly from his predecessor's edict. Finally, in the second century C.E. the emperor had the praetor's edict fixed permanently. Several other officials of the Roman government also issued edicts explaining how they would carry out their respective offices, and some of these touched on specific judicial areas (e.g., the "aediles" were in charge of the markets, so their edict had some effect on commercial law). However, the urban praetor's edict was much broader and in any case tended to serve as a model for the others. Under the empire, the word of the emperor, in several formal guises, naturally became a crucial source of law.

Juristic Opinion. A third source of law, and at least equally important, was the work of legal scholars known as "jurists." Authoritative interpretation of statutes and edicts was carried out not by courts but by these jurists. Moreover, "interpretation" was capable of changing the meaning of laws drastically. For instance, an early law stated that a son who was sold by his father three times (presumably he came back home in between sales) would thereby be emancipated or freed from paternal control. Later jurists interpreted this law to mean that a daughter (not covered by the original law at all) would be emancipated by being sold only once. A few jurists of the early empire are known to have been granted a "right of responding" to legal questions by the emperor. It is not clear what this right meant, but in general, individual jurists did not have formal, legal authority. Nonetheless, judges sought out their advice, and where the jurists were in agreement, that consensus seems to have had the practical force of law.

Sources:
John Anthony Crook, *Law and Life of Rome* (Ithaca, N.Y.: Cornell University Press, 1967).

Barry Nicholas, *An Introduction to Roman Law* (Oxford: Clarendon Press, 1962).

O. F. Robinson, *The Sources of Roman Law: Problems and Methods for Ancient Historians* (London & New York: Routledge, 1997).

TRIAL PROCEDURES UNDER THE EMPIRE

Cognitio. The republican procedures continued to be used in the early years of the empire. Over the course of the first two centuries C.E., however, they began to be displaced. Criminal trials of senators came to be held before the senate itself. Other cases, in both public and private law matters, came to be tried by a process generally called *cognitio* today. The case was heard directly by a state official. These were still not professional judges

in the modern sense but were perhaps a step in that direction. The presiding official also had considerably more control over the direction of the case than under Republican rules. He could impose legal terms, compel persons to appear, and conduct independent inquiries without the advice of the parties. With the new procedure also came increased substantive flexibility. The presiding officer had freedom to accept claims of justification or impose nonstandard penalties. *Cognitio* coexisted for some time with the earlier procedures. There were perhaps still jury trials for adultery being held in the early third century C.E. Eventually, however, it displaced the earlier forms. Also, it was the sole procedure for some offenses, such as tampering with the grain supply, which were created only under the empire.

Provinces. The above procedures were viable only near the city of Rome, since they required access to the praetor there. Outside Rome, his role was taken up by governors in the respective provinces. However, there were other complications there. For most of the Republic and early Empire many people were subject to Rome but were not themselves citizens. From the Roman point of view (as in most ancient legal thinking) this situation meant that they were not, or not automatically, subject to Roman law. Thus suits between two Egyptians generally continued to be heard under Egyptian law even after the kingdom was annexed by Rome. While there was probably no circumstance in which a governor felt he had no *right* to intervene in a case within his province, he ordinarily saw no *need* to do so. And even if he did intervene, he might only order a case to be decided under a particular local law.

Extended Reach of Roman Law. Nonetheless, the reach of Roman law extended steadily over time for at least four reasons. First, from the end of the Republic, grants of Roman citizenship were made to individuals and whole communities. This automatically brought more people under the scope of Roman law, though some local jurisdiction persisted even after universal Roman citizenship was granted in 212 C.E. Second, Roman political authorities increasingly used their own law to settle disputes in which the two parties were not both from the same foreign state, e.g., cases between a Roman and a provincial, between provincials from two different cities, or including persons from outside the empire entirely. We also know of cities that decided smaller cases themselves, but had to refer more important matters to the Roman authorities. Third, even communities that retained formal judicial independence sometimes changed their laws to resemble those of Rome, especially in the western half of the empire. This conformity seems to have been encouraged but not required by the central government. Finally, the losing party in any dispute might appeal to Roman authority just to have a second chance to win. In these last two instances, subjects and subject states colluded in weakening their own legal systems.

Archaeologists have recently found a cache of legal documents stored by a woman named Bathaba in a cave near the Dead Sea in the early second century C.E. On the one hand, she was involved in a dispute with her husband's other wife. Such a polygamous marriage was impossible under Roman law; it was an indigenous phenomenon. Yet, when she wanted to appeal (or considered appealing) to the Roman governor in her disputes, she prepared documents in Roman form. Other documents were just similar to Roman types. This one archive shows both the continued coexistence of local and Roman law and their commingling.

Source: Andrew W. Lintott, *Imperium Romanum: Politics and Administration* (London & New York: Routledge, 1993), pp. 156–157.

Sources:

Andrew W. Lintott, *Imperium Romanum: Politics and Administration* (London & New York: Routledge, 1993).

O. F. Robinson, *The Criminal Law of Ancient Rome* (Baltimore: Johns Hopkins University Press, 1995).

Robinson, *The Sources of Roman Law: Problems and Methods for Ancient Historians* (London & New York: Routledge, 1997).

TRIAL PROCEDURES UNDER THE REPUBLIC

In Iure **Phase: Determining the Legal Issue.** Broadly speaking, a private law trial took place in two parts. In the first phase, the parties appeared before the urban praetor. The praetor had nearly complete discretion to allow the case to proceed or not. If it did go forward, the praetor had to assign a judge (*iudex,* plural *iudices*) to hear the case and give a formula that summarized the issue(s) to be decided at trial. This process seems to have involved considerable negotiation among the parties and the praetor. The *iudices* were not state officials or even, generally, legal professionals. Instead, they were drawn from a roster of prominent citizens. In some important cases, more than one *iudex* was assigned to hear a given case.

Apud Iudicem **Phase: Deciding the Facts.** The trial proper was then held before the *iudex.* Both sides (as well as the judge himself) were normally assisted by legal and/or oratorical professionals. The sides presented long speeches, then evidence and testimony, and there was opportunity not only for cross-examination of witnesses but also for direct argument between the advocates on either side. There were essentially no procedural or evidentiary rules, so the parties could say whatever they wished within their allotted time. The *iudex* had nothing to decide (no motions, no objections) until the end of the case. The decision was guided by the formula, but his was often quite vague, hence the need for assistance from jurists. Nor was there any clear statement of the burden of proof, so individual *iudices* were left considerable latitude. A verdict was rendered quickly, and, where necessary, specific damages were assessed by the *iudex.* Awards were cash sums or, in some circumstances, other property; *iudices* did not, broadly speaking, order performance of particular actions, such as community service.

Early Public Law Procedures. In the earliest years of Rome, public law offenses were tried by the same popular assemblies that enacted the laws. Beginning around 400 B.C.E., this clumsy procedure came largely to be displaced by special commissions of inquiry led by magistrates. Eventually, starting in 149 B.C.E., the Romans began to establish permanent courts, roughly similar to those for private law, to try these offenses. Within a few decades this practice became the norm.

Initiating Prosecutions. Here, too, the procedure began when someone brought a complaint before the urban praetor. A distinctive feature of the public procedure, however, is that this complaint did not have to come from an injured party; any free person, even a noncitizen, could in theory prosecute a violation of public law. There was no state prosecutor, so the system required private individuals to come forward. If there were more than one potential prosecutor (and assuming the praetor allowed the case to go forward), the first task of the jury was to select whoever they thought would conduct the strongest case. The jury was of variable but considerable size (roughly between twenty-five and seventy-five men), and as in the private law courts, the jurors (also called *iudices*) were drawn from the most prominent citizens. In addition, there was a presiding officer (*quaesitor*), who might be the praetor himself or his delegate. However, the absence of procedural rules made the *quaesitor* something of a figurehead.

The Trial Proper. As in private law cases, both sides gave speeches, followed by evidence and testimony, then confrontation. In some cases, the prosecution (but not the defense) could subpoena a limited number of witnesses. At the end of the proceedings, the jurors voted immediately and apparently without the legal assistance available to private law *iudices.* In general, legal technicalities seem to have been much less important in public cases than in private ones. The majority vote won.

Sources:

John Anthony Crook, *Law and Life of Rome* (Ithaca, N.Y.: Cornell University Press, 1967).

Barry Nicholas, *An Introduction to Roman Law* (Oxford: Clarendon Press, 1962).

Andrew M. Riggsby, *Crime and Community in Ciceronian Rome* (Austin: University of Texas Press, 1999).

SIGNIFICANT PEOPLE

GAIUS JULIUS CAESAR OCTAVIANUS (AUGUSTUS)

63 B.C.E.–14 C.E.
EMPEROR

Master of the Roman World. Born as Gaius Octavius in 63 B.C.E., he was adopted by Julius Caesar in his will (this type of adoption was not an unusual procedure at Rome). Informally, he also inherited much of Caesar's political and military support. For several years he had an uneasy alliance with Caesar's lieutenant Mark Antony, but eventually (31 B.C.E.) he defeated Antony in a naval battle to become undisputed master of the Roman world. He held various offices and honors (including the name Augustus given in 27 B.C.E.) but wisely avoided any title such as "king" or "dictator," which would have rubbed his superiority in the face of other nobles too much. Over the course of his forty-five-year reign Augustus's generals acquired new territory in Egypt, Spain, and North Africa for the empire. He also instituted reforms in provincial administration, marriage law, manumission of slaves, and other areas. Augustus had no son and outlived many potential successors among allies and family. Eventually, he was succeeded by Tiberius, the son of his wife Livia by a previous marriage. Like his father, he was made a god after his death in 14 C.E.

Sources:
P. A. Brunt and J. M. Moore, *Res gestae divi Augusti: The Achievements of the Divine Augustus* (London: Oxford University Press, 1967).

Fergus Millar and Erich Segal, eds., *Caesar Augustus: Seven Aspects* (Oxford & New York: Clarendon Press, 1984).

K. A. Raaflaub and M. Toher, eds., *Between Republic and Empire: Interpretations of Augustus and His Principate* (Berkeley & Los Angeles: University of California Press, 1990).

Paul Zanker, *The Power of Images in the Age of Augustus* (Ann Arbor: University of Michigan Press, 1988).

GAIUS JULIUS CAESAR

100–44 B.C.E.
GENERAL, STATESMAN

Dictator for Life. Gaius Julius Caesar was born in 100 B.C.E., descended from an ancient and noble Roman family that could allegedly trace its ancestry back to the goddess Venus. His early career as a politician and public speaker was successful but unremarkable. It began to accelerate when he unexpectedly won election to the chief priesthood in 63 B.C.E. and, after serving as praetor, conducted successful military operations in Spain in 61 B.C.E. He then formed an alliance with the great general Gnaeus Pompeius (Pompey) and the wealthy Marcus Crassus. Caesar was elected consul for 59 B.C.E. (during which time he passed a large legislative program) and then made military governor of southern France for ten years after this. During this time he conquered the rest of France and fought campaigns in Britain as well. His political alliance broke down and he faced strong opposition from political conservatives at Rome. Returning from France, he marched on Rome with his army. His forces defeated Pompey's in 49 B.C.E., and he spent the next several years mopping up other senatorial resistance. Since he was in control of the city, he was able to have himself made dictator, originally for a year at a time, but eventually for life. Eventually hostility grew among some of the remaining senators to the point that Caesar was assassinated in 44 B.C.E.

Sources:
Matthias Gelzer, *Caesar: Politician and Statesman* (Cambridge, Mass.: Harvard University Press, 1968).

Michael Grant, *Julius Caesar* (New York: M. Evans, 1969).

Arthur D. Kahn, *The Education of Julius Caesar: A Biography, A Reconstruction* (New York: Schocken, 1986).

Erik Wistrand, *Caesar and Contemporary Society* (Göteborg, Sweden: Vetenskaps–och Vitterhets–samhället, 1979).

Zwi Yavetz, *Julius Caesar and His Public Image* (London: Thames & Hudson, 1983).

MARCUS PORCIUS CATO (CATO THE ELDER)

234-149 B.C.E.
STATESMAN, WRITER

Old-Fashioned. Born into a relatively modest family and a veteran of the Second Punic War (218–201 B.C.E.), Marcus Porcius Cato, or Cato the Elder, was one of the most important political and cultural figures of his age. (He is called "the Elder" in contrast to his great-grandson of the same name, famous for his opposition to Caesar.) His political career culminated in the consulship in 195 B.C.E. and the censorship in 184 B.C.E. Even after leaving office, he remained an influential figure in the Senate for decades; most notably he brought about the Third Punic War in the year of his death (149 B.C.E.). His reputation was as an "old-fashioned" moralist and strident nationalist, though at least the latter was partly a matter of public posturing. Cato was also the first significant writer of Latin literary prose. He published more than a hundred of his speeches (he may have been the first Roman to do so), a history of Rome, and a treatise on agriculture.

Sources:
Alan E. Astin, *Cato the Censor* (Oxford: Clarendon Press, 1978).

Ward W. Briggs, "Cato the Elder," in *Ancient Roman Writers, Dictionary of Literary Biography*, volume 211, edited by Briggs (Columbia, S.C.: Bruccoli Clark Layman / Detroit: Gale Group, 1999), pp. 35–40.

Howard Hayes Scullard, *Roman Politics 220–150 B.C.* (Oxford: Clarendon Press, 1951).

MARCUS TULLIUS CICERO

106-43 B.C.E.
ORATOR, STATESMAN, PHILOSOPHER

Indispensable Man. Cicero was born in 106 B.C.E. in the town of Arpinum, north of Rome. His family's connections in the Roman nobility secured him a rhetorical education and an apprenticeship in law and practical politics. His exceptional skills as a public speaker became apparent in his career as a courtroom advocate. This ability allowed him to run for and win a series of magistracies, all the way up to the consulship in 63 B.C.E. (he was only the second person in a century to reach the highest office without having an ancestor who had held any office). His greatest public achievement was putting down an attempted coup during his consulship. During the course of this coup, however, he executed some of the conspirators without trial, and he was later (58 B.C.E.–57 B.C.E.) briefly exiled for having done so. His legal career continued, but he was overshadowed in politics for the rest of his life. In 43 B.C.E. he spoke out strongly against Marc Antony, who seized power after the assassination of Caesar, and was one of many of Antony's opponents who was executed. Fifty-eight of his orations and more than nine hundred of his letters are extant.

Sources:
Paul MacKendrick, *The Speeches of Cicero* (London: Duckworth, 1995).

Thomas N. Mitchell, *Cicero: The Ascending Years* (New Haven: Yale University Press, 1979).

Mitchell, *Cicero: The Senior Statesman* (New Haven: Yale University Press, 1991).

Ann Vasaly, *Representations: Images in the World of Ciceronian Oratory* (Berkeley: University of California Press, 1993).

TIBERIUS CLAUDIUS MAXIMUS

LATE FIRST-EARLY SECOND CENTURIES C.E.
SOLDIER

Consummate Professional. Tiberius Claudius Maximus was a legionnaire whose career reflects the professionalism inherent in the Roman military machine. He began his service as a cavalryman and treasurer in Legion VII Claudia and was soon assigned as a guard of the legion commander and standard-bearer of the cavalry. During the Dacian uprising of 85–88 C.E. Emperor Domitian awarded him military decorations for bravery. Afterward, he was promoted to "double-pay" soldier (in the second *ala* of Pannonians) and scout by the Emperor Trajan. He received two more decorations for bravery during the First and Second Dacian wars (101–102 C.E. and 105–106 C.E.) and the Parthian War (114–116 C.E.). Because he had captured the Dacian king Decebalus and brought his head back to Trajan at Ranisstorum, the emperor promoted him to decurion. After voluntarily serving beyond his required enlistment of twenty-five years, he was honorably discharged by Terentius Scaurianus.

Sources:
J.B. Campbell, *The Roman Army 31 B.C.–A.D. 337* (London & New York: Routledge, 1994).

Peter Connolly, *The Roman Army* (London: Macdonald Educational, 1975).

DOMITIUS ULPIANUS (ULPIAN)

DIED 223 C.E.
LEGAL SCHOLAR

Trusted Counsel. Domitius Ulpianus (Ulpian) was from Tyre in modern Lebanon. He was one of the latest (and one of the greatest) of a series of lawyers in public service in the middle years of the Roman Empire. He served in several civil service posts, and, as praetorian prefect to the emperor Alexander Severus, he was responsible for imperial responses to judicial appeals that shaped the law of the time. As a legal scholar, he also wrote extensive treatises on such subjects as trusts, laws, and magistracies and commentaries on legal texts such as the praetor's edict and Sabinus's treatise on the civil law. These writings became authoritative, and Ulpian is the most frequently-quoted author in the eventual *Digest* of Justinian. He was killed during a mutiny of the Praetorian Guard in 223 C.E.

Sources:

Bruce W. Frier, *A Casebook on the Roman Law of Delict* (Atlanta: Scholars, 1989).

Tony Honoré, "Domitius Ulpianus," in *The Oxford Classical Dictionary*, edited by Simon Hornblower and Antony Spawforth, third edition (Oxford: Oxford University Press, 1999), p. 493.

James Muirhead, *Historical Introduction to the Private Law of Rome* (London: A. & C. Black, 1916).

DOCUMENTARY SOURCES

Ammianus Marcellinus, *Res gestae* (History, circa 360–395 C.E.)—Intended to be a continuation of Tacitus's *History*, which had ended with the assassination of Domitian in 96 C.E. Ammianus's history was written in thirty-one books and covered the period from the beginning of Emperor Nerva's reign in 96 B.C.E. to the Battle of Adrianople in 378 C.E. Only books 14–31 are extant.

Gaius Julius Caesar, *Commentarii de bello civili* (Civil Wars, circa 47 B.C.E.)—A war commentary and the companion volume to the author's *Commentarii de bello Gallico* (Gallic War), justifying his actions to the Roman people.

Caesar, *Commentarii de bello Gallico* (Gallic War, 51 B.C.E.)—A history of Caesar's military exploits against the Cherusci, Belgae, and other barbarian tribes. It is also, in part, a defense of the legality of his actions in Gaul and of his personal dignity.

Marcus Tullius Cicero, *Philippicae* (Philippics, 44–43 B.C.E.)— Fourteen orations attacking Mark Antony following the assassination of Julius Caesar. Cicero is considered to be the greatest orator in Roman history.

Constitutio Antoniniana (Antonine Constitution, 212 C.E.)—The name given to an edict of Caracalla that made all free men and women in the empire Roman citizens.

Sextus Julius Frontinus, *Stratagemata* (Stratagems, late 80s C.E.)—Different examples of effective military strategy presented in four books. It was evidently written as a guide for military officers. The first three books examine skillful generalship on and off the battlefield. The last book, which some modern scholars doubt was indeed written by the author, discusses discipline, determination, restraint, and troop morale.

Titus Livius (Livy), *Ab urbe condita libri* (History)—A monumental work of 142 books. Only books 1–10 and 21–45 survive intact, although there are fragments and summaries of the rest. Livy meant this history to span the period between Rome's founding and his own day (Livy died in 17 C.E.).

Marcus Annaeus Lucanus (Lucan), *De bello civili* (The Civil War) or *Pharsalia* (circa 62 C.E.)—An epic about the conflict between Caesar and Pompey.

Cornelius Nepos, *De viris illustribus* (On Famous Men, 35–34 B.C.E.)—Nepos is the founder of the technique of parallel biography. This text includes sections on significant foreign leaders and Latin historians. Some of the other works attributed to him are *De Romanorum imperatoribus* (On Generals of the Romans) and *De regibus* (On Kings).

Plutarch, *Parallel Lives*—A Greek biographer who traveled widely and taught in Rome. In *Parallel Lives*, he presents character studies of distinguished Greeks and Romans in pairs, from the age of Theseus (legendary king of Athens) and Romulus and Remus (mythical founders of Rome) down to the second century C.E.

Gaius Sallustius Crispus (Sallust), *Catilina* (The War of the Catiline, circa 42 B.C.E.)—An account of the events surrounding Catiline's conspiracy to overthrow the government in 63 B.C.E.

Sallust, *Jugurtha* (The War with Jugurtha, 40 B.C.E.)—A narrative of the conflict with the Numidian king between 111 B.C.E. and 104 B.C.E.

Gaius Suetonius Tranquillus (Suetonius), *De vita Caesarum* (On the Life of the Caesars, circa 119 C.E.–122 C.E.)—Twelve biographies presented in eight books.

Cornelius Tacitus, *Annales* (after 116 C.E.)—A history of the Julio-Claudian emperors who ruled from 14 C.E. to 68 C.E. There were approximately sixteen or eighteen books.

Tacitus, *Historiae* (Histories, 100 C.E.–110 C.E.)—Covers the period between 69 C.E. and 96 C.E. in twelve books. (Only four complete books and a portion of a fifth survive.) The Civil War of 68 C.E.–69 C.E., in which there was a quick succession of four emperors, is viewed by Tacitus as the greatest calamity ever to befall the Roman people.

Tacitus, *De origine et situ Germanorum* or *Germania* (On the Origin and Homeland of the Germans, 98 C.E.)—An essay written to inform the Romans about the lands and peoples of Germany. While Tacitus clearly admires the morals and political freedoms of the inhabitants, he also warns of the danger a united Germany would pose to Rome.

Domitius Ulpianus (Ulpian), *Libri ad edictum* (Praetorian Edicts, before 228 C.E.)—A legal commentary by a scholar who had an exalted opinion of a lawyer's calling. According to Ulpian, lawyers were "priests of justice" devoted to "the true philosophy."

Ulpian, *Libri ad Sabinum* (Civil Law, before 228 C.E.)—Another legal commentary.

Ulpian, *De officio proconsulis* (On the Duties of the Provincial Governor, before 228 C.E.)—A manual on the responsibilities associated with high government office.

Gaius Velleius Paterculus, *Histories to the Consulship of Marcus Vinicius* (30 C.E.)—A short history of Rome written by an Augustan loyalist.

A tetradrachma with a depiction of Zenobia, ruler of Palmyra from 267 to 272 C.E. (British Museum)

Relief showing Hadrian's triumphal entry into Rome following one of his military campaigns against the barbarians, second century C.E. He is being greeted by the guiding spirits of the Senate and the Roman people (from Donald Kagan and others, *The Western Heritage*, 1998).

CHAPTER SEVEN

LEISURE, RECREATION, AND DAILY LIFE

by BRYAN DALEAS

CONTENTS

Sidebars and tables are listed in italics.

264 B.C.E.	• Three pairs of gladiators fight at the funeral games of Decimus Brutus Pera, the first gladiatorial combat displayed at Rome.
246-241 B.C.E.	• First Punic War; Rome gains control of Sicily in the first thrust of Roman expansion outside of the Italian peninsula. Romans come into greater contact with Greek culture. Works of Greek art are brought from Sicily to Rome, and Romans also develop a taste for Greek theatrical productions.
254-184* B.C.E.	• Titus Maccius Plautus translates and adapts Greek comedies for the entertainment of Latin-speaking audiences.
218-201 B.C.E.	• Second Punic War; Rome repels Hannibal's invasion of Italy and conquers Spain; Rome gains control of precious metal mines in Spain; new wealth begins to arrive in Rome.
215 B.C.E.	• The tribune Gaius Oppius sponsors a sumptuary law (*lex Oppia*) forbidding women to own more than half an ounce of gold, wear multicolored clothing, or ride in two-horsed vehicles in Rome. The law is meant to curb extravagant personal behavior during the period of the Punic Wars.
195 B.C.E.	• The *lex Oppia* is repealed.
190-159* B.C.E.	• Publius Terentius Afer (Terence) writes Latin comedies based on Greek models.
186 B.C.E.	• Marcus Fulvius Nobilior produces the first wild beast hunts at Rome for public entertainment.

*Denotes Circa Date

181-141 B.C.E.

- Four different laws (*lex Orchia, lex Fannia, lex Didia,* and *lex Licinia*) and a senatorial decree are enacted to prevent conspicuous consumption and display by members of the wealthy classes. These measures attempt to limit expenditures on private entertainments, the numbers of guests at private entertainments, individual dress, and other personal concerns.

179 B.C.E.

- Opening at Rome of the *macellum,* a food market that brings several previously separate markets into the same building.

174 B.C.E.

- Circus Maximus is rebuilt by the censors Quintus Fulvius Flaccus and Aulus Postumius Albinus. They overhaul the entire complex, rebuild the starting gates, and set up a system of lap-counters in the form of large wooden eggs to indicate to the spectators the number of laps run by each team.

149-146 B.C.E.

- Third Punic War; Rome destroys Carthage in 146; Africa becomes a Roman province.

146 B.C.E.

- Rome sacks Corinth; the first temple built of marble, the Temple of Jupiter Stator, is constructed in Rome; spoils of war and tributes give Rome new monetary resources.

144-140 B.C.E.

- The aqueduct, Aqua Marcia, is built by Quintus Marcius Rex, the urban praetor. This structure was a great engineering accomplishment that brought water to the top of the Capitoline Hill. The water provided by the Aqua Marcia was considered the best in Rome.

73-71 B.C.E.

- An uprising is led by the Thracian gladiator Spartacus at Capua. The brave and powerful gladiator attracts many fugitives and leads his huge army around Italy, defeating several Roman armies and destroying various regions in his path.

55 B.C.E.

- The opening of Rome's first permanent theater, the Theater of Pompey in the Campus Martius. Built by Gnaeus Pompeius Magnus, this theater is estimated to have accommodated eleven thousand spectators.

*DENOTES CIRCA DATE

46 B.C.E.

- Julius Caesar institutes a reformed calendar that reconciles the traditional agricultural year with the complete revolution of the moon around the earth. He also produces the first gladiatorial games not associated with the funeral of a deceased relative.

40* B.C.E.

- The first regular medical school is established at Rome by Asclepiades of Bithynia.

25 B.C.E.

- The Baths of Agrippa are begun in the Campus Martius. Agrippa's bath complex is the first of the imperial baths at Rome. Upon his death in 12 B.C.E. Agrippa wills the baths to the Roman people for their free use.

13 B.C.E.

- Dedication of the Theater of Balbus at Rome. This theater, the smallest of the permanent theaters in Rome, seats approximately 7,700 spectators.

13 OR 11 B.C.E.

- Dedication of the Theater of Marcellus. This theater accommodates about thirteen thousand spectators.

59 C.E.

- A riot erupts between the inhabitants of Pompeii and the nearby town of Nuceria in the amphitheater of Pompeii during a gladiatorial display. The city of Pompeii is forbidden to produce gladiatorial spectacles for the next ten years.

64 C.E.

- Fire destroys large sections of Rome during the reign of the emperor Nero.

79 C.E.

- The eruption of the volcano Mt. Vesuvius destroys the southern Italian cities of Pompeii and Herculaneum. Pompeii, covered mostly with pumice and volcanic ash, is preserved well enough to provide excellent evidence for various aspects of life in a Roman city, including domestic architecture, public buildings, and trade. Herculaneum suffers a more drastic fate, being covered in volcanic mud whose durability has made excavation of the city difficult.

*DENOTES CIRCA DATE

80 C.E.
- Dedication of the Flavian Amphitheater (Colosseum) at Rome. Built by the Flavian Emperors (Vespasian, Titus, and Domitian), the Colosseum seats approximately 45,000 spectators at large-scale public events such as gladiatorial combats.

104* C.E.
- The Baths of Trajan are built over one section of Nero's Golden House, which has been destroyed by fire and become the most important of the imperial baths. This complex sets a precedent for the symmetrical design of future baths.

100–110* C.E.
- The Markets of Trajan are built. (The function of this network of buildings has been much disputed by modern scholars. Possible uses include office space and a spice market.)

216 C.E.
- The first great imperial baths built in more than one hundred years, the Baths of Caracalla, are lavishly decorated with fine works of art, many of which are later plundered when the baths fall into disuse. (Many of the statues taken from the Baths of Caracalla can be seen today in the National Archaeological Museum in Naples.)

404 C.E.
- The last gladiatorial games are held in the Flavian Amphitheater (Colosseum).

*DENOTES CIRCA DATE

Model of a typical Roman apartment house found at the port of Ostia in the first and second centuries C.E. (from Donald Kagan, and others, *The Western Heritage,* 1998)

OVERVIEW

The Nature of the Sources. The question "What was daily life like in Roman antiquity?" is in some respects easy to respond to, yet, in other ways difficult to answer. It is easy to point to the sources at our disposal; works of art, ruins of buildings, and passages of literature. The difficulty lies in distinguishing between the experiences of those for whom the sources reveal the most, and the experiences of those for whom the sources reveal the least. The majority of people living in the Roman world must have been members of the latter category. Therefore, we can describe the lives of only a fraction of Rome's population with a great degree of detail and accuracy. That fraction consisted of the economic, social, and political elite—for whom works of art were produced and luxury homes were built, and by whom much literature was written.

Common Experiences. It is not impossible, however, to describe experiences that were common to both the elite and the nonelite of the Roman world. Large public buildings, for example, were intended to accommodate members of all Roman classes. Therefore, members of all classes witnessed the same public spectacles, the same public entertainments in the same buildings at the same time. We know that members of all classes derived essentially the same benefits from public works such as paved roads and public access to water supplied by the aqueducts. We know that the same public bathing experience was available to all Roman citizens wherever there existed public bathing facilities. The process of "Romanization" (the assimilation of Roman culture by peoples outside of the city of Rome proper) fairly guaranteed the consistency of these experiences throughout the Roman world. The experiences that were peculiar to the lower classes are documented less fully, and therefore are known mostly from inference. Such experiences were certainly no less "Roman" or culturally valid for their lack of evidence, and certainly have a place in any general study of Rome.

Roman Calendar. Whether an individual was a senator, farmer, or slave did not change the fact that the sun rises and the sun sets, or the fact that the length of daylight hours changes seasonally. All Romans had to rise at dawn to take advantage of the natural light if they intended to accomplish anything. The position of the sun was precisely the same for all classes in any given location, and so the Roman calendar, with all its faults and peculiarities, was faulty and peculiar to all Romans alike. Still, Romans across the Roman world divided the year into months, the months into days, and the days into hours as best they could. Their market days were held at regular intervals, and they observed religious holidays by ceasing all business and legal activities.

Class Distinctions. Other truly daily activities, such as eating, could certainly reveal distinctions of social and economic class. The poor person's diet was restricted by cost, and therefore was less elaborate and perhaps less appealing than the diet of wealthy individuals who could afford a wider range of foods than just grain and simple vegetables. The manner of taking one's meal was also determined by class; who but the rich could afford the space to accommodate the requisite number of dining couches for a formal dinner party, not to mention the expense? It is no surprise that fine silver plate and utensils have been discovered in the urban houses of wealthy families, while the poor no doubt ate from simple earthenware or wooden vessels.

Various Living Arrangements. Living arrangements in the Roman world were as diverse in size, comfort, and decoration as the population was diverse in socio-economic class and individual tastes. Again, the evidence for domestic experience is skewed in favor of the rich, the remains of whose villas and townhouses can be seen in almost all parts of the world where Romans established provinces and colonies. The surviving remains of apartments and tenements, however, give a glimpse into the lives of the more populous lower classes. Nevertheless, we can learn a great deal about the daily life of the Romans from what survives, particularly in the cities of Pompeii and Herculaneum, which were frozen in time in 79 C.E. because of the eruption of the volcano Mt. Vesuvius. Ostia, Rome's port city at the mouth of the Tiber River, shows some remarkable differences in housing preferences from those of Pompeii and Herculaneum. Archaeological evidence from these and other Roman cities gives us insight into the layout of Roman houses and trends in their decoration, the nature of ancient apartment complexes, and the conditions of small rental units in buildings otherwise occupied by single families or various businesses.

Combined Evidence. The combination of archaeological and literary evidence helps us to understand certain aspects of living arrangements more fully than we would from either source alone. While we can see how Romans built and decorated their homes from the physical remains around Europe and Africa, we know something of the Romans' attitudes toward their own domestic experience from literature. Authors such as Pliny, Cicero, and Martial reveal thoughts about living conditions, the distractions of city life, the calm of country life, and the hazards of being a landlord. Without their intellectual contributions we cannot understand houses as homes, or lives as lifestyles.

Documentary Media. In addition to the remains of public and domestic buildings, and existing literature, Romans documented their lives in various artistic media. Traditional Roman households kept portrait busts of deceased relatives, as well as wax death masks, which were then worn by participants in funeral processions. Larger statuary depicting prominent Roman citizens, as well as art commissioned by the Roman state, allow us to see a more public side of Roman life. From these sources details about Roman clothing come to life. We are able to re-create among other items the forms of the Roman gentleman's *toga*, the lady's *palla*, and the soldier's boots. The materials and colors, however, are known mostly through their descriptions in Latin literature, and from what few articles survive of ancient Roman clothing. Careful comparison of the many statues produced throughout Roman history and across the Roman world helps us to understand how clothing differed by region and era.

Contemporary Attitudes. Other aspects of Roman life, such as education, have a narrower range of documentary media. Individuals with a vested interest in education describe the nature of the ancient Roman curricula and the quality of instruction. These same authors also reveal contemporary attitudes about schooling, as well as how some students responded to their instructors. Likewise, the Roman diet has fewer documentary sources than architecture, for example, and what we know comes primarily from literary sources.

Leisure Activities. Some of the most fully documented activities are those leisure-time pursuits enjoyed by crowds around the entire Roman world. As the influence of Rome encroached upon native cultures outside of the capital city and the Italian peninsula, the Romans placed their stamp of *Romanitas* ("Roman-ness") everywhere they went. Town planning was standardized to include public baths, a theater, an amphitheater, and a town center or *forum*. Aqueducts ensured a continuous supply of water for drinking, bathing, laundering, and anything else that required it. Paved roads ensured efficient transportation, particularly of Roman soldiers. Cities on the Italian peninsula and in Gaul, Britain, and Africa displayed the unmistakable characteristics of mother Rome.

Free Time. The large public buildings where all classes of Roman society gathered to relax, to exercise, or to be entertained provide the most obvious evidence of how they spent their leisure time. Various artistic media portray circus races, wild beast hunts, gladiators, and theatrical performances. Many Roman authors discuss these same topics in various literary genres. All these sources combined provide so fully detailed a description of leisure pursuits as to suggest that Romans had too much leisure time at their disposal. Such a suggestion is not entirely inaccurate, but must be considered within a well-defined historical context.

War and Change. The era of the Punic Wars (246–146 B.C.E.) was a dramatic turning point in the development of Roman culture. As a result of the First Punic War (246–241) Rome gained control of the island of Sicily, the first thrust of expansion beyond the Italian peninsula. More importantly in terms of cultural development, Romans were now engaging more actively with societies whose cultural origins were Greek rather than Italian. Until this time, Roman contact with Greek culture was scant and confined to the Greek cities of southern Italy and whatever Rome's Etruscan neighbors had managed to assimilate. The conquest of Sicily, however, brought Roman soldiers into full contact with things Greek. They naturally had the opportunity to view Greek-style theater and art, both of which found a new home in Rome. They also witnessed the luxury of Greek court life, and the amenities of Greek cities. During the era of the Punic Wars the first playwrights began to work at Rome. The Greek playwright Livius Andronicus was brought from Tarentum to Rome, where he translated the works of Homer and Greek plays. Plautus and Terence were also active during this era and wrote comedies in Latin based on Greek models but intended for a Latin-speaking audience.

Traditions Threatened. As a result of the Second Punic War (218–201 B.C.E.), Rome gained control of Spain and therefore the desirable resources of precious metal mines on the Iberian peninsula. Roman interest and affinity for Greek culture continued to grow as a result of wars fought in the East, particularly with Macedonia (215–147 B.C.E.), and the conquest of these areas had a significant impact on the course of cultural development back at Rome. Many educated Greeks were brought back to Rome, usually as slaves, and they found new homes within the families of Rome's socially and economically privileged upper classes, where they often functioned as tutors to their owners' children. Many such Greeks brought with them their philosophical principles and trades, including the practice of medicine. With the destruction of Carthage (146 B.C.E.) following the Third Punic War and the fall of the Greek city-state of Corinth in the same year, Rome's dominance in the Mediterranean was fixed. The newfound wealth of material resources from the East lined the coffers of both state and private citizens, and from this era forward Romans enjoyed an increase in purchasing power for luxury goods on a scale previously unknown to Rome.

Acceptance of Change. As a result of wars of conquest, Rome's economic power grew within the last two centuries of the old, traditional Republic, and therefore many of the traditionally elite classes were slow to accept changes that they perceived as a threat to the traditional ways of Roman life. Not every Roman embraced the Hellenistic Greek culture that was seeping into a traditionally conservative, practical Roman society. Marcus Porcius Cato, who advocated the destruction of Carthage, was no enthusiastic supporter of Greek culture, and although he understood the value of learning the Greek language he remained scornful of Greek tutors and disdainful of Romans who affected Greek ways. Such xenophobia explains in part why Romans, who had been enjoying Greek-style entertainment in the form of theatrical productions, did not have a permanent theater in which to produce them until 55 B.C.E. The conservative Roman suspicion of mass public gatherings, particularly of the lower classes, also explains their reluctance to provide a permanent place in which crowds of people might gather. By the time of the Augustan era, Rome had three permanent theaters, at least two circuses, and its first large public bathing facility. Any reservations about public assemblies seem to have been shed by the end of Augustus's reign (14 C.E.).

Greek Influence. Rome's growing fondness for large public buildings gleaming with marble exteriors is a direct result of her contact with the Hellenistic cities where Greeks had long been erecting such structures. In spite of such changes in attitudes toward public gathering places, Romans continued to impose upon public audiences a hierarchical structure to reflect the socio-economic distinctions of class and gender. Romans in attendance at the theater and amphitheater sat according to rank; the first fourteen rows of seats were reserved for senators, with *equites* (knights) behind them, and so on. Women and slaves could occupy the seats furthest from the stage. Only at the circus did men and women mingle freely.

Changing Tastes. As Rome conquered the Mediterranean and beyond, she grew not only rich but also more sophisticated in matters of taste and elegance. The outward appearance of Rome's large public buildings received aesthetic attention, and so too did private homes, wardrobes, and dinner tables. Many works of Greek art found their way into Roman public buildings and the private homes of Roman generals responsible for subjugating Greek cities. As more territory was amassed in the form of provinces, more Roman men had opportunities to engage in foreign service, and the less scrupulous of them extorted money and property from their provinces. Some of this wealth was spent on expensive building materials in private homes, including various marbles from outside of Italy that were not previously used in domestic architecture.

Cutting Edge. Although the basic shape of clothing did not change radically during the Roman Empire, different fabrics and colors came in and out of fashion as the rich often expressed their affluence by displaying the most recent developments in materials and pigments. Perhaps the most outrageous display of wastefulness was found in Roman dining rooms. At least from the time of Augustus onward we find many literary references to food and con-temporary dining practices. Just as some Romans strove to be on the cutting edge of fashion, some also exerted a great deal of effort to create new culinary delights from a host of exotic ingredients. Romans not only served strange new foods but also hosted large dinner parties with entertainment. The host tried to combine a menu of enticingly diverse dishes for a guest list of equally interesting friends and acquaintances.

Conspicuous Consumption. From the era of the Punic Wars onward, Rome periodically enacted sumptuary laws that were meant to curb conspicuous consumption and extravagant personal appearance. The first of these ordinances, the *lex Oppia* of 215 B.C.E. (Oppian Law), was sponsored by the tribune Gaius Oppius and forbade women to own more than half an ounce of gold, to wear multicolored clothing, or to ride in two-horsed vehicles within the city of Rome. Although this particular law was associated with efforts to reduce the consumption of resources during a period of warfare, not every sumptuary law could claim such an excuse. Naturally these measures were directed at people who could afford to spend a great deal of money on food, houses, and clothing, namely the upper class. The *lex Oppia* was subsequently repealed in 195, but other laws followed during the next fifty years. Further legislation attempted to regulate the amount of money people could spend on private entertainment, the number of guests at such entertainments, and other aspects of personal conduct. It seems that outside of efforts to conserve resources in times of war, efforts to enforce conformity and adherence to more traditionally frugal Roman customs were the causes for these legal restrictions.

Public Entertainment. Toward the end of the Republic, Romans were spending huge amounts of money not only for their personal comfort but for public entertainment as well. As tastes became more sophisticated along with the expansion of the Roman world, there was a corresponding development in the scale and variety of public entertainment produced at Rome. Entertainment paid for by a public official was deemed necessary to ensure that man's future political success as he moved up the *cursus honorum*. Novelty and variety were desirable qualities. Theatrical productions of comedy in the third and second centuries B.C.E. competed with various other attractions, including gladiatorial combat. Although gladiatorial combat was originally associated with funeral rites, and probably of Etruscan origin, eventually the producers of public spectacles realized the potential to please a Roman audience with the violence of bloody sport. Gaius Julius Caesar was the first Roman to produce gladiatorial combat not actually affiliated with the funeral of a deceased family member. Instead, he put on a show to honor the memory of his deceased daughter; a subtle slight of hand that would change the course of public spectacles forever.

Animals and Sport. Before the end of the Republic, Roman officials were trying hard to exhibit animals not native to Italy in order to produce truly novel spectacles. The first exotic animals came in 275 B.C.E. when Marcus

Curius Dentatus brought the first elephants to Rome. The animals were captured from the Greeks fighting under the direction of Pyrrhus in southern Italy, and their display in Rome set the precedent for the use of exotic animals for the entertainment of Roman audiences. A mere display, however, did not hold an audience's attention for long. Soon these animals were expected to die a bloody and painful death for the delight of the Roman people. Gladiators were trained in large numbers and fought in public spectacles. Just as the Roman appetite for exotic foods grew with the growing hegemony of Rome, so too did the Roman appetite for violent spectator sports.

Public Spectacles. Even though lions were dying by the hundreds by the end of the Republic, the number of public spectacles produced and their variety would reach unprecedented highs during the Roman Empire. As early as the reign of Augustus the emperor realized that the production of public entertainment was a valuable device to keep the masses of Roman people occupied, and therefore less concerned about a government in which they were taking less and less of an active role. Animals were shipped to Rome from all areas of Roman influence. Gladiators were pitted against one another in various combinations of expertise and training. The *naumachia* or staged naval battle re-created historical maritime events on lakes and artificial bodies of water created for this purpose. Criminals condemned to die by exposure to wild beasts became featured attractions. The spectrum of different displays was limited only by human imagination, for human ingenuity solved any technical issues.

Cruelty Popular. Ironically, one of the crowning achievements of Roman architecture was meant to house public spectacles on an unprecedented scale. The Flavian Amphitheater, better known as the Colosseum, was dedicated in 80 C.E. and was not only a tremendous feat of Roman engineering but a marvel of technical wizardry as well. The Colosseum employed various sub-arena devices to ensure the greatest variety of stage tricks and the continuous appearance of animals throughout the many hours of frequently produced games. From the surviving literature of Roman antiquity it appears that few people spoke out against the games until the Christian era. Thus, violent and bloody public spectacles continued for generations, and in the Colosseum gladiatorial games continued until 404 C.E. In addition to the Colosseum, the survival of ancient amphitheaters in other cities such as Pompeii, Verona, Corinth (in Greece), and Arles (in France), attests to the widespread popularity of these cruel spectacles throughout the Roman world.

Opposition. While public displays of violent sport were popular and always attracted large audiences, some Romans did not enjoy them and even wrote about their feelings of disgust at the violence. Romans who spoke (or wrote) against the games were few and far between, especially in the pagan era. As Christianity spread in the Roman world, the newly enlightened began to voice their concerns about the violence and meaningless death associated with mass public entertainment. The public arena, of course, had been used to execute Christians beginning in the first century C.E.

Rest and Relaxation. Not every leisure activity necessarily involved viewing violent and bloody sport. Just as the Roman amphitheater provided the most suitable setting for the production and viewing of spectator sports, the Roman baths provided the setting for indulging in comfort and relaxation. The act of public bathing as a social pastime is largely unknown to modern Americans. To a Roman, however, going to the baths was more than a mechanical cleansing routine; it was a social opportunity during which one indulged in pampering oneself, and incidentally an opportunity to take some exercise. The first large imperial bath complex at Rome was constructed by Marcus Vipsanius Agrippa during the reign of Augustus, but his contribution to the ritual of bathing pales in comparison to the truly mammoth and opulent facilities that were to follow. Some of the later complexes could accommodate more than one thousand bathers at a time. The comfort and luxury of the imperial *thermae* can only be approximated by modern health spas. Although Roman baths offered space for exercise, the primary object in patronizing the baths was to relax, socialize, and maintain personal hygiene. The lack of baths in private homes ensured a steady clientele of patrons who used the public baths frequently. Outside of the arenas for public spectacles, the baths were probably the only other place a Roman citizen was sure to be found with any regularity during the Empire. Maintaining the *thermae* was a huge undertaking that required not only human resources but also enormous quantities of water and fuel for heating. The baths therefore could stay active only so long as these resources were available. During the Gothic War of the sixth century C.E., the aqueducts to Rome were cut, thus leaving many baths out of order.

TOPICS IN LEISURE, RECREATION, AND DAILY LIFE

CLOTHING

Layers of Clothing. In the modern world we are accustomed to wearing several layers of clothing; we wear undergarments, pants, dresses, skirts, shirts, sweaters, jackets, suits, coats, and other items depending upon the weather and what individual circumstances dictate. The Romans also wore multiple layers of clothing as the seasons and their own occupations and status required.

The Man's *Tunica*. Roman men wore a basic garment called a *tunica* (tunic) over simple undergarments. The tunic was a rectangular slip with an opening at the top to allow the garment to fit over the head, and openings on either side for the arms. The ordinary tunic was woven in two pieces, and sewn together at the shoulders, though tunics woven in one piece are known to have existed. Throughout the Republic and into the High Empire, tunics were either sleeveless or had short sleeves, and the length was adjusted to fall just below the knee by means of a belt at the waist. By the early third century C.E., as a result of Eastern cultural influences, the Roman *toga* assumed the longer sleeves and greater body length of similar garments found in Eastern societies. More than one tunic could be worn in response to cooler weather. Men of the upper classes typically wore white tunics, while working men perhaps wore darker colors. The usual material was wool woven in a variety of textures to accommodate the needs and resources of the wearer, though fine thread was used to weave more elegant fabric for more luxurious tunics. Men of senatorial rank wore a broad purple stripe on their tunics, while equestrians wore a narrow purple stripe to indicate rank.

The *Toga*. For formal occasions and appearances in public the Roman man wore a *toga* (toga) over his tunic. The privilege of wearing a toga was reserved for male Roman citizens; slaves could not wear the Roman toga. The toga consisted of a large piece of cloth (in the first century C.E. typically almost twenty feet long), elaborately draped around a man's body, and the help of a second person was often necessary to dress a man properly in his toga. This piece of clothing gave the Roman man an air of dig-

---

A GENTLEMAN'S WARDROBE

Whenever a male Roman citizen appeared in public, custom dictated that he wear his toga. This one piece of clothing was so important that, by itself, it visually proclaimed the distinction between slave and free, as well as between Roman and foreign. Their more conservative peers frowned upon Roman men who declined to dress according to their station. In his work concerning the decline of oratory, Cornelius Tacitus makes a derogatory reference to Romans appearing in public wearing only their tunics:

Again, is there an accomplishment, the fame and glory of which are to be compared with the distinction of an orator? Whom, as he passes by, do the ignorant mob and the men with the tunic oftener speak of by name and point out with the finger?

Source: Cornelius Tacitus, *Dialogue on Orators 7*, translated by Alfred John Church and William Jackson Brodribb (New York: Random House, 1942).

---

nity, but it could also impede his movement, and therefore the toga was not a garment worn by common laborers who needed to move freely. The usual color of the toga was white, though the Emperor and select individuals could wear a purple toga. Individuals in mourning often wore a black or darkly colored toga (the *toga pulla*).

Changing Styles. The size of the toga, and thus the method of draping it around one's body, changed across Roman history. From statues we can see these changes and reconstruct the history of the Roman toga. From the earliest representation of a toga in statuary, we can assume that in the third century B.C.E. the toga was less voluminous than those of the later Republican period, which are also represented in statuary. The earlier toga seems to have reached to the middle of the shin, while statues dating later in the Republic show that the toga reached to the feet. By far the most voluminous example of the Roman toga came from the period of the Empire. The proportions of the imperial toga required slightly

By the time of Augustus, Roman men were appearing regularly in public without their togas. Augustus tried to revive the traditional Roman dress and to enforce the wearing of a toga in and around the Forum:

Augustus set himself to revive the ancient Roman dress and once, on seeing a group of men in dark cloaks among the crowd, quoted Virgil indignantly: 'Behold them, conquerors of the world, all clad in Roman gowns!' and instructed the aediles that no one should ever again be admitted to the Forum, or its environs, unless he wore a gown (toga) and no cloak.

Source: Gaius Suetonius Tranquillus, *De uita Caesarum* (*Augustus* 40), translated by Robert Graves (London: Penguin, 1957).

Statue of Emperor Titus dressed in a toga, circa 80 C.E. (Vatican Museum, Rome, Braccio Nuovo, Inv. No. 2282)

different methods of draping to accommodate the mass of material, which can be seen in statuary of the imperial era.

Wearing the Toga. The toga was fashioned from an expanse of material roughly semicircular in shape and was draped around the body in such a way that the right shoulder and arm were left uncovered while the bulk of the toga was carried over the left shoulder and arm. The wearer could pull the toga over his right shoulder and arm, and even over his head, as we can see from statues depicting such styles. Wool was the typical material, since it could be spun and woven in a variety of weights appropriate for differing climates and weather. High Roman officials had the privilege of wearing a purple border (*latus clavus* or "laticlave") on their toga, like the *toga praetexta* that (perhaps surprisingly) Roman boys were allowed to wear until they officially donned the pure-white *toga virilis* (toga of manhood) at about the age of sixteen.

Cloaks. Since the toga was a formal garment and not entirely practical, various cloaks of a more utilitarian nature were worn in antiquity. Cloaks were generally draped about the shoulders and fastened in front by means of strings or a garment pin called a *fibula*, which was sometimes used to fasten the cloak on the shoulder. The shape of the cloak varied from rectangular to semicircular and like most garments was made of wool. Some cloaks also had a hood or a cowl for further protection from the elements.

The Woman's *Tunica*. The woman's tunic, worn over basic undergarments, was longer and wider than the man's, and generally had longer sleeves, though sleeve length was often determined by weather. Women of all classes around Roman Europe wore similar tunics, though the quality and weight of the fabric varied according to individual circumstances. The length of the tunic was adjusted by controlling excess material with a belt at the waist. Slaves and other working women would naturally wear their tunics higher so as not to impede their movement. The tunic worn by Roman matrons in public differed from tunics worn by the lower classes, and was called a *stola* from the first century B.C.E. on. The *stola* was long enough to cover the lady's feet and bore a border sewed to the lower edge of the garment.

Proper Roman women did not appear in public unless they were dressed as *pudicitia* (modesty) dictated. In practical terms, this meant that almost no part of her body was visible to an onlooker except for her face and hands, which could in any case be shielded within the folds of her *palla*. Quintus Horatius Flaccus (Horace) mocks the sexual indulgence of his generation, saying how difficult it is to get a really good look at a proper Roman lady when she is fully dressed.

With a married lady you can't see a thing except her face. The rest is covered by her long dress . . . if you want forbidden fruit protected by a wall (and that, I may say, is what drives you crazy) you'll find a host of snags . . . a dress (*stola*) reaching to the ankles, and on top of that a wrap (*palla*)—a hundred things prevent you from getting a clear view.

Source: Horace, *Sermones* 1.2.94–100, in *Horace: Satires and Epistles; Persius: Satires*, translated by Niall Rudd (London: Penguin, 1987).

Statue of a woman and a little girl wearing pallas, circa 50 B.C.E. (Palazzo dei Conservatori, Rome, Braccio Nuovo, Inv. No. 2176)

The *Palla*. Outside of their homes Roman women wore a type of shawl called a *palla*, which was the Roman lady's equivalent of the toga. This outer garment was typically made of wool, though lighter material might have been used for hot weather. Roman matrons were expected to wear the *palla* in public, much as Roman men were expected to appear in a toga. The *palla*, though varying in size, was usually large enough to extend to the knees and could be brought over the head. This garment was a necessary staple in the Roman woman's wardrobe and did not seem to change for several centuries. However, by the end of the third century C.E. women preferred a smaller version of the *palla* when the weather did not require the warmth of the larger garment. Statuary from Italy and the provinces show women dressed in a very similar fashion. While the shape of these garments was rather static, women used color and decoration to vary their wardrobes.

Children's Garments. Children dressed much as their fathers and mothers, but freeborn Roman boys were allowed to wear the *toga praetexta*, a child-sized toga with a purple border indicating their status as Roman citizen children. Roman boys also wore a good luck charm called a *bulla*, which like the toga was a sign of a freeborn Roman citizen. When Roman boys officially entered adulthood, at about the age of sixteen, they stopped wearing the *toga praetexta* and the *bulla*, dedicating the latter to their household gods; they then assumed the plain white toga of manhood, the *toga virilis*. Just before they were married, Roman girls put aside their childhood clothes as well.

Tunics and Cloaks for Children. Roman boys wore tunics with narrow purple stripes. These tunics were essentially the same in form as those of the Roman adult male, and similarly girt about the waist to control the length of the garment. Girls' tunics were stylistically the same as the boys' though typically worn longer. Roman children probably wore cloaks of the same type as those worn by Roman adults.

Sources:
Judith Lynn Sebesta and Larissa Bonfante, eds., *The World of Roman Costume* (Madison: University of Wisconsin Press, 1994).

Lilian M. Wilson, *The Clothing of the Ancient Romans* (Baltimore: Johns Hopkins University Press, 1938).

TRADITIONAL SIMPLICITY IN THE ROYAL HOUSEHOLD

Augustus, always vigilant in his revival of traditional Roman customs, kept an ordinary wardrobe of clothing made for him by the women of his family.

On all but special occasions he wore house-clothes woven and sewn for him by either Livia, Octavia, Julia, or one of his grand-daughters.

Source: Gaius Suetonius Tranquillus, *De uita Caesarum* (*Augustus* 40), translated by Robert Graves (London: Penguin, 1957).

Wedding ring, gold with a cameo, from the late third or fourth century C.E. and reportedly found in France (Walters Art Gallery, Baltimore, 57.1824)

CLOTHING: HEAD WEAR, FOOTWEAR, AND JEWELRY

Covered Heads. Throughout much of the Republic, Roman women customarily covered their heads in public. In addition to using the *palla* to cover her head, a Roman matron had a variety of other small garments specifically for this purpose. Small mantles and kerchiefs were also typical head coverings, and wives of certain priests had special garments for this purpose. By the time of Augustus, however, we see in statuary women with their heads either covered or uncovered, and thus the practice of covering the head seems to have become a matter of personal choice.

Hair-Grooming. Details of the Romans' personal grooming habits were often similar to those of the modern world. Men and women patronized barbers (*tonsor*) and hairdressers (*ornatrix*), and wealthy Romans even owned slaves trained in these occupations. Large imperial bath complexes sometimes offered these services, and many Roman men even had excess body hair removed by a professional at the baths. Dyeing hair was a common practice, and both men and women did it. But hair dye must have been far more harsh in antiquity without the benefit of scientific research. Ovid devotes an entire poem (*Amores* 1.14) to the damaged hair of his mistress, who used hair dyes so imprudently that her hair fell out.

Jewelry. Women wore cosmetics and jewelry, and changed their hairstyles to keep up with current fashions. During the Empire it was fashionable for women to wear elaborate hairpieces that added height to their stature. Statues from this period show us what Roman women looked like with such hairstyles. Jewelry for men consisted almost exclusively of finger rings, and anything more was considered effeminate. The typical man's ring was a symbol of his citizen status, and only members of the upper classes could wear such a ring made of gold. Other men wore the citizen's ring fashioned from iron. Women's jewelry included earrings, finger rings, bracelets, armlets, necklaces, brooches, pendants, pins, and gems for the adornment of their hair. Gold was the precious metal of choice, and many examples of superbly worked gold jewelry from Roman antiquity have been discovered, though silver and bronze were also used to fashion jewelry. Metal was often engraved, and could also be set with precious stones or gems.

Footgear. The footgear Roman men and women wore reflected their social status as well as their occupations. Archaeological and artistic evidence from around the entire Roman world reveals that Romans used leather, wood, cork, felt, metal, and plant fibers to construct footgear. Many types of sandals, shoes, boots, and slippers were worn by the ancient Romans. Naturally, climate as well as local custom determined in part the type of footgear and the materials from which it was made. Socks, or other kinds of linings, are known to have existed from archaeological and literary evidence, though few examples have survived from antiquity.

Necklace with a gold medallion of a marriage scene (early fifth century C.E.) and a hematite intaglio of Abrasax, a cock-headed deity with serpent legs (second–third centuries C.E.) (Metropolitan Museum of Art, New York, Rogers Fund, 1958, 58.12)

Sandals, Shoes, and Boots. Both men and women wore sandals, *soleae* or *sandalia,* with various strap and thong arrangements for keeping the sole of the sandal attached to the foot. Sandals were typically worn only indoors, and they were not considered appropriately formal for appearing in public. A type of sandal called *sculponae* was favored in Germany and England. This slip-on sandal consisted of a high wooden sole with a leather strap to keep it in place. In the damp conditions of northern Europe *sculponae* probably lasted longer than sandals made entirely from leather. Sturdier shoes called *calcei* fully enclosed the foot, as opposed to the open sandals, and were the standard shoe appropriate for wear in public. *Calcei,* therefore, were worn with the *toga* and *palla* as part of the formal dress of Roman citizens. Peasants and farmers, and probably slaves who worked on farms, wore footgear called *perones,* which were either a simple boot or shoe of leather. The appearance of such shoes is uncertain.

Caligae. Roman soldiers wore military boots called *caligae* (singular *caliga*). These boots were made from a single piece of leather and consisted of an innersole and a thicker hobnailed outer sole, as well as a network of straps over the ankle. The toes were left open. *Caligae* were the regulation footgear of all soldiers up to the rank of centurion, and were worn in all areas of the Empire through the first century C.E. By the second century C.E. soldiers in the northern provinces stopped wearing the *caligae,* probably in favor of boots that more fully covered the entire foot. Statues and paintings depicting generals, emperors, horsemen, and deities show these figures wearing high boots, often with elaborate decorations, although no examples of such boots have been found.

Sources:
Judith Lynn Sebesta and Larissa Bonfante, eds., *The World of Roman Costume* (Madison: University of Wisconsin Press, 1994).

Lilian M. Wilson, *The Clothing of the Ancient Romans* (Baltimore: Johns Hopkins University Press, 1938).

CLOTHING: LEATHER AND TEXTILES

Preparing Leather. Leather used in making footwear came from various animals and was prepared by scraping and tanning. Color could be added to the leather, but since dyeing material of any kind could be expensive, much footwear was left in the natural color of the leather. The process of preparing leather for use in clothing and dyeing produced terrible smells, and therefore tanneries seem to have been located around the margins of Roman cities, at least as far as the archaeological evidence in Rome and Pompeii shows. In Rome, the tanning industry was located across the Tiber, away from the heart of the city. In Pompeii, it was near one of the city gates away from the center of the city.

Materials and Coloring. Wool was the most common material used for clothing, and it came mostly from domestic sheep. In the early days of the Republic, most wool was used without dyeing, the only color variation being the result of naturally occurring differences in the color of the

---

WHY PAY TOP DOLLAR?

In the third book of his mock-didactic poem, the *Ars amatoria* (*Art of Love*), Publius Ovidius Naso (Ovid) instructs women how to use artistic skill to produce beautiful looks when nature has not supplied sufficient beauty. He also warns against spending too much money on expensively dyed clothing, such as the *dibaphos* or "double-dipped" cloth that was consecutively dyed in two types of purple dye:

What now of dress? Put rich brocades aside and stuffs in Tyrian purple double-dyed. Now that of cheaper colours there's no lack, it's mad to bear one's fortune on one's back.

Source: Publius Ovidius Naso, *Ars amatoria* 3.169–172, in *Ovid: The Love Poems,* translated by A. D. Melville (Oxford: Oxford University Press 1990).

---

wool right off the sheep. Southern Italy was the center of the wool industry in Italy, but as Rome continued to come into contact with other nations and cultures, by the late Republic Romans began to use the wool of sheep from other parts of the world. The spinning of wool into yarn or thread and the weaving of cloth were occupations almost every Roman girl learned from the women of her family.

Fabrics. Linen was always produced in Italy, but a finer product was available from Egypt. Spain and Sicily also had thriving fabric industries and provided Italians with another source of linen and other fabrics. Cotton was also known from eastern civilizations, and so too was silk. Silk remained the most expensive of fabrics, and therefore most silk was sold in thread form, which was then interwoven with other kinds of threads.

Fabric Dyes. Most clothing was white but could be decorated with simple details, particularly around the borders. The ancients used a vast array of plant, animal, and mineral extracts to make dyes for their clothing. Materials and equipment used for making dyes were expensive, and the dyeing process required great amounts of water and fuel. Therefore people would not have made dyes and dyed their cloth at home. Rather, dye shops specialized in providing such services. The most expensive color to produce was purple, and was often associated with the elite classes of Roman citizens. By the time of the Empire fabric and color had become indications of the wealth of those wearing them. The spectrum of luxury colors continued to grow in the Empire, and the rich continued to pursue the newest and most expensive colors in a gaudy display of materialism.

Fullers. Special tradespeople known as fullers operated shops where cloth was cleaned, shrunk, and softened. Fullers also laundered and repaired soiled and worn clothing, as well as re-dyed faded clothes. Alkaline soil was used as a type of soap to launder cloth and clothing. Urine, too, was an important chemical for the cleaning of woolen garments. Fullers washed clothing by treading upon the items in large vats, a practice that existed not only in Italy but also in other areas of the Empire. Fullers bleached white fabric by means of burning sulfur. Clothing to be bleached was stretched on a wicker frame while still damp, then subjected to the fumes of the burning sulfur, and then washed a second time.

Sources:
Judith Lynn Sebesta and Larissa Bonfante, eds., *The World of Roman Costume* (Madison: University of Wisconsin Press, 1994).

Lilian M. Wilson, *The Clothing of the Ancient Romans* (Baltimore: Johns Hopkins University Press, 1938).

EDUCATION

Parental Supervision. The type of education Romans received depended largely upon their gender and socio-economic status. Although many Romans remained illiterate, many others learned basic reading and writing skills. For the children of wealthy families, the study of reading and writing often began at home and then continued when the children attended school. Both fathers and mothers took an active interest in their children's education.

Tutors. Roman men often took pride in teaching their own children rather than entrusting them to foreign slaves or poor instructors. However, sometimes circumstances prevented fathers from instructing their children regularly. Men pursuing a military career could be absent from home for long periods of time, while politicians constantly worked in the Forum or Senate house. Therefore, a carefully chosen tutor was more often the favored method of educating children.

Gendered Education. By the age of twelve, girls stopped attending school while those boys who showed intellectual promise continued their education. Girls were expected to learn domestic economy from the other women in their families. The skills of spinning and weaving were taught to all Roman girls at all levels of society, since Roman women were expected to produce cloth and make clothing for the family.

The Basics. As a result of the wars with Eastern nations during the second century B.C.E., many educated Greeks were enslaved, brought to Rome, and employed as tutors in the homes of wealthy Romans. They often set up their own schools where they taught Roman children for a fee. Children whose families could not or did not have tutors at home attended primary schools to learn the fun-

damental principles of reading, writing, and arithmetic. Boys and girls often attended school together for several years beginning at the age of seven, though not all schools were necessarily coeducational. Slaves called "pedagogues," whose duty it was to accompany children outside their homes, monitored the children's progress and helped them with their studies.

School Furnishings. Students did not have comfortable chairs and desks; instead, they sat on wooden benches and wrote their lessons on tablets, which they held on their laps. The tablets consisted of planks of wood covered with wax. One wrote on the tablet by scratching words into the wax with a *stylus*. The writer could smooth over the wax to correct mistakes, or to "erase" what was written in order to use the tablets over again. Playing games with the letters of the alphabet fashioned out of ivory or wood helped children to recognize letters, while teachers taught their students to write letters on their tablets. Typically a teacher would make an outline of a letter on a tablet and the student then traced over the letter with his own stylus. Children used their fingers and pebbles to learn to count, and eventually learned to use an abacus for more complex reckoning. Not every Roman child attended school, however. Although parents might have taught their children the rudiments of reading, writing, and arithmetic, many Roman boys and girls began to learn a trade at a fairly young age.

Educational Standards. Much was learned through rote memorization and recitation, which must not have been very exciting for young students. The letters of the alpha-

Detail from a third-century C.E. sarcophagus depicting a young girl listening to a teacher (Oronoz, Palazzo Rondanini, Rome)

Cato the Elder (Marcus Porcius Cato) would not allow his son to be taught by a slave, and so he undertook the child's education himself.

As soon as the boy had reached the age of understanding, Cato took him over and began to teach him to read and write. As a matter of fact, he did have a slave called Chilo who had taught plenty of children reading and writing, but, as he himself says, if his son was slow on the uptake, he did not want him to be told off or have his ear pulled by a slave, and he did not think it right for his son to be indebted to a slave for such important information.

Cornelius Tacitus wrote a biography of his father-in-law, Gnaeus Julius Agricola, a governor of Britain, in which he indicates that Agricola's mother, Julia Procilla, closely supervised her son's upbringing and education. According to Tacitus, she did not allow him to indulge his interest in philosophy at a young age.

His mother was Julia Procilla, a lady of singular virtue. Brought up by her side with fond affection, he passed his boyhood and youth in the cultivation of every worthy attainment. He was guarded from the enticements of the profligate not only by his own good and straightforward character, but also by having, when quite a child, the scene and guide of his studies, Massilia, a place where refinement and provincial frugality were blended and happily combined. I remember that he used to tell us how in his early youth, he would have imbibed a keener love of philosophy than became a Roman senator, had not his mother's good sense checked his excited and ardent spirit.

Traditionally, Roman men oversaw their sons' education, teaching them basic reading and writing skills before the children entered a school or before engaging the services of a tutor. Fathers also desired that their daughters learn to read and write, and many fathers took just as much care to see their daughters educated properly as they did for their sons. Often widowed women oversaw their children's education, or they relied upon the help of male relatives.

Sources: Plutarch, *Cato maior* 20, in *Plutarch, Roman Lives: A Selection of Eight Roman Lives,* translated by Robin Waterfield (Oxford: Oxford University Press, 1999).

Tacitus, *Agricola* 4.2–3, translated by Alfred John Church and William Jackson Brodribb (New York: Random House, 1942).

bet, as well as addition and multiplication tables, were learned in singsong chants. The Romans did not have state-enforced educational standards and curricula as we do today; the quality of Roman education therefore varied greatly from school to school. Since there were no state-appointed and -funded teaching positions in Rome until the time of the Emperor Vespasian, teachers depended upon the fees they collected to earn a living and pay for rented space where they taught. Often teachers held class in open, outdoors spaces where they were likely to attract the attention of adults who wanted to find a teacher for their children. If the teacher was lucky, he managed to use space near the Forum, where he was visible to the many Romans passing by or engaging in activities nearby. Eventually, if the teacher attracted enough students, he could afford to rent a more suitable location for his classes. Furthermore, there were no laws that prevented teachers from beating their students.

Secondary Education. In their secondary education, boys studied both Greek and Latin literature taught by a *grammaticus.* Greek was considered a useful language not only for the purposes of communication but also to build a solid foundation for further studies in rhetoric and oratory. Boys left these secondary schools when they assumed the *toga virilis,* at which time they became attached to an adult mentor who guided the young man's political education. Ideally, the young Roman man accompanied his father, or another male relative or close

family friend, and from him learned details of political and social protocol, as well as moral deportment. A young man usually served an apprenticeship in the army for military training (*tirocinium*), even if he had no intention of making his career in the military. Young men who hoped to pursue careers in law or politics furthered their formal education by studying rhetoric and oratory under the direction of a *rhetor* and attending lectures by well-known philosophers. From the late Republic on, gentlemen of the ruling classes often took a tour of the intellectual centers of the Greek world, visiting such places as Athens and Rhodes where they would become better acquainted with Greek philosophy.

Sources:

Stanley F. Bonner, *Education in Ancient Rome: From the Elder Cato to the Younger Pliny* (London: Eyre Methuen, 1977).

Teresa Morgan, *Literate Education in the Hellenistic and Roman Worlds* (Cambridge & New York: Cambridge University Press, 1998).

Thomas Wiedemann, *Adults and Children in the Roman Empire* (New Haven: Yale University Press, 1989).

ENTERTAINMENT

Leisure Activities. A great variety of leisure activities occupied the free time of Romans from every class of society. Men, women, boys, and girls enjoyed social activities ranging from playing simple board games to viewing competitive spectacles (*spectacula*) in the arena. Leisure time was most often spent in daily trips to public baths and attending theatrical productions and other large public spectacles in the circus or amphitheater. Competitors in public spectacles were almost exclusively slaves, freedmen, or foreigners. Roman citizens did not feel it was proper for citizens to appear in public spectacles.

The Baths. Since most Romans did not have bathing facilities in their homes, public bathing became the usual method of maintaining personal hygiene. Bath complexes, which came to be called *thermae* during the reign of Augustus, were either state-funded or run by private companies. Although bathing was originally a practical activity for keeping clean, eventually public bathing became a popular social activity among all classes and both sexes. By the fourth century C.E. there were approximately one thousand public baths in the city of Rome itself. Almost every town in Italy and the Roman Empire had at least one public bathing facility. Bath establishments not only housed rooms for bathing, but some large and well-appointed complexes also included areas for exercise, swimming, massage, hair removal, and reading.

Various Temperatures. A complete bathing regimen involved passing through several rooms whose temperatures varied. A bather left his or her clothing in the dressing room, or *apodyterium*. The *caldarium*, or hot room, was the first room of the baths visited after disrobing. The heat of the *caldarium* was maintained by hot air piped into hollow spaces built into the walls and under the floors. The *caldarium* also contained tubs filled and kept hot with water from a furnace. The temperature of the next room, the *tepidarium*, was lower than that of the *caldarium*. The coolest room in the sequence was the *frigidarium*. *Thermae* sometimes also included a sweat room called either a *laconicum* or *sudatorium*. The warmer rooms were often outfitted with cold plunge pools to allow the bathers to cool themselves periodically during their bathing activities. People who took exercise before bathing used a curved, hand-held scraper called a *strigil* to remove the dirt, sweat, and oil from their bodies before entering the baths.

A REAL CROWD PLEASER

Even though gladiatorial combat had become a means of keeping crowds of Roman citizens occupied in their leisure hours, some people still produced these games in honor of their deceased releatives. Pliny the Younger writes to his friend Valerius Maximus about the games that Valerius gave in Verona, in honor of his deceased wife. These games not only honored her, but also repaid the people of Verona for their support of Valerius and the honors they had bestowed upon him.

You did well to put on a show of gladiators for our people of Verona, who have long shown their affection and admiration for you, and have voted you many honors. Verona was also the home-town of the excellent wife you loved so dearly, whose memory you owe some public building or show, and this kind of spectacle is particularly suitable for a funeral tribute. Moreover, the request came from so many people that a refusal would have been judged churlish rather than strong-minded on your part. You have also done admirably in giving the show so readily and on such a lavish scale, for this indicates a true spirit of generosity. I am sorry the African panthers you had bought in such quantities did not run up on the appointed day, but you deserve the credit although the weather prevented their arriving on time: it was not your fault that you could not show them. (6.34)

Seldom did anyone speak out against the savagery of arena sports until the spread of Christianity in the Roman world. Saint Augustine, in his *Confessions*, tells the story of a man who attended the amphitheater with a friend, though the man went under protest and did not intend to watch or enjoy the spectacle. However, once the games were in full swing, the loud excitement of the crowd overwhelmed the man's resistance.

As soon as he saw the blood, he at once drank in the savagery and did not turn away. His eyes were riveted. He imbibed madness. Without any awareness of what was happening to him, he found delight in the murderous contest and was inebriated by bloodthirsty pleasure. (6.8)

Sources: *Pliny: Letters*, translated by Betty Radice (London: Penguin, 1963).

Augustine, *Confessions*, translated by Henry Chadwick (Oxford: Oxford University Press, 1992).

Bath Complexes. The style and sophistication of a bath complex depended upon the region and era in which the baths were built. Pompeii and other Campanian towns show baths from the late Republic and early Empire differing in size and technical design. Baths from this region and era typically had an exercise court called a *palaestra*, which functioned as the main entrance to the facility. Marcus Vipsanius Agrippa built the first of the imperial bath complexes at Rome, which were begun around 25 B.C.E., and required the building of the *Aqua virgo*, an aqueduct meant to supply these baths with the necessary huge quantity of water.

Relief depicting a chariot race in the Circus Maximus, 180–190 C.E. (Archaeological Museum, Foligno, Italy)

Grand Scale. Several emperors from Nero to Constantine built lavishly decorated baths on a grand scale. In addition to the usual bathing rooms, grand Imperial *thermae* had *palaestrae,* libraries, fountains, and various other rooms flanking the courtyards to satisfy different functions. The plans of Imperial *thermae* were usually symmetrical, which suggests that men and women had separate, yet comparable, facilities. Marble was featured prominently in the decoration of Imperial *thermae,* as were statuary and mosaics. Clearly, during the Empire, public bathing had developed into a popular leisure activity far beyond its basic purpose of cleansing the body. Bathers enjoyed not only splendid bathing facilities but also many other recreational activities of both physical and social varieties.

Spectator Events. Romans enjoyed many varied spectator events throughout the Republic and Empire, and the reiteration of the architectural settings for these events around the Roman world shows their widespread popularity. The three types of buildings used by the Romans for sporting events were the circus, stadium, and amphitheater. While the Roman circus and stadium were derived from the Greek stadium, the amphitheater was an entirely Roman creation.

Circus Games. The circus was designed specifically for chariot races. Romans viewed races of chariots drawn by either two or four horses (*bigae* and *quadrigae,* respectively). Its shape was long and narrow, and had one curved and one rectangular end. Spectators sat in rows of seats built along both long sides and around the curved end of the circus. The first rows of the spectators' seats were reserved for senators and *equites* (knights), which was a tradition honored in the theater as well. Unlike the theater, however, men and women were free to mingle at the circus. The races began at the starting gates (*carceres*) built at the rectangular end of the track. The chariots raced along and around a long narrow island called a *spina* where counters were

located to indicate the number of laps each chariot had completed. Four teams distinguished by colored tunics (red, blue, green, and white) competed, and some spectators engaged in betting while others participated in activities characteristic of loyal fans. Rivalries between factions were common and are known to have led to mischief.

Circuses and Games. Although several different circuses are known to have existed at Rome, the oldest and most prominent was the Circus Maximus. Tradition tells us that Romulus founded the Circus Maximus in the valley between the Palatine and Aventine Hills. In addition to chariot races, a great variety of contests were produced in the Circus. The *Ludi circenses,* or Circus Games, included different types of races, gladiatorial combat, staged animal hunts called *venationes,* and other sorts of athletic contests. Besides the *Ludi romani* (Roman Games) held in September, and the *Ludi plebei* (Plebeian Games) held in November, circus games could be decreed throughout the year to celebrate military triumphs and the dedications of new buildings.

Exotic Animals. Exotic animals were displayed as early as 275 B.C.E., when Marcus Curius Dentatus brought to Rome elephants taken from Pyrrhus in southern Italy. In subsequent years triumphant Roman generals displayed animals captured from the lands they conquered, and thus continued a tradition of displaying exotic animals as part of their war booty. The *venatio* first included simply capturing or killing the animals in a staged "hunt." If the animals were not to be killed, then they were sometimes kept and trained to perform tricks. By the end of the Republic, Romans had come to expect truly exotic animals to appear in public spectacles sponsored by Roman magistrates. When Marcus Caelius Rufus was aedile in 50 B.C.E., he asked his friend Cicero (who was governor of Cilicia at the time) to send him panthers to use in the spectacles he intended to produce at Rome. As aedile, it was important for Caelius to impress the voters sufficiently to earn and keep their support. Apparently, however, Cicero did not easily fulfill Caelius's request, as he is scolded in a letter from Caelius that is preserved along with the corpus of Cicero's own letters (*Epistulae ad familiares* 8.9).

Athletic Contests. The stadium held various athletic contests, of which foot races were most frequently featured. The stadium was similar in shape to the circus, but it was shorter and had no *spina*. Several stadia were built in Rome, and seem to have been a feature of some Imperial bath complexes. The best example is the Stadium of Domitian, whose system of entrances and exits allowed the building to handle large crowds of spectators efficiently. The general shape of Domitian's stadium has been preserved by the modern-day Piazza Navona, which was developed directly on top of it.

Fan-Clubs and Riots. The ancients could be as fanatical about their spectator sports as modern Americans are about baseball and football. Romans formed associations that were the ancient equivalent of our fan clubs. The rivalries between different associations sometimes led to trouble, as Tacitus attests in the *Annales,* his history of the Julio-Claudian era of Imperial Rome (14.17). In 59 C.E. the rival factions of Pompeii and Nuceria created a riot in the amphitheater at Pompeii. The disruption and hysteria of the riot were severe enough to warrant punishment from Rome: the Pompeiians were forbidden to have any such public gathering for the next ten years, and all the associations had to be dissolved.

Amphitheaters and Gladiatorial Games. By far the most widely recognized arena associated with Roman spectator sports was the Flavian Amphitheater, which we now call the Colosseum. Although the Colosseum is the largest and most grand of Roman amphitheaters, it is not the oldest. The amphitheater at Pompeii is the oldest known amphitheater, and dates at least to the time of Sulla (circa 80 B.C.E.). The amphitheater was invented specifically to view gladiatorial combat, and seems to have its origins in Etruria and Samnite Campania, where such games existed in pre-Roman times. There, modestly scaled fights to the death were staged to honor their dead. This practice originally involved combatants who were either slaves or criminals. The fight probably took place at the burial site, and seems always to have been associated with religious ritual. Tertullian, a Christian author writing in the late second or early third century C.E., criticized the development of such games (*De spectaculis* 12).

Growth of Popularity. During the Roman Republic, gladiatorial games were not normally produced as part of the traditional public games (*ludi*) sponsored by Roman magistrates. Rather, private individuals produced gladiatorial spectacles in honor of a deceased relative (*munera*). As these games became more frequently and grandly produced, gladiatorial schools were established in Rome and Campania to train the numbers of gladiators necessary to fulfill the increasing demand. While gladiatorial spectacles were produced during the Republic as part of the funeral rites in honor of important citizens, during the Empire such games became popular spectator activities produced by the state for the purpose of mass entertainment. The construction of the Colosseum during the reigns of the Flavian emperors illustrates the prominent place that bloody spectacles came to hold in Roman leisure time pursuits.

The Flavian Amphitheater. The so-called Colosseum, begun by the emperor Vespasian and finished by his sons Titus and Domitian, could accommodate approximately fifty thousand spectators in three seating sections and one standing room section at the top. The Colosseum is said to have had an awning that could be spread and retracted by means of rigging worked by sailors. A complicated system of doors, corridors, and staircases made the facility more efficiently filled and emptied of its audience. The floor of the arena was made of wood and covered a network of animal cages and elevators used to raise beasts to floor level. Fine-grained sand covered the arena floor to absorb blood shed from combatants and animals. The term "arena" comes from the Latin word *harena,* for the sand used on the stage-level floor.

Types of Gladiators. In the early history of gladiatorial games, combatants were slaves or criminals condemned to death by fighting one another. However, the gladiators of the late Republic and the Empire could be either involuntary participants (slaves, condemned criminals, or war captives) or individuals who voluntarily bound themselves by oath. Gladiators trained in schools (also called *ludi*) under the direction of a *lanista*, who was often a former gladiator. Some slaves who trained and fought as gladiators earned their freedom and then continued to compete for high fees. Four types of gladiators existed: the *Murmillo* wore a Gallic helmet with a metal fish as a crest, and was heavily armed with an oblong shield and short sword; the *Samnite* was also heavily armed with Samnite-type weapons and a visored helmet; the *Retiarius* was lightly armed and fought with a net and trident; and the *Thracian* fought with a round shield and curved scimitar. Not all combatants, how-

---

A DAY AT THE RACES

Not all Romans were fond of horse-racing. Pliny the Younger expresses his scepticism about the originality of the races, claiming that one viewing was sufficient to satisfy his own interest.

I have been spending all the last few days amongst my notes and papers in most welcome peace. How could I in the city? The races were on, a type of spectacle which has never had the slightest attraction for me. I can find nothing new or different in them; once seen is enough, so it surprises me that so many thousands of adult men should have such a childish passion for watching galloping horses and drivers standing in chariots, over and over again.

Source: Pliny, *Epistulae* 9.6.1–2, translated by Betty Radice (London: Penguin, 1963).

Mosaic of gladiatorial combat from the Torre Nuova, Rome, fourth century C.E. (Galleria Borghese, Rome)

ever, were trained gladiators. People condemned to the beasts were often left without weapons or any other form of protection against the wild animals.

Theatrical Productions. Throughout the Republic and Empire, Roman audiences enjoyed a variety of theatrical presentations including comedies and tragedies modeled on Greek sources, as well as mime, pantomime, and farcical plays called *Atellanae* that were native to the Italian town of *Atella*. Even though Romans viewed comedy and tragedy from at least the second century B.C.E., the first permanent theater at Rome was not built until 55 B.C.E. The popular comic dramas were often disdainfully viewed as "low-brow," and actors were typically considered socially inferior. Furthermore, many Romans were initially skeptical about constructing a permanent building where the Roman masses might gather and potentially create trouble. Nevertheless, shortly after Gaius Pompeius Magnus (Pompey) dedicated his theatre in the Campus Martius in 55 B.C.E., two other theaters were constructed in the same vicinity; the theater of Balbus and the theater of Marcellus. Clearly by the end of the Republic, theatrical entertainment had become a popular and permanent leisure time pursuit. In fact, theaters begin to appear with great frequency throughout northern and central Italy during the Augustan era. The Greek cities of southern Italy and Sicily had permanent theaters from a much earlier time, since dramatic productions were long viewed by the audiences in those places. Pompeii, for example, enjoyed a stone theater as early as the second century B.C.E., and it is assumed that the Pompeiians also viewed their gladiatorial games in the theater until they built an amphitheater in the first century B.C.E. Throughout the Empire, every Roman town included a theater among its public buildings, and many of these facilities can still be seen today.

Comedy and Tragedy. The Romans adopted (and adapted) Greek models in writing comedy and tragedy. In the earliest stages of Latin language drama, the plays were probably little more than translations of the Greek originals. Performances took place during the day, out of doors on temporary wooden stages until the construction of Pompey's theater. A legal reform in 194 B.C.E. reserved the best seats for senators, which indicates that from at least this time seating was arranged as part of the temporary theater facility. Dramatic performances were part of the religious festivals such as the *Ludi romani* and the *Ludi plebeii* that also included spectator sporting events. The production of these events was the responsibility of the aediles, who depended upon the success of their festivals to ensure political support from the Roman people. Latin dramas were presented with the actors wearing Greek costumes, and most likely also wearing the masks always associated with Greek drama. Women did not perform in comedy and tragedy; thus, all actors were male. Musical accompaniment seems to have always been a feature of Roman dramas.

Open-Air Distractions. Before Rome had permanent theaters, drama was performed in the open. The lack of a physical structure within which to perform left the audience and the cast prone to distraction. In spite of the success of his comedies, Terence had to compete with other kinds of performances for the attention of his audience. In the prologues to his play *Hecyra*, the producer informs the audience that the first two productions of the play were ruined by the distractions of other performances, including gladiatorial contests, and he is trying to introduce the play at Rome for the third time.

Other Theatrical Genres. In addition to comedy and tragedy, Romans enjoyed viewing several other dramatic forms of which mime, pantomime, and Atellane farce are the most significant. The participants in these presentations could be either male or female. Atellane farce (*Atellana*) is a native Italian genre whose name comes from the Campanian town of Atella. Like Greek and Roman comedy, these farcical presentations utilized stock characters and themes. The setting was typically a small Italian town, and the drama satirized country life in crude language. Originally presented in the Oscan dialect, the *Atellanae* eventually became a Latin language drama, and was sometimes performed after the presentation of a tragedy.

Mime. Originally a Greek art form, mimetic performance found its way to Rome by the second century

of low moral character by Roman standards. By the second century C.E. pantomime had become preferred to comedy and tragedy.

Sources:

Richard C. Beacham, *The Roman Theatre and Its Audience* (Cambridge, Mass.: Harvard University Press, 1992).

Michael Grant, *Gladiators* (London: Weidenfeld & Nicolson, 1967).

John H. Humphrey, *Roman Circuses: Arenas for Chariot Racing* (Berkeley: University of California Press, 1986).

Thomas Wiedemann, *Emperors and Gladiators* (London & New York: Routledge, 1992).

LIVING ARRANGEMENTS: ROMAN HOUSES AND APARTMENTS

Houses. The types of homes the Romans inhabited depended upon several factors, including their social and economic status, their preference for urban or rural environment, and their professional occupations and needs. Poor farmers, for example, needed to live close to the land they cultivated, while Roman politicians needed to live close to or even in the cities where they worked. Although city dwellers typically lived and worked in the same place, wealthy Romans often had more than one house so that they could enjoy both the convenience of living close to their workplace as well as the peace and quiet of life outside the cities. Also, when wealthy Romans traveled, it was convenient to stay in one of their own houses or the houses of their wealthy friends rather than at an inn. Poor Romans did not have such a luxury. Peasant farmers stayed on their farms just as poor city folk stayed in the cities, often for their entire lives.

Ruins of the Circus of Maxentius, one of Rome's largest arenas for chariot races, originally erected along the *Via Appia* in 309 B.C.E.

B.C.E. and became firmly established in theatrical festivals throughout the Republic and Empire. Mimes worked either solo or in troupes and "told" the plot of their dramas through imitative movements and sounds. They wore costumes but apparently did not use masks in their performances of scenes from daily life, mythology, and assorted improbable themes. The nature of such drama was often farcical and indecent, yet very popular among Roman audiences.

Pantomime. Like mime, pantomime relied upon gestures to reveal a story, yet pantomime also involved conventional dances associated with specific themes. Dancers of pantomime worked solo to the accompaniment of music, a chorus, and sometimes an assistant who might have narrated the performance. The dancer wore a loose fitting costume to allow free movement, and a mask with closed lips, as no sounds were uttered by the pantomime. A change of mask indicated a change of character when necessary. The themes presented in pantomime were taken from mythology and history, and they could often be erotic in nature. While pantomime was introduced to Rome rather late compared to comedy and tragedy, 22 B.C.E., the profession of pantomime was a lucrative one, though considered to be

SOME THINGS NEVER CHANGE

Marcus Tullius Cicero, who owned several villas for his own use, was also a landlord. To judge from his own writings, Cicero seems to have been guilty of neglecting his rental properties.

Two of my shops have collapsed and the others are showing cracks, so that even the mice have moved elsewhere, to say nothing of the tenants.

More than one hundred years after Cicero admitted his negligence as a landlord, Romans still complained about poor living conditions in urban tenements. Decimus Iunius Iuvenalis (Juvenal), in one of his satires attacking the vice and social problems of his society, indicates clearly the magnitude of this housing issue:

Here we live in a city which, to a large extent, is supported by rickety props; that's how the landlord's agent stops it falling. He covers a gap in the chinky old building, then 'Sleep easy!' he says, when the ruin is poised to collapse.

Sources: Cicero, *Epistulate ad Atticum* (14.9), translated by D. R. Shackleton Bailey, Loeb Classical Library (Cambridge, Mass.: Harvard University Press, 1999).

Juvenal, *Saturae* 3.193–6, from *Juvenal: The Satires*, translated by Niall Rudd (Oxford: Clarendon Press, 1991).

House of Diana at Ostia, an example of a brick-faced tenement of the mid second century C.E.

Types of *Villa*. A wealthy Roman family might have had a fine townhouse (*villa urbana*) as well as one or more villas outside of the city (*villa suburbana*). These villas included the same features as their urban counterparts, but also had certain details peculiar to their locations and functions. A villa in the country could serve not only as a home but also as a working farmhouse (*villa rustica*) with rooms for food storage and spaces to accommodate grain mills and oil or winepresses. The country houses were often luxurious retreats, and typically included baths for the comfort and convenience of the owner, his family, and friends. Many villas were built in beautiful locations close to the sea where the occupants could enjoy wonderful views of the ocean, as well as the refreshing breezes during the hot Mediterranean summer.

Financial Resources. The size, style, and decoration of a house could reflect the financial resources of its owner, and thus domestic architecture was a material sign of social and economic status. Marcus Vitruvius Pollio, a Roman architect and military engineer of the late Republic and early Augustan era, expresses in his work *De architectura* the need for domestic architecture to reflect the status and occupation of its owner.

Self-Sufficiency. Men and women who lived in the country usually relied upon the self-sufficiency of their living arrangements to satisfy most or all of their needs. Working rural villas produced the food required by the owner's family and staff. Cattle could be raised on the property, and sheep's wool could be harvested and used to make clothing. Any other peculiar or luxury goods would have to be brought from the city. Year-round inhabitants such as farmers and farm slaves of rural areas probably did not have many opportunities to get to cities and towns where they could enjoy public baths and public entertainment. Roman cities also offered to their inhabitants the convenience of water supplied by aqueducts, while those people living outside of cities and towns relied upon well water.

Urban Life. Large urban centers have always attracted people from other areas to settle down and take advantage of economic and social opportunities. Many Roman citizens who were not native to the city of Rome moved there as they advanced in their public careers or business ventures. The same is true of other urban centers such as Ostia and Pompeii. Cities throughout Italy, Europe, Africa, and Asia that had been "Romanized" offered the same amenities such as luxurious public baths, public entertainment at the theater or amphitheater, and public welfare programs in the form of a grain dole. In addition to the allure of such attractions, cities, and especially Rome, suffered the same problems that modern cities continue to fight. Overcrowding in unsafe tenements, fire, crime, poverty, and political corruption were all aspects of urban life the ancients tolerated for the sake of living in the big cities. The wealthy, naturally, could insulate themselves more successfully against these problems, and found periodic if temporary relief from city life by spending vacations in their luxury villas outside of the cities.

Archaeological Evidence. While Vitruvius offers much information concerning the plans of Roman houses, we can also learn a great deal about Roman houses from archaeological work in the city of Rome and all around the Roman world. The southern Italian cities of Pompeii and Herculaneum offer some of the best evidence for Roman domestic architecture. Situated on the Bay of Naples, these two cities were buried by the eruption of the volcano Mount Vesuvius in 79 C.E. Fortunately, so many architectural details were preserved that we can describe accurately the common features of Roman houses.

Typical Floor Plan. By the time of the Late Republic, the atrium-style house had become the traditional form of architecture for single-family houses. The *atrium* was the principal room around which other rooms opened. The doorway into a house was usually set back from the street, and entered through a *vestibulum*, or vestibule. The passage leading from the door into the *atrium* was called the *fauces*. Around the *atrium* were usually arranged *cubicula*, or bedrooms, which were often small and probably used for nothing more than sleeping. Windows in general were few, and artificial lighting in the form of oil lamps was not terribly effective. Consequently, the *cubicula* must have been dark, and could not have been useful for much else besides sleeping.

Water and Light. In the center of the atrium floor was found the *impluvium*, a basin for catching rainwater that fell through the *compluvium*, an opening in the roof directly above the *impluvium*. The houses of only a few wealthy families were ever fitted with plumbing to supply water directly from aqueducts. Therefore it was important for families to save in cisterns buried on their property whatever water could be gathered in the *impluvium*, or to fetch water from wells or public fountains fed by aqueducts. The roof of the house sloped towards the *compluvium* to facilitate the process of gathering water. Another important function of the *compluvium* was to allow light to enter the atrium.

In the Atrium. Romans usually placed in the atrium a shrine to their household gods (the *lares*) called a *lararium*. This shrine might be as simple as a painting on the wall, or

as elaborate as a miniature temple with figurines. A strongbox for the safekeeping of family valuables was usually placed somewhere in the atrium, too. To ensure the safety of the house and its contents, strong wooden doors that swiveled on pins and were locked from the inside closed the doorway.

Other Rooms. The *tablinum* was an important feature of the Roman *domus*, particularly for wealthy families. This

Exterior view of Hadrian's Villa at Tivoli, built 124-133 C.E.

room, just at the back of the atrium, could be used for several purposes including the *salutatio* when a patron met his clients. The *tablinum* might also have served as a dining room, or even a study. Rooms called *alae* were featured at the back of the atrium and to the sides of *tablinum*. In these *alae* the Romans displayed their ancestral busts, or kept chests or strongboxes to store valuables. Formal dining took place while diners reclined on couches arranged in a group of three, each couch accommodating as many as three diners comfortably. This arrangement, as well as the dining room itself, was called a *triclinium,* of which large and well-appointed homes sometimes included more than one. The larger and more elegant houses also had a *peristylium* located beyond the atrium portion of the building. The *peristylium* was an open area, not roofed, where the homeowner might have a formal garden. Just as rooms were arranged around the atrium, rooms could be arranged around the peristyle. Like the term *peristylium,* the names of the rooms associated with this back portion of the house are of Greek origin. An *oecus* was either a reception room or dining room, often elaborately decorated. The *diaeta* was an open sitting room, while the *exedra* was more of a recess situated typically at the back of the *peristylium.* One might have a *triclinium,* or some other space used for sitting or perhaps reading. While the *atrium* portion of the house was entirely roofed over, except the *compluvium,* and offered little natural lighting, the *peristylium* was open to the sky except perhaps for the roofed colonnade around it, and offered light and air. Houses that were large and well-appointed enough to have these two distinct areas were clearly meant to provide for the owner and his family a variety of rooms to use and enjoy during the different seasons of the year.

Cooking. Romans did most of their cooking over a fire in the hearth of their homes. The hearth was more or less open, rather than the enclosed fireplaces found in modern homes. The hearth, made of stone, was raised off the floor, and under it could be stored fuel for the fire. Since Roman houses lacked a chimney, smoke escaped through a small hole in the kitchen roof, which must have made the Roman kitchen a smoky and smelly place to be. Some houses appear to have had their own ovens for baking, but this is the exception rather than the rule; most people must have purchased their bread from commercial bakeries.

AN INSURANCE SCAM REVEALED!

Destroying one's own property in order to collect insurance money is not a scam unique to the modern world. The same trick was used in Rome, as the poet Martial (Marcus Valerius Martialis) pointed out in the late first century C.E.

You had bought a house, Tongilianus, for two hundred thousand. An accident, all too common in Rome, took it away. A million was subscribed. I ask you, Tongilianus, couldn't it look as though you set fire to your own house?

Source: Martial, *Epigrammata* 3.52, translated by D. R. Shackleton Bailey, Loeb Classical Library (Cambridge, Mass.: Harvard University Press, 1993).

After settling the positions of the rooms with regard to the quarters of the sky, we must next consider the principles on which should be constructed those apartments in private houses which are meant for the householders themselves, and those which are to be shared in common with outsiders. The private rooms are those into which nobody has the right to enter without invitation, such as bedrooms, dining-rooms, bathrooms, and all others used for like purposes. The common are those which any of the people have a perfect right to enter, even without invitation. . . . Those who do business in country produce must have stalls and shops in their entrance-courts, with crypts, granaries, storerooms, and so forth in their houses, constructed more for the purpose of keeping the produce in good condition than for ornamental beauty. For capitalists and farmers of revenue, somewhat comfortable and showy apartments must be constructed, secure against robbery; for advocates and public speakers, handsomer and more roomy, to accommodate meetings; for men of rank who, from holding offices and magistracies, have social obligations to their fellow-citizens, lofty entrance-courts in regal style, and most spacious atriums and peristyles, with plantations and walks of some extent in them, appropriate to their dignity. They need also libraries, picture-galleries, and basilicas, finished in a style similar to that of great public buildings, since public councils as well as private lawsuits and hearings before arbitrators are very often held in the houses of such men.

Source: Vitruvius, *De architectura* 6.5.1–2, translated by Morris H. Morgan (New York: Dover, 1960).

Kitchen and Bathrooms. The kitchen was often grouped with slaves' quarters and a latrine in a portion of the house designated as a service area. Not all houses necessarily had quarters for slaves on the main floor of the house. Some houses must have had rooms for slaves on an upper story away from the parts of the home occupied and used by the owner's family. The latrine was small and situated near the kitchen, so as to be easily fitted with plumbing if the house brought water in from the public supply. If a house had its own baths, they too would be located in this area for ease of supplying water.

Furniture. Romans owned comparatively little furniture, and most rooms remained fairly empty until needed. Then a slave or two would move whatever furniture was required into the appropriate room. Except for beds and larger couches, most Roman furniture was small and light and could be moved easily from place to place. The Roman bed was small and narrow, consisting of a mattress stuffed with fibers such as straw, and a wooden frame to support the mattress. Cushions or pillows and blankets would make the bed more comfortable. Slaves, who usually lived in the house along with their owner's family, often slept in the peristyle without the privacy of their own *cubicula* or the comfort of a bed. Everyone would have slept fully clothed, particularly in the winter months, since Roman heating devices in the form of braziers were not as efficient as the central heating systems we enjoy today.

Construction Materials. The basic construction materials used to build houses were stone, mortar, and wood. The type of stone used depended to a large extent on the geographical location. Volcanic stone was a common resource throughout Italy, and its qualities varied by region. The exterior walls of a house could be fitted with a finer stone such as marble to give a more elegant appearance to the building. Interior walls were typically covered with plaster and decorated with frescoes, a type of painting that consists of pigment applied directly to the wet plaster, which then becomes a permanent part of the plaster wall. Floors could be left plain or decorated with cut stone or intricate mosaics made up of small stones or bits of colored glass called *tesserae*. Rugs of natural animal skins were expensive and therefore used mainly by wealthy homeowners.

Sanitary Facilities. The lack of indoor plumbing and a constant supply of fresh water to individual residences meant that personal hygiene was often not as fastidious as our own. Romans of course needed to bathe, but they did not usually do so at home. Rather, people frequented public baths where they not only attended to personal grooming but also indulged in exercise and social interaction. Just as most Roman houses lacked baths, most houses lacked toilets as well. Even when a house had its own toilet, it was not necessarily connected to a sewer system with running water to flush it clean. At home, people used chamber pots that they emptied into the streets or city sewers. Large public latrines with open seating-arrangements were a convenience in many Roman cities.

The Notion of Privacy. The ancient Roman concept of personal privacy must have been very different from our own. Daily activities occurred in the open areas of the house, namely the atrium or peristyle, where individuals could take advantage of natural light. Also, Roman houses accommodated more people than the owner and his immediate family. Other relatives as well as slaves might have lived with the owner's family. This idea of *familia* is more extensive and inclusive than our modern notion of a "nuclear family" consisting solely of two parents and their children. Furthermore, spaces adjacent to the house were often rented out as shops and apartments to people unrelated to the homeowner. Typical Roman houses usually consisted of a single story, but some two-story houses did exist.

Renting an Apartment. Although we find many houses in Roman cities, the majority of the urban population actually lived in apartments. Simple rooms in a larger house could be rented as an apartment, either along the street fronts or above the shops that lined Roman streets. Sometimes individual houses were divided into multifamily

Iulia Felix, daughter of Spurius, known only by name, was the proprietor of an establishment in Pompeii that was apparently a dining and bathing club. The property covered an entire city block, and included baths, dining facilities, and a very large kitchen-garden. As many property owners did, Iulia Felix rented to tenants the spaces adjacent to her property. According to the following inscription on a building in the ill-fated city, it seems that the entire property was available, including shops and apartments that were not part of the club proper.

FOR RENT

FROM AUGUST 13, WITH A 5-YEAR LEASE

ON THE PROPERTY OF IULIA FELIX,

DAUGHTER OF SPURIUS:

THE ELEGANT VENUS BATHS,

STREETFRONT SHOPS AND BOOTHS,

AND SECOND-STORY APARTMENTS.

dwellings. The majority of apartments, however, were probably to be found in complexes, which the Romans called *insulae*. Romans rented apartments just as we do, and the landlords could advertise vacancies by painting rental notices on the walls of the buildings.

Crowded Arrangements. Apartment buildings often rose to six or seven stories and were cramped. As in Roman houses, the lighting and plumbing of apartment buildings were never very sophisticated, and tenants often shared cooking and sanitary facilities. Such crowded arrangements must have been dark, noisy, and fairly uncomfortable even for an average sized family. *Insulae* were also notoriously unsafe; buildings were prone to catch fire and even collapse on account of their flimsy construction.

The Evidence of Ostia. The city of Ostia, which lies on the mouth of the Tiber River, bustled with commercial activity in antiquity. Ostia is so well preserved that we can learn a great deal about the construction of apartment buildings, and the living arrangements within them. The apartment buildings of Ostia, however, may not be representative of the Roman world at large; Ostia enjoyed relative affluence, particularly during the Empire, and therefore seems to have lacked the slums and tenements known to have existed at Rome. Nevertheless, Ostia provides important evidence that contrasts with the remains of Pompeii and Herculaneum where houses were the rule.

Strategic Location. Ostia's importance as a port city began as a result of its strategic location at the mouth of the Tiber River, especially during the First Punic War (246–241), and the business of importation grew following Roman victories over both Carthage and eastern cities. The

increasing population of Ostia relied upon the developing importation business to supply staples and luxury goods. During the reign of Augustus and other Julio-Claudian emperors, Ostia enjoyed several new building programs, and also constructed an aqueduct and a permanent theater. Rome's continuing reliance upon Ostia's commercial activities ensured a stable economy and further stimulated the growth of Ostia's population.

Growing Population. The geographical spread of Ostia's population was limited by the city walls, and by the second century C.E. the inhabitants of the city could be accommodated only by the upward expansion of domestic architecture. Large, multiple-family, brick apartment blocks came to replace the atrium-style houses known from the excavations at Pompeii and Herculaneum. The style of the apartments reflected contemporary practices at Rome. City dwellers enjoyed many public bath complexes, a theater, an amphitheater, public sewers, and, located throughout the city, many public cisterns fed by aqueduct. While the city of Ostia housed an expansive middle class, wealthy Romans built luxury villas along the shore to the south of the city.

Economic Decline. In the third century C.E., Ostia experienced a decline in trade, and the Roman world at large was distressed by the rapid changes in government. The large apartment buildings formerly occupied by the working classes were neglected and abandoned; many were destroyed by fire and not rebuilt. The number of large luxury houses built in this era attests to the continuing presence of wealthy families in the city. However, by the fourth century the middle class of merchants no

Garden at the house of M. Lucretius at Pompeii with examples of early-imperial "bourgeoisie" decorative statuary

longer had business to sustain them in Ostia, and their economic demise left a huge gap between the rich and poor. Invading armies and sea raids threatened Ostia during the fifth century, and the population was diminished throughout the following centuries.

Sources:

Ian M. Barton, ed., *Roman Domestic Buildings* (Exeter, U.K.: University of Exeter Press, 1996).

A. G. McKay, *Houses, Villas and Palaces in the Roman World* (Ithaca, N.Y.: Cornell University Press, 1975).

L. Richardson Jr., *Pompeii: An Architectural History* (Baltimore: Johns Hopkins University Press, 1988).

MEDICAL ISSUES

The Medical Profession. There were no organizations in Roman antiquity that governed the study and practice of medicine. One learned to be a doctor as an apprentice to an established authority. Until very late in the Republic, slaves and other members of the lower classes practiced medicine more as a trade than a science. In 46 B.C.E. Julius Caesar extended Roman citizenship to those practicing medicine at Rome, and Asclepiades of Bithynia founded the first regular school of medicine at Rome around 40 B.C.E. Thus, the status of medicine and the people who practiced it became elevated, and by the time of the Empire, doctors enjoyed a more prestigious place in Roman society. Romans in general were suspicious and skeptical about doctors, who were typically slaves, freedmen, and foreigners.

Low Success Rates. The practice of medicine did not always involve the precise application of knowledge developed through careful observation, experimentation, and exploration. Ancient medicine was intimately bound up with superstition, folk remedy, and magic as well as scientific methodology. Many people who called themselves doctors did not enjoy high success rates in terms of curing their patients. Poorer people may not have ever seen a proper doctor, but received their care from people who dispensed drugs (*pharmocopolae*), or they may have entrusted their health and lives to the gods rather than to trained medical practitioners. Romans believed that particular deities governed particular parts of the body, and by praying to those gods they could mend their ailments.

Social Distinction. Both doctors and druggists were notoriously incompetent and fraudulent, charging exorbitant rates for their services and supplies. In an attempt to attract business, doctors often lectured to city crowds. Educated Romans preferred doctors whose methods were philosophically based rather than medically proven. Consequently, the education and training of a patient's medical professional was often directly related to the social class and education of the patient himself. Nevertheless, Roman society esteemed the best doctors who could treat their patients successfully, and such physicians enjoyed social distinction among the aristocratic homes of Rome. Some physicians were famous on account of their vast wealth, rather than their skill. State funding for physi-

Relief depicting workers making soap and salve, second or third century C.E. (Epinal Museum, France)

cians seems to have begun in the early Empire and continued from that time.

Homecare. The head of the Roman household, the *paterfamilias,* was expected in his great wisdom to know something about medical problems and their solutions. The remedies consisted of combinations of food and drugs and ritual magic, the application of which did not rely upon the practitioner's expertise; so long as the ingredients were correct and the ritual performed correctly, the cure was supposed to follow. When the *paterfamilias'* expertise was not sufficient, Romans could take recourse to either the *pharmocopolae* or a medical man (*medicus*) or woman (*medica*) for their ailments. Whether the head of household or a doctor or a druggist treated the ill, all needed to know something about botany since drugs were derived mostly from plants.

Women in Medicine. Pregnant women usually gave birth with the aid of a midwife. Although some ancients were interested in gynecology, it was not a specialty of the same importance as it is today. Women often employed a nurse (*nutrix*) to breast-feed their children. Although this practice seems strange by modern standards, many women of Rome's upper class did not breast-feed their own children. A wet nurse was often responsible for breast-feeding children from more than one family, and this activity of

Relief from the mid second century C.E. of a midwife performing a delivery. A colleague holds the patient who is seated in an "obstetrical chair" grasping the special handles (Ostia Museum, Italy).

nursing unrelated children was thought to develop strong bonds between them.

Sources:

Karl Christ, *The Romans: An Introduction to Their History and Civilization,* translated by Christopher Holme (Berkeley: University of California Press, 1984).

Ralph Jackson, *Doctors and Diseases in the Roman Empire* (Norman: University of Oklahoma Press, 1988).

John Scarborough, *Roman Medicine* (Ithaca, N.Y.: Cornell University Press, 1969).

A ROMAN DAY

Dividing the Day. Unlike our modern practice of using watches and clocks to keep track of time, the Romans did not have devices that could accurately divide an entire day (our twenty-four-hour period) into smaller parts. Instead, they observed the position of the sun during the day, and with the use of a sundial the Romans could divide the daytime into twelve equal portions called *horae* (hours). Since the hours of the day during winter are shorter than the hours of the day during summer, the length of a Roman hour fluctuated accordingly. The three principal moments in any day were sunrise, noon, and sunset, and all further subdivision took place between these points in time. The hours of the night were also divided into twelve equal parts.

No Roman "Week." The Roman concept of a "week" was not based upon a cycle of seven days. Rather, the Romans had a tradition of holding market days (*nundinae*) at eight-day intervals. The ancient Jews and Christians, however, marked their weeks by observing a festival at seven-day intervals, the Sabbath or Sunday, respectively. Certain days were designated for various festivals, both religious and others. Days that were designated as appropriate for the transaction of business and proceedings of court were called *fasti*, while days on which these activities could not occur were called *nefasti*.

Dividing the Month. The Romans observed lunar months with an average of 29.5 days. Their twelve-month year, therefore, naturally fell short of the solar year. The discrepancy necessitated the periodic insertion of an extra month to bring the calendar year into alignment with the solar year. There were three points of reference in every month. The *kalendae* (calends) was always the first day of the month. The *ides* (*idus*) was the fifteenth day of months consisting of 31 days, and on the thirteenth of the other months. The *nonae* (nones) was always on the ninth day before the ides. Years were dated in relation to the founding of Rome, which according to Roman tradition is set at 753 B.C.E. in modern reckoning. Thus, events in Roman history were chronologically described by the Romans in terms of their happening in years before or after the founding of the city, *Ab urbe condita*, abbreviated to *AVC*.

Morning Rituals: The *Salutatio*. A Roman day typically began at sunrise in order to take advantage of the daylight hours. Breakfast (*ientaculum*) consisted of cheese and fruit, perhaps leftovers from the previous day, and since bread was a common food item, then surely bread was eaten as part of the first meal of the day. The hours before noon were filled with social calls paid to patrons by their clients. During this greeting ritual (*salutatio*) members of one social class visited a patron (*patronus*) of higher social status to pay their respects, perhaps ask for favors, and receive a basket of provisions or money (*sportula*). The *salutatio* took place in the atrium of the patron's house, where clients and patron met formally dressed in their togas. The patron-client system took strict consideration of the socio-economic status of both patron and clients, and a man who functioned as a patron could also be a client of a more prominent citizen. Clients who sought favors from their patron would also be expected to accompany their patron in public, even on visits to his own patron. The crowd of clients accompanying their patron lent an air of prestige to the man, and created a visible token of his power and importance.

Keeping Time. In the origins of the patronage system, patrons were members of patrician families, and clients were plebeians. As some plebeians amassed their own wealth, they, too, could become patrons. While slaves did not take part in the *salutatio,* freed slaves did become the clients of their former masters. In the Republic, Roman men active in politics relied upon their clients to provide political support in return for their patronage, while clients relied upon the financial generosity and protection of their patrons. Patrons expected their clients to campaign and vote for them, as well as appear with them in public. Clients could expect to receive legal advice or representation from their patrons, in addition to their daily allotment of provisions. The relationship between patron and client was useful for both parties. However, when the practice of popular elections waned in the Empire, the patron-client relationship largely degenerated into the pursuit of economic benefits that clients might derive from their patrons. Therefore, clients often became fickle sycophants who pursued patrons based upon the possibility that they might inherit property. If a patron was a childless gentleman, he was often the target of an unscrupulous client's attention.

Lunch. The next meal after *ientaculum* was *prandium*, or lunch, which Romans consumed at midday. *Prandium* was not a heavy meal. Rather, the Roman lunch was more of a snack, eaten on the go. City dwellers might either return home for their lunch or purchase something at a tavern or

Fragments of a Republican-era calendar, the Fasti Antiates, covering the months Martiu to Junius (March to June). Painted on plaster, it recorded feast days (Museo Nazionale Archeologico delle Terme, Rome).

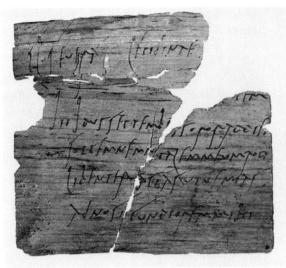

Pen-on-wood birthday invitation (100 C.E.) from Claudia Severa to Sulpicia Lepidina found
at Vindolanda, the site of a Roman fort in Britain (British Museum)

from a vendor. Although many Romans often ate at home, they could also pick up a quick meal, a drink, or snack in a *thermopolium*, or *popina*, which were similar in function to our fast-food restaurants. These shops became popular around the public baths during the Empire when Romans enjoyed a much greater variety of commodities and more leisure time than their ancestors did earlier in the Republic.

Dinner. The main meal of the day (*cena*) took place in the late afternoon or early evening. What individuals ate for dinner depended upon their financial resources and the formality of the occasion. For example, a poor person or family might have eaten simple dishes of vegetables or fruits, soups made of grains, perhaps some meat, and of course bread. Meat was always expensive and may not have been a featured course of a common meal. The very poor ate a great deal of grain, which could be baked as bread or ground and boiled into porridge called *puls*. Although drinking water was available, wine mixed with water was the preferred beverage, or vinegar mixed with water in poor homes.

Dinner Parties. Fancier meals and dinner-parties could be quite elaborate and involve several courses. Formal dining took place while the diners reclined on couches arranged in a group of three called a *triclinium*. Each couch could accommodate three diners comfortably. Wealthy Romans often had more than one room in their houses that they could use for dining, and sometimes they ate outside, much the way we do when the weather permits. Poorer people did not have the space in their homes for such dining arrangements, so they probably ate while sitting.

Family Time. The *cena* was the one meal of the day that brought family members together at the table. The children of the household participated in making sacrifices to the gods, which involved a small offering of food and drink from the family table. *Cena* also gave parents

the opportunity to teach their children proper manners so that they might learn to conduct themselves suitably as adults when they eventually became established in their own homes.

The *Convivium*. When a rich person or family entertained guests at dinner, the *cena* became a *convivium*, or banquet. This *convivium* involved several courses, including appetizers (*gustum, gustatio,* or *promulsis*), a main course (*mensa prima* or *caput cenae*), and dessert (*mensa secunda*). A patron often entertained his social equals as well as his clients at dinner parties; this meal gave the patron the opportunity to maintain social and political contacts as well as perpetuate the reciprocal obligations of the patron-client relationship. Guests usually brought their own large cloth napkins to dinner so that they could take home leftovers from the party. If

TRADITIONAL EXPECTATIONS NO LONGER VALID

By the time of the Julio-Claudian emperors, the patron/client relationship was very different from that during the Republic. Lucius Annaeus Seneca, tutor to the emperor Nero in the first century C.E., expresses a more jaded assessment of this system than Cicero had done nearly a century earlier.

Your clients? But none of these men courts you for yourself; they merely court something from you. People used to hunt friends, but now they hunt pelf; if a lonely old man changes his will, the morning-caller transfers himself to another door.

Source: Lucius Annaeus Seneca (Seneca the Younger), *Epistulae morales ad Lucilium* 19.4. translated by Richard M. Gummere, Loeb Classical Library (Cambridge, Mass.: Harvard University Press, 1917).

Gaius Valerius Catullus, a poet of the first century B.C.E., wrote a poem attacking a certain Asinius Marrucinus for his gauche behavior during a dinner party at which the poet was also a guest. Catullus was apparently a victim of Marrucinus' thieving hand!

Asinius Marrucinus, you do not make a pretty use of your left hand when we are laughing and drinking; you take away the napkins of people who are off their guard. Do you think this is a good joke?

Source: Catullus, *Carmina* 12.1–4, translated by Francis Ware Cornish, Loeb Classical Library (Cambridge, Mass.: Harvard University Press, 1988).

a patron did not wish to dine with his clients, he could simply provide food items for the client's basket (*sportula*) to be taken home.

Going to Market. Many items familiar to the modern diet were also popular in antiquity. Vegetables, including asparagus, lettuce, onions, and cucumbers; meats, such as pork, lamb, and hare; and poultry, such as chicken, duck, and pigeon were all available in the ancient marketplace. Seafood, in varieties no longer available to us, tempted the ancient Roman palate. Cheeses, cured hams and sausages, mushrooms, truffles, and assorted breads found their way into Roman meals. Apples, pears, and plums were some of the fruits enjoyed by Romans, usually eaten at the end of a meal. A particularly Roman condiment made of fermented fish, called *garum* or *liquamen*, was used to flavor almost any dish, and does not really have an exact parallel in modern, western cuisine.

Grow Your Own. Inhabitants of rural areas and those who owned large estates could grow or produce their own food. Citizens living in Rome and in the urban centers around the Roman world, however, bought much of their food in shops and specialized markets such as the vegetable and cattle markets. In Rome during the Republic, these food shops were established around the Forum and other locations within the city. In 179 B.C.E. the separate food shops were consolidated in one large market building called the *macellum*, which was demolished during the reign of Augustus and replaced by other similar structures in the city. The standard characteristics of a *macellum* included a central circular structure called a *tholos*, which was supplied with water and drains for the sale of fish, and a ring of shops around this central structure. The *macellum* at Pompeii serves as a good example of this type of building. It is a large rectangular building with a central *tholos* and a row of shops along one interior wall. The drains of the *tholos* were found to be full of fish scales, which shows the *tholos* to have housed a fish market.

Sources:

Ilaria Gozzini Giacosa, *A Taste of Ancient Rome*, translated by Anna Herklotz (Chicago: University of Chicago Press, 1992).

Antony Kamm, *The Romans: An Introduction* (London & New York: Routledge, 1995).

L. Richardson Jr., *Pompeii: An Architectural History* (Baltimore: Johns Hopkins University Press, 1988).

SIGNIFICANT PEOPLE

MARCUS GAVIUS APICIUS (APICIUS)

FIRST CENTURY C.E.
GASTRONOME

Exotic Foods and Culinary Arts. Apicius lived during the reigns of Augustus and Tiberius. Not much is known about him, except that he was proverbially associated with exotic foods and the culinary arts. Although the book *De re coquinaria* is attributed to Apicius, it is more likely to be a collection of recipes compiled well after his death. In any case, the recipes are little more than lists of ingredients without specific measures or exact cooking instructions. In spite of the shortcomings of *De re coquinaria* when compared to modern cookbooks, the dishes it describes provide valuable insight concerning the Roman diet during the early Empire. Melon, goose liver, and oysters all appear as appetizers on the Roman menu, much as they might today. However, some dishes go beyond what modern dining practices include. In addition to the less-surprising items such as anchovies, chicken, and pig, one finds peacock tongue, camel heels, and sow's udder. Apicius is also credited with being the first to serve what the French call *foie gras*—the livers of geese that had been force-fed on figs.

Source:
laria Gozzini Giacosa, *A Taste of Ancient Rome,* translated by Anna Herklotz (Chicago: University of Chicago Press, 1992).

(? TITUS) PETRONIUS

DIED 65 C.E.
AUTHOR

Pursuit of Pleasure. Credited as the author of *Satyrica,* a satirical narrative of hedonistic life in Rome, Petronius was a friend of the emperor Nero's court. His birth date is uncertain. Petronius served as governor of Bithynia and was consul in 61 C.E., appointments that he successfully fulfilled. Petronius seems to have dedicated the remainder of his life to writing, sleeping, and the pursuit of pleasure. Petronius's sense of style was considered so refined that he was unofficially called the emperor's "arbiter of elegance." Nero considered nothing charming or elegant without Petronius' approval. Such favoritism incurred the jealousy of other courtiers, and soon Petronius came under Nero's suspicion. Without waiting for official orders, Petronius committed suicide in a long, protracted process that involved variously cutting open his veins and binding them up again while he conversed with friends, ate, and slept so that his death might appear natural. His last act was to send a letter to Nero, not flattering him as was the custom for those about to perish under imperial order, but detailing Nero's debaucheries and the names of his male and female companions. Petronius died in 65 C.E.

Sources:
Philip B. Corbett, *Petronius* (New York: Twayne, 1970).

Froma I. Zeitlin, "Petronius as Paradox: Anarchy and Artistic Integrity," *Transactions of the American Philological Association,* 102 (1971): 631–684.

GAIUS PLINIUS CAECILIUS SECUNDUS (PLINY THE YOUNGER)

CIRCA 61-112 C.E.
POLITICIAN AND AUTHOR

Domestic Architecture. Pliny the Younger was a native of Comum in the Tuscan countryside to the north of Rome. He held the consulship in 100 C.E. and was active in forensic work his entire life. His nine books of literary letters recount political, social, domestic, and other events of his era. Many of these letters are truly essays about contemporary life, and were probably written as such rather than as strictly personal correspondences. In some of his autobiographical letters Pliny writes of his various villas, their situation, construction, and decoration, and thus he attests to the importance of domestic architecture to a Roman of his status and economic resources. Pliny was also a patron of his native Comum. When he discovered that local children were going elsewhere for school, Pliny helped to endow local positions to attract teachers to Comum so the native children could study in closer proximity to their families. In a letter to his friend Cornelius Tacitus, Pliny writes, "I was visiting my native town a short time ago when the young son of a fellow-citizen came to pay his respects to me. 'Do you go to school?' I asked. 'Yes,' he replied. 'Where?' 'In Mediolanum (Milan).' 'Why not here?' To this the boy's father (who had brought him and was standing by) replied: 'Because we have no teachers here.' 'Why not? Surely it is a matter of great importance to you fathers (and luckily there were several fathers listening) that your children should study here on the spot? Where can they live more happily than in their native place? Where can they be brought up more strictly than under their parent's eye or with less expense than at home?'"

Sources:
Pliny, *Epistulae* 4.13.3–5, translated by Betty Radice (London: Penguin, 1963).

W. Jeffrey Tatum, "Pliny the Younger," in *Ancient Roman Writers, Dictionary of Literary Biography,* volume 211, edited by Ward W. Briggs (Columbia, S.C.: Bruccoli Clark Layman / Detroit: Gale Group, 1999), pp. 243–250.

MARCUS FABIUS QUINTILIANUS (QUINTILIAN)

FIRST CENTURY C.E.
PROFESSOR OF RHETORIC

A State Employee. Quintilian was born around 30 C.E. at Calagurris in Spain. Educated at least in part at Rome, he became a well-known teacher of rhetoric and among his pupils was the younger Pliny. Quintilian is said to be the first teacher whose salary was paid by the state. Also a legal advocate, Quintilian defended the Jewish Queen Berenice. His writings include *Institutio oratoria* (Oratorical Training), from which we learn a great deal about contemporary expectations regarding the education of children and young men. Quintilian had hoped that his two sons might live up to these expectations, but sadly they died at the ages of 5 and 9. Quintilian's works are often considered in light of their contribution to ancient literary criticism.

Sources:
George A. Kennedy, *The Art of Rhetoric in the Roman World* (Princeton: Princeton University Press, 1972).

Kennedy, *Quintilian* (New York: Twayne, 1969).

LUCIUS ANNAEUS SENECA (SENECA THE YOUNGER)

CIRCA 4 B.C.E.-65 C.E.
AUTHOR, PHILOSOPHER, AND IMPERIAL TUTOR

Exile and Redemption. Seneca was born circa 4 B.C.E. at Corduba in Spain, and educated at Rome. Seneca became a well-known author and orator, and was long associated with the Julio-Claudian family. Accused of adultery with Caligula's sister Julia Livilla, Seneca was exiled to Corsica in 41 C.E. until Agrippina (also sister of Caligula, and wife of the emperor Claudius) instigated his recall in 49 and made him tutor to the future emperor Nero. Seneca served as adviser to Nero during the first five years of his reign, and after falling into disfavor with Nero he retired in 62. A charge of complicity in the Pisonian Conspiracy of 65 led to Seneca's suicide on Nero's order. Seneca's great literary contributions span several genres and much of his adult life. He is a fascinating study in human compliance during an era when many members of the educated upper class were no longer participating actively in Roman government. The Neronian age was both a renaissance of cultural activity and a turbulent pool of intrigue and corruption. For a while, Seneca successfully managed to work within the imperial system as a close associate of the imperial family. His untimely death, however, was symptomatic of the vicissitudes of Nero's reign. His philosophical writings display an affinity for Stoicism, yet his lifestyle and great wealth betrayed qualities inconsistent with his philosophical persuasion. Perhaps a hypocrite, Seneca succeeded where most Romans of his generation and background would not have dared to attempt.

Sources:
C. D. N. Costa, ed., *Seneca* (London: Routledge & Kegan Paul, 1974).

Miriam T. Griffin, *Seneca: A Philosopher in Politics* (Oxford: Oxford University Press, 1976).

Villy Sørensen, *Seneca: The Humanist at the Court of Nero*, translated by W. Glyn Jones (Edinburgh: Canongate, 1984).

SPARTACUS

EXECUTED 71 B.C.E.
SLAVE, GLADIATOR, AND REVOLUTIONARY

The People's Champion. The Thracian-born slave Spartacus had once served as an auxiliary in the Roman army and had been sent to Capua to train as a gladiator. In 73 B.C.E. Spartacus escaped from the training school. With several companion escapees, Spartacus led a revolt, having attracted Thracian, Celtic, and German fugitives. His army, numbering approximately ninety thousand, defeated several Roman armies. The renegade gladiators and fugitives plundered Italy as they moved up and down the peninsula until Crassus caught and executed Spartacus in 71 B.C.E. All of Spartacus's followers who had been caught were then crucified along the Appian Way. Although the gladiators who escaped from Capua had been slaves, they did not attempt to recruit runaway slaves from the towns around Italy. Instead they attracted downtrodden and disillusioned country folk. The experience is a reminder that gladiators, whether criminal or slave, were human beings whose dignity was compromised in the interest of mass entertainment.

Sources:
Edward T. Salmon and Andrew William Lintott, "Spartacus," in *The Oxford Classical Dictionary*, third edition, edited by Simon Hornblower and Antony Spawforth (Oxford: Oxford University Press, 1999), p. 1433.

Joseph Vogt, *Ancient Slavery and the Idea of Man* (Cambridge, Mass.: Harvard University Press, 1974).

QUINTUS SEPTIMIUS FLORENS TERTULLIANUS (TERTULLIAN)

CIRCA 160-225 C.E.
CHURCH FATHER

African Christian Community. Tertullian was born in Carthage in North Africa. He studied law and philosophy, and as a young man Tertullian was attracted to Christianity. Tertullian was disenchanted with pagan immorality and admired the early Christian martyrs. He is the earliest of the Latin Church authors, and one of the only Romans of his era to express feelings of horror at the practice of gladiatorial games and other public spectacles. Tertullian lived in an era when Latin literature was becoming less focused on a Rome-centered audience and more concentrated upon provincial Roman life and problems. For Tertullian, the growing African Christian community was the center of his life rather than the city of Rome itself. In spite of the invective Tertullian raises against pagan immorality in his writings, his works are informative regarding contemporary provincial Roman society. In particular, his *De spectaculis* reveals many details about public spectacles that one might not learn about otherwise, including the gory, painful, and protracted deaths of participants in these events.

Sources:
William Hugh Clifford Frend and Mark Julian Edwards, "Tertullian," in *The Oxford Classical Dictionary*, third edition, edited by Simon Hornblower and Antony Spawforth (Oxford: Oxford University Press, 1999), pp. 1487–1488.

E. Allo Isichei, *Political Thinking and Social Experience: Some Christian Interpretations of the Roman Empire from Tertullian to Salvian* (Christchurch: University of Canterbury, 1964).

DOCUMENTARY SOURCES

Note: The following list includes archaeological monuments.

Baths of Caracalla—huge Imperial bath complex at Rome dedicated in 216 C.E. The impressive remains are sufficient to indicate the monumental luxury of bathing as a leisure activity during the Roman Empire.

Catullus (Gaius Valerius Catullus) circa 84–circa 54 B.C.E.; *Carmina* (Poems or Songs). Poems written in a variety of lyric meters on a variety of themes. In addition to his well-known love poetry, Catullus's subjects are often contemporary political and private figures whose behavior and customs he mocks.

Cicero (Marcus Tullius Cicero) 106–43 B.C.E.; *Epistulae ad Atticum* (Letters to Atticus). Letters to and from Cicero's friend Atticus, discussing current events and personal concerns.

Cicero, *Epistulae ad familiares* (Letters to Friends). Letters to a variety of friends and acquaintances discussing current events and personal concerns. Cicero's extensive corpus of letters is one of the greatest resources documenting the final years of the Roman Republic. Much is said about politics in addition to culture and society.

Corpus inscriptionum latinarum (Corpus of Latin Inscriptions). This collection of Latin inscriptions encompasses the entire Roman world. Inscriptions are found on many different types of monuments including public buildings, triumphal arches, and graves, and cover many different themes. Some inscriptions record items of interest in the daily lives of Romans including such things as vacancy notices for rental apartments.

Flavian Amphitheater (also known as the Colosseum)—Amphitheater at Rome dedicated in 80 C.E. The remains are possibly the most impressive of all monuments from Roman antiquity. It is a marvel of engineering of the Roman Empire, as well as a reminder of the prominent place mass entertainment held in Roman society.

Herculaneum—City in the region of Campania in southern Italy. Lying on the Bay of Naples, Herculaneum was buried in the eruption of Vesuvius in 79 C.E. The well-preserved remains of Herculaneum reveal details of life in a Roman city, including styles of architecture.

Horace (Quintus Horatius Flaccus) 65–8 B.C.E.; *Sermones.* (Literally Conversations, but often called Satires). Satirical poems on a variety of subjects. Horace often includes details of daily life activities such as dining.

House of the Faun, Pompeii—Built in the second century B.C.E., this luxurious townhouse is an outstanding example of the influence of Hellenistic Greek aesthetics on Roman decorative arts and domestic decoration.

Juvenal (Decimus Iunius Iuvenalis)—*Saturae* (Satires). Satirical poems that attack the customs and vices of contemporary Rome. Juvenal's works are more caustic than those of Horace, and include the names of well-known contemporary figures.

Martial (Marcus Valerius Martialis) circa 60–circa 130 C.E.; *Epigrammata* (Epigrams). Short poems on a variety of subjects. Martial's poems are primarily satirical, and reveal interesting details about Roman society of the first century C.E. The first book of poems deals with the spectacles produced by the emperor Titus in the Colosseum to celebrate its opening in 80 C.E.

Ostia—Rome's port city at the mouth of the Tiber River, on the coast of Italy. Ostia provides a useful study of daily life in a busy commercial city of Roman antiquity. While Ostia has typical public buildings of the Roman world (theater, baths, etc.), the domestic architecture of Ostia contrasts sharply with that of Pompeii and Herculaneum.

Ovid (Publius Ovidius Naso) 43 B.C.E.–circa 18 C.E.; *Ars amatoria* (Art of Love). A mock-didactic poem about finding and winning over a beloved. In the third book of this poem Ovid gives advice to women about enhancing their appearance through the application of cosmetics and wearing clothing of suitable color.

Ovid, *Amores* (Love Poems). A collection of poems mainly about love. One of these poems is entirely devoted to berating his mistress for her abuse of hair dyes, which gives us insight into hair care practices in the early Roman Empire.

Petronius (Titus Petronius Arbiter) d. 65 C.E.; *Satyrica*. A satirical novel written in both poetry and prose. The remains are fragmentary, but the longest section, known as "Trimalchio's Dinner," is a funny portrait of a rich yet vulgar freed slave's dinner party. The episode is a commentary upon the contemporary excesses of the class of former slaves, many of whom became wealthy in service to the emperors of Rome.

Piazza Navona—modern name of the area in Rome developed directly over Domitian's stadium. The shape of the modern piazza follows precisely the outline of the stadium, whose foundations are still visible under the current structures.

Pliny the Younger (Gaius Plinius Caecilius Secundus) 61 or 62–circa 114 C.E.; *Epistulae* (Letters). Pliny's letters are almost essays about current events, and provide valuable insight into the history and society of Rome in the late first and early second centuries C.E. One of the most famous of these letters describes the eruption of Vesuvius in 79 C.E., which Pliny witnessed.

Plutarch ([L.?] Mestrius Plutarchus) circa 46–circa 120 C.E.; *Parallel Lives*. Biographies dealing mostly with political and military figures. We can learn much about the upbringing, including family life and education of Romans such as Tiberius and Gaius Gracchus, and Cato.

Pompeii—City in the region of Campania in southern Italy. Lying on the Bay of Naples, Pompeii was buried in the eruption of Vesuvius in 79 C.E. The remains of Pompeii are some of the most informative sources regarding life in a Roman city. Many of the typical characteristics of a Roman city can be seen, including an amphitheater, two theaters, a forum with *macellum*, and a number of bath complexes. The townhouses of Pompeii teach us much about the construction, layout, and decoration of Roman houses.

Pont du Gard—Three-tiered Roman aqueduct built circa 14 C.E. near Nîmes, France. This aqueduct is testimony not only to the durability of Roman architecture, but also to the process of "Romanization" in areas of Europe conquered by Rome. The aqueducts were necessary not only for bringing drinking water into Roman cities but also for supplying the quantities of water necessary to run Roman bathing facilities.

Suetonius (Gaius Tranquillus Suetonius) circa 70–circa 140 C.E.; *De vita Caesarum* (On the Life of the Caesars). Biographies of Roman emperors from Julius Caesar to Domitian. Many valuable details about Roman society and history are to be found here, particularly about the education and daily habits of Rome's elite families.

Tacitus (Cornelius Tacitus) circa 55–circa 117 C.E.; *Dialogus de oratoribus* (Dialogue on Orators). A conversation that the author claims to have witnessed concerning the decline of Roman oratory in the first century C.E. The speakers discuss standards of education, poor teaching, and loss of political freedom as the causes for the decline.

Terence (Publius Terentius Afer) circa 195–159 B.C.E.; *Hecyra* (The Mother-in-Law). Latin comedy based upon a Greek model. In the prologue to this play we learn how difficult the production of drama was in Rome of the second century B.C.E. Before Rome had a permanent theater in 55 B.C.E., drama was performed in the open and often had to compete with other forms of entertainment for the same audience. The prologues to other plays as well as the plays themselves offer information about daily life and manners, and theatrical productions in the second centuries B.C.E.

Tertullian (Quintus Septimius Florens Tertullianus) circa 160–circa 240 C.E.; *De spectaculis* (On Spectacles). Christian attack on the vices and moral concerns associated with entertainment spectacles including gladiatorial combat. Tertullian is one of the few Romans of his era who criticized the games.

Villa of the Mysteries, Pompeii—This building is a wonderful example of a luxurious seaside villa complete with its own baths and working farmyard. The original portions of the complex date to the first century B.C.E.

Vitruvius (Marcus Vitruvius Pollio) late first century B.C.E.–early first century C.E.); *De architectura* (On Architecture). Handbook on Roman architecture that treats principles of symmetry and proportion, the designs of public and domestic buildings, and other aesthetic concepts of Vitruvius's era.

Gold Roman engagement ring from the third century C.E. (Yale University Art Gallery, New Haven, Connecticut)

THE FAMILY AND SOCIAL TRENDS

by T. DAVINA McCLAIN

CONTENTS

Sidebars and tables are listed in italics.

218-201 B.C.E.

- The Second Punic War, also known as the Hannibalic War, occurs. The First and Second Punic Wars take many men out of Rome, leaving women to take care of the family and the city. The large number of captives provides Roman families with greater access to slave labor.

216 B.C.E.

- After the battle of Cannae, so many women are in mourning that the festival for Ceres cannot be held. The Senate limits the period of mourning to thirty days and prohibits mourning in public.

215 B.C.E.

- The *lex Oppia* (Oppian Law) is passed to restrict the amounts of luxury items, such as gold and colorful expensive cloth, that women can possess. This measure is either a sumptuary law or a law to provide funds for the war against Hannibal.

204 B.C.E.

- The *lex Cincia de donis et muneribus* regulates the value of the gifts that husbands, wives, and other kin can exchange and forbids payment to lawyers or advocates.

200 B.C.E.

- The *lex Plaetoria* prevents minors from engaging in and being held responsible for financial arrangements.

195 B.C.E.

- Women successfully demonstrate for repeal of the Oppian Law.

169 B.C.E.

- The *lex Voconia* limits the amount of real estate that men in the highest social class can leave to women as their heirs and limits the amount one can leave to a nonrelative.

161 B.C.E.

- The *lex Fannia* limits the types of food, the number of guests, and the overall amount one can spend on a dinner party.

131 B.C.E.

- The censor Quintus Caecilius Metellus Maecedonicus urges the Senate to make marriage mandatory because it is a necessary evil.

* DENOTES CIRCA DATE

90 B.C.E.	• The *lex Iulia* grants to all Italians citizenship and *conubium*, which is the right to contract legal marriages.
82-79 B.C.E.	• Sulla's dictatorship and proscriptions bring the death of more than two thousand men. The slaves of these men (more than ten thousand) are freed by Sulla and become his freedmen. The sons of proscribed men are prohibited from running for public office.
59 B.C.E.	• Julius Caesar passes laws making public land available for fathers of three or more children.
55 B.C.E.	• Gaius Pompeius Magnus (Pompey the Great) completes and dedicates Rome's first stone theater.
46 B.C.E.	• Cicero urges Caesar to encourage larger families.
44 B.C.E.	• Caesar is assassinated.
43 B.C.E.	• The Second Triumvirate (Octavius, Lepidus, and Antony) is formed and compiles a proscription list naming three hundred senators and two thousand equestrians for execution. Among these are Lepidus's own brother and the orator Marcus Tullius Cicero.
27 B.C.E.- 14 C.E.	• The reign of Augustus begins the Roman principate.
18 B.C.E.	• The *lex Iulia de maritandis ordinibus* makes adultery a crime for both men and women, provides incentives for men and women to have children, and imposes restrictions on those who do not marry by a certain age (twenty-five for men; twenty for women): men cannot hold public office; neither men nor women can attend public games; nor can they receive inheritances except from close relatives.

*DENOTES CIRCA DATE

2 B.C.E.

• The *lex Fufia Caninia* limits the number of slaves one can free in his or her will.

**2 B.C.E.-
37 C.E.**

• The *Lex Junia* places slaves who were freed, but not by any official means or in a number in excess of that established by the *Lex Fufia Caninia,* in the Latin class. Members of this status cannot make wills, so all of their property returns to their former masters. Members of the Latini can become full citizens by performing certain public services or by having a legitimate child who survives at least to his or her first birthday.

9 C.E.

• The *Lex Papia-Poppaea* reinforces the *Lex Julia* of 18 B.C.E.

32 C.E.

• The senate debates a proposal that would prohibit provincial governors from taking their wives with them on their tours of duty. The measure does not pass.

50 C.E.

• The *senatusconsultum Velleianum* prohibits women from pledging to cover the debts of any other person.

64 C.E.

• The burning of Rome displaces many citizens. Emperor Nero begins rebuilding the city.

68 C.E.

• Nero commits suicide. His childhood nurse and his former mistress, Acte, wrap up his body and ensure that he is buried in his family tomb. The death of Nero ends the reign of the Julio-Claudian family.

69 C.E.

• The year of the four emperors (Galba, Otho, Vitellius, and Vespasian) is one of turmoil and uncertainty.

70-79 C.E.

• Vespasian returns Rome to political and financial stability.

*DENOTES CIRCA DATE

79 C.E.

- The eruption of Mount Vesuvius on 24 August buries Pompeii, Herculaneum, and Stabia as well as many of the inhabitants of these cities.

80 C.E.

- Titus completes and dedicates the Flavian Amphitheater (better known as the Colosseum).

81-96 C.E.

- Domitian rules autocratically. Unlike previous emperors, he does not consult the Senate about his decisions or decrees.

98-117 C.E.

- Trajan sets up a system whereby the imperial treasury makes loans to Italian landowners. The landowners pay the principal back to the state, but pay the interest (5 percent) into a fund in their own areas. The money in these funds is used to provide assistance to help poor families raise their children. Trajan also sets aside part of the grain supply to feed five thousand poor Roman children.

142 C.E.

- Antoninus Pius extends the scope of a fund begun by Trajan by providing assistance for dowries for girls of poor Italian families. Because he does this in honor of his wife Faustina after her death, the girls are known as the *puellae Faustinianae,* "The Girls of Faustina."

175-180 C.E.

- During the reign of Marcus Aurelius, an order of the senate prohibits guardians from marrying their wards under the age of twenty-five.

193-235 C.E.

- Septimius Severus comes to power and the Severan dynasty continues through the authority of the Severan women.

197 C.E.

- Severus revokes the ban on marriage for soldiers.

212 C.E.

- Caracalla grants citizenship to all free men within the borders of the empire.

* Denotes Circa Date

THE FAMILY AND SOCIAL TRENDS

251 C.E.	• The Goths and other barbarians begin invading the Roman Empire.
286 C.E.	• Diocletian divides the empire and shares power equally with Maximian.
301 C.E.	• Diocletian regulates wages and prices in an attempt to deal with poverty and stabilize the economy.
315 C.E.	• Constantine passes a law providing public assistance for the poor who do not have the means to care for their children in an effort to curb the selling or exposing of infants.
390 C.E.	• Theodosius allows women to serve as *tutores*, or guardians.
476 C.E.	• The last recognized Roman emperor, Romulus Augustulus, is deposed.

* **Denotes Circa Date**

Wall painting of a woman playing a cithara, from the villa of Publius Fannius Synistor at Pompeii, first century B.C.E.
(Rogers Fund, 1903, Acc. # 03.14.5, Metropolitan Museum of Art, New York)

OVERVIEW

The Roman Family—What Is It? What was a family for the Romans? Was a family a group of people related by birth, or by marriage, or by the fact that they lived together? For the Romans, the answer would include all of these. The basic Roman *familia* consisted of everyone, including slaves, who lived in a household. Within that household could be a variety of in-laws, more likely from the husband's family, but a wife on a rare occasion might bring her widowed mother or orphaned siblings to live with them as well. *Familia,* the Latin word from which the word "family" derives, therefore more accurately corresponds to the idea of a household, in which a nanny or housekeeper or a gardener might also be included, than to the modern word "family," which more often means people related by birth or by marriage, many of whom might live in different places. Certainly the Romans recognized those bonds, but they used another term, *gens,* to designate people who share the same family name, whether by birth or adoption. Each freeborn Roman, therefore, was a member of a *familia* and a *gens.* While a slave might be a member of his or her master's *familia,* the state did not recognize a slave as a member of a *gens.* If a slave were freed, he would then become part of his master's *gens,* but would most likely leave behind the *familia.* "Family" in this chapter will be used primarily to designate those people related by marriage and blood living together. *Familia* will refer to the whole household.

The Family and/in Society. What did it mean to be a member of a *familia* or a *gens* in day-to-day life? What demands did the household unit place on a man? a woman? children? slaves? Likewise, what did it mean to men and women to be born into a particular *gens?* And how did life change through the passage of time? There has always been a sense that family was stronger in the past than in the present. Even the ancient Romans felt that the family was so important that at times they urged people to marry and raise children, offering rewards for those who did and punishments, or at the least restrictions, for those who did not. There was a sense that the state could not survive if the family was not strong. Most important, the example set by Aeneas—devotion to the family (father, son, wife), devotion to the gods (in bringing the household gods from Troy to Italy), and his devotion to the state (in founding a new city)—established the concept of *pietas. Pietas* as a concept

helped hold the Roman people together, especially in times of turmoil.

Patrons and Clients. In addition to the relationships established in the *familia* and in a *gens,* members of Roman society were also bound together through a system of patronage. Every Roman was either a patron or a client. Patrons were wealthy and influential people—both men and women, although men appear to have been in the majority—who offered financial and material support, as well as legal and personal protection. Clients were those who received help from patrons and in return provided services, goods, votes, and support in the form of being part of a visible entourage in public arenas. The patron/client relationship was one that was passed down from generation to generation. New clients came from freedmen and freedwomen and their descendants. As the form of government changed, however, the nature of the patron/client relationship changed as well: under the monarchy and the empire the king or emperor was the ultimate patron, with the upper classes serving as patrons for the lower classes, but also as clients of the kings or emperors. During the republic, the patron/client relationship was outside the governmental structure and became more of a personal obligation. Just as the changes in governmental system affected the nature of patronage, so also did the changes affect the family.

Family and the State. Rome as a state began its existence as a monarchy. From the founding in 753 B.C.E. to 509 B.C.E., Rome was ruled by kings who were chosen at first by the people and approved by the Senate, an advisory body of *patres,* or fathers, established by the first king, Romulus. The second, third, and fourth kings were chosen for their individual characters and capabilities. Two of these kings, in fact, did not even live in Rome at the time of their elections: Numa Pompilius (the second king) and Ancus Marcius (the fourth king and Numa's nephew) were Sabines who lived in Sabine towns. This respect for character, regardless of place of birth, allowed the Romans to benefit from that which was best in other cultures. It also meant that Rome became a place to which people came in search of better opportunities for themselves and their families. The fifth king, Lucius Tarquinius Priscus, was an Etruscan who, on the advice of his wife, moved his household from Tarquinia to Rome. In Tarquinia, Lucius was just the son of a foreigner who had no access to power or prestige because his father was not Etruscan. But in Rome, as Tanaquil (his wife) pointed out, there was respect for the individual regardless of his family background: the Romans had even put foreigners on the throne. Somehow, however, the perception of the monarchy changed: the sons of Ancus Marcius, the man Lucius succeeded, felt cheated, as if they had a right to rule because their father and their great-uncle had been kings. They assassinated Lucius, but Lucius's son-in-law took the throne at the encouragement of Tanaquil and later with the support of the people. The kingship became something associated with a family, rather than an elected office. Just like Lucius, his son-in-law Servius Tullius was assassinated by the son of his respective predecessor. The seventh and final king, Lucius Tarquinius Superbus, killed his father-in-law at the insistence of his wife, Tullia. Superbus's own reign ended because of a similar act of violence against the family: his son raped Lucretia, a noblewoman and the wife of his own cousin. After Lucretia named her attacker to her husband and father, and made them swear to avenge her honor, she committed suicide to seal her reputation as a chaste woman.

Revolution and a New Government. Although Superbus had long treated the people as slaves, it took this violation of a family to move the people to revolution. The people threw the Tarquins out of Rome and established a new government in which officials were elected each year, with two consuls at the head of the state. A division that occurred during the monarchy began even more to dominate Roman society and divide one group of families from another: when Romulus created the Senate, the descendants of these *patres* ("fathers") became known as patricians. The rest of the free population were known as the plebeians ("the people"). All of the new offices (consul, praetor, aedile, quaestor, censor, dictator, and magister equitum) were open only to the patricians, even though the plebeians constituted the majority of the population. Tension grew within the society because patrician families had access to power and plebeian families did not. Although patrician families did help plebeian families through patronage, it was not enough.

The Twelve Tables. Part of the strength of the patricians' power lay in the fact that Rome did not yet have a set of written laws. Finally a plebeian revolt forced the patricians to begin the process of writing down the laws. The result was a codification of Rome's laws on twelve *tabulae* (the so-called Twelve Tables, perhaps originally of wood) placed in public for all to see. Although the plebeians had hoped that this action would benefit them, in reality they only learned in what a powerless position they were. The patricians looked down on them so much that the two groups were not even allowed to intermarry.

The Rise of the Plebeians. As time passed, the plebeians began to make greater and greater inroads into the power structure. Their first office of political power was the tribune of the *plebs*. The function of this office was to defend the people's rights. They quickly gained the right to intermarry and, in time, they were able to run for any of the elected offices. Tradition still favored the patricians, but as patrician families began to lose their wealth and even to die out, the plebeians began to be more prominent in politics, in religion, and as guardians of tradition.

Fighting for Plebeians. One area in which plebeian families continued to be at a disadvantage was in the ownership of land. Patrician families, even poor ones, held onto their property. In addition, patrician families gained access to public lands owned by the state, which they farmed as if they owned the property and for which they paid only a nominal rent, if any at all. Although agitation for a more-equitable distribution of land was a part of every age of the Republic, the tensions came to a head in 133 B.C.E. A tribune of the plebs, Tiberius Sempronius Gracchus, used his veto power and the plebeians' right to pass laws in the assembly to push through legislation limiting the amount of land that patricians could own or use. But because he also used nontraditional ways to push through the law, and because he made it known—contrary to the law—that he would run for consecutive terms as tribune, the patricians had him and several hundred of his followers killed. The Sempronius Gracchus family continued the fight, and ten years later Tiberius's younger brother, Gaius, also held the tribunate and aroused the populace. When it became clear that the senatorial forces were again going to use violence, Gaius committed suicide, but three thousand of his followers were still killed. In the midst of all of this upheaval, Cornelia, the mother of these two men, became an influential and remarkable figure. A patrician by birth and the daughter of Publius Cornelius Scipio Africanus, she had been married to the influential plebeian Tiberius Sempronius Gracchus and borne him twelve children, of which only three survived to adulthood. As a mother, she referred to her sons as her "jewels." As a widow, she refused the proposal of Ptolemy VIII Euergetes, the king of Egypt. As a literary figure, she wrote letters worthy of the attention of later generations—they were praised by Cicero and Quintilian—and her home became a center of literary discussion and cultural exchange. One of her letters reportedly urged Gaius not to follow in his brother's footsteps but to pursue reform in ways that would help the state and not endanger it. Clearly he did not listen to her advice. After his death, however, Cornelia shaped the reputations of her sons as champions for the people.

The End of the Republic. The last one hundred years of the Republic were filled with turmoil for many families. The civil war of Sulla and Marius left many dead and divided the state. When Sulla prevailed, he initiated proscriptions to rid himself of political enemies. This systematic campaign of execution left many families without fathers, without a male to lead the family. Sulla confiscated properties, leaving families without homes or the means to take care of themselves. Although these actions directly affected the upper classes, the results must have harmed the lower classes, too, because they were left without patrons to protect them or customers for their wares. When Sulla stepped down from his dictatorship in 79 B.C.E., a brief period of peace followed. Two critical changes in the Roman attitude about family began to be more evident and more pervasive during this period of the Republic. First, people began to marry later or not at all, and when they did marry, they had few children, if any. Because of this new pattern, the population began to decrease, particularly in the upper classes. A second change was in the behavior of the young men raised during this period. Many of them, because they lacked interest in marriage or in politics, spent their time and their fortunes in leisure activities—horses, prostitutes, gambling, and drinking. When the money ran out, and the expectation that these young men should begin to take their place in society by marrying, having children, and running for office became insistent, they had neither the means nor the inclination to follow the usual path. In the year 63 B.C.E. one of these young men, Lucius Sergius Catilina (Catiline), ran for the consulship. When he lost, he organized a conspiracy of fellow outcasts and, with a makeshift army of poor men and opportunists, plotted to kill the consuls and many of the senators. When the plot was revealed to one of the consuls (Cicero) by the "girlfriend" of one of the conspirators, the result was the execution of the leaders—more deaths of young men, more hardship for families. Not long afterward, the first triumvirate—Caesar, Pompey, and Crassus—was formed. Politics became more important than family, and Caesar (the father-in-law of Pompey) eventually defeated Pompey and began to rule alone as dictator.

The Principate Begins. With Caesar's assassination in 44 B.C.E., the second triumvirate was formed: Gaius Julius Caesar Octavianus (formerly Gaius Octavius, Caesar's nephew, heir, and now adopted son), Marcus Antonius (Mark Antony—Caesar's right-hand man), and Marcus Aemilius Lepidus. They sealed their pact by creating a list of victims—men each member wanted killed. Lepidus even allowed his own brother's name to be put on the list! Like the first triumvirate, this group attempted to build an alliance through marriage: Antony married Octavia, Octavian's sister, but he soon abandoned her for other women, most notably Cleopatra. Again a dispute grew between the three leaders, until ultimately Octavian won out and, after the death of Antony and the exile of Lepidus, began to rule alone. In 27 B.C.E., Octavian received the name Augustus from the Senate and began his rule as *princeps* ("first man [among equals]"), although he kept all of the institutions and appearances of the Republic. Augustus's actions with regard to family were hypocritical at best: at the same time that he passed laws forcing people to marry and rewarding them for having children, he himself made and broke marriages among his relatives to suit his political needs. The consistent notion throughout was that marriage and the production of legitimate children were good for the state; the happiness of the individuals involved was not relevant. The people responded to his laws and dictates by finding ways to circumvent them: women registered as prostitutes so that they could not be prosecuted for adultery; some men became engaged to babies to avoid having to marry; others just refused to marry and paid the price politically and financially.

The Family in the Empire. As Rome grew and changed, a variety of elements affected the nature, function, and life of the family. More people from outside the city and even outside Italy moved to Rome, bringing their religions and customs with them. Rome's policy of accepting difference, allowing different practices and different beliefs so long as a person was also willing to support the state and to participate in the state religion, opened the way for Mithraism, the worship of Isis and other Egyptian gods, and Christianity to become part of the Roman landscape. While this policy was not a problem for most people, for Christians it was impossible to worship God and Jupiter, or worse yet, the emperor. Beginning with Augustus, the cult of the emperor had become an ever-present part of Roman religion. Although Augustus forbade worship of himself unless it was in conjunction with worship of Rome, other emperors were less restrained and less tolerant. Attacks on Christianity sent many families into living something of a double life: politics became separate from religion and religion became more of a family-focused or family-oriented experience. Most importantly, Christianity challenged Roman *pietas* (duty to the gods, state, and family) by reorienting one's devotion to God alone.

Families in the Frontiers. As the empire spread, more Romans were living outside the city and Italy. Since the time of Augustus, soldiers had been forbidden to marry while they served in the army. In practice, however, many soldiers had families with women from the areas around Roman outposts. In 197 C.E. the Emperor Septimius Severus ended the ban against marriage for soldiers. He likewise lifted the ban on provincial governors and officials marrying during their term of office, a ban that also dated from the reign of Augustus. It may have been because Severus was himself a military man—born in northern Africa, with a wife from Syria (Julia Domna)—that this new emperor showed concern for the personal lives of soldiers. It may also have been because he had recently defeated the last challenger to his rule and he wanted to ensure the support of the military. Reportedly, his deathbed words to his sons were to "get along and be kind to the soldiers." They did not listen.

The Strength of the Family. Although the world around the Roman family changed over the centuries, the belief that the family was the strength of the society remained a part of Roman thinking even after there was no longer a recognized Roman Empire. Throughout the changes in religion—the acceptance of Christianity by Constantine, the return to traditional Roman religion brought by Julian, and finally the ratification of Christianity as the state religion by Theodosius—and the changes in government (monarchy, republic, principate, empire, tetrarchy; capitol in Rome, capitol in Constantinople), the family continued to garner the attention of the emperors and legislators.

CHILDREN

Pregnancy. In Roman literature and culture, having children, especially a son, was a sign that the gods had blessed the marriage. In reality, getting pregnant was not always so easy. Part of the difficulty of conceiving came from a misunderstanding about the menstrual cycle and periods of fertility. Some women wore amulets, used potions, and prayed to various goddesses for children. Likewise, some women did not want to have children and therefore used a variety of means to prevent pregnancy, ranging from wearing talismans, to using concoctions that they inserted before or after intercourse, to instrumental or medical abortions or mistaken techniques such as riding horses or jumping up and down vigorously when they discovered, to their dismay, that they were pregnant. Men may have used slaves or prostitutes to satisfy their sexual desires in an effort to limit the number of legitimate children, but it was unlikely—and was considered improper—for husbands to avoid their wives' beds altogether.

Raising Children. If a couple had a child, the father made the decision about whether or not to raise the baby. A father did not officially acknowledge the baby until it was nine days old, if a boy, or eight days, if a girl, because so many babies died soon after birth. On the appropriate day, the baby was placed at its father's feet. If the father walked away, the baby was put out in the elements to die. If he picked up the child, he signaled that they would raise the baby. The baby now received its name. How often were babies rejected and exposed? It is a hard question to answer. Deformed babies were almost always exposed. Legal texts suggest that poor families exposed children for whom they could not provide adequate care. During difficult times in the empire, some families refused to raise their children. During the reign of Nero a parent abandoned an infant son in the midst of the Roman Forum with the note "I will not raise you, lest you slit your mother's throat," in reference to Nero's recent murder of his mother, Agrippina the Younger. Emperors such as Trajan, Hadrian, and Constantine passed decrees providing public assistance to poor families who had children they could not afford to keep. Such measures suggest that infanticide was a practice driven more by poverty than by a disregard for human life.

Gold bulla, a circular charm worn by children to protect themselves from evil spirits, circa first century C.E. (from Denise Dersin, *What Life Was Like When Rome Ruled the World*, 1997)

Rites of Passage. Freeborn boys wore the *toga praetexta* (the toga with a purple border) and an amulet called a *bulla* until they reached an age and maturity that made them ready to assume the *toga virilis* (toga of manhood). At that point, the boy took off his child's clothes and his *bulla* and dedicated them to the household gods. Then he, his family, and friends went to the Roman Forum, where he would be introduced as a citizen and his name would be recorded in the register of his family's tribe. Many families chose the festival of the Liberalia on 17 March as the day for their sons to become men. After the dedication of the Forum of Augustus in 2 B.C.E, boys assumed the *toga virilis* on the steps of the Temple of Mars Ultor. Girls were recognized as women on the eve of their marriage. They would dedicate their childhood toys and child's garb to the household gods and put on the *stola* (gown) of a married woman. They would also begin to wear their hair in styles up on top of their heads, rather than down and loose.

Adopted Children. The process of adopting children in ancient Rome was different from modern processes of and reasons for adopting. There is no evidence that Romans adopted babies or very young children or daughters, except for foundlings. Adoption first and foremost was to provide an heir for a family that had no son to carry on the family name or receive the family's property. Therefore, a family would adopt a young man, someone whose character they could judge and who appeared strong and healthy enough to provide the family with a future. A family with several sons had a dilemma because the law required that each son inherit an equal amount of the family property. This meant dividing land and resources and decreasing the overall wealth of the family. Adoption, therefore, provided a benefit for both families involved: the adopting family gained an heir and ensured that their family would not die out; the birth-family of the adoptee was better able to provide for the rest of the children.

Sources:
Suzanne Dixon, *The Roman Family* (Baltimore: Johns Hopkins University Press, 1992).

Beryl Rawson, ed., *The Family in Ancient Rome: New Perspectives* (Ithaca, N.Y.: Cornell University Press, 1986).

Jo-Ann Shelton, *As the Romans Did: A Sourcebook in Roman Social History* (New York: Oxford University Press, 1998).

DAILY LIFE

Morning. The family would rise early in the morning. The father would greet clients, then head off to visit his patron and to see to any business that he had for the day. Among the lower classes, the father would go to visit his

Relief of a potter and his wife, circa 110 C.E. (Adolph D. and Wilkins C. Williams Fund, 60-2, Virginia Museum of Art, Richmond)

patron and then go to work. If it was a family-owned business, his wife would go as well. The upper-class women would prepare for day. The paedogogue and other slaves would take care of the children, taking them to school or watching them. Since families who owned businesses often lived above or behind the shop, the parents were never far away.

Farm Families. Families living and working on a farm would follow a similar pattern. Fathers would head to the fields or meet with the farm manager. If it were a market day, he might go into the nearest town himself with the produce, both to sell the items and catch up on the latest news. His wife would work at home. The children would either go to school, work with a tutor, or perform chores.

Festivals. If it was a day for games or a festival, the family would prepare to attend. Certainly many of the working poor—those who provided concessions or necessary services—still worked on these days, but many people would have a day of relaxation. Since there was no such thing as a weekend, these festival days provided the only relief from what was otherwise a continuous string of work or school days.

Afternoon. Romans did not have a lunch hour, but they tended to close their shops (as some still do today) in the midafternoon, the real heat of the day, to relax and grab a bite. There were many shops where one could buy some bread and cheese and something to drink. They would then head to the baths, or to some sort of relaxation. Children would return to their studies.

Evening. The day ended early for most Romans because they had such poor lighting that they needed the sunlight to carry out most tasks. The family would come together again for the only substantial meal of the day. If the couple were throwing a party, the elaborate preparations would have been completed and the children would have been fed and kept in the servants' care. These parties might go on into the night.

Little Interaction. This brief look at daily life suggests that many families did not spend much time together. Mothers would have more time with their children than fathers, but even that was limited if a woman also worked. Although in modern times holidays are considered family time, in most forms of entertainment families were separated by gender and did not enjoy the spectacles together. Men and women of the upper classes did have more leisure time and could, if they chose, spend time with their children, but servants such as the paedogogue and nurse often spent more time with the children than did their parents.

Sources:

Suzanne Dixon, *The Roman Family* (Baltimore: Johns Hopkins University Press, 1992).

Jo-Ann Shelton, *As the Romans Did: A Sourcebook in Roman Social History* (New York: Oxford University Press, 1998).

DEATH

Funeral Rites. When a member of the family died, the family held a funeral that was partly a private and partly a public event. The death of an infant often received little

---

TRIMALCHIO'S TOMB

In Petronius's *Satyrica*, Trimalchio describes to his dinner guests the tomb he has ordered in his will. His is a particularly ostentatious example and something few Romans would have equaled:

"Tell me my dearest friend," he said, "will you order my tomb according to my instructions? My earnest request is that you set my little dog below my statue, and put in garlands, perfumes, and all the contests of Petraites, so that through your kindness my life can continue after death. Build it a hundred feet wide at the front, and two hundred feet from front to rear. I'd like fruit trees of all kinds surrounding my ashes, and lots of vines; it's quite wrong for a man to have an elegant house in life, and not to give thought to our longer place of residence. So before all else I want an inscription with the words 'This tomb must not pass to an heir.' I'll be careful to stipulate in my will that I come to no harm when dead; I'll appoint one of my freedmen to mount guard over my tomb, to ensure that people don't make a beeline to shit against it.

"I want you also to depict ships in full sail, and myself sitting on a dais wearing the toga with a purple stripe and five gold rings, dispensing coins from a wallet to the people at large; you know that I laid on a dinner for them at two *denarii* a head. If you will, incorporate dining-halls as well, and all the citizens having a good time in them. On my right erect a statue of my Fortunata holding a dove, and leading along her puppy with its jacket on. Put in my boy-favorite, and some big winejars sealed with gypsum to ensure that the wine doesn't leak out. You can show one of the jars as broken, with a slave weeping over it. Put a sundial in the middle, so that whoever wants to know the time will read my name, whether he wants to or not. Oh yes, and give some thought to whether this inscription strikes you as suitable enough: 'Here rests Gaius Pompeius Trimalchio of the household of Maecenas.' He was formally declared Priest of Augustus in his absence. Though he could have claimed membership of every Roman guild, he refused. He was god-fearing, brave and faithful. He grew from small beginnings and left thirty million, without ever hearing a philosopher lecture. Farewell, Trimalchio; and fare well, you who read this."

Source: Petronius, *The Satyricon*, translated by P.G. Walsh (New York: Oxford University Press, 1997).

---

ceremony, other than the private grief of the family. Graves of babies were rarely marked. The nature of funeral proceedings varied depending on the means of the family. No one was buried inside the city walls. Most burials were along roadways. The large size of family tombs created something of a villagelike atmosphere, and the area where such tombs were found became known as a *necropolis*, literally, a "city of the dead." Poorer families would have the body taken out of the city, accompanied by the family members who would display their mourning

Relief of a funeral cortège, late first century B.C.E. (Museo Nazionale D'Abruzzo, L'Aquila)

by dirtying their clothes and faces and leaving their hair uncombed. The monument would reflect what they were able to pay and would express some sentiment about the departed. Often the epitaph included the age of the deceased and whether or not he or she had been married. Wealthier families would have a more-elaborate funeral. A particularly famous man—a politician or general—would lie in state so that the citizens could pass by and pay their respects. A member of the family would deliver a eulogy in the Roman Forum so that as many people as possible could hear. A funeral procession would wind through the city with family, friends, clients, and slaves following the body. Family members would carry the wax death masks of their ancestors as emblems of the glory of the *gens*. The group would proceed to the family tomb. They would either cremate the body or place it in an ash urn, or sarcophagus. The sarcophagus would then be placed in the tomb. The family would read the person's will and distribute the wealth according to his or her wishes. Women wrote their own wills, but they had to be approved by their guardians unless the women were Vestal Virgins or independent of another's control (*sui iuris*). It was certainly expected that parents would leave their possessions to their children or to family members. Some chose to free slaves or to leave property to their freedmen and freedwomen. In the empire, it became common to name the emperor as an heir, as evidence of one's esteem.

Sources:

Henry C. Boren, *Roman Society: A Social, Economic, and Cultural History* (Lexington, Mass.: D. C. Heath, 1977).

Jo-Ann Shelton, *As the Romans Did: A Sourcebook in Roman Social History* (New York: Oxford University Press, 1998).

EDUCATION

Teachers and Subjects. In the early years both boys and girls were educated at home. Both learned how to read and write and perform basic mathematical functions under the guidance of a *litterator*, the equivalent to the present-day elementary schoolteacher. The *litterator* was either an educated slave who belonged to the family or a freedman who would find an area, often an outdoor and somewhat noisy space, where for a fee he would teach the children sent to him. In the third century B.C.E. is the first recorded instance of a *litterator*, the freedman Spurius Carvilius, setting up a school and charging a fee. Each morning a *paedagogus*, a slave whose job was to care for the children, would lead them from home to the school. Study with the *litterator* lasted five to six years. Next, if the family could not afford more education, the boy began working in a family business or was sent out as an apprentice to a skilled craftsman or tradesman. One contract for such an apprenticeship showed that the craftsman, in this case a weaver, was responsible for the boy's upkeep during his year of service and that in return the boy worked for him while he learned his craft. The contract stipulates that the weaver is supposed to teach the boy all aspects of his trade within that year's time:

> Pausiris, son of Ammonius, and Apollonius, a weaver, son of Apollonius, have reached the following agreement: Pausiris has given as an apprentice to Apollonius his son Dioskus, who is still under age, so that he may learn the weaver's trade, all of it, as he himself knows it, for a period of one year from the present day. And Dioskus shall work for Apollonius and do everything he is told to. Apollonius has received for the boy, who will be clothed and fed by the weaver for the whole period of the agreement, 14 drachmas to cover the costs of clothing, and Pausiris will give him 5 silver drachmas a month to cover the costs of food. And Pausiris, the father, is not allowed to take the boy away from his master within that period of time. If the boy does not do all his work, he must pay his master one silver drachma for each day on which he is negligent and lazy, or he may offer to remain an equal number of days longer. The penalty for taking the boy away before the end of the period agreed upon is 100 drachmas and an equal sum payable to the Treasury office. If the master weaver should fail to instruct the boy, he must pay the same penalty.

TRIALS OF A TEACHER

The biographer Suetonius wrote about lives of teachers in his work *On Famous Men*. Although most of the work is lost, one part that survives offers some information about a *grammaticus*:

Lucius Orbilius Pupillus was born in Beneventum. He was left an orphan when both his parents were killed on the same day by a treacherous plot of their enemies. First he obtained a job as a menial servant for the town magistrates. Then he joined the army, was decorated, and eventually was promoted to the cavalry. When he had completed his years of service, he returned to his studies and thus filled an ambition he had had since boyhood.

For a long time he lived as a teacher in his hometown, but then in his fiftieth year (the year of Cicero's consulship), he moved to Rome and taught there. However, he earned more fame than money. In one of his books, written when he was an old man, he complains that he is "a pauper, living in an attic." He also published a book called *My Trials and Tribulations* in which he complains about the insults and injuries done to him by negligent or ambitious parents.

He had a fiery temper which he unleashed not only on his rival teachers, whom he castigated on every occasion, but also on his students. Horace called him "the teacher who loved the whip," and Domitius Marsus wrote that many of his students suffered floggings and whippings. Even men of rank and position did not escape his scathing sarcasm.

He lived to be almost 100 years old. . . . In the Capitol at Beneventum, in the area to the left, there is a marble statue of him on display. He is seated, and holds in his hands two books. He left a son who was also named Orbilius and who was also a schoolteacher.

Source: Jo-Ann Shelton, *As the Romans Did: A Sourcebook in Roman Social History*, second edition (New York: Oxford University Press, 1998), p. 103.

Further Education. In those families that could afford to provide their sons further education or chose to continue the education of their daughters, children progressed to the instruction of the *grammaticus*, who continued the work of the *litterator* but raised it to a new level. Quintilian defined the work of the *grammaticus* as to teach "the art of speaking correctly and the interpretation of poetry." This study was not so narrow as it might appear: for the Romans, speaking and writing were intertwined, so a student needed to practice his writing and to read widely in prose and poetry in order to develop his vocabulary. A knowledge of music helped a speaker to develop a rhythm, and the study of history gave the speaker examples of past actions to support his arguments. To interpret poetry required a background in mythology, religion, art, astronomy, philosophy, and history.

Study of Rhetoric. Only the wealthiest or the most politically oriented of the families could send their sons on to study with a *rhetor*, whose purpose was to train public speakers. In the early Republic, young men learned this skill by a sort of apprenticeship: they would attach themselves to a well-respected political figure from whom they could learn by observation in the Senate and in the law courts. Cicero's own education, in the late Republic, combined the formal training with the apprenticeship.

Decline of Oratory. In the Empire, as the political influence of individuals became determined more by imperial favor than by personal talent, the nature of rhetorical training changed, emphasizing style over content. Both Quintilian and Tacitus bemoaned the deterioration of rhetorical education: Tacitus, because boys were assigned speeches on outlandish topics; Quintilian, because rhetoric had become a means of display rather than a vehicle for conveying important truths.

Imperial Interest. Although education remained primarily a private matter for families, some emperors did

Teacher and students, from a late second century C.E. funerary monument (Rheinisches Landesmuseum, inv. 9921, Trier)

One of the characters in Petronius's *Satyrica* is Agamemnon, a teacher of rhetoric. In the passage below, he gives his view of the problems teachers face in meeting parents' expectations and in holding the attention of their students:

It's no wonder that teachers go astray with these exercises: they're forced to rave, because everybody else has gone crazy. Unless they said what the darling pupils wanted to hear, they'd be "standing in empty classrooms" as Cicero says . . . the teacher of oratory is like a fisherman: if he didn't put on his hook something he knew the little fishies would like, he'd wait on his jutting rock with no hope of profit.

So what are we going to do? We should be blaming the parents because they won't let us offer a strict curriculum. They do the same thing with their children as with everything else, sacrifice them for some short-term advantage. In their rush for rewards, they shove raw pupils into the forum. They say that there's nothing more important than eloquence, but they force it on their offspring before the mothers have finished giving birth. If they would let us gradually increase the difficulty of the work and cultivate the boys with demanding reading; if we could form young minds on the precepts of philosophy; if pens could root in the words, the Athenian way, for anything substandard, and dig it out; if the pupils could listen for a long time before imitating, if they could be convinced that nothing that children like is great literature; then the eloquence of the past would reemerge with its proper weight and grandeur.

Later in the *Satyrica*, Echion, a rag seller, talks about his son to Agamemnon and about the sort of education he wants his son to have and why:

That little squirt of mine's growing up. He'll be a student for you soon. He can already recite his times tables up to four. If he lives, you'll have a little servant by your side. Any time he's free, he's got his head bent over his writing tablet. He's bright, he's good stuff. . . . He's done with the Greeks now, and he's coming at Latin literature, not doing so bad neither, even if his teacher thinks the world of himself and never sticks to the point. There's another teacher, though, who doesn't know much but takes some trouble, and he teaches more than he knows himself. He spends the holidays at the farm, and he's happy with any tip you give him.

Now I've bought the boy a bunch of them law books, 'cause I want him to learn a little law to use in the family business. That kind of thing buys groceries. He's already had more literature than's good for him. If he doesn't cooperate, I've decided to get him trained in a trade: barber or herald or at least advocate. Nothing but death can take your trade away. Every day, I yell at him, "Primigenius, believe me, whatever you learn, you're learning it for yourself. You've heard of Philero the advocate? If he hadn't learned a trade, he'd be hungry every day. He used to carry peddler's goods around on his back. Now he's squaring up against Norbanus."

Source: Petronius, *Satyricon*, translated by Sarah Ruden (Indianapolis: Hackett, 2000).

---

take a public interest in promoting the value of education. Vespasian was the first to establish official professorships of rhetoric—one of Latin and one of Greek—and to appoint men to these positions and pay them from the imperial treasury. He chose Quintilian for the first chair of Latin rhetoric in the 70s C.E. Marcus Aurelius added to Vespasian's contribution by establishing four professorships of philosophy and by creating a professorship of rhetoric at Athens, as well. During the military upheaval of the third century C.E., state-supported education in the more-populated cities of North Africa and in Rome and Athens survived, but the instability of the time interfered with education in many other areas of the empire. When Diocletian brought the empire some measure of peace, he and his successor Constantine also restored education to its place of importance. In his Edict on Prices, Diocletian even established a pay ratio for the *litterator, grammaticus,* and *rhetor* at 1:4:5. The state again began to provide funds for professorships of rhetoric and philosophy in many areas of the empire.

Schools. In the early Republic, most education took place in the home under the guidance of the family. This private aspect of education never changed for the Romans. There was never a fully organized, state-supported educational system. Some wealthy men helped provide funds for schools, but the best example, Pliny the Younger, still assumed that the school and the selection of teachers should be under local control. In a letter Pliny requests the historian Tacitus's help in finding applicants for a teaching position in Comum, his hometown, where he has offered to pay one-third of the expenses for building a school so that the children do not have to continue going to a neighboring town for their education. Pliny specifically states that he offered only one-third of the cost because he believes the parents would stay more actively involved in caring for the school and overseeing the teacher if the financial burden rested primarily on them.

Places to Teach. Many teachers, especially *litteratores,* had no permanent building in which to teach classes. Lessons were conducted in open spaces, under awnings, or in the sun, often near noisy shops or along busy streets. *Grammatici,* in part because they were paid more, often had a place—although it may have been a room in their own homes—to offer classes. *Rhetores* were the most fortunate, with more formal schools and facilities to offer their students the comfort they needed to concentrate on their studies.

Sources:
Henry C. Boren, *Roman Society: A Social, Economic, and Cultural History* (Lexington, Mass.: D. C. Heath, 1977).

Judith P. Hallett, *Fathers and Daughters in Roman Society: Women and the Elite Family* (Princeton: Princeton University Press, 1984).

Jo-Ann Shelton, *As the Romans Did: A Sourcebook in Roman Social History*, second edition (New York: Oxford University Press, 1998).

FAMILIAL INTERACTIONS

Mothers and Daughters. Both mothers and fathers were involved in their children's lives to varying degrees, but mothers were expected to have more direct contact with their children in the early years. They supervised their children's upbringing, either by taking care of the children themselves or by supervising the slaves who were assigned to take care of them. As daughters grew, mothers took more responsibility for teaching them what they needed to know to prepare them for marriage. In a poem by Propertius, Cornelia expressed special affection for her mother and for her daughter. Scribonia, the mother of Cornelia and of Augustus's daughter Julia, went of her own free will into exile with her daughter in 8 C.E. Julia Maesa looked to her daughters Julia Mamaea and Julia Soaemias in order to maintain control of the empire after the death of the Emperor Caracalla in 217 C.E.

Mothers and Sons. Sons spent more time away from the home as their education progressed. Yet, mothers stayed close to their sons and worked on behalf of their political careers. Cornelia, mother of the Gracchi, was noted for guiding the development of her sons throughout their lives. Aurelia, the mother of Julius Caesar, kept a close eye on her son's wife Pompeia and it was through her testimony to her son that Caesar divorced her. Servilia, the mother of Marcus Junius Brutus (famous for assassinating Caesar), raised her son after his father's death. Although there were male figures in his life—his uncle, Cato the Younger; his stepfather, Decimus Junius Silanus; and his mother's lover, Julius Caesar—Servilia took an active role in his life and in the family. She worked through the powerful men who were her friends to secure political opportunities for her son. She tried to arrange an advantageous marriage for Brutus, but he chose to marry Porcia, his cousin, contrary to Servilia's wishes. Sometimes sons had to assert their independence. Yet, the fact that Servilia was the only woman who knew beforehand about Brutus and Cassius's plot to assassinate Caesar demonstrates the closeness between mother and son. And even though she was Caesar's mistress, she chose to support her son. Livia, the wife of Augustus and mother of Tiberius, was, according to Tacitus, an overbearing influence on her son's actions once he became emperor. Similarly, Agrippina the Younger was infamous

Tombstone relief of a family at dinner, second century B.C.E. (Musee Calvert, Avignon)

THE LIFE AND DEATH OF CORNELIA

Propertius, one of the great love poets of the age of Augustus, closed his final book of odes with a long poem (4.11) written from Cornelia (the half sister of Julia, Augustus's daughter) to her husband after her death. Propertius creates the image of a man weeping over a new grave, with the ghost of his wife standing nearby, attempting to console him:

Paullus, cease burdening my grave with tears:

No prayers will open the gate of darkness. . . .

Early, when my bordered dress was put away

Before my marriage-torch, and a new head-band

Caught up and bound my hair, then I was brought

To your bed, Paullus—soon to be separated thus.

On this stone it may be read engraved that I

Have been married to one alone. I call

To witness my ancestors' ashes, tended by Rome,

Beneath whose inscriptions stricken Africa lies. . . .

That the censor's law was never relaxed for me,

No spot in me has made your hearth-fire blush;

Cornelia was never a stain on spoils so great,

But rather set an example to a noble house.

My life was constant, the whole was free from reproach:

We lived respected from the marriage to the funeral torch.

Nature gave me laws that are drawn from ancestors:

From fear of judgement, no higher could be attempted.

Let the urn deal me whatever harsh votes it may.

Yet she shall not be shamed who sits by me:

Not you, who towed with rope the lagging Cybele,

Claudia, rare priestess of the tower-crowned goddess;

Not you, whose fine white linen showed a living hearth

When Vesta demanded back the fire damped down.

Nor have I done you wrong, sweet source, my mother

Scribonia: except for death, would you have me changed?

I am praised by a mother's tears, and civic grief,

And the groans of Caesar are my ashes' defense:

He bewails the passing of his own daughter's

Worthy sister, and we see a god's tears flow.

I earned, moreover, the stole of fertile honor:

My kidnap was not made from a sterile home.

You, Lepidus, you, Paullus, are my comfort

In death: I closed my eyes in your arms.

And I saw my brother twice in public office:

In the festive time, when his consulship began,

His sister was taken. My daughter born to mirror

Your father's time as censor, make sure you cleave

By my example to one sole husband. In turn secure our line.

The ferry puts out for me, and I assent,

So many tending the growth of my good deeds.

This is the last reward of a woman's triumph,

That uninhibited talk should praise her well-earned tomb.

I commend you to our children—our mutual pledge—

This care still breathes, is fired in my ashes.

The father must fulfill the mother's role: your neck

Will have to take the weight of all my mob.

When you kiss their tears away, you must kiss for me.

The whole domestic load is henceforth yours.

And if you will grieve at all, let it be alone—

When they come, guile them with dry-cheeked kisses.

Paullus, enough for you the nights you wear out

For me, and the dreams you often believe have my face:

And when in secret you speak to my picture,

Deliver each word as though I shall reply.

Yet should our marriage bed be made afresh,

A tentative stepmother occupy my couch,

Speak well of and bear with your father's wife,

My sons: she will surrender to your manners.

Don't praise your mother overmuch. Loose speech

That makes comparisons will cause offence.

But if, content with my shade, he remembers me,

And still esteems my ashes as myself,

Learn promptly to perceive advancing age

And leave no access for a widower's cares.

May the years subtracted from me be added to you:

Thus may my children gladden Paullus' age.

All's well: as a mother, I never was in mourning—

The entire family came to my funeral.

I rest my case. Arise, my grieving witnesses,

While kindly Earth weighs out my life's reward.

Heaven is open to virtue: may I be found deserving,

And my shade be carried to join my honored ancestors.

Source: Sextus Propertius, *The Poems*, translated by W. G. Shepherd (Harmondsworth, U.K. & New York: Penguin, 1985).

for her manipulations of Nero and Nero's advisers. When Nero tired of her attempts to control him, he had her killed. Monica, the mother of St. Augustine, was a formidable figure in the family. As a Christian, Monica was determined that her son, too, would be a Christian. She oversaw his education, ended his longtime affair with the woman who bore his son, arranged a marriage that never happened, and followed him to Rome when he left Africa. Although Augustine took his own path to Christianity, he considered himself deeply indebted to his mother's persistence and intelligence.

Fathers and Daughters. Contrary to the popular opinion that daughters were a disappointment, or were considered a burden or less desirable than sons, evidence suggests that fathers took great pride in their daughters. Fathers often used their daughters to create political alliances through marriages, but they also came to their defense if needed. Likewise, some daughters followed in their fathers' footsteps. In 42 B.C.E. Hortensia, the daughter of the great orator Hortensius, used her speaking abilities to persuade the triumvirs not to place an exorbitant tax on wealthy widows. Cicero had two children, but he was clearly more devoted to his daughter, so much so that grief at her death overwhelmed him. Augustus depended on his daughter Julia to bring him an heir. After making Agrippa divorce Marcella and marry Julia, Augustus thought her sons Gaius and Lucius would follow him to the throne. When they died, Augustus forced his stepson Tiberius to divorce his wife and marry Julia. When Julia's behavior became unbearable, Augustus ordered her into exile. Although he needed her for his attempts at building a dynasty, he could not forgive her actions. Pliny the Younger writes of the intense grief of his friend Fundanus at the death of his teenage daughter, who was the image of her father. Yet, Vibia Perpetua's father so disapproved of her conversion to Christianity that he took her infant son away from her while she was in prison.

Fathers and Sons. Fathers looked to their sons to carry on the family name, the family reputation, and the family fortune. At the same time, there was a certain amount of tension between fathers and sons because of these expectations. Some scholars suggest that this tension—caused by worries about family property and reputation—existed only in the upper classes, that the lower classes, with less to pass on, did not suffer from the same pressures. The gaps in evidence make it difficult to draw conclusions about the lower classes, but we have information about the relationships between many fathers and sons. Cato the Elder was particularly famous for his devotion to his son from the time he was a baby: he sat nearby while the child was being nursed. He taught the boy his letters by writing out his own history of Rome (the *Origines*) in large letters for his son to copy. The orator Cicero was delighted by his son's birth and made sure that his son had the opportunity to get the best education, so that he, too, could be an orator, but they were apparently never

---

GRIEF OF A BROTHER

The poet Catullus expresses a deep grief at the death of his brother (101):

Through many nations and through many seas

I have come, brother, for these poor funeral rites,

So that I might render you the last dues of the dead

And in vain comfort your silent ashes,

Because Fortune has robbed me of you, alas,

Poor brother, unfairly taken from me.

But now, meanwhile, accept these gifts which by ancient custom

Of the ancestors are offered in sad duty

At funeral rites, gifts drenched in a brother's tears,

And forever, brother, goodbye and farewell.

Source: *Catullus: The Complete Poems*, edited by Guy Lee (New York: Oxford University Press, 1998).

---

close. The poet Horace, the son of a freedman, expressed gratitude for the opportunities that his father provided and the way that his father raised him. Horace's father worked as an auctioneer and saved enough money to send his son to Rome in style—with slaves—to get a gentleman's education. The orator Quintilian mourned the loss of his two sons, who both died as children. He found special comfort in the fact that his older son, ten years old at his death, loved him even more than he loved his paedogogue and nurse. Quintilian's words give some indication of the distance that existed between fathers and their children during the early years of a child's life. St. Augustine's recollection of his father in his *Confessions* offers the picture of a rather distant man who had mixed success in providing for his son financially, but who left his son's spiritual well-being in the hands of his mother.

Siblings. Evidence about the relationships between brothers and sisters, brothers and brothers, or sisters and sisters comes from poetry, inscriptions, and inferences from cooperation in the political realm. What we know comes from actions between adult siblings. The Gracchi brothers, Tiberius and Gaius, the sons of Tiberius Sempronius Gracchus and Cornelia (daughter of Scipio Africanus), worked together on their political agenda: both wanted to expand rights to the Italians, provide land for the poor, and lessen the power of the wealthy, but both used means that circumvented normal political channels and led to violence and ultimately to their deaths. Marcus Aemilius Lepidus, the triumvir, consigned his brother to death by allowing his name to be placed on the proscription list compiled by the second triumvirate (Lepidus, Octavian, and Antony). Although Paullus was allowed to escape and to go into exile, the fact that his brother was willing, maybe even eager, to sacrifice him for his own political gain suggests a less than amicable relationship. In contrast, when Marcus Tullius Cicero was forced into exile for executing the members of the conspiracy led by Catiline, which sought to murder Rome's consuls and senators, his brother Quintus worked to have him cleared and recalled. An inscription about a woman named Turia details how she and her sister worked together to hunt down and convict the murderers of their parents and how she provided a dowry for her sister.

Women and Their Natal Families. When a woman married under the system known as *manus*, she legally became part of her husband's family. As *manus* grew more rare, women married and moved into the homes of their husbands, but legally they and their property were under the control of their fathers, either until the father's death or until he had declared them independent—in Latin, *sui iuris*, "under one's own law." Familial affection, not legal status, determined a married woman's interaction with her father, mother, and siblings. Evidence suggests that daughters maintained close relationships with their mothers. Sempronia and her mother Cornelia were close enough to be suspected of causing the death of Sempronia's husband. Turia's devotion to her sisters after her marriage made her take over their care after the deaths of their parents.

Sources:

Suzanne Dixon, *The Roman Family* (Baltimore: Johns Hopkins University Press, 1992).

Dixon, *The Roman Mother* (Norman: University of Oklahoma Press, 1988).

Judith P. Hallett, *Fathers and Daughters in Roman Society: Women and the Elite Family* (Princeton: Princeton University Press, 1984).

Paul Veyne, ed., *From Pagan Rome to Byzantium*, volume 1, in *A History of Private Lives*, edited by Philippe Ariès and Georges Duby (Cambridge, Mass.: Belknap Press of Harvard University Press, 1987).

Wall painting from the luxurious Boscoreale villa on the outskirts of Pompeii, mid first century B.C.E. (Rogers Fund, Metropolitan Museum of Art, New York)

FAMILY IN ROMAN SOCIETY

Life Outside the Home. The interaction of different members of the *familia* or *gens* with other members of society depended on a variety of factors: social status, gender, age, rank, marital status, and profession, to name a few. Although one of the ideals toward which a *familia* would strive was independence, ultimately one family was intertwined with several others through marriage and through political beliefs and religious duties. Looking at the family in the broader context of society and social change provides a better sense of the nature of Roman society.

Divisions in Roman Society. The two broad social divisions in Roman society were the patricians and the plebeians. Traditionally the patricians were the descendants of the first Roman senators, the *patres*, chosen by Romulus at the beginning of Rome's history. The plebeians were the remaining free citizens. The original division was based on lineage. As the society progressed, and as the economy began to include commerce and crafts along with agriculture, another group, the *equites* ("horsemen" or "cavalrymen") emerged. At first the *equites* were linked only by the fact of their being at the same economic level and sharing military duties. Throughout the Republic the group gained prestige, but it was not until 129 B.C.E. that a ruling that prevented senators from being enrolled in equestrian centuries, or divisions, in the army marked the *equites* as a separate division of society. An additional proposal by Gaius Sempronius Gracchus excluded senators from certain courts, allowing only those in the new economic class to serve. The *equites* were a mixed group of plebeians, businessmen, former freedmen, or the sons of freedmen. Socially they had much in common with patricians and the two groups intermarried with little hesitation.

Distinctions. In addition to these legally recognized classes, Roman society was also in practice divided into the *honestiores* and the *humiliores*—the more honorable men and the more humble men. In the empire, distinction began to be made in the penalties and punishments assessed Romans, based on their status in one of these two groups: *honestiores* suffered milder penalties than *humiliores* for their crimes. These distinctions were based on a combination of one's personal wealth and family name. As time passed, the distinction became wholly

Although slaves were legally possessions, there were Romans, such as the Stoic philosopher Seneca, who looked at slaves as human beings who just happened to be placed in an unfortunate circumstance. In this letter to Lucilius, Seneca expresses his view and reflects on the relationship between slaves and their masters (*Letters* 47):

I'm glad to hear, from these people who've been visiting you, that you live on friendly terms with your slaves. It is just what one expects of an enlightened, cultivated person like yourself. "They're slaves," people say. No. They're human beings. "They're slaves." No, they're friends, humble friends. "They're slaves." Strictly speaking they're our fellow-slaves, if you once reflect that fortune has as much power over us as over them.

This is why I laugh at those people who think it degrading for a man to eat with a slave. Why do they think it degrading? Only because the most arrogant of conventions has decreed that the master of the house be surrounded at his dinner by a crowd of slaves, who have to stand around while he eats more than he can hold. . . . And all this time the poor slaves are forbidden to move their lips to speak, let alone eat. The slightest murmur is checked with a stick; not even accidental sounds like cough, or a sneeze, or a hiccup are let off a beating . . . The result is that slaves who cannot talk before his face talk about him behind his back. The slaves of former days, however, whose mouths were not sealed up like this, who were able to make conversation not only in the presence of their master but actually with him, were ready to bare their necks to the executioner for him, to divert onto themselves any danger that threatened him;

they talked at dinner but under torture they kept their mouths shut. It is just this highhanded treatment which is responsible for the frequently heard saying, "You've as many enemies as you've slaves." They are not our enemies when we acquire them; we make them so.

How about reflecting that the person you call your slave traces his origin back to the same stock as yourself, has the same good sky above him, breathes as you do, lives as you do, dies as you do? It is as easy for you to see in him a free-born man as for him to see a slave in you. Remember the Varus disaster: many a man of the most distinguished ancestry, who was doing his military service as the first step on the road to a seat on the Senate, was brought low by fortune, condemned by her to look after a steading, for example, or a flock of sheep.

I don't want to involve myself in a endless topic of debate by discussing the treatment of slaves, towards whom we Romans are exceptionally arrogant, harsh and insulting. But the essence of the advice I'd like to give is this; treat your inferiors in the way in which you would like to be treated by your own superiors. And whenever it strikes you how much power you have over your slaves, let it also strike you that your own master has just as much power over you. "I haven't got a master," you say. You're young yet; there's always the chance that you'll have one. Have you forgotten the age at which Hecuba became a slave, or Croesus, or the mother of Darius, or Plato, or Diogenes? Be kind and courteous in your dealings with a slave; bring him into your discussions and conversations and your company generally.

Source: Seneca, *Letters from a Stoic*, translated by Robin Campbell (Harmondsworth, U.K.: Penguin, 1969).

---

based on wealth. In 361 C.E. the Emperor Julian issued an edict about punishments for crimes, but he used the terms *locupletes* and *per egestatem abiecti sunt in faecem vilitatemque plebeiam*—"the wealthy" and "those who have through poverty fallen into impurity and the worthlessness of common people."

Priests and Priestesses. Religious offices in Roman society took many forms. Most, especially the *Flamen Dialis* (the priest of Jupiter), the *Flamen Martialis* (the priest of Mars), the *Flamen Quirinalis* (the priest of Quirinus), and the *Rex sacrorum* (the king of sacred things) were lifetime responsibilities. To be eligible for the *Flamen Dialis* and the *Rex sacrorum*, both the man and his parents had to have been married by a special ceremony called a *confarreatio*, and his wife had to be alive. She automatically became the *Flaminica Dialis*, or the *Regina sacrorum*, with religious duties of her own. If the wife of the *Flamen* died, he had to step down from the priesthood. The *Flamen* and *Flaminica Dialis* were never allowed to leave Rome. Candidates to fill these four priesthoods were chosen by the pontifical college, a group

made up of the three major priests (*Flamen Dialis, Flamen Martialis, Flamen Quirinalis*), the *Rex sacrorum*, the twelve lesser *flamines*, the *pontifex maximus*, the lesser pontiffs, and the Vestal Virgins. At first the three major *Flamines* were barred from holding political office. In the late Republic, only the *Flamen Dialis* still faced this limitation. The office appears to have gone vacant during the late Republic, until Augustus revived it in 11 B.C.E. The twelve lesser *flamines* were each assigned to one of the lesser gods or goddesses. Like the major *flamines*, the lesser *flamines* were noted for their distinctive dress. Unlike the major *flamines* who were all patrician, the minor *flamines* were plebeian.

Vestal Virgins. The Vestal Virgins were Rome's only independent priestesses. The *Flaminicae* and the *Regina sacrorum* held their positions only by virtue of being married to the priests. Vestals were specifically independent of any other member of Roman society. Upon being chosen, they immediately because *sui iuris* (independent), but the *pontifex maximus* served as something of a father figure for them. When Vestals needed to be chosen, families

Banquet scene from a mural in a building at Pompeii, 60 B.C.E. (Museo Nazionale, Naples)

in the Republic the *pontifex maximus* appears to have been chosen by the pontifical college, but by 300 B.C.E. the *pontifex* was chosen through popular election. When the Emperor Augustus assumed the office of *pontifex maximus* after the death of Lepidus, the office became part of the powers associated with the emperor, clearly joining the state and its religion. By 383 B.C.E. the Emperor Gratian had dropped the title.

Lesser Pontiffs. In addition to the *pontifex maximus* there were lesser pontiffs assigned to perform the rituals at festivals. Although there were originally only three pontiffs, the number grew as high as sixteen under the guidance of Julius Caesar. In the early and middle Republic, men were chosen by the pontifical college, but in 104 B.C.E. they were elected to office by the people and usually served for life. Pontiffs determined the proper dates for festivals, days when one could conduct business (*dies fasti*), and days when one could not (*dies nefasti*). They kept records of events and strange occurrences that happened throughout the year and supervised burial procedures and laws governing tombs. Like all the other offices, pontiffs were originally patricians, but by 300 B.C.E. half were plebeians.

Slaves. Slaves were an ever-present part of Roman society. In the early Republic, Roman citizens might end up as slaves through debt-bondage, a practice by which they worked for those to whom they owed money for a specific period of time to pay off the debt. In the fourth century B.C.E. a law prevented one Roman citizen from enslaving another to satisfy a debt. Thereafter, slaves were primarily prisoners of war or individuals brought from other countries by slave traders or pirates. Slaves had only the rights granted to them by their owners, so the lives slaves experienced varied considerably depending on the character of the families who owned them and the sort of work for which they had been purchased.

Work-Conditions. The conditions in which slaves worked were sometimes harsh, especially for those slaves who worked hard labor. Those sent to the silver mines in Spain were often convicted criminals. In *The Golden Ass*, Apuleius describes the slaves in a grain mill: "Good gods, what scrawny little slaves they were! Their skin was everywhere marked with purple welts from their many beatings. Their backs, scarred from floggings, were shaded, as it were, rather than actually covered by their torn patchwork garments. Some wore only flimsy loincloths. All of them, decked out in these rags, carried brands on their foreheads, had their heads half-shaved, and wore chains around their ankles. Their complexions were an ugly yellow; their eyes were so inflamed by the thick smoke and the steamy vapor that they could barely see."

Freedmen. Because Romans routinely freed slaves or allowed them to purchase their freedom, freedmen were a substantial part of Roman society. Many freedmen received citizenship along with their freedom; others had to earn it by having legitimate children or serving the state. The sons of freedmen were, however, auto-

were supposed to offer their daughters' names. Then lots were drawn to see which girl (usually between the ages of six and twelve) would serve Vesta for the next thirty years. The state provided the girls with a generous amount of money that was strictly under their own control and with which they could do as they pleased. Although being chosen a Vestal was considered an honor for the girl and her family, it also meant that the family lost its child to the state. By the time of the late Republic, fewer and fewer families were willing to offer their daughters as candidates. The Emperor Augustus considered the cult so important that he established a new shrine to Vesta on the Palatine Hill as part of his home and announced that if any of his own family were eligible, he would put their names forward. The cult continued to be an important part of Rome's culture until 394 C.E. when it ceased to exist. Even though these girls grew up away from their families and under the care of the older Vestals, one incident in the Republic suggests that a strong family bond remained. In 143 B.C.E. Appius Claudius Pulcher had asked for, but not been granted, a triumph for his victory over the Salassi. When a tribune of the plebs threatened to use his veto to stop the triumphal procession, the Vestal Claudia (Appius's daughter) leaped into the chariot with her father and rode with him to prevent the tribune from interfering. Since anyone was allowed to enter the Atrium of Vesta in the Roman Forum during the day, it seems likely that the families of these girls visited their children and maintained familial affection, if not the physical family unit.

Pontifex Maximus. The *pontifex maximus* was head of the pontiffs and oversaw all aspects of state religion. Early

matically citizens. Freedmen gained greater importance in the early Empire because so much of the bureaucratic structure that kept the state running began to be handled either by slaves or freedmen. The Emperor Claudius considered two freedmen, Narcissus and Pallas, as trusted advisers and raised them to public positions of authority and wealth.

Sources:

Apuleius, *The Golden Ass,* translated by P. G. Walsh (Oxford: Clarendon Press; New York: Oxford University Press, 1994).

Peter Garnsey and Richard Saller, *The Roman Empire: Economy, Society, and Culture* (Berkeley: University of California Press, 1987).

Finley Hooper, *Roman Realities* (Detroit: Wayne State University Press, 1979).

Beryl Rawson, ed., *The Family in Ancient Rome: New Perspectives* (Ithaca, N.Y.: Cornell University Press, 1986).

HOUSING

The Home—City and Country. Where did the family live? In the city, especially in Rome, crowded conditions meant that most people lived in small apartments in an *insula,* or apartment building. These multistoried buildings (as high as seventy feet) provided small rooms, few windows, no indoor plumbing on the upper floors, and little in the way of comfort. Worse, these buildings easily caught fire. Those who lived on the upper floors often lost all of their possessions, if not their lives, in conflagrations. During the Republic there were no firemen, so the fire was put out only by those who volunteered to help at the moment. Plutarch records that

Marcus Licinius Crassus, one of the Republic's richest men, used to send agents to a burning building to offer to buy it from the owner at a greatly reduced price. And then the agent would buy any neighboring buildings—especially those threatened by the fire—as well. The poet Martial (3.52) suggests that one landlord, who had insured his building for much more than he paid, torched the place himself!

Better Accommodations. Wealthier families lived in nicer, larger houses that provided the family with a greater amount of living space away from the bustle of the street. These homes resembled the villas that many of these families also owned out in the country. The layout of these more elaborate houses varied, but basic components were present in each. The door from the street entered into an *atrium,* or receiving hall. Here guests would wait to be greeted by their host. Likewise, clients gathered in the *atria* of their patrons. The *atrium* was decorated with painting from the floor to the ceiling, with the more elaborate painting from eye level to the ceiling, so that it could be seen above the heads of a crowd. In the center of the ceiling was the *compluvium,* which was a rectangular hole through which sunlight and rain came into the *atrium.* Immediately below the *compluvium* was the *impluvium,* a small pool or basin for catching rain. The other three rooms that any house had were the *tablinum* (a general purpose area immediately beyond the *atrium*), the *triclinium* (dining-room), and the *cubiculum* (bedroom or private meeting room). More elaborate houses would have a courtyard or peristyle that provided a garden area within the confines of

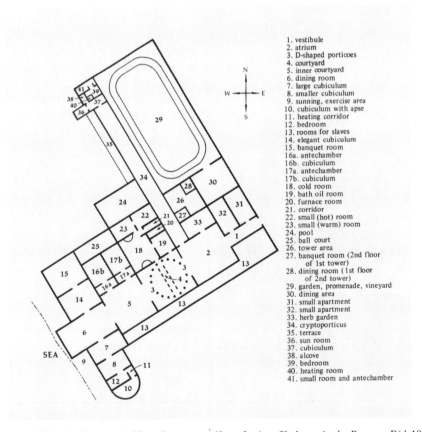

1. vestibule
2. atrium
3. D-shaped porticoes
4. courtyard
5. inner courtyard
6. dining room
7. large cubiculum
8. smaller cubiculum
9. sunning, exercise area
10. cubiculum with apse
11. heating corridor
12. bedroom
13. rooms for slaves
14. elegant cubiculum
15. banquet room
16a. antechamber
16b. cubiculum
17a. antechamber
17b. cubiculum
18. cold room
19. bath oil room
20. furnace room
21. corridor
22. small (hot) room
23. small (warm) room
24. pool
25. ball court
26. tower area
27. banquet room (2nd floor of 1st tower)
28. dining room (1st floor of 2nd tower)
29. garden, promenade, vineyard
30. dining area
31. small apartment
32. small apartment
33. herb garden
34. cryptoporticus
35. terrace
36. sun room
37. cubiculum
38. alcove
39. bedroom
40. heating room
41. small room and antechamber

Diagram of Pliny the Younger's villa at Laurentum (from Jo-Ann Shelton, *As the Romans Did,* 1998)

Street in the town of Herculaneum, which was buried in ash following the eruption of Mount Vesuvius in 79 C.E.

the house. The peristyle was surrounded by a covered walkway off of which would be rooms, such as the *cubicula,* to allow privacy. The *culina,* or kitchen, was placed at the far back of the house to keep the heat and smoke away from the living areas and to minimize the danger of fire. Storerooms and *cubicula* for slaves would also be in the back near the kitchen. Houses without a peristyle might still have a *porticus* (covered area) and a garden for flowers or produce. Rooms that faced the street might be used or rented as shops.

Country Houses. The *villa,* or country house, for the wealthy provided an escape from the noise and heat of the city. Many of the old and wealthy families owned large tracts of land worked by slaves or tenant farmers who answered to an overseer who lived full-time on the farm. The land provided income for the family through produce (olives, grapes, grain) and livestock (sheep, horses, cattle) and provided much of the food and supplies the family needed both in the country and in the city. Places such as Pliny's elaborate villa at Laurentum were built solely to provide comfort for the family and whatever friends came to visit. Rural families who spent their lives working on the farm had less elaborate and more practical homes. Some farmhouses included the stables and workrooms for processing grain and olives within the same walls as their living quarters.

Sources:

Henry C. Boren, *Roman Society: A Social, Economic, and Cultural History* (Lexington, Mass.: D. C. Heath, 1977).

Jo-Ann Shelton, *As the Romans Did: A Sourcebook in Roman Social History* (New York: Oxford University Press, 1998).

LOVE

Husbands and Wives. What was the relationship between a husband and wife? The legal relationship depended upon whether or not the marriage conveyed *manus.* The personal relationship depended on much more. Because the husband was usually older than his wife, especially if this was her first marriage, there was some expectation that the husband took over the wife's education about domestic matters. As the wife (and possibly *materfamilias*) her duties included managing all aspects of the household: overseeing cleaning, cooking, giving orders to slaves, and preserving the *pax deorum* (peace with the gods) inside the home by attending to the household gods (the *Lares* and *Penates*) and outside the home by attending religious festivals and by behaving appropriately in public.

The Marriage-Relationship. The relationship that developed between a husband and wife ranged from complete dislike to a genuine love. Obviously, marriages in which the couple could develop no working relationship often ended in divorce, but there is no reason to believe that bonds of love never developed in arranged marriages, or even that a son's or daughter's expression of love had not convinced a father to arrange the marriage in the first place. Much more has come down about what a wife owed to her husband within the bonds of marriage, but some of these expectations were reciprocal. What, then, did a husband owe to a wife, and vice versa? The first expectation

This inscription from the *Corpus of Latin Inscriptions* (*CIL* 6.1527, 31670), dating to the early part of the first century C.E., offers an account of the life of a woman known as Turia. Her story demonstrates the close bonds between all members of a family and the devotion married couples had for each other, even in times of peril. In addition, we see the destructive effects of political turmoil on the family.

. . . Rare indeed are marriages of such long duration, which are ended by death, not divorce. We had the good fortune to spend forty-one years together with no unhappiness. I wish that our long marriage had come finally to an end by my death, since it would have been more just for me, who was older, to yield to fate.

Why should I mention your personal virtues—your modesty, obedience, affability, and good nature, your tireless attention to wool making, your performance of religious duties without superstitious fear, your artless elegance and simplicity of dress? Why speak about your affection toward your family (for you cared for my mother as well as you cared for your parents)? Why recall the countless other virtues which you have in common with all Roman matrons worthy of that name? The virtues I claim for you are your own special virtues; few people have possessed similar ones or been known to possess them. The history of the human race tells us how rare they are.

Together we diligently saved the whole inheritance which you received from your parents' estate. You handed it all over to me and did not worry yourself about increasing it. We shared the responsibilities so that I acted as the guardian of your fortune and you undertook to serve as protector of mine. . . .

When my political enemies were hunting me down, you aided my escape by selling your jewelry; you gave me all the gold and pearls which you were wearing and added a small income from household funds. We deceived the guards of my enemies, and you made my time in hiding an "enriching" experience. . . .

Why should I now disclose memories locked deep in my heart, memories of secret and concealed plans? Yes, memories—how I was warned by swift messages to avoid present and imminent dangers and was therefore saved by your quick thinking; how you did not permit me to be swept away by my foolhardy boldness; how, by calm consideration, you arranged a safe place of refuge for me and enlisted as allies in your plans to save me your sister and her husband, Gaius Cluvius, even though the plans were dangerous to all of you. If I tried to touch on all of your actions on my behalf, I could go on forever. For us let it suffice to say that you hid me safely.

Yet the most bitter experience of my life came later. . . . I was granted a pardon by Augustus, but his colleague Lepidus opposed the pardon. When you threw yourself on the ground at his feet, not only did he not raise you up, but in fact he grabbed you and dragged you along as if you were a slave. You were covered with bruises, but with unflinching determination you reminded me of Augustus' Caesar's edict of pardon. . . . Although you suffered insults and cruel injuries, you revealed them publicly in order to expose him as the author of my calamities. . . .

When the world was finally at peace again and order had been restored in the government, we enjoyed quiet and happy days. We longed for children, but spiteful fate begrudged them. If Fortune had allowed herself to care for us in this matter as she does others, we two would have enjoyed complete happiness. But advancing old age put an end to our hopes for children. . . . You were depressed about your infertility and grieved because I was without children. . . . You spoke of divorce and offered to give up your household to another woman, to a fertile woman. You said that you yourself would arrange for me a new wife, one worthy of our well-known love, and you assured me that you would treat the children of my new marriage as if they were your own. You would not demand the return of your inheritance; it would remain, if I wished, in my control. You would not detach or isolate yourself from me; you would simply carry out henceforth the duties and responsibilities of my sister or my mother-in-law.

I must confess that I was so angered by your suggestion that I lost my mind. I was so horrified that I could scarcely regain control of myself. How could you talk of a dissolution of our marriage before it was demanded by fate! How could you even conceive in your mind of any reason why you should, while still alive, cease to be my wife, you who remained very faithfully with me when I was in exile, indeed almost in exile from life! How could the desire or need for having children be so great that I would break faith with you!

I wish that our old age had allowed our marriage to last until I, who was the elder, had passed away; it would have been fairer for you to arrange a funeral for me. . . . But by fate's decree, you finished the race of life before I did, and you left me all alone, without children, grieving and longing for you. . . . But inspired by your example I will stand up to cruel fortune, which has not stolen everything from me since it allows the memory of you to grow brighter and stronger through praise. . . .

I conclude my oration with this: you have deserved all, and I can never repay you completely. I have always considered your wishes my command. I will continue to do for you whatever I still can.

May the Manes grant to you and protect your eternal peace, I pray.

Source: Jo-Ann Shelton, *As the Romans Did: A Sourcebook in Roman Social History* (New York: Oxford University Press, 1998).

was *fides:* faithfulness or trustworthiness for the wife in sexual matters but also in economic and personal matters. The wife ran the household, and access to her husband's financial affairs gave her a certain amount of power. Likewise, a husband needed to demonstrate his trustworthiness in managing his own finances to ensure that he could provide for their children, in using his wife's dowry, and in developing his own reputation so that their children would benefit from the public appraisal of their parents. Although a wife could not require sexual fidelity from her husband, some epitaphs testify to the husband's faithfulness in sexual matters. Both the husband and wife owed each other a certain measure of respect, *reverentia,* but only the wife was expected to behave with *obsequium,* dutifulness or cooperation, toward her husband. Kindness, *comitas,* might also characterize the relationship on both sides. A husband could show kindness by indulging his wife with material comforts or with genuine gentleness in his treatment of her and discretion in any extramarital alliances. A wife might equally allow her husband his indulgences without complaint. *Societas*—partnership, alliance—was a word the first king of Rome, Romulus, used to describe what the Sabine women would share with their Roman husbands. He particularly stated that the women would be partners of all of their husbands' possessions and of citizenship and children. *Amor* is more difficult to trace. Certainly husbands and wives are described as loving each other, but there is little direct evidence. The writings of Cicero (at times), Quintilian, and Pliny the Younger express heartfelt affection for their wives. Inscriptions on tombstones provide what seem to be personal sentiments, but can also be somewhat formulaic: for example, there are certain things that one expects to find on tombstones, and thus the sentiments might have more to do with what was expected than what was felt. At the same time, enough monuments give the barest of epitaphs, recording only that "X gave this monument to Y who was well deserving"; to say more was a conscious choice on the part of the surviving spouse.

Courtesans, Prostitutes, Slave Women, and Mistresses. According to an anecdote, one day Cato the Elder saw a young man coming out of a brothel and praised him for spending his sexual energies there. When Cato saw the same young man coming out of the brothel several days in a row, he expressed his dismay: he told the young man that it was fine to visit a brothel, but not to take up residence there. This anecdote provides a glimpse of the role that prostitution played in Roman society. Ideally, prostitutes, courtesans, and slave women provided acceptable options for men's sexual exploits and need for companionship without compromising freeborn Roman women or other men's wives. But "ideally" and "in reality" are two different

Statue of a wealthy married couple, circa first century B.C.E. (Vatican Museum)

things. Although Cato himself was well known for spending his nights with a slave girl after the death of his wife, other men, such as Julius Caesar, spent their time with the wives or former wives of their peers.

Social Levels. It is important to note the different social levels within the world of prostitution itself. Slaves, both men and women, were subject to the desires of their owners. Streetwalkers, women who had no set place of operation and who stationed themselves in areas where men could easily find them, had little choice about their clients. At the next level might be those who worked in brothels. Although their conditions were still deplorable and these women had no control over the men who bought their time, they did not have to have sex in alleyways, and they did have some protection by the brothel owner against abusive clients. For the most part, streetwalkers and brothel workers would have been frequented by lower-class men or young men with little money of their own.

A Different World. Courtesans lived in a different world. They often had houses or apartments provided for them, or enough money to buy their own property. They had more control over the men with which they associated. These women could provide a distraction as well as sexual pleasure. All prostitutes had to register with the *aedile* (city commissioner) and all paid taxes on what they earned.

Legal Loophole. Because prostitutes were immune to legislation that punished adultery, some upper-class women who wanted the freedom to have affairs registered as prostitutes, thereby circumventing the laws that Augustus had passed. During the reign of Tiberius, however, a measure was passed that prohibited the descendants of senators (down to the great-grandchildren) and the immediate relatives of members of the equestrian class from engaging in prostitution.

Homosexuality. Ancient sexuality existed in a world free from the moral issues that Christianity attached to sexual relations between men and women, men and men, and women and women. In Rome there were two primary concerns with sexuality: the first was the need to know the paternity of one's children without a doubt; the second was a matter of dominance. The Romans felt that no man should willingly be dominated sexually (or in any other way, for that matter) by another man. Homosexual behavior (this is a modern term and notion, not an ancient one) was not rejected but was considered appropriate and acceptable within certain limitations: men were free to penetrate slaves and prostitutes (male and female), but just as they were supposed to abstain from sex with freeborn women or girls, so also were they supposed to avoid sexual contact with freeborn boys. Information about lesbian relationships is exceedingly scarce and most problematic, since it comes primarily from poetry and especially from satires that aim at condemning the women who would take the dominant role in sexual intercourse with another woman. Again, the issue was one of role, rather than homosexuality itself. To the Roman way of thinking, men, not women, should play the aggressive and penetrating partner in sexual intercourse. Thus, poet Martial objects to Philaenis, not because she engages in sex, but because she "devours girls" and challenges men to competitions in satisfying sexual appetites. The true emotional devotion one man felt for another, so evident in the Emperor Hadrian's attachment to his lover Antinous, has no visible public parallel for love between two women, but that does not mean that no such love existed.

Sources:

Suzanne Dixon, *The Roman Family* (Baltimore: Johns Hopkins University Press, 1992).

Dixon, *The Roman Mother* (Norman: University of Oklahoma Press, 1988).

Judith P. Hallett, *Fathers and Daughters in Roman Society: Women and the Elite Family* (Princeton: Princeton University Press, 1984).

Susan Treggiari, *Roman Marriage: Iusti Coniuges From the Time of Cicero to the Time of Ulpian* (Oxford: Clarendon Press; New York: Oxford University Press, 1991).

MARRIAGE

Finding a Spouse. Marriages among the upper-class Romans tended to be arranged by the woman's father and the young man or his father. Sometimes the betrothal took place years before the actual marriage. The bride-to-be may have had little say in the matter, but a mother clearly expected to be consulted, expressed her opinion, and even made marriage arrangements in her husband's absence. An anecdote in Plutarch's *Life of Tiberius Sempronius Gracchus* recounts that one day Appius Claudius Pulcher hurried into his home and announced to his wife that he had arranged a marriage for their daughter. His wife, somewhat annoyed and surprised, asked why he was in such a hurry, unless the young man was Tiberius Gracchus. Pulcher was pleased because Gracchus was indeed just the man he had chosen. These marriages tended to have political or economic purposes, as well as to satisfy the desire to continue the husband's family line. Less is known about marriage among the lower economic classes, but arranged marriages took place among them as well, perhaps more for economic than political reasons. Tombstones indicate that men and women who worked together as slaves and developed an affection for each other married upon gaining their freedom. Slaves could declare that they were husband and wife and often masters would respect the bond and not separate the family, especially in the case of slaves living in the household. If a husband or wife received freedom, often he or she worked to secure the freedom of his or her spouse and children.

Personal Choices. This is not to say that upper-class marriages never evolved from mutual affection, but opportunities for such acquaintance were unlikely considering the difference in ages between women (twelve to sixteen) and men (twenty to thirty) for a woman's first marriage. Subsequent unions were more likely to be personal choices. Finding a husband was not always easy. When Cicero began looking for Tullia's third husband in

51 B.C.E, he asked the help of various friends in finding suitable candidates, in part because he was out of the country serving as the governor of Cilicia. Only a few men were available who met Cicero's political needs, personal inclination, and his daughter's approval. Publius Cornelius Dolabella, although not Cicero's first choice, was the favorite of Tullia and her mother Terentia. In Cicero's absence they were able to take the lead and arrange the engagement. Even though he had his doubts, Cicero gave his approval.

The Right to Marry. Only men and women who had *conubium,* the legitimate right to marry, were able to enter into a union that could produce legitimate children. Slaves did not possess *conubium;* so, although they entered into unions that they valued, their marriages did not have to be recognized by their owners, until the Emperor Constantine issued an edict at the beginning of the third century C.E. that prohibited owners from separating slave families and required those who had to reunite them as quickly as possible. All Roman citizens possessed *conubium* and could, therefore, marry each other without question about the legitimacy of their children. Roman citizens could marry Latins (residents of the Italian peninsula who had been given special rights by the Roman government), who had been awarded *conubium* along with their other privileges. Foreigners as well might be awarded *conubium* and could, therefore, marry Roman citizens. Among Roman citizens there were concerns about and even bans against marriage between certain classes at different times in Rome's history. According to the historical tradition, there was a time in the early Republic when a law prevented patricians (families who were descended from the first *patres,* or senators) and plebeians from intermarrying. In 445 B.C.E., however, the *lex Canuleia* allowed patricians and plebeians to marry, but practice may have kept the two groups separate. During the reign of Augustus, the emperor promoted a law that forbade senators and their children and grandchildren to marry freedwomen or the children of freedmen and women who had been actors or actresses. Augustus also prohibited soldiers from marrying while they served in the army. The Emperor Septimius Severus ended this practice in 197 C.E. By that point Romans had permanent military outposts scattered around the Empire. A Roman man serving as an administrator in a province could not marry a woman from that province during his term of office. Prostitutes also did not have *conubium.* Finally, the parties also had to be of an appropriate age to marry: the bride had to be at least twelve; the groom, although often in his twenties, had to be at least fourteen. For those who did not have the right to marry but who chose to live together as husband and wife nonetheless, their relationship was called *contubernium* (literally, "the state of being tent-mates"). A freeborn man or a freedman might live as husband and wife with a slave woman. Likewise, a male slave might have a freedwoman as a wife. The state offered limited recognition to these relationships, even if they could not produce legitimate children.

Betrothal and the Dowry. Two agreements might precede a marriage, especially among the upper classes: an arrangement of *sponsalia,* or betrothal, and an agreement about the amount of the dowry (and the means for its return should the marriage end in divorce). The betrothal might be as simple as a verbal agreement between the girl's father and the young man that a marriage would occur at a certain time, or it might be as elaborate as a large family party at which the young man would present the bride-to-be with a ring. The betrothal was sealed with a kiss and the joining of right hands by the couple. There was no specific amount of time between the betrothal and the marriage, until Augustus passed legislation limiting the length of a betrothal to two years. The most important event before a marriage, however, was the arrangement concerning the dowry (an amount given a woman by her father at her marriage). Although the dowry may have been a part of early Roman marriage, the first mention of the dowry in legal texts comes in 230 B.C.E. In this year a procedure was established for returning the dowry upon the divorce of the couple. The passage of this law may indicate that divorce was becoming frequent enough to need legislation, rather than provide any indication about the history of the dowry. Although the dowry belonged to the woman, her husband was allowed to treat the property as his in order to increase the value and use the revenue. Before the marriage the woman's father and the prospective groom decided on the amount and how it would be paid. For instance, when Cicero agreed to the marriage between Tullia and Dolabella, he arranged to pay her dowry in three equal payments over three years. In theory, revenue from the dowry helped the husband provide for his wife, but evidence, again from the marriage of Tullia, suggests that was not always the case: at one point Tullia was reportedly in such financial difficulty that Cicero (who was out of the country because of the civil war between Caesar and Pompey) had to apply to his friend Atticus to take care of Tullia's needs; apparently Terentia had mishandled the family finances or refused to help her daughter. When Cicero began divorce proceedings on Tullia's behalf, Dolabella had to return the dowry in the same manner as he had received it. A husband could keep part of the dowry only if he proved his wife had committed adultery.

The Wedding. When a woman married, she did not alter her name. She did, however, change where she lived, what she wore, and possibly whom she looked to as a guardian. In most instances, however, a marriage occurred by the declaration that a man and woman were going to live together as husband and wife. The event was celebrated with a party for friends and family that began at the bride's house. One ritual that the bride performed was the dedication of her childhood toys to the household gods, so signifying that she was no longer a child, but an adult. The bridal outfit consisted of a white dress with saffron-colored veil and shoes. Not all families could afford such expensive preparations, so the girl may merely have exchanged her child's garment for the *stola* ("gown") of the Roman matron. Once the celebration was over, a procession of friends and family carrying torches would accompany the new bride to the house of her husband, who was most likely still living with his parents. In addition, three young boys whose parents were still living accompanied the bride, two holding each of her hands and one carrying a special torch, the *spina alba* ("white wood"). The celebrants made jokes, said suggestive things, and threw nuts—all to encourage fertility for the couple. The groom left the party before the bride in order to meet her at the door of his house. When the bride arrived, she decorated the doorway with oil and wool. Some believe that the bride may have expressed her devotion to her husband by uttering the phrase "*ubi tu Gaius, ego Gaia*" ("Where you are Gaius, I am Gaia") to mark her arrival to his house. The bride's attendants (including the *pronuba*, or matron of honor) carried the bride across the threshold so that she would not trip and therefore bring a bad omen to the beginning of the marriage. The bridegroom then offered her a torch and water, symbolizing his willingness to provide for her well-being. A small ritual marriage-bed might be set up in the atrium of the house, and there she would place an image of her *genius*, in essence, her soul. The day after the wedding, the new couple was expected to provide a dinner party for the wedding guests. In their presence the new wife made her first offering to her husband's household gods. In the days following the wedding, the couple was expected to attend other parties together. This public demonstration, like the procession on the wedding day, made it known to all that they were married.

Marriage and *Manus*. There were three different types of ceremonies associated with marriage that determined the degree to which a woman and her dowry came under her husband's authority. Although a woman could own property and could buy and sell that property, she did so with the approval of her *tutor*, or guardian, unless she had been declared independent (*sui iuris*). For a married woman, her guardian was either her father or her husband. For a divorced, widowed, or orphaned woman, another man, usually a relative from her *gens*, served as her guardian. His job was more to protect the family's resources than to hinder a woman from buying and selling property.

Confarreatio. The *confarreatio* (literally, "a sharing of *far*," a sort of grain made into bread) was the most elaborate and most rare of the three ceremonies associated with marriage and was practiced only by patricians and likely substituted for the basic wedding ceremony described above. If a man wanted to serve as the *Flamen Dialis*, the high priest of Jupiter, the *Flamen Quirinalis*, the high priest of Quirinus, the *Flamen Martialis*, the high priest of Mars, or the *rex sacrorum* (the king of sacred matters), both he and his parents had to have been married through

Relief of a newly-married couple joining hands to symbolize their union, first century C.E. (Museo Nazionale, Rome)

confarreatio. In this ceremony, the husband received *manus*, or authority over his wife, from her father. In the ceremony itself, the bride and groom sacrificed a loaf of bread made from *far* to Juppiter Farreus. They performed rituals and repeated a given set of vows in front of ten witnesses, including the *Pontifex Maximus* and the *Flamen Dialis*. One account states that a sheep was sacrificed and skinned and that the couple sat on the sheepskin with their heads covered. A couple married by *confarreatio* could not divorce. If one of the spouses should die, the other had to step down from his or her priesthood.

Usus. The second way to establish *manus* was called *usus*. In this instance, after a man and woman announced that they were husband and wife, a husband gained *manus* only if his wife was never away from his home for more than three consecutive nights each year. If she did not stay away from her husband's house, he received *manus* over her and her dowry. *Manus* became less common as the Republic came to a close but still existed enough in the early empire that a procedure (*emancipatio*) existed to free a woman from her husband's control. *Usus* faded out as a means of marriage by the end of the second century C.E.

Coemptio. The third procedure affecting a marriage, was *coemptio*, a sort of ritual sale that placed a woman and her property in a man's control in the presence of a minimum of five adult Roman male citizens as witnesses. That man could become her husband, but *coemptio* in and of itself did not constitute a marriage; it only conveyed *manus*. A man and woman who had previously married might at some point, therefore, perform *coemptio* to establish the husband's *manus*. A woman could, in fact, make a *coemptio* with a man who was not her husband in order to make that man her *tutor*, or guardian. Understanding *coemptio* is difficult because its focus is more on control of property than on establishing a marital relationship between a man and a woman. For that reason, a woman's guardian or guardians had to approve any *coemptio*, but their approval was not necessary for marriage.

Purpose of Marriage. The explicit purpose of marriage was for the procreation of legitimate children. A husband could, therefore, divorce his wife if the marriage produced no children (the assumption was always that a lack of children resulted from a defect in the woman's ability to conceive). Although some men divorced their wives for being barren, other men, such as the husband of Turia, refused to divorce their wives just because of a lack of children. The writer Pliny the Younger had a young wife who, although she became pregnant once but miscarried, never bore him any children.

Alliances. Marriage could create political and economic alliances, as well. After Caesar, Pompey, and Crassus formed the first triumvirate, Pompey married Julia, Caesar's daughter, to add a personal dimension to their political arrangement. Likewise, Antony married Octavia, the sister of Octavius, one of his partners in the second triumvirate. Since he had produced no male heir, the Emperor Augustus used marriage to try to establish a successor to his rule. When all the other choices had died, he forced his stepson, Tiberius, to divorce the wife he loved and to marry Julia, Augustus's only daughter. This marriage made Tiberius both his son-in-law and stepson and, therefore, his closest male relative. It also made him miserable.

Marriage Legislation. Like other governmental officials before him, Augustus became concerned because fewer people were marrying and having children. He therefore passed laws in 18 B.C.E. and 9 C.E. that favored men and women who had legitimate children and that urged men and women to marry. For Roman citizens, Augustus required men to be married by the age of twenty-five and women by the age of twenty. If a woman's husband died or divorced her, the legislation required that she remarry within two years or a year and a half, respectively. These lengths of time allowed for the appropriate period of mourning and ensured that any children the woman might bear were recognized as her husband's. Men, on the other hand, were expected to remarry quickly, although those whose wives had died most likely would have observed a year of mourning. Augustus required that men be married, up to the age of sixty, and women, up to the age of fifty-five, under the assumption that those were the outer limits of childbearing age.

Special Consideration. Augustus also expected the couple to have children and to raise them. Therefore, he gave special consideration and privileges to men and women who had three or more children. The children had to reach a certain age (puberty for boys and marriageable age for girls) to count. Children who were killed in war counted, regardless of their age. The more children men

had, the more privileges they received: when two men were elected consul, the one with more children became the senior consul. Before Augustus's reign, seniority was determined by age. In Rome, a man with three children no longer had to serve as a woman's guardian. (A man who lived outside Rome had to have four or five children, depending on whether he lived in Italy or in the provinces.) Women who had three children no longer had to have a guardian. For freedwomen, four children released them from the guardianship of their former owner, or three children if they had already transferred their guardianship to someone else. Freedmen no longer owed work to their former owners once they had two children. Slave women could gain their freedom by producing four children, but because any children born while the woman was a slave were automatically also slaves and stayed in the master's household, even if she left, the idea of consigning children to servitude for their own benefit may have prevented many slave women from pursuing the matter.

Divorce. In the early Republic, when most (if not all) marriages conveyed *manus*, only husbands could initiate a divorce, and only with a just cause such as adultery, poisoning children, or compromising the security of the *familia*. If he divorced his wife for any other reason, his property was confiscated and half was given to his wife, half deposited in the temple of Ceres. In the earliest recorded divorce, in 307 B.C.E., Lucius Annius was removed from the Senate by the censors because he did not properly consult his friends before divorcing his wife. (The loss of his property would also have ended his eligibility for the Senate.) The expectation that Lucius should have consulted others about a private matter suggests that a husband needed some external support for his decision. A divorce in 230 B.C.E. reveals a new development: Carvilius Ruga divorced his wife because she had failed to have a child. Since the stated purpose of marriage was to produce legitimate children, the perceived sterility of a wife was deemed as just cause for a divorce. In this instance, the wife was able to reclaim her dowry and Carvilius suffered no other penalty. As marriage with *manus* became less common, women's fathers or even the women themselves, if they were *sui iuris* (independent), were able to initiate divorce with full recovery of the dowry. In general, a father could not initiate a divorce against his daughter's or son's will. The exception was the emperor. Augustus acted rather freely, ordering divorces and arranging marriages to further his dynastic aims and satisfy his personal needs. He forced Agrippa, and then Tiberius, to divorce their wives to marry his daughter Julia. He commandeered Livia from her husband while she was pregnant with her second child.

Social Class. Social class also affected one's ability to divorce: a freedwoman could not divorce her patron without his consent. Only upon a formal agreement of divorce or upon the patron's second marriage did a freedwoman gain the right to remarry.

Divorce Procedure. The divorce procedure appears to have been rather informal—an announcement that the marriage was over and the other person should have his or her property—*tuas res tibi habeto*. In the late Republic, a more-formal declaration involved one party sending a freedman—someone who could testify in court, if need be—to deliver the message of divorce to the other party. Although in the late Republic and early empire one party had to inform the other of the intention to divorce, in 294 C.E. the Emperors Diocletian and Maximian ruled that formal notice did not have to be given for a divorce to be valid. It was not until 449 C.E., during the reign of Theodosius and Valentinian, that divorce again required a formal notification, this time in the form of a *repudium*—a statement of rejection—by one spouse or the other.

Sources:

Suzanne Dixon, *The Roman Family* (Baltimore: Johns Hopkins University Press, 1992).

Dixon, *The Roman Mother* (Norman: University of Oklahoma Press, 1988).

Jane Gardner, *Women in Roman Law and Society* (Bloomington: Indiana University Press, 1986).

Judith P. Hallett, *Fathers and Daughters in Roman Society: Women and the Elite Family* (Princeton: Princeton University Press, 1984).

Susan Treggiari, *Roman Marriage: Iusti Coniuges From the Time of Cicero to the Time of Ulpian* (Oxford: Clarendon Press; New York: Oxford University Press, 1991).

THE NATURE OF THE FAMILY

Members of the *Familia*. A *familia* included everyone who lived in the same household. The oldest male in the house was known as the *paterfamilias*. The *paterfamilias* had ultimate authority over the whole *familia*. Likewise, the oldest woman in the house was the *materfamilias*. Unlike the *paterfamilias,* the authority of the *materfamilias* was not legal; rather, she held a position of respect and was able to exercise the authority that this respect gave her. A husband and a wife (*vir* and *uxor* respectively, or *coniunx*, a word like "spouse") were not the *paterfamilias* or *materfamilias*, if they lived with the husband's parents. Children, *liberi* ("the free ones"), were members of the *familia*, but only of their father's *gens* ("family"). Likewise, a wife remained a member of her *gens* even after her marriage, unless she married with *manus*, a condition that placed her under her husband's control and therefore made her a member of his *gens*. Other members of the *familia* include the household slaves, particularly ones who took care of the children. The *nutrix*, or nurse, cared for children from their birth. Some children developed a long-lasting affection for their nurses, and evidence suggests that nurses remained in the household long after the children had grown. When the Emperor Nero committed suicide in 68 C.E., it was his nurse and former lover, Acte, who cared for his body and buried him in the family tomb. Once a child became a little older and began attending school outside the home, a *paedagogus* ("a child escorter") was assigned to accompany and protect the child.

LIST OF PRAENOMINA

Because there was a limited number of *praenomina*, or first names, often the first name appears only as an abbreviation in literary works and in inscriptions. The abbreviations, with the corresponding names, are as follows:

A. Aulus	Mam. Mamercus
App. Appius	N. Numerius
C. Gaius	P. Publius
Cn. Gnaeus	Q. Quintus
D. Decimus	Sex. Sextus
K. Kaeso	Ser. Servius
L. Lucius	Sp. Spurius
M. Marcus	T. Titus
M'. Manius	Ti(b).Tiberius

Some of the names, such as Quintus, Sextus, and Decimus, come from numbers (for example, fifth, sixth, and tenth). Spurius was a name often given to sons who were born after their father's death or whose paternity might have been in question. (Or they were given the *cognomen* Postumus, "after burial.") Other abbreviations one might see in inscriptions are:

f or F—*filius* or *filia* (son or daughter)

n or N—*nepos* (grandson)

l or L—*libertus* or *liberta* (freedman or freedwoman)

Source: William G. Hale and Carl D. Buck, *A Latin Grammar* (Boston & London: Ginn, 1903; reprinted, Tuscaloosa: University of Alabama Press, 1966.)

Members of a *Gens*. A *gens* refers to all individuals born or adopted into the same family and who, therefore, had the same family name. All males had at least two names: the *nomen*, which was the family name, and the *praenomen*, which corresponds to a first name. Some men also had a *cognomen*, an honorary name or a sort of nickname that had become part of the family tradition. Take, for example, the orator Marcus Tullius Cicero: his *gens* name is Tullius, the name he shared with his father, his brother, his son, and his daughter (the latter in a modified form, to show feminine gender). Marcus is his *praenomen*. His brother's *praenomen* was Quintus. Cicero is his *cognomen*, a nickname that had become hereditary in the Tullian *gens*. Because there was a relatively limited number of *praenomina*, men were usually identified not only by their full name but also by the *praenomina* of their fathers and their grandfathers. For instance, the orator was known as Marcus Tullius M. f. M. n. Cicero: Marcus Tullius Cicero, son (*filius*) of Marcus, grandson (*nepos*) of Marcus. In modern times scholars tend to refer to Roman men by their *cognomina*: Brutus (Marcus Junius Brutus), Caesar (Gaius Julius Caesar), Augustus (Gaius Julius Caesar Octavianus Augustus). Notice the last example, the name of the emperor Augustus. Because Julius Caesar had no male heirs, he adopted his sister's son, Gaius Octavius. When a young man was adopted, he took his adopted father's name; hence Gaius Octavius became Gaius Julius Caesar. The name of his *gens* was retained in a slightly different form: Octavius became Octavianus, and his full name became Gaius Julius Caesar Octavianus. In 27 B.C.E. the Senate awarded the new leader and *de facto* emperor an honorific name, Augustus. Thus, Gaius Octavius became Gaius Julius Caesar Octavianus Augustus.

Women's Names. Women's names were much simpler. There were no *praenomina* for women. At first their only name came from the *gens* name, the *nomen*. Marcus Tullius Cicero's daughter, therefore, was named Tullia. Gaius Julius Caesar's daughter was named Julia. Marcus Fabius Ambustus had two daughters, both named Fabia. To distinguish them, they were referred to as Fabia Maior ("the elder Fabia") and Fabia Minor ("the younger Fabia"). If a family had three or more daughters, they might be known as Claudia Prima ("First"), Claudia Secunda ("Second"), Claudia Tertia ("Third"), Claudia Quarta ("Fourth"), and so on. At the end of the Republic and the beginning of the Principate, women began to have *cognomina*. Livia, the wife of Augustus, was actually Livia Drusilla. Nero's mother was Julia Agrippina. The wife of the Emperor Septimius Severus was Julia Domna; her sister was Julia Maesa; her nieces, Julia Soaemias and Julia Mamaea. Notice that women did not change their names at marriage: a woman kept the name of the family into which she was born throughout her life.

Sources:

Suzanne Dixon, *The Roman Family* (Baltimore: Johns Hopkins University Press, 1992).

Beryl Rawson, ed., *The Family in Ancient Rome: New Perspectives* (Ithaca, N.Y.: Cornell University Press, 1986).

Paul Veyne, ed., *From Pagan Rome to Byzantium*, volume 1, in *A History of Private Lives*, edited by Philippe Ariès and Georges Duby (Cambridge, Mass.: Belknap Press of Harvard University Press, 1987).

PUBLIC SPACES

Temples. Strictly speaking, the word *templum* referred to a sacred area and not just to the building dedicated to a god or goddess. Families would go to *templa* for several reasons, most often to ask the god or goddess for something and to offer the deity a sacrifice in return. If a family member were sick, someone might go to the temple of Asclepius to offer a sacrifice for the person's recovery. A married woman who had not yet produced children would go to the temple of Juno or Diana to ask the goddess's help in becoming pregnant. Businessmen or travelers would appeal to Mercury to protect their interests and their journeys, whereas sailors or merchants might sacrifice to Neptune before a voyage.

Fora. Every town of any size had a *forum*—an open area surrounded by shops or temples that served as a political, religious, and commercial space. Rome had several *fora*—some serving all three purposes, some with more limited functions. The best known of the fora, the Forum Romanum, or Roman Forum, was originally an open market with shops, but was also a place with reli-

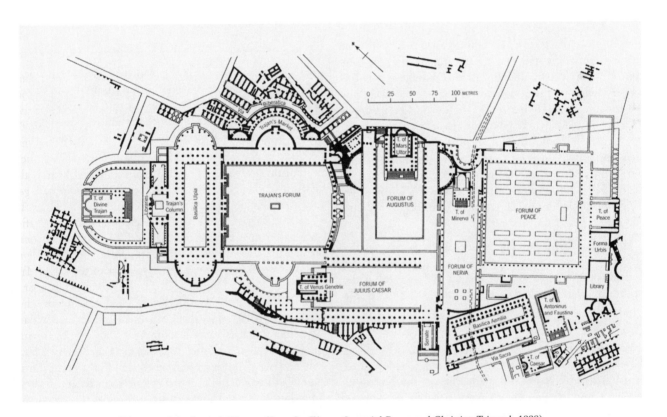

Diagram of the Imperial Forum (from Jas Elsner, *Imperial Rome and Christian Triumph*, 1998)

gious importance and of political convenience. Bordered on one end by the Capitoline Hill and on one side by the Palatine Hill, the Roman Forum contained the state treasury, law courts, the Senate House, many temples, the House of the Vestals, and the Rostra—a platform from which speeches could be delivered to all those who gathered in the flat, open space in front of it. In times of turmoil and war, families flocked near the Rostra or to the steps of the *curia* (senate house) to hear news of victories and defeats. They watched from the Roman Forum as triumphal processions passed down the Sacred Way. Since the Roman Forum quickly became less of a marketplace and more of a political and religious area, other fora took over the commercial aspects: the Forum Boarium, located near the Tiber, was a cattle market; the Forum Holitorium (also near the Tiber) was a vegetable market; and the Forum Piscarium (near the Forum Boarium) was a fishmarket. These four fora were all in place near the beginning of the Republic and even as far back as the monarchic period. As the Republic ended and the Empire began, individuals began adding new fora. The Forum of Julius Caesar was dedicated in 46 B.C.E., even though it was not complete at that time. (Octavian finished the construction after Caesar's death.) This area, adjacent the Roman Forum, was bordered on all sides by a colonnade with a series of shops on one side and a temple to Venus Genetrix (Venus the Producer) dominating the middle. The Forum of Augustus was dedicated in 2 B.C.E. and surrounded the temple to Mars Ultor (Mars the Avenger), which Octavian had vowed to build at the battle of Philippi when he defeated Brutus and Cassius. This forum functioned as a place dedicated to Rome's glorious past and to the belief in a glorious future. The people could come and gaze on the statues of great men from Roman history and from the Julian *gens*. In the temple itself stood the statues of Venus, Mars, and their descendant, the Divine Julius Caesar. This temple became the place where boys became men as they publicly assumed the *toga virilis*. Roman officials who had been appointed governors of foreign provinces began their journeys from this temple as well. And the Senate moved from the *curia* to the temple of Mars Ultor when it began deliberations about declaring wars, military strategy, and awarding triumphs.

Forum of Vespasian. The Forum of Vespasian was the next area enclosed by an emperor. The centerpiece for this space was the Temple of Peace, begun in 71 C.E. after the capture of Jerusalem and completed in 75 C.E. The area around the temple appears to have functioned as a park-like setting in the midst of the bustling city.

Forum of Nerva. The Forum of Nerva was begun, and almost completed, by Domitian, but was not dedicated until 97 C.E. by Nerva. Located between the Forum of Augustus and the Forum of Vespasian, the Forum of Nerva organized the last open area bordering the northern side of the Roman Forum. At the end near the Roman Forum stood the Temple of Janus. At the opposite end

LIVING OVER A BATHHOUSE

In one of his philosophical letters (56 C.E.), Seneca describes what it is like to live over a bathhouse. Although it is doubtful that Seneca himself lived in such a place, and the point of his letter is to prove that the true Stoic scholar has enough self-discipline and self-control to block out the noise, the description offers a powerful view of life in the city.

Here am I in the middle of a roaring babel. My lodgings are right over a bath! Now imagine every sort of outcry that can revolt the ear. When the more athletic bathers take their dumb-bell exercise, I hear grunts as they strain or affect to strain, hissing and raucous gasps as they expel their breath after holding it: when I run against some sedentary soul, who is content with the mere humble massage, I catch the smack of the hand as it meets his shoulders, with a different note according as it alights flat or hollowed. But if a tennis-professional comes along and starts scoring the strokes, all's up. Next add the quarrelsome rowdy and the thief caught in the act and the man who loves his own voice in a bath: after that, the people who jump into the plunge-bath with a mighty splash. Besides those whose voices are the real unvarnished thing, if nothing else, you must imagine the remover of superfluous hair emitted from time to time a thin falsetto. . . . Then there is the cordial-seller with a whole gamut of yells, and the sausage-vendor, and the puff-pastry-man, and all the eating-house hawkers crying their wares each with a distinctive melody of his own.

Source: Michael Grant, *Latin Literature: An Anthology* (Harmondsworth, U.K. & New York: Penguin, 1978).

was a Temple to Minerva. Doorways in the walls between the Forum of Nerva and the Forum of Augustus on one side and the Forum of Vespasian on the other earned the Forum of Nerva another name: the Forum Transitorium (The Passageway Forum), by which it was most commonly known from the third century C.E. on.

Forum of Trajan. The final large imperial forum, the Forum of Trajan, was actually begun by Domitian but completed in phases, first by Trajan and then by Hadrian. The first half of the Forum of Trajan was dominated by a new law-court, the Basilica Ulpia. The second part contained the Column of Trajan, libraries, and the Temple of the Divine Trajan. The primary purpose of the area, demonstrated by the Basilica Ulpia, was to provide a new venue for the growing number of legal cases being processed in the city. The Basilica Ulpia also provided a place to store official records, display laws, and for emperors to make public declarations: Hadrian used the venue to burn the records of those who owed money to the state; Aurelian also burned some of the public records; and Marcus Aurelius auctioned imperial gold to raise money for his war efforts. In the fourth century C.E. the Emperor Constantine began to dismantle the Basilica Ulpia to use some of its architectural details for his own triumphal arch.

The Baths of Caracalla, dedicated in 216 C.E., covered 156,000 square yards and could accommodate 1,600 people.

Baths. Part of one's daily routine was a visit to the baths. The wealthiest Romans had private baths in their houses, but the majority of people living in cities went to the public baths to wash the dirt off their skin and to meet up with friends and neighbors to catch up on the gossip. In the Republic the baths were primarily a place for cleaning and exercising. As the complexes grew in size, they added other spaces for leisure activities and other means for improving one's physical appearance. There were libraries, rooms to sit and talk, and places one could hear music or play games. Seneca describes all the sounds he heard—the masseur, the hair-plucker, the hot-waxer, and the snack-seller. Important figures such as Augustus's military adviser Agrippa and the emperors Nero, Titus, Trajan, Caracalla, and Diocletian built baths in the city of Rome and around the empire.

Theater. Throughout most of the Republic, theaters were temporary buildings set up only for certain games at which plays were performed. In 55 B.C.E. Gnaeus Pompeius Magnus built the first permanent stone theater. Now plays could occur year-round. Children went to plays with their parents—one playwright complains about the disturbing sound of crying babies—but families did not sit together in the theater. Women and men sat in separate sections, so the children sat with one parent, probably their mother. Boys close to the age of maturity might have joined their fathers. In addition to offering plays as part of the state-sponsored games, individuals paid for plays and other entertainment to be provided for the people to mark military victories or in honor of the death of a family member. Romans of all classes attended plays.

Nero. Among the emperors, Nero alone is known for having performed onstage. Romans considered acting a lower-class and demeaning profession. For an emperor to appear onstage was shocking, to say the least. That Nero forced upper-class Roman citizens and even women to appear onstage as well did not help his popularity.

Bread and Circuses. All emperors, however, learned the importance of providing plays and other spectacles for the people as a means of keeping them happy and occupied. Because Rome was full of idle poor, emperors needed to find something for them to do. In the Republic, political figures—those holding the office of *aedile* in particular—had used games to gain popularity. In the Empire, the emperor used them as a way to pacify the people. From this practice came the saying that "bread and circuses" were what the mob wanted.

Amphitheaters. In the amphitheaters men and women watched gladiators fight and battles between animals and between humans and animals. In the Republic, gladiator fights were given in the Roman Forum, where spectators watched from seats constructed just for the event. The first wooden amphitheater in the city was built in the Campus Martius (the Plain of Mars) in 29 B.C.E. The most famous such structure, the Flavian Amphitheater (better known as the Colosseum) was begun in 79 C.E. by Vespasian and completed by the emperor Titus in 80 C.E. From the time of Augustus, men and women sat separately in the amphitheater (as in the theater): men had the better, lower seats; women had the upper seats. Boys had their own section, with their paedogogues seated nearby. Behind the women's seats was an open area for the standing crowd who could not pay for a place to sit. During most shows, some sort of awning was drawn over the crowd to protect them from the sun.

Circuses. Circuses in Rome are not what modern people think of—traveling animal shows; rather, the circus was an oblong racetrack around which horses and chariots raced. The oldest in Rome, the Circus Maximus, dates from the period of the monarchy. The Circus Flaminius was added around 220 B.C.E. in the Campus Martius. The Circus of Nero (known now as the Vatican Circus) provided the venue for his persecution of the Christians (not the Colosseum, as one sees in the movies). The Circus of Maxentius, first dedicated in 309 C.E., still remains in good condition outside the city along the Appian Way. Only at these races did women and men sit together to watch and cheer for their teams—the Reds, Greens, Blues, and Whites. (The emperor Domitian added Gold and Purple to the list, but they disappeared with his reign.) The poet Ovid in the *Ars amatoria* (Art of Love) talks about the races as the best place to meet potential lovers, but they also served as an opportunity for a family outing.

Sources:

L. Richardson Jr., *A New Topographical Dictionary of Ancient Rome* (Baltimore: Johns Hopkins University Press, 1992).

Jo-Ann Shelton, *As the Romans Did: A Sourcebook in Roman Social History* (New York: Oxford University Press, 1998).

RELIGION

Household Gods. Every Roman had an interest in maintaining the *pax deorum,* or peace with the gods. For the family, that meant daily attention to the images of its guardian gods, the *Lares* and *Penates,* at a small shrine, a *lararium.* The *Lar familias* represented the spirit of the family and especially its ancestors. The *Lar,* therefore, became associated with ghosts, both inside and outside the home. The *Penates* (from *penus,* "pantry") were deities who protected the interior of the house. The honoring of the *Lares* of a region in the city took place at a public festival (the *Compitalia*) in which people hung up dolls representing each member of the household in the hopes that the spirits would vent any anger at the dolls and not at the human beings. There were also *Lares publici* or *Lares* associated with the whole city of Rome. Inside the home, the members of the family propiti-

Portion of the south side of the *Ara Pacis* showing flamines, or priests, 9 B.C.E.

ated the *Lar* every morning. In addition, any food that fell on the floor during a meal was burned at the *lararium* as an offering. The *Penates* were worshiped in the temple of Vesta as well as in the home. Every important family event—birth, birthday, marriage, death—involved the household gods. The notion of the household gods goes all the way back to Aeneas's flight from Troy: he carried his father and the household gods out of the burning city. Each family also worshiped Vesta in their homes by daily offering a small sacred cake to the fire. Certain other features of the house had their deities: Janus governed the doorway; Limentinus, the threshold; Cardea, the door hinge. For rural families there was the god of the boundary stones, Terminus, and various spirits of springs and crops that needed attention.

Public Festivals. The Romans celebrated several festivals (*feriae*) dedicated to various gods at specific times of the year. These public celebrations allowed the whole city to share in propitiating the gods and goddesses. The *pontifex maximus* would assign the days for the festivals, but they tended to fall at the same time each year. Priests and priestesses performed all the rituals while the people watched in silence. It was of the utmost importance that each ritual be performed accurately; otherwise the deity would not accept the sacrifice, and the ritual would have to be performed all over again to avert dire consequences. Many of the festivals specifically concerned family issues: the Lupercalia on 15 February included a ritual whereby young men would flick women with a whip to encourage fertility. The Matralia on 11 June was set aside for women to pray for the well-being of their sisters' or brothers' children. The Lemuria, celebrated on three nonconsecutive days (9, 11, and 13 May) gave the *patresfamilias* the opportunity to propitiate the spirits of the dead ancestors. During the days of the Saturnalia in late December, the whole family relaxed, children did not go to school, and masters and slaves exchanged places.

Religion—Roman and Christian. Throughout its history, Rome prospered because of its willingness, even eagerness, to accept new and different ways of thinking and creating. The philosophical schools of Greece and religions of Egypt all had places in the Roman world at one time or another. Yet, on rare occasions, times of stress in particular, Roman officials ordered the foreign beliefs out of the city, in an effort to regain the *pax deorum*, the peace with the Roman gods. The bans were never permanent. Therefore, when the Romans came in contact with Christianity, they treated it in a manner similar to how they reacted to the cults of Isis or Cybele. Christianity was different, however, and caused deep divisions within families and between families and the state. From the reign of Claudius until the reign of Theodosius, Jews and Christians (for the most part, the Romans saw little difference between the two groups) became easy targets and scapegoats on whom the state could blame an apparent disruption in Rome's peace with its gods. Under some emperors, such as Trajan, Christians fared a little better: they were not hunted out, but if confronted, they had to renounce their faith or suffer for their devotion.

Imagine the distress of a mother and father raised in the traditional beliefs when confronted with the fact that their child had chosen to reject Roman gods in favor of this strange practice. The famous example of Perpetua demonstrates well the effect that this new faith had on familial relationships and loyalty: Perpetua was one of three children raised by loving parents in Northern Africa near Carthage. At some point after her marriage, she turned to Christianity. There is no hint that her religious beliefs were a problem until she was arrested along with other Christians. Despite the repeated requests of her parents, especially her father, she refused to renounce her faith. For a while she was allowed to nurse her infant son in prison, but when she again refused her father's pleas to sacrifice to the emperors, her father refused to bring her son to her. On 7 March 203 C.E. she and other Christians were killed by animals and gladiators as part of the games given by the magistrate in honor of the birthday of Geta, son of the Emperor Septimius Severus.

Shifting Restrictions. As imperial attitudes changed, so did the fates of Christians and those who worshiped Roman gods. During the turmoil of the third century C.E., Christians were actively pursued and persecuted. During the reign of Constantine, Christians experienced freedom of religion. When the Emperor Julian came to power in 361 C.E., he restored Roman traditional religion to its place of prominence. The Emperor Theodosius declared Christianity the state religion in 391 C.E. and turned his persecution against heretics (people who rejected some aspect of Christianity) and those who preferred the traditional religion. Although it became difficult for families to know what to think or believe with regard to the gods, the family continued to be the central unit of society, the structure within which men and women came together to produce legitimate children, to educate those children, and to share all that life in their age—Republic, Empire, traditional, or Christian—had to offer.

Sources:

Lesley Adkins and Roy A. Adkins, *Dictionary of Roman Religion* (New York: Facts On File, Inc., 1996).

Mary Beard and John North, eds., *Pagan Priests: Religion and Power in the Ancient World* (Ithaca, N.Y.: Cornell University Press, 1990).

Robert B. Kebric, *Roman People* (Mountain View, Cal.: Mayfield, 1992).

H. H. Scullard, *Festivals and Ceremonies of the Roman Republic* (Ithaca, N.Y.: Cornell University Press, 1981).

SLAVES

Slaves in the *Familia*. There were many slaves who could figure in the daily life of a family, depending on its wealth and living situation. Families who lived outside the city on a farm might have several slaves who helped with the cultivation of crops and the care of the animals. Most likely, slaves built the house and took care of any repairs. Slaves worked in the granaries, mills, and bakeries that provided bread for many of the people in the city. Slaves built the baths, aqueducts, theaters, amphitheaters, and temples that were a part of the lives of all families. Slave auctions took place in the ports and

Funerary bas-relief (circa first century C.E.) from the tomb of a slave couple who had gained their freedom, denoted by the letter *L* written after their names (Staatliche Museum, Berlin)

in the marketplaces. In the *familia* itself, a family with children might have a nurse and a paedagogue. Slaves who had been born in the household (*vernae*) had strong bonds with the family, and were less likely to be sold and more likely to be freed. These slaves often grew up with the children of the household, becoming their companions as well as their guardians and helpers. Other slaves served as the sexual partners or "pet" slaves of the master.

Liabilities. Having a large number of household slaves was a sign of wealth because it was expensive to feed, clothe, and house slaves who brought no produce or profits into the house. Slaves in the house also created a certain tension, a fear that the slaves might revolt or kill the family. There are many instances in which slaves rose up against reportedly cruel masters and killed them. The punishment for such an action was severe: every slave belonging to the family was executed without exception, until the Emperor Hadrian ordered capital charges against slaves to be handled by the courts rather than by the families.

Freedom. If a slave had a skill, the owner might provide the slave with the equipment—for crafts work, for instance—and take the majority of the profits in return. But such a slave also had the possibility of eventually buying his or her freedom from the money—*peculium*—that he or she was allowed to keep. If a slave bought his freedom or was freed by her owner, the newly freed person became a citizen and changed his or her name to include that of the family to which they had belonged. These freedmen were essential for carrying on the family name.

Sources:

Suzanne Dixon, *The Roman Family* (Baltimore: Johns Hopkins University Press, 1992).

Jo-Ann Shelton, *As the Romans Did: A Sourcebook in Roman Social History* (New York: Oxford University Press, 1998).

ADVICE FOR NURSES

The author Quintilian, in his work on the proper education of an orator, begins with advice about almost every aspect of the child's care. He advises parents (*The Elements of Oratory* 1.1.4-5):

Above all, make sure that the infant's nurse speaks correctly. . . . Of course, she should without doubt be chosen on the basis of good moral character, but still make sure that she speaks correctly as well. The child will hear his nurse first, and will learn to speak by imitating her words. And by nature we remember best those things which we learned when our minds were youngest.

The author Pliny the Younger, as a grown man, writes to the caretaker of a farm that he has given to his nurse (*Letters* 6.3)

Thank you for taking over the management of the little farm which I had given to my nurse. It was worth 100,000 sesterces when I gave it to her, but it has decreased in value as production dropped. Now, under your care, it will recover its value. Please remember that I have entrusted to you not just trees and soil (although I mean these, too), but my little token of appreciation (for my nurse). It is of as much concern to me who gave it, as to her who received it, that it be as profitable as possible.

Pliny gave the farm to his nurse to show his regard for the care that she gave him not just as a child, but throughout his life. The profit from its crops provided her income so that she no longer had to work and did not have to worry about providing for herself.

Source: Jo-Ann Shelton, *As the Romans Did: A Sourcebook in Roman Social History* (New York: Oxford University Press, 1998).

SIGNIFICANT PEOPLE

CORNELIA

CIRCA 187 - BEFORE 100 B.C.E.

WIFE AND MOTHER

Early Years. Cornelia was one of four children, two sons and two daughters, born to Publius Cornelius Scipio Africanus and Aemilia. Between 175 and 170 she was married to the plebeian Tiberius Sempronius Gracchus, a man some twenty years her senior and an opponent of her father in political matters. Tiberius himself had a distinguished political career that may have led Cornelia's guardian to choose him as her husband, or perhaps it was at Cornelia's bidding.

Widowhood. According to Plutarch, there was a story that Tiberius once found a pair of snakes on his bed. When he consulted the augurs about what he should do, they told him that he had to choose to let one live and to kill the other, but if he killed the female snake, Cornelia would die; if he killed the male snake, his death would soon follow. Plutarch says that because he loved his wife and because he was much older than she, Tiberius killed the male snake and let the female go free. He died not long afterward, in 150 B.C.E., leaving Cornelia with twelve children, only three of whom—two sons, Tiberius and Gaius, and a daughter, Sempronia—lived to adulthood. After Tiberius's death, Cornelia chose not to remarry, even though she received a proposal from Ptolemy VIII Euergetes II, ruler of Egypt.

Devoted Mother. Cornelia devoted herself to her children. She took an active role in their education and in the shaping of their political views. She stayed involved in the political activities of her sons, writing letters to advise them and guide their actions. The quality of her thought and style earned praise from Cicero, but her letters seem to have disappeared by the time of Quintilian. After the death of her son Tiberius in 133 B.C.E., at the hands of his political enemies, Cornelia left Rome and moved to her home at Misenum. Her villa there became a center of culture, a place where learned men gathered to discuss literature and philosophy. In 123 B.C.E. Cornelia also lost

Gaius to his political enemies, leaving her with only her daughter Sempronia, who had married Publius Cornelius Scipio Aemilianus. She was also a widow: her husband, who had apparently approved of the murder of Tiberius in 133 B.C.E., had died mysteriously in 129 B.C.E. Rumor suggested that Sempronia and Cornelia were responsible for his death, in retaliation for Tiberius's murder. (Cicero's *Dream of Scipio* implies this scenario is the case.) Cornelia died sometime before 100 B.C.E.

Sources:

Alan E. Astin and Ernst Badian, "Cornelia," in *The Oxford Classical Dictionary*, edited by Simon Hornblower and Antony Spawforth (Oxford: Oxford University Press, 1999), p. 392.

Elaine Fantham and others, *Women in the Classical World: Image and Text* (New York: Oxford University Press, 1994).

LIVIA DRUSILLA

58 B.C.E. - 29 C.E.

EMPRESS

Unsettled Life. Livia was born into a patrician family with a long history of active political involvement. In 43 or 42 B.C.E., at the age of fifteen or sixteen, she married Tiberius Claudius Nero. In 40 B.C.E. Livia and Claudius had to flee Rome because Claudius had chosen to support Lucius Antonius, the enemy of Octavian, in the war in Perusia. Livia, Claudius, and their young son Tiberius returned to Rome after the pact of Misenum granted clemency in 39 B.C.E. Octavian soon persuaded Claudius to divorce Livia so that he could marry her. Even though Livia was pregnant with their second child, Claudius consented and even betrothed her to Octavian himself. Livia's second child, Drusus Julius Caesar, was born in 38 B.C.E., three months after her marriage to Octavian.

A Good Match. Contrary to Octavian's hopes, Livia produced no more children and thus did not give him the heir that he desired. Yet, Octavian (soon known as the

Emperor Augustus) and Livia were an excellent match, both politically astute and able to work together to convey a family image, even without children of their own. As part of Augustus's rebuilding project, she helped to restore temples and to reestablish the dignity of Roman religion. Perhaps because she presented such a strong and capable persona, she developed a reputation as a crafty and manipulative woman who was determined to see her own sons in places of power.

Scheming Matriarch. Rumor had her involved in the deaths of Augustus's chosen successors (Marcus Claudius Marcellus, Gaius Julius Caesar, and Lucius Julius Caesar) and in the deaths of rivals for Tiberius's power (Agrippa Postumus and Germanicus, her own grandson) even after he had assumed the throne at Augustus's death. She and Tiberius alone were present at the death of Augustus, after which she was adopted into the Julian *gens*, becoming Julia Augusta. She lived through the first fifteen years of Tiberius's reign. Her determination to maintain her position of power and prominence did not sit well with her son. He left Rome in 26 C.E. to get away from the city and his mother. He did not return before her death in 29 C.E.

Sources:

Nicholas Purcell, "Livia Drusilla," in *The Oxford Classical Dictionary*, edited by Simon Hornblower and Antony Spawforth (Oxford: Oxford University Press, 1999), p. 876.

MARCUS TULLIUS TIRO

104 B.C.E. - 4 B.C.E.

SLAVE, SECRETARY, FREEDMAN, FRIEND

Unfree Roots. Born a slave, Tiro was raised in the household of Marcus Tullius Cicero, the father of the famous orator. Because Tiro was only two years younger than Cicero (the orator), he likely became Cicero's companion in childhood. That Tiro's master had him educated in Latin and in Greek as well is evident from his service to Cicero as a secretary. Tiro assisted Cicero in his career as an orator by taking down his speeches in a special shorthand (Tironian notation) that he developed himself. Cicero often credited Tiro with the care and editing of his manuscripts. As part of the family, Tiro looked after Cicero's children and associated with the friends of the orator on a regular basis.

A Special Client. In May or June of 53 B.C.E Cicero freed Tiro, but that did not end his association with the orator. Now as Marcus Tullius Tiro he was a client of Cicero, but more importantly he was a devoted friend. Letters between Tiro and Cicero's son Marcus (while Marcus was away studying in Athens) suggest that the friendship extended to all generations of the family, even after he was freed. Quintus, the orator's brother, praised Cicero's decision to free Tiro, a man to be valued for "his literary talents, charming conversation, and wealth of knowledge." In 51 B.C.E Tiro contracted malaria but lived for another fifty years with the affliction. After Cicero's death in 43 B.C.E. Tiro, together with Cicero's best friend Atticus, published volumes of Cicero's letters to his friends and family. Tiro himself wrote a biography of Cicero, but the work has not survived.

Sources:

Ernst Badian, "Marcus Tullius Tiro," in *The Oxford Classical Dictionary*, edited by Simon Hornblower and Antony Spawforth (Oxford: Oxford University Press, 1999), p. 1564.

John Percy Vyvian Dacre Balsdon and Miriam T. Griffin, "Marcus Tullius Cicero," in *The Oxford Classical Dictionary*, edited by Simon Hornblower and Antony Spawforth (Oxford: Oxford University Press, 1999), pp. 1558–1560.

DOCUMENTARY SOURCES

Cicero (Marcus Tullius Cicero), *Letters* (circa 40 B.C.E.)— As Rome's greatest orator, Cicero addressed many topics, but it is in his letters that one sees so much about the life of the family: his relationships with his brother and his wife, his devotion to his daughter, his hopes for his son, his fears about the state, and his need for friendship.

Livy (Titus Livius), *The History of Rome from the Founding of the City* (circa 25 B.C.E.–14 C.E.)—Livy's history of Rome covered the earliest period before the founding of the city down to 9 B.C.E. His work gives us an important sense of who the Romans thought they were and what mattered to them as Romans.

Lucan (Marcus Annaeus Lucanus), *Pharsalia* (circa 63 C.E.)—Lucan's poem on the civil war between Julius Caesar and Pompey the Great emphasizes their relationship as one-time father-in-law (Caesar) and son-in-law. Lucan's description of the battles cast the death and destruction in personal terms—what war costs families.

Petronius ([Gaius?] Petronius Arbiter), *Satyrica* (before 66 C.E.)—The *Satyrica* is our earliest example of a Roman novel. Its narrative follows characters in their travels and encounters with teachers, freedmen, slaves, prostitutes, priestesses, and poets.

Pliny the Younger (Gaius Plinius Caecilius Secundus), *Letters* (circa 99–109 C.E.)—Pliny's letters were written for publication and published by him during his own lifetime. From them one learns about social, domestic, legal, religious, and political issues during his time.

Plutarch (Lucius Mestrius Plutarchus), *Lives* (circa 105 C.E.)—Plutarch's biography of great Romans provides details about the lives and perceptions of the men who rose to prominence during the Republican period.

St. Augustine (Aurelius Augustinus), *Confessions* (circa 397–400 C.E.)—Augustine's *Confessions* offer a personal insight into family life, education, and faith in the late Empire.

Seneca the Younger (Lucius Annaeus Seneca), *Philosophical Letters* (circa 63 C.E.)—These letters, addressed to his friend Lucilius, explore all aspects of life in Rome from the point of view of a Stoic living in the time of Nero.

Suetonius (Gaius Suetonius Tranquillus), *On Famous Men* (circa 100–110 C.E.); *The Lives of the Twelve Caesars* (circa 120–130 C.E.)—Suetonius's biographies of men such as Horace, Vergil, and Orbilius often provides the only information about the lives of these writers. His accounts of the lives of the emperors provides the sort of personal details that a standard historical approach does not.

Tacitus (Publius Cornelius Tacitus), *Agricola* (98 C.E.); *Dialogue on Orators* (circa 102 C.E.); *Histories* (circa 110 C.E.); *Annals* (circa 120 C.E.)—Tacitus's works reveal the difficulties of living in the Empire. *Agricola* tells about the life and career of his father-in-law, a good man who did what he could during the reign of Domitian. The *Dialogue* addresses the changes in education. The *Histories* and the *Annals* examine life under the emperors who followed Augustus.

Terence (Publius Terentius Afer), *The Girl from Andros* (166 B.C.E.); *The Mother-in-Law* (165 B.C.E.); *The Brothers* (160 B.C.E.)—In these three of Terence's six plays, he addresses various relationships between family members and issues such as infant exposure, the power of a father over his son, and adoption.

Vergil (Publius Vergilius Maro), *Aeneid* (circa 19 B.C.E.)—Vergil's epic poem gives Rome a glorious past that links the city of his own day with the renown of ancient Troy.

Third-century C.E. mosaic depicting gladiators fighting wild beasts (Borgese Museum, Rome)

Fresco depicting rites to the goddess Isis, found in Herculaneum, circa 50 C.E. (Museo Nazionale, Naples)

RELIGION AND PHILOSOPHY

by PETER COHEE

CONTENTS

Sidebars and tables are listed in italics.

IMPORTANT EVENTS OF 264 B.C.E. TO 476 C.E.

262 B.C.E.

- The Temple to Minerva, the goddess of arts and handicrafts, skilled tradesmen and artisans, is dedicated on the Aventine.

249 B.C.E.

- The Sibylline Books, a collection of oracular verses consulted in times of emergency, recommend the celebration of Century Games (*ludi saeculaves*).

238 B.C.E.

- The Temple to Flora, the goddess of flowering plants, mainly cereals, is dedicated near the Circus Maximus.

235 B.C.E.

- The consul Manlius Torquatus closes the Janus Gate, signifying that no Romans were at war in the world.

215 B.C.E.

- The Temple to Venus of Eryx, a goddess of mediation, is dedicated on the Capitoline.

212 B.C.E.

- The Sibylline Books order the establishment of Apollo's Games.

205 B.C.E.

- Twin shrines are built to Honor and Virtue at the Capena Gate.

204 B.C.E.

- The Sibylline Books order the Great Mother of the Gods to be brought to Rome.

194 B.C.E.

- The Temple to Juno the Savior, the city guardian and goddess of procreation, is dedicated.

191 B.C.E.

- A temple is dedicated to the Great Mother on the Palatine.

*DENOTES CIRCA DATE

186 B.C.E.

- Private worship of Bacchus, the Roman version of the Greek god Dionysus, the god of wine and intoxication, whose followers often participated in bacchanals, is ruthlessly suppressed by the Senate.

181 B.C.E.

- A Shrine to Venus of Eryx is dedicated near the Colline Gate.

155 B.C.E.

- Greek philosophers, including the Stoic Diogenes of Babylon, Carneades of the Academy, and the Peripatetic Critolaus, visit Rome.

146 B.C.E.

- The Sibylline Books order celebration of Century Games.

114 B.C.E.

- The Temple to Venus Changer of Hearts, established in an attempt to make women remain chaste to their husbands, is dedicated.
- The trial of three Vestals accused of having sex with men is held.

55 B.C.E.

- The Temple to Venus Victrix, Pompey's personal god, is dedicated in the Theater of Pompey.

46 B.C.E.

- The Temple to Venus Genetrix, established in honor of Caesar's victory over Pompey, is dedicated in the Forum of Julius Caesar.

45 B.C.E.

- Caesar reforms the Roman calendar.

29 B.C.E.

- The Temple to Divine Julius, part of the deification process of Caesar, is dedicated in the Forum.
- Octavian closes the Janus Gate, in honor of peace in the empire.

*DENOTES CIRCA DATE

28 B.C.E.
- The Temple to Apollo, Augustus's favorite deity, is dedicated on Palatine Hill. The cult of Apollo is eventually elided with that of the emperor.

17 B.C.E.
- Augustus celebrates the *ludi saeculares* (Century Games).

2 B.C.E.
- The Temple to Mars the Avenger, restoring this god's place of prominence in the Roman pantheon and celebrating Augustus's defeat of the enemies of Caesar, is dedicated in the Forum of Augustus.

35* C.E.
- The Temple to Isis, the Egyptian goddess seen as a dispenser of life and healing, is dedicated.

37 C.E.
- The Temple to Divine Augustus is dedicated on the Palatine.

38* C.E.
- The Jewish religious leader Jesus is crucified by the order of Roman governor Pontius Pilate in Jerusalem.

47 C.E.
- Emperor Claudius celebrates the *ludi saeculares.*

64 C.E.
- The Great Fire of Rome destroys major portions of the city; emperor Nero blames and punishes Christians for the disaster.

88 C.E.
- Emperor Domitian celebrates the *ludi saeculares;* he bans Jews and philosophers.

112 C.E.
- The governor Pliny discovers the Christian church in Bithynia.

*DENOTES CIRCA DATE

121 C.E. • The Temple to Venus and Rome, representing success in war and natural productivity, is built by emperor Hadrian on the Sacred Way.

204 C.E. • Emperor Septimius Severus celebrates the *ludi saeculares.*

218-222 C.E. • The Temple to Elagabalus, the Unconquered Sun, based on the Syrian god, El Gabal, is dedicated.

250* C.E. • The Temple to Serapis, the Egyptian companion god to Isis, is dedicated.

312 C.E. • Constantine sees a vision of a cross superimposed on the sun, and believes the vision helped his forces defeat Maxentius; the emperor tolerates Christianity and converts himself just before his death.

340* C.E. • Eusebius of Caesarea dies. He authored such important Christian works as *History of the Church* and *Preparation of the Gospel.*

363 C.E. • The last known consultation of the Sibylline Books.

391 C.E. • The patriarch Theophilus destroys the Egyptian Temple of Sarapis in Alexandria.

395 C.E. • Christianity becomes the state religion.

398 C.E. • John Chrysostom, who advocates such things as care for the poor and improved education, becomes the bishop of Constantinople.

*DENOTES CIRCA DATE

400* C.E.

- The Palestinian Talmud, the Jewish collection of rabbinical opinion and stories, is compiled and written down in the form of commentaries.

403 C.E.

- John Chrysostom is deposed by the Synod of the Oak, and dies in exile in 407.

420 C.E.

- The biblical scholar and ascetic Jerome (Eusebius Hieronymus) dies.

451 C.E.

- The Council of Calcedon the Monophysites is held. These Christians, who argue that Jesus Christ was both human and divine (as opposed to having two separate natures), later form the Egyptian Coptic Orthodox Church, the dominant form of Christianity in Africa until the nineteenth century.

476 C.E.

- The *Lupercalia,* a festival that will later be transformed into the feast of the Purification of the Virgin, is still celebrated in Rome. It will be banned by the bishop of Rome, Gelasius I, in 494.

***DENOTES CIRCA DATE**

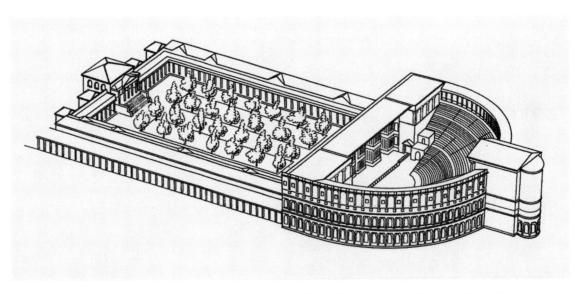

Drawing of Pompey's theater complex (dedicated in 55 B.C.E.) on the Campus Martius in Rome; the Temple of Venus Victrix is on the far left (from Mary Beard, and others, *Religions of Rome,* 1998)

OVERVIEW

What is Religion? What we might call religion appeared along with *homo sapiens sapiens* in the Paleolithic era, about fifty thousand years ago. These people left signs of belief in some supernatural reality beyond the physical experience. They buried their dead together with personal belongings such as jewelry, weapons, and clothing. They also painted pictures of animals they hunted on the walls of caves and ritually preserved the remains of animals they killed and ate. We deduce from these remains that early human hunters identified with the animals they killed, that they felt anxiety about killing and eating "one of their own," and that they tried to restore them to life. Early religion therefore seems marked by concern with hunting, food, death, and a wish to restore the dead to life. We do not have enough evidence to speak about the origins of religion, however. Nor can we speak of the purpose of religion, for that assumes that religion was deliberately invented; we can only observe its features and qualities. But we can say that it is universal: wherever we find human beings, we find religion too. We might even define man as *homo religiosus.* The elements of religion are also universal: prayers and hymns, sacrificial offerings, sacred places, and images of divine beings. We must try to account for the universality and common structure of religion. The answer to this search lies in the way human beings, regardless of time, place, or race, live together.

Religion is Communal. We tend to think now that religion is mostly a private matter, between an individual person and his or her god or gods. But when we consider religion as practiced from the most remote antiquity, we must note first that religion is *communal,* that is, religious acts belong to communities, not to isolated individuals. Religion is shared—first by families and kinship groups, then it is extended to include others not related—thus creating a kind of artificial family. Religion is one of the most important ways by which human beings organize themselves into societies. It seems to do this by forming a system of mutual responsibilities and privileges around the common concerns of food, death, and preservation of life. Religion assures an individual of receiving a proper funeral by requiring him or her to attend to these duties for others, and it involves community members in the hunting, gathering, and preparing of food through the ceremonial sharing of a meal. We might

say that religion defines a family and a community by establishing customs and standards of right action. These customs and standards allow us to live together productively in relative peace.

Religion is Ceremonial. We also tend to think that religion is mostly a matter of personal belief. But again, when we look at religion over the long span of time and consider its universal qualities, we see that it is also essentially *ceremonial,* for group participation requires outward signs of inner belief. An individual's religious beliefs are complex; we often hold conflicting views simultaneously, and our thoughts change greatly over the course of our lives. The individuals within a group of people celebrating a religious rite may have different ideas about the reality behind the ritual, but they participate in the same actions. And this too is a critical point: one's personal beliefs vary and change, but a group's ceremonies tend to remain quite constant. In fact, a community's religious identity is practically the same thing as the ceremonies they perform. Thus, it is important for these rituals to be taught to each succeeding generation and in such a way that they tend to be performed with little change. Participation in religious acts binds individuals to a group, one generation to the next. Such rituals become traditional, carefully passed from age to age, and shape the group's idea of itself over a long period of time.

Religion is Conservative. Religion therefore is *conservative* and necessary in maintaining a society's stability; it tends to promote a society's success. In any community there is political strife; there are hostilities, enmities, and jealousy. Feuds between individuals may escalate to involve clans and may threaten the society's survival. But religious obligations and traditional standards of behavior tend to keep societies from destroying themselves over temporary or individual issues. It does so by constant reference to the society's common, age-old acts of worship, its religious duties. Ritual also serves to distinguish the different roles of a society's members, such as male and female, young and old, parent and child, and to give each role its honor. Religion is no guarantee of order, but it does tend to preserve order.

Religion at Rome. If we keep in mind that religion is essentially communal, ceremonial, and conservative, we can understand more easily why Sallust (86–35 B.C.E.), an historian of the time of Julius Caesar (100–44 B.C.E.), called the Roman people *religiosissumi mortales,* the most religious beings. It is also necessary to understand that in the Romans' view of themselves every civic act had a religious justification. Elections, meetings of the Senate, declarations of war, a general's decision to commence battle—all these and more began with sacrifices, prayers, vows, and the consultation of the will of Jupiter Best and Greatest, the supreme god of the Roman people. If these acts were correctly performed, and if the permission of Jupiter was obtained for a given act, then, in effect, the Romans, under the leadership of their public officials and military commanders, were carrying out the will of the gods. That is a powerful force in the creation of an empire.

Religion and Government. This importance of religion does not mean, however, that the Romans practiced "theocracy," a government of priests devoted exclusively to governing for religious purposes. Educated Romans certainly understood the difference between politics and religion; the question for them was more a matter of what relationship existed between these two institutions. In the United States we have become used to an ideal of "separation of church and state," that is, that government will not involve itself in matters of religion. To the Romans this separation would have seemed insane. The orator and philosophical essayist Cicero (106–43 B.C.E.) wrote:

> Our ancestors wanted the same persons to be responsible for the cult of the immortal gods and for the most important affairs of state; in this way the best and most outstanding citizens might preserve our religion by their good political administration, and preserve the state by their wise management of our religious affairs. (Cicero, *On His House* 1.1)

Cicero elsewhere argued that religion was the foundation of the state, an opinion expressed by many other Roman writers. They all agree that the Romans' painstaking attention to every detail of ritual, prayer, and ceremony was what made the Roman people worthy of empire. Polybius, a Greek historian of the third to second centuries B.C.E., agreed, though he was more matter-of-fact in his opinion:

> The respect in which the Roman constitution is most markedly superior is their behavior towards the gods. It is, I think, the very thing that brings reproach amongst other peoples that binds the Roman state together: I mean their superstitiousness. For nothing could exceed the extent to which this aspect both of their private lives and of their public occasions is dramatized and elaborated. Many would find this astonishing. To me at least it seems clear that all this has been done for the sake of the common people. For if you could form a state entirely out of wise men, then perhaps it would not be necessary to adopt this course. But since the mass of every people is fickle and full of lawless desires, irrational anger and violent impulses, it is essential that they should be restrained by invisible terrors and suchlike melodramas. That is why I do not accept that the ancients were acting irrationally or at random when they introduced the notion of the gods or ideas about the terrors of Hades; it is rather our contemporaries who are being rash and unreasonable in banishing these. (Polybius, *Histories* 6.56.6–12)

Religion and Politics. The Romans were skilled at using religion to gain political advantage. For example, Julius Caesar, after he had defeated his political rivals in a bloody civil war and assumed dictatorial power, dedicated in triumph a temple to Venus Genetrix, or Venus the Mother, in 46 B.C.E. Romans generally considered themselves descendants of Venus through the Trojan hero Aeneas, her son by a mortal man. In particular, Caesar claimed direct personal descent from Venus through Aeneas's son Iulus, the legendary founder of the Julian family. Caesar had this temple built right next to the Senate House, the center of Roman political activity. In doing so, he made it clear that, by the will of the divine mother of the Roman race and his own ancestor, he was entitled to assume full and personal control over Rome and its empire. To worship Venus Genetrix was virtually to worship—certainly to venerate—Julius Caesar. There are many other such examples, both before and after Caesar's time.

Religion and Citizenship. Did the Romans cynically exploit religion for political ends? From our perspective, maybe, but not necessarily from theirs. To be a Roman citizen meant chiefly to worship the gods of the Roman people and to receive the protection of those gods in turn. The public religion was a "civic polytheism," that is, that the number and variety of gods not only reflected the various backgrounds of the people but united them. The long-lasting success of the Roman empire was due, as they themselves recognized, to the way their religion organized them into a cohesive society; it justified their political and military acts and preserved their customs and values. From this point of view it is easier to understand why Rome was hostile to such foreign religions as Judaism or Christianity, which forbade their members from participation in the Roman public religion. But it is also easier to see how important that religion was in making one coherent whole out of all the many races and cultures that made up the Roman empire.

Kinds of Evidence. That having been said, however, an important question must now be asked: how can we know if the Romans really were the "most religious beings?" What evidence supports the claim that religion was so important in the Roman world? After all, religion exists only in the moment: prayers vanish on the wind, and beliefs are intangible. We need something more concrete and permanent by which to evaluate their claim. We have two kinds of evidence for Roman religiosity: literary and physical.

Literary Evidence. It is essential to bear in mind that Roman religion was not a "scriptural" religion. Unlike most modern "revealed" religions such as Christianity, Islam, or Judaism, it did not have a body of sacred writings that served to conduct a community of believers in living their lives. In that sense, at least, ancient Roman religion did not have a literature. But precisely because of its ceremonial, communal, and conservative nature, Roman religion produced—even required—a body of what we would consider technical writings. The most important of these writings came to be known as the *annales maximi,* "The Yearbooks of the Pontifex Maximus," that is, of the chief priest of one department of the public religion. According to our sources, the Pontifex Maximus would each year mount a painted white board, or *album*, on an outside wall of the Regia, the office of the pontifical priesthood in the Roman Forum. On this board would be painted all the important events of each year: election of public officials, military matters, and important religious occurrences such as prodigies and omens, and what official actions were taken concerning them. Their style was simple and matter-of-fact, not what is generally thought of as "literary." These yearbooks eventually became the standard reference for Roman historians. While the yearbooks themselves no longer survive, the religious portions of these records were preserved in later historical works. Livy, an historian of the first century B.C.E. under Augustus, the successor to Caesar and the first emperor (63 B.C.E. to 14 C.E.), is a leading example of this method of historical writing. Livy is an invaluable source of information about religious institutions and actions before Rome had a written history.

Priestly Records. There were several public priesthoods, each responsible for a different area of the people's religion. They each kept records of their activities, such as election of priests, ceremonies performed, and, in the case of the more important priesthoods, decisions they made on technical questions of religion or advice they gave to the Senate on such occasions. These decrees and responses probably formed a large part of their archives. They tended to be conservative, for they established precedents or examples to follow in similar instances in the future. For a Roman the *mos maiorum*, "the way of our ancestors," was always the surest guide to right action. In no area was this more important than in religion.

Handbooks. These priestly records in turn served as the source for unofficial technical handbooks on religious practices. It is important to remember the words of Cicero. Roman religion, with a few notable exceptions, did not have a special caste or class of hereditary priests. The very same men served simultaneously as lawmakers, generals, and priests. In fact, almost all important religious acts undertaken on behalf of the Roman people were performed not by priests but by elected public officials. It might be the case that these men also belonged to one or several priesthoods, but they performed sacrifices, vows, gave games, dedicated temples, and took auspices as magistrates, not as priests. As such, they needed to have a convenient source of information on the correct wording of a certain prayer, or the correct procedure to carry out a sacrifice, and so on. For this purpose they kept handbooks, derived and excerpted from the priestly archives. These works in turn tended to become more generally available to educated private Romans.

Authority on Religion. Cicero again deserves special notice for his interest in Roman religion. In addition to revealing much about the details of Roman public religion in his letters and speeches, Cicero also wrote, among his philosophical works, two that concern us: *On Divination* and *On the Nature of the Gods*. These books treat the subject of religion more from a theoretical and intellectual point of view, but they give us an invaluable and intimate look at the some-

times conflicting attitudes of a traditional Roman who is also a well-educated and rational thinker. Cicero is especially important for another reason: from the age of fifty-three until his death ten years later, he was a public augur and knowledgeable about augural matters.

Antiquarian Writers. Finally, the Romans' great interest in their traditions led to the composition of what is called antiquarian literature, in which certain public institutions, including religion, were systematically collected and treated. An important example of this kind was the *Investigations of Human and Sacred Things* by Marcus Terentius Varro (116–27 B.C.E.), one of ancient Rome's greatest scholars. This work exists now only in the form of excerpts and quotations found from later writers, but enough remains to give us an idea of the interest in religious antiquities among educated Romans. Other such examples are the much later *Attic Nights*, by Aulus Gellius (born circa 125 C.E.), and the *Saturnalia*, by Macrobius (third–fourth centuries C.E.), which attest to the popularity of matters of pagan religious ceremony long into the Christian era. Their sources were indirect: histories, such as Livy's, poetry, and religious handbooks. Still, they often preserve important information.

Inscribed Evidence. Epigraphy includes inscriptions (records carved on stone or bronze), calendars, and coins; in fact, calendars and coins are only special kinds of inscriptions. We have some two dozen ancient Roman calendars, mostly in fragmentary form, including one from the time before Caesar undertook a major reform of the Roman calendar in 45 B.C.E. These works are important because they tell us how the Romans regulated the passage of time by observing annually recurrent holidays. They also record changes in Roman religion, the addition of new gods, and so on. Coins tell us about the importance of priesthoods and the political aspect of public religion, and they often give us miniature illustrations of temples that no longer exist.

Art and Architecture. Roman art and architecture are temples, shrines, statues or sculptures of the gods, and especially frescoes and mosaics that preserve many important details of sacrifice, worship, and ritual. By studying the archeology of a temple we can learn a great deal about how the cult of a particular god or goddess changed—or remained the same—over long periods of time. We can learn much about the rituals of sacrifice and priestly costumes from sculptures such as those on the Altar of Peace constructed by Augustus. Statues tell us something about how Roman people imagined their gods and how closely they were identified with the Roman people as a whole. But it is important to note that, wherever possible, literary evidence must be supported by physical evidence, and vice versa. Relying on one or the other source exclusively can lead to misunderstanding.

Historical Growth. The evidence we have, taken all together, documents the history of Roman religion. It is not a perfect history, unfortunately; many questions must remain unanswered until we acquire more evidence. Still, we do have enough information for a good outline with considerable detail in some areas. We can see fairly clearly that

Roman religion developed over a long period of time through the alternate tendencies of *continuity* and *change*. This religion was extremely traditional, but it also had to serve the needs and purposes of real people in real times of changing circumstances. As Rome's political power grew to become an empire all around the Mediterranean Sea and all of western Europe, the people of Rome acquired new gods, symbols of their world domination. There was therefore an extraordinary increase in their pantheon. Gods came and went, but ceremonies tended to stay the same. For example, a traditional rite would be adapted to accomodate a newly adopted deity, or the basic structure of a public holiday would be modified to serve the cult of the imperial families in later Roman history, or the ancient priestly titles of the pre-Christian religion would be applied to Christian priests and bishops. In fact, the Pope, head of Roman Catholicism, is still called Pontifex Maximus.

"Original" Roman Religion? Can we find an "original" Roman religion? Can we peel back all the historical layers to get down to the authentic religion? Some great scholars have tried, but with only limited success. They began with the evidence of the calendars. They noted that some gods' names and holidays are written in larger letters, and that these gods tended to be those worshiped throughout Roman history. Their theory was that some deities were "native-born," others "newcomers," and that each group was worshiped differently from the other. But other scholars observed from literary and physical evidence that there was never any such distinction in the Romans' own ideas about their gods.

Early Latins and Rome. We know from physical evidence that from the late Bronze Age, about 1000 B.C.E., an ethnic group called the Latini inhabited the broad plain known as Latium, "The Wide Place," in central Italy. They spoke a common language and were loosely united under a common worship of Iuppiter Latiaris, "Jupiter of the Latin People," who allegedly lived on the top of the Alban Mountain, about fifteen miles southeast of the later site of Rome. Rome itself began to emerge as a permanent Latin settlement during the mid eighth century B.C.E., agreeing pretty well with the legendary founding of Rome by the hero Romulus on 21 April 753 B.C.E. It was inhabited by several groups of people, probably shepherds who lived in palisaded hill-forts on rocky outcrops of the Apennine Mountains, the hills of Rome.

Importance of the Forum. The early inhabitants of "Rome" deposited their dead in a marshy low-lying area between these hills—the later Roman Forum. The oldest layer of graves was of cremated dead, followed in later times by inhumed, or buried, corpses. The different burial customs do not necessarily indicate a change in religious beliefs, however. The remains also reveal that essentially the same rites were performed over the graves: the sacrifice of a pig, the consumption of a ritual meal by the family of the deceased, and offerings of grains and vegetables. This area, then, served as a common village burial ground for hundreds of years. The Forum and the hills overlooking it would later become the religious heart of the city, the place for all the most important temples and ceremonies. If you stood in the center of the Forum you would be entirely surrounded and looked down on by all the most powerful gods of the Roman people. Eventually, it became illegal to cremate or bury anyone within the *pomerium*, the sacred limit of the city, especially in the Forum. In a way, we can say that the whole city within this sacred limit became a holy area. Thus, it was highly significant that Julius Caesar, after he was assassinated on 15 March 44 B.C.E., was cremated in the Forum and, when he was declared a god, that a temple was established on the site of his cremation.

Religious Diversity. Throughout Roman history we find repeated testimony of the willingness of the Romans to accept new ways and new people into their society. Early legends of the founding of Rome speak of the first citizens as runaway slaves, thieves, and refugees from other nations. The early inhabitants of the new city were soon joined by people from neighboring Italian tribes, who no doubt brought with them their ancestral religious practices. For example, Roman foundation legends (though probably not systematically composed until the mid third century B.C.E.) speak of the earliest period of Rome's history, the Monarchy or Regal Period (753–509 B.C.E.), as a series of seven kings, each bringing religious institutions to the new community from their different ethnic backgrounds. Romulus, the Alban founder, instituted the practice of taking auspices. His successor, Numa Pompilius, was a Sabine who is said to have established the calendar, the cult of Vesta, the priesthood of the pontifices, and so on.

The Etruscan Contribution. Later kings, the Tarquins, were Etruscan, and of a different ethnicity entirely. The first Tarquin king had the Forum drained by means of a sewer, thus making the ancient cemetery a real city center, but keeping its sanctity intact. Other kinds of augury, especially the observation of lightning and the entrails of sacrificed animals (haruspicy) were added to Roman religion from the Etruscans, as were gladiatorial contests—originally a funeral custom. Servius Tullius, ethnically a Latin but raised in the household of the Etruscan kings, is said to have brought the goddess Diana from her ancient Latin sanctuary of Aricia in the Alban hills and to have established her in a new temple on the Aventine Hill in Rome. By so doing he increased Rome's authority over other Latin states. The last of these kings, Tarquinius the Arrogant, established the cult of Jupiter Best and Greatest on the Capitoline Hill. Though the Romans forcibly removed this Tarquin from the throne and set up a republican government in 509 B.C.E., they still maintained his religious institution for a thousand years thereafter.

Influence of Individuals. This long process of bringing gods to Rome also served to heighten the prestige of individuals and families within Rome's ruling elite. For example, in 204 B.C.E., during Rome's desperate struggle against the Carthaginian general Hannibal, a goddess from Asia Minor, the Great Mother of Gods, was brought to Rome through the personal initiative of Publius Cornelius Scipio, who at that time was Rome's leading general in the war against

Carthage. This was a very public confirmation, not only of Rome's extension of power into the far Greek East but especially of the importance of the Scipios in Roman politics at that time. This process continued with the adoption by Augustus of Apollo as his personal protective deity. The public worship of Apollo developed into a close identification with the worship of the emperors and their families—another example of a private cult becoming public. Rome had long had interest in Egypt, which became the private province of the emperors from the time of Augustus. This acquisition led to the spread of Egyptian cults, especially those of the gods Isis and Serapis, throughout the Empire, largely by soldiers in Rome's armies. We might say that this process culminated in the adoption by the emperor Constantine (272–337 C.E.) of Christianity. His successors made the new religion the "official" one of the whole Roman world. Gradually the ancient pre-Christian gods disappeared, but many elements of the traditional religion were absorbed into Roman Catholic and Orthodox Christianity.

Greek Influences. From the earliest times, perhaps well before Rome was a unified city in any sense, the Greek hero-god Herakles, known to the Romans as Hercules, was worshiped at his Greatest Altar in another forum, the Cattle Market, between the Palatine Hill and Tiber River. According to his mythology, Herakles, as he was driving the magical cattle of Geryon back to Greece from the otherworldly Red Island, killed the monster Cacus near that spot. Soon after the Republic was established, the Greek god Hermes, called Mercurius by the Romans, was included among the people's gods, as were Ceres, Liber, and Libera, the Roman names for the Greek deities Demeter, Dionysus, and Kore, a few years later. At that time Greek civilization, especially in Athens, was nearing its highest point. It was Rome's Etruscan kings who had developed commercial and political contacts with the Greek world. Though Rome would not reach such a height for another four hundred years, the adoption of Greek gods was a way for the young Republic to assert itself as an emerging power to be recognized in the larger Mediterranean world. Later, during its wars with the African city of Carthage throughout the third century B.C.E., Rome adopted many other gods from Greece. In this way Rome increased and demonstrated her influence over Greek cities, especially those in southern Italy and Sicily, whose loyalty shifted continually between Rome and Carthage.

Greek Myth and Roman Religion. Here we must distinguish between Greek mythology and real Roman religion. The culturally advanced Greeks were distantly related to the Romans. Both peoples belonged to what is called the Indo-European family, a race of people who originally spoke dialects of the same language and shared essentially the same religious systems. The Greeks maintained the traditional Indo-European mythology, including stories of the gods' adventures among themselves and mortals. In general, Greek myths were more closely related to actual Greek religion. The Romans, on the other hand, converted many of those myths into their early political history. Properly speaking, we have no Roman mythology. Varro tells us, furthermore, that there was not even a statue of a god in Rome until almost two hundred years after the city was established. Much later the Romans adopted Greek gods and goddesses into their religion and consciously imitated the Greeks in their art and literature, especially in poetry of the first centuries B.C.E. and C.E. What is important to note is that the Greek myths do not represent what most Romans thought about their gods, nor do they tell us much at all about how the Romans practiced their religion.

Greek Philosophy and Roman Religion. We can also say that the Romans did not have any philosophy of their own; this they likewise learned from the Greeks. Greek thinkers from the sixth century B.C.E. on tried to discover the physical nature of the universe, including the nature of the gods. They sought to find the few essential elements of which all things are composed. On that basis they inquired about the best way for humans to live in order to be happy. Human ethics, they felt, had—or perhaps did not have—something to do with the way the gods had structured the physical universe. Greek thinkers sought the relationship between human reason, or science, and human good.

Roman Attitudes toward Greek Philosophy. The Romans were suspicious of Greek philosophy for a long time; to them it seemed unmanly and a waste of time. Roman contact with Greece became much more intense and permanent during the wars with Carthage, and after about 150 B.C.E. it became more respectable for Roman families to send their sons to cities such as Athens, Pergamum, and Antioch, where they studied for several years in one or several Greek philosophical schools. One might expect that philosophy would have had a harmful influence on traditional Roman religion, making it more rationalistic and secular; but in fact, educated Romans such as Cicero were able simultaneously to maintain both the intellectual views of the gods proposed by Greek thinkers as well as the traditional ceremonies and customs of the ancestral Roman religion. To understand this practice, it is important to remember that ancient religion did not depend as much on dogmatic systems of belief, prescribed in written texts, as modern religions. Still, it is also well to remember that the Romans periodically expelled philosophers from Rome.

The "Pre-Socratic" Thinkers. Socrates of Athens (469–399 B.C.E.) has come to represent an epochal change in the history of Western thought. In fact, the term "philosophy" seems to date from the time of Socrates' follower Plato; thus, it is erroneous to use it of thinkers before Socrates' time. Historians of philosophy therefore give the name "Pre-Socratics" to a dozen or so Greek thinkers who were active before or no later than Socrates. The earliest of these is Thales, who lived in the early sixth century B.C.E., and the latest is perhaps Democritus, who was born around 460 B.C.E. Thus, they represent more than a century of sustained energetic speculation about nature, the gods, and man's experience and knowledge of reality. In fact, the Pre-Socratic tradition is really a kind of evolved form of Greek myth in a more rational age; many of the Pre-Socratic thinkers wrote in poetic verse.

Pre-Socratic Thought. There is no one "school" of thought among the Pre-Socratics. Most of them were highly original and independent thinkers. We do not have much left of what they wrote; for the most part we have only fragments preserved in the form of quotations by later writers. So it is risky to assume that we know exactly what, for example, Empedocles thought about this or that. Still, we can say that there were a few essential questions that they debated: is the physical universe a unity, or composed of separate elements? If it is a unity, how do we explain the unlimited variety of observable things? If the universe is composed of elements, are these elements in harmony with one another, or in a state of perpetual conflict? Are the physical elements of nature everlasting, or do they perish? Is existence a permanent state, or are there cycles of coming-into-existence and destruction? They were also concerned with what we call epistemology: How do we know what we know? What are the senses, exactly? How does our knowledge correspond to external reality?

Monism vs. Atomism. Gradually, though, we can trace the outlines of two opposite views: monism and atomism. Monism is the belief that all things are really only forms of an original unity, the One. The Atomists, on the other hand, beginning with Leucippus, held that the universe was composed of an almost endless number of tiny elements, atoms or "seeds of things," out of which everything we observe is composed. Even the senses were only streams of matter. Both schools struggled to discern the relationship between matter and space, or Void. The concept of Void was especially problematic, for it suggested that "Nothing" can be. If there can be Nothing, does that not suggest that the gods are limited, since there is an area of the physical universe where they do not exist? If the gods are limited, what does that mean for human relations with the divine? Are the gods involved in human affairs, or do they belong to another realm entirely?

Pythagoras: Religion and Science. One of the most influential of the Pre-Socratics was Pythagoras (mid sixth century B.C.E.), for he established the idea of "philosophy" as a way of life. To him is attributed a cluster of semireligious ideas, especially that of *metempsychosis,* the transmigration of souls into new bodies after death, or reincarnation. Followers of Pythagoras formed themselves into communities and lived according to rules of discipline, including vegetarianism. Pythagoras is also closely associated with the discovery of certain principles of mathematics; he and his followers believed that mathematics in nature was the result of the divine creation of the universe. Pythagoreanism, then, was a combination of science, religion, and ethics. He was thus a precursor to the philosophic schools of the fourth century. Most important for our purposes, Pythagoras settled in southern Italy, where his influence was widely spread long before Roman power extended into that area.

The Sophists. Into this arena of searching enquiry entered a generation of men known generally as the "Sophists." They came to Athens primarily from Greek colonial cities on the west coast of Asia Minor, southern Italy, and Sicily. Like the Pre-Socratics (in fact, some of the Sophists are included among the Pre-Socratics), they formed no single homogeneous "school" of thought. Most of them gave lessons in rhetoric, the art of speaking persuasively to achieve legal and political success, but their interests varied widely. Several of them, especially Protagoras and Gorgias, seem to have challenged prevailing moral views.

Uncommon Philosopher. Socrates was not really a philosopher in the common sense. He did not conduct a school where he taught a system of philosophical principles, nor did he leave any written work. But he had a profound influence on aristocratic young Athenian men of his day. This is important to note, because Athens at this time was at the peak of its cultural and political majesty. What we know of Socrates comes chiefly from the works of his followers Plato (circa 429–347 B.C.E.) and Xenophon (born circa 430 B.C.E.), who wrote their works after Socrates' death. From these we learn that Socrates, in reaction to the challenges posed by certain Sophists, began a life of intense self-examination and the critical scrutiny of the ideas of others. Socrates had heard from an acquaintance that the god Apollo, through his human spokeswoman the oracle at Delphi, had said that "Socrates of Athens was the wisest of mortals." Not knowing how that could be, Socrates went about the city of Athens conversing with men such as the Sophists, who had a reputation for being wise and knowledgeable. In these conversations, or dialogues, Socrates would question the other person closely about the subject of which he claimed to be an expert. They were not debates, for Socrates himself did not take a given position in an argument. He put every idea of the other person to demanding tests of consistent logic and rational principles. This style of teaching and learning by conversation is still called the "Socratic Method." Socrates often exposed that in fact these experts were frauds, that they knew nothing. Socrates concluded that he must be the wisest of mortals after all, if only because he alone knew that he knew nothing.

Socrates' *Daimonion*. Naturally, Socrates offended many Athenians by his lifestyle and his often embarrassing examinations of others' ideas. He was finally tried on charges of introducing new gods to Athens and of corrupting the youth of the city. We have a version of the speech he made in his self-defense in Plato's *Apology*. In it he explains how, in the course of his life, he had learned to listen to an inner voice within him, a *daimonion* or divine spirit, which must also be in every man. It was this *daimonion*, he said, that drove him incessantly to search out the truth of all things, though it might mean incurring others' disfavor. He did not mean to disobey the laws; but this inner voice spoke a higher law, which we must obey. The unexamined life, Socrates said, is not worth living for a human being. He did not convince the jury, which then sentenced him to death. After conversing, as always, with his friends, Socrates drank a cup of hemlock poison and passed away.

Plato and the Academy. Socrates had many aristocratic young followers, including the brilliant Plato (circa 429–347 B.C.E.). Plato imitated Socrates to a certain extent, retiring from the active political life of his city and devoting his life to the pursuit of wisdom, *philosophia*. But he formalized what was only casual in Socrates, for he established a permanent school of philosophic inquiry. He would meet his students in the sacred grove of the Athenian hero Akademos; thus, Plato and his followers and their characteristic thoughts are known as the Academy, from which we derive the term. His students ranged in age from the late teens to early middle age. Plato's writings, as mentioned, are in the form of dramatic dialogues, most (but not all) involving Socrates in conversation with others. These talks concern, in one form or another, the right way for human beings to live in order to be happy. Plato never introduces himself as a participant in these dialogues, so it is difficult to learn from them exactly what Plato himself actually thought. Plato invites the reader to engage in an ongoing and never-completed discussion about what the highest values are, convinced that there are such values and that they are objective and knowable, though there may never be one simple, clear definition of them. Plato is most closely identified with a certain idealism: the things we observe in our reality are but images of original, divine, and perfect "forms" that we cannot see in this life. Plato's struggle was to discover what the highest good in each thing is, so that one can live one's life according to a principle of moral priorities. We make ourselves unhappy, he might say, by putting lesser things, such as money and physical pleasure, ahead of things that are really most important. The *scholarchs* (or heads) of the Academy continued in an unbroken line from Plato until the first century B.C.E.; the influence of the school may be seen in the philosophical writings of Cicero.

Aristotle and the Lyceum/Peripatos.

Aristotle (384–322 B.C.E.), one of the world's greatest geniuses, was a student of Plato for more than twenty years. After serving as tutor for a while to the young Alexander the Great, Aristotle established his own school in the *Lukeion,* a precinct sacred to Apollo. They met in the shaded portico of the sanctuary, called the *peripatos,* or "strolling place"; his school of thought is now generally known as the Peripatetic. Aristotle developed Plato's theory of objective reality and priorities, that is, that all things can be known, and that, by establishing the highest type of each thing, one can then classify all things in a rational, hierarchical order. This system depends on careful observation of things as they really are and on the ability to make fine distinctions between the qualities of things. Aristotle is associated with the "teleological" method, that is, that everything in nature has an ultimate end or *telos* toward which its own inner nature, derived from its divine creation, directs it. Knowing the *telos* of each thing is the only way we can classify things and know the best type of each class; this in turn allows us to organize our knowledge. Aristotle really sought a method of universal or encyclopedic knowledge. He turned his and his students' talents and energies to collecting data from all areas of experience: biology and other sciences, literature, politics, ethics and morals, and so on. His influence on Western thought has been enormous, and his methods really formed the basis of the modern educational system. As a rhetorician, for example, he profoundly influenced Roman theorists such as Cicero and Quintilian.

Cynicism and Scepticism.

Diogenes (circa 412–403 to circa 324–321 B.C.E.) challenged assumptions about customary ethics. As he saw it, man should live closer to his natural state, without laws, nations, marriage, social institutions, and so on. He lived on the street as a beggar and shamelessly performed all natural functions in public. Cynicism is important for two doctrines: "cosmopolitanism," the belief that the world is one whole entity, that there are no states or countries, and that all men are "citizens of the world"; and "philanthropy," a natural love of one's fellow man. These concepts, especially the former, later became essential principles of Stoicism, an influential philosophy in Rome. Pyrrhon of Elis (circa 365–275 B.C.E.) also challenged conventions by reverting to questions posed by earlier Pre-Socratics about the validity of knowledge of reality. Pyrrhon and his followers, known as Sceptics, held that nothing can be known for certain; it is therefore wise to withhold one's judgment about things.

Epicurus and the Garden.

Epicurus (341–270 B.C.E.) followed Leucippus and Democritus in the "atomistic" school of thought. According to this view, all nature is composed of atoms falling ever downward through the vacuum of infinite space. As they fall, they bond together randomly to form physical bodies. Even the senses, thoughts and feelings can all be explained as chance collections of atoms. Thus, there is no divine plan of creation. To be wise and happy in this life, one must free oneself from superstitious fears of gods and eternal punishments, and live in such a way as to neither do harm to others nor suffer pain oneself. This belief involves a retreat from active public life. Epicurus bought a large house and grounds in Athens, where he lived with his disciples, an early kind of communism, preceding that of early Christianity by several centuries. His school is therefore often referred to as the Garden. Epicurus's philosophy found adherents later in Rome, especially among poets, such as Lucretius and Horace. Lucretius even wrote a long hexameter poem, *On the Nature of Reality,* in which he attempted to explain Epicureanism to a Roman audience.

Zeno and the Stoa.

Zeno of Citium (335–263 B.C.E.) used to meet his students in a long covered portico in Athens called the *Stoa;* thus, the names Stoic and Stoicism. This philosophy belongs much more to the "monistic" view of reality, that is, that all things are part of a Unity and are directed by some divine plan toward some predetermined end. The wise person, then, will employ reason in his observation of physical nature to understand human ethics, the highest kind of study. As it developed, Stoicism came to express the view that each person's life is determined by fate, and that God's will pervades all things. The task for man is to accept that fate and divine will and live his life in accordance with them. Divine Providence will reveal its intentions only in the long course of time, in history. Stoicism was brought to Rome by Diogenes of Babylon, his student Panaetius, and the historian Polybius in the 150s B.C.E., and a little later by Panaetius's student Posidonius, who was also an historian. Stoicism matched well the Romans' own view of the divine and of human responsibility to divine will. Stoicism became a powerful intellectual force justifying Rome's imperial ambitions. There were several important Stoic writers in Rome and Rome's empire, such as Seneca, Musonius Rufus, Epictetus, and the emperor Marcus Aurelius.

Christianity. Elements of traditional Roman religion and Greek philosophy were combined (and still survive) in Christianity. Pagan philosophers such as Socrates, Diogenes the Cynic, Epicurus, and Epictetus all served as models for early Christian saints and martyrs, whose lives, committed to the uncompromising search for truth, were often spent suffering poverty and persecution. The organizational system of priesthoods, and the ritual practices of Roman religion, were taken over when Christianity was adopted by later Roman emperors. It is impossible to understand Christianity without a knowledge of these important antecedents.

TOPICS IN RELIGION AND PHILOSOPHY

DISTINCTIONS AND DEFINITIONS

Public vs. Private Religion. When studying ancient Roman religion, we must make some fundamental distinctions and define some basic terms. The first distinction, that between *public* and *private* religion, is in fact somewhat false, for Roman public religion was to a great extent an outgrowth of private religion. That is, as different clans joined to form the early Roman political state, some cults originally belonging to families, such as the worship of Hercules at the Greatest Altar, or, much later, Christianity, were eventually adopted as public cults, belonging to the whole people. It would seem best, therefore, to begin a study of Roman religion with private cults. It is important to keep in mind, though, that the systematic examination of a religion does not necessarily give us a complete or accurate picture. Real life, including religion, is not very systematic. The Romans' whole experience was thick with gods, forces, and powers of which we can know only a little. Whereas we tend to think of religion as only one aspect of our lives, religion permeated every aspect of the lives of the Romans. Even if we had much more evidence for Roman religion, the reality was far more complex. Still, a presentation arranged by deities, holidays, sacred places, and priesthoods gives us some useful outline of that reality. After all, that is exactly how Marcus Varro, a Roman scholar and a real expert in Roman religion, decided to examine the subject.

Polytheism. Ancient Roman religion, as most ancient and many modern religions, was polytheistic, meaning that many gods were worshiped by the same people. Some scholars of religion used to consider polytheism a primitive state of religion, believing that monotheism, the exclusive worship of one god, was a higher form of religious experience. This view is no longer generally held. Of course, the ancient Egyptians, Babylonians, Greeks, and Romans acknowledged the concept of one supreme god. But, they felt, mortals, with limited insight, could best understand the divine in the plural, not the singular: the "gods," so to speak, were but aspects of God. To say that there is "one God" would have suggested to them that the divine is somehow physically limited to one body, one form. To aid our understanding, poets and artists represent these gods anthropomorphically, for example, in human shape, which makes the divine more accessible to human intelligence. Further, in a polytheistic religion the same god or goddess may even be worshiped under several names or epithets, which individualizes his or her special powers and interests. This system makes it easier to approach the god for specific help in specific circumstances. A multiplicity of gods, each with several separate identites, also reflects the complex nature of human civilizations, in which people organize themselves by the kind of work they do or the power and status they have. As in a city, so in the divine world there is a structured hierarchy of abilities, qualities, and responsibilities.

Civic Polytheism. Polytheism was thus an essential fact of the Roman state's integration of many peoples into one political entity. The history of Roman religion is the story of a centuries-long process of adding gods to the Roman pantheon. This collection of gods was a potent symbol, not only of the original complexity of Roman society, but also of its increasing political power. As the Roman people extended their influence, first in Latium, then throughout Italy, and finally around the whole Mediterranean world and western Europe, they brought the gods of conquered and subject nations back to Rome. This practice made their city the spiritual capital of its world empire, a new kind of Olympus, where the gods were regarded as "first citizens" dwelling in their preferred home. These gods thus gave their own city spiritual power and protection. This multitude of deities made it possible for new Roman citizens, from Britain to Egypt, from the shores of the Black Sea to the Atlantic, to belong to the Roman world. The Roman Empire without this civic polytheism is simply inconceivable. Again, the "separation of church and state" would have been incomprehensible to people of antiquity: to be a citizen was to honor the gods of the city. Now, an individual could certainly have one's private religion and worship his or her favorite deity, as long as one did not ignore—and thus insult—the others. To refuse to worship the public gods was to anger those gods and to risk not only losing their protection, but even calling down their anger on the whole people. In this light it is much easier to understand the Romans' suspicion of Greek philosophy and their hostility to obstinately monotheistic religions—superstitions, the Romans called them—such as Judaism and Christianity.

Trend toward Monotheism? Some scholars see a gradual trend toward monotheism in Roman religion. They feel that this trend was a reflection of political changes. During the Republic (509–31 B.C.E.), power was more or less distributed and limited through traditional and constitutional checks and balances, including religion. Auspices, for example, or the scheduling of religious holidays, could be used to block legislation or postpone public debate. Beginning with the emperor Augustus in 27 B.C.E., ever-greater power was concentrated in the hands of one person, which, the theory holds, finds its religious expression in the predominant cult of one deity over others. This theory is attractive on the surface, but there are several arguments against it.

Sacra and *Auspicia*. Both public and private religion in ancient Rome can be further divided into two areas: sacral and auspical. *Sacra* are all the things a nation, city, family, or individual might offer to a god: sacrifices of animals, plants, wine, and incense; temples and other sacred places; holidays and games; vows and votive gifts; prayers; and hymns. It is important to remember that sacrifice, the return to the gods of some of the good things one got from them, including the lives of animals, was an absolutely essential fact of ancient religion. *Sacra* also include *praedictio*, the examination by special priests of prodigies, portents, and the entrails of sacrificed animals in order to determine a god's wishes or to learn the outcome of an intended action. *Auspicia*, on the other hand, was the set of ritual observations of such things as the flight, song, and eating habits of birds, or the sound or appearance of lightning, by which one might learn whether or not Jupi-

Catacomb of the Jordani in Rome, built by the early Christians and used as an underground cemetery and haven from persecution

ter—and Jupiter alone—permits an action, such as a meeting of the Senate, an election, a vote on a law, or a wedding, to be undertaken on a given day. It was not the action itself but the time of its undertaking that Jupiter approved. Auspices were not prophecy or fortune-telling; rather, they were a one-time approval from Jupiter for one action only, though he may at any moment thereafter change his mind from positive to negative. There was, however, a special kind of auspice known as *augurium*, or augury. Augury was the use of auspical observations to permanently designate a place or a person for perpetual service of the divine; this was called inauguration.

Religion and Imperium. In Roman public life, the right to perform sacrifices in the people's name, to vow and dedicate gifts, temples, and games to the gods, as well as the right to request Jupiter's permission through auspices, was granted only to certain officials elected in auspicated, or religiously sanctioned, public elections. (Priests took auspices only for the purpose of inauguration and on a few other ceremonial occasions.) This fact conferred on such magistrates supreme civil and military authority or *imperium* (for a limited time only, usually one year), and validated the people's choice by reference to the divine will.

According to Cicero, the Roman state was firmly founded on the twin supports of *sacra* and *auspicia*. Speaking of the first two kings of Rome, Romulus and Numa Pompilius, he says:

> And while the religion of the Roman people, taken as a whole, is divided into *sacra* and *auspicia*, a third element may be added as a support, namely, whatever the interpreters of Apollo's oracle or the Etruscan seers might advise by way of prediction from portents and signs. I am convinced that Romulus founded our state on the basis of auspices, Numa by the establishment of sacral rites. (Cicero, *On the Nature of the Gods*, 3. 5)

By performing the sacrificial rites in the correct ways and at the correct times, by obtaining Jupiter's permission for all their acts as a civil society, the Roman people maintained the *pax deorum*, that good relationship with the gods of their city who in turn preserved them and their empire.

Sources:

Mary Beard, John North, and Simon Price, *Religions of Rome,* 2 volumes (Cambridge & New York: Cambridge University Press, 1998).

Georges Dumézil, *Archaic Roman Religion,* translated by Philip Krapp (Chicago: University of Chicago Press, 1970).

GODS OF THE ROMAN PEOPLE

Too Many Gods to Name. Early Christian writers, such as St. Augustine and Tertullian, mocked the traditional Roman religion, in which there was a separate deity for every single, minuscule aspect of human life and experience. In agriculture, for instance, there was a god to watch over seeds, one to keep mice from eating them, one concerned with the plowing of furrows, another with the sowing of seed, yet another with irrigation, or mildew, or drought, or the harvest, and so on, almost without end.

Wall painting of the lararium (house shrine) from the House of Vettii, Pompeii, circa 63–79 C.E. The deity Genius is in the center, and two lares (lesser protective gods) are on either side.

While this polytheism certainly offended monotheistic Christians, it still tells us much about the Romans and their gods. The Roman pantheon was a celestial bureaucracy, with major and minor divinities overseeing human life in fine detail. The Roman belief was that every human action was guided by an expert divinity. Even the most mundane aspects of human life thus became suffused with divinity. It is not possible to discuss the almost infinite number of gods of the Roman people; there are simply too many. But a survey of the principal deities will help us see something of the Roman religious experience in both its private and public dimensions.

Jupiter. Even polytheistic religions generally recognize one highest god who creates and governs all things mortal and divine. This god is usually concerned with the organization of all reality and the administration of authority and power; he is thus usually a patron of kings and the ruling classes in a society; but he may have other, narrower interests as well. The Latin name of the supreme god of the Roman people, Iuppiter, is originally a compound of two nouns, *Dyeu-pater,* literally, Day-Father, lord of the bright daytime sky. The *Dyeu-* element is in fact identical with the name of Jupiter's Greek equivalent, Zeus, and is the base of the Latin word for "god," *deus.* Jupiter was associated with natural phenomena of the sky, especially weather and the fearsome power of the thunderbolt. He was also especially interested in wine harvests, triumph in warfare, obligations of hospitality, and sacred oaths. In general, Jupiter as sovereign god was concerned with all things that are first, best, and greatest. We know from plentiful remains of temples that Jupiter was worshiped all over the Italian peninsula, and not in Rome only. His temples were always situated on the highest hill around, such as that of Jupiter of the Latin Race on the Alban Mountain. In Rome we find sites dedicated to Jupiter on nearly all principal hills. But his oldest sanctuary, the one most important to the religious and political life of ancient Rome, was that on the hill called the Capitoline, or Hill of the Head (*caput*).

Jupiter the Striker, Jupiter the Stayer. According to Roman legend, Romulus, the founder and first king of Rome, established the first temple of his new city to Iuppiter Feretrius, or Jupiter who Strikes, for example with his lightning, those who break oaths. Soon thereafter Romulus and the young men he had gathered abducted girls and women from their neighbors the Sabines because they needed wives to confirm and civilize their new town. The Sabines came to get their women back, and there was a battle in the area later know as the Forum. The Roman fighters began to panic and flee; Romulus prayed and vowed a temple to Jupiter, who caused the Romans to stay and fight. So Romulus established a temple near the old Palatine Gate to Jupiter the Stayer. Certainly these temples are very old, whether or not there was an historical Romulus.

Jupiter Best and Greatest. The most important form of Jupiter, and the most prominent temple, was that of (Iuppiter Optimus Maximus) the Best and Greatest on the

Capitoline Hill. The temple was actually vowed and begun by the last king of Rome, the Etruscan Tarquin the Arrogant, in 510–509 B.C.E. It is characteristic of the Romans that, even though they removed Tarquin from the throne, vowing never again to have a king and establishing a republican government, nevertheless they upheld the religious obligation undertaken by Tarquin and gave it the greatest honors. This Jupiter was thus the principal god of the Roman people in their civic capacity, that is, as a constitutional entity. As the Roman Republic grew, Jupiter assumed more and more importance. Roman magistrates took the auspices to obtain his permission to act on the people's behalf; to him they sacrificed on the day they took office; and to him they presented, upon their successful return from war, some of the loot captured from defeated enemies, at the conclusion of their triumphal parade through the city up to the Capitoline. The middle day of each month, the Ides, being the "highest point" of the month, was a feast day in honor of Jupiter Best and Greatest.

Other Jupiters. Other aspects of Jupiter were recognized and separately worshiped. In 295 B.C.E. the temple of Jupiter the Victor was established; a year later another temple to Jupiter the Stayer was placed on the Palatine Hill. In the time of Augustus, in 22 B.C.E., Jupiter the Thunderer was honored on the Capitoline, and in the middle of the third century C.E. a strange Eastern form of Jupiter, called Dolichenus, received a temple on the Aventine Hill.

Juno. The temple of Jupiter Best and Greatest was actually shared with two female deities, Juno and Minerva, who each occupied their own sanctuaries on either side of Jupiter's central hall. These three gods are thus usually referred to as the Capitoline Triad. Juno is later thought to be the wife of Jupiter, though that position may not have been part of her original identity. Like Jupiter, she was worshiped throughout Italy but especially in Latium; in her case we can easily see the process of Roman borrowing of the cults of other peoples. Her name seems related to *iuventas,* the Latin word for youth, and she gives her name to the month of June. She seems to have been originally associated with the opening of the monthly cycle of the moon, for the first day of each Roman month, the Kalends, was sacred to her. She shares this function with Janus, the god of openings. Juno is generally associated with the women of Rome in their status as wives and mothers, and in the protection and increase of Rome's population. Because chastity was considered essential for legitimate marriage and children, Juno was also concerned with the sexual purity of young girls.

Juno the Queen. When the Romans were besieging their Etruscan enemies of the city of Veii in 392 B.C.E., the Roman general prayed to the protective deity of that city, Juno Regina, or Juno the Queen. He asked her to give victory to the Roman army, to leave the city of Veii, and to move to Rome, a religious procedure known as *evocatio,* or "calling out." She seems to have agreed, for the Romans soon thereafter captured the city and sold its inhabitants into slavery. But the Romans were anxious about laying hands on her cult statue; they were afraid of committing sacrilege. At that moment one of the Roman soldiers said, somewhat jokingly, "Juno, do you want to go to Rome?" Bystanders were shocked to see the statue nod, as if to say yes. The statue was then easily moved, and this Juno was given a new home on the Aventine Hill. In 207 B.C.E., after a series of dread prodigies and portents, the pontifices decreed that twenty-seven maidens should go through the city singing a hymn of expiation. The historian Livy relates what happened then:

While they were rehearsing the hymn, composed by Livius Andronicus, in the temple of Jupiter the Stayer, the temple of Juno the Queen on the Aventine Hill was struck by lightning. The Etruscan seers responded that this prodigy concerned the married women with children, and that the goddess must be appeased with a gift. By an edict of the curule aediles those women who had residence in the city and within the tenth milestone were assembled on the Capitoline. They chose 27 of their number, to whom they would each make a contribution from their dowries. From that a gift of a golden bowl was made and carried to the Aventine, and purely and chastely offered by the women. Immediately thereafter the ten priests of Apollo decreed a day for an additional sacrifice to that same goddess. This was the order of procession: from the temple of Apollo two white female oxen were led through the Carmental Gate into the city; behind them two cypress-wood statues of Juno the Queen were carried; then the 27 maidens, dressed in long gowns, sang in procession the hymn to Juno the Queen. . . . The ten priests of Apollo, crowned with laurel and dressed in purple-bordered togas, filed behind the maidens. From the Gate by way of the Altar of Juno of Marriage they came into the Forum, where the procession halted. The maidens, passing a rope from hand to hand, sang as they danced in step, keeping time with the beat of their feet. From there they went by way of the Etruscan Quarter and the Ridge, through the Cattle Market, up the Publician Slope and reached the temple of Juno the Queen on the Aventine. There the two victims were sacrificed by the ten priests of Apollo and the cypress-wood statues were taken into the temple. (Livy, *From the Founding of the City,* 27. 37. 11–15)

Juno Lucina. An outstanding example of how private Roman cults gradually became public is that of Juno Lucina. While childbirth is an intimate family matter, any society, to survive and prosper, must have children and care for them; the delivery of healthy babies is as important for the community as for the private family. Juno Lucina protected women through the dangerous moments of labor and childbirth. Her name resulted from the fact that she helped mothers bring newborns into the light, or *lux* in Latin. This function may be related to her aspect as goddess of openings and beginnings. She had an ancient sacred grove on the Esquiline Hill, where her temple was founded in 375 B.C.E. There she was worshiped both publicly and privately, especially during the Matronalia, the Romans' Mothers' Day, and when new babies were born. Expectant women (and their husbands as well) would make votive offerings to Lucina to win her help in the easy birth of healthy babies.

Juno the Warner. Shortly after the Roman defeat of Veii, the city of Rome itself was attacked by marauding tribes of Gauls from across the Alps. They besieged the lower part of the city, so the Roman people crowded for protection onto the Arx, or Citadel, a steep promontory on the north side of the Capitoline Hill. Some Gaulish warriors discovered an unknown path up one side of the Arx, and one night a band of them climbed up, intent on murder and pillage. At that moment Juno's sacred geese began to honk, thus alerting the Romans, who drove the enemy off the hill. This Juno was thereafter known as Moneta, the Warner, and her temple was established in 344 B.C.E. Centuries later the first public mint was established on the Arx; the modern words "mint" and "money" reflect the fact that coins were first stamped in Rome next to the shrine of Juno Moneta.

Juno Savior Mother Queen. For the Romans, the acquisition of political power over other peoples meant the assumption of responsibility for maintaining all their traditional religious observances, though under the supervision of priesthoods at Rome. In 338 B.C.E. Rome finally won control of all Latium, subjecting the other Latin towns to its political leadership. One of these towns was Lanuvium, home of the ancient cult of Juno Savior Mother Queen. This Juno, unlike Juno the Queen from Veii, did not move to Rome but kept her home in Lanuvium: priests and magistrates were sent from the capitol and local priests were appointed to maintain her cult. She did eventually have a temple established in Rome in 194 B.C.E., the remains of which still stand. We also know what this Juno looked like, for we have statuary remains, coins, and relief sculptures of her. She was dressed in a goatskin cape, wore a kind of goat-horn helmet, and carried a spear and a shield. These articles of clothing represent her dual function of city guardian and goddess of procreation.

Minerva. Though she was the third deity of the Capitoline Triad, Minerva does not seem to have been as prominent as Jupiter and Juno. Evidence indicates that she first came to Rome at the founding of the Capitoline temple complex in 509 B.C.E., though she was well known throughout Italy. In general, Minerva was understood to be the goddess of arts and handicrafts, thus she was especially cultivated by artisans, skilled tradesmen, musicians, and actors. For this reason a separate temple was established for her on the Aventine Hill around 262 B.C.E., which served as a meeting hall for associations of craftsmen.

Mars. In antiquity, warfare was an almost annual occurrence. It was seasonal, usually taking place from spring to autumn only, when weather permitted marching, transport of troops by ship, and the launching of navies. Even so, war was not simply accepted as a fact of life; it had exceptional importance. From the Romans' perspective, every war they engaged in, century after century, had religious justification; they called it *bellum iustum*, "religiously sanctioned war." War was the just vengeance for wrongs committed against the Roman people. In their view, if another city or state had violated an oath or a treaty with Rome, things that were protected by Jupiter, god of oaths and fidelity, then war had to be declared. Not only did generals lead men into battle only after taking auspices to obtain Jupiter's permission, but the very declaration of war itself was a religious act. It is not surprising, then, that war in Rome was cultivated as a god, Mars, and that he was the most important god after Jupiter himself. In fact, Mars seems to have been the principal god of the ancient Italian peoples before Jupiter came to prominence. We can tell this from several kinds of evidence. First, the names of our months still reveal that the original Roman calendar year recognized only ten: December, the twelfth month, means "tenth." Thus, the ancient Roman year began on the first day of March, the Month of Mars. Secondly, the *suovetaurilia*, a boundary-purification procession and sacrifice of a pig, a sheep, and a bull, originally special to Mars, was gradually adapted to the worship of Jupiter, suggesting that Jupiter took over some of the ancient functions of Mars. It is interesting, too, that Mars was also worshiped by farmers as a protector of boundaries, as shown in this ritual prescribed by Cato the Elder (234–149 B.C.E.):

> This is the way to purify a field. Order a *suovetaurilia* to be led around the area (then pray), "With the good will of the gods and that it turn out successfully, I order you, Manius, that you purify my farm, field, and land with that *suovetaurilia*, from whatever direction you decide either to drive them around it or lead them around it." Address Janus and Jupiter with a wine-offering, saying, "Father Mars, I beg you and beseech you to be favorable and propitious to me, my house, and our household. For this purpose I have ordered a *suovetaurilia* to be led around my field, land, and farm: that you keep away, ward off, and sweep away illnesses seen and unseen, barrenness, destruction, and bad weather; and also that you allow the crops, the grains, vineyards and orchards to flourish and have good yields; to keep my shepherds and flocks safe; and to give good health and strength to me, my house, and our household. For these purposes, for the sake of purifying my farm, land, and field, and for the sake of making purification, just as I have said, be blessed, Father Mars, with these suckling *suovetaurilia* which are to be sacrificed." (Cato, *On Farming*, 141)

Model of the Temple of Mars the Avenger, which was consecrated in 2 B.C.E. (Museo della Civilta Romana, Rome)

Mars an Agricultural God? There is some further and very old evidence that seems to connect Mars with agriculture. Many scholars have used this information to argue that Mars was originally a god of crops, grains, and fruits, and only later became a war god. One piece of evidence that suggests this connection was the priesthood devoted to the agricultural goddess Dea Dia. These were the Arval Brethren, the first term of which is clearly related to the Latin word for cultivated land, *arva.* We have in fragmentary form the text of an Arval hymn in very ancient Latin, which seems to associate Mars more closely with farming than fighting. The hymn's meaning has been much debated, but its general sense is "Do not allow destruction, plague to invade. . . . Be satisfied, wild Mars. Leap on the boundary. Stand as watchman (?). Help us, o Mars. Triumph, triumph, triumph triumph, triumph!" Naturally, the seasonal nature of ancient warfare coincided, somewhat, with that of farming. But we also have to remember that the climate in the Mediterranean was then, even more than now, much different from the temperate seasons we experience in the Northern Hemisphere. In fact, many grain crops were planted in the fall and harvested in the spring. The key words in the prayers cited are those that refer to borders and boundaries. Mars guards them so that peaceful productive life can continue safely within them. Warfare lies outside the area of daily human life.

Domi/Militiae. Rome was the home of its divine citizens, its gods. It was a sacred space, marked out by a sacred boundary, the *pomerium.* The shedding of human blood being a kind of pollution, war in any form was customarily prohibited within the *pomerium.* A commander returning from war, for example, had to disband and purify his army and himself and relinquish his power before entering the sacred city. The Romans made a clear distinction between the civil sphere of action, which they called *domi* (literally "at home"), and being at war, *militiae.* Therefore, for all Mars's importance to the Romans, he did not have a temple within the sacred boundary. Rather, Mars's place lay outside it, to the west of the Capitoline Hill, on the river plain known as the *Campus Martius,* the Field of Mars. Whereas other deities tend to have their temples on hills and elevated places, Mars, the god of war, does not. For Mars was concerned with the totality of male citizens organized as a military entity: to assemble men as an army and to fight a battle requires a flat place. The earliest temple of Mars was that outside the Capena Gate, founded in 388 B.C.E. when Rome was in the midst of a serious struggle against its hostile neighbors for control of Latium. Another was established two centuries later in the *Campus Martius* near the ancient Altar of Mars.

Father Mars and the Romulus Legend. The Romans derived their ancestry from the divine beings Venus and Mars, though separately. According to Homer's *Iliad,* composed about the same time as the historical founding of Rome, Aphrodite, the Greek goddess of love, was the mother by a mortal man of the hero Aeneas in Troy, in northwest Asia Minor. The Romans later developed this myth, referring to the goddess as her Latin equivalent, Venus, and making Aeneas the founder of a new race of Trojans in Italy after the destruction of Troy, traditionally held to have occurred around 1185 B.C.E. But Aeneas himself did not found Rome. His son Ascanius, also called Iulus, founded the hill-town Alba Longa ("Long White") in the Alban Hills south of the later site of Rome. One of Ascanius's distant descendants, Procas, had two sons, Numitor and Amulius. Amulius was wicked and forcefully removed his elder brother from the throne. To make certain that no male descendants of Numitor would later claim the throne, Amulius made Numitor's daughter and only child, Rhea Silvia, a Vestal Virgin so that she would never have children. The historian Livy tells us what happened then:

> In my opinion the origin of such a great city and the beginning of the greatest empire—next to the gods' power—was determined by fate. The Vestal virgin was raped. When she had given birth to twin sons, she named Mars the father of her illegitimate offspring, whether she believed it was really

so, or whether a god as father made her sin more respectable. But neither the gods nor human beings protected her or her children from the king's cruelty. The priestess was bound and put under close watch, while he ordered the boys to be thrown into the water of the Tiber river flowing by. (Livy, *From the Founding of the City,* 1.4.1–3.)

Of course the babies, Romulus and Remus, were saved. The basket in which they had been placed upon the river washed up near a fig tree at one end of the later Roman Forum. They were at first reared by a she-wolf, an animal sacred to Mars. They were then raised by a kindly shepherd, Little Lucky, and his wife. Upon coming to young manhood, they discovered their ancestry, killed the tyrant Amulius, and restored their grandfather to the throne of Alba Longa before going down into the plain of Latium to establish their own towns where they had been reared as babies. The brothers quarreled over whose settlement had the greater approval of Jupiter, and Romulus killed his brother Remus with a shovel. We see in this legend two ideas important to Roman culture: the confirmation of warfare as the just revenge on wrongdoers and that violence lies at the foundation of civilization.

Mars the Avenger. The dictator Julius Caesar traced his family line back to Venus: Iulus, son of Aeneas, had originated the Julian clan, it was said. When Caesar was assassinated on 15 March 44 B.C.E., his nephew and adopted son Octavian (later Augustus) took command of one side in a civil war against his adoptive father's killers. Many years later, in 2 B.C.E., Augustus brought Mars into the sacred limits of the city: he established a huge temple to Mars the Avenger in the new Forum of Augustus, immediately adjacent to Caesar's Forum and temple of Mother Venus. In a highly political way, Augustus exploited ancient mythological associations of Venus and Mars with his own family, restored Mars to his original preeminence in Roman religion, and justified his brutal suppression of Caesar's enemies.

Mars and the Census. It is important to remember that ancient citizen armies were arranged according to wealth and social status. The wealthiest citizens, those who could afford horses, body armor, weapons and so on, and who thus had the most to risk in war, took the first rank; others followed them in order of property qualifications, called centuries by the Romans. Every five years they conducted a census, a reckoning of the personal worth of all citizens, not only to know the size of the general population and the total wealth of the community, but also in order to organize the army. This gathering was called a *lustrum* (from *lustrare,* to purify), and again a purificatory *suovetaurilia* was involved. The male citizens, arranged in centuries, would stand in the Field of Mars while the animal victims were led around it three times before being sacrificed to Mars. The god would be thanked for keeping the people safe for the past five years and asked to do the same during the next. In a sense, the male citizen body was then dedicated to the protective god Mars.

Mars, Awaken! Though Mars did not have a temple within the sacred boundary of the city, sacred implements of war that represented him symbolically were kept in the Regia, the office of the pontifical priesthood in the Forum. Mars was "present" not in the form of a statue but of a simple war-lance. Together with it were the *hastae Martis,* the javelins of Mars, and his sacred *ancilia.* The latter were twelve archaic shields of figure-eight shape, one of which was said to have fallen from heaven; the other eleven were made to protect the identity of the original. Warfare is an altered state of human experience, and must be ceremonially acknowledged. When the time for war came and the general had "awakened Mars," then the god's special priests, the *Salii* (Leapers), would take out the *ancilia* and with them perform an ancient war dance and sing hymns that were so old that people in Caesar's day could already no longer understand them. In the fall, when the armies had returned, the *Salii* would put the *ancilia* away again. So it was that the months of March and October were full of cult acts for Mars, especially purifications of the army and its weapons. Such acts set fighting men temporarily outside the everyday experience of citizens, and then return them to that world after the killing.

Honor and Virtue. The Romans were quite inclined to deify abstract human qualities. In the honor of Jupiter, for example, they erected a small temple to Fides, or Trustworthiness, on the Capitol, this being a quality essential to the faithful keeping of oaths and promises. Honor and Virtue were elevated to divine status and attributed to the god Mars, for these traits are the essential qualities of a good citizen soldier. There was an ancient shrine and altar to Honor outside the Colline Gate, and another outside the Capena Gate near the temple of Mars. This latter site was made a double temple to Honor and Virtue in 208 B.C.E. It was the site of the *transvectio equitum,* the review of the cavalry on its way to wars to the south of Rome. We have a large number of dedicatory inscriptions to either of these deities made by soldiers all over the Roman world.

Bellona and the Fetial Law. As Honor and Virtue, the goddess Bellona, whose name simply means War (the ancient spelling is Duelona), was worshiped as an aspect of Mars. When the Romans were in serious difficulties fighting the Etruscans and Samnites in 296 B.C.E., a temple to Bellona was established in the Campus Martius near the ancient Altar of Mars. The grounds of this temple were used in a unique way. From remote antiquity on, the Roman declaration of war was a religious ceremony. When an enemy nation had done wrong to the Roman people, a public priest known as a fetial was sent as ambassador. He would go to Rome's border with the offending nation, call on Jupiter and the enemy territory itself as witness, then recount all his demands for satisfaction. He would repeat this demonstration to any passersby, then go to the city gate and to the forum of the enemy state. If satisfaction was not made within thirty-three days, he would return to Rome, and after debate, war would be formally declared. Again, Livy tells us about the rite (the Ancient Latins were the enemy in this particular case):

Marble head of Juno Sospita from Lanuvium. Possibly a cult image from a temple, it dates from the middle-late Republican era (Deutsches Archaologisches Institut, Rome).

The custom was that the fetial priest would carry an iron-headed spear, or a blood-red one fire-hardened at the tip, to their border, and with no fewer than three adults present he would say: "Inasmuch as the peoples of the Ancient Latins and individual Ancient Latins have acted against and cheated the Roman people, the Quirites; inasmuch as the Roman people has ordered war with the Ancient Latins and the senate of the Roman people, the Quirites, has decreed, agreed, voted that there be war with the Ancient Latins, for that reason I and the Roman people declare and make war on the peoples of the Ancient Latins and on individual Ancient Latins." When he had said this, he hurled the spear into their territory. (Livy, *From the Founding of the City*, 1. 32. 12-14.)

Of course, as Rome's power grew and its conflicts were with nations far away, it was no longer possible to send fetials to demand satisfaction and declare war. They therefore resorted to a legal fiction. During the wars with the mercenary Greek general Pyrrhus of Epirus in the early third century B.C.E., a captive Greek soldier was made to purchase a plot of land in the Campus Martius near the temple of Bellona. This ownership made it perpetually "enemy territory." When war was declared, the fetials would then go to the temple of Bellona and carry out their traditional rite.

Janus Two-Face. The Latin word for door is *ianua*, from which, with a slight change of spelling, comes the word "janitor," originally a doorkeeper or doorman. A doorway is a place of transition, a boundary where one enters a different space and, possibly, a different experience. In many religions of the world, and particularly in Roman religion, boundaries of all kinds were sacred. They required the particular attention of a deity. In Rome that god was Janus, the god of beginnings. He thus shares this interest with Juno. When the Roman calendar was modified and the year no longer began on the first of March, the beginning month was named after Janus. His own priest, the King of Sacrifices, performed for him a special sacrifice, the Agonium, in the Regia or "King's House" in the Forum on 9 January each year. Together with Juno he was honored on the beginning day of each month, the Kalends. He is also called Matutinus, God of Morning, for he is there at the beginning of each day. When a long list of deities was invoked in prayer, Janus was called on first, even before Jupiter. Because of later poetic inventions, it came to be believed that Janus was the first principal god of the Romans, and was later superseded by Jupiter, but this is not so. As Varro put it, "The first things are in Janus's power, the highest things in Jupiter's." Because every door both opens and closes and because every beginning is also an ending, Janus is called *Bifrons,* "Two-Face," with one bearded face looking forward, the other backward. We see this image on the earliest Roman minted coins, which has nothing to do with the fact that a coin has two "faces," but simply because of Janus's function as god of firsts.

The Twin Janus Gate. The Forum was originally a swamp; several streams ran through it on their way to the Tiber River. It was from very early times a graveyard, eventually becoming the religious center of the new city. The crossing of streams, especially on such hallowed ground, was felt by the Romans to require extra-careful ritual precautions. One of the principal streams that ran through the Forum area was the Cloaca. In the time of the Tarquin kings this stream began to be directed through a huge sewer in its drainage course down to the Tiber River. Even earlier a covered wooden bridge had been constructed over the Cloaca, by which the Sacra Via, the Sacred Road, might continue uninterrupted from one area of the Forum to the other. This bridge consisted of two parallel passageways, each with a door at either end. It was called the Ianus Geminus, the Twin Janus Gate. Though the Cloaca itself was over time completely channeled through its sewer and no longer even visible, Roman conservatism and religious scrupulousness required the maintenance of the Twin Janus. A custom developed whereby, as long as a Roman army was out in the field and the Roman people were somewhere at war with an enemy, the doors of the Twin Janus were left open. When the Romans were completely at peace, with no war anywhere in their domain, the gates of one passageway were closed, a concrete symbol of the benefits of Roman civilization. Tradition held that the legendary King Numa had built the Janus and had been the first to close its doors. In 235 B.C.E. the consul Manlius Torquatus also closed them. After that, however, it was not until the reign of Augustus that the Janus Gate was again closed, in 29 B.C.E.; in fact, Augustus boasted that he had closed it three times in his long rule.

Venus. The goddess Venus at Rome evolved from a protectress of gardens, vegetables, and vineyards to a highly politicized divinity. Venus gradually adopted the mythology of Aphrodite, the Greek goddess of sexual love, and was eventually paired with the deified goddess Roma herself. The name Venus means simply "charm" or "seductive pleasure" (though some connect it with *vinum*, wine). We know that she did not have a place in the original Roman calendars, which tells us she was not included in the oldest Roman pantheon. There is much evidence that she was especially worshiped at Lavinium and Ardea, and it is likely that she was borrowed from there and worshiped at Rome. Her holidays coincided generally with the Vinalia, wine-harvest festivals, and over time much of the month of April was devoted to the worship of Venus, especially by women. The earliest known temple of Venus in Rome was located on the Esquiline Hill in the sacred grove of Libitina, goddess of burials.

Venus the Favorable. The earliest datable temple to Venus was that for her aspect as Obsequens, Favorable, in 295 B.C.E., near the Circus Maximus. It was paid for out of fines assessed on married women who had committed adultery.

Venus Erycina. The Roman Venus began to be merged into the mythology of the Greek goddess Aphrodite, for political reasons, during Rome's wars with Carthage in the third century B.C.E. Atop a mountain known as Eryx on the northwest coast of Sicily was an ancient temple to Aphrodite, where sacred prostitution was practiced. The temple and town surrounding it made a strategic fortress, overlooking the cape of Drepanum, extremely important for the naval warfare waged between Rome and Carthage. To win the town from control of Carthage, the inhabitants and the Romans politicized the myth of Aphrodite, mother by a mortal man of the Trojan hero Aeneas. According to this myth Aeneas, escaping the destruction of Troy, established the cult to his mother at Eryx, then went on to found Lavinium, from which the city of Rome would eventually be founded. This religious connection justified Roman occupation of that part of Sicily beginning in 248 B.C.E. In 217 B.C.E. disturbing events caused the Roman Senate to order a consultation of the Sibylline Books, the public oracle through which the god Apollo spoke to the Roman people. Among other things, Apollo instructed them to build a temple to Venus Erycina. This was accordingly vowed to her and dedicated on the Capitoline Hill two years later. Again in 181 B.C.E., following yet another consultation of the Sibylline Books, a second temple was established for Erycina outside the Colline Gate in north-central Rome. This area became well-known as a place of prostitution.

Venus Changer of Hearts. Sometime in the mid to late third century B.C.E., upon consultation of the Sibylline Books because of the frequency of adulteries committed by women, a statue was dedicated to Venus Verticordia, Venus Changer of Hearts, by Sulpicia, recognized as the most chaste woman in Rome at that time. The belief was that this form of Venus would change women's thoughts of other men back to their wedded husbands. In 114 B.C.E. a dread prodigy occurred: a girl was riding a horse when they were both struck by lightning. She was found on the road, stripped nearly nude, with her tongue sticking out of her mouth. Wishing to know the meaning, the Senate summoned the Etruscan seers. They interpreted the prodigy as a sign that some act of unchastity had been committed by the Vestal Virgins. Evidence pointed to three Vestals, Aemilia, Licinia, and Marcia, who were alleged to have been having sexual relations with a man. They were tried in a special court; two were convicted and one was acquitted. Again the Sibylline Books were consulted, and it was decreed that two Gauls and two Greeks should be buried alive and that a temple to Venus Verticordia should be established. Vestals guilty of unchastity were buried alive within the city wall near the Colline Gate.

Venus and the First Men. From the time of the wars with Carthage, Venus came to be more and more closely identified as the mother and special protectress of the Roman race. The Epicurean poet Lucretius (circa 94–51 B.C.E.), though himself virtually an atheist, nevertheless began his long philosophical poem *On the Nature of Reality* with a hymn to Venus Genetrix, Venus the Mother:

> Mother of Aeneas' people, pleasure of men and of gods,
> nourishing Venus, you who fill the constellations gliding
> under heaven, the ship-bearing sea, and the crop-bearing

MAJOR GREEK GODS AND THEIR ROMAN EQUIVALENTS

GREEK	ROMAN
Zeus	Jupiter
Hera	Juno
Apollo	Apollo
Artemis	Diana
Athena	Minerva
Poseidon	Neptune
Aphrodite	Venus
Hermes	Mercury
Hephaestus	Vulcan
Ares	Mars
Hades	Pluto
Dionysus	Liber
Hestia	Vesta

Source: R. M. Ogilvie, *The Romans and Their Gods in the Age of Augustus* (London: Chatto & Windus, 1969).

earth with life, since through you every kind of living being is conceived and, coming into existence, sees the sunlight, you, goddess, the winds flee, the clouds of heaven flee you and your approach, for you the multi-patterned earth sends up sweet flowers, for you the level plains of the sea smile and the peaceful sky glows with radiant light. (Lucretius, *On the Nature of Reality*, 1–9)

The political use of Venus was manifest during the last century of the Republic, when ambitious individuals competed for supreme military and civil power at Rome. It was a turbulent era, marked by unconstitutional acts and political violence. The first of these men was Lucius Cornelius Sulla, known as Felix, "Lucky" (circa 138 to 79 B.C.E.). Believing himself especially favored by Venus (he was quite fond of women), he called himself Ephaphroditus, "Son of Aphrodite," and added to his power by cultivating Venus Felix. He had images of her stamped on coins. He was followed in this activity by Gnaeus Pompeius Magnus (106–48 B.C.E.), one of the great generals of the period. To secure his eminence in the city, he built the first stone theater, located in the Campus Martius. Atop the theater's rows of seats he constructed a small temple to his personal deity, Venus Victrix, Venus of Victory. But she did not bring Pompey success against his chief rival for power, Julius Caesar, who began a civil war in 49 and defeated his rival at the battle of Pharsalus the following year; Pompey fled to Egypt, where he was assassinated upon landing. Prior to the battle at Pharsalus, Caesar vowed a temple to Venus Victrix if she would desert Pompey and help him instead. But when Caesar dedicated the temple two years later, he established it to the mythological mother of his own clan (Iulus was another name for the son of Aeneas), Venus Genetrix.

Venus and *Roma*. Because in Greek mythology Ares, the god of war, and Aphrodite are represented as lovers, it was relatively easy to point to the dual ancestry of the Romans, to Venus through Aeneas and to Mars through Aeneas's descendant Romulus. These deities became abstract representations of qualities the Romans valued: success in war and natural productivity. As an abstract concept Roma was represented in deified form on coins from fairly early times. Eventually Venus and Rome were closely identified by the emperor Hadrian (117–138 C.E.), who in 121 C.E. built a large temple for these goddesses, each with her own compartment.

Vesta. The worship of the goddess Vesta at Rome is a good example of how public and private religion operate simultaneously. Vesta's name, which corresponds to that of the goddess Hestia in Greek mythology and religion, means simply "hearth" or "fireplace." This fireplace provides physical comfort and the sharing of food. The preparation of food requires cleanliness and purity, which Vesta also represents. The fireplace, or *focus* in Latin, was the innermost center of the round Roman house of earliest times; it remained a symbol of the sanctity and security of the home and family life, of which Vesta is the deified form. The Romans understood very well that individual

morality and the integrity of the family were the core of their state and world empire. Vesta has a close relationship with Janus: as he watches over the entrance to the house, she guards its innermost area. As prayers must open with Janus, they must close with Vesta. The King of Sacrifices, Janus's special priest, also has a special relationship with the Vestal Virgins.

Public Vesta of the Roman People as Citizens. *Vesta Publica Populi Romani Quiritium* is Vesta's full name in her public cult. Her center was in a round building in the heart of the Forum, directly across from the Regia. It is probably the oldest preserved building in the Forum, though it was destroyed or damaged by fire and rebuilt many times over the centuries. The Christian emperor Theodosius had it closed in 394 C.E. It is likely that the round structure purposely reproduced the shape of the ancient Roman private house. In fact, it was called the "house" or the "atrium" of Vesta, not her "temple," for that word means an inaugurated place, where auspices can be taken and public business can be undertaken. But no men could enter the house of Vesta: she is a virgin, as are her attendants, and a man's presence would violate that status. The one exception was the Pontifex Maximus (or any pontifex representing him), who must necessarily enter on occasion. In the center of the house of Vesta was a hearth in which a fire was kept burning constantly. On the first day of March, the ancient New Year's Day, under careful ritual conditions, the fire was allowed to go out and then renewed. Also at the center of the house of Vesta was the "pantry" or "cupboard," where certain materials used for sacrifice and purification were kept, together with seven mysterious symbols of Roman power. These probably included the Palladium, a wooden or perhaps stone image of the goddess Athena that, according to legend, had been brought from the innermost part of that virgin goddess's temple at Troy by Aeneas and preserved by his descendants ever afterward. It was the responsibility of the Vestal Virgins to keep the fire burning, to bring fresh water from the sacred spring of Egeria in special containers, to make the sacrificial and purificatory materials, and above all, to maintain their own sexual purity. The virgins lived in an apartment complex immediately adjoining the house of Vesta.

Di Penates. The communal responsibilities and sharing of food have been an essential part of religion from earliest times. We may thus easily understand the importance of the Di Penates, the gods of the pantry, in both private and public religion at Rome. The pantry, or food storage cupboard, was called the *penus*, and in the oldest form of the Roman house it was situated close to the hearth and the dining table. For this reason the Di Penates are closely connected with Vesta. Once the meal was prepared and set on the table, a portion of each article of food was placed on a platter, carried to the fire, and offered up in sacrifice to the Di Penates. The pantry gods were identified with the health and well-being of the family and gradually came to be worshiped as the collective, protective deities of the whole house. This devotion becomes especially significant in the Imperial era, for the Di Penates of the Roman People as Citizens, as part of the cult of Vesta, becomes practically identical with the worship of the imperial dynastic households. It was generally believed that the Di Penates were brought by Aeneas from Troy, that their cult was established at Lavinium, his first settlement in Italy, and taken from there by his son Iulus to Alba Longa, and finally, centuries later, to Rome. The Di Penates were understood to be a pair of young men, and appeared on coins in the iconogaphy, or standard pictorial representation, of the Dioscuri, the twin Greek heroes Castor and Pollux. This fits a pattern well known throughout the ancient eastern Mediterranean world, especially from such places as Thebes and Samothrace in Greece, where two young heroes, the Cabiri, are worshiped as the protective gods of a family.

The Lares. The Lar (later plural *Lares*) was another tutelary or protective deity of the family. Originally he was the guardian spirit of the plot of a household's land. At the juncture of lands owned by different families, called a *compitum*, often also a crossroads, each family erected a small shrine on its own land to its own Lar. Every year in early January, families of neighboring farms would jointly celebrate the *Compitalia* or *Laralia*, in honor of these gods. On the night before, the altars would be decorated with dolls and balls of wool hung with string. The next day there would be offerings, games, and a day off and an extra measure of wine for the slaves who worked the land.

The Lares and Slavery. In fact, the cult of the Lares was most closely associated with slaves, chiefly because it was they who worked the land. The health and well-being of field workers was of vital importance in an agricultural economy, and the Lar was concerned with slaves, who were regarded as part of the equipment necessary for farming. The word *familia*, family, originally meant all the slaves, or *famuli*, owned by a household. This association of the cult of the Lares and slaves was a permanent feature of Roman religion until the Christian emperor Theodosius banned all pagan practices in 392 C.E.

Lar Familiaris. With increasing prosperity and the urbanization of the wealthy, slaves came more and more from the rural into the domestic life of a household. Though they had nothing to do originally with the hearth or food, they became an integral part of the worship of Vesta, the Di Penates, and the family Genius. This change is probably a result of the fact that a slave woman, the *vilica*, wife of the overseer-slave, was also chiefly responsible for the fire, water supply, and food preparation in the house. She was charged with decorating the hearth with garlands on the Kalends, Nones, and Ides of each month and with praying to the Lar of the house. In this way the Lar became synonymous with the household as a whole. In the atrium or entrance room of a Roman house was a shrine, the *lararium*, a kind of cabinet at which the Lares, the Di Penates, and the Genius of the family were honored. The Lar eventually became plural, represented as two dancing children with curly hair and dressed in togas tied up high. They were worshiped daily, but especially at all recurring or extraordinary events in the family's life, such as birthdays, births, deaths, and weddings. When girls and boys reached puberty they dedicated, respectively, their dolls or *bullae* (good-luck charms worn around the neck on a string) to the Lar. When a family member went away on a journey or returned from one, the Lar was honored. At street junctions in the city the cult of the Lares Compitales was maintained as in the country, and around these neighborhood shrines there developed a kind of religious club, with annually elected officers, who were either slaves or freedmen. These clubs became political factions in the turbulent civil strife of the first century B.C.E., and were at times suppressed. They were reconstituted by the first emperor, Augustus, but the cult thereafter became politicized by being officially associated with the worship of the Genius of the imperial family.

Diana. The name Diana shares the same root as Jupiter and means "bright," because of her aspect as a goddess of the shining moon. The regularly recurring cycle of the moon's phases associates Diana with women in their menstrual cycles and thus in pregnancy and childbirth. Like her Greek equivalent Artemis, Diana was invoked by women, especially young mothers in labor, as Eileithyia. She shares this concern with Juno Lucina, with one important difference: Diana is a virgin goddess. Diana also seems to be the divine agency responsible for conferring political leadership on individuals and states. She is a *liminal* goddess, that is, one concerned with the protection of those in transition from one area of human experience to another. Diana's cult centers, always in sacred groves in wild forests, were extraordinarily frequent in Latium and neighboring states. Her most important pre-Roman sanctuaries were at Mt. Tifata near Capua and at Aricia, overlooking a small volcanic lake known as the Mirror of Diana. There a primitive custom was maintained. Diana's priest, known as the *rex nemorensis*, King of the Grove, retained his "kingship" by dueling with anyone who contested him. A branch from a certain tree was used as a weapon, and the winner either remained king or became the new one. In historical times this honor was sought chiefly by runaway slaves.

Diana at Rome. Sometime in the middle of the regal period (753–509 B.C.E.) the ancient capital city of Latium, Alba Longa, was destroyed by a Roman army and its citizens were forcibly removed to Rome. The remaining independent Latin cities formed a confederation in response to the Roman threat, making Aricia their headquarters. According to semihistorical legend the Roman king Servius Tullius, born of a slave mother, arranged to transfer the cult of Diana from Aricia to Rome, thereby establishing Rome's political supremacy in Latium. Her new altar and temple were established on the Aventine Hill, and her sacred founding day was 13 August. An archaic inscription laid out the regulations for the maintenance of the temple, and this guide became the legal model for all later temple establishments.

Goddess of Three Forms. Diana was gradually assimilated to her Greek equivalent, Artemis, the Mistress of Animals and midwife. Diana had three dimensions: in the sky she was Luna, the moon; on earth she was Diana protectress of women; and in the underworld, she was Hecate, a goddess of the dead and of witchcraft. Diana, as deity of marginal or transitional places, was especially honored at crossroads, or *trivia*, by which name she was also sometimes known.

Apollo. The god Apollo was already well established in ancient Greek religion and mythology by the time of Rome's founding in 753 B.C.E. His areas of concern were chiefly prophecy, healing, and the entry of young men into adult life. He also became associated with music and poetry and the ideal of clear reason. As Phoebus, the Brilliant One, he was also identified with the sun, as his sister Artemis was with the moon. His principal cult centers were on Delos, his island birthplace in the Aegean Sea, and at Delphi on the slope of Mt. Parnassus near the Gulf of Corinth. Greek colonists of Neapolis (present-day Naples) in southern Italy established at nearby Cumae an oracular center of Apollo, where his priestess, an old woman called a Sibyl, would answer people's questions about present problems or future events. She did this by falling into a trancelike state and scattering palm leaves on which prophetic verses were written; the verses on the leaf selected would answer the question posed.

The Sibylline Books. According to legend, sometime during the reign of Tarquinius the Ancient, the fifth king of Rome (616–579 B.C.E.), the Cumaean Sibyl came to Rome and offered the king nine books of prophetic leaves for sale. He scoffed at her, at which she threw three books into the fire. She then offered the remaining six books, but at the original price. Again the king declined, and again the Sibyl burned three books. The Sibyl offered the remaining three books, again at the original price, and this time the king, aware that something valuable was at stake, purchased them. Whether this story is true or not, some collection of such oracular verses formed the core of an official oracle at Rome, to be consulted only in times of extreme emergency, and then only on orders of the Senate. A special priesthood was established for this consultation, consisting first of two, later ten, and finally fifteen men. The earliest certain consultation of the Sibylline Books was in 496 B.C.E., during a crop pestilence and famine. The books ordered the introduction to Rome of the divine triad of Ceres, Liber, and Libera. In fact, the books were chiefly responsible for practically all subsequent innovations in Roman public religion thereafter, always in response to some portent or crisis such as plague. The books were last consulted publicly in 363 C.E.

Apollo Medicus. Apollo at Rome was thus worshiped mostly as a god of healing. His only temple, until the time of Augustus, lay outside the *pomerium*, or sacred city boundary, in the Campus Martius, probably because of concerns about spreading illness. It was vowed in 433 during a plague and dedicated two years later by the consul C.

The goddess Ceres sitting on her throne, from Aricia in central Italy, circa 300 B.C.E. This terracotta figure is reconstructed from fragments (Antiquarium, inv. no. 112377, Museo Nazionale Romana [Terme Museum], Rome)

Iulius. In 212 B.C.E., again on instructions from the Sibylline Books, new public games were instituted in Apollo's honor, at which theatrical performances first became important in Rome.

Apollo Palatinus. Since the founding of the temple of Apollo Medicus, the Julian clan had always had a particular interest in Apollo. When Augustus came to power, he established a new cult center on the Palatine Hill near his own home, dedicating it to Apollo in 28 B.C.E. He thus symbolized the preeminence of his own family's god (and legitimized his own rule and new political order) over that of Jupiter Best and Greatest, the Capitoline god of the Republic and its magistrates. The Sibylline Books, formerly housed in the Capitoline temple, were transferred to that of Apollo on the Palatine. Even after Augustus's death, Apollo continued to play a significant role in the Imperial period. We can see a long trend whereby the first emperor's personal god, in his aspect as sun god, leads to the introduction by emperors in the third century C.E. of the Unconquered Sun. This Eastern god, in the time of Constantine the Great (272–337 C.E.), was rather easily replaced by Jesus Christ. Thus, Christianity became virtually the official religion of the Roman empire.

Aesculapius. We have grown used to a comfortable expectation of high-quality medical care in times of illness or accident. In antiquity, people were much more anxious about disease and health. The mysterious, often hidden, nature of disease was regarded as supernatural. It was Apollo who revealed the hidden causes of illness and provided their remedies. Apollo's healing capacity was personified in the god Aesculapius, his son by the nymph Coronis, according to Greek mythology. In 293–292 B.C.E. a serious plague struck much of Italy and Greece. In Rome all usual methods of cure were tried, without success. The Senate ordered the Sibylline Books to be consulted; they revealed that Aesculapius was to be brought from the Greek city Epidaurus to Rome. Ten men were dispatched to bring him. When their ship docked, a snake, Aesculapius's symbolic animal, slithered on board. The ship returned to Rome and as it came up the Tiber River the snake slipped overboard and swam onto Tiber Island, just under the Capitoline and Palatine Hills. Aesculapius's temple was dedicated there in 291, thereafter the chief healing center in ancient Rome, and it continues as the site of hospitals even today. A serpent curled around a walking-stick remains a symbol of the medical practice. Sick persons were cured through "incubation," that is, they would lie in the temple at night under the supervision of priest doctors. If they were pious, the god would come to them in dreams and reveal the cause and the cure of their illness. Apollo's prophetic and healing powers are thus integrated.

Tellus Mater, Ceres, Liber, Libera. To societies almost entirely dependent on agriculture, gods of the earth, crops, and harvesting are important. Since agriculture was invented in what is presently Iraq in about 10,000 B.C.E., we have some idea of the age and the place of origin of these kinds of religion. Once again the sharing of food in the preservation of life is central to religious practice. It must be kept in mind that, in antiquity, meat did not make up much of the total diet and was only consumed as part of religious observance and sacrifice. Grains, beans, fruits, vegetables, and dairy products made up most of the diet. Very ancient deities of the Roman people were Saturnus and Consus, deified forms of the acts of sowing seed and storing the harvest, respectively. Two goddesses to whom the Romans especially looked for agricultural success were Tellus Mater, Mother Earth, and Ceres, goddess of cereal grain crops. Tellus had her temple on the Esquiline Hill and was usually celebrated together with other deities, especially Ceres. The worship of Ceres and her two associates, Liber and Libera, came to Rome as a result of a plague and the consultation of the Sibylline Books in 496 B.C.E. Her temple was dedicated on the Aventine Hill three years later, and it soon became an organizing and administrative center for the plebeian, or nonaristocratic, segment of Roman society. After 449 B.C.E. copies of all decrees of the Senate were kept there. The cult of Ceres and Libera adopted some of the elements of the Greek mystery religion of Demeter and her daughter Persephone at the famous sanctuary of Eleusis, near Athens, while Liber's worship took on some of the forms of the religion of Dionysus, the Greek god of wine. Bread and wine were potent religious symbols of the renewal of life through the act of sacrificing and sharing of food and drink, even borrowed into the new Christian religion.

Castor and Pollux. Another pair of gods who represented a segment of Roman society were Castor and his twin brother Pollux, though Castor was by far the predominant object of worship. The two brothers were also known as the Dioscuri, Sons of Zeus, represented in the heavens by the constellation Gemini, the Twins. Castor was outstanding as a horseman, Pollux as a boxer. In their Greek mythology the brothers represent the undying loyalty soldiers have for one another. In 499 B.C.E. a coalition of Latin cities had formed against the new Republic in Rome. In a battle at Lake Regillus the Roman ranks began to give way. The general made a vow to Castor and Pollux. According to one source two glorious young men on white horses and dressed in purple cloaks suddenly appeared on the Roman side, giving them courage and causing the enemy to panic. Shortly thereafter these same two horsemen were seen, many miles away, in the Forum at Rome, watering their horses at the Spring of Juturna near the House of Vesta. They announced the Roman victory and suddenly disappeared. In 484 the temple of Castor was dedicated; its remains are still evident.

Borrowing and Adaptation. In fact, stories of the miraculous appearance of Castor and Pollux were already well known in Greece. The Romans had adapted the story as a means of demonstrating the vital importance of their cavalry—and the social class of which it was made—at that time. The *ordo equester*, the Equestrian Order, was a property class of citizens, those who had enough wealth to maintain horses and the equipment necessary for cavalry combat, but who did not, for various reasons, hold public offices that would gain them entry into the Senate. Castor was the divine patron of this social class. Beginning in 304 B.C.E., on 15 July, every five years a census was taken and a public review made of all those who were included in the Equestrian Order. Dressed in their full armor and military decorations, they would ride from the temple of Mars at the Capena Gate, pass before the censor, who was seated on the steps of the temple of Castor, and continue up to the temple of Jupiter Best and Greatest on the Capitoline.

Castores and the Di Penates. In that part of their cult that concerns the equestrian class, Castor eclipses Pollux. The two brothers are usually called the "Castors" in this respect. But much of their cult derived from the ancient town of Lavinium, where they were very early combined symbolically with the Di Penates, also represented as twin young men.

Sources:

Mary Beard, John North, and Simon Price, *Religions of Rome,* 2 volumes (Cambridge & New York: Cambridge University Press, 1998).

Ken Dowden, *Religion and the Romans* (London: Bristol Classical Press, 1992).

J. H. W. G. Liebeschuetz, *Continuity and Change in Roman Religion* (Oxford: Clarendon Press, 1979; New York: Oxford University Press, 1979).

R. M. Ogilvie, *The Romans and Their Gods in the Age of Augustus* (London: Chatto & Windus, 1969).

Robert Turcan, *The Gods of Ancient Rome,* translated by Antonia Nevill (Edinburgh: Edinburgh University Press, 2000).

W. Warde Fowler, *The Religious Experience of the Roman People, from the Earliest Times to the Age of Augustus* (London: Macmillan, 1911).

LIGHT FROM THE EAST

Change within Tradition. Roman religion evolved along with Rome's increasing political influence throughout the Mediterranean world. Gods from Greece, Asia, Egypt, and finally Palestine all took their places in Rome's pantheon. Many cults, often emerging from the east and concerning self-sacrifice, death, and resurrection, began as private or as family religious practices and then assumed a public status. We also notice a general tendency toward imagery of the sun and monotheism.

Cybele, the Great Idaean Mother of Gods. Sometime in prehistory a meteorite struck the earth in Asia Minor, presumably near Mt. Ida. In a temple at Pessinus it was an object of religious awe and veneration. Over time it came to be identified with the Phrygian goddess Cybele, who was concerned with fertility, healing, prophecy, the protection of cities, and wild nature. This range of powers caused her to be worshiped as the Great Mother of the Gods. As Greek influence extended into Asia Minor, she came to be represented in human form, wearing a crown of a turreted city wall and seated in a chariot drawn by a pair of lions. During the third century B.C.E. tribes of invading Gauls from western Europe settled in that part of Asia Minor, thereafter named Galatia. The priests of Cybele were then known as *galloi,* Gauls.

Cybele Goes to Rome. King Attalus I of Pergamum in Asia Minor had defeated the Galatians, and, to secure his rule, he brought the meteorite to Pergamum and set up a new cult center there. He was also a firm defender of Roman interests in Asia Minor. During his reign, in 205 B.C.E., a consultation of the Sibylline Books at Rome revealed that Cybele should be brought from Pergamum and given a new home. Under the direction of Publius Cornelius Scipio, a member of Rome's leading family at that time and one with strong connections to Attalus, the black stone was brought by ship. A new temple, along with public games, was dedicated to the Great Mother in 191 B.C.E. This location on the Palatine, and her own origin on Mt. Ida, was especially important to the Julian clan, for Venus and the mortal hero Anchises, so the myth said, had mated on Mt. Ida. Their offspring was the Trojan hero Aeneas, founder of the Roman people in Italy through his son Iulus. Augustus, the first emperor and a member of the Julian family, established his home on the Palatine several centuries later, making the connection quite clear.

The Worship of Cybele. Only part of Cybele's worship was administered by Roman officials: they supervised her games, offerings, and the annual bathing of her cult statue.

ATTIS, DEVOTE(E) OF CYBELE

In what is perhaps his most remarkable poem, Catullus describes the ecstatic experience of Attis, a young man seized with the desire to worship Cybele. Like all *galloi,* Attis castrates himself; this change of anatomical gender is marked in the Latin by an actual change of grammatical gender that is almost impossible to represent in English, though it would have been arresting to its original Roman readers:

Attis, carried over the high seas in a swift ship, as he reached the Phrygian grove with eager desire and approached the goddess's dark places shadowed in woods, there aroused by a mad rage, his mind wandering, he sheared off his genitals with a sharp flint. And then, as s/he perceived he/r limbs were left without manhood, even then spotting the soil of the earth with fresh blood, aroused, s/he took in he/r snow-white hands a light tambourine—your tambourine, Cybele, the instrument, Mother, of your mystery. And shaking the hollow bullhide with delicate fingers, trembling, s/he began to sing this song to he/r companions: "Come, Gallic women, go at once to the deep groves of Cybele, go at once, wandering flock of the Lady of Dindymus, you who, as exiles, seeking foreign places, quickly following my sect, under my leadership, companions to me, endured the destructive salt sea and the cruel ocean, and who have unmanned your bodies out of your excessive hatred of Venus, delight our Lady's mind with your swift mistakes. Let your slow delay yield to your inclination. Go at once, seek the Phrygian home of Cybele, the Phrygian groves of the goddess, where the voice of the cymbals rings out, where the tambourines resound, where the Phrygian flute-player plays deep on the curved reed, where the ivy-bedecked Maenads toss their heads violently, where they carry out their sacred rites with piercing screams, where that errant herd of the goddess usually flits about; we must rush to that place with our swift dances." (Catullus, *Poems* 63)

Source: *The Poems of Catullus,* translated by James Michie (New York: Vintage, 1971).

Other activities were considered indecent for a Roman. Cybele's priests, the *galloi,* were eunuchs, that is, men who had castrated themselves in order to serve the goddess. Her cult was orgiastic, involving wild and uninhibited dancing by men and women, accompanied by clashing cymbals, rattles, and flutes. After about the mid second century C.E. a new element was added to her cult, the *taurobolium.* In this form of sacrifice a worshiper would lie in a pit dug in the ground, a kind of grave, while over him a bull would be slaughtered so that the devotee would be bathed in its blood. The bull would then be castrated and its testicles offered in sacrifice. In this way it was believed one was "reborn into eternal life." Cybele's cult incorporated the Near Eastern myth of the beautiful young man Attis, beloved of Cybele, who either was castrated by her out of jealousy or who castrated himself. In this myth Attis experiences the recurrent cycle of self-sacrifice, death, and resurrection. She and he eventually figured as lunar and solar beings, respectively.

Suppression of Foreign Religions. All the examples of foreign cults introduced to Rome should not disguise the fact that there were also many official suppressions and expulsions of them over the course of time. On several occasions soothsayers, philosophers, astrologers, and Jews were expelled from the city. In 186 B.C.E. the private worship of Bacchus had spread from Greece and Egypt to southern Italy and thence to Rome. It had already gained a large, and apparently fanatic, following there when the chief magistrates discovered its existence. Several thousand people were executed and strict limits were placed on its future practice. The causes of such strong reactions were moral, religious, and civil. Though it does not always seem so, the Romans were an extremely serious and moral people, concerned about proper and decent behavior. It greatly offended the Roman sense of propriety that, in the worship of Bacchus, for example, men and women were meeting, together, in secret and at night. Rumors of cannibalism, promiscuous sex, murder, and conspiracy to crime were taken seriously. In 17 B.C.E., on the other hand, when Augustus celebrated the recurrent Century Games, some parts of which took place at night with both men and women present, he formally authorized this activity in a decree, which still exists in the form of an inscription. Religion also played a part in such suppressions. Unless a deity had expressed through some prodigy or oracle his or her wish to be celebrated in Rome, the private or individual worship risked provoking the anger of the traditional gods of the people. Finally, the Roman state did not welcome free and private association of its citizens in large numbers. In such circumstances, they felt, revolutions and crimes against the state were plotted. Unauthorized private religious "clubs" were a type of illegal association. These attitudes explain the harsh measures taken against such foreign religions as that of Isis or Christianity.

Isis and Serapis. It took a long time for the Egyptian goddess Isis to become officially accepted at Rome. Isis was, like Cybele, a goddess who gradually accumulated many powers over different aspects of human life, especially that of women. Like Juno, she was concerned with marriage; like Diana, with pregnancy and childbirth; and like Ceres, with agricultural success. Her Egyptian mythology is old and varied. She was the sister and wife of the god Osiris, whom the god Set had murdered and dismembered, scattering the pieces of his body all around the world. Isis, weeping, went looking for the pieces; when she had collected them all she restored Osiris to life. The actual cult practice made this mythological labor a recurrent event, a dramatization of the natural cycle of birth, sacrifice, death, and rebirth. After the time of Alexander the Great (356–323 B.C.E.), Egypt came under the rule of the Ptolemies, a Macedonian Greek royal dynasty. By at least the third century B.C.E. there was a vigorous cult of Isis on the Greek island of Delos, an important trading center. Trade and traffic between Delos and the Greek city of Naples brought the worship of Isis to Italy by at least the second century B.C.E., and it was known at Rome by 80 B.C.E. Between the years 59 and 49 B.C.E. the private altar of Isis, and her Egyptian companion Serapis, on the Capitoline Hill was destroyed at least five times by the authorities, an indication of her enduring and increasing popularity. There was an official acceptance of the cult in 43 B.C.E., but because of the love affair between the Roman general Marcus Antonius and the Ptolemy queen Cleopatra in Egypt, and their ambitions to set up a rival empire in the East, the worship of Egyptian gods was suddenly forbidden. Augustus defeated Antonius and Cleopatra at Actium in 31 B.C.E., and three years later he still prohibited any private shrines to Egyptian gods within the *pomerium*, the sacred boundary of the city of Rome. Thereafter, though, all Egypt became the private province of the emperor. Sometime in the reign of Caligula (37–41 C.E.) the cult was finally accepted as part of the public religion, and a joint temple to Isis and Serapis was constructed on the Campus Martius. The religion of Isis was of great importance throughout the Roman world. It played a significant part of life at the city of Pompeii before its destruction by the eruption of Mt. Vesuvius in 79 C.E. and was the subject of a novel by Apuleius called *Metamorphoses,* in which he describes his transformation into a donkey by witchcraft and his restoration to human form by Isis.

Mithras. The cult of Mithras originated in ancient Persia, present-day Iran. It first came to the Romans' attention when the general Pompey the Great (106–48 B.C.E.) was sent to destroy the fleets of pirates operating from Cilicia on the southwest coast of Asia Minor in 67 B.C.E. It was not of much importance at Rome until the mid second century C.E. From that point on, until the dominance of Christianity, its popularity was immense, especially in Rome and Ostia. Mithraism cut across all sections of Roman society and was widely practiced particularly among Roman soldiers in western Europe. Its popularity among the ruling class helps explain why it escaped official suppression.

The Practice of Mithraism. Mithraism was one of many "mystery" religions of the ancient world. The term "mystery" (Greek *mustêrion*, something that must be revealed) in this context means that worshipers progress by degrees in their knowledge of certain cult secrets. For each level or degree of advancement there were corresponding titles, costumes, and so on. In Mithraism, for example, an initiate began as a "crow," and advanced through six degrees of knowledge until he became a "father." There were tests, oaths, strict secrecy, and sacramental communion. We have abundant physical evidence of Mithraism, but because of the secrecy of the cult, there is hardly any literary evidence to help us interpret the physical remains. Mithraism was a kind of men's religious social club. Their meeting places conformed to a standard type, which depended on the mythology of Mithras. Called *spelaea*, "caves," these were long narrow chambers, often underground or made of a natural cave, with a vaulted ceil-

Marble relief from Sidon, Asia Minor, showing Mithras slaying a sacrificial bull while surrounded by signs of the zodiac, circa 400 C.E. (Louvre, Paris)

ing. Along each side ran a continuous bench on which the celebrants reclined when partaking of the ceremonial meal. At the far end of the hall was a statue or carved relief of the young hero/god Mithras, who is always depicted the same way: dressed in Persian clothing and hat, he is kneeling over a bull whose head he is pulling upward and whom he is stabbing with a knife. He is surrounded with mysterious symbols and animals associated with the cult. Above, a hole let sunlight illuminate the statue or relief. The "cave" was supposed to be a replica of the universe, arranged according to an astrological or zodiacal plan. As one advanced in the rites, he moved further up the bench in ever-increasing places of honor, a sign of his expanding knowledge of the secrets of the universe.

The Unconquered Sun God. At the same time that Mithraism was at its height, another Near Eastern religious cult gained great popularity in Rome, that of the Unconquered Sun God. It even combined with Mithraism in many instances, a process known as "syncretism." In fact, the worship of the sun—and the moon as well—as a deity had a long history in Rome, perhaps beginning in the time of the kings. There were several temples to Sol and Luna in Rome, and it was understood that the Circus Maximus, where horse and chariot races were held, was part of the worship of the sun: as the sun appeared to go around the earth, so the horses and riders ran in laps around the Circus. Apollo and his sister Diana also came to be closely identified with Helios and Selene, the Sun and Moon, respectively. Augustus's special devotion to Apollo and Diana established a long-lasting pattern of imperial cult of these two gods. In the time of the emperors Elagabalus

(218–222 C.E.), who took this name from the Syrian name of the god, El Gabal, and Aurelian (270–275 C.E.), whose mother was a priestess of the Unconquered Sun God, this cult reached its high point. The emperor himself was represented as the sun in human form: seated on his throne with a radiant halo around his head. This iconography, or standard pictorial representation, was adopted by Christians, especially as Christianity attained imperial acceptance with Constantine the Great (272–337 C.E.)

Consistency. We have grown used to a distinction between "pagan" and "Christian," meaning that Christianity was the end of the ancient Roman religion. This is partly true, but it is equally true that Christianity was also a continuation of Roman public religion. The history of Roman religion was a large pattern of change and innovation, but within the limits of a conservative tradition. Gods came and went, names and terms changed, but the elements of religious practice remained essentially the same.

Historical Background. The Hebrew people, a distinct ethnic group with a common religious tradition, inhabited a central part of what is today Israel, from perhaps as early as 2000 B.C.E. Their religion was strictly monotheistic and scripturally revelatory. This means that the people's epic literature, composed over a long period of time, was regarded as a guarantee by their god, Yahweh, that they were a chosen people, destined to rule in their own land. The geographical location of this land, and the relatively small population of the Hebrew people, meant that they suffered frequent domination by larger and more powerful civilizations of the Near East. In the fifteenth century B.C.E., for example, the Jews were forced to migrate to Egypt as slave workers for the pha-

Hellenistic bronze statue of the Phrygian goddess Cybele in a chariot being drawn by lions, circa third century B.C.E. (Metropolitian Museum of Art, New York)

raohs. They were led back by their prophet Moses. From the sixth to fourth centuries they were under the control of the Persian empire. The conquest of Alexander the Great followed. After his death in 323 B.C.E., Macedonian kings ruled large districts in that part of the world and imposed a Hellenistic, or Greek, culture on the native populations. Many aspects of this culture were deeply offensive to Jewish traditions, and there were a series of revolts against it. As Roman interests began to extend to Asia Minor, Egypt, and the Near East, especially after the campaign of Pompey the Great in 67 B.C.E., the Romans and Jews began a long, uneasy relationship. The Romans were very traditional people themselves and admired the antiquity and traditionalism of Judaism, the religion of the Hebrews. But they were baffled by the Jews' monotheism, especially their belief in a god who could not be represented by an image, and by their extreme reluctance to adapt. Jews were from time to time expelled from Rome.

The Historical Jesus. The person Jesus, later known as the Christ, "The Anointed One," was born in Palestine to a Jewish mother during the reign of the emperor Augustus, perhaps as early as 4 B.C.E. Just at this time, in Rome and elsewhere in Rome's empire, there were fervent expectations of the dawning of a new age. In 17 B.C.E., for example, Augustus had celebrated the Century Games, associated with the idea of *palingenesis,* that an old order of things in the world was passing away and the world was

being renewed. Augustus himself promoted this belief by a kind of revival of traditional Roman religious customs, rebuilding of temples, and reinstituting of old priesthoods and establishing new ones. After a century of civil war, the Peace of Augustus did indeed appear to be the dawning of a new age. Among the Jews there was a strong belief that Yahweh was soon to fulfill his promise to his people. For many this meant political as well as religious renewal: the removal of the Roman military and government presence in Palestine and the appearance of the Messiah, the Savior whom their prophetic scriptures had long foretold. Some of the most traditional and conservative Jews were forming themselves into strict religious communities in anticipation of the Messiah's arrival. It was into this political and religious fervor that Jesus was born. Sometime in his early adulthood, during the reign of the emperor Tiberius (14–37 C.E.), Jesus began a life imitating the ancient Jewish prophets. He went about from town to town, working miracles, delivering sermons, and teaching. As he did so, he acquired a following of disciples. His popularity and notoriety increased, and he began to be regarded as a threat by the Jewish priestly classes. To them he seemed a usurper, a renegade, and a blasphemer. They eventually arranged to have him arrested and brought before the Roman governor Pontius Pilate, who sentenced him to death by crucifixion. According to eyewitness accounts, the body of Jesus was not in its tomb several days later, and Jesus began appearing to his disciples, instructing them to spread the message of his life and resurrection.

The Early Christian Church. After the death and reappearances of Jesus his disciples began to zealously preach his story to other Jews, soon even to the Gentiles, that is, non-Jews, throughout Palestine, Asia Minor, Egypt, Greece, and Italy. The worship of Christ was popular chiefly among slaves and soldiers at first, but quickly gained favor among wealthier citizens and inhabitants. The early Christian community, as with other mystery religious groups, was a kind of social club, but it also was a form of welfare. Members often lived in communal arrangements, sharing food and property. They depended on written texts, later grouped together and called the New Testament, in which the mystery of Jesus the Anointed One and his resurrection were told and explained. The original disciples of Jesus, who now called themselves Apostles, "the ones who were sent," were energetic in establishing new communities of believers. Peter, who had known Jesus, had even gone to Rome. Paul, at first a zealous Jewish persecutor of the new sect, who then miraculously converted after Jesus' resurrection, was arrested and sent to Rome to plead before the emperor.

Rome and the Christians. Religious cults were common in the ancient world, and as long as adherents obeyed the law and honored the gods of Rome, they were left alone. But the Christians easily attracted attention. First, they greatly annoyed the priestly classes of traditional Jewish religion, who saw them not only as religious renegades but also as competitors for Roman acceptance. Secondly, they were regarded with suspicion as an overzealous new sect of Judaism at a time when other such groups were agitating for political independence from Rome. The historian Tacitus records that the emperor Nero blamed the great fire of 64 C.E., which destroyed much of Rome, on the Christians. Though he has little good to say about them, Tacitus remarked on the unusually cruel treatment of them by Nero: they were tied to poles and set on fire to illuminate public games he put on at night. As the early church grew, it experienced periodic spates of hostility from Jewish communities and from the Roman state. In 112 C.E. the presence of a cell of Christians was reported to the Roman governor of Bithynia in north central Asia Minor, Gaius Plinius Secundus. Their obstinacy and fanaticism caused him to write to the emperor Trajan for advice about the proper way to interrogate and punish them. Trajan's reply is interesting:

> In prosecuting the cases of those who have been reported to you as Christians, my dear Secundus, you have followed an appropriate course of action. For a procedure having, so to speak, a fixed form, applicable in all cases, cannot be established. They are not to be hunted out. If they are reported and convicted, they are to be punished, but in such a way that anyone who denies that he is a Christian and gives manifest evidence of this by giving thanks to our gods, although suspect in the past, he is to obtain pardon by his repentance. But anonymous written accusations are to play no part in any criminal case. For that sets a very bad example and is not in keeping with our age. (Pliny, *Letters* 10. 96 and 97)

Christianity and Greek Myth and Philosophy. After the Apostles died, a second generation of leaders took their place; they were typically wealthier and much better educated. These individuals began to organize the church communities in a more systematic way, to circulate the Apostles' letters and their written accounts of Jesus' life, and to explain the new religion to a population steeped in Greek literature and philosophy. These men, called collectively the Fathers, wrote voluminous works in which they argued how the miraculous life and death of Jesus was in fact not only in keeping with, but even the fulfillment of, the philosophical life so central to Greek culture. As for traditional Greek mythology, they explained it as God's preparation of the minds of men for the mystery of the Christ. The historical Socrates and the mythological Hercules were examples of preparation. By integrating Greek philosophy and Christian belief, the Fathers—who wrote in both Greek and Latin, for readers throughout the Roman Empire—were able to attract converts from the upper levels of society and thus to make Christianity more respectable. This practice also served to make Greek philosophy more accessible to ordinary people.

Persecution and Acceptance. The followers of Christ were at first persecuted by the Jewish priestly classes. The latter informed against them to the Roman authorities, accusing them of cannibalism, promiscuous sex, corruption of morals, murder, and other criminal activities. The Christians countered these accusations, insisting that they lived virtuous and law-abiding lives and that the love that they expressed for one another was not of an immoral kind. The chief difficulty was that the Christians would not offer sacrifice and pray to the gods of the Roman people, in particular to the dead and deified emperors or to the divine powers that protected the person and family of the living emperor. This stand essentially was an act of treason. All that Rome wanted was a minimal show of respect for its religious traditions. It did not help that there were recurrent Jewish separatist revolts, for the Romans did not distinguish Christians from other Jews for some time. Gradually, however, Christianity made its way into the uppermost level of Roman society. The emperor Constantine the Great, whose mother and sister had already converted, ascribed his victory in battle over Maxentius in 312 C.E. to the miraculous appearance of the sign of the cross superimposed on the sun, and a heavenly voice that declared "Under this sign you will conquer." In other words, the Cross was replacing the Sun (associated with Apollo) as the symbol of the emperor's personal religion. Constantine did not himself convert until just before his death in 337, but his toleration had already made Christianity virtually an official religion. This acceptance was made decisive when the emperor Theodosius banned all pagan religious practices in 391. At this point the tables were turned: Christians began looting and destroying pagan temples and violently persecuting those who did not subscribe to the new creed.

Sources:

Mary Beard, John North, and Simon Price, *Religions of Rome*, 2 volumes (Cambridge & New York: Cambridge University Press, 1998).

Walter Burkert, *Ancient Mystery Cults* (Cambridge, Mass.: Harvard University Press, 1987).

Georges Dumézil, *Archaic Roman Religion*, translated by Philip Krapp (Chicago: University of Chicago Press, 1970).

J. H. W. G. Liebeschuetz, *Continuity and Change in Roman Religion* (Oxford: Clarendon Press, 1979; New York: Oxford University Press, 1979).

Ramsay MacMullen, *Paganism in the Roman Empire* (New Haven: Yale University Press, 1981).

H. H. Scullard, *Festivals and Ceremonies of the Roman Republic* (Ithaca, N.Y.: Cornell University Press, 1981).

PUBLIC PRIESTHOODS

Religion as a Part of Government. Religion is communal, ceremonial, and conservative. In practical terms this means that a community will authorize certain individuals, priests, to maintain its religious customs. In some societies the priests form a special caste, dedicated exclusively to religious affairs. With a few notable exceptions, this structure was not the case at Rome, where religion was an integral part of government. Their priests were at the same time active in politics and military service. For the Romans, it was proof of their veneration for their gods that they had as priests persons who were competent in all areas of public life. This practice meant that known individuals were accountable for correctly tending the gods of the people and for conducting public business with divine favor. It was also a great honor to belong to a priesthood. Originally, new priests were selected only by the existing members of a priesthood, or *collegium,* "college." The priesthoods were also the exclusive domain of the patrician class; plebeians were excluded. Over time this system became democratized. Beginning in the fourth century B.C.E. plebeians began to gain access to priesthoods, and after 104 B.C.E. priests of the more important colleges were elected by representatives of the people in a special voting assembly. Some priesthoods were held for life, others for a limited term.

Auspical vs. Sacral Priests. As Roman religion was divided into *auspicia* and *sacra,* Roman public priesthoods were similarly organized. One could hold priesthoods in both areas simultaneously, however. The priests of the auspical sphere were the *augures.* Sacral priests, generically called *sacerdotes,* literally "those who render something sacred," formed a much more complex group.

Augures Publici. The term *augur* means "he who increases something, makes something successful with divine authority." The augurs of the Roman people, also called Interpreters of Jupiter Best and Greatest, were really concerned with just two things: *auspicia* and *inauguratio.* Auspices were signs of approval (or disapproval) of a public action sent by Jupiter. Inauguration was the ritual use of auspices to confirm places or persons intended for permanent religious service, such as sacred areas for temples or shrines and priests. Auspices and the augurs should not be confused with *extispicium* (innards-examining) and the *haruspices* (Etruscan innards-consulters), though both kinds of priests are now generally referred to as "seers," and both were concerned with the interpretation of lightning and thunder as signs.

What are Auspices? *Auspicium* means literally "bird-watching." In actual practice, auspices were the observation of the flight, singing, and eating habits of birds and of the location in the sky of lightning or thunder. Auspices were either *impetrativa,* requested signs, or *oblativa,* signs sent by Jupiter unasked. Auspices were not a command from Jupiter, however; they simply indicated that Jupiter did or did not permit a given action on a given day. Certainly the report of negative auspices could be used to obstruct an action by a political opponent, an important piece of legislation, say, or a meeting of the Senate. In time of war, a Roman general in the field or an admiral at sea would take a curious kind of auspices called *auspicia ex tripudiis.* Wherever he went he had several sacred chickens in portable

Fragmentary relief of a *suovetaurilia* (purificatory sacrifice) of the Julio-Claudian period, circa 31 B.C.E.–68 C.E. (Scat. Somm. 1096 Louvre, Paris)

Temple of Vesta, Roman goddess of the hearth-fire, first century B.C.E.

cages. When he had to take auspices he instructed the handlers to sprinkle feed on the ground and release the chickens. If the chickens ate greedily it was a sign of Jupiter's approval; if not, that action was not to be undertaken on that day. In one famous incident in 249 B.C.E., the Roman admiral Appius Claudius was eager to meet the Carthaginian fleet in a naval battle. But the chickens would not eat, despite repeated attempts. In frustration and rage Claudius threw the chickens overboard saying, "If they won't eat, let them drink!" His entire fleet was destroyed that day. Auspices were an integral part of the Republican constitution of Rome. After the reign of Augustus and the beginning of the Imperial period, when all power was in the hands of one man, and elections, legislation, and meetings of the Senate had less and less real importance, the auspices lost their significance.

What Did the Augurs Do? Except for inaugurations, the augurs did not take auspices. That was done by elected public officials of the highest level, those with *imperium*, supreme civil and military authority. An augur might be on hand to advise about correct procedure, or the college of augurs might jointly advise the Senate in cases of incorrect auspices. For example, if the presiding magistrate at an election did not take the opening auspices in the right way, the augurs would give their opinion; if he had not, the election would be nullified and a new one held. The college of augurs was chiefly an expert advisory board. The history of their decision in such cases formed the augural discipline, which they were responsible for conserving.

The Pontifical College. The sacral area of Roman religion, both public and private, was administered, or at least overseen, by the pontifical college. The term *pontifex* is much disputed. The prevailing theory is that it means "bridge- (or path-) maker" (Latin *pons* "bridge"), for example, one who guides the people across eerie supernatural boundaries. An older view has equal claim, however: the *pont-* element is an ancient form of the word "five" (cf. Greek *pente* "five"), thus a pontifex would originally have been "one of five men who sacrifice." Properly speaking, the pontifical college included the King of Sacred Rites, the flamens, the pontifices, the Vestal Virgins, and the Feasters of Jupiter; the Leaping Priests of Mars seem also to have been closely attached. Except for the pontifices, all the sacral priests were concerned with the cult of one particular deity. The King of Sacred Rites was dedicated to the service of Janus; each of the flamens to Jupiter, Mars, Quirinus, and other gods; the Vestals to Vesta; and the Leaping Priests to Mars. But a pontifex could stand in for these priests (except of course for a Vestal), especially for a flamen, at any time.

What Did the Pontifices Do? Religion belongs to the community. In Rome this meant that sacrifices made on behalf of the people to its gods must be made by someone elected, under auspices, by the people. The pontifices were chiefly advisers and supervisors. If a magistrate were to make a prayer of dedication, for example, a pontifex might read it first, letting the magistrate repeat after him. This scrupulousness was critical in Roman religion. If a prayer, a sacrifice, or public game was performed in any detail incorrectly, however slight the flaw might be, it would have to be repeated either wholly or in part. This was known as *instauratio,* restoration. To ensure that the deity was not offended by the mistake, additional expiatory sacrifices would have to be made. If a prodigious event occurred or was reported to the Senate, the pontifices would advise the Senate whether or not to accept responsibility for it. If so, they would recommend the proper expiatory measures and oversee their correct performance. In all of these and similar matters the pontifical college were the recognized experts.

The Pontifices and Private Religion. This scrupulousness also applied in the area of private religion. For instance, if it was necessary for a family to move the buried remains of a kinsman, they had to obtain the pontifices' permission first, as seen in this inscription:

> The college of pontifices has decreed that, if the facts of the matter are as contained in the letter of application, it is permitted, in the case of the girl who is mentioned, to remove her from the tomb and to lay her down again as prescribed and to restore her epitaph to its original form, having first made an expiation of a black sheep for the work to be done.

The eldest male of a family, called the *paterfamilias,* was responsible for seeing that his family's traditional religious duties were maintained. If there was no male descendent to assume these responsibilities, it was necessary to adopt one from another family. But the pontifices had to approve such an adoption, making sure that *that* family would not be left without a male head, thus jeopardizing its traditional *sacra.* If a family dies out, its *sacra* also die out; this affects the Roman people as a whole and must be prevented.

Sources:

Mary Beard and John North, eds., *Pagan Priests: Religion and Power in the Ancient World* (Ithaca, N.Y.: Cornell University Press, 1990).

Alan Watson, *The State, Law and Religion: Pagan Rome* (Athens: University of Georgia Press, 1992).

RENEWING GREEK PHILOSOPHY AT ROME

No "Roman" Philosophy? Greek mythology was the matrix, the inexhaustible store of material out of which evolved not only Greek literature but also Greek science and philosophy. The people who would become the Romans were related to the Greeks, and they originally shared that mythology, but they converted much of it into their founding legends and early political history. Lacking that core material and the productive contacts that the Greeks had with the East and Egypt, Rome had no native philosophy.

Awareness of Greece. Classical Greek culture flowered during the mid fifth century B.C.E., especially in Athens. Greek influence extended to southern Italy through the many Greek colonial cities there, and to central Italy through trade and political contacts with the Etruscan aristocracy. At that very time Rome was still a small rural town, struggling to preserve its recently established republican government after expelling its last Etruscan king. A political crisis then erupted between the patrician and plebeian social classes. The plebeians, who felt increasingly excluded from positions of power in the new state, demanded the written codification of Roman law, until then the exclusive property of the patricians. A plebeian revolt brought about the establishment of a committee to write such a code. According to Roman historical legend, these men travelled to Athens to study the laws composed in 594 B.C.E. by the Athenian lawgiver Solon, who had them inscribed on revolving pillars and set in a public place. The Romans' journey to Athens for this purpose is probably fictitious, but the kernel of the story seems true: that aristocratic Romans were aware of Greek culture and looked to Greece as a model for some of their own institutions, even at that early time. Certainly, Rome's wars with Carthage, beginning in the third century B.C.E., brought the Romans into increasing contact with the wider Greek world throughout the Mediterranean basin. By then the classical Greek philosophical schools begun in the fifth and fourth centuries had evolved into many distinct sects, each with a fairly clear set of doctrines, but also with much mutual borrowing of ideas.

Greek Philosophy Comes to Rome. By the mid second century B.C.E. Rome was clearly the center of power throughout the Mediterranean. States in Greece, Asia, and Africa had to go to Rome to settle any international affairs. In 156–155 B.C.E. a delegation was sent from Athens to speak to the Roman Senate on some diplomatic matters. This delegation included the heads of the three most important schools of Greek philosophy: the Stoic Diogenes of Babylon, Carneades of the Academy, and the Peripatetic Critolaus. While there they gave demonstrations of their knowledge. Carneades, for example, known for his criticism of belief in the gods, delivered two show-speeches on successive days, one on behalf of Justice, the next against it. Such events sparked, according to Cicero, a remarkable desire for learning among the Roman youth, and we might say that Greek philosophy really had its firm beginnings in

Rome at this time. But they also aroused deep suspicions, for Romans generally disapproved of idle intellectual activity as unfit for proper gentlemen. Cato, a traditional Roman statesman of the time, was worried about the effect philosophy might have on morals, so he arranged for the Athenian delegation to leave Rome as soon as possible. Certain Romans, however, most notably the family of the Scipios, admired Greek culture and welcomed it more warmly. Even so, Roman moral sensibility always felt it necessary to justify the study of philosophy by the practical value it might bring in the management of the state. Thus at Rome those aspects of Greek philosophy that had a more direct bearing on ethics and the practical virtues were most attractive, while the merely theoretical aspects tended not to be of such interest.

Development of Stoicism. Panaetius of Rhodes (circa 185–109 B.C.E.), a student of Diogenes of Babylon, was another Stoic who was favorably received by Scipio Aemilianus and who had an impact on Roman thought, particularly on Cicero. Like Polybius, Panaetius insisted on the role of divine providence in world affairs. He also emphasized the everyday practice of ethics and morals in fulfillment of that divine plan. Posidonius (circa 135–circa 51 B.C.E.), Panaetius's student in turn, visited Rome in the 80s before establishing his school on the island of Rhodes, to which many young Romans came to further their education. Posidonius taught that all knowledge is interconnected, and he sought to integrate it all in a universal world history. The physical sciences, and history, too, he argued, should serve to instruct mankind in moral virtue.

Development of Scepticism. A successor, after one generation, of Carneades to the directorship of the Academy, the philosophical school begun by Plato, Philon also was at Rome in the 80s at the same time as Panaetius of Rhodes. While there he taught many well-to-do Roman youths, most importantly Cicero. Since none of Philon's writings survives, we depend on Cicero for our knowledge of his teachings. Between the time of Plato and Carneades, a sect of the Academy had formed under Pyrrhon the Sceptic. The Sceptics held, as certain Presocratics had earlier, that certain knowledge of things in this world is not possible. Therefore, to avoid error, they held that it is best to withhold judgment at all times. Philon modified this radical view somewhat. He said that, in the absence of absolute knowledge, one must at least rely on the *plausible* in order to make informed decisions and to act morally. In some respects he moved the thought of the Academy closer to that of the Stoic school, which held that absolute knowledge was not only possible but essential.

Cicero as Philosopher. Marcus Tullius Cicero (106–43 B.C.E.), one of the leading political figures during the collapse of the Roman republican government in the first century B.C.E., is also the man most closely associated with philosophy at Rome. Cicero enjoyed an excellent education in his youth and studied in the leading schools of the Epicureans, Academics, Stoics, and Peripatetics. After Julius Caesar defeated Pompey, his chief rival for personal control

of Roman politics, in the civil war that ended in 48 B.C.E., Cicero's public career was over, for he had long supported Pompey's interests. In 45 B.C.E. his beloved daughter Tullia died in childbirth, an event that deeply affected him. He retired and committed himself to the writing of philosophy as a consolation for his grief.

Cicero's Philosophic Works. Almost all of Cicero's philosophical writings are in the form of dialogues, that is, fictional conversations between persons of Cicero's own time or earlier on some given topic. In doing this Cicero deliberately imitates Plato and Aristotle, who wrote many of their treatises in this same style. A dialogue between two or several persons allows the alternate presentation and criticism of ideas, a process that brings the participants closer to the truth. In Cicero's dialogues the debt to Greek thinkers is always acknowledged, and his characters usually outline the doctrines of one school of philosophy or another on the given topic. Cicero was no mere translator or paraphraser of Greek philosophers, however. One of his greatest achievements was his creation of a Latin philosophical vocabulary. Compared to classical Greek, Latin has an archaic, almost primitive quality, but in Cicero's hands it became the equal to Greek in its refined philosophical terminology. His philosophical works can be organized into three groups: rhetoric, political philosophy, and ethics.

Cicero's Rhetorical Works. Cicero was especially attracted to those lines of philosophical inquiry that included rhetoric, the art of persuasive public speaking. Ever since Socrates' critical questioning of the Sophists in fifth-century Athens, rhetoric had always been a branch of philosophy, for Greek thinkers had long been interested in the relationship between fact and word. To gain power and prestige in Greco-Roman antiquity, one had to be able to speak well and convincingly in public assembly. Oratory, having a practical application for the common good, was thus more acceptable to many Romans than "idle" philosophical speculation. Much of Cicero's surviving writings consists of speeches he delivered as a politician and a private lawyer; many of them reflect his philosophical training as well. Cicero felt that the orator must use his abilities wisely and for the greatest good. Therefore he must develop not only his speaking ability but also his soul in moral virtue. In such works as *On the Orator, The Orator,* and *Brutus,* Cicero explored various arguments about the relationship between moral philosophy and rhetoric. In these works he follows Plato, who had dealt with the topic in several of his dialogues.

Political Philosophy. Oratory, of course, makes sense only in the context of active politics. Cicero also devoted himself to the study of political philosophy, that is, of the philosophical foundations of a good state. In his *On the Republic,* which exists now only in fragmentary form, Cicero dealt with the problem of the ideal state and its constitution. He resumed a topic dealt with earlier by Aristotle and Polybius, the theory of the mixed constitution, but he incorporates an element of Platonic thought, that a state should be guided by a wise man thoroughly trained in philosophy. Though it contains elements of the thought of several schools, this work is greatly influenced by Stoicism, especially in its concluding vision of Rome, its place in the divine plan of the universe, and of the rights of all men for justice and good government. His dialogue *On Laws* is a critique of Roman law from the point of view of the schools of philosophy. It is influenced greatly by Stoic thought, derived from Diogenes of Babylon.

Moral Philosophy or Ethics. Cicero was also interested in the more private or personal application of philosophy, that is, in the conduct of one's own life. *Concerning the Purposes of Good and Evil Things* is an examination of the proper response to success and adversity. His *Concerning Duties* is an outline of moral obligations to one another and how one must train in philosophy to meet them. The *Tusculan Disputations,* on the other hand, concerns those things that make for a happy life. Two dialogues on more intimate subjects are *On Growing Old* and *On Friendship.* Cicero used famous characters from earlier Roman history, such as Cato and Scipio Aemilianus, as examples of Roman moral virtue in composing these works. Finally, in two dialogues, *On the Nature of the Gods* and *On Divination,* Cicero attempts to reconcile traditional Roman religious customs and beliefs with Greek rationalism. It is a difficult task, which Cicero does not quite succeed in, but he does reveal that human beings are really capable of that kind of inner contradiction: belief in the divine is something that cannot always be rationally justified. Certainly, Cicero says, the traditional practice of religion and veneration of the gods confers many benefits on a state.

Epicureanism in Verse. Though Stoicism had the greatest influence on Roman philosophy, the opposing school, Epicureanism, also had its adherents. Epicurus (341–270 B.C.E.) derived his theories from earlier Greek thinkers such as Leucippus and Democritus, men whom we would call "atomists." They held that all physical reality is simply a result of the random joining of particles falling in infinite space. Even the gods are merely composites of atoms, and they too, like everything, will eventually decompose and reform in different ways. The object for human beings, then, is to overcome the fear of death, of the gods, of divine punishment for sin, and to live in such a way as to avoid either causing or experiencing pain. Lucretius (circa 94–circa 55 B.C.E.), a contemporary of Cicero, was the chief proponent of Epicurean philosophy in Rome. In a long epic poem, *On the Nature of Reality,* following the tradition of some Pre-Socratic thinkers, Lucretius sets out the principles of Epicurean philosophy. His poem is meant to be a "protreptic," that is, an invitation to philosophy. Lucretius explains all physical and mental phenomena, including dreams, emotions, and other insubstantial forces, in this materialistic way. There is no divine plan; if the gods exist, they are far removed and take no interest in human affairs and troubles. The wise man, he says, is like a person sitting on a hillside near the sea, watching a naval battle far in the distance. He is unconcerned about their agony and observes all with complacency. Epicureanism and Stoicism were diametrically opposed, and Cicero regularly finds fault with the Epicurean school of thought.

Imperial Stoicism. The Roman Stoic philosopher and writer Seneca was born in Spain at the close of the first century B.C.E. Of a wealthy family, he was taken to Rome for his education, where he was attracted to philosophy at an early age. He became private tutor to the young man who would eventually become the emperor Nero. Upon Nero's accession to power, Seneca became his speechwriter and personal adviser. As Nero's personality began to disintegrate and he engaged in more and more serious criminal activity, Seneca grew disgusted and retired. By 64 C.E. he occupied himself solely with writing philosophy and tragedy. Accused by Nero of participating in an assassination plot, he was forced to commit suicide. His philosophical works include *Dialogues, On Mercy, On Acts of Kindness, Natural Questions,* and *Moral Letters.* He was very influential, especially on some of the Christian Fathers.

Sources:

Brad Inwood, *Ethics and Human Action in Early Stoicism* (Oxford: Clarendon Press, 1985; New York: Oxford University Press, 1985).

Inwood and L. P. Gerson, eds., *Hellenistic Philosophy: Introductory Readings* (Indianapolis: Hackett, 1988).

A. A. Long, *Hellenistic Philosophy* (London: Duckworth, 1974; New York: Scribners, 1974; second edition, Berkeley: University of California Press, 1986).

Long and D. N. Sedley, eds., *The Hellenistic Philosophers,* 2 volumes (Cambridge & New York: Cambridge University Press, 1987).

Phillip Mitsis, *Epicurus' Ethical Theory: The Pleasures of Invulnerability* (Ithaca, N.Y.: Cornell University Press, 1988).

Martha C. Nussbaum, *The Therapy of Desire: Theory and Practice in Hellenistic Ethics* (Princeton: Princeton University Press, 1994).

Malcolm Schofield and Gisela Striker, eds., *The Norms of Nature: Studies in Hellenistic Ethics* (Cambridge & New York: Cambridge University Press, 1986).

SIGNIFICANT PEOPLE

Note: Biographical entries for Lucretius and Cicero, both centrally important figures in the history of philosophy at Rome, may be found at the end of Chapter 3 and Chapter 6, respectively.

AURELIUS AUGUSTINUS (ST. AUGUSTINE)

354-430 C.E.
TEACHER, BISHOP, SAINT

An Educated Youth. Augustine was born in 354 C.E. to a pagan father, Patricius, and a Christian mother, Monica, in the town of Thagaste in Numidia in Northern Africa. After learning the basics while living in Thagaste with his parents, brother, and sister, Augustine went to Madaura to study with a *grammaticus* from 366 C.E. until 370 C.E. From the *grammaticus,* Augustine learned Cicero and Vergil, but he never developed an appreciation for Greek. Sometimes he slipped away from classes to the amphitheater to see games. When his father no longer had the funds to pay for his schooling, Augustine had to return to Thagaste, where he became involved with a gang. In his *Confessions* he recounts an incident when he and the members of his gang stole pears from a man's tree. It was also during this time that he began his long-term affair with a woman whose name he never mentions. In 371 C.E. Augustine moved to Carthage to begin his higher education. In 371 or 372 his mistress bore him a son, named Adeodatus ("given by god"), although Augustine had no desire for children. His own distant relationship with his father may have made him hesitant to become a father himself. Patricius also died in 371 C.E. In Carthage, Augustine continued his study of Cicero, particularly of his rhetorical work *Hortensius.*

Teacher. During this period he also developed an interest in Manicheism and converted to this philosophical religion. In 374 C.E. Augustine returned to Thagaste to teach and remained in Thagaste for three years. From 376 to 383 C.E. Augustine returned to Carthage to teach. In 383 C.E. he took his mistress and his son to Rome, where he lived for a year before taking over the chair of rhetoric at Milan at the request of Quintus Aurelius Symmachus. His mother, Monica, who had followed him to Rome and Milan, arranged a marriage for Augustine and forced him to send his mistress and son away (they returned to Thagaste).

Changing Beliefs. Augustine had become disillusioned with Manicheism when he had spoken with one of the leading minds from the sect (Faustus) and found him less intelligent than he had hoped. In Milan he found Ambrose, the bishop of the Christian church. Although Ambrose did not bring about Augustine's conversion to Christianity, he did bring Augustine into contact with Simplicianus, the person who had mentored Ambrose; Simplicianus advised Augustine to read the letters of Paul, and told Augustine the stories of others' conversions. Monica also played a part, not by imposing her will, but by sharing in philosophical conversations that impressed Augustine with her intelligence. In 387 C.E. Augustine escorted Monica to Ostia from where she intended to sail back to Thagaste. She never made it, dying in Ostia with her son Navigius by her side. She bemoaned the fact that she would not be buried in Thagaste beside Patricius. Augustine remained in Italy until 388 C.E., when he returned to the family farm at Thagaste. Shortly afterward, his son Adeodatus died. In 391 C.E. he was ordained as a priest and then bishop (in 395 C.E.) of Hippo. It was at Hippo that he wrote his best known works: the *Confessions* and *The City of God.* He remained the bishop of Hippo until his death in 430 C.E.

Sources:

Peter Brown, *Augustine of Hippo: A Biography* (London: Faber & Faber, 1967; Berkeley: University of California Press, 1967).

Garry Wills, *Saint Augustine* (New York: Viking, 1999).

MARCUS AURELIUS

121–180 C.E.

EMPEROR, STOIC PHILOSOPHER

Student of Philosophy. Originally named Marcus Annius Verus, the future emperor called Marcus Aurelius was raised by his grandfather and mother. He was attracted to the study of philosophy when he was only twelve years old. Epictetus was a great influence on him, which is evident in his work commonly called the *Meditations*, though probably called by him *Notes to Himself.* This was probably a kind of philosophic diary, not intended for publication, which probably was written as an older man and possibly during his campaigns against the Germanic tribes. He seems also to have incorporated elements of Platonism. In fact, the diary was lost and recovered only in the fourth century C.E. Like Epictetus, Marcus Aurelius was concerned with the making of moral choices in life and with the role of divine providence in events. He believed that one is to avoid those things that distract him from making correct choices, including power and glory, which are transitory anyway, and to forego his personal satisfaction for the sake of a greater good.

Philosopher Emperor. Aurelius became co-emperor, along with his half brother Lucius, when Antoninus died in 161. The new emperors were immediately faced with revolts in the borderlands and sent armies to quell the disturbances. Lucius, then known as Verus, died of plague while both emperors were leading Roman armies in Dacia. After several serious military setbacks, the Romans were able to push northern incursions out of Italy, but Aurelius had spent much treasure in the effort. He spent nearly the rest of his rule dealing with warfare in the borders, until his death in the north in 180.

Sources:
Anthony Birley, *Marcus Aurelius: A Biography,* revised edition (New Haven: Yale University Press, 1987).

Mark Forstater, *The Spiritual Exercises of Marcus Aurelius* (New York: Harper-Collins, 2000).

EPICTETUS

MID FIRST TO SECOND CENTURIES C.E.

SLAVE, STOIC PHILOSOPHER

Practical Philosopher. Epictetus was born in Phrygia in the middle of the first century C.E. and taken to Rome, where he was sold as a slave. He was later freed and studied philosophy under Gaius Musonius Rufus the Stoic. When the emperor Domitian banished philosophers from the city in 89 C.E., Epictetus went across the Adriatic Sea to Nicopolis on the west coast of Greece and established his school there. His disciple Arrian published his teachings, contained in the *Discourses* and the shorter *Manual*. Epictetus was very much a practical philosopher. He argued that philosophy must be applied in daily lives, not undertaken as an abstract study only. The moral choices one makes, how one comes to

terms with those things that are not in their power, how one forms their character, these were the issues that most concerned Epictetus. On these points Epictetus looked back to Panaetius as his model. In many ways the Stoicism of Epictetus was highly compatible with the tenets of early Christianity, and had considerable effect on the future emperor Marcus Aurelius.

Sources:
Jonathan Barnes, *Logic and the Imperial Stoa* (Leiden & New York: E. J. Brill, 1997).

Adolf Friedrich Bonhöffer, *The Ethics of the Stoic Epictetus: An English Translation,* translated by William O. Stephens (New York: Lang, 1996).

Iason Xenakis, *Epictetus: Philosopher-Therapist* (The Hague: Martinus Nijhoff, 1969).

EUSEBIUS HIERONYMUS (SAINT JEROME)

CIRCA 347–420 C.E.

BISHOP, BIBLE TRANSLATOR, SAINT

Bible Translator. Jerome was born into a Christian family in Strido, near the Adriatic coast in northern Italy. As a boy he was sent to Rome, where he was taught by the scholar Donatus, among others. In 373 he went on a pilgrimage to Jerusalem. On the way he fell ill, and stayed in the desert for three years. Ordained as a priest in 379, he accompanied the bishop of Antioch to the Council of Constantinople in 382 and then to Rome. There he became Pope Damasus's secretary and received the task of revising the old Latin translation of the Bible. This assignment took him until about 406, but it became the version used in western Christendom until the time of Martin Luther. After Damasus's death, Jerome returned to Asia Minor, accompanied by a rich widow and her daughter, settling eventually in Bethlehem, where he died in 419 or 420.

Sources:
Adam Kamesar, *Jerome, Greek Scholarship, and the Hebrew Bible: A Study of the Quaestiones hebraicae in Genesim* (Oxford: Clarendon Press, 1993; New York: Oxford University Press, 1993).

J. N. D. Kelly, *Jerome: His Life, Writings, and Controversies* (London: Duckworth, 1975).

MARCUS MINUCIUS FELIX (MINUCIUS)

FLOURISHED 200–240 C.E.

CHRISTIAN APOLOGIST

First Apologia in Latin? The exact dates of Minucius Felix's life are unknown. There is a tendency to think the more forceful Tertullian wrote his Latin apologies first, in which case

Felix's work would have been written at the beginning of the third century C.E. However, it is not absolutely necessary to consider Minucius's stylistically polished work as derivative of Tertullian's. A reference to a speech of Fronto (who died around 170) may therefore give us a closer date for the lawyer Minucius, in which case he antedates Tertullian. Minucius is primarily known for his *Octavius,* a dialogue between two Christian converts and an educated pagan. The work is modeled on the philosophical dialogues of Cicero.

Source:

Henry Chadwick, "Minucius Felix, Marcus," in *The Oxford Classical Dictionary,* edited by Simon Hornblower and Antony Spawforth (Oxford: Oxford University Press, 1999), p. 988.

PLOTINUS

205-270 C.E.

NEOPLATONIC PHILOSOPHER

A Deep Thinker. Although a Roman, Plotinus was possibly born in Egypt, though he also seems to have been fluent in Greek. He became a philosopher in his late twenties, and even traveled east to improve his knowledge of philosophies in that region. Around 235 he settled in Rome. A teacher and social activist, he had a large following during his years in Rome. A late member of the Academy, in the period of thought known as "Neoplatonism," Plotinus composed his teachings into a comprehensive work called the *Enneads,* or *The Book of Nines,* when he was about fifty. Plotinus's conception of reality held that all things proceeded outward from the "One" in concentric circles, like the ripples on water when a stone is thrown in a pool. These rings represent the various states of reality as they progress further and further from their origin. In the innermost ring, for example, is "Mind," the next "Soul," and finally, furthest out, "Nature," that is, simple material reality with neither mind nor soul. Plotinus's revival of Platonic thought remained the principal philosophical influence in late antiquity, until the emperor Justinian closed down the Athenian schools of philosophy in 529 C.E.

Sources:

Émile Bréhier, *The Philosophy of Plotinus,* translated by Joseph Thomas (Chicago: University of Chicago Press, 1953).

Lloyd P. Gerson, *Plotinus* (London & New York: Routledge, 1994).

John Peter Kenney, *Mystical Monotheism: A Study in Ancient Platonic Theology* (Providence, R.I.: Brown University Press; Hanover, N.H.: University Press of New England, 1991).

PORPHYRY

234-CIRCA 305 C.E.

NEOPLATONIC PHILOSOPHER

Devoted Student. Probably of Syrian background and originally named Malchus, Porphyry was likely born in Tyre. He studied with Plotinus in Rome in the 260s and attempted to integrate systematic Aristotelian logic with Plotinus's new interpretation of Plato. He wrote commentaries on the works of Plato and Aristotle and saw to the posthumous publication of Plotinus's *Enneads.* He was critical of the Christians and wrote a work against them. He was, however, respectful of traditional forms of religious ritual and belief.

Sources:

John J. O'Meara, *Porphyry's Philosophy from Oracles in Augustine* (Paris: Etudes Augustiniennes, 1959).

Andrew Smith, *Porphyry's Place in the Neoplatonic Tradition: A Study in Post-Plotinian Neoplatonism* (The Hague: M. Nijhoff, 1974).

SEXTUS EMPIRICUS

SECOND CENTURY C.E.
SCEPTIC PHILOSOPHER

Sceptical Philosophy. Pyrrhon of Elis (365–275 B.C.E.) established a branch of the Academy known as the Sceptic school. The central theory of the Sceptics was the impossibility of absolute knowledge of anything. Socrates, in fact, was the model of this teaching, for in Plato's dialogues Socrates never arrives at a positive answer, but only refutes false views. Philon of Larissa dealt with this problem through the willingness to accept the probable in the absence of absolute certainty. The Skeptics, however, held that the wise thing to do was to withhold judgment about the reality of things.

Philosopher-Doctor. This approach was resumed in Rome by Sextus Empiricus, who lived in the middle of the second century C.E. Little is known about his life, other than that he was a doctor. His radical scepticism, sometimes called Pyrrhonism, set it apart from Stoicism, which tended to insist on absolute knowledge. He wrote two major works, *Outlines of Pyrrhonism,* discussing the differences among philosophical schools of thought, and *Against the Professors,* critiquing dogmatic philosophies.

Sources:

Jonathan Barnes, *The Toils of Scepticism* (Cambridge & New York: Cambridge University Press, 1990).

Tad Brennan, *Ethics and Epistemology in Sextus Empiricus* (New York: Garland, 1999).

DOCUMENTARY SOURCES

St. Ambrose, *Hexaëmeron* (On the Six Days of Creation, circa 380 C.E.)—An allegorical explanation of the Old Testament.

Aurelius Augustinus (St. Augustine), *Confessiones* (Confessions, 397 C.E.)—Primarily an autobiographical work. Augustine takes the opportunity to promote Christianity, including his thoughts on sin and redemption.

St. Augustine, *De civitate Dei contra paganos* (The City of God, 413–426 C.E.)—One of Augustine's refutations of pagan thought, he adapts classical thinking to Christianity, laying the foundation for Christian theology. Responding to the turmoil of a Roman world under attack, he called for Christians to look to Christian beliefs over the laws of Rome.

St. Augustine, *Retractationes* (Reconsiderations, 426–427 C.E.)—A reconsideration and validation of his life's work, Augustine explains his development and explains the thought process in much of his writing.

Marcus Aurelius, *Meditations* (circa 170 C.E.)—A private collection of the thoughts of an aging emperor, Aurelius philosophizes on the nature of man, remembers his teachers and their lessons, and contemplates on the temptations and responsibilities of rule.

Cicero, *De divinatione* (On Divination, circa 43 B.C.E.); *De natura deorum* (On the Nature of the Gods, circa 44)—Two works revealing the nature and pratice of Roman religion.

Epictetus, *Discourses* (circa mid second century C.E.)—A collection of Epictetus's Stoic teachings, gathered by his student Arrian, in which he calls for the use of stoicism to improve moral reform.

Aulus Gellius, *Noctes Atticae* (Attic Nights, circa 180 C.E.)—A collection of essays on many topics, including philosophy.

Lucretius, *De rerum natura* (On the Nature of Things, circa first century C.E.)—Expounds an Epicurean (atomic) explanation of life, arguing that there is nothing beyond death, and life should be lived to the fullest.

Macrobius Ambrosius Theodosius, *Saturnalia* (circa 383 C.E.)—A dialogue among guests at a party the night, and during the three days, celebrating a pagan holiday, which reveals many insights into Roman thought on philosophy, religion, and religious celebration.

Marcus Minucius Felix, *Octavius* (circa 200 C.E.)—One of the first Christian apologies written in Latin, written in the form of a dialogue between a Christian and a pagan.

Plotinus, *Enneads* (circa 300–305 C.E.)—A collection of philosophical essays collected by Plotinus's student Porphyry dealing in everything from ethics to metaphysics.

Porphyry, *Against the Christians* (circa 300 C.E.)—An attack on Christianity.

Lucius Annaeus Seneca (Seneca the Younger), *Epistulae morales* (circa 55 C.E.)—A collection of more than one hundred philosophical essays concerning moral issues.

Sextus Empiricus, *Against the Professors* (circa third century C.E.)—A critique of several disciplines, including dogmatic philosophy, mathematics, and rhetoric.

Sextus Empiricus, *Outlines of Pyrrhonism* (circa third century C.E.)—A discussion of the different philosophical schools of thought of the time.

Tertullian (Quintus Septimius Florens Tertullianus), *Ad martyres* (circa 197 C.E.); *Ad nationes* (circa 197 C.E.); *Apologeticus* (circa 197 C.E.)—One of the first defenders of Christianity to write in Latin, these works refute charges of pagan activity and sorcery in Christianity.

SCIENCE, TECHNOLOGY, AND HEALTH

by JOHN M. RIDDLE

CONTENTS

Sidebars and tables are listed in italics.

300-250* B.C.E.

- The Romans develop concrete mortar.

280* B.C.E.

- The Greek astronomer Aristarchus of Samos observes the summer solstice; he promotes the heliocentric theory of the solar system. He is also credited with inventing a sundial and correctly estimating the length of the year.

272 B.C.E.

- Construction begins on the first aqueduct in Rome.

265-194* B.C.E.

- Eratosthenes of Cyrene, a Greek who studied and taught in Alexandria, writes several books on mathematics, including *Platonicus*, a treatise on mathematical properties in music; *On Geometrical Means* and *On the Duplication of the Cube*, in geometry; and *Geographica*, a work of mathematical and ethnographical geometry.

250-200* B.C.E.

- Large estates become more common in Italy, as do commercial farming and animal husbandry.
- Greek physicians bring theoretical medicine to Rome.
- Aratus of Soli writes *Phaenomena*, a poem that helps spread Greek ideas on astronomy to Rome.

212-211 B.C.E.

- The inventor Archimedes, whose mathematics and mechanics—including a planetarium and a screw to remove water—influenced Rome, dies at the hands of the Romans during the siege of Syracuse.

200-100 B.C.E.

- Apollonius of Perga writes major works on conics and mathematical astronomy.

174 B.C.E.

- The first Roman map, allegedly of Sardinia, is placed in a temple.

*DENOTES CIRCA DATE

160* B.C.E.
- Marcus Porcius Cato (Cato the Elder or Cato the Censor) writes *De agricultura,* an agricultural treatise emphasizing proper management of large villas with slave-labor.

159 B.C.E.
- Crates of Mallus, as an envoy of Pergamum, visits Rome; his lectures, which may have included Homeric geography, help promote scholarship in astronomy and geography.

153 B.C.E.
- The Romans add two months to their earlier ten-month calendar.

147-127* B.C.E.
- The Nicean astronomer Hipparchus, who lived primarily in Rhodes, is credited with making astronomy a practical science.

140* B.C.E.
- The Greek historian Polybius, who chronicled Roman domination of the Mediterranean, uses geography to help explain their expansion.

140s-120s* B.C.E.
- The Scipionic Circle, a group of prominent men loosely gathered around Publius Cornelius Scipio Aemilianus, advocates the promotion of Greek learning and culture in Rome.

100-1* B.C.E.
- The mathematician and musicologist Nicomachus of Gerasa writes *Introduction to Arithmetic,* covering the Pythagorean concept of numbers, which will heavily influence later Roman scholars.
- The global shape of the earth is acknowledged by most Roman scholars.

87-86 B.C.E.
- The Syrian Stoic philosopher Posidonius, as a member of an embassy of Rhodes, visits Rome; his school in Rhodes attracts many Roman intellectuals, who are introduced to his teachings in such subjects as mathematics, astronomy, geography, and biology. He teaches that the universe is governed by reason, believes the moon affects the tides, and introduces the use of latitudinal lines to measure the circumference of the earth.

* DENOTES CIRCA DATE

55 B.C.E.

- Cicero proclaims that mathematics is necessary for general education in *De oratore* (On the Orator).

50* B.C.E.

- Cleomedes writes *On the Circular Motions of the Celestial Bodies*, an astronomical treatise based on the work of Posidonius and Eratosthenes. (The book, however, may have been written as late as the early second century C.E.)
- Geminus of Rhodes popularizes basic concepts of positional astronomy and mathematical geography in *Introduction to Astronomy*.

46 B.C.E.

- Julius Caesar revises the calendar with the "long year" and thereafter introduces a shorter February with a leap-year addition.

44 B.C.E.

- Caesar commissions four Greeks to survey and produce a map of Asia, Europe, and Africa; the project was assigned to Agrippa and was completed during Augustus's reign.

40s-30s* B.C.E.

- Strabo of Amaseia, who had studied at Rome, writes the seventeen-part *Geographia* and influences Roman leaders in the usefulness of geography.

37 B.C.E.

- One of Rome's greatest scholars, who excelled in many areas—ranging from literature to history, humor to architecture, logic to history—Varro (Marcus Terentius Varro) composes *De re rustica*, a treatise on agriculture, aimed at an audience of upper-class Romans.

30* B.C.E.

- The military engineer Vitruvius Pollio writes *De architectura*, a treatise on architecture and construction.

1-100* C.E.

- The Asclepiadian school of medicine, based on the Bithynian physician Asclepiades's work, appears in Rome. He taught that the movement of corpuscular bodies within humans could be controlled through noninvasive treatments.
- The Romans' health is good because of hygiene, nutrition, and exercise.

*Denotes Circa Date

1-100*
C.E.
(CONT'D)

- Aulus Cornelius Celsus writes a Latin treatise on medicine.

- The Claudian aqueduct, an arched structure that brought water to Rome, is completed.

40s-50s*
C.E.

- Pliny the Elder writes the encyclopedic *Naturalis Historia,* a thirty-seven book compendium of geographical and medicinal descriptions.

- Dioscorides writes *Materia medica,* a treatise largely covering pharmacy, including information on more than one thousand drugs.

43-44
C.E.

- The first work in Latin on geography, *De chorographia,* is written by Pomponius Mela.

52 C.E.

- The *Aqua Claudia,* an aqueduct providing water to Rome, is completed.

60-65 C.E.

- Lucius Iunius Moderatus Columella writes a twelve-book treatise on agricultural science, largely for the villa owner with a large slave workforce.

62* C.E.

- Seneca the Younger writes *Natural Questions,* explaining his stoic views on astronomy, including his arguments that comets have circular orbits.

97 C.E.

- Frontinus is appointed *curator aquarium* (superintendent of aqueducts) and will later write a treatise on aqueducts, the *De aquis urbis Romae.*

98-138
C.E.

- The physician Soranus of Ephesus serves under Trajan and Hadrian, writing many medical treatises that include works on hygiene, disease, surgery, and gynecology.

100-200
C.E.

- Municipalities begin to emphasize hygiene and public health.

* DENOTES CIRCA DATE

150 C.E.
- Ptolemy writes the *Almagest*, a textbook of astronomy, largely based on his earlier *Canobic Inscription* (146–147).

152-162 C.E.
- Vettius Valens writes a nine-book astrology, the *Anthologies*, that includes many horoscope charts.

157 C.E.
- Galen, the greatest medical writer of antiquity, begins his practice in Pergamum. From 169 until his death in 216, he is permanently in service to the emperors.

170* C.E.
- Rome suffers its first pandemic plague.

200-300 C.E.
- The average life span of a Roman peaks at around forty-seven years of age.

200* C.E.
- Solinus writes an encyclopedia on geography, the *Collectanea rerum memorabilium*.

300-400* C.E.
- Calcidius, a Christian translator and commentator, produces works on Plato and mathematics.
- Marcellus Empiricus writes *On Medical Matters,* a treatise in forty-two books on folk medicine.

364* C.E.
- Theon of Alexandria writes commentaries on Ptolemy's *Almagest* and *Handy Tables.*

400-500 C.E.
- Macrobius writes a summary of Roman astronomy and mathematics, the *Commentarii.*
- Theodorus Priscianus, Gratian's personal physician, writes *Euphoriston,* a treatise on medicine.

*Denotes Circa Date

| 415 C.E. | • | Hypatia, the first woman mathematician and last of the pagan scientists, dies at the hand of a Christian mob. |
| 475-500* C.E. | • | Martianus Capella writes a textbook on Roman science. |

*Denotes Circa Date

Relief from the second century C.E. showing the interior of a butcher shop (Museo della Civilta Romana, Rome)

OVERVIEW

Greek Legacy. "Let others better mould the running mass / Of metals, and inform the breathing brass, / And soften into flesh a marble face; / Plead better at the bar; / describe the skies, / And when the stars ascend, and when they rise. / But Rome! 'tis thine alone, with awful sway, / To rule mankind, and make the world obey. / Disposing peace and war they own majestic way; / To tame the proud, the fetter'd slave to free; / These are imperial arts, and worthy of thee," (Vergil, *Aeneid* 6. 15–21). When Aeneas foretold Rome's contribution in these lines by Vergil, he was conceding that its genius would not be in the sciences but in governance. Vergil acknowledges that other cultures will be the better metallurgists, artists, mathematicians, astronomers, and lawyers. Vergil was born during the Late Republic, but the words that he chose for Aeneas's pronouncement were prophetic for the Imperial period that followed. The Romans mostly borrowed their physics, mathematics, astronomy, and medicine from the Greeks. Another poet, Horace, put it aptly: *Graecia capta ferum victorem cepit* ("Captive Greece took her fierce captor captive"). To what the Romans borrowed from the captive Greeks, they proudly added native Roman lore, especially observations about agriculture and animal husbandry. In applied knowledge the Romans were superior to the Greeks and other ancient peoples. They were marvelous in construction engineering, including massive public buildings and well-designed houses, as well as advanced in developing central heating, transportation, hygiene, and public health. In addition to having a Hellenistic theoretical basis for their sciences, they absorbed learning where they could find it: from Egypt, Persia, and other cultures whom they encountered and conquered. In doing so, the Romans produced a new synthesis by refining Greek science, extracting and reconciling contradictory elements, and logically constructing theoretical explanations, where the Greeks were content with controversy and adding to science from their own advances and that of other cultures. Faithfully the Romans passed their *scientia* to the Western Middle Ages and, to a lesser degree, to the Byzantines and Muslims.

Astronomy and Mathematics. Each area of Roman science has its own history. Astronomy and mathematics were inextricably linked together. To most Romans astronomy meant little more than knowledge of the major celestial bodies—sun, moon, planets, and star constellations—and the calendar. If they were sailors, the knowledge had to be greater because of navigation. Closely connected to the heavens were weather signs. Early Roman astronomy was simplistic, that of farmers who knew by the signs when to plant and to harvest. As early as the third century B.C.E., some Romans became aware of the more refined, learned astronomy of the Greeks. Hellenistic science connected mathematics, most especially geometry, to astronomy on a theoretical level. Some Romans saw the theory as having no practical application. In astronomy, mathematics, and, indeed, all areas of the sciences, the Romans were attracted to an easily learned, textbook format—the handbook, which were summaries of knowledge that the writers in Latin and Greek found useful for synthesizing and simplifying Greek learning. The handbooks did not necessarily fairly and evenly present all knowledge. Often authors pushed their own particular viewpoints. For easy memory, some handbooks were in verse; an important example is the handbook by Aratus of Soli (died circa 240 B.C.E.), one of the earliest works on astronomy known to the Romans. Reflecting the Roman interest in the subject, he was more concerned with celestial observations of star movements, the positions of the constellations, than he was in epicycles or "horse-fetters," technical terms employed to explain planetary movement. Particularly appealing to the Romans were Greek writers who regarded Homer's view of the universe as essentially correct. The Romans understood Homer, just as they did Vergil. They avoided the higher mathematics necessary to explain how planets move in orbits around their circumferences around the earth and how each circumference's center is different from the position of the earth.

Cosmic Theories. Some educated Romans were familiar with the great Greek philosophers who proposed cosmic theories. They knew of Aristarchus's geometrical proof of the relative distances between the sun, moon, and earth. They knew also of his theory that the earth and planets moved around the sun, but they, like most Greeks, rejected such notions. Hipparchus's mathematical demonstration about planets moving on epicycles and deferents was too attractive for them. His geocentric universe was harmonious with Empedocles' and Aristotle's theory of the elements, and, equally important, Hipparchus's theories were a mathematical predictive of celestial movements. Much of the astronomy came to the Romans through Posidonius, the Syrian philosopher who visited Rome in 87–86 B.C.E. who blended astronomic theory with Stoic philosophical ideas in a way attractive to Roman thought. Through handbooks by Cleomedes, Nicomachus, and Geminus, as well as Calcidius's translation and commentary on Plato's *Timaeus,* the Romans learned of higher mathematics and geometry necessary to calculate and prove Hipparchus's theories. Educated Romans knew Euclid's plane geometry, Archimedes' mathematical mechanical principles, and Apollonius's conic geometry. Even by being somewhat familiar with higher mathematics, the Romans did not embrace, integrate, and apply Euclid's, Archimedes', and Apollonius's sophisticated approaches to learning. The exception was Ptolemy's textbook on astronomy, primarily an eclectic summary of accepted Greek mathematical and astronomical data fitted within a geocentric concept. Perhaps, because Ptolemy's works were so carefully elucidated, the Romans and scholars in the later Middle Ages regarded the world as best described by Ptolemy. Later Roman writers such as Pappus, Theon, and Hypatia, the first known woman mathematician, built on Ptolemy's pronouncements. Only through the adoption of Greek mathematical astronomy could the Romans, under Julius Caesar, have made the necessary changes in 46 B.C.E. to produce the calendar that, with a minor correction in the sixteenth century, is still in use.

Geography. Geography was closely related to astronomy in Greek learning, but less so in Roman thought. The Romans' idea of geography was more what would be called physical geography and, above all, cartography (mapmaking). Primarily to advertise the valorous deeds of their ancestors, the Romans embraced geography because they wanted to display their conquests of far-flung regions. In the third century B.C.E. in Alexandria, Eratosthenes devised an ingenious mathematical hypothesis of the circumference of the earth, very close to what it actually is, and with it the global lines of longitude and latitude so necessary for computations of distances and relative positions of landmasses. The Scipionic Circle, a group of leading learned Romans associated with the Scipio family, accepted and encouraged studies of distant regions, not only for their curiosity but also for intelligent Roman expansion. Polybius, a Greek with strong ties to Rome, popularized geographical study with his descriptions of the western European and African regions. Augustus Caesar sponsored a geographical commission to map the empire. Inspired by Eratosthenes, Pomponius Mela, Agrippa, Strabo, and Ptolemy, mapmakers made the Romans aware of locations such as India, China, East Africa, the British Isles, and the Atlantic and Pacific Oceans, as well as the North, Persian, and Caspian Seas. Some Roman temples had wall, and even floor, maps so that the public could see and learn.

Engineering. Engineering is the science in which the Romans were truly great innovators. Roman houses were well built and centrally heated; their temples and public buildings were constructed to last and to beautify the city; their aqueducts brought clean water abundantly for drinking, washing, hygiene, and many industrial and commercial uses. Their city streets were paved, as were the highways that reached to the outermost areas of the Roman Empire—the moors of Scotland, the fields of the Ukraine, the desert regions of the Persian Gulf, and the desolate sands of the Sahara Desert in north Africa. Bridges traversed wide rivers, and mountain ranges such as the Alps and Pyrenees were no obstacles to their engineering feats. Roads ran straight and were so well constructed that even today some sections remain and are now carrying motor-vehicle traffic. The Romans' greatest innovation was the invention of mortar to cement bricks and other construction material. Some functioning churches and mosques today are simply converted Roman basilicas. All these achievements notwithstanding, the Romans did not celebrate engineering as a profession. The army used many of the engineers to design ingenious war machines such as catapults.

Public Health. Comparable to their construction techniques were the Romans' achievements in public health. When graves are found, modern paleopathologists can determine the age of the person at death. On this evidence, clearly the average Roman life span was almost fifty years. Nothing in Roman medical practice in dealing with diseases could have achieved that longevity, so one is left to ascribe the accomplishment to good public health, nutrition, and hygiene. Like Greek culture, Roman culture emphasized fitness and cleanliness. The aqueduct systems that brought clean water also flushed the sewers so that wastes were removed from populated areas. Exercise was recommended. Nutritional rules were inculcated and followed. An important part of the Roman diet was *garum,* a fermented fish oil rich in vitamins and readily digested amino acids. Fruits, vegetables, and whole-grain cereals made their diet wholesome.

Agriculture. While the Romans did not embrace the physical sciences with the gusto of the Greeks, in one area—agriculture—they surpassed all. As early as the late third century B.C.E., Cato the Elder wrote about how to manage a farm. Essentially agriculture is a science, even when conducted by illiterate peoples. The knowledge of plants, soils, climate, and other complex factors developed out of cumulative experience, and the application of human reason enhanced it. Romans prided themselves in rationally run farms and in the understanding of market conditions affecting production and profits.

Medical Science. In the sense of combining cumulative experience with the application of human reasoning, the knowledge of medicine was similar to agriculture. Early Roman medicine was built on the experience of adults, especially fathers and mothers of households, based on what they learned from their parents and "wise" people and tested by their own experiences. This empirical approach was applied to disease prevention as well as to therapy. What foods to eat, how much is too much, what herbs or substances are good for digestion, upset stomachs, diarrhea, constipation, cuts, and bruises—these concerns were the matters of early medicine. In the third century B.C.E. Greek physicians came to the Roman towns and brought a learned medicine based on the tradition of Hippocrates. The application of empirical cures became irretrievably conjoined with theory and concepts of physiology that the Romans heretofore had not conceived. Greek medicine significantly modified Roman medicine. Far from producing a consensus, however, Greek medicine introduced controversy. Romans wondered about which among the competing schools of medicine were to be believed and followed. Were the old traditional Roman remedies to be preferred to the newer, prestigious, and learned medicine? Newer schools developed in a period under Roman influence that joined the Empiricist and the Dogmatist Schools that came earlier, and they were called the Methodists, the Pneumatists, and, finally, the Asclepiadians. Under the Romans, Dioscorides, Soranus, and Galen wrote the best works in Greek medicine written in antiquity—at least, those works surviving. Also, writers in Latin contributed richly to medicine, especially Celsus, whose books on medicine compare favorably with most writings in Greek. Following the Hippocratic injunction, regimen (diet, exercise, and bathing) was the first course of therapeutic address as well as prophylactic (or preventative) medicine. If a regimen proved impracticable or ineffective, the second address

was drugs. Many of the same drugs employed by the Romans continued to be used through the nineteenth century, and some of those prescriptions are experiencing a return to favor in the twenty-first century. The physician's last resort was surgery. Surgical instruments found in archaeological sites attest to the sophisticated skills of Roman surgeons. Medical education was conveyed through the traditional apprenticeship method, there being no formal institutions of medical training. In the Roman Empire, cities contracted for physicians supported by public money to administer medical services to the poor, who were unable to afford private physicians' fees. Essentially, municipal governments provided a public health system.

The Transmission of Knowledge. In the late empire, Roman science continued to favor the handbook as a means of relating science. Beginning in the third century C.E. and ending with Isidorus Hispalensis, or Isidore, bishop of Seville, in the seventh century C.E., several writers in Latin codified scientific knowledge in easily digested textbooks. They are called the Transmitters because much of what was known about Greek and Roman science was incorporated in their works. They became the textbooks for the Middle Ages. They were diverse works, such as encyclopedias, as well as specific works on medicine and mathematics. Some Transmitters were original in their presentations and explained the subjects even better than their classical models, such as Euclid and Ptolemy. More often than not, however, the Transmitters oversimplified, misunderstood, and poorly explained complex subjects.

TOPICS IN SCIENCE, TECHNOLOGY, AND HEALTH

AGRICULTURAL SCIENCE

Roman Farming. Early agriculture was a science whose techniques and lore were transmitted orally. The Romans were the first people to make agriculture a subject for technical discourse, systematically presented. "Cato first taught agriculture to speak Latin," said Columella, himself a writer on agriculture. First through its legions, then through its ploughs, the Romans transformed the face of western Europe. Early Roman agriculture consisted of small farms whereon a family could sustain itself with few goods purchased at the markets. As Rome expanded, many developments in agriculture trans-

formed the small farm into large, cash-crop corporate enterprises that were rationally run. The Mediterranean soils of Italy were thin in topsoil. Ploughs were scratch devices pulled by animals. Never producing the abundant yields of modern farms, Roman farms were increasingly specialized according to the area, the nature of the soil and climate, and market conditions. As Rome expanded by annexing contiguous areas, soldiers and urban landless were often granted agriculturally productive areas. The Romans fostered the notion that the strength of the Republic lay in its small farmers and landowners. The urbanization of Italy and internationalization of markets caused farms to grow in size, with smaller farmers marginalized and eventually virtually eliminated. Cereal crops were more competitively grown in Sicily and North Africa. Large areas of public land (*ager publicus*) became available to wealthy Romans who occupied tracts that left production during and just after the Second Punic War (218–201 B.C.E.). They were transformed into private land (*ager privatus*) and made into large estates, called *latifundia*. Italian agricultural production turned primarily toward viticulture, olive orchards, animal husbandry (mostly cattle), and fresh vegetables for local markets. The Gracchi brothers (133–121 B.C.E.) were only partially successful when they attempted agricultural reforms to reinstate small farms. In the long run, they did not succeed in reducing the growth of large capital farming with slave and low-wage laborers. Rome's expansion beyond Italy resulted in large markets for grain, wool, leather, and wine, especially through government contracts for military supply.

Farms West and East. Julius Caesar found Gaul, northern Europe, and Britain to be largely forest lands with small clearings, where on small plots grew vegetable and cereal supplements for the Celtic and Germanic diets. A century later, large farms in those same regions were run as businesses, and they pushed back the forest. Essentially, in western and northern Africa, the large units of agricultural production in the Roman Empire became the medieval manors with few changes. Were one to have flown over Gaul in the second century and then again in the eighth century, one might well have seen the same farms, little changed in the intervening years. In the Roman east, farming did not change much from the Hellenistic era that preceded it. The Romans treated agriculture as an area of science where reason and business were applied to production for maximum yields. They employed organic fertilizers, crop rotations, and systematic periods to allow fields to recover by allowing them to be fallow.

Agricultural Handbooks. The first surviving work on agriculture was by the famous Marcus Porcius Cato, the Censor (234–149 B.C.E.), who wanted his sons and all Romans of ambition to run good, productive, efficient farming estates. He described his own villa and what features are necessary for a good farm, with horticultural and viticultural advice, as well as practical business procedures, such as how to store wine and olive oil until the prices are high. Somewhat disjointed in presentation, this work interspersed recipes and extolled the virtues of cabbage. Gardens, he said, not only nourish but cure as well. Two later writers on agriculture helped establish agriculture as a science, worthy of study as well as application. Varro (116–27 B.C.E.) wrote a work called "On Cultivating the Land," which dealt with agriculture in general and especially with animal husbandry, notably cattle, sheep, and small animals. Varro recognized the importance of bees in crop production and advised on how to keep hives. The most systematic agricultural treatise was written by

Columella (flourishing mid first century C.E.), who was born in Gades in Spain but owned farms in Italy. He is known for his thoroughness, precision with detail, and systematic arrangement. Subjects covered include farm organization, viticulture, arboriculture, animal husbandry, fish farming, poultry and small animals, surveying, climatic factors, soil conditions, and how to employ various land formations. He recognized the existence of contagious diseases among animals. Viticulture received the most emphasis, partly because of its complexity and partly for its profitability.

Sources:
W. E. Heitland, *Agricola: A Study of Agriculture and Rustic Life in the Greco-Roman World from the Point of View of Labour* (Westport, Conn.: Greenwood Press, 1970).

K. D. White, *A Bibliography of Roman Agriculture* (Reading, U.K.: University of Reading, 1970).

White, *Roman Farming* (London: Thames & Hudson, 1970; Ithaca, N.Y.: Cornell University Press, 1970).

ASTRONOMY AND MATHEMATICS

Closely Related. With few exceptions, mathematics and astronomy were closely related in the ancient writings on science. From the first century B.C.E. and throughout the Roman Empire, learning, teaching, and practical application was exegetical, that is, dispersed through the

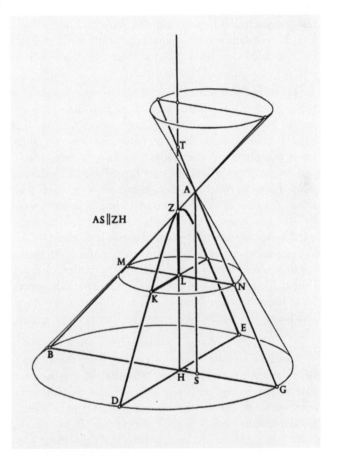

Diagram illustrating a problem in Apollonius's Conics that shows planes ZDE intersecting a parabola and MKN in a circle (from G. J. Toomer, "Apollonius of Perga," in *Dictionary of Scientific Biography*, edited by Charles Coulston Gillispie, volume I, 1970)

The numerous stars, scattered in different directions, sweep all alike across the sky every day continuously forever. The axis, however, does not move even slightly from its place, but just stays forever fixed, holds the earth in the centre evenly balanced, and rotates the sky itself. Two poles terminate it at the two ends; but one is not visible, while the opposite one in the north is high above the horizon. On either side of it two Bears wheel in unison, and so they are called the Wagons. They keep their heads forever pointing to each other's loins, and forever they move with shoulders leading, aligned towards the shoulders, but in opposite directions.

Source: Aratus, *Phaenomena*, 19–30, translated by Douglas Kidd (Cambridge & New York: Cambridge University Press, 1997).

interpretation of texts, often through easily understood handbooks. Mathematics was not an isolated pursuit but was considered a part of what a learned person should know. Cicero (*On the Orator* 1.10, 3.127), for example, claimed that mathematics was an exact, abstruse, and obscure field, but one that an educated person could master, many scholars having obtained perfection in its study. Far from mastering mathematics, the Romans did not indulge in its study in depth, and their contributions to it were more superficial than profound.

Three Distinct Categories. Early Romans knew well the celestial signs—those that told the best times to plant and to harvest, that signaled changes in season, and that gave directions to travelers in unfamiliar regions. They knew the phases of the moon, the major constellations, and the positions of various stars throughout the calendar year. Indeed, roughly, they knew what a year was, although the early Roman year was imprecise compared to later adoptions of more-sophisticated calendars developed by the ancient Egyptians, Babylonians, and Greeks. When astronomy is discussed, there are three somewhat distinct areas: the primitive astronomy of the everyday Romans (as opposed to scholars); mathematical astronomy, learned primarily from the Greeks; and astrology, also learned from the Egyptians, the Babylonians, and, to a lesser degree, the Greeks.

Roman Calendar. Prior to learning from the Greeks, the Romans had an awkward calendar. March was the first month of the year, and there were at that time ten months in all (hence, September from *septem*, "seven," October from *octo*, "eight," November from *novem*, "nine," and December from *decem*, "ten"). In 153 B.C.E. they added the two months of January and February, and moved consular elections to the first of January. Again, practicality was the reason. With Rome engaged in a protracted war in Spain, the Roman consular elections, traditionally held on 1 March, did not allow time for the

consul charged with command to organize, assemble, and transport an army to Spain in time for a full campaign. By the time the consular army arrived, the rebels had encroached on Roman territory. The remainder of the season was wastefully expended in pushing them back to the point where they were at the beginning of the previous winter when the consul's term was over. The solution was to move the elections to January so that the consul could assemble and transport an army in time for the spring—the fighting season. March, May, Quintilis (July), and October had thirty-one days, February had twenty-eight, and the remaining months had twenty-nine. The total number of days in a year was therefore 355. To adjust to the inevitable discrepancies, February was shortened to twenty-three or twenty-four days and an "intercalary" month of twenty-seven days was added. By the time of Julius Caesar, the solar calendar was off the actual solar value by three months. Finally, in 46 B.C.E. Caesar revised the calendar by making that year 445 days in length. His reform was based on the Egyptian lunar calendar, with Greek astronomical calculations that allowed a twelve-month year by inserting days into the shorter months to bring them to thirty days. February alone was the exception: every fourth year an extra day was added between 23 and 24 February (the "leap-year" addition to the end of February is a modern adaptation). Not until 1582 were subsequent calendar changes made, when Pope Gregory XIII promulgated the reform.

Mathematical Astronomy. The Romans fixed upon the wrong Greek writer for their earliest authority on mathematical astronomy, but his work suited the needs of the Romans because of its simplicity. Also, he was relatively concise and practical—all qualities the Romans admired. This scholar was Aratus of Soli (circa 310–circa 240 B.C.E.), who wrote in Greek a poem on astronomy and meteorology (or weather signs). Aratus was not a scientist but a person of literature; his poem *Phaenomena* was popular with the Romans, whose introduction to learned astronomy came through this work. At least four Latin translations were made. Cicero translated 769 lines when he was a young man, and he based much of his worldview on Aratus. Drusus Germanicus, nephew of Emperor Tiberius and adopted son of Augustus, translated 857 lines. In the fourth century C.E., Avienus paraphrased in Latin most of the long poem. Early in the eighth century an anonymous writer designed a poorly written translation that heavily influenced the astronomy of the Middle Ages.

Concentric Spheres and Horse-Fetters. Aratus based his composition on the astronomy of Eudoxus of Cnidus (circa 400–circa 347 B.C.E.), who was more of a mathematician than an astronomer, although he wrote on both subjects. Perhaps intended more as a geometrical exercise than a description of the physical world, Eudoxus proposed a universe of twenty-seven concentric spheres revolving around the earth. The perplexing motion of planets was explained through a *hippopede*, or "horse-fetter," a fig-

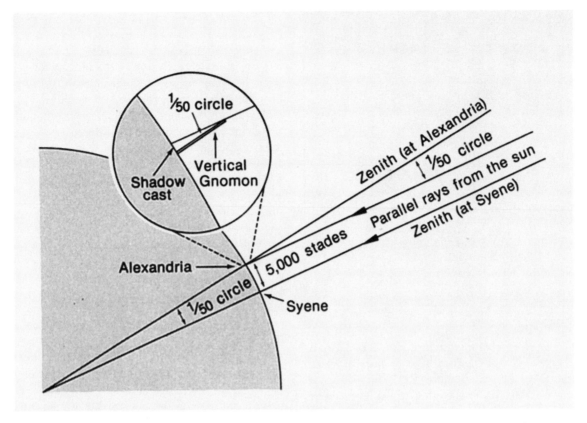

Diagram of Eratosthenes's measurement of the Earth (John Campbell, *Introductory Cartography,* 1984)

ure-eight-shaped curve, that represented the movement of a planet in latitude and retrograde wobbles. Eudoxus's theory could not explain the obvious variations in size and brightness the planets exhibit. A later modification by Callippus (flourishing 330 B.C.E.) added to Eudoxus's concentric spheres two more spheres for the sun and moon, and one more for the planets, but still his theoretically constructed cosmos was irreconcilable with observational data. The Greek word *planê* meant "wandering," because, unlike stars whose progressive movement across the sky was even, planets wandered, each with its own pattern. Sometime after Callippus, a theory of unknown authorship solved the problem by using epicyclic and eccentric forms. One saw planets moving in circles in their own orbits, thereby explaining why a planet's path appeared to have sudden rapid movements that were nearly linear, and then appear to circle back in a retrogressive manner.

Positional Astronomy. Aratus chose not to relate the more technical aspects of Eudoxus's astronomy in his poem, but instead relied upon him for the celestial observations of star movements. After beginning with a hymn to Zeus, he described the northern and southern constellations. Aratus postulated the existence of a South Pole, based on earlier logical inferences by Aristotle and Eudoxus. In *De caelo* (285b) Aristotle put the South Pole on "top," but later he altered this view. Aratus mentioned it first but, without more ado, moved to a discussion of the two Bear constellations, also called Wagons (the Big and Little Dipper). After describing them, he noted that

the Greeks relied on the Great Bear for navigation, whereas the Phoenicians depended on the Little Bear. Aratus described the northern and southern constellations and planets but refrained from a discussion of their movements. Based on Eudoxus's model, he explicated the circles of the celestial sphere before moving to a discussion of the calendar: days in a lunar month, hours of the stars as they arise and set, and the Metonic cycle, a nineteen-year lunar cycle discovered by the Athenian astronomer Meton (flourishing 432 B.C.E.). The final part—a distinct, almost separable section—concerned weather signs. Probably inspired by Hesiod's poem on farming, *Work and Days* (which includes much important early Greek information on astronomy), Aratus's work was read and admired by the Romans, who were introduced to astronomy through this nontechnical, easy-to-read poem that was, above all, practical.

Astronomy, Homer, and Stoicism. Homer was the Greek poet the Romans knew best, and Homer's geography was readily understood: landmasses surrounded by a vast ocean. Like Aratus, Crates was a scholar of literature who wanted to interpret Homer's universe according to Stoic principles. As the likely founder of King Eumenes II's library in Pergamum, Crates was devoted to Stoic values based on what he regarded as Homer's prescient theories of cosmic arrangements. He visited Rome probably in 159 B.C.E. (where he broke his leg stepping into a sewer) and may have inspired the Romans to provide public libraries and perhaps more pedestrian-friendly streets. In

the history of science an important question is not only
what written works were known but the order in which
each came to be known. Because the Romans learned
astronomy from Aratus and Crates, whose works were
practical and simplistic, they tended either to disregard,
to misunderstand, or, at best, to depreciate the better
Hellenistic astronomers, such as Aristarchus and Hipparchus.

Heliocentric Universe. Some educated Romans were
aware of a proposal by Aristarchus of Samos (flourishing
280 B.C.E.) that the earth was one of seven planets cir-
cling the sun. The work where he made his proposal has
not survived, no doubt in part because it was disbelieved.
Aristarchus has only one surviving work, called *On the
Sizes and Distances of the Sun and Moon*, in which he proposed the relative distances between the earth, sun, and
moon. He assumed that the moon receives its light from
the sun. When the moon appeared in the sky as a half
moon, he postulated that the angle formed by the sun's
rays and the visual line from the earth would be ninety
degrees. He applied the geometrical theorems that (1) the
square of the hypotenuse is equal to the sum of the
squares of both sides and (2) the angles within a square
triangle equal 180 degrees. He determined that the angle
formed by the moon to the earth and by the sun to the
earth was 87 degrees (whereas it is actually 89' 52"). He
concluded that the ratio of relative distances from the
earth to the moon is more than eighteen times, but less
than twenty times, the moon's distance from the earth.
Because he lacked the instruments for a more accurate
measurement of the angle, his calculation, based on true
values, was inaccurate, the actual ratio being about 400:1.
Aristarchus proposed a heliocentric universe, possibly
elaborating on a Pythagorean notion that the earth
revolved around the sun, but the work in which his proposition appeared was lost. Nonetheless, the Romans and
the people of the Middle Ages knew Aristarchus's precur-

sor theory to Copernicus in the 1540s. Like the Greeks,
the Romans rejected such a radical idea that seemed to
contradict common sense. Although details are lacking,
one can surmise that some of the reasons for this stand
were the same objections handed (much later) to Copernicus: namely, if the earth revolved around the sun and it
took a day to complete a revolution, one who jumped up
should land slightly to the west. Moreover, if, in explaining day and night, man observed that the earth revolved
around its axis daily, then why is there not such a wind-
force so strong as to level the surface of the earth? Finally,
and critically, if the earth revolved around the sun and the
sun was motionless like other stars, there ought to be an
angle between the earth and a star relative to the sun as
the earth changed position, but this is not the case. The
angle should especially be apparent every six months
when the earth was on the opposite side of the sun. This
phenomenon is known as the stellar parallax. It was not
until the 1830s that sufficiently powerful and accurate
telescopes made it possible for the angles to be seen. To
the Greeks, and later the Romans, the inability to make
such an observation doomed Aristarchus's theory. Not
until the eighteenth century, with the work of English
scientist James Bradley, was the proposition broached
that the *minimum* distance to the stars was on the order of
four hundred thousand times the distance to the sun.
Such magnitudes defied common sense to the Romans
and, besides, such information would have had no practical application.

Geocentric Universe Proven Mathematically. Ptolemy
wrote that Hipparchus (circa 192–120 B.C.E.) objected to
Aristarchus on the grounds of the stellar parallax. Ironically, were it not for his commentary on Eudoxus and
Aratus, Hipparchus's more important work in astronomy would have gone uncelebrated among the Romans.
Hipparchus's astronomical calculations were based on
personal observations on the island of Rhodes made
during the period from 141 to 127 B.C.E., and from
access to the now-lost Babylonian Tables that contained
centuries of celestial data. Hipparchus's genius was
relating astronomical data to practical application and,
in doing so, his theoretical basis rejected Aristarchus's
heliocentric cosmos in favor of a traditional geocentric
view. Employing trigonometric functions, he constructed tables for the sun and moon with the use of
ingenious instruments. He could compute and predict
lunar and solar eclipses, and his calculation for the average length of the lunar month comes within one second
according to modern computation. In many respects it
is not known precisely what Hipparchus did, because
what is known of him primarily came through others,
notably Ptolemy (flourishing 150 C.E.). Even before
Ptolemy, the Romans celebrated Hipparchus but did
not fully understand him. They even exaggerated his
influence, as did the Elder Pliny, who thought that
Hipparchus had swept the heavens clean of supernatural
nonsense and left rationality in its place. Despite lavish

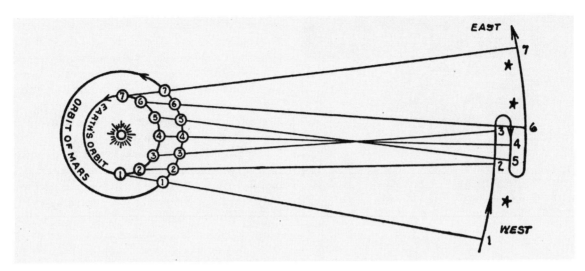

Retrograde motion of Mars explained on the basis of Copernican theory (from Marshall Clagett, *Greek Science in Antiquity*, 1955)

praise on one hand, Pliny saw Hipparchus as intellectually arrogant for attempting to discover that which even the gods did not know: the number of stars and their courses. Cicero accepted Hipparchus's criticisms of Aristarchus's heliocentric universe, although he likely read about Hipparchus in Serapion (flourishing first century B.C.E.). Serapion's now-lost work on astronomy and geography argued that the sun was nineteen times larger than the earth.

The Gods and the Universe. The Romans learned and based much of their astronomy and philosophy of cosmic purpose on the Stoic philosopher Posidonius, who attempted a coherent doctrine that the Romans found intriguing. Cicero, Pompey the Great, and other Romans traveled to Rhodes to hear him lecture. Posidonius taught that God manages the universe through reason and there were three causes: matter, the soul (prime active power), and reason (the principle or directive of activity). The finite universe he regarded as a single sphere within eternal time and indefinite space or void. The cosmos was a living, sentient entity with a soul and it operated through reason. Heavenly and earthly bodies were composed of the fifth element, ether, and the four elements were of god or reason. The latter was separated from the physical world, and, at the same time, pervasive within it. The earth nourished heavenly bodies as they revolved around it in spherical orbits, a concept on which astrology was built in the Roman Empire. The sun was pure fire, around three million English miles in orbital diameter, while the smaller moon was approximately two millions stades from the earth and five hundred million from the sun. Posidonius's calculations were accepted by the Romans and have importance in history because his figures were employed by Christopher Columbus in the fifteenth century.

Human Limits. The Romans incorporated Greek astronomy and mathematics within their handbook traditions for compacting knowledge in easily understood formats. The theories of the cosmos were too tedious and impractical for Roman tastes. Even the indefatigable Pliny, who absorbed learning like a sponge and whose praise of Hipparchus was lavish, thought that man's attempt to know the deepest cosmic secrets was beyond his capacity to understand. Pliny said Hipparchus "dared to give the number of stars to posterity and to enumerate the heavenly bodies by name," an exercise *etiam deo improbam* ("unseemly even for a god") (Pliny, *Natural History* 2.24.95). Similarly, when he described attempts to fix the proportions of pharmaceuticals, Pliny argued that such attempts were "beyond the capability of man" (Ibid. 29.8.25). Stoic philosophers, including Pliny, increasingly saw the universe as *divina natura*, or Divine Nature, in contrast to *imbecillitas humana*, or "limited human intelligence."

Handbook Astronomy. The handbook format for science in general, astronomy in particular, appealed to the Romans, although many of the handbook writers were Greeks whose works were written or known in Latin translation. Cleomedes (flourishing from the early first century B.C.E. or as late as the early second century C.E.) wrote a handbook that primarily relied on Posidonius. Heavily influenced by Stoic philosophy, Cleomedes was concerned with astronomical calculations based on a geocentric model. For the earth, he explained remarkably accurately the equator, tropics, "arctic," and "antarctic" circles, the values for the astronomical seasons, the sun's eccentric orbit that makes it closer to earth during certain seasons, and the sidereal day being shorter than the solar day (indirectly from Hipparchus). He described the moon's phases, thereby dispelling many superstitions, and gave the approximately correct zodiacal periods (except for Mars) for Mercury, Venus, Jupiter, and Saturn. Fortunately, he recorded the methods that Eratosthenes and Posidonius employed for measuring the surface of the earth.

Number Theory. Following the handbook tradition, Nicomachus of Gerasa (flourishing 100 C.E.) presented an arithmetic that was less inclined toward astronomy than to

Hypatia, daughter and pupil of Theon, enjoys the distinction of being the first known woman mathematician and the last of the ancient mathematicians. She assisted her father in the commentary on Ptolemy's *Almagest* and the revisions to Euclid's *Elements*. She supposedly wrote commentaries (now lost) on Diophantus's *Arithmetica* and Apollonius's *Conic Sections*. She is the last-known lecturer at Alexandria, where her teachings on mathematics and Neoplatonism, a philosophy she propounded, won for her the admiration of her students and the enmity of the Christians. Likely her works were among those burned in frequent pillages of libraries by Christian mobs and she was killed by one of the mobs around the year 415.

Source: Maria Dzielska, *Hypatia of Alexandria*, translated by F. Lyra (Cambridge, Mass.: Harvard University Press, 1995).

number theory, a subject the Romans found intriguing. The Pythagoreans heavily influenced Nicomachus, especially in regard to music theory and the mathematical harmony of the scales. Nicomachus's eclectic work combined philosophy and pure mathematics, for example, even and odd, prime (including an explanation of Eratosthenes' "sieve" method to find prime numbers), and uncompounded numbers, as well as Euclidean problems and the derivation of superparticulars from successive multiples. His connecting the mathematical harmony of a rational universe together with the Pythagorean mystical truth was appealing to later medieval thinking.

"No One Ignorant of Geometry." Above the portal of Plato's Academy were the words: "Let no one ignorant of geometry enter." Plato's theory of ideas and advocacy of mathematics are best explained in his dialogue, *Timaeus*. Only the Romans who read Greek were stimulated by Plato's emphasis on geometry, until Calcidius (fourth to fifth centuries C.E.) partially translated *Timaeus* into Latin and provided an extensive commentary. Calcidius's discussions of geometry and astronomy were very important in the transmission of Graeco-Roman science to the Middle Ages.

Astronomical Handbook. Geminus (flourishing in Rhodes, circa 70 B.C.E.) wrote a handbook on positional astronomy and mathematical geography that greatly influenced the Romans. He wrote an *Introduction to Astronomy* and a larger, six-book work on the mathematical sciences, largely appealing to the Romans because of the application of his calculations for the calendar. Without originality or ingenuity, he discussed the zodiac, the moon and planetary orbits, and the constellations. He wrote about the inequalities of the solar orbit, thus accounting for seasonal variations ranging from 88.125 days to 94.5 days, the celestial equator, tropic and arctic circles, and various Greek lunar and solar calendar schemes.

Astrology. Babylonian priests marked the heavens according to twelve imaginary belts, thirty degrees wide (hence, 12 x 30 = 360°), based on prominent stars and constellations. They were: Aries (ram); Taurus (bull); Gemini (twins); Cancer (crab); Leo (lion); Virgo (virgin); Libra (balance-scales); Scorpio (scorpion); Sagittarius (archer); Capricornus (goat); Aquarius (water bearer); and Pisces (fishes). By around 500 B.C.E. the Babylonian priests had defined and marked these bands as the zodiac (Greek *zôidion*, "[small] living creature," for example, probably small carved or painted figures of these signs) and observed how the planets (including the sun and moon) moved in relation to the zodiac and fixed stars. They noticed the relationship between when the signs appeared and events on earth, such as weather changes, the tides, and seasons. Postulating that heavenly objects impinge on earthly events, they developed elaborate means of forecasting the future. Horoscopes were used to determine a person's birth and/or conception and to predict the individual's future. Similarly for the kingdom or community, the positions of celestial bodies could indicate short-term calamities and fortuitous events. Whereas today one relegates astrology to magic and superstition, in fact the astrologers made astronomical, mathematical, and calendar computations that bordered on what is now called science. One practical example is the charting of the tides that was truly predictive. Astrology found receptive, although controversial, support in Rome as early as the first century B.C.E. In the empire, Roman emperors from Tiberius through Vespasian, and many other emperors throughout the second and third centuries, consulted with astrologers. Indeed, at times political and military decisions were influenced and determined by astrological predictions, but not without controversy. Augustus Caesar regulated astrologers who read horoscopes in private, and periodically astrologers were expelled from Rome. Between 152 and 162 C.E. Vettius Valens, a Greek, wrote a nine-book astrology, called the *Anthologies*, that had many horoscope charts. Early Christian Church Fathers excoriated astrologers. Although their influence diminished in succeeding centuries, it is fair to say that astrology and astronomy were closely linked, each influencing the other and both emphasizing mathematics for computations.

Elements of Plane Geometry. Euclid (flourishing 295 B.C.E., in Alexandria) wrote (in Greek) the *Elements*, a well-explained text that the Moslems and Christians in the Middle Ages employed. The first section on plane geometry (hence, the name "Euclidean" geometry) was little altered through the nineteenth century as a text for teaching. Even now, high-school texts on geometry embody the same problems in much the same order. Book 1 begins with the postulates that it is possible to define a point and a straight line. In addition to *Elements*, Euclid wrote *Phenomena*, devoted to spherical geometry as applied to astronomy. The Romans appear to have learned more indirectly than directly from Euclid's texts.

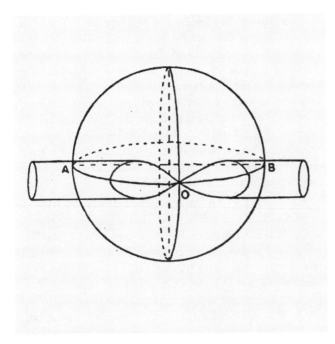

Diagram of Eudoxus's "horse-fetter," shown here at the intersection of the cylinder's surface with the surface of a sphere (from Marshall Clagett, *Greek Science in Antiquity,* 1955)

Some Greek scholars produced commentaries on it. The earliest extant commentary was written by Proclus (410–485 C.E.), who refers to several predecessors who wrote on Euclid but whose works did not survive.

Mechanics, Mathematics, and Astronomy. The Greek Archimedes (circa 287–212 B.C.E.) was the better scholar, yet less well known to the Romans than Euclid. The Romans knew Archimedes through his clever inventions, said to have delayed the fall of Syracuse, his native city, to the Romans in the Second Punic War. Several Romans (Livy, Plutarch, and Valerius Maximus) told of his death. When Rome took the city in 212, a Roman soldier found Archimedes teaching a class and dispatched him—a teacher's equivalent of dying with one's boots on. Judging by Latin sources, however, the Romans rarely read, commented on, or reflected on his works. Archimedes was a first-rate mathematician and astronomer, but they knew him indirectly through Greek writers such as Hero, Pappus, and Theon. For many of his calculations one would employ integral calculus today, but he adopted the Greek method of bypassing infinitesimals. Whereas he wrote on astronomy, those works were lost, but his method for determining the sun's diameter is incorporated in the *Sand-Reckoner.*

Solid Geometry and Conic Sections. What Euclid did for plane geometry, Apollonius of Perga (third to second centuries B.C.E.) did for solid geometry and conic sections. Born in Perga in Asia Minor, Apollonius studied in Pergamum and may have worked in Alexandria, although that is uncertain. The influence of his contributions to mathematics is certain and highly regarded. Even though Apollonius did not mention him by name, he appears to

have built on Archimedes' ideas. Apollonius's enduring work was the eight-book *Conics* that developed the geometry of parabolas, ellipses, and hyperbolas. His mathematical propositions based on geometry had direct application to mathematical astronomy. His proofs were especially important to Ptolemy in establishing the stationary point of the earth in relation to orbiting bodies in epicyclic and eccentric movements.

Stoic Views of Astronomy. In late Republican and early imperial times, many Romans regarded the universe and the god(s) as being the same or nearly the same. Penetrating the cosmic mysteries was impractical, disrespectful, and, possibly, blasphemous. Like Pliny, Seneca (first century C.E.) regarded astronomy as instructive about Nature's rational functions in order to free humans from superstition. Although he based his knowledge on Greek learning, primarily on Posidonius, Seneca's views were more astrology than astronomy. Heavenly bodies cause effects on earth, and it was the earth that received Seneca's attention. In astronomy, Seneca rejected the conventional view (derived from Aristotle and Posidonius) that comets exist between the moon and earth, thereby combining the rectilinear motion of the four earthly elements (air, earth, fire, and water) with the circular motion of ether-composed heavenly bodies. According to this view, comets travel in a combination of rectilinear and circular motions, thus, elliptical orbits. Seneca regarded comets, like other heavenly bodies, as traveling in circular orbits. Seneca's major work on astronomy and meteorology is called *Natural Questions;* written in Latin, it was popular during the Middle Ages. The integration of philosophy and physics with a Stoic emphasis made the message appealing to medieval thinkers. The close relationships between the earth and heavenly bodies appealed to those who were inclined to accept as truth the science that made the heavens and earth, god and man, linked more closely.

The Ancients' Universe as Passed to Later Ages. The work of one man, Ptolemy, was the means by which most people in the Islamic world and Christian West knew of mathematics, especially as applied to astronomy. Ptolemy supplied the theoretical basis upon which later ages founded their own observational researches down to Copernicus in the mid sixteenth century. Little is known of his life; much is known about his influence. He flourished 150 C.E. and did his work in Alexandria. His greatest work is known through its Arabic name, the *Almagest,* because no Greek to Latin translations of it were made until after the Western Europeans discovered it through an Arabic to Latin translation by Gerard of Cremona (circa 1175).

Almagest. The *Almagest* has been described as a synthesis of Greek astronomy and mathematics, not an original compilation; however, modern scholars see genius and innovation in his presentations. Books 1 and 2 are an introduction whereby Ptolemy describes the universe as understood by the consensus views of Eudoxus, Aristotle, and Hipparchus, *inter alia.* The universe is centered around a stationary, spherical earth with the celestial bodies moving from east to west in circles, just as Aristotle postulated, and making one revolution per day. In the observational data of how the seemingly irregular movements occur, Ptolemy employs trigonometrical calculations that he uses throughout his work. While bodies appear to have nonuniform and irregular motion, the reality, according to Ptolemy's account, is truly uniform, perfect motion, albeit not simple. A body travels in a circle around the earth, but the earth is eccentric to the center of the orbit. This motion accounts for some bodies, such as the sun and moon, appearing closer to the earth seasonally and more distant in other seasons. On the other hand, planets wobble and, at times, appear to slip back in a retrogressive movement; at other times, they speed up, moving almost in a line. Building on Hipparchus and other previous Greek astronomers (many unknown), Ptolemy explained how planets follow in a circle around their own orbit, an epicycle, thus creating the illusion of a retrograde motion to a stationary observer on earth. The relative position of the earth to a planet would vary according to whether the planet was in its epicycle farther from the earth or closer to the earth, this variation known as a deferent.

Planetary Orbits. Essentially this model explained mathematically many planetary orbits. The explanation was not only rational but also predictive, an essential characteristic of science. The eccentric and epicycle-on-deferent model could not predict all planets' orbits, thus another model was required. Some planets move around their orbits in ways that appear to be at varying speeds. Ptolemy related that these planets move to cover equal angles in equal times as measured from an equidistant point that is centered in neither the orbit's center nor the location of the earth.

Enduring Models. Ptolemy's three models (eccentric circle, epicycle-on-deferent, and equant) served as the explanation for celestial movements until Copernicus's reversion to the heliocentric hypothesis in 1543 and Kepler's three laws for planetary motion published in 1609. The perfection of the universe was preserved: a perfect circular motion as is required by celestial bodies composed of the fifth element, ether. Thus, the hypothesis for cosmic behavior as known to the Middle Ages was a combination of Empedocles' elements (earth, air, fire, and water), Aristotle's circular motion (celestial bodies composed of ether with rectilinear motion on earth of matter composed of the first four elements), and Ptolemy's mathematical explanation for celestial motion. In the remaining books Ptolemy explained solar and lunar theory, eclipses, parallax, a catalogue of fixed stars visible at Alexandria, planetary latitudes, and a theory of planets in longitude. His genius was in the organization, description, and application of trigonometrical methods for proofs. Another work, on geography, was ascribed to Ptolemy as well.

Late Roman Mechanics and Mathematics. Greeks living within the Roman Empire continued the study of mathematics, again through handbook and commentary formats. Pappus of Alexandria (flourishing 320 C.E.) asserted that mechanics was a part of mathematics. Also, in separate works he wrote commentaries on Ptolemy's *Almagest* and Apollonius's *Conics*. Even the eighteenth-century English physicist Isaac Newton was appreciable of Pappus's ingenuity in relating mathematics of his predecessors and making his own contributions, especially concerning loci on planes and conics.

Commentaries on Ptolemy. Ptolemy's works were not known in Latin, and it was through commentaries on his works that his contributions were kept alive in the West for a long period. These commentators were themselves talented and, occasionally, original. Theon of Alexandria (flourishing 364 C.E.) wrote an extensive commentary on Ptolemy's *Almagest* and two commentaries on his *Handy Tables* that provided a means to compute celestial positions. Along with his daughter, Hypatia, he was among the last of the researchers and teachers at the Museum in Alexandria. The only reference to his dates place him as living in the reign of Theodorius I (379–395 C.E.). As an explanation of Ptolemy, Theon's commentary is unoriginal, being a simplistic explanation to students on an elementary level. The *Almagest* commentary is in thirteen books, corresponding to the Ptolemy work, but book eleven and part of book five are lost. Also, he wrote an edition of Euclid's *Elements*, where he explained, altered, and, infrequently, corrected the Euclid text in such a way that the edited text enjoyed more popularity for a period than Euclid's original. Theon's mathematics were competent, although unoriginal, but they were well explained in a pedagogical way, thereby making his work on Ptolemy and Euclid popular for Byzantine science and, through Arabic, for Islamic science.

Sources:
Bernard R. Goldstein, *Theory and Observation in Ancient and Medieval Astronomy* (London: Variorum, 1985).

O. Neugebauer, *A History of Ancient Mathematical Astronomy*, 3 volumes (Berlin & New York: Springer-Verlag, 1975).

Liba Chaia Taub, *Ptolemy's Universe: The Natural Philosophical and Ethical Foundations of Ptolemy's Astronomy* (Chicago: Open Court, 1993).

ENGINEERING AND TECHNOLOGY

Technological Innovations. As in the imposition of political order, the Roman genius was especially evident in engineering and technological innovations. Under their rule the life spans of peoples within the Empire increased, and their health improved as well. In part these changes were because of good nutrition, but perhaps to a greater degree they were attributable to improvements in hygiene and, above all, clean water supplies.

Attitudes Toward Engineering. To a degree the Romans adopted the Greeks' attitude toward work. Simply stated, a virtuous person, one with intelligence, does not work with his hands. Indeed, success is indicated by the absence of work. Plutarch (died circa 120 C.E.)

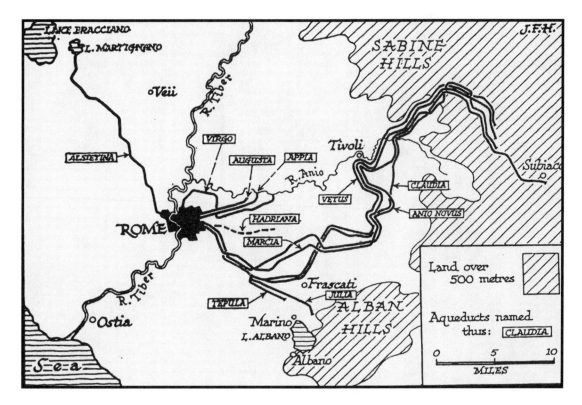

Map of the principal aqueducts serving Rome (from K. D. White, *Greek and Roman Technology*, 1984)

summed up the aristocratic attitude toward work when he connected Plato's notion of the aspiring soul longing for abstract truth to Archimedes' aversion to being associated with engineering. Plato reviled the engineer who took abstract geometry and applied it to practical things. For posterity Archimedes wanted only to be known for his contributions to abstract geometry and mathematics. He was reluctant to acknowledge his invention of several amazing mechanical devices, such as the water-screw for lifting water in mines, compound pulleys for lifting heavy objects, and ingenious military machines for the defense of his native city of Syracuse.

Suspicion of Technology. Two reasons advanced for the fall of the Roman Empire are: first, the Romans afforded little social prestige for the engineer; and second, concerns about the employment of the urban proletariat and their labor-intensive system in reliance on slave labor blocked necessary innovative technological solutions for their economy. The attitude is reflected in an incident during Vespasian's rule (69–79 C.E.) when some enterprising inventor designed a machine that could haul huge columns up to the Capitol at a minimum expense. Vespasian offered the inventor a reward and asked the perplexed man to destroy the machine, because "I must always ensure that the working classes earn enough money to buy themselves food" (Suetonius, *Vespasian* 18). The very fact that Roman historians did not record details of the machine is one indication that such inventions were unwelcome. For all of the physical remains of Roman construction and engineering, we have surprisingly little of the actual works from these engineers. There are two

notable exceptions: Vitruvius Pollio (died circa 25 B.C.E.), who wrote on architecture, and Sextus Julius Frontinus (flourishing 100 C.E.), who wrote on aqueducts.

The Ideal Architect. With these aristocratic, paternalistic attitudes notwithstanding, the Romans were proud of their material achievements—roads, public buildings, aqueducts, gigantic bathhouses, and centrally heated homes, for example—and they did afford some prestige to the engineer. Vitruvius said that an ideal engineer or architect ought to "be a man of letters, a skillful draftsman, a mathematician, familiar with historical studies, a diligent student of philosophy, acquainted with music; not ignorant of medicine, learned in the responses of jurisconsults, familiar with astronomy and astrological calculations" (Vitruvius 1.1.3). All the same, Vitruvius lamented that architects could practice without training or experience, there being no licensing procedures—such as would be established in the modern world—or guild control in the Middle Ages. Even so, his ideal architect (virtually the same as an engineer), who directs the laying of bricks, should be familiar with how matter was expected to change, as enunciated by the Presocratic philosophers. Vitruvius's ideal was unlikely to have been realized in only a few of those individuals who engaged in the professional activity during the Roman Republic or Empire.

Construction Technology. Wherever the Roman legions went, there followed durable roads, bridges, aqueducts, centrally heated houses and public buildings, and scrupulous attention to hygiene. When tourists

Colonnaded street built in the late second century C.E. looking toward the Arch of Trajan at Timgad in present-day Algeria

Europe, Asia, and Africa, where once was Rome's empire, they see the visible remains of Roman construction-engineering. Ancient Roman bridges not only majestically traverse rivers and streams but now carry the burden of automobile and truck traffic as well.

Concrete Mortar. Perhaps the greatest Roman innovation was the invention of concrete mortar. Early Roman buildings were constructed of wood, stone, clay, and brick, both mud and baked. In the third century B.C.E. Roman builders found deposits of ash near the volcano Vesuvius. To the natural ash they added lime mortar and water. When the mixed substance dried it was hard and durable. Slowly they perfected the formula. The result was cement that they called *pulvis puteolanus* (Puteolian powder), Puteolia being a city near where the ash was found. Employing the mortar between baked brick, they constructed well-designed buildings, some of which still stand. Many a Roman basilica, standing in the center of a city, was converted into a mosque or Christian church and still functions today. Without mortar the Romans could not have built the aqueduct systems that supplied clean water to public buildings and houses. For most public and some private buildings, marble slabs were placed on the cemented brick as a veneer, thereby giving the appearance of pure marble. The pockmarks that one sees, for instance, on the Roman Colosseum are the holds for marble slabs. Many of the marble slabs are now in the medieval churches of Rome, to which they were recycled from pagan buildings. Augustus boasted that he found Rome a city of mud bricks but he left her clothed in marble. Pliny

the Elder marveled at Roman ingenuity but was apprehensive about their manipulation of nature.

Roads and Bridges. Beginning in 312 B.C.E., when the first stretch of the famous road called the Appian Way was constructed, the Romans developed a system of roads designed to get the military forces to far-flung places as rapidly as possible. Digging deeply for foundation and drainage, the roads were constructed to be durable with smooth hard surfaces of stone. Most roads consisted of four to five layers and varied from four to six feet beneath the surface. With picks and shovels the legionaries traversed plains, rivers, deserts, and mountain ranges. Bridges on brick and concrete piles spanned rivers. Although built for the military by the military, roads were also used by civilian and commercial vehicles. Moving straight up inclines, grades could be as much as 20 percent. Heavy wagons would have to find zigzagged, parallel roads near the paved surface in order to negotiate uphill climbs and to brake for descents. Cities were connected to one another, and all major Italian roads to Rome, in whose center was the golden milestone. Along the roads were milestones placed at intervals called "miles" (from *mille passuum*, a "thousand paces"), based on a standard number of steps. Typically the inscriptions told of the distances to Rome, the provincial capital, the nearest city for administration of the district, the name of the legion constructing the site, and the emperor at the time of construction.

Houses. Roman houses were sturdy, usually of brick and mortar, and well designed for the comfort afforded by

Modern painting by Zeno Diemer of the great aqueduct intersection outside the city of Rome during the imperial era (Deutsches Museum, Mainz)

Mediterranean climates. Many, if not most, had central heating from ducts in the floors. A furnace was constructed on the side of the house where a fire, usually burning wood, was fed by a draft taking in outside air, which was heated in the ductlike furnace and flowed through passageways under the floors (called *hypocausta*). On the other side or through walls an upper duct led out to the open air, thereby providing well-circulated conductive heat. Similar arrangements were made for public buildings. Much-larger and more-elaborate furnaces furnished heated water in great volumes for the bathhouses, as well as radiated heat through the floors. Construction-engineering evolved with innovative use of arches to span distances for roofs, bridges, and aqueducts. Many houses were attached to the municipal water system that had main lines down the streets. The water was clean and used for drinking, cooking, bathing, decorating (fountains in courtyards), and for toilets, which were constantly flushed with running water beneath the seats. Even those people unable or unwilling to live in individual houses had good apartment houses called *insulae* (islands). With increased population densities, there was a tendency toward higher, multistoried dwellings, but a series of disastrous collapses resulted in building codes and height limitations. Similar provisions were made in housing codes for protection against fires with firewalls required between units. Public sanitation was the consequence of deliberate, rational town planning. Awareness of sanitation, especially clean water and location of sewage disposal, is notably seen not only in town planning but also in the way that the Roman army constructed their camps, even for one-night stays.

Water Consumption. Contributing immeasurably to public health was the availability of an abundance of clean water. With ingenuity and pride the Romans furnished towns with clean water transported from springs and mountain streams many miles away; some towns consumed more gallons of water per citizen than modern cities. Sextus Julius Frontinus, appointed commissioner of the City of Rome's water supply in 97 C.E., did not restrain his pride when he wrote, "With such an array of indispensable structures carrying so many waters, compare, if you will, the idle Pyramids or the useless, though famous, works of the Greeks!" (Frontinus, *Aqueducts of Rome* 1. 16).

Aqueducts. The *Anio vetus*, Rome's earliest aqueduct system, was begun in 272 B.C.E. and, when it was completed, moved water 63.6 kilometers (almost entirely below ground). In the course of three centuries, Rome added six more systems that totaled 386.2 kilometers, of which 49.6 kilometers were above ground and 336.6 kilometers below ground. The *Aqua Claudia*, completed in 52 C.E., ran some 68.7 kilometers (42 miles). Stone bridges with sturdy arcades transported water in pipes that were laid in a trough atop the aqueducts. Not confined to Rome, aqueducts supplied clean water to cities throughout the empire. Almost always transported using a gravity flow, water was gradually led downhill from mountains or higher altitudes to neighboring cities. It is said that one could roll a bowling ball from beginning to end on the aqueduct that ran from the Eifel mountains to the Roman city of Colonia Agrippina (modern-day Cologne). Rarely was water conveyed in open channels; normally, the channel was covered to reduce evaporation and contamination. Waterproof cement was used to form the troughs. Frequently, pipes carried the water and were placed in the troughs. Made of lead, wood, stone, and, most often, terra-cotta (earthenware), the pipes were required for siphons in order for water to move uphill. In areas where the softness of the water caused absorption of lead, Roman engineers avoided lead pipes because they were aware of its toxicity. Pipes would negate minor bumps in level, whereas the uneven bumps would be a problem for open channels. The troughs normally had three or more small pipes, rather than one large one. At the delivery point in the city, the aqueduct would have to enter the highest point to ensure distribution throughout the city. Water was employed to flush the public and private toilets, for public and private baths, for city fountains, for the irrigation of gardens in and around the city, and even in a few instances to turn water wheels for mills. A large municipal basin with distribution pipes exiting at different levels, the lowest being the highest priority, solved the problem for droughts when the water was low at its source. Politically, city councils could determine whether, for example, private houses had priority over public baths. At least, priorities may have been the intent; however, on the basis of some archaeological finds it appears that, in some cities, the pipes may have been arranged to ensure equal distribution to private houses, public fountains, baths, and theaters.

Water Bill. Private homes were supposed to pay dues for tapping into the municipal supply by purchasing a pipe with a city seal on it. In archaeological finds, however, it was discovered that some homeowners secretly tapped into the city main without paying. The construction and operation of aqueducts were maintained by both public taxation and private philanthropy.

Sanitation Engineering. The water systems did not operate with valves; rather, the water flowed continuously. For example, the public toilets had water running beneath the seats themselves; in front of the seats, a foot or so from the wall (allowing a person's foot to rest), ran a small stream of water. When the act was completed, one would cup one's hand and splash water to clean oneself. Deliberate care was exercised in ensuring that waste would be discharged sufficiently downstream so as not to contaminate access waters. No system of sewerage processing was developed, but the relatively small population sizes did not present such problems as would compromise comparable modern systems.

Sources:

L. Sprague DeCamp, *The Ancient Engineers* (Garden City, N.Y.: Doubleday, 1963).

Donald Hill, *A History of Engineering in Classical and Medieval Times* (London: Croom Helm, 1984).

A. Trevor Hodge, *Roman Aqueducts & Water Supply* (London: Duckworth, 1992).

Henry Hodges, *Technology in the Ancient World* (London: John Lane, 1970; New York: Knopf, 1970).

K. D. White, *Greek and Roman Technology* (Ithaca, N.Y.: Cornell University Press, 1984).

GEOGRAPHY

Theoretical Aspects. While mathematical astronomy was mostly a matter for Greeks writing in Greek, the Romans were more receptive to geography. As the Romans extended their domain, they were curious about foreign lands, peoples, and cultures. In the second century B.C.E. Polybius, who visited and entertained the Romans with learned discourse, stressed geography as an aid to understanding politics and history. Even more to the point, the ever-expanding empire called for knowledge of the world beyond the borders of Roman control. Although the Romans' contributions to geography were considerable when it came to places, peoples, and distances, nonetheless, the Greeks continued to provide the theoretical aspects. Nowhere can this case be more clearly seen than in the contrast between Eratosthenes (whose brilliant method resulted is a fairly accurate calculation of the circumference of the earth) and Marcus Agrippa. Eratosthenes wanted to calculate the circumference employing geometry and mathematics. When Agrippa wanted to know about Rome's world, he simply added up the distances between the milestones along the roads to map the region by determining distances.

Circumference of the Earth. A librarian and geographer at Alexandria devised an ingenious calculation for the circumference of the earth that challenged and astounded the Romans. Eratosthenes (circa 276–circa 195 B.C.E.) wrote a three-book *Geography* that was brilliant in conception. Julius Caesar read it for information on the German regions and Strabo, a later geographer in the Roman world, based much of his work on Eratosthenes, although he disliked his mathematical theory. Through the application of plane geometry to a well-conceived experiment, Eratosthenes computed the circumference of the earth to the equivalent of 250,000 *stades*, or 29,000 English miles, and, by another interpretation, to 25,000—the actual circumference is 24,902.45 miles. Pliny the Elder wrote that this figure is "an audacious venture, but achieved by such subtle reasoning that one is ashamed to be skeptical" (*Natural History.* 2.112.247). Acting on his hypothesis, Eratosthenes calculated the parallel of Rhodes (36° N) to be under 200,000 stades in circumference. By simple arithmetic each degree of latitude is around 541 *stades* (195,000 ÷ 360 = 541.66 stades). This calculation permitted him to map the globe with fairly accurate coordinates for the Mediterranean world that they knew, including much of north Africa, Europe (including Britain and Ireland, but excepting northern and Scandinavian regions), and Asia as far as India and the Himalayan mountains.

Scipionic Circle. Unlike the theoretical aspects of astronomy, geography was valuable to the Romans because it directly related to the ever-expanding empire. In the second century C.E. the so-called Scipionic Circle, a coalition of thinkers who were intellectually and internationally minded, were sold on the ideas of Polybius, a visiting Greek, as to the importance of knowledge of both geography and politics. Following the destruction of Carthage in 146 B.C.E., Polybius explored the western Mediterranean and adjacent Atlantic Ocean regions, including northwestern Africa, and his accounts stimulated the Roman imagination as well as their practicality.

Fanciful Notions. Roman politicians read Homer and, through Crates, they celebrated Homer's geography. According to Crates, Homer (although more aptly the Pythagoreans) conceived of the earth as consisting of four inhabited landmasses, transversely and diagonally opposite to one another, separated in the Western and Eastern hemispheres by two oceans running longitudinally from the northern and southern poles. The turbulence caused by the clash of ocean streams at the poles resulted in the ebb and rise of tides. Crates's fanciful notions of Homer's universe influenced Posidonius and Cicero. Later, Macrobius and Martianus Capella borrowed from Crates, and their works inspired Western medieval thought, especially regarding the landmasses in the Western hemispheres.

Roman Maps and Cartography. As early as 174 B.C.E. a Roman politician reportedly erected a map of Sardinia in a temple to visualize his family's military exploits. The tradition was established to display regional maps in temples and public places. Varro (116–27 B.C.E.) described a painted map where political leaders spoke to the public. In 44 B.C.E. Julius Caesar commissioned four Greeks, each of whom was assigned a region, to survey and produce a map of Asia, Europe, and Africa, but the project was never brought to fruition. Based on Caesar's earlier project, Augustus assigned Agrippa to produce a new map of the inhabited world. The undertaking was a major project, one that Agrippa did not live to conclude, but Augustus had it completed. It was erected on a wall of a portico named after Agrippa. Some have speculated that the map was circular, but, judging by its location, that seems unlikely. Although it does not survive, Pliny the Elder employed it in detail for the sections on geography, but Pliny's account ranged from criticism to admiration. Pliny's lengthy descriptions of geography, especially his focus area of northern Europe and Germany, were typically Roman in outcome; he rejected theoretical geography (*ratio*, "reason") and emphasized the practical and empirical (*usus*, "habit," and *observatio*, "observation"). A reduced version of Pliny's description of the three continents was incorporated into Martianus Capella's textbook and served the early Middle Ages for much of its geographical knowledge.

Far and Near Lands Described. In the familiar pattern, a Greek, Strabo of Amasia (64/63 B.C.E.–25 C.E.), completed the best work on Roman geography in sixteen books, called *Geographia*. Strabo traveled widely from Armenia and the Black Sea to Ethiopia along the Nile and from Italy to Syria; he combined what he knew and saw with a wealth of information drawn from earlier writers, now lost, and, we presume, personal accounts of travelers. Even though his interests were more along the lines of human geography, his work was influenced by the scientific geography of Eratosthenes, Eudoxus, and Hipparchus (mathematics and cartography). He employed Posidonius (information on Spain and Gaul), Caesar

(Gaul and the Germanies), Artemidorus (Asia Minor and Egypt), and Apollodorus of Athens (Greece). He was, however, unfamiliar with Agrippa's map and survey. Like Eratosthenes, he believed the three continents to be surrounded by a single ocean. He accepted the 360 degrees for marking coordinates by latitude and longitude, with the prime meridian at Rhodes, and described earthquakes, volcanoes, and various geological activities, such as the upheaval of landmasses from seabeds, proven by images of sea animals in rock quarries high in the mountains. Clearly Strabo's interest was in descriptive or regional geography and not mathematical geography, although in one chapter he discussed the shape of the earth and methods for measuring distance on the earth. His contributions were primarily with a description of peoples and regions, a discourse made all the better by his extensive travels. Westward he traveled only as far as northern Italy, and he had to rely on others' accounts for information about Spain, Gaul, and northern Europe. His habitable world was between the Caspian, Arabian, Persian, and Mediterranean Seas and the Atlantic Ocean. Strabo's extensive geography does not appear to be known or, at least, widely disseminated to western Romans and may have been published only in the Greek-speaking world.

Geography in Latin. Pomponius Mela (flourishing 44 C.E.) wrote the first and only treatise in Latin dedicated to geography. Systematically he described the habitable world with its three continents (Asia, Africa, and Europe). Being a native of southern Spain, he started with Atlantic Europe and moved eastward. Uninterested in mathematical geography, Mela assumed the spherical shape of the world. His descriptions of northern Europe (including Britain, Ireland, and northern Germany) were superior to Strabo's account. Along with good narrations about peoples and places, occasionally he relied on previous authorities to relate fantastic accounts of customs and habits of curious peoples.

Geography and "Natural History." Writing in Latin, although he employed many Greek sources, Pliny the Elder (circa 23–79 C.E.) wrote the *Natural History*, in which books three through six are devoted to geography. Much of their value lies with his relating data from Agrippa's map with some harsh criticisms and occasional lapses of praise. Pliny's pen, like his tongue, had a sting that hurt many a writer whom he freely criticized. Like Mela, Pliny was primarily concerned with descriptive geography. Pliny had served in the Roman army along the German frontiers, and he wrote a history, now lost, of the German wars and peoples; his account of Germany is restricted to less than two pages in modern print. Pliny regarded nature as divine and *terra* ("the earth") largely as *benignitas naturae* ("the kindness of nature") and man's friend; he excused nature for making some areas poor in rainfall, with inadequate soil, and subject to severe weather. Such conditions, he argued, should instruct people how to live within the rules established by nature. Ironically, Pliny died in one of nature's less benign moments, the eruption of the volcano Mount Vesuvius, during a daring rescue attempt.

The World According to Ptolemy. Around 150 C.E. Ptolemy wrote a *Geographia* (Geographical Manual) in eight books that was antiquity's greatest expression of world geographical knowledge. The text consists of place-names, each with longitudes and latitudes. It was written with maps, including a world map, but likely some alterations were made during the centuries following. The area of the Roman map was fairly accurately depicted, whereas northern European regions, Africa (especially western coastlines), and India have major errors. India, for example, has its triangular shape between its east and west coasts depicted less acute than it is, and the tip of the island of Sri Lanka is drawn far too large. To the north, in Asia he has China and what may be the Malay Peninsula. The easternmost site identified is Cattigara, which some scholars believe may be modern Hanoi. The continuation of a wraparound between China and Africa is cause for speculation that the continent of South America is implied, but there is no direct evidence for the assertion.

Sources:

Mary Beagon, *Roman Nature: The Thought of Pliny the Elder* (Oxford: Clarendon Press, 1992; New York: Oxford University Press, 1992).

O. A. W. Dilke, *Greek and Roman Maps* (Ithaca, N.Y.: Cornell University Press, 1985).

Roger French and Frank Greenaway, eds., *Science in the Early Roman Empire: Pliny the Elder, His Sources and Influence* (Totowa, N.J.: Barnes & Noble, 1986).

J. B. Harley and David Woodward, eds., *The History of Cartography*, volume 1, *Cartography in Prehistoric, Ancient, and Medieval Europe and the Mediterranean* (Chicago: University of Chicago Press, 1987).

HEALTH AND HYGIENE

Longevity. The Romans lived longer than ancient peoples before them and, for that matter, medieval peoples who lived after them. When one studies Roman medicine, no matter however sympathetically, one cannot conclude that the reason for an extended life was because of medical intervention. Skeletal evidence of people buried in ancient cemeteries, as well as other evidence, indicates that the average life span for Romans may have peaked at about forty-seven years, a figure not reached again until modern times. Medicine not being the reason, speculation focuses on nutrition and public health. Probably the greatest single factor is one already described: good water. Some medical historians regard good water and nutrition as the primary factors for longevity in both ancient and modern periods. Even in the last century, the practice of medicine did not appreciably affect gross demographic statistics nearly as much as public health and nutrition.

Nutritious Diet. The Romans' diet was highly nutritious. Customarily there were three meals a day: breakfast (*ientaculum*), usually a light amount of bread and fruit; lunch (*prandium*), often consisting of eggs, cold meats, vegetables, fish, and bread; dinner (*cena*), which could begin as early as the ninth hour (3–4 P.M.) and which continued into the darkness. Dinner was the largest meal of the day and often consisted of several courses. Fruit, vegetables, and whole-grain breads gave the Romans a well-balanced diet. Poor and rich alike ate as a mainstay of their diet a pottage of meal called *polenta*, normally made of barley, with a fish sauce on top. The fish sauce, generically called *garum*, was commercially prepared by layering fish catches in a large pit, using the fish whole without any cleaning. For days the fish would be allowed to deteriorate and the oils were drained off for the sauces, with the highest quality coming near the end. The last of the oils was clearer and less smelly than the less expensive oils that came earlier in the process. *Garum* contained basic, easily digested amino acids and as high in B vitamins and other nutrients.

Roman Culinary Science. A collection of 470 Roman culinary recipes was edited in the fourth century and attributed to Apicius, the author of the earliest extant cookbook. Several persons with a reputation for culinary art may have been the author, one of whom lived in the time of Julius Caesar, a second during the reigns of Augustus and Tiberius, and, finally, a third, Apicius, in the time of Trajan. The recipes reveal highly refined culinary tastes that must have reflected the eating habits of the upper socioeconomic classes. The variety of foods is amazing, with spices, fruits, and condiments being delivered to Rome from North Africa, Black Sea regions, the Near East, and the Far East.

Regimens. In addition to a healthy diet, part of the reason for the Romans' successful lifestyle was attention to hygiene and exercise. At the bathhouses—a regular part of most Romans' day—there was exercise (including some ball sports) as well as bathing, massage, lectures (on health and diet), and medical personnel performing much the same services as sports medical personnel do today. The Roman emphasis on diet, exercise, hygiene, and cleanliness doubtlessly was a major health factor. A cultural trait was an aversion to unpleasant body odors. Cosmetologists,

FEMALE LONGEVITY		
Date	**Site**	**Average Age at Death**
11,000 B.C.E.	North Africa	31
5,800 B.C.E.	Nea Kikomedeia	29.9
2,400 B.C.E.	Karatas (Greece)	29.7
1,750 B.C.E.	Lerna (Greece)	30.8
650–350 B.C.E.	Athens/Corinth	36.8
100–200 C.E.	Early Rome	34.6
100 C.E.	Britain	45

Source: John M. Riddle, *Eve's Herbs: A History of Contraception and Abortion in the West* (Cambridge, Mass.: Harvard University Press, 1997).

Two-seat toilet with decorative dolphin armrests at Timgad in North Africa, circa 100 C.E.

perfume vendors, and pharmacists were common among the many street vendors; sometimes one person sold all such items.

Public Medicine. The Roman government enhanced public health by providing free, publicly paid medical services for the poor. During the Roman Empire, many if not most municipalities contracted physicians, who were appointed and paid by the city council to provide medical services for the poor. Appointment as a public physician was prestigious and competitive, although the stipend was not sufficiently large to provide entirely for the physician's livelihood. In addition to the public clinic the physician conducted a clinic for private patients who paid their own fees. The feature of governmental health care was borrowed from the Greeks and was embraced not only in Greek-speaking areas of the East but in Latin-speaking areas of the western empire as well.

Sources:

Apicius, *The Roman Cookery of Apicius: A Treasury of Gourmet Recipes & Herbal Cookery,* translated by John Edwards (Port Roberts, Wash.: Hartley & Marks, 1984).

Robert I. Curtis, *Garum and Salsamenta: Production and Commerce in Materia Medica* (Leiden & New York: E. J. Brill, 1991).

MEDICINE

Diseases Then Unknown. Diseases were common in the ancient world, but, because medical practitioners of these times described symptoms rather than grouping diseases by classification, and because infectious disease-causing microorganisms alter through mutation, many diseases with which we are afflicted were not known or experienced. Some diseases of this period one cannot identify, probably because the organisms causing them mutated or the human immune system became invulnerable to their infections. Likely the Romans were not affected by smallpox, measles, diphtheria (although this malady was possibly described by Aretaeus of Cappadocia, circa 150–200 C.E., but osteological evidence for it is not found), scarlet fever, and influenza. Neither were they afflicted with the ravaging plagues of pandemic diseases, such as the notorious bubonic plague of 1347 C.E. or syphilis, introduced to Europe in the late fifteenth century. The greatest exception came with a plague that arrived in Rome in 170 C.E., supposedly spread by Roman troops transferred from the eastern frontier. Mortality rates were high, but data or even detailed descriptions are lacking. Modern scholars generate various hypotheses as to what type of disease it was—a microorganism ancestor to smallpox and typhus are two leading contenders—but no definitive answer has been forthcoming. Leprosy, identified in biblical and classical texts, is not the disease known in modern times by that name (the organism for which evolved during the Middle Ages). The ancients' leprosy was elephantiasis in some cases, and other nonfa-

APICIUS'S RECIPE FOR CAULIFLOWER OR BROCCOLI IN CELERY MINT SAUCE

(Adapted for the modern kitchen: *t = teaspoon, equivalent to 6 Roman scruples; T = tablespoon, equivalent to 1 Roman cyathus*):

1 cauliflower, cabbage, or
bunch of broccoli

First Sauce:

1/4 t. cumin

pinch of salt

2 T. white wine

1 T. olive oil

Take cauliflower, cabbage, or broccoli, quarter them, and put in a saucepan. For the first sauce, combine the cumin, salt, wine, olive oil, and enough water to steam the vegetables. Add the vegetables, bring to a boil, then simmer gently.

Second Sauce:

1/4 t. ground pepper

1/2 t. celery seed (or lovage)

1/2 t. mint

pinch of rosemary (or rue)

1/4 t. coriander

1/2 c. vegetable stock

2 T. white wine vinegar

1 T. olive oil or butter

Meanwhile, in a mortar, grind pepper, celery seed (or lovage), mint, rosemary (or rue) and coriander. Add to stock, vinegar, and olive oil or butter. Bring to a boil, then simmer to reduce for 25 minutes. Serve over the cooked strained vegetables.

Source: Apicius, *The Roman Cookery of Apicius: A Treasury of Gourmet Recipes & Herbal Cookery*, translated by John Edwards (Port Roberts, Wash.: Hartley & Marks, 1984).

---

tal skin afflictions as well. Helping to understand why the Romans had a less-restrictive attitude toward sexuality is the fact that they were not subject to potentially fatal venereal diseases. Certainly the Romans were inflicted with pneumonia (in various forms), cancer, typhus, gout (although a cluster of afflictions passed under its name, *podagra*), tuberculosis, pinta, yaws (the microorganism of which eventually evolved into the one causing endemic syphilis), and malaria, the latter being prevalent. Indeed, one theory for the fall of the Roman Empire was the sustained, corrosive effects of malaria as it sapped lives and energies, especially in the Mediterranean areas. Additionally they had many degenerative chest, skin, and eye diseases. Nothing that we know about ancient Roman medicine indicates that their physicians could have intervened to the extent of curing most major diseases. In those cases, the most that they did was to provide symptomatic relief and comfort.

Medical Knowledge. Two features characterize early Roman medicine: the ideal of the head of the family (*paterfamilias*) having sufficient medical knowledge to treat his family, slaves, and clients; and the handbook tradition of summarizing empirical cures for written transmission to supplement oral lore. Knowledge passed from father to son, mother to daughter, and wise woman to young woman or man probably accounted for medical therapies that most Romans received, especially those living during the Republic. Supplementary medical knowledge derived from herbalists and other pharmaceutical vendors as they plied their wares. Beginning in the third century B.C.E., Greek physicians established medical practices in Rome and other Latin-speaking areas, and, with them, the face of Roman medicine was altered—not without protest, however, from conservative-minded Romans, such as Cato the Elder and Pliny the Elder. Part of the reason for the Romans' negative reaction to Greek medicine might be attributed to the fact that early Greek physicians tended to be slaves or freedmen.

Ambivalence to Greek Medicine. Easily, Cato the Elder (234–149 B.C.E.) epitomizes Rome's love/hate relationship with Greek medicine. On one hand, he warns his sons to beware the Greeks bearing medicine, and yet, in his handbook on agriculture he proudly displays his knowledge of theoretical medicine from Greek authorities. Pliny the Elder exhibited the same ambivalence. Caustically, Pliny charged that the physicians are the only people who can murder with impunity. Greek medicine had some advantages, Cato thought, but the father of a Roman family ought to have enough native intelligence together with experience with illnesses, injuries, and cures to be able to practice medicine effectively. Cato's only surviving work, *De agricultura* (160 B.C.E.), contains some of the medical lore expected to be known by a Roman. The older Romans considered the maintenance of good health an individual responsibility. Echoing Cato, Marcus Terentius Varro (116–27 B.C.E.) gave practical advice on farming that included medical and nutritional lore. Varro's work, *De re rustica* (37 B.C.E., three books), exemplified the Roman handbook tradition with respect to medicine.

Surgery. A procedure that ancient physicians considered the last resort, surgery was used only when regimen or drug therapy was deemed not to be effective. Most physicians practiced minor surgery, but, at least in populous areas, there were specialized surgeons—some of whom had reputations for certain procedures. Celsus, in a first century C.E. treatise on medicine, described the ideal surgeon. Surgical instruments found in archaeological sites have familiar functions, such as scalpels, forceps, hooks, and probes, designs similar to those used in modern surgeries. Anesthetics were not totally lacking, although patients must have experienced pain in many instances. Physicians employed plants containing atropine and hyoscyamine to reduce pain, and Dioscorides mentions the Memphis stone that surgeons employed so that

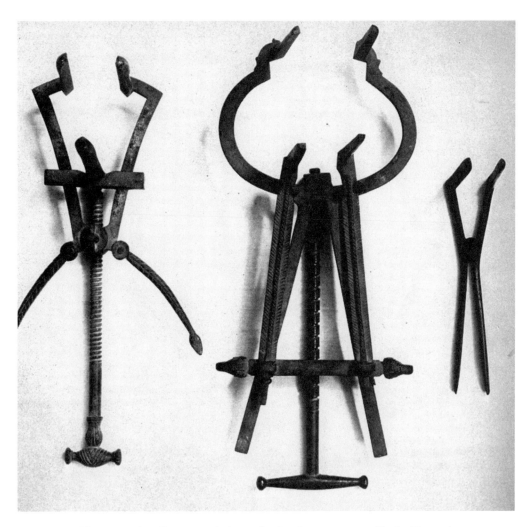

Three examples of bronze vaginal specula, circa first century C.E. (Naples Museum)

the patients would have no pain during operations. It is not known what that mineral was. Although powerful antiseptics were lacking, surgeons used plant resins to treat wounds and heal sutures, and these had mild antiseptic qualities.

The Humors. By the third century B.C.E. many physicians had adopted an evolving theory of medicine based on humors, or body fluids. Blood, phlegm, yellow bile, and black bile were believed to correspond respectively to the four elements of air, water, fire, and earth.

Schools of Medicine. Medical education in Rome, before and after Hellenistic influences, was achieved the same way as all the craftsmanship skills, namely, with master practitioners training young men as apprentices. A school of medicine, not as the familiar institution for medical education in the late medieval and modern worlds, was a group of like-minded people who shared common perspectives and theories. Despite some measure of agreement, not all physicians accepted the existence of four humors—some espousing the existence of more humors, some fewer, as well as disputing their relative importance. After the great medical researchers Herophilus and Erasistratos, Greek medicine broke up into com-

peting, and often contentious, schools, beginning with the conflict between the Empiricists and the Dogmatists. Empiricists insisted that it was impossible for the physician to penetrate the mysteries of the body and, consequently, viewed each disease as a unique event. They based their therapies on empirical cures and, along the way, rejected anatomy as irrelevant to medical practice. Autopsies could not inform one about a live body, they argued, and, besides, dissections were disgusting. In contrast, the Dogmatists appealed to theory and reason, regarded rigorous study as necessary, especially in anatomy, and believed that ultimately diseases had causes that were ascertainable.

Methodists and Empiricists. Between these two poles of the Empiricists and the Dogmatists, other schools of medicine developed whose influence was felt in Rome and, presumably, throughout the empire. One such school was that of the Methodists, who, like the Empiricists, rejected causation and anatomy but embraced a theory that all illnesses were based on an imbalance of moisture. An affliction caused too great an increase in wetness or dryness, either generally throughout the body or in specific locations. The physician's duty was to learn

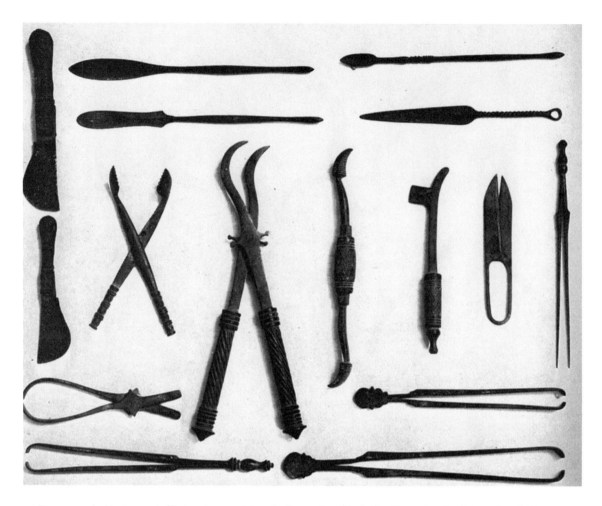

Bronze surgical instruments (first century C.E.) found at Pompeii and including flat probes (top), large "uvula" forceps (center left), scalpels (far left), and small forceps (bottom) (Naples Museum)

the cause and restore the balance by the administration of diet and/or drugs, according to opposites. Thus, a drying drug would restore an excessively moist condition. Allegedly Thessalus, a leading Methodist, claimed that he could train a full-fledged physician in six months!

Pneumatist School. Athenaeus of Attaleia (dated variously in the first centuries B.C.E. or C.E.) founded another school, the Pneumatists, but, although influential, none of its early adherents' works have survived. Closely associated with the Stoic school of philosophy, the Pneumatists postulated the existence of *pneuma* (literally, "breath") that gave vital spirits to all forms of animal life. Medicine, as they regarded it, was an essential part of a liberal education. The Pneumatists influenced Roman medicine specifically by an emphasis on diet.

Asclepiadian School. Practicing in Rome for at least part of his career, Asclepiades of Prusias and Mare (first century B.C.E.) developed a corpuscular theory of physiology. He believed that the body functioned through its composition of tiny, fragile corpuscles that moved through ducts. When the free movement was halted through injury or disease, the blockages caused morbid elements. Asclepiades and his followers attempted to employ noninvasive therapies that opened these ducts.

Diet, fasting, massage, exercise, and baths were preferred to drugs and were considered the first avenues of address. Drugs could be administered in critical afflictions, however, and surgery was rarely prescribed. Their theme was "To cure, safely, swiftly, and pleasantly." Needless to say, the Asclepiadian school had some popularity among the Romans.

Cold Baths. A follower of Asclepiades, freedman Antonius Musa (flourishing 20s B.C.E.) achieved a celebrated reputation as a physician. He devised a cold-bath therapy that attained fame when he cured Augustus Caesar in 23 B.C.E. So successful was he with his cold hydrotherapy that he won not only a fortune but also immunity from taxation both for himself and his profession. He wrote on pharmacy, but his work does not survive.

Greatest Medical Authority. Interestingly, Rome's greatest native writer on medicine in Latin may not have been a physician. A member of the famous Cornelian family, we know that Aulus Cornelius Celsus (flourishing 25 C.E.) wrote a large encyclopedia titled *Artes* and, as part of it, there were eight books on medicine. The only sections of the work surviving are the medical books. The technical skill with which he presented medicine causes modern scholars and physicians to believe that only a practitioner of medicine could have written with such clinical exactitude. Pointing to the fact that medical learning was expected of Senatorial and Equestrian class Romans, other scholars argue that, despite the sophisticated, practical erudition, Celsus's work indicates the level of knowledge that at least one well-educated Roman had. Whatever their persuasion on this dispute, Celsus is generally regarded as the best general medical writer in Latin.

History of Medicine. The surviving section of his work is called *De medicina* ("On Medicine"). After a learned introduction, Celsus gave an extraordinarily valuable history of medicine, especially concerning the Greek Alexandrians, Herophilus and Erasistratus. He had an ambivalent attitude toward the Greeks, among whom "this art [of medicine] has been cultivated much more than in other nations." In the introduction to his work, however, he asserted that even "the most uncivilized nations have had a knowledge of herbs, and other things to hand for the aiding of wounds and diseases" (1–2). After the introductory historical section, Celsus begins his summary of medicine with general dietetics and discusses pathology, general and special therapies, drugs, surgery, and bone diseases. The work is so well written that some scholars were led to claim that Celsus must have simply translated an unknown, lost work from Greek to Latin. Most scholars now agree that the work reflects no indications of having been a translation and that Celsus was an author of great literary and medical skills.

Greek Medical Writers. Even during the empire, if elite attitudes are indicated from surviving works, the Romans distrusted Greek medicine, and yet, the greatest medical writers of antiquity in terms of influence on later generations lived and practiced medicine in Greece. Most of what we know of Roman medicine comes through the writings of three such persons: Dioscorides, Soranus, and Galen.

Pharmacy. Nothing is distinctive about the actual drugs that the Romans employed. Generally, the Romans used many of the same drugs that were known by ancient Mediterranean peoples. The various plants, minerals, and animal products were much the same whether found in Greek or Latin texts. Indeed, most of the drugs are the same as those found in the various medical papyri of the ancient Egyptians, some of which date back to the New Kingdom, circa 3000 B.C.E., and various Sumerian, Akkadian, and Assyrian pharmaceutical tablets. Laxatives are one example. Most of the laxatives employed today are the same as those used for four thousand years. Among the drugs the Romans used were almond oil, aloes, ammoniacum, belladonna, calamine, calcium hydrate, castor oil, cherry syrup, cinnamon, copper oxide, coriander, galbanum, galls, ginger, St. John's wort, juniper, lavender, lead acetate, marjoram, mastic, mercury, olive oil, opium, pepper, pine bark, storax, sulfur, terebinth, thyme, willow bark, and wormwood. Cato the Censor and Pliny the Elder both championed old-fashioned Roman home remedies in preference to the drugs of foreigners, especially Greeks, but in truth most of the drugs were herbs, and most of them were similarly used regardless of culture. The Romans employed drugs primarily to treat symptoms, and they had few drugs that truly were pathological cures. Occasionally new drugs or new uses for known drugs, were discovered. For example, sometime in the Roman period, likely during the Roman Empire, they discovered that the plant autumn crocus cured gout. This plant contains colchicine, the drug currently employed for gout. Colchicine functions to break the chemical chain reaction that leads to inflammation in joint tissue. Many of the drugs the Romans employed came from east Africa, India, and even Malaysia and China, thereby producing an unfavorable balance of trade and causing money to flow out of the empire. The only drug that East Asians imported from Rome was saffron, but soon the Indians and Chinese learned to cultivate it themselves, so it was no longer imported.

Standard Authority. The empirical science of taking certain drugs for specific maladies constituted most of pharmaceutical medicine until Pedanius Dioscorides of Anazarbus (flourishing 50–70 C.E.), a Greek physician, traveled widely in search of new drugs among various ethnic groups. Dioscorides was the author of a five-book work on pharmacy called *Peri hulēs iatrikēs*, or, in Latin, *De materia medica*. So thorough, precise, and authoritative was Dioscorides that his work remained the standard authority on pharmacy through the sixteenth century. While in a medical practice, his keen observational powers, diligence in scholarship, and critical faculties resulted in a study of around one thousand *pharmaka*, or drugs. Most of the drugs were from the plant kingdom, loosely called herbs, but two sections (part of book 4 and all of book 5) discuss drugs derived from the animal and mineral kingdoms, respectively. His method, as he explained it, was to read in the libraries what every authority had written on the subject of a particular drug, to observe the drug in its environment, in particular habitats and growing conditions, to inquire among the natives of each region where he traveled regarding their use and experiences with the drug, and, finally, to test the drugs himself in clinical trials. Only when a detail had received that level of attention did he have a "fact" to relate. In library research, Dioscorides names some twenty-seven authorities. Each chapter of his work is devoted to a single plant, although he would group related "kinds," or what we would call species or subspecies, within the same genera. He followed (or devised) a method for relating the material that would subsequently be adopted as the format for herbals: (1) picture; (2) name of plant, sometimes with synonyms; (3) botanical descriptions; (4) habitats; (5) drug properties or types of actions, such as "astringent," "drying," and "cooling"; (6) medicinal uses; (7) harmful side effects; (8) quantities and dosages; (9) harvesting, preparation, and storage instructions; (10) adulteration, methods, and tests for detection; and (11) veterinary uses. In his introductory letter, Dioscorides boasted that his work surpassed previous pharmaceutical writings because of his superior organization. He did not explain what his organizing scheme was; thus, it was left to readers to discern. The overall organization is apparent: book one, for example, begins with aromatic herbs, followed by oils, ointments, resins, shrubs, trees, and fruit trees; book two starts with animal drugs, first with specific animals and ending with animal products (such as milk, fats, and blood), then cereals, pot herbs, and sharp herbs. Within each category, however, there appears some order, foreshadowing the modern scientific binomial classification scheme devised by the Swedish botanist Carolus Linnaeus in the eighteenth century. Dioscorides appeared to have classified plants by linking together related species within the same genus. At other times there are inconsistent interruptions in how the chapters are arranged. Recent scholarship discloses that Dioscorides was arranging his chapters by how the total medicinal uses related to other similar drugs, or, in other words, by drug affinities. This organization explains why there appears some botanical scheme, because related plants tend to have similar chemistries. Because Dioscorides' scheme was little appreciated or understood by later imitators who otherwise followed his methods, his organizational genius had little subsequent influence.

Gynecology. During the period of the writings attributed to Hippocrates, circa 460–330 B.C.E., there were several gynecological works produced. They were written by men and were mostly compilations of midwife practices. During the Roman Empire, a writer on gynecology truly elevated the art of women's medicine. In the words of Owsei Temkin, Soranus of Ephesus (flourishing early second century C.E.) was "one of the most learned, critical, and lucid authors of antiquity." He wrote on many medical subjects, such as acute and chronic diseases, causes of diseases, medicaments, surgery, bandages, ophthalmology, and, more philosophically, on the soul. None of those works survived except for portions preserved in the texts of later writers. What survived was influential—a masterful treatise on gynecology, called *Gynaecia*, in four books. Details of his life are few: we know that he practiced in Rome during the reigns of Trajan and Hadrian and that he received some medical training in Alexandria. Indirect evidence indicates that he learned medicine also in Ephesus. Clearly he subscribed to the Methodist School, but he was not dogmatic in applying its theoretical constructs when he saw clinical evidence pointing elsewhere. Soranus used some theoretical constructs derived from the Alexandrian physiologists and anatomists as a basis for his observations.

Women's Health. Book one defines the ideal midwife (sober, literate, displaying integrity, free from superstition, knowledgeable both in theory and practice, compassionate, and charging no excessive fees). Soranus eschewed the magic and superstition that pervaded midwifery practices, but he said that such practices, when they resulted in no harm, could be useful in gaining a

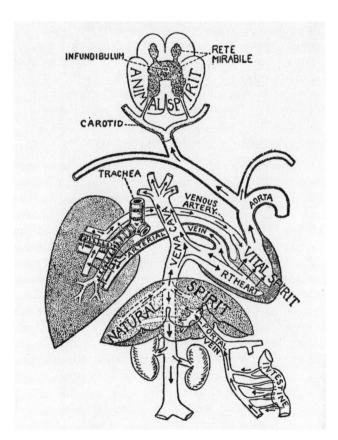

Schematic representation of Galen's concept of physiology showing the function of the three principal organs: brain, heart, and liver (from John Scarborough, *Roman Medicine,* 1969)

patient's confidence and reducing stress. The remainder of his book discusses feminine physiology and hygiene, menstruation, conception, pregnancy, and birth control. About the latter, Soranus clearly distinguished between contraception and abortion, saying that the former was safer than the latter. He said that pessary birth-control agents are less safe and effective than oral drugs. Book 2 deals with obstetrics, including regular and abnormal deliveries, nursing, infant hygiene, and childhood diseases. Book 3 concerns women's diseases, where he asserts that women have some afflictions that men do not. The fourth and final book concerns diseases that are addressed pharmaceutically and surgically. During the Middle Ages, Soranus's gynecology was not translated into Latin, and so his influence was confined to derived influence through other writers, that is, until the Renaissance.

Medicine, Physiology, and Anatomy. Most of the ancient medical theory regarding physiology and therapeutics we know through the incredibly detailed works Galen of Pergamum (circa 129/130 C.E.–post 204). Galen was the practitioner who casts the greatest shadow on Western, Islamic, and Hellenistic medical science. Because of his dominance and strongly stated, somewhat egocentric opinions, we often do not know what is original in Galen and how much he was summarizing consensus opinions about medicine. In reading Galen's works, one can be certain that medicine after him was dominated by his assertions. Son of Nikon, an architect and geometer, Galen began studies in philosophy at the age of fourteen but two years later turned to what was to be his life's profession. His grounding in geometry is said to have guided his logical mind in a life of practice, research, and writing. Galen came to value the anatomical and physiological studies of Herophilus and Erasistratus, as well as the earlier basic studies attributed to Hippocrates. Although human dissection was no longer a permissible study in his era, Galen conducted comparative anatomical studies on a variety of animals, including monkeys, sheep, and, once, even an elephant. When he was twenty-eight, he returned to Pergamum where he was engaged as a physician to a gladiator company. His practice enabled him to explore human anatomy as he attempted to reconstruct and heal the injured and maimed. Galen's intense interest in anatomy and physiology extended to some experimentation such as ligating or severing a spinal cord and inserting a tube in an artery to test for pulse. Galen not only accepted the scheme that included the four humors, but also he gave logical structure and evidence for their operation, such that medical science was persuaded by his theories for the next fifteen hundred years. Galen connected some illnesses with the mind and said that it could make a healthy body sick and a sick body healthy. Dreams, he stated, were one of the means by which the body informed the mind about what was wrong with it.

Distinguished Career. Galen's greatest anatomical writings were produced in Rome, where he went to practice in 161; there he acquired a great reputation. Galen regarded the body as centering on three organs, with ancillary dependence on them by other organs. The heart, brain, and liver control systems throughout the body. While borrowing from his predecessors, Galen was at once a synthesizer of previous works, a marvelous organizer, a severe critic, and a true contributor to medicine through his own research. He explained well the processes of digestion, assimilation (what is called metabolism), nerve and respiration function, blood formation, and embryological developments.

Circulatory Theory. While accepting Erasistratus's assertion that the arteries function to provide *pneuma* (literally, "breath," but more broadly, "vital spirits") pumped by the heart from the left ventricle, Galen added that the arteries normally carried blood as well. The Alexandrians believed that arteries contained blood in times of disease and that the spurts of blood apparently issuing from a severed artery were the consequence of a vacuum and venal blood rushing to fill it. Galen claimed that the arterial and venal systems exchanged blood through tiny, invisible pores in the ventral walls. Not until English anatomist William Harvey's theory of blood circulation published in 1628 was Galen disproved.

Drug Dosage. In many ways Galen disrupted Dioscorides' organization of drugs by affinities, when in three major works on pharmacy he proposed an alternate theory of drug behavior, one closely related to the Empedoclean theory of the four elements. Galen noted that minute amounts of drugs have little or no perceptible effect, but with increased amounts, benefits are perceived. Continue increasing the amount, he argued, and at some point the benefits diminish. This phenomenon is called dosage. According to Galen each drug had a potential of up to four degrees of activity in each of two ways: either warming or cooling (derived from its active quality) and either moistening or drying (its passive quality). The strongest drugs had four degrees of activity either actively or passively. A fourth-degree drug was potentially life-threatening and should be employed for only the most severe cases, whereas one degree of activity was almost imperceptibly mild. Thus, applying by opposites, a fever needed a cooling drug. A high fever in a child required a less strong drug than the same fever in an old person. To complicate the matter—nature is not simple—a drug that is, for example, three degrees cooling will have a passive quality that is one of four degrees of moistening or cooling. In prescribing medicines, Galen's theory is intellectually challenging, but it worked according to the ancients' perceptions of healing and curing. Galen warned that only experience demonstrated a drug's actions, not logic derived from sense perception. Seawater, for example, is sensibly moistening, and yet, internally as a drug it is drying. This pharmaceutical theory replaced Dioscorides' more clinical approach. Finally, Galen organized his order in relating drugs by the alphabet, a system that medieval copyists and simple medical personnel found more attractive because of its convenience.

Lasting Influence. Galen's influence was tremendous because of the volume of his writings, the logical structure of his observations (fitting within the framework of accepted scientific or philosophical principles), and the authority with which he wrote. Even serious attacks on his systems during the sixteenth century did not eliminate his influence on medicine altogether.

Late Roman Medicine. Toward the end of the Roman Empire, more public support was given to medical education. Alexander Severus (208–235 C.E.) granted privileges for medical instruction, and those who taught it were granted citizenship. In the fourth century C.E., medical students were supervised and required to attend lectures in the *gymnasia*. Julian (361–363 C.E.) decreed that physicians needed to be a member of a guild and licensed to practice. Although seemingly progressive, such measures were doubtlessly a response to abuse and a general decline in medical practice. After Galen, Roman medicine declined along with the infrastructure of the ancient state. This deterioration of medical practice is not to say that there were not physicians who delivered learned and dedicated services, nor was there a lack of medical writers who contributed to knowledge.

Medical Advances. Rufus of Ephesus (second century C.E.) wrote a Latin work on anatomy, dietetics, and pathology from which came important contributions on the pulse, kidney diseases, satyriasis, jaundice, gout, and gonorrhea. Oribasius (circa 320–400 C.E.), a friend and physician to the Emperor Julian, wrote a medical encyclopedia in the Roman handbook tradition that preserves large sections of medical writings that otherwise would have been lost. For example, the contributions to surgery by Archigenes (flourishing under Trajan) and Heliodorus (dates unknown), both advocates for the Pneumatic school, were incorporated in Oribasius's work. Portions of Heliodorus's surgery are known in Latin manuscript texts. Antyllus (second century C.E.) described aneurysms; these contributions would have been unknown or unattributed were it not for the references in Oribasius. He even included some works by Galen that were otherwise lost.

Acute and Chronic. In the early Roman Empire several medical works were produced on acute and chronic diseases—the latter supposedly being untreatable. Themison (late first century B.C.E.) of the Methodist School first set forth treatments for chronic diseases. Whereas Themison's works did not survive, those of his followers did, among which were Aretaeus of Cappadocia (flourishing during the time of Trajan, 98–117 C.E.), Caelius Aurelianus (circa fifth century C.E.), and an anonymous author whose influence was felt strongly in the Middle Ages. Although some ancients recognized a bifurcation of diseases, by the time Aretaeus wrote, both types received therapeutic intervention by physicians. Written in Greek, Aretaeus's nosology (the science of disease description) was especially good (for example, his description of pleurisy), and he is the first physician to describe elephantiasis. Aretaeus's devotion to a physician's compassionate duty earned for him a high reputation. Caelius wrote separately on acute and chronic diseases. Both Aretaeus and Caelius were also reportedly members of the Pneumatic School. An unknown author wrote a similar treatise, perhaps around the fifth century C.E. He is known as Anonymous Parisinus, because the major surviving manuscript is located in Paris. Similar in arrangement with Aretaeus and Caelius, the text begins by concentrating on sixteen acute diseases, followed by thirty-nine chronic diseases, with both sections arranged by the "from head to foot" format. The acute diseases are: head (phrenitis, lethargy, epilepsy, apoplexy, cephalea), neck (angina, tetanus), chest (pleuritis, peripneumonia, syncope), esophagus (hydrophobia), peritoneum (cholera), intestines (ileus, colic), and sexual organs (satyriasis). Chronic diseases begin with vertigo, madness, fanaticism, and various forms of paralysis (for the head) and end with sciatica, arthritis, gout (joints), and elephantiasis.

Head-to-Foot Pharmacology. Marcellus Empiricus (flourishing late fourth century C.E.) wrote a work on pharmacy that combined learned Greek and Roman medical knowledge with traditional Roman lore and popular Celtic and other folk knowledge. Cassius Felix (died circa 447 C.E.) wrote a similar work, but one that was more based on learned medicine especially derived from Galen. Theodorus Priscianus served as a physician to the emperor Gratian (367–383 C.E.) and wrote *Euphoriston*,

in three books. Organized "from head to foot," book one deals with external ailments, two with internal medicine, and three with female disorders. Primarily, Theodorus's value lies in the variety of his pharmaceutical prescriptions. With the pseudonym of Apuleius, an anonymous writer, probably in the fourth century, wrote a Latin herbal, with colored drawings of the plants, that enjoyed great popularity in the Middle Ages. Similarly, another writer about the same time composed an illustrated herbal titled *De herbis femininis* (On Female Herbs) that was popular and passed under the name of Dioscorides.

Women's Issues. Enjoying popularity during the Middle Ages was a medical poem in hexameters, called *Liber medicinalis*, written by Quintus Serenus (Sammonicus) in the late second to fourth century C.E. In gynecology, Moschion (sixth century C.E.) wrote *De mulieribus passionibus*, largely based on Soranus. Passing under the erroneous name of Cleopatra (in an allusion to the famous Egyptian queen), an unknown author (possibly fourth or fifth century C.E.) wrote a treatise in Greek called *Genesia;* an early Latin translation listed several abortifacients but, curiously, no contraceptives.

Sources:

Lawrence J. Bliquez, *Roman Surgical Instruments and Other Minor Objects in the National Archaeological Museum of Naples* (Mainz, Germany: Verlag Phlipp von Zabern, 1994).

Mirko D. Grmek, *Diseases in the Ancient World,* translated by Mireille Muellner and Leonard Muellner (Baltimore: Johns Hopkins University Press, 1989).

Ralph Jackson, *Doctors and Diseases in the Roman Empire* (London: British Museum Publications, 1988).

John M. Riddle, *Dioscorides on Pharmacy and Medicine* (Austin: University of Texas Press, 1985).

Guy Sabbah and others, eds., *Bibliographie des textes médicaux latins: antiquité et haut Moyen Age* (Saint-Étienne: Université de Saint-Etienne, 1987).

John Scarborough, *Roman Medicine* (London: Thames & Hudson, 1969; Ithaca, N.Y.: Cornell University Press, 1969).

TRANSMISSION OF LATER ROMAN SCIENCE

The Transmitters. The handbook format was the most enduring form for the contributions that the Romans made to science. From the third century C.E. a group of writers in Latin wrote handbooks that served as textbooks for the Middle Ages. Prominent among them were Solinus, Calcidius, Macrobius, Martianus Capella, Boethius, and Isidore of Seville. Roman mathematics was transmitted by Calcidius and Boethius, astronomy and geography by Macrobius, the seven liberal arts by Martianus Capella, and an encyclopedia by Solinus and Isidore.

Transmitting Mathematics and Astronomy. Calcidius (or Chalcidius, flourishing fourth century C.E.) is virtually unknown as a person, but his Latin translation of Plato and commentary were widely used. He dedicated his work to Osius (or Hosius), who is speculatively identified with the person of the same name who attended the Council of Nicea in 325 C.E. Calcidius made a partial translation into Latin of Plato's *Timaeus* and was the primary means through which Plato was known to the Middle Ages. In addition, he provided a commentary on Plato that incorporates higher mathematical concepts (for example, Pythagorean notions of varying units or numbers, and numerical rations of the harmonic intervals in the musical scale) and theoretical discussions of planetary and stellar motions. To explain Plato, Calcidius borrowed heavily from Theon's *Manual* (circa 364 C.E.).

Boethius. Boethius (circa 480–524 C.E.) was the most influential of all Roman writers in transmitting Roman mathematics. Unlike many of the transmitters, we know Boethius through many details of his life as a Roman senator and intellect in the court of Theoderic (454–526 C.E.). The English historian Edward Gibbon said of Boethius that he is the last of the Romans whom Cato or Cicero would have acknowledged as a fellow countryman. Boethius was fluent in Greek and availed himself of Greek texts, but wrote in Latin. Perhaps Boethius is best known for *The Consolation of Philosophy*, a Platonic dialogue between him and Lady Philology, an important avenue by which Stoicism came to Christianity. It was long thought, although not by present scholars, that Boethius was a Christian and, in reading Stoicism, medieval persons thought it was Christian philosophy. Among his writings, three were on mathematics. *On Arithmetic* was, Boethius acknowledged, a free, improved version of Nicomachus's *Introduction to Arithmetic* (circa 100 C.E.), clearly written and suitable for teaching. Boethius disagreed with Martianus Capella that the first position belonged to geometry. Arithmetic underlies the mathematical sciences, Boethius proclaimed. He asserted that there was a fourfold path—arithmetic, geometry, astronomy, and music—and, for the first time, employed the now-famous word, *quadrivium*, destined to organize the medieval curriculum. His second work, *On Music*, served as a textbook as late as the eighteenth century in Oxford. His restoration of music placed it in the curriculum from which it had fallen. He employed Nicomachus's *Manual on Harmony* and Ptolemy's *Harmonics*, both explications of Pythagorean axioms of musical chords and theories of the harmony of the spheres, involving numerical ratios of consonance and dissonance, analogies between the musical scales and planetary movements, and music theory—the ancient counterpart of modern musicology. The third contribution is a manual of geometry, but the surviving copies have emendations, and scholars have not isolated Boethius's text from the additions. Likely he completed the fourth of his *quadrivium*, a manual on astronomy, but, if so, it is lost. Much of what the Middle Ages learned about arithmetic and music came from Boethius.

Macrobius. Macrobius was central in transmitting Roman science. Ambrosius Theodosius Macrobius (flourishing early fifth century) was a high government official in North Africa. Probably in the 430s he wrote a series of works that were destined to be important to medieval thought regarding science. His seven-book *Saturnalia* is the last example of the ancient genre called "banquet" literature, among the earliest being Plato's *Symposium*. A fictional banquet conversation is portrayed by attendees who were "real" people but whose dialogue was devised by Macrobius. Fittingly, *Saturnalia* begins with a discussion about the proper date on which the ancient holiday was to begin. This discussion led to a discourse on the Roman calendar in which the authorities of Varro, Aulus Gellius, and Plutarch were invoked. Macrobius's greatest work in terms of scientific influence was *The Dream of Scipio*, where dreams, mathematics, cosmology, and world geography were subjects of learned discourse. The framework of the work was ostensibly Cicero's dream. Macrobius had no hesitation about attributing Neoplatonic concepts to Cicero, who lived approximately three hundred years before Plotinus (205–circa 270 C.E.) founded the Neoplatonic School. Number lore was summarized intriguingly from the Pythagoreans. Macrobius employed pseudo-Iamblichus's *Theology of Arithmetic* and Nicomachus's work (now lost), by the same name, to explore numbers as an asserted means of understanding the physical world. Much of the cosmology came from Porphyry's lost commentary on the *Timaeus*. He argued that the earth was a sphere and around it revolved the moon, sun, and five planets, and that the outmost sphere rotated daily from east to west. Each of the planets had its motion caused by being dragged by the outer sphere of fixed stars. The more distant a planet was from the earth, the greater the time required for its earthly circuit. He connected planetary movements with Pythagorean musical scales in a theory appealing to medieval thought. The zodiac, Milky Way, and eclipses are explained. Asserting that his authority was the ancient Egyptians, Macrobius was critical of Eratosthenes' and Posidonius's calculations regarding the circumference of the earth and the relative distances of sun, moon, and earth. Falsely he quoted Eratosthenes as claiming the sun was twenty-seven times greater than the earth and that Posidonius's figure was "many, many times greater." In invoking the "ancient Egyptians" Macrobius was likely influenced by, if not copying from, the popular Hermetic literature that purportedly reclaimed lost Egyptian "secrets." The cone of the earth's shadow as cast by the sun extended, he claimed, sixty earth-diameters, a number double Hipparchus's estimate. He adopted without attribution Eratosthenes' figure of 252,000 stades as the circumference of the earth, and the diameter as 80,000 stades. Multiplying the latter by 60 (the apex of the earth's shadow), he arrived at 4,800,000 stades as the distance between the earth and sun. In these and other calculations Macrobius attempted to impress his readers with his authority in devising elaborate mathematical calculations by using simple geometry. In what today is refered to as "cooking the data," Macrobius wanted to connect ratios and celestial movements in a way that proved harmony and order. Among his authorities for his "data" were Cleomedes, Geminus, Posidonius, Pliny, and Vitruvius.

Seven Liberal Arts. What became the core educational curriculum for Western Europe was based on the work of

Martianus Capella (circa fifth century). Little is known about his life, although he is truly one of the most important Roman writers on science. It is hardly an exaggeration to say that he wrote a textbook that lasted for a thousand years, the envy of any modern writer. The nine-book work, symbolizing the combination of pagan and Christian learning, is presented allegorically as a wedding. It is titled *The Marriage of Philology and Mercury*, with Lady Philology the symbol for Christian learning and Mercury, the pagan messenger god, for pagan learning. Each of the bridesmaids was a "subject" in the curriculum. First down the aisle and constituting book one was Lady Grammar, followed by Dialectic and Rhetoric, each containing a discussion with the spokesperson for that art. Grammar was a stern old woman ready to whack those not learning her rules, whereas Dialectic was a woman "whose weapons are complex and knotty utterances" and Rhetoric was of "outstanding beauty" and "abounding in self-confidence." Next came four bridesmaids—geometry, arithmetic, astronomy, and harmony (for example, music). The first three will come to be called the *Trivium* and the last four, the *Quadrivium*. Together they constituted the seven liberal arts (*artes liberales*, or *studia liberalia*, the pursuits befitting a free man), the curriculum for monastic and cathedral schools, the latter of which evolved into modern universities. In the last four books, Martianus Capella summarizes Roman science.

Roman Encyclopedic Tradition Transmitted. A tradition of compiling all kinds of informational data in an encyclopedia began with Pliny's *Natural History* (circa 75 C.E.). Two writers in the late Roman period summarized Pliny, with additions and subtractions according to the different disposition of the Christian era. Iulius Solinus (flourishing third century C.E.) and Isidore of Seville (circa 560–636 C.E.) summarized general knowledge of the ancients, and their works were those principally relied upon during the early Middle Ages. Little is known of Solinus's life, but his work had great appeal because it preserved various facts about the world in an almost encyclopedic manner. Primarily, Solinus's work is a compilation about geography, customs, and places. Although largely without original material, Solinus introduced the name "Mare Mediterraneum" for the sea known in English as the Mediterranean.

Schoolmaster of the Middle Ages. Isidore of Seville wrote a twenty-book encyclopedia, titled *Origines* (Origins), which summarizes the learning of antiquity through Latin authors. In 1999 a Pontifical Council of the Roman Catholic Church officially designated Isidore as the patron saint of computer technicians and users, computers, and the Internet. This assignment is appropriate, because like the Internet, Isidore had a fund of knowledge, but he uncritically presented it in such a way that fact and fiction are difficult to distinguish. The *Origines* was based on the hypothesis that the meaning of a word informs one about its original significance. In twenty books he dealt with astronomy, mathematics, geometry, medicine, mineralogy, human anatomy, zoology, meteorology, geography, botany, and agriculture. He asserted that originally there was primordial matter that changed according to the elemental qualities of coldness, dryness, wetness, and hotness. All elemental qualities created matter and were constantly in flux. Things on earth arranged themselves by weight, such as birds in the air, fish in water, and animals on earth. Humans were the central purpose for creation. Astronomy was a ticklish subject for a Christian writer who attempted to summarize the subject. It is not surprising that the first printed map in Europe is from Isidore, showing a flat, tripartite world with heaven above, Jerusalem in the center, Asia accounting for one-half of the land surface, Europe and Africa equally divided, and all continents surrounded by the ocean. Even so, Isidore's encyclopedia contained much of the learning of Roman science.

Sources:
Margaret Gibson, ed., *Boethius, His Life, Thought, and Influence* (Oxford: Blackwell, 1981).

David C. Lindberg, *The Beginnings of Western Science: The European Scientific Tradition in Philosophical, Religious, and Institutional Context, 600 B.C. to A.D. 1450* (Chicago: University of Chicago Press, 1992).

William Harris Stahl, *Roman Science: Origins, Development, and Influence to the Later Middle Ages* (Madison: University of Wisconsin Press, 1962).

SIGNIFICANT PEOPLE

ARATUS OF SOLI

CIRCA 310–CIRCA 240 B.C.E.
POET, ASTRONOMER

Influential Poet. Little is known of Aratus's life. Four letters allegedly written by him appear in an edition collected by Suidas, a Byzantine biographer, but likely they are spurious. This much can be reconstructed: he left his home of Soli in Cilicia for Athens, where he became intrigued by Stoic philosophy. Later he appeared in the courts of Antigonus Gonatas of Macedonia and Antiochus I of Syria. He prepared editions of Homer's *Odyssey* and *Iliad* and a poem celebrating the marriage of Antigonus Gonatas to Phile. His most influential work was the poem *Phaenomena*, which introduced Romans to Greek astronomy and meteorology. A celebrated piece of literature, it was translated into Latin and Arabic.

Sources:
Emma Gee, *Ovid, Aratus, and Augustus: Astronomy in Ovid's Fasti* (Cambridge & New York: Cambridge University Press, 2000).

G. J. Toomer, "Aratus," in *The Oxford Classical Dictionary,* edited by Simon Hornblower and Antony Spawforth, third edition (Oxford: Oxford University Press, 1999), p. 136.

ARCHIMEDES

CIRCA 287–212 B.C.E.
SCIENTIST, MATHEMATICIAN

Inventor. The Son of Phidias, an astronomer, Archimedes lived in the Greek city-state of Syracuse. Probably the greatest scientist and mathematician in antiquity, Archimedes's contributions to mechanics, physics, and mathematics were admired by later scientists, including the eighteenth-century English physicist Isaac Newton. His fame became legendary when he was attributed as saving his city from Roman sieges during the Second Punic War (218–201 B.C.E.). He was allegedly bathing when the mathematical formula for the displacement of water occurred to him and caused him to run through the streets of Syracuse shouting, "*Hêurêka* [I have found it]!" Among his inventions were a screw for lifting water, a planetarium, and a star globe. While there is no evidence that he visited Alexandria, he corresponded with Eratosthenes and other researchers at the Museum. Ultimately, despite his mechanical inventions, Syracuse fell to the Romans and Archimedes, while teaching, was killed by a Roman soldier.

Contributions. Archimedes developed and wrote about mathematical formulae to determine the volume of such shapes as cones and spheres, the properties of spirals and parabolas, and large-number theory. He broke boundaries in mathematics, wrote treatises in mechanics and mathematics, was an astronomer, and may even have invented a game.

Sources:
E. J. Dijksterhuis, *Archimedes,* translated by C. Dikshoorn (Princeton: Princeton University Press, 1987).

Sherman Stein, *Archimedes: What Did He Do Besides Cry Eureka?* (Washington, D.C.: Mathematical Association of America, 1999).

AULUS CORNELIUS CELSUS

FLOURISHING 25 C.E.
MEDICAL WRITER

Advanced Ideas. The only established biographical information on Celsus is that he was alive in Rome in 25/26 C.E., during the reign of Tiberius. He was a member of the illustrious Cornelian family. His eight-book work on medicine is the only surviving part of a larger encyclopedia, *Artes.* Modern scholars debate without conclusion whether he was a physician or simply a brilliant scholar who wrote in clear, concise Latin, and they also disagree on what school of medicine he appears to have been a member of. Some of his instructions reveal that medicine was advanced in some areas, as he advocated cleanliness and oils that may have worked as antiseptics. Later knowledge about ancient medical history relies heavily on his first surviving work.

Sources:
John Scarborough, *Roman Medicine* (London: Thames & Hudson, 1969; Ithaca, N.Y.: Cornell University Press, 1969).

J. T. Vallance, "Cornelius Celsus, Aulus," in *The Oxford Classical Dictionary*, edited by Simon Hornblower and Antony Spawforth, third edition (Oxford: Oxford University Press, 1999), pp. 392–393.

LUCIUS IUNIUS MODERATUS COLUMELLA (COLUMELLA)

FLOURISHING MID FIRST CENTURY C.E.
AGRICULTURAL WRITER

Specialist on Villas. Columella was born in Gades in Spain, but owned farms in Italy. His writings, which were aimed for upper-class literate farmers, show that he knew firsthand about agricultural practices all over Italy. He defended large slave-intensive villas as being efficient farming units and advocated efficient business practices as well as rationally applied farming practices. He was critical of astrologers and religion in agricultural management. His work emphasized viticulture over that of cereals.

Source:
M. Stephen Spurr, "Columella, Lucius Iunius Moderatus," in *The Oxford Classical Dictionary*, edited by Simon Hornblower and Antony Spawforth, third edition (Oxford: Oxford University Press, 1999), p. 367.

CRATES OF MALLUS

FLOURISHING 160 B.C.E.
ASTRONOMER

Stoic Inquiry. Born in Cilicia, Crates was the son of Timocrates. A contemporary of Aristarchus, but unlike him, Crates was less interested in mathematical astronomy than in relating astronomy to Homer. He sought to interpret Homer's universe according to Stoic principles. Crates visited Rome as part of King Eumenes' delegation in 159 B.C.E. and gave several lectures there that intrigued the Romans. Later he may have helped King Eumenes II to establish the library at Pergamum that subsequently was second only to Alexandria's library in fame.

Source:
Peter Barr, Reid Forbes, Robert Browning, and Nigel Guy Wilson, "Crates," in *The Oxford Classical Dictionary*, edited by Simon Hornblower and Antony Spawforth, third edition (Oxford: Oxford University Press, 1999), p. 406.

PEDANIUS DIOSCORIDES OF ANAZARBUS (DIOSCORIDES)

FLOURISHING 50-70 C.E.
MEDICAL WRITER

Early Pharmacist. Born in Cilicia, Dioscorides studied in Tarsus under Areius and subsequently traveled extensively while gathering information about drugs. A Byzantine report that he was a physician in Nero's army is erroneous. From places he identified in his work, it can be postulated that he visited extensively in Greece, Asia Minor, Syria, and Egypt and he frequented major libraries where he researched on writers on pharmacy and medicine. Likely that research included studies at the library at Alexandria. His work is dated by the latest authority whom he cited and the fact that Pliny, who was writing about the same time, did not know Dioscorides' work.

Sources:
John M. Riddle, *Dioscorides on Pharmacy and Medicine* (Austin: University of Texas Press, 1985).

M. M. Sadek, *The Arabic materia medica of Dioscorides* (Quebec: Les Editions du sphinx, 1983).

EUCLIDES (EUCLID)

FLOURISHING CIRCA 295 B.C.E.
MATHEMATICIAN

Uncertain Biography. Although Euclid is one of the more identifiable and enduring writers in classical antiquity by giving his name to a branch of geometry—Euclidean—little is known about his life. Only two biographical details can be established: he was intermediate between Plato (died circa 347 B.C.E.) and Archimedes (born circa 287 B.C.E.); and he taught in Alexandria in Egypt. Earlier scholars believed that Euclid came after Archimedes because Euclid's *Elements* 1.2 is cited in Archimedes' work, but the passage is regarded as an interpolation. Mathematical commentator Pappus of Alexandria (flourishing 320 C.E.) records that Apollonius lived in Alexandria with Euclid's students and this time period was probably between 246 and 221. One anecdote reveals the only personal detail, recorded by the Lycian Neoplatonist philosopher Proclus, who tells us that King Ptolemy (which Ptolemy is not stated) asked Euclid whether there was an easier way to learn geometry other than reading the whole of *Elements*. Euclid is said to have replied that "there is no royal road to geometry."

Mathematical Contributions. In addition to Euclid's contributions to the study of geometry, which were substantial because of the influence of *Elements*, considered the standard textbook for more than two thousand years, he also wrote on conics, optics, and music (although some of the authorship of these works is disputed). He also wrote another work on geometry, *Data*.

Sources:
Benno Artmann, *Euclid: The Creation of Mathematics* (New York: Springer, 1999).

Ian Mueller, *Philosophy of Mathematics and Deductive Structure in Euclid's Elements* (Cambridge, Mass.: MIT Press, 1981).

G. J. Toomer, "Euclid," in *The Oxford Classical Dictionary*, edited by Simon Hornblower and Antony Spawforth, third edition (Oxford: Oxford University Press, 1999), p. 564.

EUDOXUS OF CNIDUS

CIRCA 390–CIRCA 340 B.C.E.
ASTRONOMER

Diverse Scholar. An outstanding mathematician, astronomer, geographer, and philosopher, Eudoxus hailed from the Dorian city of Cnidus in Asia Minor; he was a pupil of Archytas, a Pythagorean philosopher from Tarentum, in geometry and Philistion, a physician from southern Italy, in medicine. He studied in Athens, where he knew Plato. At some point he visited Egypt, where he learned astronomy from the priests. On astronomy he lectured in Cyzicus and in various courts before returning to Athens. Eudoxus is credited with inventing the theory of proportions in geometry, as well as working on limits. He pioneered in mathematical explanations for planetary motion, general observations of constellations, and work on developing calendars.

Sources:
R. M. Dancy, *Two Studies in the Early Academy* (Albany: State University of New York Press, 1991).

G. J. Toomer, "Eudoxus," in *The Oxford Classical Dictionary,* edited by Simon Hornblower and Antony Spawforth, third edition (Oxford: Oxford University Press, 1999), pp. 565–566.

GALEN OF PERGAMUM

CIRCA 129/130–POST 216 C.E.
MEDICAL WRITER

Mathematical and Philosophical Roots. Galen was the practitioner of the art who casts the greatest shadow on Western, Islamic, and Hellenistic medical science. The son of Nikon, an architect and geometer, Galen began studies in philosophy at the age of fourteen, but two years later he turned to medicine, which was to be his life's profession. Never, however, did he forsake philosophy and, indeed, throughout his life Galen wrote extensively on the subject. His grounding in geometry is said to have guided his logical mind in an incredible life of practice, research, and writing. A modern, printed edition of Galen's medical works encompasses some twenty-two, small-print volumes. Alas, his philosophical writings were housed in a temple library that burned during his lifetime and, consequently, his philosophical writings are tragically lost to posterity. He also wrote on grammar and ethics.

Physician to Gladiators and Emperors. Galen studied medicine in several major medical training centers, including Pergamum, Smyrna, Corinth, and Alexandria. When he was twenty-eight, he returned to Pergamum, where he was engaged as a physician to a gladiator company. Working with the wounds on injured combatants allowed him special insight into the treatment of these injuries. Galen's greatest anatomical writings were produced in Rome, where he went to practice in 162; there he acquired a great reputation. By his own assertion, it was his medical successes, not the public lectures he gave, that established Galen's fame. He tells us not only that he left Rome for Pergamum as the plague made its way there from the East, but also that he was "Rome-weary" even before that. Later, Galen responded to a call from Marcus Aurelius to cure his medical problems. From time to time he treated various emperors, including Commodus and Septimius Severus.

Sources:
Rudolph E. Siegel Basel, *Galen's System of Physiology and Medicine,* three volumes (New York: Karger, 1968–1973).

Rebecca Flemming, *Medicine and the Making of Roman Women: Gender, Nature, and Authority from Celsus to Galen* (Oxford & New York: Oxford University Press, 2000).

Fridolf Kudlien and Richard J. Durling, eds., *Galen's Method of Healing: Proceedings of the 1982 Galen Symposium* (Leiden & New York: E. J. Brill, 1991).

NICOMACHUS OF GERASA

FLOURISHING 100 C.E.
MATHEMATICIAN, ASTRONOMER

Pythagorean. Nicomachus was a famous writer on mathematics and astronomy, but practically nothing is known of his life. The Gerasa associated with his birth is likely the city by that name in Palestine. The philosophical lecturer Lucian of Samosata, a fortified city on the Euphrates, said, "You calculate like Nicomachus." Lucian (born circa 120) indicates that when he wrote this line, Nicomachus was a famous man. A specialist on Pythagorean theory, Nicomachus wrote *Introduction to Arithmetic,* a text that influenced scholars in the Middle Ages. He also contributed to the study of harmonics, and several of his other mathematical works are lost.

Sources:
Flora R. Levin, *The Harmonics of Nicomachus and the Pythagorean Tradition* (University Park, Pa.: American Philological Association, 1975).

G. J. Toomer, "Nicomachus," in *The Oxford Classical Dictionary,* edited by Simon Hornblower and Antony Spawforth, third edition (Oxford: Oxford University Press, 1999), p. 1042.

SORANUS OF EPHESUS

FLOURISHING EARLY SECOND CENTURY C.E.
PHYSICIAN, MEDICAL WRITER

Prolific Medical Writer. Some confusion arises about the biography of Soranus because of the presence in the records of several physicians with this common Greek name. This much is established: he learned medicine primarily at Ephesus, where there was a center for medical training. There he had a teacher, Magnus Ephesius, to whom he frequently refers in his writings. Soranus became a member of the Methodist School of medicine that rejected the humoral theory. He studied also in Alexandria in Egypt and practiced medicine in Rome in the reigns of Trajan and Hadrian. He produced approximately twenty works on medicine, covering such topics as hygiene, chronic diseases, fractures, and surgery. He wrote a valuable work on gynecology and midwifery.

Source:
Helen King, "Soranus," in *The Oxford Classical Dictionary,* edited by Simon Hornblower and Antony Spawforth, third edition (Oxford: Oxford University Press, 1999), p. 1426.

MARCUS TERENTIUS VARRO

116-27 B.C.E.
STATESMAN, LIBRARIAN, POLYMATH

Prolific Author. Varro was one of Rome's most prolific writers, having written some 490 books, of which only two have survived. The rhetorician Quintilian called him "the most learned of the Romans." His family was a member of the middle, or equestrian, class. Born at Reate in the Sabine region of Italy, he studied in Rome under L. Aelius Stilo, who was a Stoic grammarian, and in Athens under Antiochus of Ascalon, a philosopher at the Academy. Elected to his first government position in 86 B.C.E., he rose in the offices until he became Praetor. He served in Spain in support of Pompey during the Civil War, but Julius Caesar pardoned him after Pompey's death. In 47 B.C.E. Caesar appointed him as director of a library, but misfortune followed him when he made an enemy with Mark Antony, who proscribed him. His life was spared but much of his property was confiscated. The remainder of his life was given over to scholarship and writing. His range of interests was astonishing, from history and rhetoric, to law and medicine, to architecture and literature. His two extant works are *De lingua Latina,* on Latin grammar, and *De re rustica,* on agriculture.

Sources:
Jens Erik Skydsgaard, *Varro the Scholar: Studies in the First Book of Varro's De re rustica* (Copenhagen: Munksgaard, 1968).

G. J. Toomer, "Nicomachus," in *The Oxford Classical Dictionary,* edited by Simon Hornblower and Antony Spawforth, third edition (Oxford: Oxford University Press, 1999), p. 1042.

VITRUVIUS POLLIO

DIED CIRCA 25 B.C.E.
ENGINEER, ARCHITECTURAL WRITER

Engineer in Service to Emperors. Vitruvius wrote a ten-book work called *De architectura,* and from that work comes most of what little is known about him and the architecture of his age. In an unspecified way he served under Julius Caesar and, under Augustus Caesar, he built a basilica at Fanum Fortunae, on the Adriatic coast. He was also entrusted with the care of siege engines and artillery or ballistic apparatus. Judging by the absence of contemporary references to him, he must have been an engineer with a modest reputation. Despite his major contribution in promoting and recording the history of architecture, he was highly conservative and had a distaste for innovation.

Sources:
George Hersey, *The Lost Meaning of Classical Architecture: Speculations on Ornament from Vitruvius to Venturi* (Cambridge, Mass.: MIT Press, 1988).

Alexander McKay, *Vitruvius, Architect and Engineer: Buildings and Building Techniques in Augustan Rome* (Basingstoke, U.K.: Macmillan, 1978).

Richard Allan Tomlinson and J. T. Vallance, "Vitruvius," in *The Oxford Classical Dictionary,* edited by Simon Hornblower and Antony Spawforth, third edition (Oxford: Oxford University Press, 1999), pp. 1609–1610.

DOCUMENTARY SOURCES

Antonius Musa, *De herba botanica* and *De tuenda vale-tudine ad Maecenatem* (circa 20 B.C.E.)—Two works on pharmacy that circulated during the Middle Ages, although modern scholars no longer regard Musa as their author, the real ones being unknown.

Aratus of Soli, *Phaenomena* (circa 200 B.C.E.)—A poem in Greek on astronomy and meteorology, or weather signs, that was popular with the Romans. At least four Latin translations were made.

Anicus Manlius Severinus Boethius (Boethius), *Consolation of Philosophy* (circa 500 C.E.)—A Platonic dialogue between Lady Philology and Boethius, supposedly written while he was in prison, which was believed to show that Boethius was Christian and the philosophy espoused therefore was Christian. He also wrote celebrated treatises on arithmetic, music, and Aristotle's logic.

Marcus Porcius Cato (Cato the Censor), *De agricultura* (On Agriculture, circa 160 B.C.E.)—The first treatise on agriculture that is extant; it conveys that the Romans considered agriculture a science.

Aulus Cornelisu Celsus (Celsus), *De medicina* (On Medicine, circa 25 C.E.)—The surviving portions of Celsus's encyclopedia titled *Artes;* they concentrate on medicine (as one of nine liberal arts), with information on general dietetics, pathology, general therapy, special therapies, pharmaceuticals, surgery, and bone diseases.

Cleomedes, *Circular Theory of the Heavens* (circa first century B.C.E. to early second century C.E.)—A two-part handbook on astronomy, written in Greek.

Lucius Iunius Moderatus Columella, *De re rustica* (mid first century C.E.)—The most systematic agricultural treatise, in twelve books, covering farm organization, viticulture, arboriculture, animal husbandry, fish farming, poultry and small animals, surveying, climatic factors, soil conditions, and how to employ various land formations. Viticulture received the most emphasis, partly because of its complexity and partly for its profitability.

Pedanius Dioscorides of Anazarbus (Dioscorides), *On the Materials of Medicine* (circa 70 C.E.)—The most extensive and authoritative treatise on pharmacy until the sixteenth century, although his organization by drug affinities was misunderstood by later physicians.

Euclid, *Elements* (circa 295 B.C.E.)—A well-explained text on geometry and mathematics that the Moslems and Christians in the Middle Ages employed. The work covers geometry, plane geometry, the theory of numbers, irrational numbers, and solid geometry. The first section on plane geometry (hence, the name Euclidean geometry) was little altered through the nineteenth century as a text for teaching. He is also credited with *Data* (on geometry); *On Divisions,* extant only in Arabic; *Porisms* (on conic sections); *Phaenomena* (a textbook on astronomy); *Optics; Catroptrica* (on mirrors, lost but with fragments preserved by later authors); *Harmonic* (on musical theory); and *Section of the Canon* (on music).

Sextus Iulius Frontinus (Frontinus), *On Water Works for the City of Rome* (circa 100 C.E.)—A firsthand account of the author's experiences with aqueducts, as well as engineers' reports, government documents, and historical accounts.

Galen of Pergamum—Between circa 145 C.E. and circa 200, he wrote more than 119 treatises on medicine in 22 volumes. Galen's extensive medical works were based on his solid education in philosophy and practical experience as a physician. Some of his works are known only in Latin or Arabic translations.

Ambrosius Theodosius Macrobius (Macrobius), *The Dream of Scipio* (circa early fifth century C.E.)—A commentary on Pythagorean number theory, cosmology, geography, and musicology. Macrobius, *Saturnalia* (circa early fifth century C.E.)—A dialogue celebrating the holiday, which includes discussions on the calendar and related astronomy.

Martianus Minneus Felix Capella, *The Marriage of Philology and Mercury* (early fifth century C.E.)—A textbook in allegory on the marriage on Christian (Lady

Philology) and pagan (symbolized by Mercury), summarizing Roman science, including the four sciences (geometry, arithmetic, astronomy, and music) that were a part of the "liberal arts."

Nicomachus of Gerasa, *Introduction to Arithmetic* (circa 100 C.E.); *Manual of Harmonics* (circa 100 C.E.)—Both works were written in Greek but translated in Latin, and became a primary means for the Romans in the later Middle Ages learning Pythagorean number theory.

Pappus of Alexandria, *Collection* (circa 320 C.E.)—Eight separate treatises on the mathematical sciences, providing commentaries on the application of mathematics to astronomy and mechanics.

Gaius Plinius Secundus (Pliny the Elder), *Natural History* (circa 75 C.E.)—An encyclopedia on nature containing around twenty thousand factual data derived from more than two thousand books.

Pomponius Mela, *De chorographia* or *De situ orbis* (circa 44 C.E.)—A largely derivative three-volume geography.

Claudius Ptolemaeus (Ptolemy), *Almagest* (circa 100–170 C.E.)—A thoroughly explained astronomical theory grounded in mathematics on cosmic theory. Some scholars credit him for the authorship of *Geography*. Other works attributed to him are: *Optics* (five books; Greek text lost but known through Arabic translation); *Planetary Hypotheses* (two books, first available in Greek, second through Arabic translation); *Astronomical Influences* (four books); *Optics* (five books, available through Latin translation of Arabic translation); and *Harmonics* (three books).

Gaius Iulius Solinus, *Collectanea rerum memorabilium* (third century C.E.)—Mostly a compilation about geography, customs, and places, primarily taken from the works of Pliny the Elder and Pomponius Mela.

Soranus of Ephesus, *Gynecia* (Gynecology, early second century C.E.)—Only extant work on gynecology and obstetrics; also wrote two surviving treatises called "On Signs of Fractures" and "On Bandages."

Strabo of Amasia, *Geography* (circa 7 B.C.E.; revised circa 18 C.E.)—An extensive geography invaluable for its descriptions, especially those based on his own travels, and for relating the mathematical astronomy and geography of Posidonius and Eratosthenes.

Marcus Terentius Varro, *De re rustica* (On agricultural matters, circa 27 B.C.E.)—A three-volume treatise on agriculture in general; animal husbandry, notably of cattle and sheep; and care of small animals. Varro recognized the importance of bees in crop production and advised on how to keep hives.

Vitruvius Pollio, *De architectura* (circa 25 B.C.E.)—A ten-volume work dealing with the personality and training of the ideal architect; with building materials; temple architecture; public buildings; domestic architecture; ancillary matters, such as flooring, paints, siding, and paving for roads; aqueducts; astronomy-related topics, including clocks and dials; and mechanics, especially as related to water engines, hodometers, and military machines and artillery.

GLOSSARY

Ab urbe condita (abbreviated A.V.C.; lit. "From the founding of the city"): The Roman system of reckoning years, measured before and after the founding of Rome, 753 B.C.E.

Academy: The philosophical school founded by Plato and continued by his followers.

Acropolis: A citadel located on elevated ground, usually containing the city's major temples and shrines. The most famous acropolis is that of Athens, Greece.

Acta diurna: Public notices of daily happenings, including ceremonies, legal cases, and speeches, posted in the Roman forum.

Acute disease: A disease having a sudden onset, sharp rise, and short course (opposite of "chronic").

Adlocutio: Formal speech, with one arm raised, often by an emperor to troops; also the pose used to depict such a speech.

Aedile: The office of aedile originated in the supervision of the temples (*aedes*) of the *plebs* but in classical times governed public events within the city, the grain supply, and markets. Usually the term refers to the four aediles of Rome, but many Italian municipalities had junior magistrates of the same name and similar function.

Affinities: *See* **Drug Affinities**

Agnate: A blood relative traced only through male lines. Early Roman law of inheritance and guardianship gave recognition to agnate's interest in their relatives' property. Later this recognition was to some extent reduced in favor of nearer relatives not necessarily traced through male bloodlines.

Agonium: The name for a sacrifice made by the King of Sacred Rites in the Regia several times a year.

Aitiology: The study of mythical causes for contemporary features.

Aition (Gk. plural = *aitia*): A story giving a mythical reason for a contemporary name, topographical feature, or custom.

Akrotêrion (plural = *akrotêria*): A sculpted figure placed on top of the apex and corners of a pediment.

Ala (plural = *alae;* lit. wing, wings): Side rooms that flank the back side of the atrium, often used to display a family's ancestral busts and to store the family strongbox.

Alemanni: A confederation of Germanic peoples. They were constantly attacking Roman borders until their defeat at the Battle of Strasbourg in 357 C.E. They settled in Switzerland and the Franks later conquered them.

Allusion: A reference or reminiscence of one literary passage in another.

Altar of Peace (Lat. *Ara pacis*): A shrine to commemorate the *Peace of Augustus,* dedicated in 9 B.C.E.

Ambitus: A criminal offense, including the offer of bribes or other inducements to voters.

Amphitheater (Lit. "theater on both sides"): An oval structure in which public spectacles, particularly gladiatorial combat, were produced. The Colosseum in Rome is perhaps the most famous example.

Amphora (plural = amphorae): A certain type of long, narrow pottery used especially for storage and transportation of goods. Some had pointed bases that enabled them to be stored conveniently in racks on board a ship. Amphorae were regularly used for transporting varieties of cargo throughout the Roman world.

Ancilia: Twelve figure-eight-shaped shields sacred to the war god Mars, kept by his Leaping Priests and carried by them in their annual processional dances through Rome.

Annales maximi: The yearbook of the Pontifex Maximus.

Annalistic: An approach to the writing of history that covers events year by year, rather than by theme.

Antefixe: A clay ornament attached to the edge or corner of the roof of a building, usually a temple, sometimes functioning for drainage purposes.

Apodyterium (Gk. *apodutêrion*): The changing room at the *thermae* (q.v.).

Apologist: An author who defends a position or school of thought. Christian apologists defend Chrsitianity against the attacks of pagan society and in so doing demolish age-old assumptions and beliefs.

Aprosdoceton (Gk. *aprosdokêton*): The rhetorical use of surprise, such as the unexpected twist at the end of an epigram.

Apse: Semicircular space at the end of a hall or basilica.

Aqueduct: A system for bringing water from its source into a city or town.

Ara pacis: See **Altar of Peace**

Arena: The floor of a public building on which games were displayed. From the Latin *harena,* or sand that was spread on the floor to absorb shed blood.

Arval Brethren: Special priests of the goddess Dea Dia; they met annually in her sacred grove about five miles southeast of Rome, where they sacrificed and celebrated games in her honor.

Arx: The northwest cusp of the Capitoline Hill, where a temple to Juno the Warner was located.

As (plural = *asses*): The *as* was a small bronze Roman coin. Because it was so small, it was worth little and it was used generically to refer to something of little value, much as today someone might say something is "not worth a cent."

Asianism: A school of oratory that advocated a flowery style of speaking. Opposite of *Atticism.*

Assembly: *See Comitia*

Atellanae: Farcical plays native to the Italian town of Atella.

Atomism: The belief that the universe is composed of an almost endless number of tiny elements, atoms, or "seeds of things," out of which everything we observe is composed.

Atrium: The principal room of an atrium-style Roman house, around which other rooms are arranged. It served as the waiting room for clients and guests.

Atticism: A school of oratory that championed a plain style of speaking. Opposite of *Asianism.*

Auctoritas: Lit. "prestige" or "authority"; it was an important measure of one's social status and political influence.

Augur: A priest of Rome whose responsibility was to maintain the science of auspices, the art of divining the will of Jupiter. See *auspicia.*

Augury (Lat. *augurium*): The performance of certain rites involving the use of auspices, especially the inauguration of priests and of land intended for permanent religious use.

Auspicia: In general, the science of observation of certain phenomena, such as lightning and the song and flight-patterns of birds, to ascertain whether or not Jupiter gives permission for a specific act.

Auspicia ex tripudiis: A type of auspices in which the permission of Jupiter is indicated by the greedy eating of food by sacred chickens kept for the purpose.

Autopsy (Gk. *autos* "oneself" + *opsis* "sight"): In discussions of historical writing and others, this term refers to firsthand experience (as opposed to relying on the accounts of others).

Autopsy, deep: An autopsy is the examination of a dead body in order to determine the cause of death or pathological condition. A deep autopsy is the dissection of the body cavity beneath the rib cage or abdominal wall for the same purpose.

Basilica: A public hall designed for large civic and administrative gatherings.

Bellum iustum: "Just war," the religious/legal concept by which the Romans declared that they were correct to initiate a state of warfare because an enemy had wronged Rome without provocation or satisfaction, because Jupiter had given his permission through auspices, and because the people had voted for it.

Bigae: Two-horse chariot.

Bulla: An amulet worn by freeborn boys to protect them from evil spirits (and which also indicated their freeborn status). When boys became men, they dedicated the amulet to their household gods. Girls may have worn the bulla as well, but the evidence is vague.

Calceus (plural = *calcei*): A sturdy shoe that fully enclosed the foot.

Caldarium: The hottest room of the public baths (*thermae*), containing a hot plunge pool and separate water basin.

Caliga (plural = *caligae*): Military boot. The diminutive, *caligula* or "Little Boot," was the affectionate childhood nickname of the Roman Emperor Gaius Caesar.

Campus martius (Lit. "Field of Mars"): A broad, flat area bounded by the Pincian, Quirinal, and Capitoline Hills. It had an altar to Mars and was used for army musters and exercises. It was the gathering point for elections and military triumphs; over time it became an area of civic importance, housing temples, shrines, and many other public buildings.

Capitoline Triad: The three gods Iuppiter Optimus Maximus, Minerva, and Juno.

Caput cenae (Lit. "head of the meal"): The main course of a Roman banquet. Also known as *mensa prima.*

Carceres (Lit. "prisons," or "enclosures"): The starting gates of the chariot race.

Carpentum: A two-wheeled wagon popular with women of the ruling class.

Casuistic: Reasoning, especially legal reasoning on a case-by-case basis rather than according to general principles or procedures. This approach was characteristic of the Roman jurists.

Cavea: The seating area in a theater.

Cella: The central room of a temple, where the cult statue was housed.

Cena: Dinner; the principal meal of the day, taken in the late afternoon or early evening.

Censor: A public official responsible for conducting the *census* and maintaining the official list of Roman citizens. Censors had the responsibility to maintain the integrity of the membership of the senatorial and equestrian orders. They also conducted the sale and lease of public property and contracts. Two censors were elected every five years.

Census: A ceremony occurring every five years in which the citizen body was counted, an account was made of the property value of each, the people as a whole were purified, and the rolls of senate members were updated.

Chronic disease: A disease marked by long duration or frequent recurrence (opposite of "acute").

Chthonic: Having to do with the earth, as opposed to the sky. Jupiter, for example, is a sky god, whereas Ceres has chthonic associations.

Cimbri: A Germanic people from Jutland near the Elbe River. They migrated in the second century B.C.E. with the Teutones and the Ambrones to Noricum; some settled in Switzerland. By the time of Tiberius only a small portion remained in Jutland.

Circus: A long, narrow racecourse for chariot racing. The most famous one in Rome was the Circus Maximus.

Citizenship: Roman citizenship was a formal designation originally available only to freeborn citizens in the city of Rome. Gradually it was extended to all free residents of the Roman Empire. It granted certain privileges, such as voting and judicial rights.

Civic Polytheism: The idea that the number and variety of a people's gods not only reflect the various backgrounds of the people but also unite them as a people.

Client: A person who owed an obligation to someone of a higher class (his *patronus* or patron).

Coffers: In architecture, these are box-shaped hollows in the dome or ceiling of an arch that reduce the mass of the vaulting.

Cognitio: An Imperial procedure for hearing civil and criminal legal cases that was more inquisitorial than Republican trial procedure, that is, more closely controlled (and sometimes even initiated) by the state rather than the parties.

Cognomen: A nickname that men either inherited or earned. In the early empire, women began having *cognomina*, too.

Collegium (plural = *collegia*): While clubs of all sorts formed in the Roman world, a *collegium* would almost always at least in name be devoted to some religious purpose. Workers in the same craft or field might form a *collegium* to pool together their resources for the funerals of members and to provide regular social occasions for members.

Colonnade: A series of columns, set at regular intervals, usually supporting a roof or covering.

Colosseum: The Flavian Amphitheater at Rome.

Comitia (singular = *comitium*, or "assembly-place"): Any of the several assemblies that voted on laws and elections. The *comitia* were composed of all adult male citizens who attended the votes in Rome. Each was divided (in various ways) into subunits, and the object was to win the votes of a majority of those units, not necessarily of individual voters. For instance, the *comitia tributa* (tribal assembly) divided voters into 35 geographical units called "tribes," and the *comitia centuriata* divided them into 193 "centuries" (perhaps related to the military unit of the same name) based on wealth and age. The people could not speak, or offer or amend proposals; they only voted on what was presented by the presiding magistrate. *See also contio.*

Compluvium: A hole in the roof of the atrium of a house, which allowed sunshine, air, and rainwater to enter. *See also impluvium.*

Coniunx: "Spouse" (Lit. "joined together"); the term could refer to either a husband or wife.

Consilium: The informal council of a magistrate or head of a household. Even persons with clear individual legal authority were expected to consult broader public opinion before taking important action. Roman emperors adopted the tradition, and the council eventually evolved into an imperial court.

Consul: The office of consul was the most powerful individual office during the Roman Republic. Beginning in 509 B.C.E., when the Republic was established, two consuls were elected annually. The Romans thus sometimes designated years in history by the names of the consuls in office that year. For example, the year 338 B.C.E. could be reckoned the year Lucius Furius Camillus and Gaius Maenius were consuls. The consuls were in charge of military and political affairs, proposing laws, and supervising other magistrates.

Contaminatio: Combining different Greek plays (or parts of them) into one Roman play. This was the practice of Terence and possibly also of Plautus.

Contio: An assembly held for magistrates (or persons sponsored by them) to address the people, but not to vote. The audience could not (formally) speak. *See also comitia.*

Controversia: A type of declamation: a rhetorical exercise in which two students argued either side of a (fictitious) legal case.

Contubernium: A domestic arrangement (not considered a marriage) between two slaves, or a slave and a free person.

Con(n)ubium: In legal terms, the right to marry.

Convivium: A banquet or fancy dinner party.

Cosmopolitanism (< Gk. *cosmos* "world" + *polis* "city-state"): The belief that the world is one whole entity, that there are no states or countries, and that all men are "citizens of the world"; one of the doctrines of the Cynic school.

Cubiculum: A small room used either as a bedroom or as a private sitting room. *Cubicula* were typically located off the atrium of an atrium-style house.

Culina: The kitchen.

Curia: The senate house on the edge of the Roman Forum.

Cursus honorum: This "Course of Honors" refers to the sequence of political offices that elite Romans were expected, or at times required, to follow in order to enter the Senate and to acquire substantial political power. Although the *cursus* changed somewhat over time, the most basic order ran quaestor, [aedile,] praetor, and consul.

Cursus publicus: The official Roman postal service established by Augustus.

Curule aedile: A public officer of the patrician class responsible for the maintenance of public streets, building safety, temples, and certain public games.

Cynics: A school of philosophy founded by Diogenes, which held that it is best to ignore social conventions and customs as false and to live as naturally as possible.

Dactyl: A poetic foot, or metrical unit, consisting of one long syllable followed by two short ones.

Daimonion (Gk. diminutive of *daimôn* "god"): A divine spirit that must, according to Socrates, be in every person.

Damnatio memoriae: Punishment whereby one's name and images are erased from public documents and monuments. In the case of emperors, their decrees and edicts would be overturned.

Decemvir: A member of a board of ten men. In the early republic, two sets of *decemviri* were elected to write down Rome's laws.

Declamation: Practice-speeches given as part of a rhetoric student's training in oratory. The two main types of declamation were the *controversia*, or fictitious law case, and the *suasoria*, or fictitious deliberative speech.

Decurion: A member of a local council, the municipal equivalent of a senator at Rome. The decurions were among the *honestiores* (q.v.), but were not high enough in the hierarchy to gain tax exemptions under the Empire.

Dediticii: Enemies who had surrendered absolutely to the Roman will.

Deep autopsy: *See* **Autopsy, deep**

Deferent: *See* **Epicycle-on-Deferent Movements**

Defixiones: Curse tablets that were sealed and deposited in the earth.

Demonetarization: *See* **Monetarization**

Denarius (plural = *denarii*): The *denarius* was the basic silver coin in the Roman world. Especially as inflation grew in the third century C.E., many transactions were reckoned in *denarii*. The Price Edict of Diocletian, for example, gives prices in *denarii*.

Deus ex machina: The "god from the machine," a divine character at the end of a tragedy who unravels the mess into which the humans have gotten themselves.

Diaeta: An open sitting room located off the *peristylium* of a Roman house.

Dictator: A man named by the consuls to serve during a time of crisis. His term of office was limited to six months or to the end of the crisis.

Didactic: Possessing the quality of teaching; a "didactic poem" purports to give instructions on any given topic.

Dies fasti: Days on which business or legal activities could be conducted.

Dies nefasti: Days on which no business or legal activities could occur.

Diocese: An administrative unit of the later Empire. The emperor Diocletian divided the former provinces into more and smaller units. These were then grouped into twelve dioceses to create a new level of organization.

Diplomata: Written certificates that guaranteed special rights and privileges for the bearer.

Divine Apparatus: The conventional episodes involving the rather humanlike gods in epic poetry; these episodes reflect the human action on a higher plane.

Domi: Literally "at home," this term came to be used of all public affairs and politics except those of a military nature; see *militiae*.

Domus: The Roman house.

Donatists: A schismatic sect in North Africa who refused to accept Caecilian as bishop because he had been an informer under Diocletian's persecution of the Christians. In spite of forcible attempts to align them with Rome, the schism remained until North Africa was conquered by the Arabs.

Dowry: An amount agreed upon by a woman's father and her prospective husband. The dowry rightfully belonged to the woman, but her husband could manage it to make it financially profitable for the family.

Drachma: A Greek monetary unit equivalent to a Roman *denarius*.

Drug Affinities: System devised by Dioscorides to arrange drugs by their physiological actions on and in the body.

Duoviri: (Lit. "[board of] two men.") Some of the Roman minor magistracies were made up of such pairs, but usually the term refers to the chief magistrates of municipalities, equivalent to the consuls at Rome.

Eccentric Movements: The center of a planet's smaller circle around its orbit deviates from the true, geometric center; thus, the planet appears to wobble as it moves in an epicycle around its own greater orbit around the earth.

Echo: In literature, a (sometimes unconscious) reminiscence of a passage in an earlier work.

Edict: The official decree of a Roman magistrate, whether to establish policy for his whole term or for a specific purpose. The most important was the edict of the urban praetor, which provided for most circumstances under which civil suits could be started.

Elegy: Poetry written in alternating hexameters and pentameters; it was originally probably accompanied by a flute player but soon acquired associations of lament.

Elements: In ancient thought, an element is a substance that is irreducible. According to the theory of Empedocles, there were four elements out of which physical forms were made: earth, air, fire, and water. Aristotle added the notion that their movements are rectilinear. Heavenly bodies were regarded as composed of a fifth element, ether, whose movement is a perfect circle. The *Elements* of Euclid in geometry were basic principles assumed to be true on which other postulates could be based.

Emancipatio: A procedure by which a father could make his sons or daughters independent or by which a slave owner could free a slave.

Encaustic: A painting technique involving the application of pigments mixed with hot wax.

Encomium: Formal rhetorical praise of someone or something.

Entablature: All parts of an architectural order above the columns.

Entasis: The vertical, convex curve of a column.

Epic Simile: A simile used in epic poetry (such as the *Aeneid* of Vergil), sometimes running for several lines, in which the comparison between two things may be quite intricately developed.

Epicureanism: An atomistic philosophy that held that all reality is simply the chance meeting of atoms falling through empty space. The responsibility of individuals therefore is to seek to minimize the pain experienced in mortal life. This school of philosophy was based on the teaching of the fourth-century-B.C.E. Greek philosopher Epicurus.

Epicycle and Epicyclic Movements: The movement of planets in circles around their own orbits. The center of the planet's circular movement forms the circumference of the larger orbit.

Epicycle-on-Deferent Movements: The appearance of retrograde motions by planets is caused by a combination of the earth being off center (or, eccentric) of the orbit formed by the planet around the earth and also by the deferent movement apparent when the planet is moving around its own epicycle. Thus, from the earth a planet may appear to slip backward, whereas it deferred around its own epicycle.

Epigram: A short poem, often with a witty twist in its final line, most often written in elegiac meter.

Epigraphy: The study of ancient inscriptions (records on stone or bronze, calendars, and coins) as part of the historical record.

Epistyle: A line of blocks extending above columns to support the upper part of the building.

Epitaph: An inscription on a tombstone.

Epode: A poem consisting of alternating longer and shorter lines, often in iambic meter.

Eponymous: Someone or something after whom something else is named. Romulus is the eponymous hero of Rome; Augustus is the eponymous emperor of the month of August.

Epyllion: A modern term, coined in the ancient Greek style, to mean "mini-epic." A famous example is Catullus 64.

Eques (plural = *equites*): Lit. "horseman"; originally the designation of a Roman citizen with enough money to maintain a warhorse for the Roman cavalry. Gradually the men of this category became a (middle) social class of some prestige, wealth, and power, predominantly businessmen, and second only to the senatorial class. Under Augustus, an *eques* had to have an estate of at least four hundred thousand sesterces (*see also sestertius*).

Equinox: Two times of the year when, because the sun has crossed the equator, days and nights are of equal length throughout the world.

Ethnography: Writing about different peoples.

Etruscans: The people who inhabited central Italy across the Tiber River from Latium; a culturally advanced race with trading and political contacts throughout the Mediterranean.

Euergetism: The contribution of gifts to a community, whether in the form of cash, services, or public buildings. It was driven both by the giver's sense of civic obligation and by a desire to achieve popularity.

Exedra: A recessed area typically situated at the back of the *peristylium* of a Roman house.

Expiation: A ritual act of sacrifice to appease the anger of a god or gods for some sin committed.

Explorator: A scout in the Roman army.

Extispicy (Lat. *exstispicium*): The consultation, by Etruscan *haruspices*, of certain internal organs (*exta*), especially the liver and heart, of sacrificed animal victims. Marks on the *exta* were regarded as omens.

Familia: The Roman concept of family that encompasses not only adults and their children but other relatives and the household slaves as well.

Fasces: A bundle of wooden rods (about five feet long) tied together around an ax, symbolizing the early punishments of beating and beheading. These were the traditional insignia of the magisterial authority of consuls and praetors and were carried by attendants (*lictors*) who marched before the magistrate.

Fasti: See Dies fasti

Fathers, Apostolic: A general term for those Christian writers, thinkers, and leaders after the generation of the original disciples of Jesus (the "Apostles").

Fauces: Lit. "jaws," "throat." The passage of a Roman house leading from the outside door into the atrium.

Feasters of Jupiter: The *Epulones,* special priests of Jupiter responsible for sacrificing to that god on the Ides (13th or 15th) of every month.

Fetial: A priest responsible for the religious rituals involved in the declaration of war and the making of treaties with foreign states. The *fetiales* sought divine approval for such events.

Fibula: A pin used to fasten clothing.

Fides: Trust, trustworthiness.

Flamen: A sacral priest dedicated to the service of one god only, such as for Jupiter, Mars, Quirinus, or other, lesser gods.

Flute: In architecture, vertical concave channels or grooves on columns.

Formula (plural = *formulae*): Instructions from the urban praetor to the judge(s) of civil suits. They gave only general guidance on the legal issues at stake.

Forum: A public place or marketplace; town center. In Rome, the Forum was the principal place of all business and legal activity.

Framing: In literary composition, the use of a word, phrase, or motif at both the beginning and the end of a structural unit.

Freedmen/Freedwomen: Slaves could, depending on the will of their master, acquire their freedom, at which point they took on the designation Freedman or Freedwoman. They retained this title for the rest of their lives, but their children were freeborn citizens.

Fresco: Wall painting produced by application of pigments to wet or damp plaster.

Frieze: The horizontal area above the main cross beam in a classical temple; the term is often used to denote the decoration within this horizontal band.

Frigidarium: An unheated room at the public baths (*thermae*) containing a cold-water basin.

Galli (Gk *galloi*): The self-castrated priests, or eunuchs, of Cybele, the Great Mother (*magna mater*) of the gods.

Garden: The school of the philosopher Epicurus, which met in the garden of his home in Athens. This was secluded from public life and included women and slaves as well as male citizens. Because of the private nature of this enclave and despite their focus on an almost ascetic simplicity, "epicurean" became a synonym for "hedonistic."

Garum: An oily sauce produced by allowing fish to deteriorate. Various stages of the process produced differing qualities of sauce. The product was served as a condiment for various foods, most especially *polenta,* a cereal.

Genius: A spirit. The *genius* was a combination of a guardian spirit and a spirit that represented each individual.

Gens: A group of relatives who all share the same name, whether by birth or adoption; thus, an extended kinship group, such as a tribe or clan.

Gracchi: Tiberius Sempronius Gracchus and his younger brother Gaius Sempronius Gracchus each challenged the authority of the Roman senate and attempted to pass legislation aimed at relieving the oppression of the poor. Each was assassinated in turn, along with many of their followers, but their legacy lived on into the final days of the Roman Republic.

Grammaticus: The teacher responsible for the second level of Roman education. After a student completed his study with the *ludi magister* (q.v.), he would proceed (at about age twelve) to the *grammaticus,* who taught him grammar, composition, and the explication of literary texts. Transfer to the *rhetor* (q.v.) came at about age fifteen.

Gustatio: The appetizer course of a Roman banquet; also *gustum.*

Hamartia: Lit. a "missing of the mark"; this is Aristotle's term for the crucial mistake made by a tragic character that leads to his or her *peripeteia* (q.v.).

Haruspicy: Also called *exstispicy* (q.v.), the Etruscan art of divination practiced by the *haruspices,* especially by means of the examination of certain vital organs of sacrificed animals; not to be confused with augury or auspices (q.v.).

Hastae Martis: The Spears of Mars, kept in the Regia (q.v.).

Hellenistic: Of or related to the era following the conquest of the known world by Alexander the Great, and the subsequent spread of Greek culture throughout the Mediterranean.

Hellenize: Lit. "Greekify"; this word refers to the importation of Greek culture and ideas into the non-Greek world (*see also* **Hellenistic**).

Hexameter: A line of verse consisting of six dactyls (q.v.) or their metrical equivalent.

Hippopede: Lit. "horse fetter"; an allusion to the shape of a figure eight on its side; the perceived movement of the looping movements of planets as they appear to move across the sky according to theory by Eudoxus.

Homeric Epic: Narrative verse by (or following the model of) the Greek poet Homer, which develops at great length a limited part of a myth.

Honestiores: Members of the upper social strata of the later Empire, including senators, *equites,* and local aristocracies. They were subject to relatively lighter punishments for criminal offenses. *See also humiliores.*

Hora (plural = *horae*): The twelve (equal) divisions of a Roman day from dawn to sundown.

Household Gods: These were of two major types, the *Lares* and the *Penates.* [1] The *lares* (singular = *lar*) were, in origin, either gods of the crossroads or deified ancestor spirits; it was certainly as the latter that they came to be worshiped in the home. Each house had a *lararium,* a cabinet in which the images of the *lares* were kept; at this shrine, which was typically in the atrium, the members of the family made offerings. [2] The *penates (di penates,* that is, gods of the *penus* or larder) were the gods of the interior part of the house. They were worshiped not only in individual households but also in the temple of Vesta, the goddess of the hearth, and in a shrine on the Velia, a hill overlooking the Forum in Rome.

Humiliores: Members of the lower social strata of the later Empire. They were subject to relatively harsher punishments for criminal offenses. *See also honestiores.*

Hypocaust: The raised floor of a room heated from below by hot air from a furnace.

Ides (Lat. *Idus*): The thirteenth day of the month, except, in March, May, July, and October, when it falls on the fifteenth. Julius Caesar was assassinated on the Ides of March.

Ientaculum: Breakfast; for a Roman, usually a light meal of cheese, fruit, and bread.

Iliadic: Of, related to, or emulating the *Iliad,* Homer's epic about the Trojan War. Cf. "Odyssean."

Imperator: Originally the semiofficial title of a Roman general, given to him by his troops after he had won a major victory. Beginning with Vespasian, *Imperator* became one of the official titles of the Roman emperor; in fact, it is the source of the English word "emperor."

Imperium: A magistrate's supreme civil or military authority. In the earliest period, *imperium* belonged to the kings; subsequently, to consuls, praetors, dictators, *magistri equitum* (q.v.), and military tribunes with consular power (*see also* **Tribune**).

Impetrativa: Auspices sent by Jupiter at the request of the magistrate or augur taking the auspices; *see also oblativa.*

Impluvium: The basin in the floor of an *atrium* directly under the *compluvium* for the purpose of gathering rainwater.

Inauguratio: The use of *auspices* (q.v.) by an augur to permanently delimit or reserve a person, or an area of land, for religious service.

Indo-European: Of or belonging to the race of prehistoric peoples who originated in south-central Asia Minor and migrated to the westernmost parts of Europe and southeast into India.

Infamia: Official legal disgrace, affecting those convicted of major crimes; those found guilty in private cases involving particularly sensitive trusts; persons dishonorably discharged from the military; and members of certain professions (such as prostitutes, gladiators, and the managers of both). Aside from the social stigma, persons under *infamia* lost most of their right to participate in the government.

Inhabited World: The landmasses that had been explored in the ancient world and were known to contain life. By the Roman period, this area extended as far westward as Spain and as far eastward as India (and to some extent China). Northward, the Romans knew of Sweden, though the landmass was not thoroughly explored. Parallel to this was the Caspian Sea. To the south, the Romans knew of Africa but never learned how far southward it extended.

Instauratio: The process whereby a rite, if done improperly, must be repeated, either in part or in whole.

Insula: (Lit. "island"). A multistory apartment building. These buildings could rise as tall as seventy feet. While the bottom floor could contain nice apartments, the top floors offered small, dingy rooms.

Iron Age: The period between 1000–700 B.C.E., when the use of iron became more widespread.

Irrational Numbers: Supposedly discovered by Pythagoras, irrational numbers are those not expressible as an integer or as the quotient of two integers. They can be expressed as an infinite decimal with no set of consecutive digits repeating itself indefinitely as, for example, $\sqrt{2}$.

Iudex (plural = *iudices*): A private citizen who decided public or private legal cases. Private cases were usually decided by one *iudex;* public ones by many. *Iudices* were not (except coincidentally) legal experts. Cf. **Jurist.**

Iuppiter Optimus Maximus: Lit. "Jupiter Best and Greatest"; the god Jupiter in his aspect as the principal and most powerful of the Roman pantheon.

Iuridici (singular = *iuridicus*): Officials who administered the justice system in the provinces and (starting in the second century C.E.) in Italy outside Rome, on behalf of the praetor and provincial governors.

Ius Latii: The "rights of Latium." After 338 B.C.E., some *Latini* (q.v.) shared the rights of marriage and trade (*conubium* and *commercium*) with Romans. Under Augustus, Latin rights were extended to people who lived in Gaul, Africa, and Spain, as well as in Italy.

Jurist: A legal expert; closer to a modern law professor than a lawyer. They advised private citizens and state officials on legal matters.

Kalendae: The Kalends; the first day of the month in the Roman calendar. The expression "On the Greek Kalends" was a whimsical way of saying "never."

Laconicum: The sweat room of the *thermae,* also called the *sudatorium.*

Lanista: A trainer of gladiators, often himself a former gladiator.

Lar (plural = *lares*): *See* **Household Gods**

Latini: An Indo-European (q.v.) people, the "Latins," who settled in Latium (q.v.) on the Tiber River.

Latitude: The angular distance of any location on the surface of the earth north or south from the equator. Cf. **longitude.**

Latium: "The Broad Place," the area of central Italy settled and inhabited by the people known as the *Latini.*

Legacies: The practice of "legacy-hunting" is the attempt to get into someone's last will and testament and thus inherit money (a "legacy").

Legati: "Deputies" appointed by provincial governors to take charge of matters to which they could not attend personally. Under the Empire many provinces were practically governed by *legati* assigned by the emperor who was technically the official in charge.

Leptosunê: Greek for "delicacy." A fashion in later Greek poetry prized subtlety and refinement, which was termed *leptosunê.* This literary value was taken over by certain Roman poets such as Catullus.

Lex (plural = *leges*): Any law passed by one of the popular assemblies.

Liberi: "Children" (from the adjective *liber,* "free," though it is not clear how the plural came to have this meaning).

Longitude: The distance of the inhabited world from east to west; the distance east or west of the earth's surface accounted for in degrees, or in time. Cf. **latitude.**

Ludi: "Games" in the ancient Roman world, which included religious festivals, dramatic performances, public rituals, as well as the more spectacular events such as gladiatorial combats, reconstruction of naval battles, and the like. Typically these were sponsored by the state.

Ludi circenses: Circus games including chariot races, gladiatorial combat, and *venationes* (q.v.).

Ludi magister: The *ludus litterarum* was the Romans' elementary school, and the *ludi magister* or *litterator* was its teacher. His task was to teach the students how to read and write, and perhaps some basic mathematics. Students began elementary education at about the age of seven.

Ludi plebei: The "Plebeian Games," public spectacles held in November.

Ludi romani: The "Roman Games," public spectacles held in September.

Lustrum: A purificatory rite involving the leading of sacrificial animals around an area or group of people to be purified, followed by the sacrifice of those animals.

Macellum: A market selling a variety of provisions.

Magister equitum: The "master of the cavalry," second in command to a dictator, was named by the dictator to assist him in times of crisis.

Magistrate: An executive officer of the Roman government, like a modern president, mayor, or cabinet secretary, though Roman magistrates were all elected. They also all served one-year terms, and shared their offices with one or more colleagues. (Not to be confused with the contemporary American "magistrate," a minor federal judge.)

Magna Graecia: "Great Greece"; the Greek colonies in southern Italy.

Maiestas: One of two forms of treason under Roman criminal law. Originally it involved a variety of ways to harm the state, but under the Empire it usually meant disloyalty to the Emperor.

Manes: Roman spirits of the dead; these might be individual souls, gods of the underworld, or the whole realm of the dead. In later antiquity, they came to be regarded as the souls of family ancestors in particular.

Manichaeism: A system of belief based on the gnostic tradition. Manicheans saw the world as being in conflict between light and darkness: Satan has stolen the light and imprisoned it in man's brain; religion, with the help of the forces of good, is to set the light free. This was thought to be achieved by severe asceticism and vegetarianism.

Manumission: The freeing of a slave, at which point the slave becomes known as a freedman or freedwoman. Former slaves of Roman citizens themselves became Roman citizens, rather than reverting to their original nationality.

Manus: The authority that a husband has over a wife in certain types of marriages. In the early republic, women passed from their father's control to their husband's. In the middle and late republic, women married more often without *manus,* meaning that they remained in the control of their fathers. Only a marriage by *confarreatio* always conveyed *manus.*

Marcomanni: *See* **Suebi**

Materfamilias: The oldest living woman of any family.

Materia medica: "The materials of medicine," or drugs.

Mediterranean Triad: Grain, grapes, and olive oil are together known as the "Mediterranean Triad" because they formed the basis for agriculture and food production all around the Mediterranean Sea (and hence the basis for the Roman economy).

Mensa prima: Lit. "first table"; the main course of a Roman banquet.

Mensa secunda: Lit. "second table"; the dessert course of a Roman banquet.

Meridian: A line that is in a plane with the axis of a circle; it is also the plane of the celestial meridian that passes through a place.

Metempsychosis: The transmigration of souls into new bodies after death; reincarnation.

Metonic Cycle: So-called after its proposer, Meton of Athens (flourishing around 430 B.C.E.), and probably borrowed from the Babylonians, a Metonic cycle is a nineteen-year cycle that supposedly reconciles nineteen tropical years with 235 lunations (the period of time averaging, according to modern calculations, of 29 days, 12 hours, 44 minutes, and 2.8 seconds between the phases of the moon). Ancient calculations were not as precise, inasmuch as accurate time measures were unavailable.

Militiae: Literally "at war," this term came to be used of foreign affairs generally (opposite of *domi,* "at home").

Monarchy: The historical period when kings ruled Rome, 753–509 B.C.E.

Monetarization: Building up an economy based on cash transactions, rather than barter or direct personal entitlements. The use of coins in the tax system and to pay the army encouraged at least some monetarization of the Roman Empire. In the late empire, financial crises and the devaluation of the currency (putting less precious metal in coins of the same face value) caused people to try to hold on to their cash, causing a partial reversal of this process (demonetarization).

Money changers: Men who made a living exchanging the coinage of one city or country for the coinage of another. They needed to weigh and know the metal constituents of coins in order to determine their value. They also had a reputation for being dishonest.

Monism: The belief that all things are really only forms or aspects of an original unity, the One.

Monotheism: The exclusive worship of one god.

Montanists: A second–third century apocalyptic movement that expected an outpouring of the Holy Spirit on the Church. The Montanists thought they saw the first signs of this in their own leaders. In Africa, the movement had strong ascetic traits.

Mos maiorum: Lit. "the custom of [our] ancestors," the Roman term for long-established customs or ancestral traditions.

Motto: A Latin translation of the opening of a Greek poem.

Munera: Games, usually in honor of a deceased relative, sponsored by a private individual for public enjoyment.

Municipium: A town that was granted Roman citizenship while retaining its own laws.

Murmillo: A gladiator, heavily armed with an oblong shield and short sword, who fought wearing a Gallic helmet.

Mystery Religion: A cult in which a worshiper is initiated by degrees into secret knowledge, usually of the afterlife, imparted to him by other members of the cult, until the full mystery is finally revealed.

Nabataeans: The people of northern Arabia. They spoke Aramaic, and their kings were subject to Rome.

Naumachia: A nautical battle staged on a lake or artificial body of water for public entertainment.

Necropolis: The series of tombs, usually along roadways, that formed something of a "city of the dead."

Nefasti: See Dies nefasti

Neoplatonism: The characteristic thought of the Platonic Academy several centuries after the death of Plato; concerned chiefly with the possibility of absolute knowledge.

Neoteroi: The "new poets" around Catullus (*neôterismos* is Gk. for "revolution") who advocated terseness and wit.

New Comedy: A form of comedy written after circa 330 B.C.E.; it deals with middle-class Greek life and uses some stock characters.

Nobiles: Latin for "nobles," this term referred in the later Republic to the wealthier, more prestigious members of the Roman citizenry, who reckoned themselves an aristocracy.

Nomen, nomen gentile: The family name (that is, name of the *gens*). The *nomen* was shared by all who were members of a family by birth or adoption but not by marriage. Freed slaves took a form of their former master's name.

Nones (Lat. *nonae*): The ninth day (counting inclusively) before the Ides of the month. Since the latter fell on the 13th or 15th, the Nones would fall on the 5th or 7th of the month.

Novus homo: Latin for "new man," this term refers to men from families not traditionally among the Roman elite who worked their way into the upper class of Roman society, especially the Senatorial order.

Nundinae: Market days held at eight-day intervals.

Nutrix: A woman, often a slave, who cared for children.

Oblativa: Auspices sent by Jupiter unasked for, especially in the form of lightning or thunder from a certain direction.

Obsequium: The dutiful obedience a Roman husband expected from his wife.

Odyssean: Of, related to, or emulating Homer's *Odyssey,* an epic about the hero Odysseus's journey back home. Cf. "Iliadic."

Oecus: A reception or dining room located off the *peristylium* of a Roman house.

Oikoumenê gê: The Gk. term, used from the time of Herodotus, to designate the "inhabited world," or the "known world." *See also* **Inhabited World.**

Optimates: These were backers of the Roman aristocracy during the later Roman Republic, in contrast to the *populares* (q.v.), who courted the will of the mass population.

Opus incertum: A masonry technique using small stones of irregular shape to retain a concrete core in a wall.

Oracle at Delphi: The priestess of Apollo at Delphi, the god's sanctuary on Mount Parnassus in Greece, to which people would go to ask for prophecy concerning their lives or important undertakings.

Oratory: The practice of public speaking.

Orbis terrae: The Latin term often used to designated either the "inhabited world" (q.v.), or the globe itself, including its mythical, unexplored regions. Also *orbis terrarum.*

Orgiastic: A term used to describe a religious experience that involves complete abandonment of oneself, usually through dancing, music, singing, sacrifice, and wine, to a god's influence.

Ornatrix: A woman who styled women's hair.

Palaestra: An exercise court, used especially for wrestling, and often associated with the *thermae.*

Palingenesis: The belief, associated with Stoic philosophy and certain religions, that reality undergoes cycles of birth, maturity, decline, death, and renewal.

Palla: A shawl or mantle worn by women for modesty and warmth.

Pantheon: A collective term for all the gods and goddesses a people recognizes.

Papyrus: A reedlike plant from Egypt, or the sheet of writing material made from such plants.

Parallel: Each of the circles drawn upon a map, separated by five or ten degrees, perpendicular to the axis. They mark the degrees of latitude.

Pastoral Verse: Verse purportedly written by shepherds about rustic themes.

Paterfamilias: The oldest living adult male in a family, head of the household.

Patres: This term, lit. "fathers," was sometimes used to refer to the senators, thus giving rise to the term "patricians."

Patrician (Lat. *patricius*): This term applies to a social class going back to the earliest days of Rome. The patricians constituted the nobility, in contrast to the plebeians (q.v.). Patrician status could be obtained only by birth, except perhaps in cases where a new city came under Roman rule: its established nobility might also be reckoned as patrician. By the late Republic the class had dwindled in population and prestige and eventually faded out. *See also* **Plebeian.**

Patron (Lat. *patronus*): A member of the upper class who provided funds and assistance for certain members of the lower classes, known as his clients (q.v.), who in turn were expected to provide him with political support as needed.

Pax deorum: "Peace with the gods." Romans worked to preserve a peaceful relationship with their gods by offering sacrifices and performing rituals meant to gain the gods' favor.

Peculium: Property held in a special account for a child or slave by the technical owner. It could be revoked, but while it existed the owner was liable for the child or slave's debts up to that amount.

Pedagogue: A slave whose job it was to escort children to and from school and supervise their studies.

Pediment: The triangular space formed by the slanting roof at the ends of a building, usually a temple.

Pelagianism: The heretical teaching of the British fourth-fifth century theologian Pelagius, which claims that man can bring about his own salvation by his own efforts, rather than God's grace. Its consequence is asceticism and the denial of original sin.

Penates: *See* **Household Gods**

Pentameter: A line of verse consisting of four dactyls (q.v.) and two long syllables thought to make up a fifth foot.

Peripatetic: Of or related to the philosophical tradition founded by Aristotle, whose school, the Lyceum, appears to have had a *peripatos* or walkway.

Peripeteia: A reversal of fortune, typically from good fortune to calamity, as in tragedy. According to Aristotle, this results from a hamartia (q.v.), or error, on the part of the tragic character.

Periplus (Gk. *periplous,* lit. "a sailing around"): Refers to a genre of geographical writing, in which observations and analysis are arranged in the same order as the geographical features. The genre is at least as old as Scylax's exploration of the Indus River. The *periplus,* coupled with mathematical geography, was the central mode of exploration in the ancient world and was often conducted by traders seeking new market goods.

Peristyle (Lat. *peristylium*): The open-roofed, garden space at the back of a Roman house.

Perones: Simple boots or shoes made of leather, worn by peasants, farmers, and farmhands.

Personal Narrator: A storyteller who relates a tale from the point of view of one of the people in it without having this character speak for him/herself.

Pharmacopola: Someone who sells medicines, a druggist; often a derogatory term.

Philanthropy: A natural love of one's fellow human being; one of the doctrines of Cynicism (q.v.).

Philhellenism: An appreciation for Greek culture.

Pietas: One's moral duty: this could be *erga parentes* (toward one's parents), *erga patriam* (toward one's fatherland), or *erga deos* (toward the gods).

Plebeian: A member of the lower socioeconomic class (Lat. *plebs*) of early Rome, as opposed to the patricians (q.v.). Membership in these groups was determined entirely by birth. From the establishment of the Roman Republic in 509 B.C.E. until the third century B.C.E., the plebeians struggled with the patricians for increased rights and power; after this so-called Struggle of the Orders ended, the distinction faded away. In the period covered by this volume it was already relatively unimportant, though a certain number of governmental positions were reserved for plebeians. (*See also* **Secession of the Plebs.**)

Polenta: Hulled grain that was ground into a meal, then cooked in water (possibly with flavoring agents); a mainstay of the Roman diet. The most frequently employed grain was barley.

Political Philosophy: That branch of philosophy which deals with the ideal form of government and its underlying principles.

Polyculture: Because certain crops had different soil requirements and harvest times, farmers in the Roman world could grow different crops on the same land, notably grain, grapes, and olives. Growing crops in this way is known as *polyculture*.

Polymetric: Poems composed of many different metrical patterns and lines.

Pomerium: The sacred limit of the city of Rome, within which it became illegal to cremate or bury anyone.

Pons: "Bridge."

Pontifex Maximus: The chief priest of the sacral department of Roman religion. The *pontifices* were a group of "priests," or more precisely experts in religious law. The *pontifex maximus* was responsible for setting feast days, overseeing the Vestal Virgins, and leading the pontifical college. In the republic, he was elected by a modified popular vote; only seventeen tribes participated in the selection. Beginning with the reign of Augustus, the emperor took over the office of *pontifex maximus* as well.

Pontifical College: The board made up of the three major priests (*Flamen Dialis, Flamen Martialis, Flamen Quirinalis*), the *Rex sacrorum*, the twelve lesser *flamines*, the *pontifex maximus*, the lesser pontiffs, and the Vestal Virgins.

Popina: A Roman snack shop.

Populares: These were politicians in the late Roman Republic who tried to amass power by invoking the will of and seeking favor from the mass population of Rome, often in the spirit of the Gracchi. They are often contrasted with *Optimates* (q.v.), who supported the elite classes.

Porphyry: Red volcanic stone quarried from Egypt.

Portico (Lat. *porticus*): A colonnade attached to a building, usually serving as a porch.

Pozzolana: Volcanic earth from near Naples; the active ingredient in concrete.

Praedictio: Divination, the science of interpreting a prodigious event, either by consultation of the Sibylline Books, or through extispicy (q.v.).

Praenomen: A Roman man's first name, which came before the *nomen gentile* (q.v.). Women did not have *praenomina*.

Praetor: The praetor governed the courts of Rome and was the second most powerful magistrate in Rome, second to the Consul. In particular the "urban" praetor (chosen from his colleagues by lot) controlled all civil litigation. There were eventually eight praetors.

Prandium: Lunch; the next meal after *ientaculum* (q.v.).

Presocratics: A modern term for Greek thinkers prior to the time of Socrates of Athens; they were scientists, mathematicians, and poets, as well as "philosophers."

Prime Number: Any positive integer that has no factor except itself and one. The earliest prime numbers perceived were 2, 3, 5, 7, 11, 13, 17, and 19. Euclid proved that there were an infinite number of prime numbers.

Princeps: A benign term, adopted as a title by Augustus, and meaning roughly "first citizen." In the Republic, the *princeps senatus* was the senior man in the senate. He spoke first on all matters. Augustus, therefore, in using the simple title *princeps,* masked his absolute power behind good Republican terminology.

Principate: The regime established by Augustus (see *princeps*); more generally, the Empire from Augustus to 284 C.E.

Private Law: One of the two major branches of Roman law, including dealings between a specific number of individuals: contract, property, inheritance, marriage and family law, personal injury and defamation, theft, and assault. Public law, by contrast, involved matters where at least one of the parties was the community as a whole: many crimes (especially those involving governmental corruption), citizenship, and structure of the government. Under the Republic, private and public law cases were decided in different kinds of courts, but under the Empire they could both come under *cognitio* (q.v.).

Proconsul: *See* **Promagistrate**

Promagistrate: Someone who was given (most of) the authority of a consul or praetor so they could carry out a specific task for the state; these were called proconsuls and propraetors respectively. Originally promagistrates were appointed mainly for ongoing wars, but by the end of the Republic of the government of the empire was done by them.

Promulsis: An appetizer or "relish."

Propraetor: *See* **Promagistrate**

Proscribe, Proscription: "Proscribing" refers to the practice of drawing up lists of Romans who were to be killed and have their property confiscated. The proscriptions of Sulla were particularly notorious, but many other powerful Romans at various times used proscriptions, especially during the civil war at the end of the Roman Republic.

Protreptic: A work of philosophical writing which seeks to attract people to the study of philosophy as a way of life.

Province (Lat. *provincia*): The area of authority of a Roman magistrate or promagistrate. This might be administrative (for instance, the urban praetor's control of civil jurisdiction), geographical (for instance, a "province," in the English sense, to be governed), or task oriented (for instance, to clear the sea of pirates).

Public Law: *See* **Private Law**

Publicans (Lat. *publicani*): Wealthy Roman businessmen who would bid on public contracts, especially to collect taxes.

Puls: Wheat that has been ground and boiled into porridge.

Pulvis puteolanus: Pulvis is the Latin word for powder or dust. The special volcanic ash found near Puteoli and Mount Vesuvius, the volcano that destroyed Pompeii, was the basic material out of which the Romans learned to manufacture concrete mortar.

Punic Wars: A series of three wars fought between Rome and the North African city of Carthage between 264 and 146 B.C.E.

Pyrrhonism: Another name for Scepticism (q.v.).

Quadrigae: A four-horse chariot.

Quadrivium: A group of four subjects—geometry, arithmetic, astronomy, and music—constituting the upper division of the seven liberal arts (being the arts befitting the *liberalis* or "free man") in the mediaeval universities. *See also* **Trivium.**

Quaestor: The first magistracy in the *cursus honorum,* the path of offices that a man had to go through to reach the consulship. Quaestors were originally inquisitors in murder cases. By the second century B.C.E. the *quaestor* became a financial office, charged with overseeing public expenses, the water supply, and paying soldiers. In the fifth century B.C.E. there were two quaestors; by the first century B.C.E. there were twenty.

Quinquereme: A warship with five banks of oars on either side.

Quirites: The technical term for the Roman people in their capacity as citizens.

Recitatio: The public reading of a literary work.

Recusatio: Lit. "refusal"; this refers to the refusal of elegiac or other poets to write epic. The refusal, however, is always made in and with another type of poetry.

Regia: The office of the pontifical priesthood in the Roman Forum.

Relief Sculpture: Sculpture in which figures emerge partly from a sunken background.

Repetundae: A criminal offense—taking too much money from provincial subjects under one's authority or, eventually, other kinds of corruption in provincial government.

Rescripts: Documents written by the emperor in response to petitions made by his subjects. They carried the force of law and were often transcribed to stone to be set up in public places.

Retiarius: A gladiator who fought with a net (*rete*) and trident.

Revelatory: A term used to describe religious texts or teachings that reveal an ultimate truth or the will of an absolute God to devoted adherents.

Reverentia: Reverence, respect. The devotion shared by a husband and a wife.

Rex nemorensis: Lit. "king of the grove," the special priest of the goddess Diana at her hilltop shrine at Aricia, southeast of Rome.

Rex sacrorum: Lit. "king of ceremonies," a priest who took over the religious duties of the king after the end of the monarchy. He was responsible for sacrifices on the first day of each month, and on the *Nones* (the 5th or, sometimes, the 7th day of the month) he would announce the festival days for that month.

Rhetor: A teacher of rhetoric and oratory. The *grammaticus* (q.v.) represented the secondary level of Roman education; the *rhetor,* the tertiary. With the *rhetor* the student studied *rhetoric,* the principles governing oratory or persuasive public speaking. Knowledge of rhetoric was important for success in both the political and the legal arenas of Roman life.

Ring Composition: In literature this refers to the repetition, at the end of a structural unit, of a sequence of words, phrases, or motifs from its beginning, but in inverse order (ABCBA). Also known as "pedimental composition."

Roman Forum: The low area, originally a swamp and cemetery, between the Palatine, Capitoline, and Esquiline Hills; it became the principal religious and civic center of the Roman world.

Roman Odes: The first six odes of Horace's third book of Odes.

Romanitas: Roman-ness; the quality of being Roman.

Romanization: The absorption (sometimes conscious, sometimes voluntary) of various elements of Roman culture (language, laws, dress, religious customs) by subject peoples. There was little forced Romanization, but the Roman government also did nothing to make life easier for persons or peoples who wanted to retain their traditional cultures.

Sacerdos: A generic, sometimes specific, term for priests of the sacral part of Roman religion, as opposed to *augur* (q.v.).

Sacra: All those things that a people or an individual might give to a god, such as the sacrifice of animals, liquid offerings, incense, a temple or shrine, or public games or holidays.

Sacralization: The making sacred of something. The later Roman emperors increasingly connected themselves to divinity (both pagan and Christian), and even in the Republic some Romans allowed themselves to be worshiped by foreign subjects.

Sacrosanct: Inviolable, secure from physical assault. The tribunes of the *plebs,* for example, were sacrosanct.

Salii: Special priests of the god Mars who, in March and October, would perform an ancient dance and song in procession through the city, carrying his *ancilia* or ancient shields.

Salutatio: Lit. "greeting," A morning ritual during which a client (q.v.) visited his *patronus* (q.v).

Samnis: A gladiator who fought with Samnite weapons.

Sandalia: Sandals; footgear with thongs or straps.

Sarcophagus: A container designed to hold a dead body; usually made of marble or other stone.

Saturnian: A native Italian meter whose exact mechanism we still do not understand; it depended on alliteration and pairing of terms.

Scepticism: The philosophical school of Pyrrhon and his followers, who held that nothing can be known for certain.

Sculpona (plural = *sculponae*): A slip-on sandal with a high wooden sole, favored in Germany and England.

Secession of the *Plebs*: During the Struggle of the Orders, the Plebeians several times went on strike against the Patricians by withdrawing from their jobs and functions. Because the city and the military needed the Plebeians, this action would force concessions from the Patricians.

Sedition: An attempt to overthrow or destabilize an existing government, often by violence.

Senate: The Senate was the most powerful and prestigious political body in ancient Rome, although eventually the Emperor and his court surpassed it. Members of the Senate, called Senators, at various times in history were born, appointed, or otherwise enrolled into the Senate (but never elected). To belong to the Senate, members had to own considerable property, and most often there was a level of financial worth required.

Sestertius (plural = *sestertii*): The *sestertius* or "sesterce" was the basic bronze coin during the Roman Empire. Many financial assessments were set in terms of sesterces. For example, the emperor Augustus set the financial requirements for membership in the Senate at one million sesterces and the equestrian order at four hundred thousand sesterces.

Sibyl: A prophetess, sometimes said to be inspired by Apollo. Sibyls were associated with various locations, including Delphi (in Greece) and Cumae (in Campania). *See also* **Sibylline Books.**

Sibylline Books: According to ancient legend, the Cumaean Sibyl offered nine books of oracles to the Roman king Tarquinius Superbus at a high price. When he refused to buy them, she burned three, and offered him the remaining six at the same price. He refused again; she burned three more, and finally he agreed to buy the remaining three—at the original price. Whatever their origin, the Romans did indeed have books of oracles, which were stored in a vault under the temple of Capitoline Jupiter. These were eventually destroyed by fire, but a new collection of oracular sayings was made, and Augustus had these stored in the temple of Apollo on the Palatine Hill. In times of dread portents and prodigies, the priests of Apollo would consult these Books in order to interpret the meaning of the signs.

Sidereal Day: The interval between two successive cycles or transits of the stars across the sky on the equinox. The "stars'" day is slightly different from the solar day.

Slaves: Residents of Rome or the Roman Empire who were not free, because, for example, they were captured in war, were slaves. Legally they were the property of their masters. Slaves might acquire their freedom, but they could never become full free citizens, just a freedman or freedwoman.

Social War: *See Socius*

Societas: "Partnership." A description of the relationship between a husband and wife, or between political or military allies.

Socius (plural = *socii*): An ally. Until the early part of the first century B.C.E., much of Italy was composed of "free" allies of Rome, bound by treaty to give military support to Roman wars. After the Social War (known as "War of the Allies") of 91–88 B.C.E., these communities were granted Roman citizenship.

Solea (plural = *soleae*): Sandal-like footgear with straps.

Solstices: The two times of the year when the sun is the furthest from the equator, after reaching its tropical points, and it appears to stand still; the summer solstice occurs around 21 June, while the winter solstice occurs around 22 December.

Sophists: Various itinerant lecturers, thinkers, and orators in Athens who taught young men to speak well in order to achieve political success.

Spectacula: Spectacles; public shows such as plays and gladiator fights.

Spina: A long, narrow island around which chariots raced in the circus.

Sponsalia: "Betrothal." A formal agreement in which a father and a young man arrange a marriage between the father's daughter and the young man. The young man would present the girl a ring, which she would wear on the third finger of her left hand.

Sportula: Provisions given by a patron to his clients.

Stadium: A structure similar in shape to the *circus,* but on a smaller scale, and used for foot races and other contests.

Statute: A law passed by a legislative body (as opposed to the decisions of courts or legal scholars, or the decrees of executive officers).

Stele: An upright stone slab, often used as a grave marker, sometimes with inscriptions and relief sculpture.

Stellar Parallax: In the heliocentric theory of the solar system, in revolving around the sun, an angle should be seen formed by a fixed star and the observer on earth as the earth changes its position around the sun. The inability of the human eye without powerful instruments to measure an angle was a point of refutation to Aristarchus's proposal that the earth revolves around the sun.

Stipulatio: A form of contract, potentially concerning any kind of legal transaction, necessarily phrased as an oral question and answer. If there was a dispute about the transaction, the judge was bound to interpret the contract literally rather than applying a "good-faith" standard.

Stoa: A long, rectangular construction with a roof extending from the back wall to a row of supports in front.

Stoicism: A philosophical school of thought, founded by Zeno, that believed in a Divine Providence governing all things. It advocated the assertion of reason over passion.

Stola: The dress of a married or adult Roman woman.

Strigil: A curved scraper used to remove sweat, dirt, and oil from a bather's body.

Stucco: Plaster used on walls and ceilings, often for ornamentation.

Stylus: A pointed writing instrument used to incise letters onto a wax tablet.

Suasoria: A rhetorical exercise in which a student delivers the speech he imagines an historical or mythical character would have delivered in a given situation. *See also* **Declamation.**

Sudatorium: The sweat room of the *thermae,* also called the *laconicum.*

Suebi: Tacitus's term for the Germanic peoples east of the Elbe River, including the Marcomanni, Quadi, and Semnones. Some entered Spain in the fifth century B.C.E.; the Visigoths defeated them in the sixth century C.E.

Sui iuris: "under one's own control." Children were under the control of their father until his death, or until he released them from his control, making them independent.

Suiones: A term used in the geographical work of Pomponius Mela to designate the inhabitants of modern-day Scandinavia.

Sumptuary Law: A law designed to restrict extravagance and excessive luxury by limiting personal expenditures.

Suovetaurilia: A ceremony involving boundary purification procession and sacrifice of a pig, a sheep, and a bull (*sus, ouis,* and *taurus* respectively, hence the name).

Suus heres (plural = *sui heredes*): The person(s) who will inherit from you if you die without a will, that is, your children, or your grandchildren whose own parents (your children) have already died.

Syncretism: The blending of elements of different religious practices and philosophical beliefs.

Synoecism: The gradual growing together of separate communities to form a single urban area.

Tablinum: The main reception room of a Roman house, located at the back of the atrium directly opposite the front door. Here a patron would greet his clients.

Taurobolium: The special sacrifice of a bull in the worship of Mithras and other mystery cults; celebrants would be bathed in the blood of the sacrificed bull.

Teleology: The belief, held by Aristotle, that everything in nature has an ultimate end, toward which its own inner nature directs it.

Tempera Technique: The use of medium such as egg yolk to bind colors in painting.

Templum: The sacred area dedicated to any god or spirit. The area might contain an altar or a temple dedicated to a god. The *templum* may also be the area marked out by an augur for the purpose of reading the signs, or a place like the Senate's meetinghouse (*curia,* q.v.).

Tepidarium: An indirectly heated warm room in the *thermae* (public baths), sometimes containing a pool of tepid water.

Terracotta: Baked clay.

Tessera (plural = *tesserae*): A piece of stone, terracotta, or colored glass used in composing mosaics.

Tetrarchy: A government of four men, two *Augusti* and two Caesars, established by Diocletian to manage the huge expanse of the empire.

Thermae: A public bath complex, typically including several rooms with waters of different temperatures, from hot to cold.

Thermopolium: A fast-food and drink bar.

Tholos: A circular structure with a domed roof.

Thrax: Lit. "Thracian"; a gladiator who fought with a round shield and curved scimitar.

Tirocinium: a period of military apprenticeship for young Roman men.

Toga: The formal garment of the Roman male citizen, made of a long oval of cloth that was elaborately draped around the body.

Toga praetexta: A toga with a purple border worn by Roman boys until they reached the age of manhood.

Toga uirilis: The toga worn by male adults.

Tonsor: A barber.

Tonstrix: A female hair cutter.

Travertine: Light-colored limestone, often used in Rome and its environs.

Tribe: Rome originally began with three tribes (said to have been established by Romulus). As the population expanded, the number of tribes expanded until there were thirty-five: four urban tribes and thirty-one rural tribes. As people were added to Rome's population, they were assigned to a tribe. Voting in the popular assembly and for the *pontifex maximus* was done by tribes, with the tribes voting in a particular order. Roman officials used the tribes to conduct the census, recruit soldiers, and collect taxes.

Tribunate: The office of Tribune (q.v.).

Tribune: [1] *Tribunus plebis* (tribune of the *plebs*): Originally the leaders of the Roman *plebs* (q.v.), the tribunes eventually became officers of the Roman state. They sponsored legislation and had the authority to block laws and magisterial decrees. Their persons were sacrosanct (q.v.). [2] *Tribunus militaris* (military tribune): One of the (up to) six staff-officers attached to a legion. These were generally young aristocrats seeking military experience. Some were elected and others were political appointees. [3] *Tribunus aerarius* (tribune of the treasury): Originally these were officials of the Roman tribes (q.v.) who collected property taxes for waging war, and saw to the payment of the soldiers. Later the term came to refer to a property class slightly below the *equites* (q.v.).

Tribunician: Of or related to a tribune. Most notably, the emperors did not technically hold the office of tribune, but they were granted "tribunician" powers.

Triclinium: Either the traditional arrangement of three dining couches around a serving table, or the room that accommodated them.

Trireme: A warship with three banks of oars on each side.

Triumph: An elaborate festival and parade of spoils that celebrated a Roman conquest. The victorious general was feted as *triumphator* and was dressed for the occasion in the garb of Jupiter.

Triumvirate: A power-sharing arrangement among the three most powerful men in Rome.

Trivium: Of the "liberal arts," the seven subjects held in the Middle Ages to befit the educated *liberalis* or free man, three were language based: grammar, dialectic (logic), and rhetoric. These were known collectively as the *Trivium*, which formed the lower division of study in the mediaeval universities. *See also* **Quadrivium**.

Tropes: Certain figurative uses of language, such as simile or metaphor.

Tropics: Each of two solstitial points, where the sun begins to move toward the equator after reaching its furthest distance to the north and south of it; each of two latitudinal parallels, the topic of Cancer and the tropic of Capricorn, at a fixed distance to the north and to the south of the equator.

Tunica: The basic garment common to Roman men, women, and children. Rectangular in shape, with holes for the head and arms, this garment was worn over underclothing, and its length was adjusted with a belt at the waist.

Tutela: Legal guardianship. The guardians of minors had considerable control over their property (subject to suit for fraud after they reached legal age). Women without a living father were also subject to a tutor, though his power was much weaker (and came to be nearly nonexistent in practice).

Tutor: Someone appointed to serve as a guardian for a woman, to conduct her legal and business affairs.

Univira: A woman who married only once.

Urban Praetor: *See* **Edict** *and* **Praetor**

Usus: A form of arrangement constituting a marriage in which a man and woman live together and announce themselves as husband and wife.

Uxor: "Wife."

Vaults: A tunnelled or barrel vault is an arched roof; a groin or cross vault involves the intersection of two such vaults.

Venatio (plural = *venationes*): Wild-beast hunts staged in public arenas for entertainment.

Verna: A slave born in the household in which his or her mother serves.

Vestal Virgin: One of six young girls chosen for lifelong service to the goddess Vesta; their duties, besides remaining sexually pure, included the keeping of the sacred hearth and fire and the providing of other ritual and purificatory supplies for public sacrifices.

Vestibulum: The vestibule, an enclosed entryway into a Roman house, serving as a lobby of sorts.

Via: "Road."

Villa: A luxurious Roman house, either in a city or outside of town.

Villa rustica: A villa in the country (*rus*) that served as a working farm.

Villa suburbana: A luxury home outside of a city (*urbs*).

Villa urbana: A luxury home in the city (*urbs*).

Vir: Latin for "man" and also "husband."

Viticulture: The cultivation of the vine, generally the grapevine for wine manufacture.

Zodiac and Zodiac Periods: From observations made by the Egyptians and more so by the Babylonians, the five planets ("wandering stars": Mercury, Venus, Mars, Jupiter, and Saturn) appear to move through the sky within a narrow band, called the zodiac. This band and its eleven constellations were marked into twelve segments of thirty degrees each, thus giving us the signs of the zodiac. The time periods for the movements were used to measure the motions of the sun and moon and could be employed for astrological predictions.

GENERAL REFERENCES

GENERAL

Mary Beard and Michael Crawford, *Rome in the Late Republic* (Ithaca, N.Y.: Cornell University Press, 1985).

Averil Cameron, *The Later Roman Empire, AD 284–430* (Cambridge, Mass.: Harvard University Press, 1993).

Karl Christ, *The Romans: An Introduction to Their History and Civilization,* translated by Christopher Holme (Berkeley: University of California Press, 1984).

Elaine Fantham, and others, *Women in the Classical World: Image and Text* (New York: Oxford University Press, 1994).

Michael Grant, *History of Rome* (London: Weidenfeld & Nicolson, 1978).

Finley Hooper, *Roman Realities* (Detroit: Wayne State University Press, 1979).

Simon Hornblower and Antony Spawforth, eds., *The Oxford Classical Dictionary,* third edition (Oxford: Oxford University Press, 1999).

E. Allo Isichei, *Political Thinking and Social Experience: Some Christian Interpretations of the Roman Empire from Tertullian to Salvian* (Christchurch, New Zealand: University of Canterbury, 1964).

Richard Jenkyns, ed., *The Legacy of Rome: A New Appraisal* (Oxford & New York: Oxford University Press, 1992).

Peter Jones and Keith Sidwell, eds., *The World of Rome: An Introduction to Roman Culture* (Cambridge & New York: Cambridge University Press, 1997).

Donald Kagan, ed., *The End of the Roman Empire: Decline or Transformation* (Lexington, Mass.: D. C. Heath, 1978).

Antony Kamm, *The Romans: An Introduction* (London & New York: Routledge, 1995).

Naphtali Lewis and Meyer Reinhold, eds., *Roman Civilization: Selected Readings,* two volumes (New York: Columbia University Press, 1951–1955).

H. M. D. Parker, *A History of the Roman World from A.D. 138 to 337* (London: Methuen, 1958).

L. Richardson Jr., *A New Topographical Dictionary of Ancient Rome* (Baltimore: Johns Hopkins University Press, 1992).

Jo-Ann Shelton, *As the Romans Did: A Sourcebook in Roman Social History,* second edition (New York: Oxford University Press, 1998).

Oliver Taplin, ed., *Literature in the Greek and Roman Worlds: A New Perspective* (Oxford & New York: Oxford University Press, 2000).

Allen M. Ward, Fritz M. Heichelheim, and Cedric A. Yeo, *A History of the Roman People,* third edition (Upper Saddle River, N.J.: Prentice Hall, 1999).

Colin M. Wells, *The Roman Empire* (Stanford, Cal.: Stanford University Press, 1984).

THE ARTS

Michael von Albrecht, *A History of Roman Literature: From Livius Andronicus to Boethius* (Leiden & New York: E. J. Brill, 1997).

William S. Anderson, *Barbarian Play: Plautus' Roman Comedy* (Toronto: University of Toronto Press, 1993).

W. G. Arnott, *Menander, Plautus, Terence: Greece and Rome New Surveys in the Classics* (Oxford: Clarendon Press, 1975).

Giovanni Comotti, *Music in Greek and Roman Culture,* second edition (Baltimore: Johns Hopkins University Press, 1989).

Gian Biagio Conte, *Latin Literature: A History* (Baltimore: Johns Hopkins University Press, 1987).

Edward Courtney, *Archaic Latin Prose* (Atlanta: Scholars Press, 1999).

Courtney, *Musa lapidaria* (Atlanta: Scholars Press, 1995).

Michael Grant, *Latin Literature: An Anthology* (Harmondsworth, U.K. & New York: Penguin, 1978).

George M. A. Hanfmann, *Roman Art: A Modern Survey of the Art of Imperial Rome* (New York & London: Norton, 1975).

Jacob Isager, *Pliny on Art and Society* (London: Routledge, 1991).

K. Jex-Blake and Eugenie S. Sellers, eds., *The Elder Pliny's Chapters on the History of Art* (Chicago: Argonaut, 1968).

George A. Kennedy, *The Art of Rhetoric in the Roman World* (Princeton: Princeton University Press, 1972).

E. J. Kenney and W. V. Clausen, eds., *Latin Literature,* volume 2, *The Cambridge History of Classical Literature* (Cambridge: Cambridge University Press, 1982).

Diana E. E. Kleiner, *Roman Sculpture* (New Haven & London: Yale University Press, 1992).

Roger Ling, *Roman Painting* (Cambridge: Cambridge University Press, 1990).

William L. MacDonald, *The Architecture of the Roman Empire I: An Introductory Study,* second edition (New Haven: Yale University Press, 1982).

MacDonald, *The Architecture of the Roman Empire II: An Urban Appraisal,* second edition (New Haven: Yale University Press, 1987).

Timothy J. Moore, *The Theater of Plautus: Playing to the Audience* (Austin: University of Texas Press, 1998).

Jerome J. Pollitt, *Art in the Hellenistic Age* (Cambridge: Cambridge University Press, 1986).

Nancy and Andrew Ramage, *Roman Art: Romulus to Constantine,* third edition (London: Laurence King, 2000).

L. Richardson Jr., *Pompeii: An Architectural History* (Baltimore: Johns Hopkins University Press, 1988).

Curt Sachs, *The Rise of Music in the Ancient World, East and West* (New York: Norton, 1943).

Donald E. Strong, *Roman Imperial Sculpture* (London: A. Tiranti, 1961).

Mario Torelli, *Typology and Structure of Roman Historical Reliefs* (Ann Arbor: University of Michigan Press, 1982).

P. G. Walsh, *Livy: His Historical Aims and Methods* (Cambridge: Cambridge University Press, 1961).

John B. Ward-Perkins, *Roman Architecture* (New York & London: Harry N. Abrams, 1977).

Timothy Peter Wiseman, *Catullus and his World: A Reappraisal* (Cambridge: Cambridge University Press, 1985).

A. J. Woodman, *Rhetoric in Classical Historiography: Four Studies* (London: Croom Helm, 1988).

COMMUNICATION, TRANSPORTATION, AND EXPLORATION

Graham Anderson, *Philostratus: Biography and Belles Lettres in the Third Century A.D.* (London & Dover, N.H.: Croom Helm, 1986).

N. J. E. Austin and N. B. Rankov, *Exploratio: Military and Political Intelligence in the Roman World From the Second Punic War to the Battle of Adrianople* (London & New York: Routledge, 1995).

Roger S. Bagnall, *Reading Papyri, Writing Ancient History* (London & New York: Routledge, 1995).

J. P. V. D. Balsdon, *Romans and Aliens* (Chapel Hill: University of North Carolina Press, 1979).

Carlin A. Barton, *The Sorrows of the Ancient Romans: The Gladiator and the Monster* (Princeton: Princeton University Press, 1993).

Mary T. Boatwright, *Hadrian and the Cities of the Roman Empire* (Princeton: Princeton University Press, 2000).

Alan K. Bowman, *Life and Letters on the Roman Frontier: Vindolanda and Its People* (New York: Routledge, 1994).

Lionel Casson, *Ships and Seamanship in the Ancient World* (Princeton: Princeton University Press, 1971).

Casson, *Travel in the Ancient World* (London: Allen & Unwin, 1974).

Jo-Marie Claassen, *Displaced Persons: The Literature of Exile from Cicero to Boethius* (Madison: University of Wisconsin Press, 1999).

Raffaella Cribiore, *Writing, Teachers, and Students in Graeco-Roman Egypt* (Atlanta: Scholars Press, 1996).

O. A. W. Dilke, *Greek and Roman Maps* (Ithaca, N.Y.: Cornell University Press, 1985).

Niels Hannestad, *Roman Art and Imperial Policy* (Aarhus, Denmark: Aarhus University Press, 1986).

William V. Harris, *Ancient Literacy* (Cambridge, Mass.: Harvard University Press, 1989).

Finley Hooper and Matthew Schwartz, *Roman Letters: History from a Personal Point of View* (Detroit: Wayne State University Press, 1991).

E. D. Hunt, *Holy Land Pilgrimage in the Later Roman Empire, AD 312–460* (Oxford: Clarendon Press, 1982; New York: Oxford University Press, 1982).

Lawrence Keppie, *Understanding Roman Inscriptions* (Baltimore: Johns Hopkins University Press, 1991).

Ray Laurence, *The Roads of Roman Italy: Mobility and Cultural Change* (London & New York: Routledge, 1999).

A. D. Lee, *Information and Frontiers: Roman Foreign Relations in Late Antiquity* (Cambridge & New York: Cambridge University Press, 1993).

Susan P. Mattern, *Rome and the Enemy: Imperial Strategy in the Principate* (Berkeley: University of California Press, 1999).

Russell Meiggs, *Roman Ostia* (Oxford: Clarendon Press, 1960).

Fergus Millar, *The Emperor and the Roman World: 31 BC–AD 337* (Ithaca, N.Y.: Cornell University Press, 1977).

John S. Morrison, *Greek and Roman Oared Warships* (Oxford: Oxbow Books, 1996).

Claude Nicolet, *Space, Geography, and Politics in the Early Roman Empire* (Ann Arbor: University of Michigan Press, 1991).

Colin O'Connor, *Roman Bridges* (Cambridge & New York: Cambridge University Press, 1993).

Henry A. Ormerod, *Piracy in the Ancient World: An Essay in Mediterranean History* (Liverpool: University Press of Liverpool; London: Hodder & Stoughton, 1924; reprint, Chicago: Argonaut, 1967).

O. F. Robinson, *The Sources of Roman Law: Problems and Methods For Ancient Historians* (London & New York: Routledge, 1997).

H. S. Versnel, *Triumphus: An Inquiry into the Origin, Development and Meaning of the Roman Triumph* (Leiden: E. J. Brill, 1970).

Paul Zanker, *The Power of Images in the Age of Augustus*, translated by H. Alan Shapiro (Ann Arbor: University of Michigan Press, 1988).

THE FAMILY AND SOCIAL TRENDS

Suzanne Dixon, *The Roman Family* (Baltimore: Johns Hopkins University Press, 1992).

Dixon, *The Roman Mother* (Norman: University of Oklahoma Press, 1988).

Jane Gardner, *Women in Roman Law and Society* (Bloomington: Indiana University Press, 1986).

Judith P. Hallett, *Fathers and Daughters in Roman Society: Women and the Elite Family* (Princeton: Princeton University Press, 1984).

Robert B. Kebric, *Roman People* (Mountain View, Cal.: Mayfield, 1992).

Beryl Rawson, ed., *The Family in Ancient Rome: New Perspectives* (Ithaca, N.Y.: Cornell University Press, 1986).

Susan Treggiari, *Roman Marriage: Iusti Coniuges From the Time of Cicero to the Time of Ulpian* (Oxford: Clarendon Press; New York: Oxford University Press, 1991).

Paul Veyne, ed., *From Pagan Rome to Byzantium*, volume 1, in *A History of Private Lives*, edited by Philippe Ariès and Georges Duby (Cambridge, Mass.: Belknap Press of Harvard University Press, 1987).

Joseph Vogt, *Ancient Slavery and the Idea of Man* (Cambridge, Mass.: Harvard University Press, 1974).

GEOGRAPHY

Karim W. Arafat, *Pausanias' Greece: Ancient Artists and Roman Rulers* (New York: Cambridge University Press, 1996).

Mary Beagon, *Roman Nature: The Thought of Pliny the Elder* (Oxford: Clarendon Press, 1992).

Hipparchus Bithynius, *The Geographical Fragments of Hipparchus*, edited by D. R. Dicks (London: Athlone, 1960).

Harry E. Burton, *The Discovery of the Ancient World* (Freeport, N.Y.: Books for Libraries Press, 1969).

Tim Cornell and John Matthews, *Atlas of the Roman World* (New York: Facts on File, 1982).

Leonard A. Curchin, *Roman Spain: Conquest and Assimilation* (London: Routledge, 1991).

J. L. E. Dreyer, *A History of Astronomy from Thales to Kepler* (New York: Dover, 1953).

Christian Habicht, *Pausanias' Guide to Ancient Greece* (Berkeley: University of California Press, 1985).

Francois Hartog, *The Mirror of Herodotus: The Representation of the Other in the Writing of History*, translated by Janet Lloyd (Berkeley: University of California Press, 1988.)

Claude Nicolet, *Space, Geography, and Politics in the Early Roman Empire* (Ann Arbor: University of Michigan Press, 1991).

Pomponius Mela's Description of the World, translated by Frank E. Romer (Ann Arbor: University of Michigan Press, 1998).

Colin A. Ronan, *Discovering the Universe: A History of Astronomy* (New York: Basic Books, 1971).

Peter Salway, *The Oxford Illustrated History of Roman Britain* (Oxford: Oxford University Press, 1993).

J. O. Thomson, *History of Ancient Geography* (Cambridge: Cambridge University Press, 1948).

LEISURE, RECREATION, AND DAILY LIFE

Apicius, *The Roman Cookery of Apicius: A Treasury of Gourmet Recipes & Herbal Cookery*, translated John Edwards (Port Roberts, Wash.: Hartley & Marks, 1984).

Ian M. Barton, ed., *Roman Domestic Buildings* (Exeter, U.K.: University of Exeter Press, 1996).

Richard C. Beacham, *The Roman Theatre and Its Audience* (Cambridge, Mass.: Harvard University Press, 1992).

Stanley F. Bonner, *Education in Ancient Rome: From the Elder Cato to the Younger Pliny* (London: Eyre Methuen, 1977).

Ilaria Gozzini Giacosa, *A Taste of Ancient Rome*, translated by Anna Herklotz (Chicago: University of Chicago Press, 1992).

Michael Grant, *Gladiators* (London: Weidenfeld & Nicolson, 1967).

John H. Humphrey, *Roman Circuses: Arenas for Chariot Racing* (Berkeley: University of California Press, 1986).

Teresa Morgan, *Literate Education in the Hellenistic and Roman Worlds* (Cambridge & New York: Cambridge University Press, 1998).

Judith Lynn Sebesta and Larissa Bonfante, eds., *The World of Roman Costume* (Madison: University of Wisconsin Press, 1994).

Thomas Wiedemann, *Adults and Children in the Roman Empire* (New Haven: Yale University Press, 1989).

Wiedemann, *Emperors and Gladiators* (London & New York: Routledge, 1992).

Lilian M. Wilson, *The Clothing of the Ancient Romans* (Baltimore: Johns Hopkins University Press, 1938).

POLITICS, LAW, AND THE MILITARY

Frank F. Abbott, *A History and Description of Roman Political Institutions* (New York: Biblo & Tannen, 1963).

Frank E. Adcock, *The Roman Art of War under the Republic* (New York: Barnes & Noble, 1960).

Alan E. Astin, *Cato the Censor* (Oxford: Clarendon Press, 1978).

J. P. V. D. Balsdon, *Julius Caesar and Rome* (London: English Universities Press, 1967).

Timothy D. Barnes, *The New Empire of Diocletian and Constantine* (Cambridge, Mass.: Harvard University Press, 1982).

P. A. Brunt and J. M. Moore, *Res gestae divi Augusti: The Achievements of the Divine Augustus* (London: Oxford University Press, 1967).

Averil Cameron, *The Later Roman Empire, AD 284–430* (Cambridge, Mass.: Harvard University Press, 1993).

J. B. Campbell, *The Roman Army 31 B.C.–A.D. 337* (London & New York: Routledge, 1994).

Peter Connolly, *The Roman Army* (London: Macdonald Educational, 1975).

John Anthony Crook, *Law and Life of Rome* (Ithaca, N.Y.: Cornell University Press, 1967).

Crook, *Legal Advocacy in the Roman World* (Ithaca, N.Y.: Cornell University Press, 1995).

Arther Ferrill, *The Fall of the Roman Empire: The Military Explanation* (London: Thames & Hudson, 1986).

Bruce W. Frier, *A Casebook on the Roman Law of Delict* (Atlanta: Scholars Press, 1989).

Karl Galinsky, *Augustan Culture: An Interpretive Introduction* (Princeton: Princeton University Press, 1996).

Peter Garnsey, *Social Status and Legal Privilege in the Roman Empire* (Oxford: Clarendon Press, 1970).

Matthias Gelzer, *Caesar: Politician and Statesman* (Cambridge, Mass.: Harvard University Press, 1968).

Adrian K. Goldsworthy, *The Roman Army at War 100 B.C.–A.D. 200* (Oxford & New York: Clarendon Press, 1996).

Michael Grant, *The Army of the Caesars* (New York: Scribners, 1974).

Grant, *Julius Caesar* (New York: M. Evans, 1969).

Grant, *The Roman Emperors: A Biographical Guide to the Rulers of Imperial Rome, 31 B.C.–A.D. 476* (New York: Scribners, 1985).

P. A. L. Greenhalgh, *The Year of the Four Emperors* (London: Weidenfeld & Nicolson, 1975).

Keith Hopkins, *Death and Renewal* (Cambridge & New York: Cambridge University Press, 1983).

Herbert F. Jolowicz and Barry Nicholas, *Historical Introduction to Roman Law* (Cambridge: Cambridge University Press, 1972).

Arthur D. Kahn, *The Education of Julius Caesar: A Biography, A Reconstruction* (New York: Schocken, 1986).

John M. Kelly, *Roman Litigation* (Oxford: Clarendon Press, 1966).

L. J. F. Keppie, *The Making of the Roman Army: From Republic to Empire* (London: B.T. Batsford, 1984).

Andrew W. Lintott, *The Constitution of the Roman Republic* (Oxford: Clarendon Press / New York: Oxford University Press, 1999).

Lintott, *Imperium Romanum: Politics and Administration* (London & New York: Routledge, 1993).

Lintott, *Violence in Republican Rome* (Oxford: Clarendon Press, 1968).

Fergus Millar, *The Crowd in the Late Roman Republic* (Ann Arbor: University of Michigan Press, 1998).

Millar, *The Emperor in the Roman World (31 B.C.–A.D. 337)* (Ithaca, N.Y.: Cornell University Press, 1977).

Millar and Erich Segal, eds., *Caesar Augustus: Seven Aspects* (Oxford & New York: Clarendon Press, 1984).

Barry Nicholas, *An Introduction to Roman Law* (Oxford: Clarendon Press, 1962).

Wilfried Nippel, *Public Order in Ancient Rome* (Cambridge & New York: Cambridge University Press, 1995).

K. A. Raaflaub and M. Toher, eds., *Between Republic and Empire: Interpretations of Augustus and His Principate* (Berkeley & Los Angeles: University of California Press, 1990).

Keith Richardson, *Daggers in the Forum: The Revolutionary Lives and Violent Deaths of the Gracchus Brothers* (London: Cassell, 1976).

Andrew M. Riggsby, *Crime and Community in Ciceronian Rome* (Austin: University of Texas Press, 1999).

O. F. Robinson, *The Criminal Law of Ancient Rome* (Baltimore: Johns Hopkins University Press, 1995).

Robinson, *The Sources of Roman Law: Problems and Methods for Ancient Historians* (London & New York: Routledge, 1997).

Chris Scarre, *Chronicle of the Roman Emperors: The Reign-by-Reign Record of the Rulers of Imperial Rome* (London: Thames & Hudson, 1995).

Howard Hayes Scullard, *Roman Politics 220–150 B.C.* (Oxford: Clarendon Press, 1951).

Ronald Syme, *The Roman Revolution* (Oxford: Oxford University Press, 1939).

Lily R. Taylor, *Party Politics in the Age of Caesar* (Berkeley: University of California Press, 1949).

Allen Mason Ward, *Marcus Crassus and the Late Republic* (Columbia: University of Missouri Press, 1977).

Alan Watson, *The Law of Obligations in the Later Roman Republic* (Oxford: Clarendon Press, 1965).

Watson, *The Law of Property in the Later Roman Republic* (Oxford: Clarendon Press, 1968).

Watson, *The Spirit of Roman Law* (Athens: University of Georgia Press, 1995).

Erik Wistrand, *Caesar and Contemporary Society* (Göteborg, Germany: Vetenskaps-och Vitterhets-samhället, 1979).

Zwi Yavetz, *Julius Caesar and His Public Image* (London: Thames & Hudson, 1983).

Paul Zanker, *The Power of Images in the Age of Augustus* (Ann Arbor: University of Michigan Press, 1988).

RELIGION AND PHILOSOPHY

Lesley Adkins and Roy A. Adkins, *Dictionary of Roman Religion* (New York: Facts on File, 1996).

Jonathan Barnes, *Logic and the Imperial Stoa* (Leiden & New York: E. J. Brill, 1997).

Barnes, *The Toils of Scepticism* (Cambridge & New York: Cambridge University Press, 1990).

Mary Beard, John North, and Simon Price, *Religions of Rome*, 2 volumes (Cambridge & New York: Cambridge University Press, 1998).

Walter Burkert, *Ancient Mystery Cults* (Cambridge, Mass: Harvard University Press, 1987).

Lucinda Dirven, *The Palmyrenes of Dura-Europos: A Study of Religious Interaction in Roman Syria* (Boston: E. J. Brill, 1999).

Ken Dowden, *Religion and the Romans* (London: Bristol Classical Press, 1992).

Georges Dumézil, *Archaic Roman Religion*, translated by Philip Krapp (Chicago: University of Chicago Press, 1970).

Brad Inwood, *Ethics and Human Action in Early Stoicism* (Oxford: Clarendon Press, 1985; New York: Oxford University Press, 1985).

Inwood and L. P. Gerson, eds., *Hellenistic Philosophy: Introductory Readings* (Indianapolis: Hackett, 1988).

J. H. W. G. Liebeschuetz, *Continuity and Change in Roman Religion* (Oxford: Clarendon Press, 1979; New York: Oxford University Press, 1979).

A. A. Long, *Hellenistic Philosophy* (London: Duckworth, 1974; New York, Scribners, 1974; second edition, Berkeley: University of California Press, 1986).

Long and D. N. Sedley, eds., *The Hellenistic Philosophers*, 2 volumes (Cambridge & New York: Cambridge University Press, 1987).

Ramsay MacMullen, *Paganism in the Roman Empire* (New Haven: Yale University Press, 1981).

R. M. Ogilvie, *The Romans and Their Gods in the Age of Augustus* (London: Chatto & Windus, 1969).

Phillip Mitsis, *Epicurus' Ethical Theory: The Pleasures of Invulnerability* (Ithaca, N.Y.: Cornell University Press, 1988).

Martha C. Nussbaum, *The Therapy of Desire: Theory and Practice in Hellenistic Ethics* (Princeton: Princeton University Press, 1994).

Malcolm Schofield and Gisela Striker, eds., *The Norms of Nature: Studies in Hellenistic Ethics* (Cambridge & New York: Cambridge University Press, 1986).

H. H. Scullard, *Festivals and Ceremonies of the Roman Republic* (Ithaca, N.Y.: Cornell University Press, 1981).

Robert Turcan, *The Gods of Ancient Rome*, translated by Antonia Nevill (Edinburgh: Edinburgh University Press, 2000).

Alan Watson, *The State, Law and Religion: Pagan Rome* (Athens: University of Georgia Press, 1992).

SCIENCE AND TECHNOLOGY

Mary Beagon, *Roman Nature: The Thought of Pliny the Elder* (Oxford: Clarendon Press, 1992; New York: Oxford University Press, 1992).

Lawrence J. Bliquez, *Roman Surgical Instruments and Other Minor Objects in the National Archaeological Museum of Naples* (Mainz: Verlag Phlipp von Zabern, 1994).

Robert I. Curtis, *Garun and Salsamenta: Production and Commerce in Materia Medica* (Leiden & New York: E. J. Brill, 1991).

L. Strague DeCamp, *The Ancient Engineers* (Garden City, N.Y.: Doubleday, 1963).

O. A. W. Dilke, *Greek and Roman Maps* (Ithaca, N.Y.: Cornell University Press, 1985).

Roger French and Frank Greenaway, eds., *Science in the Early Roman Empire: Pliny the Elder, His Sources and Influence* (Totowa, N.J.: Barnes & Noble, 1986).

Bernard R. Goldstein, *Theory and Observation in Ancient and Medieval Astronomy* (London: Variorum, 1985).

Mirko D. Grmek, *Diseases in the Ancient World*, translated by Mireille Muellner and Leonard Muellner (Baltimore: Johns Hopkins University Press, 1989).

J. B. Harley and David Woodward, eds., *The History of Cartography*, volume 1, *Cartography in Prehistoric, Ancient, and Medieval Europe and the Mediterranean* (Chicago: University of Chicago Press, 1987).

W. E. Heitland, *Agricola: A Study of Agriculture and Rustic Life in the Greco-Roman World from the Point of View of Labour* (Westport, Conn.: Greenwood Press, 1970).

Donald Hill, *A History of Engineering in Classical and Medieval Times* (London: Croom Helm, 1984).

A. Trevor Hodge, *Roman Aqueducts & Water Supply* (London: Duckworth, 1992).

Henry Hodges, *Technology in the Ancient World* (London: John Lane, 1970; New York: Knopf, 1970).

Ralph Jackson, *Doctors and Diseases in the Roman Empire* (London: British Museum Publications, 1988).

O. Neugebauer, *A History of Ancient Mathematical Astronomy*, 3 volumes (Berlin & New York: Springer-Verlag, 1975).

John M. Riddle, *Dioscorides on Pharmacy and Medicine* (Austin: University of Texas Press, 1985).

John Scarborough, *Roman Medicine* (London: Thames & Hudson, 1969; Ithaca, N.Y.: Cornell University Press, 1969).

Liba Chaia Taub, *Ptolemy's Universe: The Natural Philosophical and Ethical Foundations of Ptolemy's Astronomy* (Chicago: Open Court, 1993).

K. D. White, *A Bibliography of Roman Agriculture* (Reading, U.K.: University of Reading, 1970).

White, *Greek and Roman Technology* (Ithaca, N.Y.: Cornell University Press, 1984).

White, *Roman Farming* (London: Thames & Hudson, 1970; Ithaca, N.Y.: Cornell University Press, 1970).

SOCIAL CLASS SYSTEM AND THE ECONOMY

Peter J. Aicher, *Guide to the Aqueducts of Ancient Rome* (Wauconda, Ill.: Bolchazy-Carducci, 1995).

Henry C. Boren, *Roman Society: A Social, Economic, and Cultural History* (Lexington, Mass.: D. C. Heath, 1977).

Lionel Casson, *Everyday Life in Ancient Rome* (Baltimore: Johns Hopkins University Press, 1998).

Annamaria Ciarallo and Ernesto De Carolis, eds., *Pompeii: Life in a Roman Town* (Milan: Electa, 1999).

T. J. Cornell and Kathryn Lomas, eds., *Urban Society in Roman Italy* (London: UCL Press, 1995).

Richard Duncan-Jones, *Money and Government in the Roman Empire* (Cambridge & New York: Cambridge University Press, 1994).

Harry B. Evans, *Water Distribution in Ancient Rome: The Evidence of Frontinus* (Ann Arbor: University of Michigan Press, 1994).

M. I. Finley, *The Ancient Economy* (Berkeley: University of California Press, 1973).

Peter Garnsey, *Cities, Peasants, and Food in Classical Antiquity: Essays in Social and Economic History*, edited by Walter Scheidel (Cambridge & New York: Cambridge University Press, 1998).

Garnsey and Richard Saller, *The Roman Empire: Economy, Society, and Culture* (Berkeley: University of California Press, 1987).

Kevin Greene, *The Archaeology of the Roman Economy* (Berkeley: University of California Press, 1986).

Greene, *Roman Pottery* (London: British Museum Press, 1992).

Sandra R. Joshel, *Work, Identity, and Legal Status at Rome: A Study of the Occupational Inscriptions* (Norman: University of Oklahoma Press, 1992).

Ralph W. Mathisen, *Studies in the History, Literature and Society of Late Antiquity* (Amsterdam: Hakkert, 1991).

Friedrich Münzer, *Roman Aristocratic Parties and Families*, translated by Thérèse Ridley (Baltimore: Johns Hopkins University Press, 1999).

D. P. S. Peacock and D. F. Williams, *Amphorae and the Roman Economy: An Introductory Guide* (London & New York: Longman, 1986).

J. Theodore Peña, *The Urban Economy During the Early Dominate: Pottery Evidence from the Palatine Hill* (Oxford: Archaeopress, 1999).

John Rich, ed., *The City in Late Antiquity* (London & New York: Routledge, 1992).

Cosmo Rodewald, *Money in the Age of Tiberius* (Manchester, U.K.: Manchester University Press, 1976; Totowa, N.J.: Rowman & Littlefield, 1976).

Matthew B. Roller, *Constructing Autocracy: Aristocrats and Emperors in Julio-Claudian Rome* (Princeton: Princeton University Press, 2001).

A. N. Sherwin-White, *The Letters of Pliny: A Historical and Social Commentary* (Oxford: Clarendon Press, 1966).

David Taylor, *Work in Ancient Greece and Rome* (London: George Allen, 1975).

John Wilkins, David Harvey and Mike Dobson, eds., *Food in Antiquity* (Exeter, U.K.: University of Exeter Press, 1995).

CONTRIBUTORS

Joel Allen received his Ph.D. from Yale University in 1999 and is now an assistant professor of History and Classics at Ohio University. He is currently at work on a book titled *Cultural Diplomacy in the Roman Empire: Hostages and Students*. His general research interests include Roman foreign relations and the imperial provinces, economic and numismatic history, and the experiences of Roman women.

Peter Cohee received his doctorate in Classics at the University of Colorado in Boulder. He was a Fellow at the Thesaurus Lingue Latinae in Munich and has taught at Washington and Lee, George Mason University, and Ohio University. His special area of interest is ancient Roman public religion, in which he has published research. He is now Program Director for Classics at the Boston Latin School.

Bryan Daleas is a graduate of Hamilton College (Clinton, New York), and earned his M.A. and Ph.D. degrees in Classical Studies at Indiana University, Bloomington. His research interests include Latin literature and Roman social history, and he has presented papers about children in Roman antiquity. He is currently revising his doctoral dissertation, "Children in the Roman World: Status and the Growth of Identity," for publication.

Martin Helzle is Associate Professor and Chair of Classics at Case Western Reserve University. He received his Ph.D. from the University of Cambridge. Apart from many scholarly articles, he has published two books: one on Ovid and the other on Roman epic poetry after Vergil. He is currently preparing a two-volume commentary on Ovid's last poems, which were written from exile.

John T. Kirby is Professor of Classics and Comparative Literature and Chair of the Program in Comparative Literature at Purdue University, where he also founded the interdisciplinary Program in Classical Studies. His books include *The Rhetoric of Cicero's Pro Cluentio* (Gieben, 1990), *The Comparative Reader: A Handlist of Basic Reading in Comparative Literature* (Chancery Press, 1998), and *Secret of the Muses Retold: Classical Influences on Italian Authors of the Twentieth Century* (University of Chicago Press, 2000). In the *World Eras* series, he has also edited volume 6: *Classical Greek Civilization, 800–323* B.C.E. (Manly/Gale Group, 2001).

Wilfred E. Major took his B.A. at Southern Illinois University at Carbondale in 1989 and his Ph.D. at Indiana University in Classical Studies in 1996. He now teaches at Loyola University, New Orleans. His research interests focus mostly on Greek and Roman drama, and Greek comedy in particular. He also specializes in new translations of ancient plays and other works.

T. Davina McClain received two Bachelor of Arts degrees in Classical Studies and in History at Trinity University in San Antonio in 1986. In 1989 she earned a Masters in Latin, and in 1994 a Ph.D. in Classical Studies at Indiana University, Bloomington. She is currently Associate Professor and Acting Chair of Classics at Loyola University, New Orleans. Her research focuses on the representation of women in the work of the Roman historian Livy. A book, *Lucretia's Sisters: Gender and Representation in Livy's Ab Urbe Condita*, is in progress.

Patrick O'Sullivan is a Lecturer in Greek literature, language, art, and philosophy at the University of Canterbury, Christchurch, New Zealand. Among his chief research interests is the intellectual history of the Archaic and Classical Greek world, with a focus on the reception of poetry, ancient psychological and cognitive theories, and visual aesthetics. He has published on aspects of Greek art and drama, especially Aeschylus, and is working on a project on Greek concepts of visual imagery from Homer to Plato.

Patrice D. Rankine has been an Assistant Professor of Classics at Purdue University since 1998. He holds Ph.D. and Masters' degrees from Yale University, where he studied Classical Languages and Literatures. He earned his B.A. in Ancient Greek at Brooklyn College in New York City. Professor Rankine's interests include Senecan tragedy and the use of classical mythology in American literature. His current projects include a book on Ralph Ellison, tentatively titled *Mythocentrism: History, Heroism, and the Classical Tradition in the Works of Ralph Ellison*, and a book on Senecan tragedy, *Facing Power: Seneca's Tragedies in the Early Roman Empire*.

John M. Riddle is the Alumni Distinguished Professor of History at North Carolina State University. He is the author of seven books, including *Eve's Herbs: A History of Contraception and Abortion in the West* (Harvard University Press, 1997). He is a past president of the Society for Ancient Medicine and of the American Institute for the History of Pharmacy. In Prague he was awarded the Urdang International Medal for the history of medicine and pharmacy, the fourth American to receive this recognition.

Andrew M. Riggsby is Associate Professor of Classics at the University of Texas at Austin. He is the author of *Crime and Community in Ciceronian Rome* (University of Texas Press, 1999) and of scholarly articles on a variety of topics. His primary research interests are in rhetoric and oratory and in the cultural history of the political institutions of the late Roman Republic and early Empire.

INDEX OF PHOTOGRAPHS

Coin depicting the personification of the *Via Traiana*, a highway built by order of Trajan, circa 109 C.E. (Hunterian Museum, Glasgow) 158

A coin minted in 137 B.C.E. with a depiction of a Roman citizen dropping a stone tablet into a voting urn (Bibliothèque Nationale, Paris) 238

Colonnaded street built in the late second century C.E. looking toward the Arch of Trajan at Timgad in present-day Algeria 394

The Colosseum in Rome, completed in 80 C.E. 82

Constantine, marble portrait, circa 313 C.E. (Palazzo dei Conservatori, Cortile 2, Inv. 1692, Rome) 126

Construction project under way, relief, circa 100–110 C.E.; a human-powered treadmill is depicted at the lower left (Lateran Museum, Vatican, Rome) 198

Crassus 211

Cybele in a chariot being drawn by lions; Hellenistic bronze statue, circa third century B.C.E. (Metropolitan Museum of Art, New York) 364

Diagrammatic plan of a typical Roman legion encampment of the second century B.C.E. (from E. Fabricius, "Some Notes on Polybius' Description of Roman Camps," *Journal of Roman Studies,* 1932) 231

Diocletian 211

Julia Domna 173

Livia Drusilla 331

Election slogans on the wall of a building in Pompeii, circa 79 C.E. 240

Engagement ring, gold, from the third century C.E. (Yale University Art Gallery, New Haven, Connecticut) 294

Quintus Ennius (Ennius) 130

Eratosthenes's measurement of the Earth (John Campbell, *Introductory Cartography,* 1984) 387

Etruscan *fasces* dating from 600 B.C.E. This ax bundled with rods was the symbol of authority of the Roman kings and later the consuls

and praetors (Soprintendenza alle Antichità dell'Etruria Meridionale, Rome). 234

Euclides (Euclid) 410

Eudoxus's "horse-fetter," shown here at the intersection of the cylinder's surface with the surface of a sphere (from Marshall Clagett, *Greek Science in Antiquity,* 1955) 391

Fasti Antiates, a Republican-era calendar, covering the months Martiu to Junius (March to June). Painted on plaster, it recorded feast days (Museo Nazionale Archeologico delle Terme, Rome). 287

Fresco depicting rites to the goddess Isis, found in Herculaneum, circa 50 C.E. (Museo Nazionale, Naples) 334

Fresco of Flagellation, from the Villa of Mysteries, Pompeii, circa 60 B.C.E. 109

A fresco from a house on the Esquiline Hill in Rome, circa 50 B.C.E., depicting a scene from Homer's *Odyssey* (Vatican Museum, Rome) 110

Frieze of a produce market in Rome, late second century C.E. (Ostia Museum, Ostia) 192

A frieze showing the census being conducted in Rome in the first-century B.C.E.. While one citizen is being registered (on the left), the others are preparing to perform sacrifices (Louvre, Paris). 199

Funeral cortège, relief, late first century B.C.E. (Museo Nazionale D'Abruzzo, L'Aquila) 307

Funerary bas-relief (circa first century C.E.) from the tomb of a slave couple who had gained their freedom, denoted by the letter *L* written after their names (Staatliche Museum, Berlin) 330

Funerary relief of men with poles stomping on grapes to extract the juice for wine production, circa first century C.E. (Museo Archeologico Nazionale, Venice) 185

Funerary relief of a Roman family, with inscription, from the late first century B.C.E. (North Carolina Museum of Art, Raleigh) 166

Funerary stele of the shipbuilder Publius Longidienus, circa first century C.E. The inscription reads: "Publius Longidienus hastens to get on with his work" (Ravenna Museum, Ravenna). 194

Galen's concept of physiology showing the function of the three principal organs: brain, heart, and liver (from John Scarborough, *Roman Medicine,* 1969) 404

Garden at the house of M. Lucretius at Pompeii with examples of early-imperial "bourgeoisie" decorative statuary 284

The *Gemma Augustea,* a cameo depicting Rome and Tiberius, late first century B.C.E. (Kunsthistorisches Museum, Vienna) 155

A geographer's interpretation of the world. The "inhabited world" is an island—including Europe, Asia, and Africa—surrounded by Ocean (from O. A. W. Dilke, *Greek and Roman Maps,* 1985) 50

Glassware from the first century C.E. (Yale University Art Gallery, New Haven, Connecticut) 188

Gold bulla, a circular charm worn by children to protect themselves from evil spirits, circa first century C.E. (from Denise Dersin, *What Life Was Like When Rome Ruled the World,* 1997) 304

Tiberius Gracchus 212

Publius Aelius Hadrianus (Hadrian) 173

Hadrian's triumphal entry into Rome following one of his military campaigns against the barbarians, second century C.E. He is being greeted by the guiding spirits of the Senate and the Roman people (from Donald Kagan and others, *The Western Heritage,* 1998). 258

Hadrian's Villa at Tivoli, built 124-133 C.E. 282

Herculaneum, which was buried in ash following the eruption of Mount Vesuvius in 79 C.E. 317

Quintus Horatius Flaccus (Horace) 131

Horace's house in the Sabine Hills near Licenza 105

House of Diana at Ostia, an example

INDEX

Page numbers in boldface refer to a topic upon which an essay is based.
Page numbers in italics refer to illustrations, figures, and tables.

Persia, war with, 243
Persius Flaccus, Aulus, 113
Petitions for imperial action, **241**
Petronius, 112, 206, **290**, 306, 309
Phaenomena (Aratus), 386, 409
Pharmaceutical drugs, 403–404, 405, 406
Philhellenism, 149
Philippics (Cicero), 232
Philosophy, **110–111**, 368–370
    Aristotle, 347
    atomism, 346, 347, 370
    Cicero's works, 369–370
    cynicism, 347
    Epictetus, **372**
    Epicureanism, 370
    ethics, 370
    Greek, 152, 345–348, **368–370**
    Marcus Aurelius, **372**
    monism *vs.* atomism, 346
    Neoplatonism, 373
    overview, **341–348**
    Plato, 346–347
    Plotinus, **373**
    political, 369–370
    Porphyry, **373**
    pre-Socratic, 345–346
    Pythagoras, 346
    scepticism, 347, 369, 373
    Seneca, 370
    Sextus Empiricus, **373**
    Socrates, 346–347
    Sophists, 346
    See also Stoicism
Physicians, 191, 193, 285–286, 399, 401–403,
    405
Physiology, 404–405, 411
Pietas, 76–77
Pilgramages, 167
Piracy, 170, 194
Plane geometry, 390–391
Planetary motion, 386–387, 392, 407
Plato, 346–347
Plautus (Titus Maccius Plautus), 92–93, **134,**
    201
Plebeians, 181–182, 204–205, 302, 313
    See also Class system and social structure
Pliny the Elder
    ethnocentric views, 56, 57–58
    geographic work, 49–50, **61**, 397
    on Hipparchus, 388–389
    limitations of ethnography, 59
Pliny the Younger, 101
    correspondence of, 163
    on the games Valerius gave in Verona, 275
    gift of farm to his nurse, 330
    on horse racing, 277
    treatment of slaves, 203
    villas of, 281, **290**
Plotinus, **373**
Plumbing, 283
Pneumatists, 402
Poetry, 73–74, 94–97, **102–105,** 154
    See also Literature; Specific writers
Poles, 386, 387
Police, lack of, 244
Political geography, 49, 55, 56, 59
Political philosophy, 369–370
Politics. *See* Government and politics
Polybius, 120, **174**

Polyculture. *See* Multiculturalism
Polytheism, 344–345, 348–349
Pompeii, 109–110, *164, 192*
Pont du Gard Aqueduct, *84*
Pontifex maximus, 315
    yearbooks of, 342–343
Pontiffs, 315, 367–368
Porphyry, **373**
Port cities, 168, 169, 194, 284–285
Port of Ostia mosaic, *167*
Portrait of a man from the Fayum, Egypt, 107
Portrait sculptures, **120–126**
Posidonius, 49, **61–62,** 389
Positional astronomy, 387
Postal service, 158, 189
Pottery, 187–188, *305*
Praenomina, 324–325
Praetorian Guard, 241, *242*
Praetors, 199–200
Prayer to Diana, 351
Pre-Socratic philosophy, 345–346
Prestige building with public inscriptions,
    165–166
Price-edict of Diocletian, 196, 197
Priests and priestesses, 314, *328,* 343, **366–368**
Prima Porta Augustus, 121, 123
Princeps, 239
Prison, Tullianum, *245*
Private law, 226, **248–249,** 253
Private religion, 348, 368
Produce market, frieze of, *192*
Propaganda, 150
Propertius (Sextus Propertius), 95, **134,** 311
Property damage, 248–249
Property ownership, 249
Prostitution, 248, 319–320, 356
    See also Brothels
Provinces
    citizenship, 148
    management, 148
    political corruption, 149
    resources of, 55–56
    rights of inhabitants, 247
    trial procedures, 252
Ptolemy (Claudius Ptolemaeus)
    astronomy and mathematics, 383, 391–392,
    398
    geographic work, 50, **62**
    world map, *47*
Public baths, 275–276, 283, 327
Public buildings, 265, 266, 325–327
Public health, 383, 399
    See also Medicine
Public inscriptions, 164–166
Public law, 226, 249, 253
Public medicine, 399
Public memorials, **164–166**
Public policy, 241
Public religion, 348, 366–368
Public spaces, **325–328**
Public spectacles, 190, 266–267, 276–279,
    327–328
Publicans, 201, 207
Punic Wars, 148, 265–266
Punica (Silius Italicus), 135
Pythagoras, 346